PRODUCTION and OPERATIONS MANAGEMENT

PRODUCTION and OPERATIONS MANAGEMENT

(Revised Second Edition)

Prof. P. Rama Murthy

B.E., M.Tech. (Heat Power)
M.I.I.E, PG. D.B.A., C.E.M., G.I.I.E.

Principal
Intell Engineering College, Anantapur, A.P.
(Formerly Professor of Mechanical Engineering
at J.N.T.U. College of Engineering, Anantapur).

PUBLISHING FOR ONE WORLD

NEW AGE INTERNATIONAL (P) LIMITED, PUBLISHERS

New Delhi • Bangalore • Chennai • Cochin • Guwahati
Hyderabad • Kolkata • Lucknow • Mumbai
Visit us at **www.newagepublishers.com**

Published by New Age International (P) Ltd., Publishers
First Edition: 2002
Second Edition: 2005
Reprint: 2015

BRANCHES

- **Bangalore** 37/10, 8th Cross (Near Hanuman Temple), Azad Nagar, Chamarajpet, Bangalore-560 018
Tel.: (080) 26756823, Telefax: 26756820, **E-mail: bangalore@newagepublishers.com**
- **Chennai** 26, Damodaran Street, T. Nagar, Chennai-600 017
Tel.: (044) 24353401, Telefax: 24351463, **E-mail: chennai@newagepublishers.com**
- **Cochin** CC-39/1016, Carrier Station Road, Ernakulam South, Cochin-682 016
Tel.: (0484) 2377004, Telefax: 4051303, **E-mail: cochin@newagepublishers.com**
- **Guwahati** Hemsen Complex, Mohd. Shah Road, Paltan Bazar, Near Starline Hotel, Guwahati-781 008
Tel.: (0361) 2513881, Telefax: 2543669, **E-mail: guwahati@newagepublishers.com**
- **Hyderabad** 105, 1st Floor, Madhiray Kaveri Tower, 3-2-19, Azam Jahi Road, Near Kumar Theater Nimboliadda, Kachiguda, Hyderabad-500 027, Tel.: (040) 24652456, Telefax: 24652457
E-mail: hyderabad@newagepublishers.com
- **Kolkata** RDB Chambers (Formerly Lotus Cinema) 106A, 1st Floor, S.N. Banerjee Road, Kolkata-700 014
Tel.: (033) 22273773, Telefax: 22275247, **E-mail: kolkata@newagepublishers.com**
- **Lucknow** 16-A, Jopling Road, Lucknow-226 001
Tel.: (0522) 2209578, 4045297, Telefax: 2204098, **E-mail:lucknow@newagepublishers.com**
- **Mumbai** 142C, Victor House, Ground Floor, N.M. Joshi Marg, Lower Parel, Mumbai-400 013
Tel.: (022) 24927869, Telefax: 24915415, **E-mail: mumbai@newagepublishers.com**
- **New Delhi** 22, Golden House, Daryaganj, New Delhi-110 002
Tel.: (011) 23262368, 23262370, Telefax: 43551305, **E-mail: sales@newagepublishers.com**

ISBN: 978-81-224-1558-2

₹ 250.00

C-15-04-8381

Printed in India at Print-O-Pack, Delhi.
Typeset at Vikas Composer, Delhi.

PUBLISHING GLOBALLY
NEW AGE INTERNATIONAL (P) LIMITED, PUBLISHERS
7/30 A, Daryaganj, New Delhi-110002
Visit us at **www.newagepublishers.com**

THIS BOOK IS DEDICATED TO MY STUDENTS

WHOM

I

LOVE AS MY CHILDREN

PREFACE TO THE SECOND EDITION

I am very happy; the book is well received by Enginnering and Management students. With in a span of 2 years, it has come for second edition. In this edition, I have added one more chapter on PERT and CPM. I have given a question bank at the end to help students.

I thank Mr. P. Issac Prasad, Assistant Professor of Mechanical Engineering and Mr. N.V. Jagadeesh Babu, Assistant Professor of Mechanical Engineering, who have helped me in preparing this book.

Anantapur

P. Rama Murthy

PREFACE TO THE FIRST EDITION

This Book, **PRODUCTION AND OPERATIONS MANAGEMENT** is brought so as to enable a teacher to cover the syllabus in a planned way. Entire matter in the book is a copy of my lecture notes prepared while I was handling the Production and Operations Management subject for M.B.A. classes and Production Planning and Control Classes for B.Tech students. I hope that students get concept of Production Management by studying this book. I would welcome suggestions for further development of the book from teachers and students.

P. Rama Murthy

CONTENTS

1

PRODUCTION AND OPERATIONS MANAGEMENT

- Introduction
- Product.
- Production.
- Management.
- Production and Operations Management an Overview.
- Definition of Production Operations Management.
- Objectives of Production Management.
- Scope of Production Management.
- Benefits derived from efficient Production Management Department.
- Functions of Production Management.
- Types of Production Systems.
- Characteristics of production systems and Production cycle.

INTRODUCTION

The Subject of Production Management is studied under different Headings-such as Production Planning and control, Production and Inventory control, production and operations control and many more. What ever may be the title of the subject, the contents of the subject are more or less one and the same. Before we discuss about production management, let us discuss about product, production and management. This will give us a rough idea about production Management and with what a production manager has to deal with.

1.1. PRODUCT

Though many authors define the product with Consumer orientation, it is better for us to deal with different angles, because it will be helpful for us to understand the subject of production and Operation Management.

***(i)* For a Consumer:** The product is a combination of or optimal mix of potential utilities. This is because every consumer expects some use or uses from the product. Hence he/she always identifies the product in terms of the uses. Say for example-Soap can be identified by complexion, cleanliness of body, freshness, fragrance or health.... etc. Because of this, many producers advertise that they are selling health, or they are selling Cine star Complexion or they are selling freshness and so on.

***(ii)* For a Production Manager:** Product is the combination of various surfaces and processes (or operations). This is because the production Manager is solely responsible for producing the product. He has to think of the various surfaces by which the product is made of, so that he can plan for processes by which a particular surface can be made and plan for required capacity of the facility by which the surface is produced. While planning he has to see that the required surface is produced by the best and cheapest method (optimally), so as to make the product to face competition in the market.

***(iii)* For a Financial Manager:** For him the product is a mix of various cost elements as he is responsible for the profitability of the product.

***(iv)* For a Personnel Manager:** For him the product is a mix of various skills, as he is the person who selects and trains the personnel to meet the demand of the skili to produce the product.

In general we can define the product as a bundle of tangible and intangible attributes, which along with the service is meant to satisfy the customer wants.

1.2. PRODUCTION

Production means application of processes. (Technology) to the raw material to add the use and economic values to arrive at desired product by the best method, with out sacrificing the desired quality. We have three ways of Production, they are:

***(i)* Production by Disintegration:** By separating the contents of Crude oil or a mixture the desired products are produced. For example the crude oil is disintegrated into various fuel oils. Similarly salt production is also an example for product produced by disintegrated. We can use Mechanical or Chemical or both technologies to get the desired product, so that it will have desired use value.

***(ii)* Production by Integration:** In this type of Production various Components of the products are assembled together to get the desired product. In this process, Physical and Chemical Properties of the materials used may change. The examples are: Assembly of Two wheelers, Four wheelers and so on.

***(iii)* Production by Service:** Here the Chemical and Mechanical Properties of materials are improved without any physical change. The example for this is Heat Treatment of metals. In real world, a combination of above methods is used.

In general production is the use of any process or procedure designed to transform a set of input elements into a set of output elements, which have use value and economic value.

1.3. MANAGEMENT

Management can be explained as an art or science, (in fact it is a combination of art and science) of getting things done by the people, by planning, coordinating, organizing, directing and controlling the activities to meet specified goals, with in the frame work of agreed policies. The above explanation put emphasis on getting things done, Planning, Organizing, Coordinating, and controlling and specific objectives and agreed policies. Today's manager needs scientific base as well as personal tactics to manage the people under him to achieve the desired goals. Above discussion about product, production and management will help us to understand what exactly the Production Management or Production, and Operations Management is.

1.4. OPERATIONS MANAGEMENT – AN OVERVIEW

Operations Management is the conversion of *inputs* into *outputs,* using physical resources, so as to provide the desired utility/utilities of form, place, possession or state or a combination there-of to the customer while meeting the other organizational objectives of effectiveness, efficiency and adaptability. It distinguishes itself from other functions such as personnel, marketing, etc. By its primary concern for *'conversion by using physical resources'*. There should be a number of situations in either marketing or personal or other functions, which can be classified or sub-classified under ***Production and Operations Management.*** For example, (*a*) The physical distribution of items to the users or customers, (*b*) The arrangement of collection of marketing information, (*c*) The actual selection and recruitment process, (*d*) The paper flow and conversion of data into information usable by the judge in a court of law, etc. Can all be put under the banner of production and operations management? '*The conversion*' here is subtle, unlike manufacturing which is obvious. While in case (*a*) and (*b*) it is the conversion of *'place'* and *'possession'* characteristic of product, In (*c*) and (*d*) it is the conversion of the *'state'* and characteristics. And using physical resources effects this 'conversion'. The input and / or output could also be non-physical such as 'information', but the conversion process uses physical resources in addition to other non-physical resources. The management of the use of physical resources in addition to other non-physical resources for the conversion process is what distinguishes production and operations management from other functional disciplines.

Production and Operations Management systems are also described as providing physical goods or services. When we say that the Central Government provides *service* and the Indian Airlines provide *service* these are two entirely two different classes of utilities and consequently the objective and criteria for reference will have to be entirely different for these two cases.

We may say that the actual production and operations management systems are quite Operations Management complex involving multiple utilities to be provided to the customer, with a mix of physical and non-physical inputs and outputs and perhaps with a multiplicity of customers.

1.5. CRITERIA OF PERFORMANCE

Three aims of performance of the Production and Operations Management system may be identified. They are,

(*a*) Effectiveness, (*b*) Customer satisfaction, (*c*) Efficiency.

The case of *Efficiency* is *productive* utilization of resources is clear. Whether the organization is in 'private sector' or in the 'public sector', is a 'manufacturing or 'non-manufacturing' organization or a 'profit' or a 'non-profit' organization, the optimal utilization of resource inputs is always a desired objective. The effectiveness has more dimensions to it. It involves optimality in the fulfillment of multiple objectives with a possible prioritization within the objectives. Modern production and operations management has to serve the target customers, the people working within, as also the region, country or society at large. Thus Production / Operations Management system, has not only to be *profitable* and / or *efficient*, but must necessarily satisfy many more *customers*. This effectiveness has to be again viewed in terms of the short and long-term horizons depending upon the operations system.

Optimum, Good, Better operations management can improve:

(*i*) Efficiency of operation system to *do things right and broader concept.*

(*ii*) Effectiveness of operation system refers to doing right things that is seven rights, they are: Right operation, Right Quantity, Right Quality, Right Supplier or Right Vendor, Right Time, Right Place and Right Price.

Basically, *efficiency and effectiveness of the operations system* can be measured by four dimensions, they are: (*i*) Cost, (*ii*) Quality, (*iii*) Dependability and (*iv*) Reliability. In fact these directly relate to the *competitiveness* of the organization, both nationally and internationally. Modern developments in better tools and techniques, methods and systems like Automation, Flexible manufacturing, CAD,

CAM, CIM at management, CADD, CIMS, Use of Robotics, TQM, OR Techniques etc, are taking place to achieve improvements in Cost, Quality, Dependability, Reliability and Flexibility and thus to help for *better management.*

1.6. DEFINITION OF PRODUCTION MANAGEMENT

It may be defined as:

(*i*) The performance of the management activities with regards to selecting, designing, operating, Controlling and updating production system.

(*ii*) It is the processes of effectively planning, coordinating and controlling the production, that is the operations of that part of an enterprise, it means to say that production and operations Management is responsible for the actual transformation of raw materials into finished products.

(*iii*) Production management is a function of Management, related to planning, coordinating and controlling the resources required for production to produce specified product by specified methods, by optimal utilization of resources.

(*iv*) Production management is defined as management function which plans, organizes, co-ordinates, directs and controls the material supply and Processing activities of an enterprise, so that specified products are produced by specified methods to meet an approved sales programme. These activities are being carried out in such a manner that Labour, Plant and Capital available are used to the best advantage of the organization.

1.7. OBJECTIVE OF PRODUCTION MANAGEMENT

The objective of Production Management is to produce the desired product or specified product by specified methods so that the optimal utilization of available resources is met with. Hence the production management is responsible to produce the desired product, which has marketability at the cheapest price by proper planning, the manpower, material and processes. Production management must see that it will deliver right goods of right quantity at right place and at right price. When the above objective is achieved, we say that we have effective Production Management system.

1.8. SCOPE OF PRODUCTION MANAGEMENT:

In fact, we apply Principles of Management; and functions of Management in our day-to-day life. We all know, from morning till night, we plan our activities; we coordinate available resources and control our activities to achieve certain goals. So also any organization must follow the Principles of Management for its survival and growth. The same is applicable to production Management also. Reading and learning Production Management will enable one to be capable of solving the problems of the organization, may be an Educational Institution, Production Shop, Hospital, Departmental shop or even a barber shop. The problems a manager face in various organizations are more or less similar to that of Production department but smaller in magnitude. Hence the knowledge of Production Management will help any professional Manager to tackle the problems of his business easily. For example: The Production Management consists of Planning, selection of materials, planning of processes, Routing, Scheduling and controlling the activities etc., Take the example of an Educational Institution/University. Here also selection of raw students, Planning of the Course Work, Educating the students and conducting the examination. Therefore this knowledge will enable one to apply the principles of Production Management to any field of life without restriction. Here, We have to remember that the above is also applicable to the management of a service organization and the management of a Project. Here it is better to distinguish between product, Service and Project, so as to help the reader to know on which particular aspect of Production Management to put much emphasis, in managing a service organization or a project.

***(i)* Product:** Manufacturing system often produces standardized products in large volumes. The plant and machinery have a finite capacity. The facilities constitute fixed costs, which are allocated to the products produced. Variable costs, such as, labour cost and materials costs. While manufacturing the product use value and economic values are added to the product. Hence the product is a store of values added during manufacture. Because the input costs and output costs are measurable, the productivity can be measured with certain degree of accuracy. Product can be transported to the markets and stored physically until it is sold.

***(ii)* Service:** Service system present more uncertainty with respect to capacity and costs. Services are produced and consumed in the presence of the customer. We cannot store the service physically. Because of this the service organizations, such as Hotels, Hospitals, Transport Organizations and many other service organizations the capacity must be sufficiently or consciously managed to accommodate a highly variable demand. Sometimes services like legal practice and medical practice involve Professional or intellectual judgments, which cannot be easily standardized. Because of this the calculation of cost and productivity is difficult.

***(iii)* Project:** Project system does not produce standardized products. The Plant, Machinery, Men and Materials are often brought to project site and the project is completed. The project is of big size and remains in the site itself after completion. As the costs can be calculated and allocated to the project with considerable accuracy, Productivity can be measured. Once the project is completed, all the resources are removed from site.

1.9. BENEFITS DERIVED FROM EFFICIENT PRODUCTION MANAGEMENT

The efficient Production Management will give benefits to the various sections of the society. They are:

- *(i)* **Consumer** benefits from improved industrial Productivity, increased use value in the product. Products are available to him at right place, at right price, at right time, in desired quantity and of desired quality.
- *(ii)* **Investors:** They get increased security for their investments, adequate market returns, and creditability and good image in the society.
- *(iii)* **Employee** gets adequate Wages, Job security, improved working conditions and increased Personal and Job satisfaction.
- *(iv)* **Suppliers:** Will get confidence in management and their bills can be realized with out any delay.
- *(v)* **Community:** community enjoys Benefits from economic and social stability.
- *(vi)* **The Nation** will achieve prospects and security because of increased Productivity and healthy industrial atmosphere.

1.10. FUNCTIONS OF PRODUCTION MANAGEMENT DEPARTMENT

The functions of Production Management depend upon the size of the firm. In small firms the production Manager may have to look after production planning and control along with Personnel,

Marketing, Finance and Purchase functions. In medium sized firms, there may be separate managers for Personnel, marketing and Finance functions. But the production planning and control and Purchase and stores may be under the control of Production management department. In large sized firms the activities of Production Management is confined to the management of production activities only. As such, there are no hard and fast rule or guidelines to specify the function of Production Management, but in the academic interest we can mention some of the functions, which are looked after by the Production Management department. They are:

***(i)* Materials:** The selection of materials for the product. Production manager must have sound Knowledge of materials and their properties, so that he can select appropriate materials for his product. Research on materials is necessary to find alternatives to satisfy the changing needs of the design in the product and availability of material resumes.

***(ii)* Methods:** Finding the best method for the process, to search for the methods to suit the available resources, identifying the sequence of process are some of the activities of Production Management.

***(iii)* Machines and Equipment:** Selection of suitable machinery for the process desired, designing the maintenance policy and design of layout of machines are taken care of by the Production Management department.

***(iv)* Estimating:** To fix up the Production targets and delivery dates and to keep the production costs at minimum, production management department does a thorough estimation of Production times and production costs. In competitive situation this will help the management to decide what should be done in arresting the costs at desired level.

***(v)* Loading and Scheduling:** The Production Management department has to draw the time table for various production activities, specifying when to start and when to finish the process required. It also has to draw the timings of materials movement and plan the activities of manpower. The scheduling is to be done keeping in mind the loads on hand and capacities of facilities available.

***(vi)* Routing:** This is the most important function of Production Management department. The Routing consists of fixing the flow lines for various raw materials, components etc., from the stores to the packing of finished product, so that all concerned knows what exactly is happening on the shop floor.

***(vii)* Despatching:** The Production Management department has to prepare various documents such as Job Cards, Route sheets, Move Cards, Inspection Cards for each and every component of the product. These are prepared in a set of five copies. These documents are to be released from Production Management department to give green signal for starting the production. The activities of the shop floor will follow the instructions given in these documents. Activity of releasing the document is known as dispatching.

***(viii)* Expediting or Follow up:** Once the documents are dispatched, the management wants to know whether the activities are being carried out as per the plans or not. Expediting engineers go round the production floor along with the plans, compare the actual with the plan and feed back the progress of the work to the management. This will help the management to evaluate the plans.

***(ix)* Inspection:** Here inspection is generally concerned with the inspection activities during production, but a separate quality control department does the quality inspection, which is not under the control of Production Management. This is true because, if the quality inspection is given to production Management, then there is a chance of qualifying the defective products also. For example Teaching and examining of students is given to the same person, then there is a possibility of passing all the students in the first grade. To avoid this situation an external person does correction of answer scripts, so that the quality of answers are correctly judged.

(*x*) Evaluation: The Production department must evaluate itself and its contribution in fulfilling the corporate objectives and the departmental objectives. This is necessary for setting up the standards for future. What ever may be the size of the firm; Production management department alone must do Routing, Scheduling, Loading, Dispatching and expediting. This is because this department knows very well regarding materials, Methods, and available resources etc. If the firms are small, all the above-mentioned functions (*i* to *x*) are to be carried out by Production Management Department. In medium sized firms in addition to Routing, Scheduling and Loading, Dispatching and expediting, some more functions like Methods, Machines may be under the control of Production Management Department. In large firms, there will be Separate departments for Methods, Machines, Materials and others but routing, loading and scheduling are the sole functions of Production Management. All the above ten functions are categorized in three stage, that is Preplanning, Planning and control stages as shown in figure.1.1.

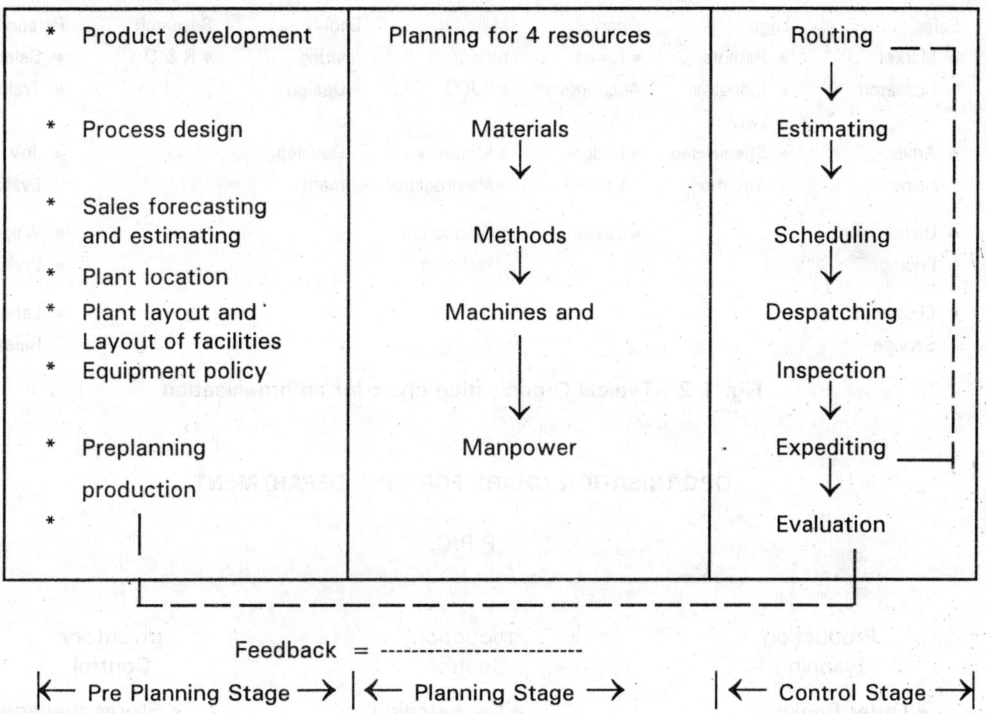

Fig. 1.1 : Production function.

1.11. PLACE OF PRODUCTION MANAGEMENT DEPARTMENT IN THE ORGANISATION

Production is the center of all actitivities of an organization. This is to say all the activities of an organization, such as: Finance, Personnel, Marketing...etc., are exists in an organization because of production activity. Hence the position of Production Management in an organization is very important. Whether it should be a line function or Staff function, more or less depends upon the corporate management policy. In small organization, Production Management is whole and sole of it. In large industries, generally it is advisable to have Production as line function, because, the decision taken by the line manager and the advices given by the Staff personnel will be based on the Production activities. The Production Manager, directly report to General Manager, who in turn report to the Board. The figure 1.2 shows a typical organization structure showing the position of Production Management. Figure 1.3 shows an organization chart for Production and Operations Management department.

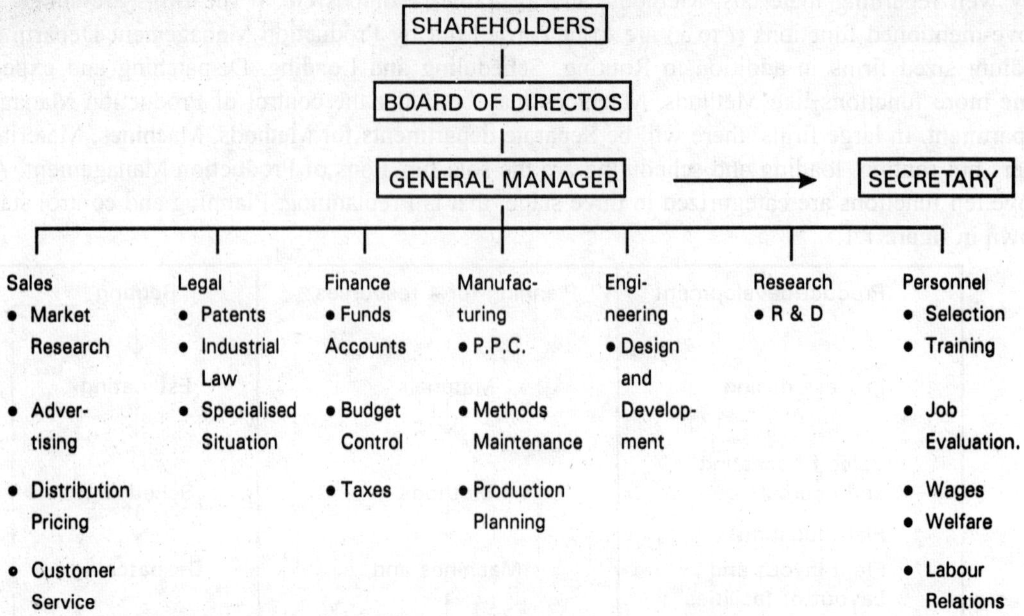

Fig. 1.2 : Typical Organisation chart for an organisation

ORGANISATION CHART FOR P.P.C. DEPARTMENT

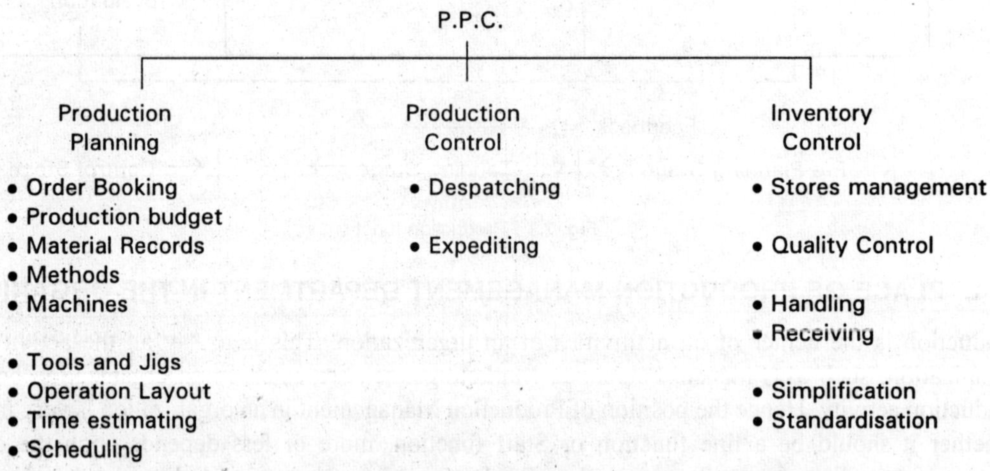

Figure 1.3 : An organization chart for production management department.

1.12. TYPES OF PRODUCTION SYSTEMS

The organization of manufacturing systems, also planning and control of production greatly depends on type of product type of the product line. Basic principles that guide the formation of planning policy and its execution may be the same for all the manufacturing concerns. But emphasis on a particular aspect of production management in fulfilling of specific requirement of the plant and the management approach to the problems of inventory, machine selection, machine setting, tooling, routing, scheduling, loading, follow up and general control will differ depending on the type of production system. Three main factors generally determine this aspect are :

- *(i)* **Type of production** i.e., quantities of finished products and regularity of manufacture. For example whether Job production or Batch Production or Continuous Production.
- *(ii)* **Size of the Plant** i.e., Small Industry, Medium sized Industry or Large Industry.
- *(iii)* **Type of Production:** In general there are three classifications in types of Production system. They are discussed below.

***(a)* Job Production:** In this system Products are manufactured to meet the requirements of a specific order. The quality involved is small and the manufacturing of the product will take place as per the specifications given by the customer. This system may be further classified as.

- *(i)* **The Job produced only once:** Here the customer visit the firm and book his order. After the completion of the product, he takes delivery of the product and leaves the firm. He may not visit the firm to book the order for the same product. The firm has to plan for material, process and manpower only after receiving the order from the customer. The firms have no scope for pre-planning the production of the product.
- *(ii)* **The job produced at irregular intervals:** Here the customer visits the firm to place orders for the same type of the product at irregular intervals. The firm will not have any idea of customer's visit. Here also planning for materials, process and manpower will start only after taking the order from the customer. In case the firm maintains the record of the Jobs Produced by it, it can refer to the previous plans, when the customer arrives at the firm to book the order.
- *(iii)* **The Jobs Produced periodically at regular intervals:** In this system, the customer arrives at the firm to place orders for the same type of product at regular intervals. Here firm knows very well that the customer visits at regular intervals, it can plan for materials, and process and manpower and have them in a master file. As soon as the customer visits and books the order, the firm can start production. If the volume of the order is considerably large and the number of regularly visiting customers are large in number, the Job Production system slowly transform into Batch Production system.

***(b)* Batch Production:** Batch Production is the manufacture of number of identical products either to meet the specific order or to satisfy the demand. When the Production of plant and equipment is terminated, the plant and equipment can be used for producing similar products. This system also can be classified under three categories.

- *(i)* **A batch produced only once:** Here customer places order with the firm for the product of his specification. The size of the order is greater than that of job production order. The firm has to plan for the resources after taking the order from the customer.
- *(ii)* **A Batch produced at irregular intervals as per Customer order or when the need arises:** As the frequency is irregular, the firm can maintain a file of its detailed plans and it can refer to its previous files and start production.

(*iii*) **A Batch Produced periodically at known Intervals:** Here the firm either receives order from the customer at regular intervals or it may produce the product to satisfy the demand. It can have well designed file of its plans, material requirement and instructions for the ready reference. It can also purchase materials required in bulk in advance. As the frequency of regular orders goes on increasing the Batch Production system becomes Mass Production System. Here also, incase the demand for a particular product ceases, the plant and machinery can be used for producing other products with slight modification in layout or in machinery and equipment.

(c) Continuous Production: Continuous Production system is the specialized manufacture of identical products on which the machinery and equipment is fully engaged. The continuous production is normally associated with large quantities and with high rate of demand. Hence the advantage of automatic production is taken. This system is classified as

(*i*) **Mass Production:** Here same type of product is produced to meet the demand of an assembly line or the market. This system needs good planning for material, process, maintenance of machines and instruction to operators. Purchases of materials in bulk quantities is advisable.

(*ii*) **Flow Production:** The difference between Mass and Flow Production is the type of product and its relation to the plant. In Mass Production identical products are produced in large numbers. If the demand falls or ceases, the machinery and equipment, after slight modification be used for manufacturing products of similar nature. In flow production, the plant and equipment is designed for a specified product. Hence if the demand falls for the product or ceases, the plant cannot be used for manufacturing other products. It is to be scraped. The examples for the above discussed production system are

(*i*) *Job Production Shop*: Tailors shop; cycle and vehicles repair shops, Job typing shops, small Workshops.

(*ii*) *Batch Production Shop*: Tyre Production Shops, Readymade dress companies, Cosmetic manufacturing companies...etc.

(*iii*) *Mass Producion Shops*: Components of industrial products,

(*iv*) *Flow Production*: Cement Factory, Sugar factory, Oil refineries...etc.,

The Table 1.1 given below and figure 1.4 will give the Characteristics of Intermittent (Job and Batch production) and continuous (Mass and flow production) Production system.

Table 1.1 : Characteristics of intermittent and continuous manufacturing system

S. No.	*Particulars*	*Intermittent production system (job and batch production)*	*Continuous production system. (mass and flow production)*
1.	Type of plant layout.	Process layout is most suitable.	Product layout designed according to a process separate line for each product is considered.
2.	Type of machine	As it necessitate frequent changes in the machine set-up required by the specification of each order, general purpose machines are more suitable. Also they have good flexibility. In batch production special purpose machines Automatic and Semi-automatic machines are used.	As production flow is permanently in the form of product line, Automatic or special purpose machines are used. In flow production specialised machines are used.

S. No.	*Particulars*	*Intermittent production system (job and batch production)*	*Continuous production system. (mass and flow production)*
3.	Type of labour	The type of production pre-supposes frequent changes in product design and machine setups; which requires highly skilled labour. Repair and maintenance of machines are to be done by these labours.	The manufacturing activity becomes a routine function and as the machines are designed to suit the process required for product and automatic in nature unskillful or semi-skilled labour is required. A specialised team of plant maintenance staff will look after the repair and maintenance of machines.
4.	Number of products and product design.	Wide range of products are manufactured in small quantities. The product design changes from lot to lot as per the product specification. Each lot produced in small size.	Few/one standard products/product is manufacutred in large quantities. Usually the product line is designed to one or two products of standard specification.
5.	Changes in machine set-up.	As specification of each order changes, the machines are to set according to the requirements of each order, frequent changes in machine setup is a common phenomenon.	In this type of manufacturing, the set-up of machines remains unchanged for a longer period. The standard products are manufactured in a continuous flow.
6.	Nature and size of orders.	Generally the size of orders is small and they are not repeated. The orders are for non-standardised products. The order may involve the production of single product or products in limited lot. Usually the production is done according to first-in-first-out principle. First orders are received and then they are translated into production.	Generally the production is carried on for stock. The production of standardised products is the nature of this type of production. Products are produced in anticipation of demand. The size of the order is large. Same type of product is produced in every cycle to satisfy the demand.
7.	Investment on machines and equipment.	As the machines are arranged in process layout and general purpose machines are required for Job production, the investment comparatively less. For batch production as automatic and semi-automatic machines are involved the investment will be higher than job production.	The machines are arranged according to process layout and because of this duplication of machines is fairly high. The machines are fully automatic, the cost is higher than intermittent production.
8.	Investment on inventories	Here the operating cycle takes more time and it is necessary to have standard materials for long period hence inventory cost per product is considerably large.	Bulk purchase of materials is done at periodic intervals. Due to continuous process, less in process inventory exists hence material cost per product is less.
9.	Material handling equipments	Because of verities of products, different routes are followed by materials also volume of order is small, mechanisation of material handling is not possible.	Mechanisation of material handling is possible. Generally, convenyors, pipe-lines, automatic material handing equipment is used.
10.	Material handling cost	Material handling per product is costlier because of long distance handling (manual) and backtracking.	Due to mechanised material handling, material handling cost per product is less.

S. No.	Particulars	Intermittent production system (job and batch production)	Continuous production system. (mass and flow production)
11.	Plant maintenance and service	It is desirable to have a maintenance department to avoid losses due to brake down of machinery.	It is essential to have a good plant maintenance department to avoid stoppage of production due to break down of machines.
12.	Balancing of production capacity	Due to different products and different types of machines with different capacity blocks, possibility of imbalance in plant capacity occurs.	The chances of imbalance in plant capacity is very much less.
13.	Production planning and control	The functions of routing, scheduling and loading becomes relatively complicated due to odd size of order, non-repetitive nature of the order, different delivery dates, etc., production planning and control is complicated.	The function of routing, scheduling and loading are carried on smoothly due to standardised products, rated capacity. Here production planning and control is simpler.

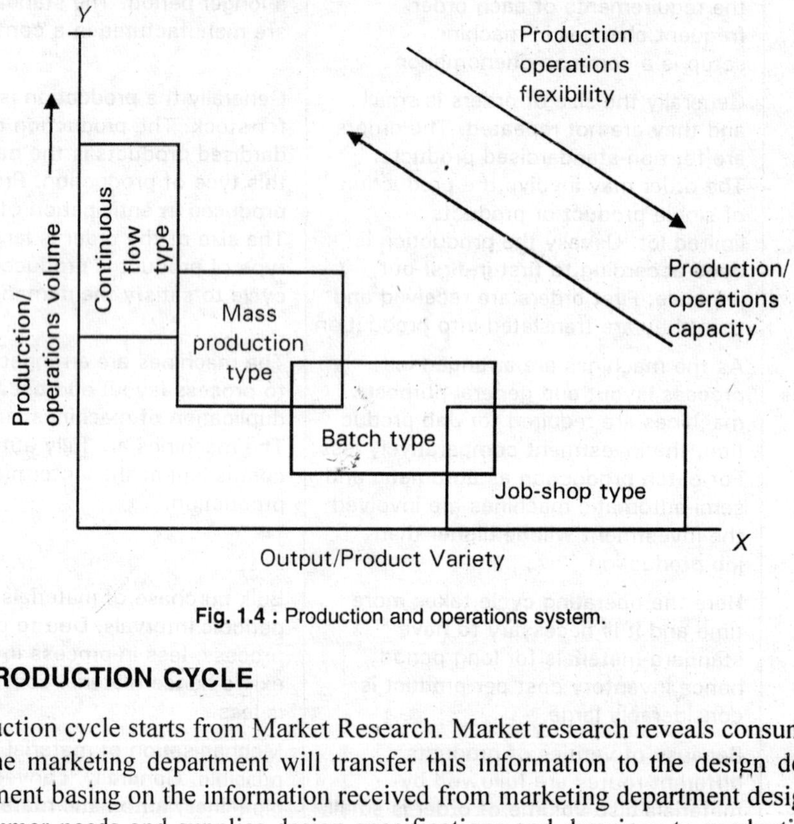

Fig. 1.4 : Production and operations system.

1.13. THE PRODUCTION CYCLE

The production cycle starts from Market Research. Market research reveals consumer preferences and needs. The marketing department will transfer this information to the design department. The design department basing on the information received from marketing department designs the product to fulfill consumer needs and supplies design specifications and drawings to production department. The production department verifies whether the product can be manufactured with the technology and skill available in the firm. If yes it will give the acceptance. Otherwise the Production Manager, Design engineer and Marketing Manager, discuss together and make alterations in the product,

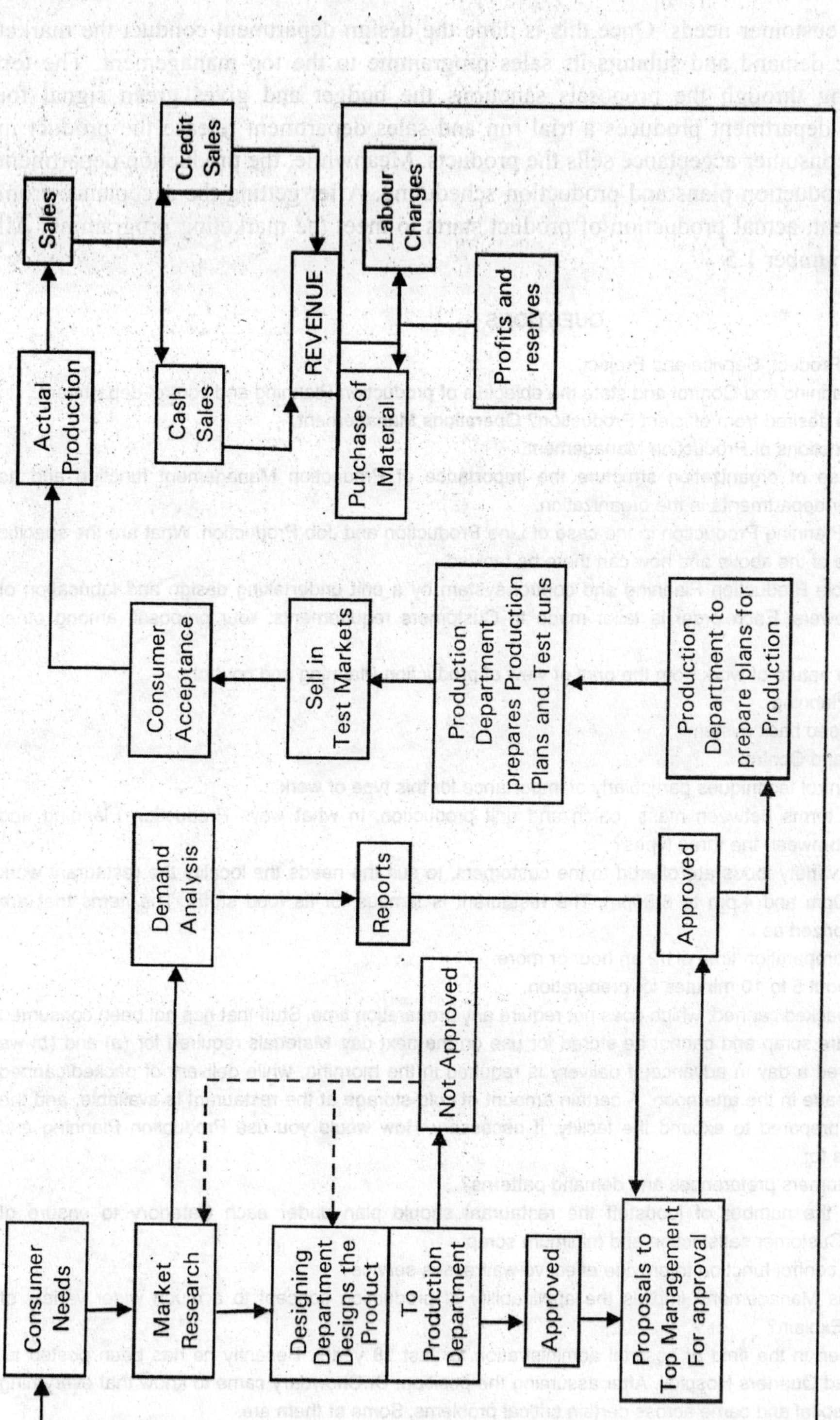

Fig. 1.5 : Production cycle.

without sacrificing the customer needs. Once this is done the design department conduct the market survey and analyze the demand and submits its sales programme to the top management. The top management after going through the proposals sanctions the budget and gives green signal for production. Production department produces a trial run and sales department release the product in the test markets to get consumer acceptance sells the products. Meanwhile, the production department prepares the detailed production plans and production scheduling. After getting the acceptance from the marketing department, actual production of product starts to meet the marketing programme. All this is shown in figure number 1.5

QUESTIONS

1. Distinguish between Product, Service and Project.
2. Define Production Planning and Control and state the objective of production Planning and control department.
3. What advantages are desired from efficient Production? Operations Management.
4. Briefly discuss the functions of Production Management.
5. Describe with the use of organization structure the importance of Production Management function and its relationship with other departments in the organization.
6. Explain the steps in Planning Production in the case of Line Production and Job Production. What are the specific problems in each one of the above and how can there be tackled.
7. Recommend a suitable Production Planning and control system by a unit undertaking design and fabrication of steel transmission towers. Each order is tailor made to Customers requirements. Your proposal, among other things, should cover
   (*a*) Production of the nature of work from the print of view of production Planning and control.
   (*b*) Pre Production Planning
   (*c*) Work order and feed back system
   (*d*) Cost estimation and Control
   (*e*) Planning and Control techniques particularly of importance for this type of work.
8. Distinguish in clean terms between mass, batch and unit production. In what ways Production Planning and control system differ between the three types?
9. In a restaurant wide variety foods are offered to the customers, to suit the needs the locality the restaurant work from 9-00am to 1-00pm and 4.pm to 8-00pm. The restaurant is famous for its food stuffs. The items that are served can be categorized as
   (*a*) Those involving preparation time of1/2 an hour or more.
   (*b*) Those require about 5 to 10 minutes for preparation.
   (*c*) Those are from packed/canned, which does not require any preparation time. Stuff that has not been consumed in any one day are scrap and cannot be stored for use on the next day. Materials required for (*a*) and (*b*) we have to be ordered a day in advance; if delivery is required in the morning, while delivery of packed/canned food is usually made in the afternoon. A certain amount of cold storage at the restaurant is available, and the management is prepared to expand the facility, if necessary. How would you use Production Planning and control procedure to:
      (i) Study Customers preferences and demand patterns?
      (ii) Determine the number of foodstuff the restaurant should plan under each Category to ensure of maximum Customer satisfaction and minimum scrap.
      (iii) Exercise a control function to provide effective waitresses service?
10. The term "Operations Management" implies the applicability of production concept to a much wider variety of human endeavours. Explain?
11. Dr.Chowdary has been in the field of hospital administration for last 18 years. Recently he has been posted as chief of a district Head Quarters Hospital. After assuming the position, Dr.Chowdary came to know that everything is not good at the hospital and came across certain critical problems. Some of them are.
   (*a*) Storage of medical and non-medical items
   (*b*) Poor patient feeding-patients have complained about the quality of food.

(*c*) Non availability of Ambulance, when needed.

(*d*) Break down of X-ray facility since long time.

Dr.Chowdary decided to take assistance of a management hand to solve the above problems and many more small problems that bother him in every day business. Dr.Chowdary gave an advertisement. Called candidates for interview and could not satisfy from the answers given by the candidates.

One fine morning a neatly dressed young man came to Dr.Chowdary and told him that he is useful to Dr.Chowdary in solving the problems in the Hospital. He told Dr.Chowdary that he is working as a production manager in local medium sized factory. Dr.Chowdary laughed at him and said, " You see young man in spite of my 18 years of experience in the hospital, I am not in a position to understand their administrative problems. You being a production manager of a manufacturing concern, how do you help me? Think that you are the young man who has approached Dr.Chowdary and explain how do you answer Dr.Chowdary.

2

PRE-PLANING STAGE OR PRODUCT DESIGN STAGE

- Factors to be considered at Product design stage.
  - ☐ Marketing Aspect.
  - ☐ Product Characteristics.
  - ☐ Economic Analysis.
  - ☐ Profitability and Competitiveness.
  - ☐ Production Aspect.

2.1 INTRODUCTION

Before preparing plans for regular production, product is to be developed and designed. When a new product is projected, the designer has to bear in mind the available resources of the plant and possible implications such as acquiring new facility, modifying the process, sub contracting etc. Therefore product design and analysis is one of the fundamental elements of management policy. While designing the Product certain factors are to be considered. Some of them are discussed below.

2.2 FACTORS TO BE CONSIDERED AT PRODUCT DESIGN STAGE

The Factors are:

(*i*) Marketing Aspect

(*ii*) Product Characteristics:

(*a*) Functional Aspect,

(*b*) Operational Aspect,

(*c*) Durability and Dependability and

(*d*) Aesthetic Aspect.

(*iii*) Economic Analysis

(*a*) The Profit Consideration,

(*b*) The effect of Standardisation, simplification and specialization and

(*c*) Break-even Analysis,

(*iv*) Profitability and competitiveness

(*v*) Production Aspect.

Now, let us discuss the above factors in detail. All the above factors are interrelated and each presents many issues that have to be carefully considered. Market research may guide the product engineers in their work to improve existing product or to develop a new product to satisfy the needs of the Consumer. The design of product and the characteristics are to be analyzed in the light of the economics of production methods, volume of Production and product varieties and so on.

2.2.1. Marketing Aspect

It is necessary to establish that wether the product will satisfy the user or not. That is, will it give the services expected by the consumer or not. If the product does not satisfy the needs of the consumer, the product cannot be sold in the market. If no consumption is there, there is no point in producing such product. In case the product satisfy the consumer, then the manufacturer has to consider, Whether similar product already exists in the market. If the demand for the product already exists in the market, its volume of sales can be assessed by market survey. If the product is altogether a new one its demand may be assessed from the demand figures of related/identical or similar products. Say for example, a type manufacturer can estimate his demand depending as the sales figure of Vehicles. Demand can also be created with the introduction of new product/product usage. Some times by giving attention to physical design or changing the design of Containers, we can create the demand. For example consider the product Horlicks. The manufacturers change the design of the container to create demand or to face competition. The figure 2.1 shows the changes in the design of container.

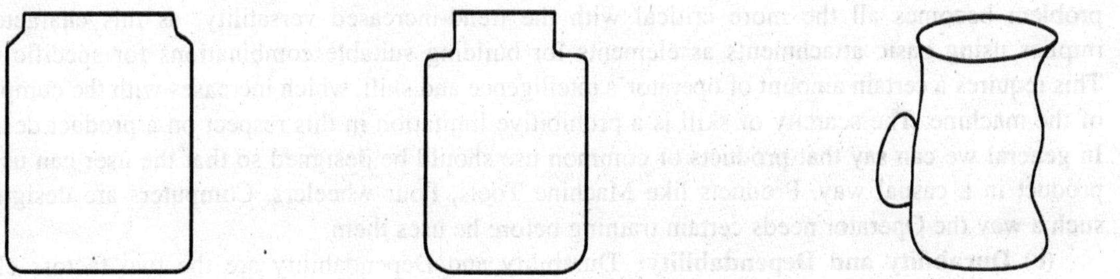

(*a*) Conventional design (*b*) Unbreakable plastic jar (*c*) Changed design of container

Fig. 2.1 : Containers of a product.

Also consider the example of soft drinks. Formerly they use to supply the drink in 250 ml bottles. Now 1 1/2 Lt bottels are available in the market. To create demand or to face competition always manufactures will think of offering new properties for their product. In market research, experience and sound judgment are required to evaluate and apply the results of such research.

Another important question one has to consider in marketing is should the customer get what exactly he needs or should he be offered what he supposed to want? Basically this is an economic question, if management wants to give maximum satisfaction and decide itself to supply the customer with what he wants, it may have to produce an infinite variety of products to suit individual user taste. On the other hand, if it decides to produce what ideally suits the customer, the sales department to educate the potential customer through advertisement compains. In practice product design is a compromise between the above two extremes.

2.2.2. Product Characteristics

As the product has to satisfy needs of a customer regarding use, appearance and life of the product the designer must see that the products will have the following Characteristics.

(*a*) **Functional Aspect:** When the marketing possibilities have been explored, the functional scope of the product has to be carefully analyzed and defined. The definition of objective itself nearly tells the customer very much about the functional scope or uses offered by the product.

Consider an example of Bathing soap; let us say that the soap has a clearly defined objective of keeping the users body clean for the day. If does not state however whether it improves complexion or not. Before a user purchases the product what he can expect from the product should be clearly defined. Take another example of Washing Machine. The defined objective is to wash clothes. How washing is carried out, what other uses offered should be clearly stated. Whether the Washer heats the Water before washing rinsing or drying the washed clothes is also done by machine? If so, how is it done? Everything should be clearly defined. A functional analysis of this kind affects the design of the machine/product, its appearance and its cost. As we go on adding more and more functions to the basic function, the design becomes complicated and maintenance of the product will be a problem. It is also possible to detach the functional aspects and usage can be left to the customer's choice. There is also a trend to offer functional versatility of the products, there by increasing the range of applications. For example, domestic grinders, sofa-cum-bed etc.

(b) Operational Aspect: After defining the functional aspect, Operational Aspect has to be considered. Not only, the product offers desired service (functions) to the customer, but it must be easy to handle and simple to operate. Sometimes the product has to be adoptable to various operational conditions and very often it is subjected to varying degree of skill of operator or user. The designer's problem becomes all the more critical with the trend-increased versatility, as this characteristic implies using basic attachments as elements for building suitable combinations for specific users. This requires a certain amount of operator's intelligence and skill, which increases with the complexity of the machine. The scarcity of skill is a prohibitive limitation in this respect on a product designer. In general we can say that products of common use should be designed so that the user can use that product in a casual way. Products like Machine Tools, Four wheelers, Computers are designed in such a way the Operator needs certain training before he uses them.

(c) Durability and Dependability: Durability and Dependability are the two factors closely realted to the selection of materials and class if workmanship which once again dictate the design of the product and the economical analysis and the cost of the product. Quality is not always a simple characteristic to define, but durability and Dependability are two factors that often determine the quality and have to be carefully considered by the designer. *Durability is defined as length of Active life of the product under given working conditions.* Durability need not always be associated with the selection of good material. The actual active life of certain products like: Matches, Rocket motors, Crackers may be rather limited, but this does not mean the materials for said products may be of low quality. Therefore additional character to be considered. That is *Dependability. Dependability is the capability of the Product to function, when called up on to do its its job.*To manufacture Rocket Motor, more dependable first class material is used in spite of its small active life. One more factor to be considered with durability is about maintenance and repair of the product. This is because the amount of repair and preventive maintenance required for certain products are closely related to quality and design policy. This is particularly important, when equipment is supposed to operate continuously and any repair due to malfunctioning or break down involves a less of production time.

(d) Aesthetic Aspect: Aesthetic quality refers to the physical appearance of the product. How does it affect the design of the product? In most cases, where the functional scope, durability and dependability have already been defined, the Aesthetic property is mainly concerned with designing and modeling the final shape around the basic skeleton. For example consider the transport busses. We have ordinary passanger busses with conventional shape of the body, where as luxury and High-Tech busses have an attractive, eye-catching body. We can quote a good number of examples such as Refrigerator, Domestic grinders, and electronic and electrical goods. Molding of shape may very often be severely limited in scope, and what finally emerges is some times termed as functional shape. This functional shape need not necessarily diverted from what is known as Aesthetic Shape. This can be identified with the examples of Consumer goods. Those who believe the functional shape argue that aesthetic shape is also as important as functional shape and it should be considered at the design stage. Others argue that Aesthetic shape is more important in marketing aspect and hence should be given more importance. In some cases this may have financial implication hence it is advisable to analyze the cost of Aesthetic aspect carefully. In some extreme cases, Aesthetic property is the governing factor in the design of a product and completely dominates it. The best example is the fancy goods, consumer goods, household equipment and so on.

When styling the shape is the dominant factor in product design, it is often used by the designer, introduction of new ideas, through which quickly out date the previous design. If the market is psychologically receptive and eager to discard old designs in favor in new ones, styling the product becomes racing against time. This race determines the salability of the product. Aesthetic value can be considerably increased by selecting desired natural, color, texture and sometimes even a line will give great economic advantage, as large verities of the product can be manufactured at comparatively low cost. The basic product remains same and variety can be achieved at low cost. Here the knowledge of materials, processes may help the designer to allow for vast number of colors and textures to be offered with little difficulty. Figure 2.2 shows functional shape of Aesthetic shape.

(*a*) Functional shape (*b*) Aesthetic shape

Fig. 2.2 : Functional and Aesthetic Shapes.

2.2.3. Economic Analysis

The economic analysis is an important factor to the management in taking decisions regarding the product design policy. After getting sufficient information about customer requirement and market potentialities on one hand and a detailed study about the functional, operational and quality aspect of the proposed product on the other, the economic analysis will start. Answering the questions below sequentially does this.

(*a*) What capital expenditure is required for manufacturing the product decided by the company?

(*b*) What is the expected production cost of the product?

(*c*) What is the reasonable margin of profit that can be expected?

(*d*) Do the price and future of the product render it competitive in the market?

(*e*) What are the expected sales?

All the above questions are interrelated. Not a single question stated above can be isolated and considered independently of others. The economic analysis is in fact a cyclic and respective procedure and the data provided by the previous question, and all the answers checked when their term comes, again to be revaluated in cycle, once a state of equilibrium is reached in the answers, no further modifications to those answers are required. But the analysis cannot be stopped.

(*a*) **Specialisation:** At the time of planning, the company has to decide to what extent it should specialize in the product line. In case company cannot fix the extent of specialization in product line, the enterprise is likely to grow to unprofitable proportions. There are companies, which add unrelated products to their product line. The optimal degree of specialization is such an important factor in the welfare of the company. The decision to add or discontiune the production outside the scope of its available resources like skill and facilities should be made by the management committee, which includes all the concerned heads of department. Good planning will of course, keep company from expanding beyond its framework of its product line i.e., specialty, manageability and profitability.

When an enterprise thinks of introducing a new product, the management has to decide whether the new product will suit their facilities available, without diluting the skills or unduly increasing the complexities of the business. Think of a company manufacturing washing soap for example. In case the company thinks of manufacturing soap powder for washing, it does not require too much of new equipments or too many new skills. But Soap Company thinks of manufacturing a television, it creates lot of difficulties. It is better to start a new company to manufacture the television than incorporating it in the same Soap Company.

(*b*) **Standardization:** Standardization in its broder sense permits almost all fields of human life. A standard in general, be defined as a model or a rule established by authority, custom or a general consent. The words standard and standardization are used more and more today in connection with Technology, Industry and Production Processes. Standardization is essential to modern mass production economy. Indian standard Institution (ISI) coordinates and promotes standardization in co-operation with various industries. Standardization is extremely useful technique designed to bring about overall economy, by increasing productivity. The aims of standardization are.

(*i*) To achieve economy in terms of cost, human effort, conservation of essential and scarce material.

(*ii*) To ensure maximum convenience by variety reduction, interchangeability of parts, reducing the inventories, elimination of waste, which are the means of increasing productivity.

(*iii*) Adopt the best possible solutions to recurring problems of economy and convenience using all the available scientific knowledge and latest technological developments.

(*iv*) To maintain the desired level of productivity.

(*c*) **Simplification:** Simplification refers to reduction of types, size, colors and other characteristics. In simple word it is reduction of varieties of finished products to obtain the lowest manufacturing and distribution cost, consistent with serving essential human wants. It can be done within companies, within industries or with in the nation. Industrial committee formed for this purpose can determine the types, sizes and varieties of products that will effectively meet consumer requirements. The benefits of adapting simplification are:

(*i*) Large amount capital is not tied up in slow moving stocks of large varieties.

(*ii*) Economical manufacturing due to simplified inspection requirements, longer runs and fewer changes in machine setups reduction in idle time of equipments, less stock to handle and reduced clerical overload.

(*iii*) Continuous employment instead of temporary or seasonal employment depending on the demand of product varieties.

(*iv*) Prompt delivery of goods to the Consumers and

(*v*) Less obsolescence of materials and machinery.

The starting of any programme of simplifcation of variety reduction is the analysis of stores ledger or purchase orders and sales records. This will reveal the situation prevailing in the stores and indicate areas where variety reduction program may be profitably started. The list of information to be collected from records for analysis is given below:

(*i*) The frequency of demand for each type of an item in terms of quantity or numbers purchased.

(*ii*) Proportion of standard items purchased.

(*iii*) Proportion of standardizable items.

The data collected from the records is systematically arranged to know, the range and variety in which each item is used. It generally happens that the demand is most frequent for some types of sizes and tapers on both sides of this type as shown in figure 2.3

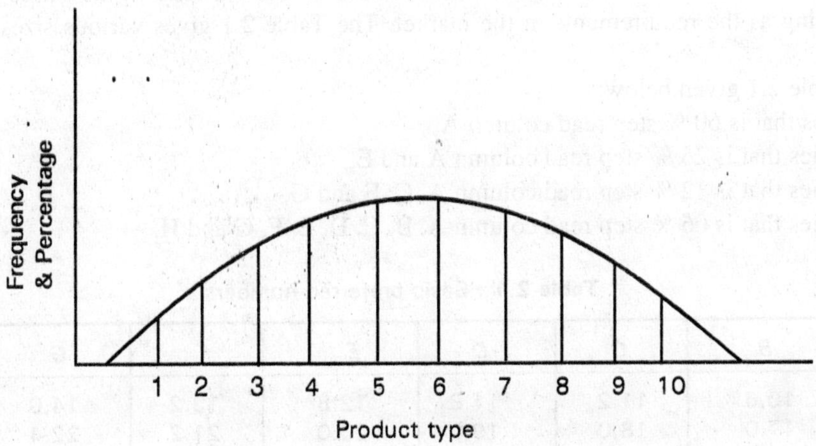

Fig. 2.3 : Frequency distribution of varieties.

Numbers 4, 5 and 6 have greater frequency and these varieties are selected for production (or purchase) and rest can be dropped. Another method of finding the varieties that is to be manufactured is by the use of preferred numbers. This method is more useful when frequency distribution is not normal, in some cases we can also notice that demand is usually concentrated around few sizes and types only. In such cases a series of standard sizes in suitable steps will be required. This series is generally determined by using preferred numbers, which are numbers derived from five series in geometrical progression. Mr. Renard, an engineer in French Army, invented these numbers. These five series are designated as R-5, R-10, R-20, R-40, and R-80 series. In each series, if the first size is 10, the last size will be 100. For example R-5 steps in geometrical progression to reach from any one size to 10 times of that size. The common ratio between steps is represented by 'r'. For example in R-5 series if first size is 10, next sizes will be 10r, $10r^2$, $10r^3$ $10r^4$ and $10r^5$.

Sizes:	10		10r		$10r^2$		$10r^3$		$10r^4$		$10r^5$
Steps:		1		2		3		4		5	

As the first size is 10, the last size is 10 r^5 = 100, therefore
R^5 = (100/10) = 10 and r = $\sqrt[5]{10}$ = 1.5849 or approximately = 1.6. The other steps are:

Step	*Series*	*Common ratio*	*Step increased by*
1	*R*-5	$r = \sqrt[5]{10}$ = 1.5549	60%
2	*R*-10	$r = \sqrt[5]{10}$ = 1.2589	25%

3	*R*-20	$r = \sqrt[5]{10} = 1.1220$	12%
4	*R*-40	$r = \sqrt[5]{10} = 1.0593$	06%
5	*R*-80	$r = \sqrt[5]{10} = 1.0291$	03%

Examples are:

(i) Wattage of electrical bulbs

(ii) Currency notes and coins

(iii) Paint tins

While finding the actual size of the product, the preferred numbers are rounded off to the nearest whole numbers. It is left to the management to produce all the varieties in the series or only few of them depending as the requirements in the market. The Table 2.1 gives various sizes in all the five series.

In the table 2.1 given below:

R-5 series that is 60 % step read column A,

R-10 series that is 25 % step read column A and E,

R-20 series that is 12 % step read column A, C, E and G,

R-40 series that is 06 % step read column A, B, C, D, E, F, G and H.

Table 2.1 : Basic preferred numbers

A	*B*	*C*	*D*	*E*	*F*	*G*	*H*
10	10.6	11.2	11.8	12.5	13.2	14.0	15.0
16	17.0	18.0	19.0	20.0	21.2	22.4	23.6
25	26.5	28.0	30.0	31.5	33.5	35.5	37.5
40	42.5	45.0	47.5	50.0	53.0	56.0	60.0
63	67.0	71.0	75.0	80.0	85.0	90.0	95.0
100	—	—	—	—	—	—	—

2.2.4. Break-even Analysis

After considering product characterstics such as functional, operational, quality, aesthetic aspects and applying specialization, standardization and simplification, management more or less arrive at a decisions as what to produce and in how many varieties. In fact, physical characteristics are decided in the above phase, before preparing the plans for regular production, the management has to decide that what is the minimum quantity that must be produced and sold so as to run the business profitably. The quantity can be found by applying break-even analysis. To understand the break-even analysis one must understand the cost structure of a product. The total cost of the product is made up of

(*a*) Fixed costs and

(*b*) Variable cost.

(*a*) **Fixed cost:** -Fixed cost consists of all those costs or expenditure, which will not vary with the quantity produced below the capacity of the plant. Examples of fixed costs are: Rent, Interest, Insurgence, Factory Power Costs, Salaries of Managers Etc.

(*b*) **Variable Cost:** -This consists of those costs, which will vary directly with the quantity produced. Examples are direct labour cost, material costs, and fuel consumption charges of Machines. When we add overhead charges to the sum of fixed costs and variable costs, we get the total cost. Figure 2.4 shows the break-up of cost structure.

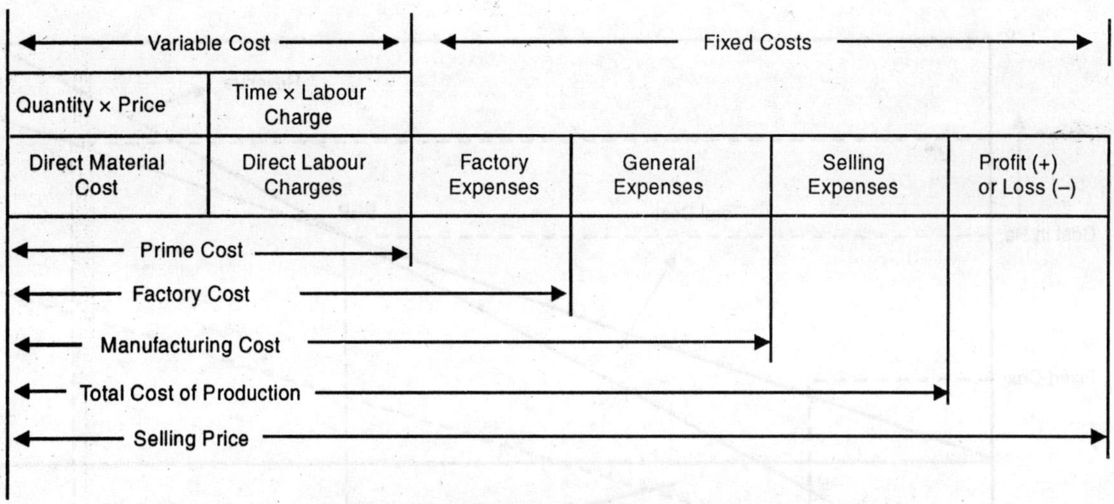

Fig. 2.4 : Elements of Cost Structure of a Product.

Break-even Analysis makes use of the fixed and variable nature of Costs to indicate the range of volume necessary for profitable operation of the plant. The part of revenue, which is absorbed by fixed costs, is known as *Contribution*. Contribution is equal to the difference between sales Revenue and variable costs. Contribution :

S = Sales Revenue and V is the Variable Costs.

$$C = S - V$$

Then

If F= Fixed costs and P=Profit in Rupees then

$$S = F + V + P \quad \text{OR} \quad P = S - F - V$$

Because $C = S - V$, $\quad P = C - F$

If C is less than F, it means to say that organization is running in loss.

Now Consider that

V = Variable cost Per Unit in Rupees.

S = Sales price per unit in Rupees.

F = Fixed costs in Rupees.

Q = Break-even point is given by,

At Break-even point the Revenue earned by the company is equals to the expenditure incurred.

There fore $F + Q \times V = Q \times S$

$$\text{or } Q \text{ in Units} = \frac{F}{(S-V)} = \frac{\text{Fixed Costs}}{\text{Contribution per unit}}$$

Figure 2.5 gives the graph showing Break-even point.

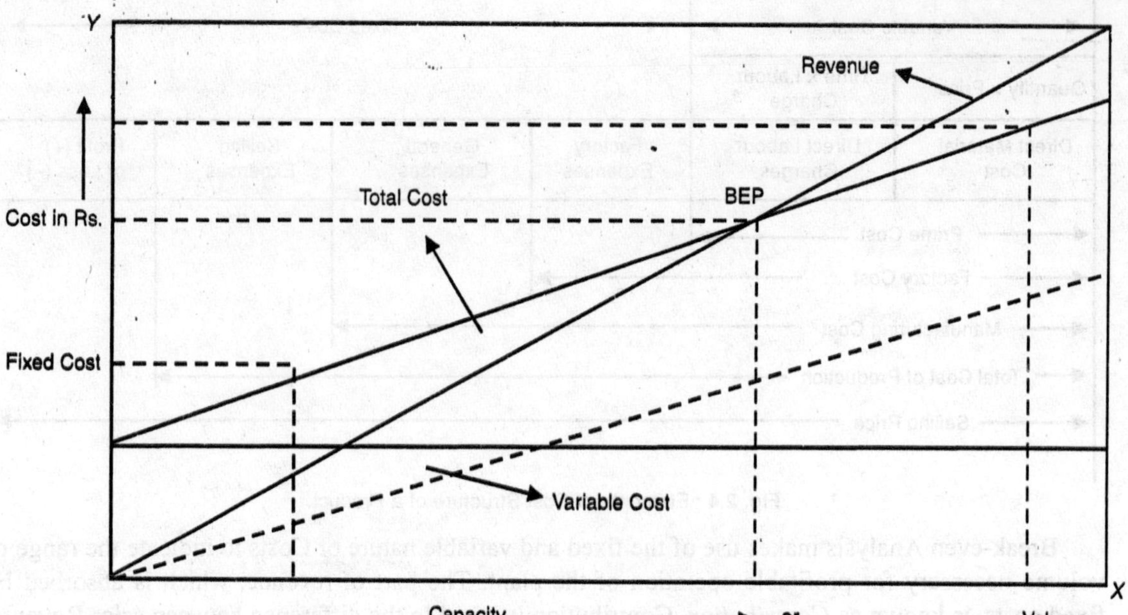

Fig. 2.5 Break Even Chart.

Break-even analysis is a part of marginal costing, basically it is concerned with finding the point at which revenues and costs agree exactly, hence the term (1) Break-even. The Break-even point is, therefore, the volume of output at which neither profit is made nor a loss is incurred.

As a result of calculating break-even point the financial department can realize that many valuable facts, all essential for operating a business enterprise, can emerge from the exercise. Some typical problems that can solved from Break-even analysis are:

(*i*) A reasonable return on capital employed.

(*ii*) To compare a number of companies by arranging probable earnings from each in order of magnitude.

(*iii*) Determination of the price of a product, which will give the desired break-even point and profit.

(*iv*) Calculation of costs and revenues for all possible volumes of output there by helping in fixing sales budget.

(*v*) Variable costs per unit can be calculated quite easily from a break-even chart.

(*vi*) The cash involved in obtaining on particular Volume of output.

Problems

Example 2.1 **: The fixed costs Per year are Rs. 40,000. Variable cost per unit for the single product is Rs. 2/- Estimated sales for the period is Rs. 1,00,000. The number of units involved coincides with the expected volume of output. Each unit is sold at Rs. 10/- each. Find the break-even point.**

Solution:

$$\text{Break even point } (BEP) = \frac{F}{1-\frac{V}{P}},$$

where
F = Fixed costs in Rupees.
V = Variable cost in Rupees per Unit.
P = selling price per unit in Rupees.

$$\text{B.E.P} = \frac{4,000}{1-\frac{2}{10}} = \text{Rs.}50,000$$

= Total sales value (= S) in Rupees.

(OR)

Break-even point is = $\frac{F}{P-V}$ Units
where F = Fixed Costs in Rupees
P = Selling Price
V = Variable cost per unit in Rupees.
40000/(10–2) = Rs. 50,000.
i.e., 5000 units × Rs. 10 = Rs. 50,000.

Example 2.2 : Variable Costs are 60% of the sales and fixed costs are Rs.30,00,000. Compute profit if total sales are Rs. 10,000,000.

Solution:

Since C = S – V, where C = Contribution in Rupees
S = Sales Revenue in Rupees
V = Variable cost in Rupees.

C = S – 60% of S   S = 40% of S

$$\therefore \quad C = \frac{40}{100} \times 10,000,000 = 40,000,00$$

P = S = V = F = C = F = 4,000,000 – 3,000,000.
= Rs. 1,000,000.

Break-even Point and Profits may change because of any one of the following:

(*i*) **Change in Volume of Production:** This has a direct effect on profits, break-even point and contribution.

(*ii*) **Change in Product Mix:** Profits, Break-even point contribution all will change.

(*iii*) **Change in Performance:** Performance of labour, quality of materials will also affect break-even point, profits and Contribution.

(*iv*) **Change in Fixed Costs:** This affects profits, break-even point.

(*v*) **Change in Selling Price:** All the there i.e., B.E.P, Profits and contribution will change.

2.2.5. Effect of Management Decision on Break-even Point

(i) To Increase in Plant Capacity: Factory fixed costs are increased. If variable costs are the same as that of the existing plant, the break-even point will go up. If we assume that the sales volume can be increased in proportion to the increased capacity, profits will go up. Often a new capacity has lower variable costs, because of improved facility and facility layout, labour savings devices and other technological improvements. This fact may partially or completely counter balance the effect of greater fixed costs on B.E.P and the effect on profit would be magnified.

***(ii)* To Replenish Obsolute Plant and Equipment:** Generally fixed costs will increase and variable costs will reduce. The effect will be same discussed above in (i).

***(iii)* To Manufacture the Components Previously Bought:** If unused capacity (idle capacity) can be utilized to manufacture the components, as is often the case, the net effect is on variable costs. Which has a direct effect on the B.E.P. If the process fixed costs are increased because of adoption of new facility the net effect as B.E.P and gross profits will depend on the direction and the magnitude of the change in the variable cost.

***(iv)* To Purchase of Components Previously Manufactured:** Effect depends upon the actual magnitude of the costs that can be disposed.

***(v)* To Retain Certain Labour Skill at the Minimum Level of Seasonal Requirements:** Some variable costs have been converted into fixed costs, the BEP may go up.

***(vi)* To Utilise Overtime to Increase the Capacity:** Variable costs increased hence B.E.P goes up. As the volume of production increased and the net effect on profit will depend upon the relationships of the beginning and ending slopes of total cost line and the magnitude of actual volume gain.

Usefulness of B.E.P.: The break-even concept is important in analyzing many business problems. Even though some times it is difficult to separate fixed and variable costs or in multi product companies. The division of fixed costs is difficult to divide product wise, the analysis makes it possible to decide economic manufacturing quantity which in term helps in budget by controls, profit planning and process selection. BEP helps to take important decision at critical stages of production planning. The break-even analysis is widely accepted and applied in product quantity (Volume of Production) analysis. Behavior of B.E.P in changed condition also shows overall effect of management decision in any business field. At the time of the dull business, a manager to reach break-even, allows certain discount, or sales promotion by reduction in selling price or offer some gifts.... etc, He can decide the magnitude of finance he can allow for the above so as to reach B.E.P at a bit higher level.

2.2.6. Profit and Competetiveness

The competitiveness of the product is measured in terms of the market share it has captured. This largely depends upon the preference (worth) the consumer is prepared to attach to the product and the ratio of worth to price. (Value=worth/price). Consumer assessment of value is not uniform and varies from person to person, time-to-time. And situation to situation. It may a time depends on preference of product features, performance, taste. A state of equilibrium is found in which the market is divided between different preferences. This equilibrium may change by the ratio of worth to price of the product becomes more favorable, when compared with other brands of similar products, the product increases its portion of the market and becomes more competitive. Such equilibrium is shown in figure 2.6. In the figure, the total cost, of a product includes set-up cost, Materials cost, overheads, storage and distribution cost. The profit expected is determined by the margin of profit per unit and by the sales volume. If the organization wants to increase its profits it can follow any one of the strategies given below.

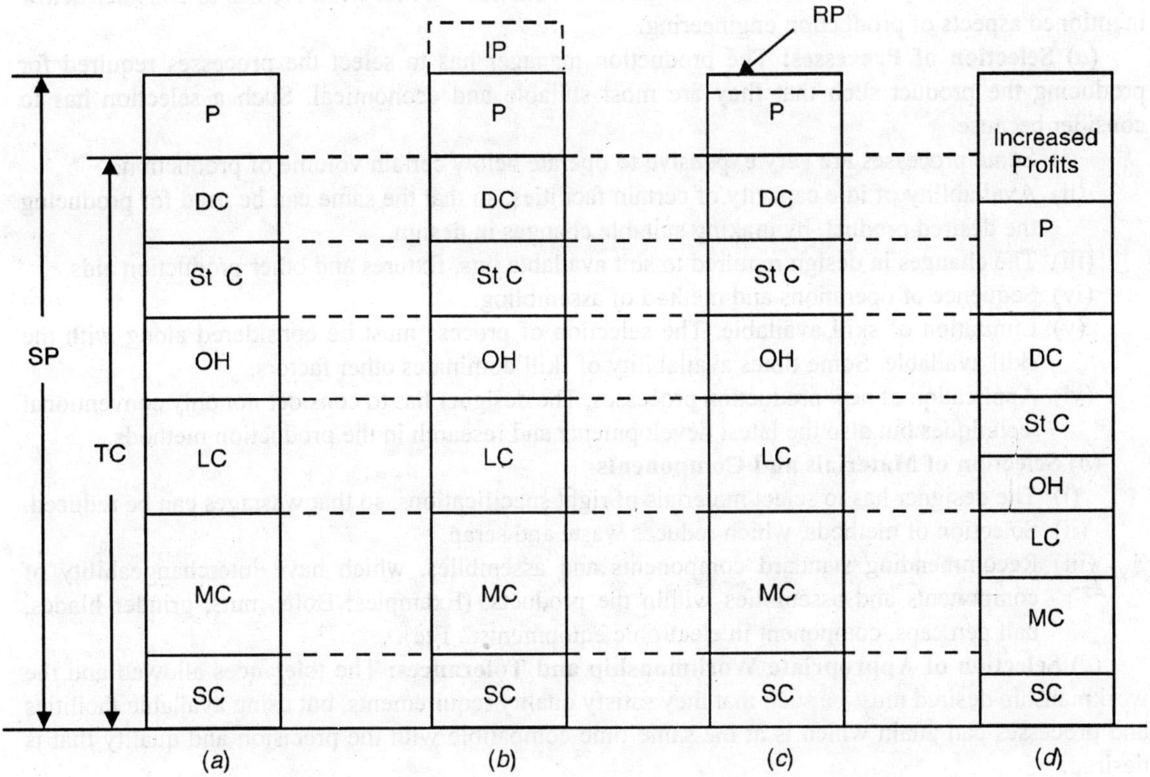

MC = Material Cost, LC = Labour Cost, SC = Set up Cost, OH = Over Heads, St C = Storage Cost, DC = Distribution Cost, P = Profit, L = Loss, IP = Increased Profit, RP = Reduced Profit Margin., SP = Selling Price, TC = Total Cost

Fig. 2.6 : Methods of increasing the profits.

Any business firm can increase its profits by :

(*i*) Increasing the sales price by increasing the profit margin. But if the firms are operating in a competitive market its sales volume may be decreased. If the customer prefers a product, which is available at lower price, then the firm has to face difficulty to sell its product. Shrinkage in the market leads to decline in total profit

(*ii*) The business can increase its sales volume by reducing the profit margin per unit. As the firm has to operate in competitive market too low margin of profit per unit will create a problem in unstable market (changes in market).

(*iii*) The best strategy is to reduce the total costs by applying cost reduction techniques or by increasing the productivity. The firm has to incur certain marginal expenditure for application of techniques. But it should see that it would not sacrifice quality.

2.3. PRODUCTION ASPECT

After dealing with all the above-discussed factors, finally it has to consider the production aspect. The product need not only be well designed and drawings are drawn but its design must also be capable of producing with the facilities available in the production shop. The designer has to keep in mind number of factors regarding production to arrive at a feasible solution. He has to design the product in such a way that the motto "Design for Production" is met with. He has to consider below mentioned aspects of production engineering.

(*a*) Selection of Processes: The production manager has to select the processes required for producing the product such that they are most suitable and economical. Such a selection has to consider because.

(i) Some processes are very expensive to operate below certain volume of production.
(ii) Availability of idle capacity of certain facilities, so that the same can be used for producing the desired product, by making suitable changes in design.
(iii) The changes in design required to suit available jigs, fixtures and other production aids.
(iv) Sequence of operations and method of assembling.
(v) Limitation of skill available. The selection of process must be considered along with the skill available. Some times availability of skill dominates other factors.
(vi) Application of new production processes. The designer has to consider not only conventional techniques but also the latest developments and research in the production methods.

(*b*) Selection of Materials and Components

(i) The designer has to select materials of right specifications, so that wastages can be reduced.
(ii) Selection of methods, which reduces waste and scrap.
(iii) Recommending standard components and assemblies, which have interchangeability of components and assemblies within the products. (Examples: Bolts, nuts, grinder blades, ball pen caps, component in electronic equipments... Etc).

(*c*) Selection of Appropriate Workmanship and Tolerances: The tolerances allowed and the workmanship desired must be such that they satisfy quality requirements, but using available facilities and processes can attain which is at the same time compatible with the precision and quality that is desired.

In general we can say the Product designed must have

(*i*) High reliability
(*ii*) Redundancy
(*iii*) Compatibility
(*iv*) Reduced verities or simplification
(*v*) Interchangeability
(*vi*) Standardization
(*vii*) Maintainability.

Reliability refers to the degree of confidence that a product will render its service under prescribed conditions. Redundancy refers to that a product taking the form of duplicate component. This is particularly true where failure of component is high. Compatibility, the property of proper assembling or joining of components. Interchangeability refers to that aspect two components of a product manufactured in different places or by different firms will assemble together to give the desired service. Standardization and interchangeability are the two important aspects of mass production. Maintainability refers to that aspect by which it will be easier for its user to maintain the product. That is to say, it should be easy for him to dissemble the component at the time of failure and repair it with reasonable amount of effort.

One more aspect that the designer has to consider is that the user must be in a position to detach the components (modules) easily and replace it by similar component (modules). The failed component may be sent for repairs, meanwhile the system, will work with the replaced module. If the failed module cannot be repaired, it can be scrapped. We have plenty of examples for this type of design, which is known as Modular design. Examples are: Spark Plug, Spare tyre, Electronic components and so an.

QUESTIONS

1. Explain the factors to be considered at product design stage. Give suitable examples.
2. Write short notes on.
   (*a*) Standardization
   (*b*) Simplification
   (*c*) Break-even analysis
   (*d*) Modular design
3. The cost of producing between 1520 units and 2,500 units of a product consists of fixed costs of Rs.25, 000/- and variable cost per unit is Rs.10/- If the selling price is Rs.20/- per unit, find the break even point.

3

FORECASTING

- Introduction
- Definition.
- Period of Forecasting.
- Accuracy of Forecasting.
- Forecasting Types
- Steps in Forecasting
- Forecasting Methods
- Method of Least Squares
- Exponential Smoothening
- Correlations and Regression Analysis for Forecasting
- Input-Output Analysis
- Econometrics

3.1. INTRODUCTION

When we hear the word forecasting, first thing comes to our mind is the image of a fortune teller or an astrologer, Every one of us forecast, no doubts we do with certain amount of skepticism and doubt, Students, when they have to write examination, by referring to old question papers, guess probable questions that may appear in examination. If such is the case of a student, going for an examination, just think of a manager dealing with the affairs of a multi product company – he is very much concerned with forecasting the sales, finance required, materials required and so on. Any business manager, generally forecast either consciously or without realizing that he is doing so .In this chapter. Let us deal with importance of forecasting and types of forecasting.

3.2. DEFINITION

Henry Fayol describes that foresight is not the whole of management, but at least it is an essential part of management. According to him to foresee in this context means " both to assess the future and make provisions for it, that is forecasting is itself action already. He describes forecasting as a kind of future picture wherein proximate events are outlined with some distinctness, while remote events appear progressively less distinct, and it entails the running of the business as foresee and provide means to run the business over a definite period.

As far as the marketing manager is concerned the **sales forecast** is an estimate of the amount of unit sales for a specified future period under the proposed marketing plan or program. It may also be defined as an estimate of sales in rupees of physical units for a specified future period under a proposed marketing plan or program and under an assumed set of economic and other force outside the organization for which the forecast is made.

When we consider the function of production management, no doubt Production department will produce goods as per the sales program given by the sales department, but it has to prepare forecast regarding machine capacity required, materials required and time required for production and so on. This needs the knowledge of what exactly happened in the production shop in previous periods.

Making of a proper forecast requires the assessment of both controllable and uncontrollable factors {both economic and non economic} inside and outside the organization.

3.3. PERIOD OF FORECASTING

The period of forecasting, that is the time range selected for forecasting depends on the purpose for which the forecast is made. The period may vary from one week to some years. Depending upon the period, the forecast can be termed as ' Short range forecasting,' Medium range forecasting' and Long range forecasting. Short- range forecasting period may be –one week, two weeks or a couple of months. Medium range forecasting period may vary from 3 to 6 months. Long- range forecasting period may vary from one year to any period. The objective of above said forecast is naturally different.

In general, short term forecasting will be of more useful in production planning. The manager who does short range forecast must see that they are very nearer to the accuracy.

In long range forecast, the normal period used is generally 5 years. In some cases it may extends to 10 to 15 years also. The purpose of long- range forecast is:

(*i*) To work out expected capital expenditure for future developments or to acquire new facilities.
(*ii*) To determine expected cash flow from sales,
(*iii*) Plan for future manpower requirements,
(*iv*) To plan for material requirement,
(*v*) Plan for Research and Development.

Here much importance is given to long- range growth factor.

In case of medium range forecasting the period may extend over to one or two years.

The purpose of this type of forecasting is:

(*i*) To determine budgetary control over expenses,
(*ii*) To determine dividend policy,
(*iii*) To find and control maintenance expenses,
(*iv*) To determine schedule of operations,
(*v*) To plan for capacity adjustments.

In case of short-term forecast, which extends from few weeks to three or six months. The purpose, is:

(*i*) Estimate inventory requirement,
(*ii*) To provide transport facilities for finished goods,
(*iii*) To decide work loads for men and machines,
(*iv*) To find the working capital needed,
(*v*) Setting up of production run for the products,
(vi) Fixing sales quota,
(*vii*) Finding the required overtime to meet the delivery promises.

3.4. ACCURACY OF FORECAST

Every one who use the forecast for one purpose or the other expects that they need that forecast should be accurate. But it is practically impossible to forecast accurately. But decisions are still made everyday to run the business by using the best information available with them. Management scientists have developed various methods for forecasting. One has to decide which method has to be used to suit the information available with him and to suit his needs. The manager, who is concerned with forecasting, must have knowledge of factors influencing forecast. Various factors that influence the forecast are:

(*i*) Environmental changes,
(*ii*) Changes in the preference of the user,
(*iii*) Number of competitive products,
(*iv*) Disposable income of the consumer.

In forecasting the production important factors to be considered are:

(*i*) Demand from the marketing department,
(*ii*) Rate of labors absenteeism,
(*iii*) Availability of materials,
(*iv*) Available capacity of machines,
(*v*) Maintenance schedules,
(*vi*) Delivery date schedules.

3.5. FORECASTING TYPES

(*a*) **Forecasting for New Products:** It is very difficult to make forecast of demand when one is involved in manufacturing a new product. To create awareness of the product in customers is essential. The marketing team has to go to potential customers and educate them regarding the uses of the new product. The various methods used are shown in figure 3.1.

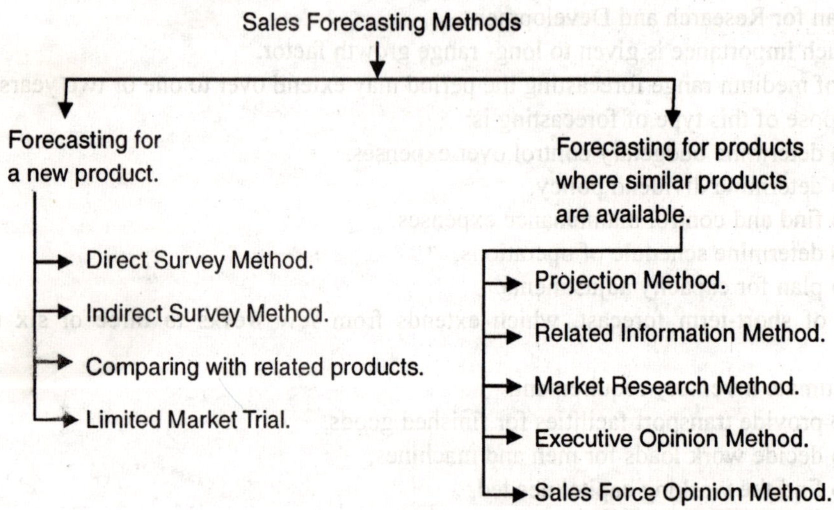

Fig. 3.1 : Sales Forecasting Methods.

3.5.1. (*i*) **Direct Survey Method :** In this method potential customers are contacted personally and information regarding what they expect from the product is collected A questionnaire is given to the customers and answers are collected. Collected data is analyzed to make the forecast. This is time consuming and bit costly method. This method is particularly useful for forecasting for capital goods.

(*ii*) **Indirect Survey Method**: The required information is collected from product representatives, whole sellers and rëtail sellers and the collected data is analyzed to get the information for making the forecast.

(*iii*) **Comparing with related products:** When the product is comparable with other products as far as uses are concerned, the sales data of that product is taken as guide lines for making forecast for the new product.

(*iv*) **Limited market trial method:** Some times a sample is manufactured (in the firm or get manufactured by other firms) and sold in the test market to get the consumer views and after knowing the pulse of the consumer, forecast can be made.

3.5.2. FORECASTING FOR ESTABLISHED PRODUCTS

(*i*) **Projection Method:** The Historical data of a product can be prepared from the data available in the company's records. Such tabulated data in terms of period and sales is known as time series. Basing on the time series data, the forecast for the product can be projected to the future period. Various methods of projection is given in the figure 3.2

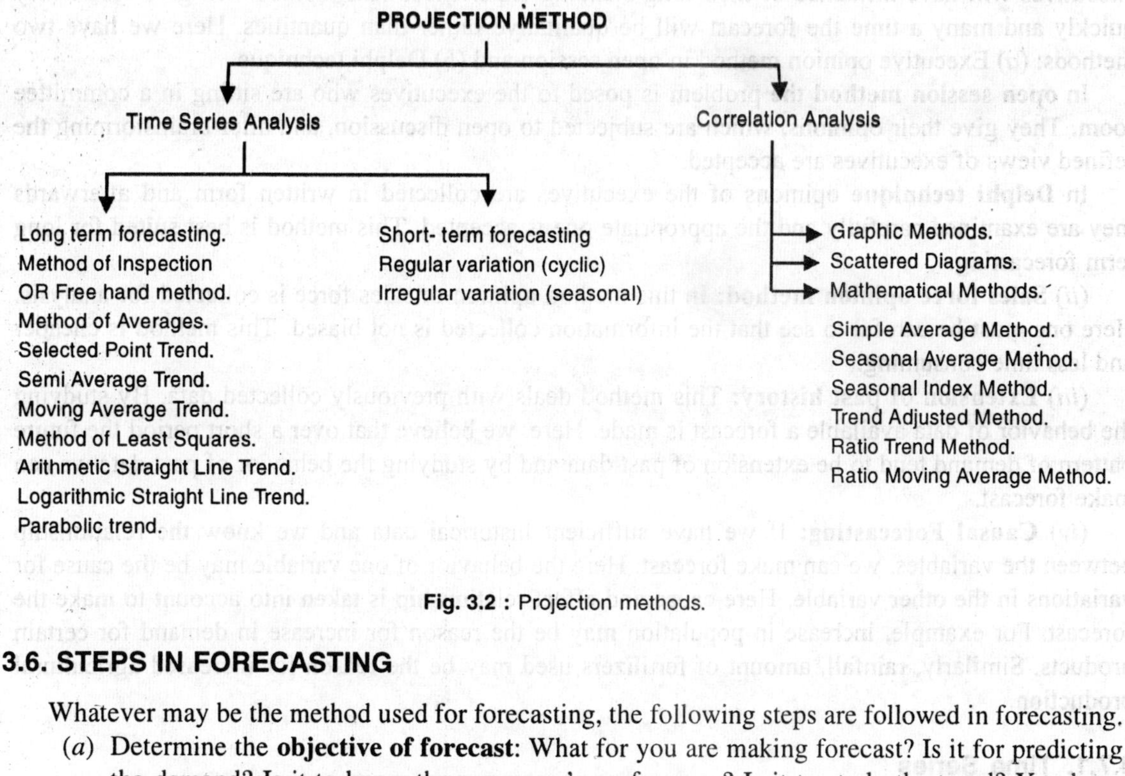

Fig. 3.2 : Projection methods.

3.6. STEPS IN FORECASTING

Whatever may be the method used for forecasting, the following steps are followed in forecasting.

(*a*) Determine the **objective of forecast**: What for you are making forecast? Is it for predicting the demand? Is it to know the consumer's preferences? Is it to study the trend? You have to spell out clearly the use of forecast.

(*b*) Select the period over which the forecast will be made? Is it long-term forecast or medium-term forecast or short term forecast? What are your information needs over that period?

(*c*) Select the method you want to use for making the forecast. This method depends on the period selected for the forecast and the information or data available on hand. It also depends on what you expect from the information you get from the forecast. Select appropriate method for making forecast.

(*d*) Gather information to be used in the forecast. The data you use for making forecast has to produce the result, which is of great use to you. The data may be collected by:

(*i*) *Primary source*: This data we will get from the records of the firm itself.

(*ii*) *Secondary source*: This is available from outside means, such as published data, magazines, educational institutions…etc.,

(*e*) Make the forecast: Using the data collected in the selected method of forecasting, the forecast is made.

3.7. FORECASTING METHODS

All the forecasting methods can be classified as:

(*i*) Judgmental forecast, (*ii*) Sales force opinion Method. (*iii*) Extension of past history, (*iv*) Causal forecasting.

(*i*) **Judgmental forecasting:** Here the opinion of senior sales managers, marketing executives is collected and analyzed to make the forecast. In many cases the opinion given by these senior executives will have influence of their long-standing experience. This method will give result very quickly and many a time the forecast will be qualitative rather than quantities. Here we have two methods: (*a*) Executive opinion method in open session and (*b*) Delphi technique.

In **open session method** the problem is posed to the executives who are sitting in a committee room. They give their opinions, which are subjected to open discussion, and after brainstorming the refined views of executives are accepted.

In **Delphi technique** opinions of the executives are collected in written form and afterwards they are examined carefully and the appropriate one is accepted. This method is best suited for long term forecasting.

(*ii*) **Sales force opinion method:** In this method opinion of sales force is collected for analysis. Here one must be careful to see that the information collected is not biased. This method is cheaper and less time consuming.

(*iii*) **Extension of past history:** This method deals with previously collected data. By studying the behavior of data available a forecast is made. Here, we believe that over a short period the future pattern of demand tend to be extension of past data and by studying the behavior of past data we can make forecast.

(*iv*) **Causal Forecasting:** If we have sufficient historical data and we know the relationship between the variables, we can make forecast. Here the behavior of one variable may be the cause for variations in the other variable. Here cause and effect relationship is taken into account to make the forecast. For example, increase in population may be the reason for increase in demand for certain products. Similarly, rainfall, amount of fertilizers used may be the reason for increased agricultural production.

3.7.1. Time Series

A time series is chronological data, which has two factors. One is some quantity such as sales in rupees, income of individual, etc., as dependent variable and second one is a unit of time as independent variable. A time series is a set of quantitative readings of some variable or composite of variables arranged in chronological order of their occurrence. A time series is simply a set of readings of values of variable quantity measured at intervals of time. The movement of variations of the dependent variable may be classified as: (*i*) Long period changes and (*ii*) Short period changes.

The long period tendency of data (increasing or decreasing) is referred as **secular** trend. The trend may be linear or non-linear. Short period changes may be regular or irregular in nature. Regular fluctuations will occur in a regular spasmodic manner. They may be seasonal or cyclical fluctuations. Seasonal fluctuations occur with same degree of regularity in the span of a year. The variations may be due to seasonal variation or social customs. Whereas irregular variations occur without any rhythm. These changes may be due to draughts, floods, famine and wars. Etc

The model accomplishes the decomposition of the time series:

$$O = T \times C \times S \times I,$$

where O = Observed value, T = Trend element, C = Cyclic variation,

S = Seasonal variation, and I = Irregular variation.

The above model is mostly used because it deals with percentage changes rather than absolute changes. The model enables us to isolate the components.

The variation in time series can be attributed a number of causes – natural, institutional and socio economic in character.

From the above we can say that the components of time series are:

(*i*) **A Trend Component,** which may be defined as a long time growth or decay.
(*ii*) **A Seasonal component,** which may be defined as a regularly occurring periodic fluctuations
(*iii*) **A Cyclic Component** defined as a wave like fluctuation about trend.
(*iv*) **An Erratic or Random or Irregular Component,** which occur in an unsystematic way.

Let us briefly deal with the above said components of time series.

(*a*) **Trend:** We find a phenomenal growth in business and industrial fields. This growth or secular trend is the outcome of population growth. In fact population growth influences the other fields of economy also. Increasing population is the potential market for all products. When we speak of growth the variables under question shows that it increases in quantity. Similarly in decaying trend, we observe decreasing quantity of the variable concerned.

Main factors responsible for an upward trend in time series may be

(*i*) Technological development,
(*ii*) Rationalization,
(*iii*) Improved productivity,
(*iv*) Better organizational methods,
(*v*) Professional management,
(*vi*) Quality control,
(*vii*) Standardization and
(*viii*) Innovative marketing.

The reasons for decreasing trend may be:

(*i*) Decline in demand
(*ii*) Price induced substitutes,
(*iii*) Scarcity of material required,
(*iv*) Changes in the habits of consumer, and
(*v*) Shift in the consumer preferences.

(*b*) **Seasonal Variations:** Periodic variations that reoccur with some degree of regularity with in a specific period are generally known as Seasonal variations. Any kind of variation, which is periodic in nature, is known as Seasonal variation. The period of season may be a week, a month, a quarter of a year or a year. Important factors that influence the seasonal variation are:

(*i*) Climate and weather conditions and

(*ii*) Customs, habits and traditions.

(*c*) **Cyclic Variations:** In economic and business activities, we see good times and bad times occur one after another and which are long term in nature. The main difference between seasonal variation and cyclic variation is degree of regularity and the time period. In any business we see four phases of changes, which are prospering phase, recession phase, depression phase and recovery phase. A business will show prosperous performance and due to influencing factors, the business shows a declining trend and finally reaches a worse state that is depression. After that due to changes in economic environment it recovers from its depressed state. This is quite natural in any business activity.

(*d*) **Erratic or Random Variations:** These variations in business activity are highly unpredictable and irregular in nature. Erratic or irregular movements of time series are either random or caused by some sporadic forces such as wars, cyclone, and earthquake, floods or fire accidents. Etc..

3.7.2. Estimation of Trend

(*a*) **Free hand method:** This method is purely an inspection method of estimating trend. The collected data is plotted on a graph paper and a line is drawn through the points, which will indicate a growth or decline of the trend. While drawing the line care should be taken to see that the line passes through the center of all scattered points, so that the lowest points and peak points are at equal distance from the line. This line is known as trend line.

Important points to be remembered while plotting graph are:

(*i*) Line should be smooth. It may be straight line or a combination of long gradual curves.

(*ii*) Sum of vertical deviations above and below the trend line should be equal.

(*iii*) The sum of squares of above said vertical deviations must be small (or zero) as far as possible.

(*iv*) Area of curve above the trend line should be equal to the area of the curve below the trend line.

The above is shown in the figure 3.3.

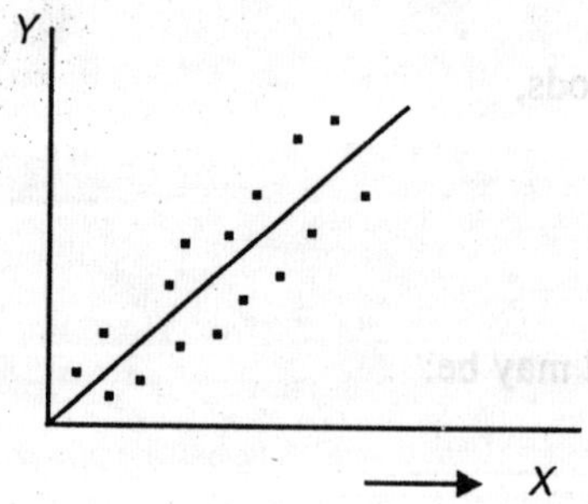

Fig. 3.3 : Free hand method.

(*b*) **Semi Average Method:** In this method, the entire time series available for a particular variable is divided into two halves. Say for example if the series has 10 entries, first five is taken as one half and next five as second half. If the series has odd number of entries, either leaving first one or last one only even number of elements is taken. This is the draw back of this method. The two averages thus calculated are marked on the graph and they are joined to know the trend.

Example 3.1 : Draw the trend line by semi average method for the following:

(*a*)	Time in years :	1	2	3	4	5	6	7	8	
	Variable units :	10	15	12	13	10	9	12	14	
(*b*)	Time in years :	1	2	3	4	5	6	7	8	9
	Variable units :	10	15	12	13	10	9	14	15	12

Solution :

(*a*) Average of first four years : $\left(\dfrac{10+15+12+13}{4}\right) = \dfrac{50}{4} = 12.5$ units.

Average of second four years $= \left(\dfrac{10+9+12+14}{4}\right) = \dfrac{45}{4} = 11.25$ units.

(*b*) Leaving last entry, average of first four years $= \left(\dfrac{10+15+12+13}{4}\right) = 12.5$ units

Average of second four years $= \left(\dfrac{10+9+14+15}{4}\right) = \dfrac{48}{4} = 12$ units.

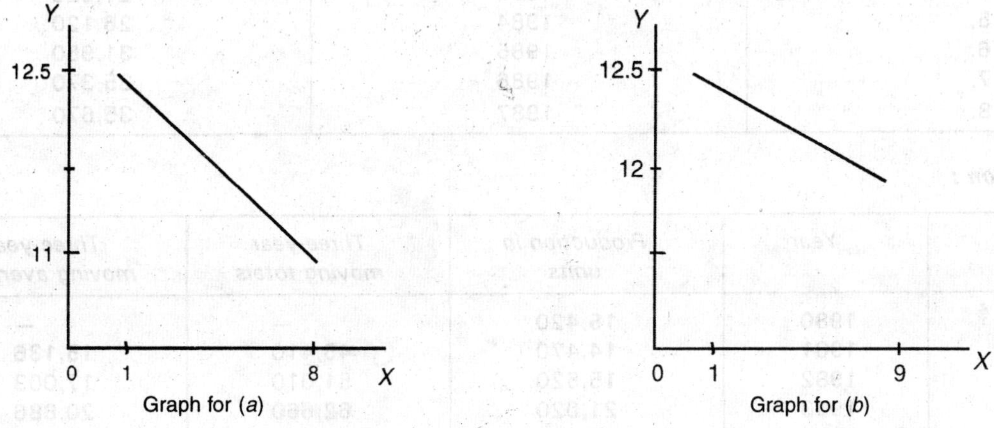

Fig. 3.4 *a* and *b* graphs for problem 3.1.

As the average falls at the center point, it should be marked at the center point on the graph. The drawback of this method is:

(*i*) We have to eliminate one element to have even number of elements in the problem,

(*ii*) In case any one half is having more heavy numbers, then the average we get will be shifted to heavy side.

(*c*) **Method of Moving Averages:** To avoid the drawback of the above two methods, moving average method is used. Moving average may be defined as the average of a fixed number of items in the series, which move through the series by dropping the top item of the previous averaged group and adding the next item below in each successive average. Adding all the values for a certain number of successive periods and then dividing the sum thus obtained by the number of items included compute-moving average. This average is written at the mid point of the group selected. This process of averaging reduces the influence of fluctuations that pull the annual figures away from the trend and helps to get smooth curve.

The selection of period for grouping generally depends on number of elements in the series and the need of the forecasting manager. When the elements in the series are small, two year moving average or three-year moving average or four year moving average is more common. When the elements in the series are large, we can go for seven year or eight year or ten year or twenty year moving averages. When we take odd number of elements, say for example 3, 5, 7.etc., the group average may be written at the center point of the group. When we take even number of elements, say for example 4, 6, 8 etc., the group average is written in the middle of the two items in the center. For example in a four year moving average, the average is written in between 2 nd and 3 rd items or centering of the average is to be done. This is explained with an example.

Problem 3.2: The data given below shows the production of certain commodity during 1980-1987. Find the trend by 3-year moving average.

S.No.	Year	Production in units.
1.	1980	15,420
2.	1981	14,420
3.	1982	15,520
4.	1983	21,020
5.	1984	26,120
6.	1985	31,950
7.	1986	35,370
8.	1987	35,670

Solution :

S. No.	Year	Production in units	Three-year moving totals	Three-year moving averages
1.	1980	15,420	—	—
2.	1981	14,470	45,410	15,136
3.	1982	15,520	51,010	17,003
4.	1983	21,020	62,660	20,886
5.	1984	26,120	79,090	26,363
6.	1985	31,950	93,440	31,146
7.	1986	35,370	1,02,990	34,330
8.	1987	35,670	--	--

Now a graph can be drawn to show the trend points.

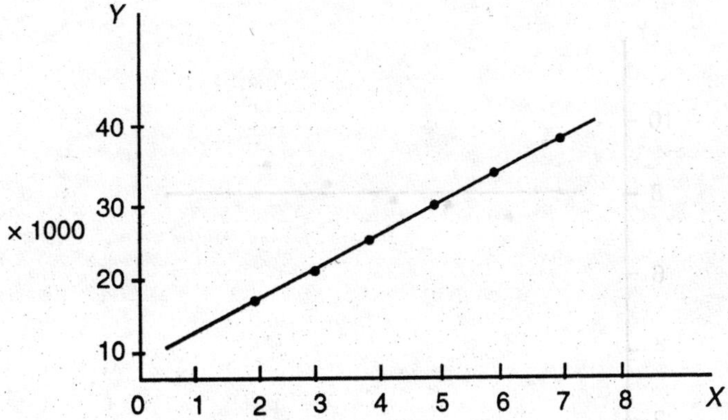

Fig. 3.5 : Trend line by three-year moving averages.

A line is drawn by free hand such that $Z = y_1 + y_2 + y_3 = y_4 + y_5 + y_6$ where y is the dauration.

We can also plot the line for actual data given in the problem, which also shows growth in the trend.

Example 3.3 : The data given below relates to production of certain commodity of M/S XYZ Company, compute 3-yearly moving averages and give the forecast for the year 1987.

S.No.	1	2	3	4	5	6	7	8
Year.	1980	1981	1982	1983	1984	1985	1986	1987
Production in units × 1000	6	7	8	7.5	6.5	7.0	9.0	

Solution :

S.No.	*Year units*	*Production to totals*	*Three-year moving averages*	*Three-year*
1.	1980	6.00	—	—
2.	1981	7.00	21.00	7.00
3.	1982	8.00	22.50	7.50
4.	1983	7.50	22.00	7.33
5.	1984	6.50	21.00	7.00
6.	1985	7.00	22.50	7.50
7.	1986	9.00	—	—

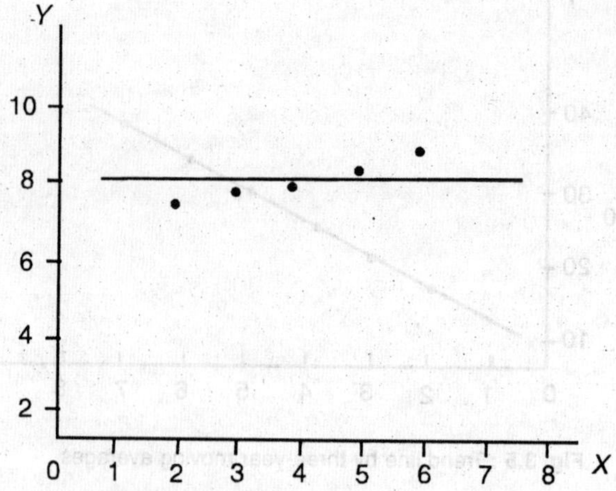

Fig. 3.6 : Trend by three-yearly moving averages.

Problem 3.3 : Calculate 7-yearly moving averages for the data given below :

S.No.	*Year*	*Number of failures in exam*	*S.No*	*Year*	*Number of failures in exam*
1.	1950	23	9.	1958	9
2.	1951	26	10.	1959	13
3.	1952	28	11.	1960	11
4.	1953	32	12.	1961	14
5.	1954	20	13.	1962	12
6.	1955	12	14.	1963	9
7.	1956	12	15.	1964	3
8.	1957	10	16.	1965	1

Solution :

S.No.	*Year*	*Failures in final exams*	*Seven-yearly moving totals*	*Seven-yearly moving averages*
1.	1950	23	—	—
2.	1951	26	—	—
3.	1952	28	—	—
4.	1953	32	153	22
5.	1954	20	140	20
6.	1955	12	123	18
7.	1956	12	108	15
8.	1957	10	87	12
9.	1958	9	81	12
10.	1959	13	81	12
11.	1960	11	78	11

Contd.

12.	1961	14	71	10
13.	1962	12	63	9
14.	1963	9	—	—
15.	1964	3	—	—
16.	1965	1	—	—

Graph for the problem :

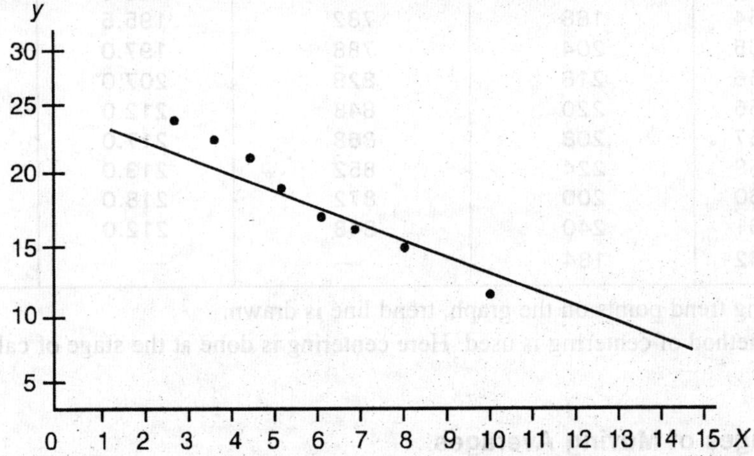

Fig. 3.7 : Trend by 7-yearly moving averages.

To find moving averages of even yaerly cycles we have to centre the averages. This method is known as *centring method.* This is explained by means of an Example.

Example 3.4 : The sales figures of a certain company are given below. Compute four-yearly moving averages.

S.No.	*Year*	*Sales in Rs. × 1000*
1.	1950	200
2.	1951	190
3.	1952	210
4.	1953	180
5.	1954	188
6.	1955	204
7.	1956	216
8.	1957	220
9.	1958	208
10.	1959	224
11.	1960	200
12.	1961	240
13.	1962	184

Solution

S.No.	Year	Sales in Rs. × 1000	4-year moving totals	4-year moving averages	4-year moving averages centered
1.	1950	200		—	—
2.	1951	190		—	—
3.	1952	210	780	195.0	193.50
4.	1953	180	768	192.0	193.75
5.	1954	188	782	195.5	196.25
6.	1955	204	788	197.0	202.00
7.	1956	216	828	207.0	209.50
8.	1956	220	848	212.0	214.50
9.	1957	208	868	217.0	215.00
10.	1958	224	852	213.0	215.50
11.	1960	200	872	218.0	215.00
12.	1961	240	848	212.0	
13.	1962	184	—	—	

After locating trend points on the graph, trend line is drawn.

One more method of centering is used. Here centering is done at the stage of calculating the four yearly totals.

3.7.4. Advantages of Moving Averages

(*i*) The method is simple and easy to use.
(*ii*) It depends on mathematical calculations.
(*iii*) Comparatively it is better than graphical method.

3.7.5. Limitations

(*i*) Choice of period of moving average is critical.
(*ii*) In case of missing observations, it will be difficult to apply this method.
(*iii*) Some trend values for the period in the beginning as well as in the end cannot be determined.

3.7A. METHOD OF LEAST SQUARES

This method is very much used in fitting trend line. The method of least **squares** is a mathematical device, which fits a line through a series of plotted points, in such away, that the sum of the squares of deviations of the actual points above and below the trend line is at the minimum. This method gives us what is known as the line of best fit. It is the line from which the sum of the deviations of various points on either side is equal to zero. In other words, if we sum up the positive and negative deviations on either side of the line of best fist, the sum will be zero. This is being so; the sum of squares of these deviations obtained will be the least as compared to the sum of the squares of the deviation obtained by using other lines. This is the reason, for calling this method as **method of least squares.**

Advantages: (*i*) Free from personal prejudice and bias. (*ii*) Trend values for all years of series may be obtained. (*iii*) This method gives most satisfactory results.

Disadvantages: It lacks flexibility of trend fitting. If one more year is added, the entire calculations are to be made freshly.

Method : The equation of straight line can be written as $Y = a + bX$ where Y is the dependent variable, such as sales, demand, etc., a and b are two unknown constants, whose values are to be found and X is the unit of time.

To determine a and b, the following equations are solved.

$$\Sigma Y = na + b\Sigma x$$

and $\Sigma xY = a\Sigma x + b\Sigma x^2$, where n = number of items in the series and $x = X - \overline{X}$.

We can take the variable from any point of time as origin, such as the first year. But to simplify the calculations, the mid-point of the time series is taken as the origin. In this process, the negative values of half of the series balance out the positive values in the series, so that $\Sigma x = 0$. As $\Sigma x = 0$, the above equations are written as follows :

$$\Sigma Y = na + 0 \text{ and } \Sigma xY = a.0 + b\Sigma x^2 = b\Sigma x^2$$

The values of constants a and b are $a = \dfrac{\Sigma Y}{n}$ and $b = \dfrac{\Sigma xY}{\Sigma x^2}$

While dealing with the method of least squares, it is better to use middle point of the time series as the origin. In case, the series has got odd number of years, the origin is the middle of the year. If the series has even number of years, the origin falls between the two middle years.

Here the value of 'a' is merely intercept or the height of the line at the origin. The other constant 'b' represents the slope of the trend line. If the value of 'b' is positive the slope is upwards (growing trend) and if 'b' is negative, the slope is downward (decreasing trend). That is the constant 'b' is the increase or decrease in Y for a unit changer in X.

- The following examples will show how to use the method.

Example 3.5 **:** Find the trend of industrial employment in a city from the data given.

Year (X) :	1960	1961	1962	1963	1964	1965	1966	1967	1968	1969
Number of Workers- Employed × 10	3.2	3.3	3.7	3.9	3.6	4.3	4.8	4.8	5.4	6.3

Year	*Number Of workers Employed*	*Deviation from 1964.5*	*Multiply by 2*	x^2	xY	*Trend value*
1960	3.2	–4.5	–9	81	–28.8	2.926
1961	3.3	–3.5	–7	49	–28.1	3.238
1962	3.7	–2.5	–5	25	–18.8	3.550
1963	3.9	–1.5	–3	9	–11.7	3.862
1964	3.6	–0.5	–1	1	–03.6	4.174
1965	4.3	0.5	1	1	04.3	4.486
1966	4.8	1.5	3	9	14.3	4.798
1967	4.8	2.5	5	25	24.0	5.110
1968	5.4	3.5	7	49	37.8	4.422
1969	6.3	4.5	9	81	56.7	5.734
n = 10	ΣY = 43.3	Σx = 0		Σx^2 = 330	ΣxY = 51.5	

Trend line $Y = a + bx$, where $a = \Sigma Y/n = 43.3/10 = 4.33$

$$b = \frac{\Sigma xy}{\Sigma x^2} = \frac{51.5}{330} = 0.156$$

Trend equation = $4.33 + 0.156x$

Trend for :

1960 = $Y = 4.33 + 0.156 \times -9 = 2.926$

1961 = $Y = 4.33 + 0.156 \times -7 = 3.238$

1962 = $Y = 4.33 + 0.156 \times -5 = 3.550$

1963 = $Y = 4.33 + 0.156 \times -3 = 3.862$

1964 = $Y = 4.33 + 0.156 \times -1 = 4.174$

1965 = $Y = 4.33 + 0.156 \times 1 = 4.486$

1966 = $Y = 4.33 + 0.156 \times 3 = 4.789$

1967 = $Y = 4.33 + 0.156 \times 5 = 5.110$

1968 = $Y = 4.33 + 0.156 \times 7 = 5.422$

1969 = $Y = 4.33 + 0.156 \times 9 = 7.734$

Example 3.6 : A survey revealed that demand for coolers in towns has given the following data :

Population in towns in 10^6	=	X	5	7	8	11	14
Number of coolers demanded	=	Y	45	65	55	75	95

Fit a linear regression of y on x and estimate the demand for coolers for a town whose population is 20×10^6.

Solution :

Population of The town (x) × 100	*Number of coolers demanded (y)*	*Size of population (x^2)*	*Product of x and y (xy)*
5	45	25	225
7	65	49	455
8	55	64	440
11	75	121	825
14	95	196	1330
$\Sigma X = 43$	$\Sigma Y = 335$	$\Sigma x^2 = 455$	$\Sigma xy = 3275$

Regression equation = $Y = a + bx$ to find a and b

$\Sigma Y = na + b\Sigma x$ 1

$\Sigma xY - a\Sigma x + b\Sigma x^2$ 2

Substituting the values,

$335 - 5a + 45b$ 3

$3275 = 45a + 455b$ 4

Multiplying the equation 3 by 9 we get,

$3275 = 454a + 455b$

$3015 - 45a + 405b$

$260 - 50b$ Therefore $b = 260/50 = 5.2$

Substituting the value of b in equation 3, we get $335 = 5a + 45\ (5.2)$

$$\text{Or } 5a = 101 \quad \text{or } a = \frac{101}{5} = 20.2$$

Now the required equation is $Y = 20.2 + 5.2x$ or $Y = 20.2 + 5.2\ (20)$
= 124.2 coolers is the demand.

(e) Logarithmic straight line or Exponential Method of Measuring the trend: Some times a smooth curve provides a better fit for data than a straight line. A smooth curve implies a uniform percentage growth or decay instead of constant increment or decrement given by a straight line. Here the equation for the curve is $y = ab^x$, which indicates that y changes at the constant rate b each period. To find the values of a and b, let us convert exponential equation into a logarithmic equation. The graph is to be plotted on a semi logarithmic paper. That is Y scale is logarithmic and X scale is arithmetic.

$$\Sigma(\log Y) = N\ (\log a) + \Sigma X\ (\log b)$$

$$\Sigma(X \log Y) = \Sigma X\ (\log a) + \Sigma X^2\ (\log b)$$

If we select the origin, such that $\Sigma x = 0$, then

$$\text{Log } a = \frac{\Sigma(\log y)}{\text{N}}, \ \log b = \frac{\Sigma(X \log y)}{\Sigma X^2}$$

Example 3.7 : The data relating to a company from 1970 to 1974 is shown below. Compute the forecast for 1975.

Year	1970	1971	1972	1973	1974
Sales in Rs. × 10^6	106	118	111	123	129

Solution :

Year X	*Sales in Rs. 10^6*	*Deviation From middle year X*	*Deviation Squared X^2*	*Log Y*	*X log Y*	*Trend*
1970	106	−2	4	2.0253	−4.0506	107.9
1971	118	−1	1	2.0719	−2.0719	112.72
1972	111	0	0	2.0453	0.0000	117.5
1973	123	1	1	2.0899	2.0899	122.8
1974	129	2	4	2.1106	4.2212	128.5
N = 5	—	$\Sigma X = 0$	$\Sigma X^2 = 10$	Σ *logy* = 10.3930	ΣX *logy* = 0.1876	

$$\text{Log } a = \Sigma \log \frac{Y}{N} = \frac{10.3930}{5} = 2.0709, \text{ therefore } a = 117.5$$

$$\text{Log } b = \frac{\Sigma(X \log y)}{\Sigma X^2} = \frac{0.1876}{10} = 0.0188 \text{ or } b = 1.0447$$

Substituting $X = -2, -1, 0, 1, 2$ and 3 in equation Log Y = Log $a + x \log b$ we get

$Y_{1970} = 2.0709 + (-2) \times 0.0188 - 2.0333, Y = 107.9$

$Y_{1971} = 2.0709 + (-1) \times 0.0188 = 2.0521, Y = 112.72$

$Y_{1972} = 2.0709 + (0) \times 0.0188 - 2.0709, Y = 117.5$

$Y_{1973} = 2.0709 + (1) \times 0.0188 = 2.0897, Y = 112.8$

$Y_{1974} = 2.0709 + (2) \times 0.0188 = 2.1085, Y = 128.5$

$Y_{1975} = 2.0709 + (3) \times 0.0188 = 2.1273, Y = 133.98$

Hence the forecast for 1975 is 133.98 units.

3.8. EXPONENTIAL SMOOTHENING

As we know, whatever method we use for forecasting, the results are not 100% accurate. Suppose that a new observation had just been made for which we have already made forecast (by any method), we find that there will be a difference between the two. That is, it is certain that if the forecast of sales for a certain item is made as 200 for a certain period, the actual sales during that period may be a bit less than 200 or a bit greater than 200. Therefore let us make our forecast for the next period from our old forecast by making provisions for the error. We shall overcompensate if we change our forecast by the full extent of the error, since some of it will be due to random fluctuations of the error. This is taken care of in Exponential Smoothening Method. The equation for exponential smoothening is:

New Forecast = Old Forecast + α(Latest Observation – Old Forecast)

The value of 'α' varies between 0 to 1, 'α' is known as **smoothening constant**, the value of which should be selected carefully. **In general 0.1 to 0.5 is reasonable.**

If F_0 = Forecast for the next period,
F_1 = Forecast for the previous period,
D_1 = Latest observation made, then
$F_0 = F_1 + \alpha (D_1 - F_1)$

Problem 3.8 **:** If the given old forecast is 350 units initially, by using exponential method compare the forecast for α = 0.1 and α = 0.5. The following series of 10 observations are given.

Observations No. :	1	2	3	4	5	6	7	8	9	10
Units :	390	390	320	370	340	330	380	340	390	310

Solution :

Initial forecast = 350 units = F_1

Actual observation = 390 units = D_1 and α = 0.5 hence using

$$F_0 = F_1 + \alpha (D_1 - F_1) = 350 + 0.5 (390 - 350) = 350 + 20 = 370$$

The second period for which the forecast is 370, the actual observation = 390, hence

$F_0 = 370 + 0.5 (390 - 370) = 370 + 10 = 380$. Similarly we can calculate for other observations.

Observation	*Forecast*	*Error*	*α × Error*	*New forecast in units*
390	350	+40	+20	370
390	370	+20	+10	380
320	350	-60	-30	350

370	380	+20	+10	360
340	350	−20	−10	350
330	350	−20	−10	340
380	340	+40	+20	360
340	360	−20	−10	350
390	350	+40	+20	370
310	370	−60	−30	340
—	340	—	—	—

When $\alpha = 0.1$

Observation	*Forecast*	*Error*	0.1 × *Error*	*New forecast in units*
390	350	+40	+4.0	354
390	354	+36	+3.6	357.6
320	358	−38	−3.8	357.6
370	354	16	1.6	355.6
340	356	−16	−1.6	364.4
330	354	−24	−2.4	351.6
380	352	+28	+2.8	354.8
340	355	−15	−1.5	353.5
390	354	+36	+3.6	357.6
310	358	−48	−4.8	353.2
—	353.2	—	—	—

3.9. METHOD OF MEASURING SEASONAL VARIATION

Many a time we see that major factors causing seasonal variations are relatively uniform and permanent, the movement may be considered as normal. It is seen that the seasonal effects on custom and social activities result in about the same month-to-month change, year after year. For example demand for cool drinks increases in summer, demand for umbrellas and rain coats increases in rainy season, demand for wool cloths will increase in winter season. Seasonal variation can be measured. Knowledge of seasonal pattern is important in business and economic analysis.

One difficulty we come across while measuring the seasonal fluctuations is imperfectness of the calendar as a device for measuring business time. Number of days in each month is different; also the number of working days will also vary depending on the number of Sundays and public holidays. Say for example day-to-day production may be same in all months. But monthly production will different due to unequal numbers of working days. In such cases taking number of working days into consideration daily average production may be worked out.

The effect of trend cycles, and irregular fluctuations must be eliminated from the original time series data to obtain an estimate of seasonal variations. Once they are eliminated, we get measures of seasonal variations in the behavior of any variable. These measures are known as Seasonal **Indexes.** By using the seasonal index, we can **deseasonalize** the time series. The deseasonlised data are known as **seasonally adjusted data,** a seasonal index for a year consists of 12 numbers, one for each month, which are expressed as percentage of their average. Two methods are generally used for estimating seasonal variation:

(*i*) Method of Simple Averages and (*ii*) Method of Moving Averages.

(*i*) Method of Simple Averages: The procedure for estimating seasonal variation by using Simple averages is:

(*a*) Average the adjusted data by years and months or quarters, if quarterly data is given.

(*b*) Calculate the average values for each month/quarter; we get monthly or seasonal averages.

(*c*) Calculate the general average of monthly or quarterly averages

(*d*) Calculate the percentage that each monthly or quarterly average bears to the general average.

(*e*) Seasonal index for a particular month or particular quarter is given by

$$\frac{\text{Monthly Average for that particular month or quarter}}{\text{General Average}} \times 100$$

Example 3.9: The data given below shows the sales data for a commodity during four quarters of the year from 1970 to 1974. Calculate seasonal index

Quarterly sales in Rs. × 1000

Year	*I quarter*	*II quarter*	*III quarter*	*IV quarter*
1970	35	39	34	36
1971	35	42	37	40
1972	35	39	37	42
1973	40	46	38	45
1974	41	44	42	45

Solution :

Quarterly sales in Rs. × 100

Year	*I quarter*	*II quarter*	*III quarter*	*IV quarter*
1970	35	39	34	36
1971	35	41	37	40
1972	35	39	37	42
1973	40	46	38	45
1974	41	44	42	45
Totals	$\frac{186}{5} = 37.2$	$\frac{209}{5} = 41.8$	$\frac{188}{5} = 37.6$	$\frac{208}{5} = 41.6$

$$\text{General Average} = \frac{37.2 + 41.8 + 37.6 + 41.6}{4} = 39.5$$

$$\text{Seasonal index} - \left(\frac{\text{Quarterly Average}}{\text{General Average}}\right) \times 100$$

$$\text{Seasonal index for I quarter} = \left(\frac{37.2}{39.5}\right) \times 100 = 94.17$$

$$\text{Seasonal index for II quarter} = \left(\frac{41.8}{39.5}\right) \times 100 = 105.80$$

$$\text{Seasonal index for III quarter} = \left(\frac{37.6}{39.5}\right) \times 100 = 95.19$$

$$\text{Seasonal index for IV quarter} = \left(\frac{41.6}{39.5}\right) \times 100 = 105.30$$

Example 3.10: The data given below belongs to monthly production of certain commodity in a production shop. Calculate average seasonal variation.

Solution :

Production in units × 1000

Month	Year 1970	1971	1972	1973
January	250	300	275	225
February	225	313	315	200
March	260	325	250	280
April	275	375	310	290
May	350	340	435	375
June	305	360	360	325
July	325	355	340	350
August	290	315	255	240
September	225	255	320	310
October	265	320	305	310
November	245	305	250	325
December	300	325	250	305

Production in units × 100

Month	*Year* *1970*	*1971*	*1972*	*1973*	*Yearly total*	*4-yearly average*	*Seasonal Index*
January	250	300	275	225	1050	262.50	$\left(\frac{1050}{1200}\right) \times 100 = 87.5$
February	225	310	315	200	1050	262.50	$\left(\frac{1050}{1200}\right) \times 100 = 87.5$
March	260	325	250	256	1115	278.70	$\left(\frac{1115}{1200}\right) \times 100 = 92.8$

Month	Year				Yearly total	4-yearly average	Seasonal Index
	1970	1971	1972	1973			
April	275	375	310	290	1250	312.5	$\left(\frac{1250}{1200}\right) \times 100=104.2$
May	350	340	435	325	1500	375.00	$\left(\frac{1500}{1200}\right) \times 100=125.0$
June	305	360	360	325	1350	337.50	$\left(\frac{1350}{1200}\right) \times 100=112.5$
July	325	355	340	350	1370	342.5	$\left(\frac{1350}{1200}\right) \times 100=114.2$
August	290	315	255	240	1100	275.00	$\left(\frac{1100}{1200}\right) \times 100=91.70$
September	225	255	320	310	1110	277.50	$\left(\frac{1110}{1200}\right) \times 100=92.50$
October	265	320	305	310	1200	300.00	$\left(\frac{1200}{1200}\right) \times 100=100.00$
November	245	305	250	325	1125	281.20	$\left(\frac{1125}{1200}\right) \times 100=93.80$
December	300	325	250	305	1180	285.00	$\left(\frac{1180}{1200}\right) \times 100=98.20$
Total					14400	3600	
Average					1200	300	

Specimen calculations :

$$\text{Seasonal Index for January} = \left(\frac{\text{Monthly average for January}}{\text{General average}}\right) \times 100$$

$$= \left(\frac{262.5}{300}\right) \times 100 = 87.50 \text{ or } \left(\frac{1050}{1200}\right) \times 100 = 87.5$$

Similarly other monthly indices are calculated.

Seasonal Index by using moving averages : Periodic fluctuations in times series are eliminated by a moving average of period equal to period of fluctuations. Procedure for finding seasonal index is :

(*a*) Calculate the moving average of the series.

(*b*) Subtract the moving average figures from the given time series figures to get short-term fluctuations.

(*c*) Tabulate the short-term fluctuations season wise for quarterly data.

(*d*) Calculate the average fluctuations for each season to get seasonal fluctuations.

Sales forecast for next season = Trend + or – Fluctuations

Example 3.11: From the data given below, which is quarterly production of a company find

(*a*) Trend values of the production by 4 quarterly moving averages,

(*b*) Seasonal movement of production,

(*c*) Irregular fluctuations in production.

Production in units x 1000

Year	*I quarter*	*II quarter*	*III quarter*	*IV quarter*
1970	60	162	124	238
1971	66	208	172	342
1972	84	306	198	442
1973	112	344	258	470
1974	134	402	272	604

Solution :

Year and quarter		*Production in units x 1000*	*Total of 4 items.*	*Averages*	*Centered average*	*Fluctuation of trend*
	1	*2*	*3*	*4*	*5*	*6 = 2-5*
1970	I	60	—	—	—	—
	II	162	—	—	—	—
	III	124	582	145.50	167	– 43
	IV	236	757	189.25	174	+62
1971	I	66	634	158.50	165	– 99
	II	208	682	170.50	184	+24
	III	172	788	197	199	– 27
	IV	342	806	201.50	214	+128
1972	I	84	904	226.00	225	– 141
	II	306	930	232.5	273	+33
	III	198	1252	313.00	289	– 91
	IV	442	1058	264.50	269	+173
1973	I	112	1096	274.00	282	– 170
	II	344	1156	289.00	293	+51
	III	258	1184	296.00	299	– 41
	IV	470	1206	301.50	309	+161
1974	I	134	1264	316.00	318	–184
	II	402	1278	319.50	336	+66
	III	272	1412	353.00	—	—
	IV	604	—	—	—	—

Calculation of average seasonal fluctuations

Year	I quarter	II quarter	III quarter	IV quarter
1970	—	—	-43	+62
1971	-99	+24	-27	+128
1972	141	+33	-91	+173
1973	-170	+51	-41	+161
1974	-184	+66	—	—
Totals	-594	+174	-202	+524
Average	-148.50	+43.50	-50.50	+131
Seasonal Number	-149		-51	

The difference between fluctuations from trend and average seasonal variations will give irregular fluctuations.

Average	-148.50	+43.50	-50.50	+131
Seasonal Number	= 149		= 51	

The difference between fluctuations from trend and average seasonal variations will give irregular fluctuations.

Year and season		Fluctuations from trends	Seasonal movement	Irregular fluctuations
1970	I	—	—	—
	II	—	—	—
	III	-43	-51	+8
	IV	+62	+131	-69
1971	I	-99	-149	+50
	II	+24	+44	-20
	III	-27	-51	+24
	IV	128	131	-3
1972	I	-141	149	+8
	II	33	44	-11
	III	-91	-51	-40
	IV	173	131	+42
1973	I	-170	-149	+21
	II	51	44	+7
	III	-41	-51	+10
	IV	161	131	+30
1974	I	-184	-149	+35
	II	66	44	+22
	III	—	—	—
	IV	—	—	—

To find the forecast for the year 1975 : Sales forecast = Trend + or – Fluctuations.

From the above solution the seasonal fluctuations for four quarters are as given below :

Quarter	*Seasonal fluctuations*
I	–149
II	+44
III	– 51
IV	+131

Hence sales forecast for 1975 = Trend + or – fluctuations.

For the year 1975

I Quarter = 1974 I quarter trend – 149 = 318 – 149 = 169

II Quarter = 1974 II Quarter trend + 44 = 334 + 44 = 378

III Quarter – 1973 III Quarter trend – 51 = 299 – 51 = 248

IV Quarter = 1973 IV Quarter trend +131 = 309 + 131 = 440

3.10. COMPUTATION OF CYCLIC VARIATION

We have seen earlier that observed value

$$O = T \times C \times S \times I.$$

When we have trend values and seasonal fluctuations, we can get cyclic variation together with Irregular fluctuation by using $\left(\dfrac{T \times C \times S \times I}{T \times S}\right) = C \times I$

Generally it is expressed as percentage rather than as values in rupees or units.

Difference between fluctuation from trends (i.e., Net sales trend) and seasonal movement gives us the irregular fluctuations.

I = (Net sales – trend) – Seasonal movements

Example 3.12 : Isolate cyclic fluctuations from the following sales figures for which the calculated trend values are given.

Year	*Sales in Rs. × 1000*	*Trend in Rs. × 1000*	*Year*	*Sales in Rs. × 1000*	*Trend in Rs. × 1000*
1970	170	228	1977	298	311
1971	231	239	1978	340	323
1972	261	251	1979	273	334
1973	267	263	1980	210	346
1974	278	275	1981	158	358
1975	302	287	1982	173	370
1976	299	285	—	—	—

Solution :

Year	Sales in Rs. × 100 = T.C.I	Trend in Rs. T	Adjusted sale (%) = TCI/T (1/2) × 100	Cyclic variation 5 = 4 – 100
1	2	3	4	5
1970	170	228	$\left(\frac{170}{228}\right) \times 100 = 74.6$	74.6 – 100 = –25.4
1971	231	239	$\left(\frac{231}{239}\right) \times 100 = 97.7$	97.7 – 100 = –3.3
1972	261	251	$\left(\frac{261}{251}\right) \times 100 = 104.0$	104 – 100 = +4.0
1973	267	263	$\left(\frac{267}{263}\right) \times 100 = 101.50$	101.50 – 100 = +1.50
1974	278	275	$\left(\frac{278}{275}\right) \times 100 = 101.10$	101.10 – 100 = +1.10
1975	302	287	$\left(\frac{302}{287}\right) \times 100 = 105.20$	105.20 – 100 = +5.20
1976	299	299	$\left(\frac{299}{299}\right) \times 100 = 100.00$	100.00 – 100 = 0.00
1977	298	311	$\left(\frac{298}{311}\right) \times 100 = 96.00$	96.00 – 100 = 14.00
1978	340	323	$\left(\frac{340}{323}\right) \times 100 = 105.30$	105, 30 – 100 = 5.30
1979	273	334	$\left(\frac{273}{334}\right) \times 100 = 81.70$	87.10 – 100 = –18.30
1980	210	346	$\left(\frac{210}{346}\right) \times 100 = 60.70$	60.70 – 100 = –39.70
1981	158	358	$\left(\frac{158}{358}\right) \times 100 = 44.10$	44.10 – 100 = –55.90
1982	173	370	$\left(\frac{173}{370}\right) \times 100 = 47.00$	47.00-100 = –53.00

3.11. CORRELATIONS AND REGRESSION ANALYSIS FOR FORECASTING:

Here we are concerned with the relationship between data possessing two measurable characteristics or attributes. For example, relationship between price and demand, agricultural yield and rainfall, wages and prices, height and weight of a person. Etc., When we analyses the relationship; between different phenomenon, such as mentioned above, we say that we are analyzing the **correlation or co-variation.**

(*i*) Correlation **or co-variation is defined as a statistical tool used for expressing the relationship between two or more variables in one single figure, referred as *Correlation co-efficient.***

(*ii*) **According to** Taro Yamme " Correlation analysis is a discussion of the degree of closeness of the relationship between two values.

(*iii*) According to A.M. Tuttle " Such analysis of the co-variation of two or more variables is usually called correlation.

A measure, which condenses in a single figure, the direction and degree of correlation, is called "coefficient of correlation".

When a group of items are recorded with respect to the values of two distinct variables and it is found that pair of values tends to be associated, the two variables are said to be correlated. The correlation between different phenomenons is a result of practical experience.

One important point we have to remember here is when we speak of correlation between two variables, we imply a CAUSAL relationship. That is the change in the values of one variable is the cause to observe change in the values of another variable. This means to say that there will be CAUSE and EFFECT relationship between two variables. Say for example the increase in rainfall is the cause and the effect is increase in the yield of crops. The raise in temperature may be the cause and the effect is increase in the demand for cool drinks. If there is no CAUSE and EFFECT relationship between two variables, which are changing in one direction or the other, we cannot say that they have correlation. Take for example increase in salaries of the employees and increase in rainfall. In such cases the variation may be due to chance. This is to say that; the presence of high degree of correlation between two variables does not essentially mean the existence of causation. Two series may show high degree of correlation, yet their close relationship may result purely from chance. The cause and effect relationship involved must be arrived at be scientific reasoning. For this, the manager making forecast must be fully conversant with the data at his command.

3.11.1. Types of Correlation

(*a*) **Positive or Negative Correlations:** The direction of variation of the variables determines whether the correlation is Positive (direct) or Negative (indirect or inverse). The correlation is positive when the values of two or more variables move in the same direction, i.e., if one variable increases (or decreases) cause the other variable also to increase (or decrease). Consider the following example:

Example 1		Example 2	
Variable X	*Variable Y*	*Variable X*	*Variable Y*
100	75	700	640
200	150	600	520
250	200	400	325
400	325	250	200

In the above-mentioned example when variable Y increases with X, because of cause and effect relationship, there exists a positive correlation. When Y decreases with a decrease in the value of X, there exists a positive correlation. If Y shows a decrease when X is increasing or Y increases, when X is decreasing, due to cause and effect relationship, there exists a negative correlation. An example for this is:

Variable X	Variable Y	Variable X	Variable Y
136	240	240	136
149	235	235	149
150	220	220	150
170	210	210	170
190	200	200	190
200	180	180	200

The figure 3.3 shows the above phenomenon.

Fig. 3.8 : Positive and negative correlation.

3.11.2. Simple, Multiple and Partial Correlation

When the relationship between two variables is studied, the correlation is termed as **simple.** For example the relationship between rainfall and yield in the crop. Suppose we study the relationship between more than two variables simultaneously, for example the yield in the crop Vs Rainfall, Fertility of land, amount of fertilizers used. Etc, the correlation is said to be **multiple**. But when we study the behavior of a variable with respect to the behavior of more than two variables (say three or four) when we are having quite a good number of variables which influences the behavior of the first variable, then the correlation is said to be **partial.** We stress only those variables, which influence each other more than others. For example, the price of a product is determined by many factors like supply, demand, export, import, money circulation, famine, wars, income of consumer. Etc, We can study the effect of variables on price, but if we study the relationship between price with demand, income of consumer and supply then the correlation is **partial.**

3.11.3. LINEAR AND NON-LINEAR CORRELATION

If the amount of change in one variable tends to bear a constant ratio to the amount of change in the other variable the correlation is said to be **linear.** In case the amount of change does not bear a constant ratio with the change in other variable, the correlation is said to be **non-linear.** Examples are:

Linear correlation:	X:	2	4	8	10	12	14	16
	Y	3	6	12	15	18	21	24

Non-Linear Correlation:	X	2	5	7	8	10	15
	Y	8	9	11	14	16	20

3.11.4. Methods of measuring correlation

There are various methods of measuring correlation. Most important of them are:

(*a*) Graphical methods: (*i*) Simple graphs, (*ii*) Scatter diagrams or Dot diagrams.

(*b*) Mathematical methods: (*i*) Karl Pearson's co-efficient of correlation, (*ii*) Spearman's Rank correlation, (*iii*) Concurrent deviation method, (*iv*) Regression equation or Least square method, (*v*) Difference method.

(a) Graphical methods:

(*i*) **Simple Graphs:** The values of two variables are plotted on a graph paper to get two curves, one for each variable. The direction and closeness of two curves shows the degree of correlation. If the curves show a parallel tendency or move in the same direction, either upward or downward, the correlation is positive. If they move in opposite direction, the correlation is negative. This method will give a rough idea of existence of correlation but it cannot give numerical measure of correlation.

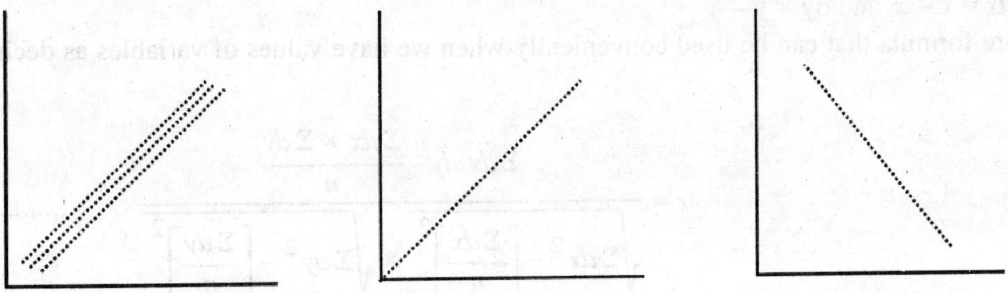

(*a*) Positive correlation. (*b*) Perfect positive correlation. (*c*) Perfect negative correlation.

(*ii*) **Scatter or Dot diagram:** The values of two variables are taken on X and Y-axis of a graph and points are located. A spread of dots appears in the diagram. Their concentration or scatter gives the idea o correlation. The figure 3.4 shows the various types of correlation.

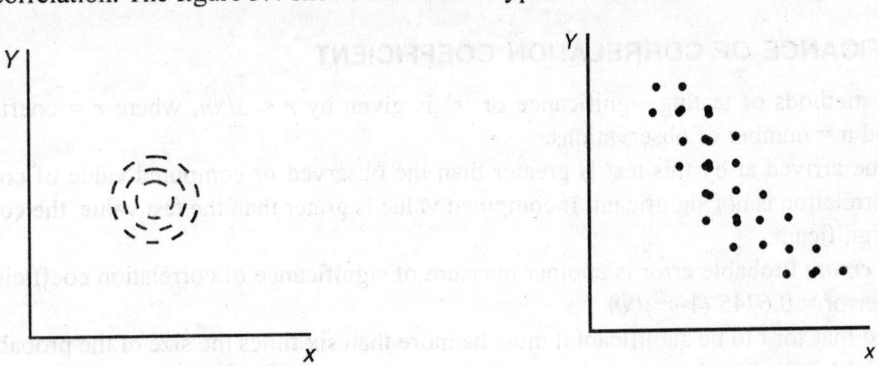

(*d*) No correlation. (*e*) Negative correlation.

Fig. 3.9 : Scatter diagram.

(b) i. KARL PEARSON'S COEFFICIENT OF CORRELATION:

This method is used extensively to study the correlation between variables. Karl Pearson's Coefficient of Correlation is denoted by 'r'. The statistical formula used for '*r*' is

$$r = \frac{\Sigma dxdy}{n\sigma x \times \sigma y},$$

where dx = deviation of items of variable x from the arithmetic average $= x - \bar{x}$

dy = deviation of items of variable y from its arithmetic average $= y - \bar{y}$

σx = standard deviation of variable x and σy = standard deviation of variable y

n = number of items paired.

In case $\Sigma dx.dy$ is positive the coefficient of correlation is positive. If $\Sigma dx.dy$ is negative, the coefficient of correlation is negative. The value of coefficient of correlation 'r' lies between +1 and –1. It cannot exceed unity. Another formula used in this method is

$$r = \frac{\Sigma dxdy}{\sqrt{\Sigma dx^2 \times \Sigma dy^2}} \qquad \text{..........(2)}$$

Where $dx = x - \bar{x}$ and $dy = y - \bar{y}$.

One more formula that can be used conveniently when we have values of variables as decimals, is:

$$r = \frac{\Sigma dx.dy - \dfrac{\Sigma dx \times \Sigma dy}{n}}{\sqrt{\Sigma dx^2 - \left[\dfrac{\Sigma dx}{n}\right]^2} \times \sqrt{\Sigma dy^2 - \left[\dfrac{\Sigma dy}{n}\right]^2}} \qquad \text{..........(3)}$$

Where, dx = deviation of items of x series from an assumed mean. i.e. $dx = (x–A)$

And dy = deviation of items of y series from an assumed mean. i.e., $dy = (y–B\}$ and n = number of items paired

One of the disadvantage of this method is it always assumes linear relationship regardless of whether the assumption is correct or not.

3.12. SIGNIFICANCE OF CORRELATION COEFFICIENT

A simple methods of testing significance or '*r*' is given by $r < 3/\sqrt{n}$, where r = coefficient of correlation and n = number of observations.

If the value arrived at by this test is greater than the observed or computed value of correlation coefficient, correlation is not significant. If computed value is grater than the test value, the correlation is said to be significant.

Probable error: Probable error is another measure of significance of correlation coefficient.

Probable error = $0.6745\ (1–r^2)/\sqrt{n}$.

It is agreed that for r to be significant it must be more than six times the size of the probable error.

Problem 3.13 Calculate the correlation coefficient between x and y from the data given below:

X	5	7	3	1	9	12	8	3
Y	8	9	5	4	9	13	7	9

Solution:

x	Dx = x – x = x – 6	Dx^2	y	Dy = y – y = y – 8	Dy^2	dx.dy
5	–1	1	8	0	0	0
7	+1	1	9	+1	1	+1
3	–3	9	5	–3	9	+9
1	–5	25	4	–4	16	+20
9	+3	9	9	+1	1	+3
12	+6	36	13	=5	25	+30
8	+2	4	7	–1	1	–2
3	–3	9	9	+1	1	–3
Σx = 48	Σdx = 0	Σdx^2 = 94	Σy = 64	Σdy = 0	Σdy^2 = 54	Σdx.dy = 58

$$\bar{x} = \frac{\Sigma x}{n} = \frac{48}{6} = 6 \text{ and } \bar{y} = \frac{\Sigma y}{n} = \frac{64}{8} = 8$$

$$\text{Now } r = \frac{\Sigma dx.dy}{\sqrt{\left(\Sigma dx^2 \times \Sigma dy^2\right)}} = \frac{58}{\sqrt{(94 \times 54)}} = \frac{58}{72.74} = +0.814.$$

X and *Y* have got high degree of positive correlation.

Example 3.14 : Sales pattern of a company given in the table below along with consumption pattern of similar goods in the market. Find the correlation coefficient between the two. Also compute the estimate of sales when consumption in the market is 20,000 units.

X = sales x 1000	1	2	3	4	5	6	7	8	9
Y = sales x 1000	9	8	10	12	11	13	14	16	15

Solution:

x = Sales × 1000	$dx = x - \bar{x}$ = x – 5	dx^2	Y = sales × 1000	$dy = y - \bar{y}$ y – 12	dy^2	dx.dy
1	–4	16	9	–3	9	12
2	–3	9	8	–4	16	12
3	–2	4	10	–2	4	4
4	–1	1	12	0	0	0
5	0	0	11	–1	1	0
6	1	1	13	1	1	1
7	2	4	14	2	4	4
8	3	9	16	4	16	12
9	4	16	15	3	9	12
Σx = 45	Σdx = 0	Σdx^2 =60	Σy =108	Σdy =0	Σdy^2 =60	Σdx.dy =57

$$\bar{x} = \frac{45}{9} = 5,\ \bar{y} = \frac{108}{9} = 12,\ r = \frac{\Sigma dx.dy}{\sqrt{\Sigma dx^2.\Sigma dy^2}} = \frac{57}{\sqrt{60 \times 60}} = \frac{57}{60} = 0.95.$$

Regression of x on y is

$$x - \bar{x} = r \times \left(\frac{\sigma_x}{\sigma_y}\right) \times (y - \bar{y}) \text{ where } \bar{x} = 5,\ \bar{y} = 12 \text{ and r} = 0.95$$

$$\sigma_x = \sqrt{\frac{\Sigma dx^2}{n}} = \sqrt{\frac{60}{9}} = 2.58 \text{ and } \sigma_y = \sqrt{\frac{\Sigma dy^2}{n}} = \sqrt{\frac{60}{9}} = 2.58$$

$$x = \bar{x} = x - 5 = 0.95 \times \frac{2.58}{2.58} \times (y - 12) \text{ or } x = 0.95y - 6.4$$

If $y = 20$, then $x = 0.95 \times 20 - 6.4 = 12.6 \times 10000$ units.

3.13. HOW TO INTERPRET THE COEFFICIENT OF CORRELATION

We know the value of 'r' lies between +1 and –1. Perfect correlation is represented by unity. The sign shows whether the correlation is positive or negative. A value zero indicates absence of correlation. Figures +1,0.and –1 occurs rarely Figures between 0.6 to 0.9 are more common. If 'r' is more than 6 times its probable error, correlation is considered to be significant. Correlation will be significant if 'r' is less than its probable error. If it is grater than 0.40, but less than 0.60, there will be a fair degree of correlation between the variables. If 'r' is less than .0.36, there will be limited correlation between two variables.

3.14. SPEARMAN'S COEFFICIENT OF RANK CORRELATION

Charles Spearman gives this method of measuring correlation between two variables in 1904. It some time happens that the characteristics, whose possible correlation is being studied cannot be measured. It will be difficult to assign numerical values to the variables. For example, when we have to compare the movie pictures regarding their ability of satisfying the customers, we can simply say this is better than the other but how much better? We have no answer. In such cases, if we prepare a scale in which we indicate ranks, then we can locate a rank for one film. To measure the degree of agreement between the two rankings given, Spearman's Rank Correlation Coefficient is employed. The formula used is:

$$R = \frac{1 - \left(6\Sigma D^2\right)}{n\left(n^2 - 1\right)} = \frac{1 - \left(6\Sigma D^2\right)}{n^3 - n},$$

where R = Coefficient of Rank correlation, D = Difference between ranks paired between two series, and n = number of observations.

The value of the rank correlation coefficient also varies between +1 and –1. When

$R = +1$, there will be complete agreement in the order of ranks. When $R = -1$, the ranks will be in opposite direction.

Example 3.15 : Find the coefficient of rank correlation between the production cost and critical appraisal of ten motion pictures

Production cost ranking.	1	2	3	4	5	6	7	8	9	10
Critical appraisal ranking.	8	6	10	7	5	2	9	1	4	3

Solution :

Production Cost ranking R_1	*Critical appraisal Ranking R_2*	*Rank difference $D = R_1 - R_2$*	D^2
1	8	-7	49
2	6	-4	16
3	10	-7	49
4	7	-3	09
5	5	0	00
6	2	+4	16
7	9	-2	4
8	1	+7	49
9	4	+5	25
10	3	+7	49
—	—	Total	266

$$R = 1 - (6\sum D^2/n\,(n^2 - 1) = \frac{1-(6 \times 266)}{10\left(10^2-1\right)} = \frac{1-1596}{10(100-1)}$$

$$= 1 - \frac{1596}{990} = 1 - 1.61 = -0.61.$$

There is fair degree of negative correlation.

3.15. COEFFICIENT OF CONCURRENT DEVIATION

This method is simple and easiest when compared to other methods. In this method direction of change or deviation is recorded from the preceding values. But in other methods we note down the deviation of the given element from the average (central tendency).. The formula used is

$$r = \left\{\sqrt{\frac{\pm(2C-n)}{n}}\right\}$$

Methodology:

(*i*) Record the direction of change of variable '*x*' i.e., take the value of first element under variable '*x*' as base and calculate whether the second element is increasing or constant or decreasing. If it is increasing the relation to first element is positive and if it is decreasing it is negative. In case no change is there put = against the value. The direction of change is denoted by a heading '*dx*'.

(*ii*) Calculate the direction of change of variable '*y*' also in the same manner and note down under the heading '*dy*'.

(*iii*) The direction of change of third element is noted by taking the second value as base. The same is continued until all the elements are over.

(*iv*) Multiply *dx* and *dy*. Care should be taken to see that proper sign (+, -, =) is noted.

(*v*) Those showing the same sign for both items of the pair are known as **'concurrence'** denoted by '*c*'.

The sign of the ultimate result depends on the sign of $(2c - n)\backslash n$.

If it is negative, this negative value multiplied by the minus sign under root i.e., $\sqrt{\pm(2c - n)/n}$ will make it positive. But the result after calculating square root will be negative. In case it is positive, then all the signs will be positive.

3.16. CORRELATION IN TIME SERIES

Time series generally show two types of fluctuations, i.e. (*i*) Long-term fluctuations and (*ii*) Short-term fluctuations. The relationship existing between two types of series must be studied separately, as the relationship between the long-term changes of two series may be entirely different from that between the short-term changes of these series. There may be remarkable difference in the degree of correlation existing between long-term changes and between short- terms changes.

Long-term changes will be more prominent and they might move in the same direction. So it is important to study the correlation between short-term changes in the values of variables. Many a time sort- term changes in two series may be in different direction. We can conveniently use modified version of Karl Pearson's formula.

3.16.1. Methodology for calculation of correlation in short–term changes

(*i*) Calculate the moving average of the values of the two variables.

(*ii*) Take the deviation of such figures of moving averages from their respective original values. These are short- term changes. Denote these short- term changes by '*dx*' and '*dy*' for variables *x* and *y* respectively.

(*iii*) Find dx^2 and dy^2 and calculate Σdx^2 and Σdy^2.

(*iv*) Multiply *dx* and dy and find $\Sigma dx.dy$. The correlation coefficient '*r*' is given by

$r = (\Sigma dx.dy)/ \sqrt{(\Sigma dx^2.\Sigma dy^2)}$

3.17. REGRESSION IN MODERN STATISTICAL LITERATURE

The coefficient of correlation between the two variables gives us an abstract form of the amount of relationship between the two variables. We may be interested in studying the change in one variable on the average for a unit change in the other. For example, if we know the relationship between the national income and tax yields for a given tax structure rates, we may be interested to estimate tax receipts at various levels of national income. The statistical device, with the help of which we estimate or predict the unknown values of one variable from the unknown values of another variable is called **'regression'.** Regression is the measure of the average relationship between two or more variables in terms of original units of the data.

Regression lines are drawn when two variables have a linear relationship. When ever there exists a linear relationship between variables *x* and *y*, the plotted dots of the scatter diagram will be found to be concentrated round a certain curve. Generally the dots on the scatter diagram lie in a zone nearer to a straight line. We can fit a straight line passing through the dots of the scatter diagram. This is the line of **best fist.** If the straight line is an adequate fit for the data, the regression is said to be linear. A line of regression gives the best mean values of one variable for any given value of the other variable. For two variables *x* and *y*, there will be two regression lines, one showing the best mean values of x corresponding to mean values of y and the other showing the best mean values of '*y*' corresponding to mean values of '*x*'. That is to say that the regression line so x and y provides the most probable values of *x* when the exact values of *y* is given and the other line *y* on *x* gives the most probable value of *y* when the exact value of *x* is known. Thus we get two lines. If two lines coincide with each other then the correlation is either perfect positive or perfect negative. We will get only one regression line on the graph and this line will give the required values of both the variables. The farther the lines are away from each other, the lesser is the degree of correlation. If the lines are nearer, the higher is the degree of correlation. If the regression lines intersect each other at right angles the variables are un- correlated.

Regression coefficient : The coefficient of regression gives the value by which one variable changes for a unit change in the other variable.

The coefficient of regression of *x* and *y* gives the value by which *x* series change for a unit change in y. it is given by: $r(\sigma_x/\sigma_y)$.

The coefficient of regression of *y* on *x* gives the value by which *y* series change for a unit change in *y*. It is given by: $r(\sigma_y/\sigma_x)$.

The coefficient of correlation between two variables *x* and *y* is given by:

$$r = \sqrt{(r\sigma_x/\sigma_y)} \times \sqrt{(r\sigma_y/\sigma_x)} = \sqrt{r^2} = r.$$

$r(r\sigma_x/\sigma_y)$ and $r(\sigma_y/\sigma_x)$ can also be written as follows :

If *y* is independent variable and *x* is dependent variable that is for a given value of *y* the value of *x* is to be measured, then regression coefficient of *x* on *y* is:

$r(\sigma_x/\sigma_y) = (\Sigma dx.dy)/\Sigma dy^2$, where *dx* and *dy* are deviations of *x* and *y* from respective means.

If deviations are taken from assumed means, then the values of regression coefficient is given by:

$r(\sigma_x / \sigma_y) = [(\Sigma\, dx.dy) - (\Sigma\, dx.\Sigma\, dy)/n]/[(\Sigma dy^2) - (\Sigma dy^2/n]$.

In case *x* is the independent variable and *y* is the dependent variable than the formula is :

$r\sigma_x / \sigma_y = \Sigma dx.dy / \Sigma dy^2$

If *dx* and *dy* are from the assumed means then :

$r\sigma_y / \sigma_x = [(\Sigma dx.dy) - (\Sigma dx.\Sigma dy)/n] / [(\Sigma dx^2) - (\Sigma dx^2/n)]$.

Example 3.16 : Find the regression equation for the data given below :

Variable *x*	18	19	20	21	22	23	24	25	26	27
Variable *y*	17	17	18	18	18	19	19	20	21	22

Solution:

Variable x	dx = x – A = x – 23	dx^2	Variable Y	dy = y – B = y – 18	dy^2	dx.dy
18	–5	25	17	–1	1	5
19	–4	16	17	–1	1	4
20	–3	9	18	0	0	0
21	–2	4	18	0	0	0
22	–1	1	18	0	0	0
22	0	0	19	1	1	1
24	1	1	19	1	1	1
25	2	4	20	2	4	4
26	3	9	22	4	16	16
27	4	16	22	4	16	16
Σx–225	Σdx––5	Σdx^2–85	Σy–189	Σdy–9	Σdy^2–33	Σdx.dy–39

$$r = \left[\frac{(\Sigma dx.dy)-(\Sigma dx.dy)}{n}\right] \div \sqrt{\left[\frac{\Sigma dx^2 - \Sigma dx^2}{n} \times \Sigma dy^2 - \Sigma dy^{2/n}\right]}$$

$$= [39 - (-5 \times 9)/10] / \sqrt{[85\text{-}(5^2/10] \times [33\text{-}(9^2/10]} - 43.5/45.5 = 0.96$$

$$\sigma_x - \sqrt{\left[\left(\frac{\Sigma dx^2}{n}\right)-\left(\frac{\Sigma dx}{n}\right)^2\right]} = \sqrt{\left[\left(\frac{85}{10}\right)-\left(\frac{-5}{10}\right)^2\right]} = \sqrt{8.25} = 2.87$$

$$\sigma_y - \sqrt{\left[\left(\frac{\Sigma dy^2}{n}\right)-\left(\frac{\Sigma dy}{n}\right)^2\right]} = \sqrt{\left[\left(\frac{33}{10}\right)-\left(\frac{9}{10}\right)^2\right]} = \sqrt{2.49} = 1.58$$

Equations for the two regression lines are

$$x - \bar{x} = r\left(\frac{\sigma_x}{\sigma_y}\right) \times \left(\frac{y}{\bar{y}}\right) = x - 23.5 = 0.96 \times \left(\frac{2.87}{1.58}\right) \times (y - 18.9) = 1.74y - 1.74 \times 18.9$$

Therefore $x = 1.74y - 9.386$

(*ii*) The regression of y on x is

$$y - \bar{y} = r\left(\frac{\sigma_x}{\sigma_y}\right)(x - \bar{x}) = \text{y} - 18.9 = 0.96 \times \left(\frac{1.58}{2.87}\right) \times (x - 23.5)$$

$y - 18.9 = 0.53x - 0.53 \times 23.5$,
Therefore, $y = 0.53x + 6.445$.

3.17.1. Difference between Correlation and Regression

(*i*) Correlation measures the degree of association between two variables x and y, where as regression brings into light the nature of relationship.

(*ii*) In regression analysis, the cause and effect relationship is more visible than in correlation. Correlation is a two way average of relationship, where as regression is unidirectional

3.18. BOX-JENKINS METHOD

This method has taken from the control theory. In a control system, there is a target, which has to be tackled, where the target itself is moving or changing its value or position. The control mechanism measures the difference between the target and the actual output. Analogues to the target are the demand in the forecasting system that is to be tracked by forecasting. Any error is used along with its derivatives and integrals for improving the forecast for the next period and so on. The equation is:

New Forecast = Old forecast + the derivative term: *A* (error in old forecast)+ time derivative term: *B* (change in error between last time and time immediately before) + the integral term: *C* (sum of the errors so far).

$F_l = F_{l-1} + (r-1)(e_{t-1} - e_{t-2}) + r_e(e_t - 1) + r_l.\ {}^{t-1}\Sigma e_t$.

3.19. METHOD OF SIMULATION

There are many problems experienced in day-to-day life. Where some mathematical model or some times the model cannot satisfactorily represent becomes so much complicated that its solution by analytical methods is not possible. In such situations Simulation or Monte-Carlo method is used. This method is generally used where distribution function are determined with the help of Random Numbers.

A Simulation model is an image of reality, which allows the solution of a problem, by trial and error approach. Monte-Carlo technique is a device for studying an artificial stochastic model of a physical or mathematical process. It is the combination of probability and sampling methods. A good simulation model should be (*i*) Accurate, (*ii*) Acceptable to the problem on hand and (*iii*) Quick to generate.

Steps in Simulation Method.

(*i*) Past behavior of the system is determined by conducting preliminary survey. This is done with past data available in records.

(*ii*) Some appropriate method is selected for the system with the help of sample observations obtained in step (*i*) above

(*iii*) The model in step (*ii*) is used to determine the probability distribution of the characteristic under study. The probability distribution can be worked out into cumulative distribution function

(*iv*) Random numbers are chosen from random number tables and are used to find the sequence of values of the variable of interest.

(*v*) Some standard mathematical function is fitted to the values obtained in the step (*iv*) above.

Problem 3.17. A newspaper dealer has collected the following data on weekend demand for papers. Simulate requirement for 10-week ends.

Number of Papers × 100	12	13	14	15	16	17	18	19	20	21
Frequency	13	9	11	15	13	17	14	12	3	2

Solution :

Demand	Frequency frequency	Cumulative intervals	Random number
12	1	1	00-01
13	3	4	02-04
14	9	13	05-13
15	11	24	14-24
16	15	39	25-39
17	13	52	40-52
18	17	69	53-69
19	14	83	70-83
20	12	96	84-96
21	3	98	96-98
22	2	100	99-100

Now for simulating the demand for 10-week ends, read the 10 random numbers from the random number tables.

Day	Random number	Random number intervals	Simulated demand
1	9	05-13	14
2	73	70-83	19
3	25	25-39	16
4	33	25-39	16
5	76	70-83	19
6	53	53-69	18
7	01	00-01	12
8	35	25-39	16
9	86	84-95	20
10	34	25-39	16

3.19.1. MARKOV PROCESS

Any stochastic process, which develops with time according to some law of probability, is known as **Markov Process.** At every point of time the process is exactly in one of its possible states. The possible states of a Monrov Process are the list of all possible outcomes at some point of time.

Its transitional matrix characterizes a Markov Process, which is a set of initial and transitional probabilities. The transitional matrix gives the step-by-step transitional probabilities of a Markov Process. The matrix has the following properties.

(*i*) Each element of the matrix should be of some probability.

(*ii*) The sum of the elements of each row in the matrix should be unity (=1), i.e. the process at some point of time should be in any one of the states

Problem 3.18. Three manufacturers *A*, *B* and *C* are competing with each other. The following matrix gives transitional probabilities that customers will move from one manufacturer to the other in any month. Interpret the matrix in terms of (*a*) Return and Loss and (*b*) Returns and Gains.

		To	
From	*A*	*B*	*C*
A	0.7	0.1	0.2
B	0.1	0.8	0.1
C	0.2	0.1	0.7

Solution: Each element of the matrix has value between 0 and 1 and the sum of elements either row wise or column wise is equal to unity. The matrix is a transitional matrix.

Each manufacturer can use each row of the matrix to interpret the monthly return on loss

Row I: It is observed that A retains 70% of its customers but looses 10% to *B* and 20% to *C*

Row II: B retains 80% and looses to *B* 10% and to C 10%.

Row III. C retains 70% and looses 20% to *A* and 10% *B*.

Suppose in the beginning we take that there are 1000 customers with *A*, 2000 customers with *B* and 3000 customers with *C*, the number of customers with *A, B* and *C* after a month is:

From	*A*	*B*	*C*	*Total*
A	700	100	200	1000
B	200	1600	200	2000
C	600	200	2100	3000
Total	**1500**	**2000**	**2500**	**6000**

Thus *A* gains 500 customers, *B* has the same number of customers and *C* looses 500 customers.

3.20. INPUT-OUTPUT ANALYSIS

Input–output analysis reflects a general theory of production based on the idea of economic interdependence. Many input – output models are useful in forecasting. Input – output analysis takes into consideration the interdependence of the different sectors in the economy. This is because; the input to one sector is output of another sector. For example, the output of coal industry will be an input to the steel plant and the output of steel industry is an input to the construction industry and so on. There are many such cyclic relations within the various sectors of economy. Taking the data of outputs and inputs and studying the relationship between these two, we will be in a position to analyze the total demand for a product and the output required from industrial units. This type of analysis is very important because it takes into account all the intricate relationships in the economy. One of the limitations in this method is that the utility of an output is restricted to economic analysis, not considering the other business, governmental, technological and internal factors. It is limited but useful analysis. The analysis need not be limited to macro-level, speaking only in terms steel sector and coal sector etc. It may be mote *'micro'*, by considering the inputs and outputs within a general product group in the total economy. This type of analysis is very much used and is found more beneficial and useful. Three major assumptions given by *W.W.Leontief* in developing this technique are:

1. The total output of an industry is consumed as input by all industries for a time period, under consideration.
2. The input bought by each industry has usually been made dependent only on the industry's level of output.

3. The ratio of an industry's input to its output, once established is fixed. This ratio is known as *input-output number* or *production coefficient*.

3.21. ECONOMETRICS

This method is also known as *statistical economics* or *empirical economics* or *quantitative economics* is based on the empirical data and economic theory. The process of developing an econometric model contains five steps. They are:

1. Specifying what is to be measured?
2. Specifying the economic variables, which have influence the items specified above in (1).
3. Collection of relevant data.
4. Constructing the model based on the collected data and theoretical relationships among the relevant variables.
5. Analysis of empirically derived results.

QUESTIONS

1. Define forecasting. List out the properties of good forecasting method. What steps you follow while making forecast?
2. List out various methods of forecasting. Explain any two methods in detail.
3. What do you mean by Time Series? Briefly explain the elements of Time series.
4. The following data is available regarding the sales of a certain product. Find the Trend of sales by using (*a*) 3-yearly moving averages and (*b*) Four yearly moving averages.

Year	1970	1971	1972	1973	1974	1975	1976	1977	1978
Sales X 1000	10	12	15	14	16	17	18	19	20

5. Fit a linear trend for the data given below and forecast for 1974.

Year	1970	1971	1972	1973
X	100	150	125	175
Y	20	38	38	62

4

PRODUCTION PLANNING

- INTRODUCTION
- Production Planning
- Factory Planning
  Process Planning,
  Operation planning.
- Factors to be considered before starting planning.
  Resource allocations
  Planning Quantity Standards.
    - Requirement Quantity
    - Write-off quantity
    - Sanction Quantity
    - Rate of Stock turn over
- Planning Specifications.
- Routing decisions:
  Make and Buy Decision
  Material form, Shape, and Quantity.
  Routing or Operation Layout.
  Planning the Assembly Line.
  LINE OF BALANCE (LOB)
  Heuristic Method
  Kilbridge Method.
  Balancing Multi-Product line
  Linear Programming Approach.
- MODULAR PRODUCTOIN AND GROUP TECHNOLOGY.

4.1. INTRODUCTION

Production Planning is the function of management, concerned with deciding what production facilities are required; how these production facilities should be laid out in the space available for production and how they should be used to produce the desired products. This function has two main aspects; first one is concerned with 'routing or planning the sequence of operations/processes/work tasks that have to be carried out to complete the required product and the second one is concerned with layout or spatial relationship between the places where the work is done. In this chapter let us discuss about the activities of production manager to fulfill the objectives of the above-mentioned two aspects.

4.2. PRODUCTION PLANNING

Production planning is the function concerned with **planning, organizing, directing and controlling** the *materials and methods* to be used to make the products, and the way in which the production facilities such as *buildings, machines and equipment, etc.,* should be laid out in the space available for production.

All functions of management will be most effective when it is done progressively. So also the production planning and control, to be more effective, should be progressive. This is to say that, best results are obtained when planning starts with a broad analysis and then proceeds, step-by-step, to fill in more details. These steps in planning or levels of planning used in production planning are named as: *i. Factory Planning, ii. Process Planning and iii. Operation Planning.*

4.2.1 Factory Planning

This is the first level of production planning. At this level the sequence of work tasks is planned in units of the process, and the spatial relationship of work places is planned. Here we decide what departments such as Foundry department, Machining department and Assembly department. Etc., are required to complete the product. Then to have a smooth flow of material we allocate a place in the factory to the department, so that materials flow from department to department sequentially. This may also be termed as *planning the department.* It is very much similar to planning the different rooms while preparing a plan for a house. Each room is situated in a right way so that inmates will have a comfortable stay.

4.2.2. Process planning

This is the second level of progressive production planning. At this level each department found in the above level is considered further and the flow of material in each department is considered. Here the requirement of facilities to get the desired physical change in the material is concerned. Then a proper place is allocated to each facility depending the flow pattern of material and a layout of facilities in the space available is prepared. The point to be considered while preparing layout is that material flow smoothly in the department. This is to say that we are planning the process in second level of production planning. It is very much similar to arranging the furniture in the room of a house, with a view to see that there will be no obstruction to do day-to-day work.

4.2.3. Operation Planning

Operation planning is the third level of production planning. Here we consider each and every production facility, particularly machinery and equipment and the work is divided into elements, then how each operation is performed and in which sequence is planned. This will help to see that maximum efficiency is achieved in producing a product. That is the available time, material, capacity of machine and labor force is utilized effectively in producing the product. This will increase the productivity and cost of production is controlled.

4.3. FACTORS TO BE CONSIDERED BEFORE STARTING PRODUCTION PLANNING

Before thinking of routing, the production-planning engineer must think of allocation of resources available in the company to maximize the profit function. If the company is manufacturing a single product he has to decide how much he has to produce and sell to maximize the profit. Also, he must think of how to utilize the idle capacity (if any) of resources/facilities available.

In case, the company is manufacturing multi products, by utilizing the available resources, say for example the company manufactures three products *X*, Y and *Z*. Depending on the profit contribution of each product demand for each product and the requirement of resources by each product, he has to work out how much of each product is to be manufactured to maximize the profit function. Here he can conveniently use the Operations Research tools—such as Linear Programming or Integer Programming to find the quantities of each product to be manufactured. Also he can plan for utilization of idle resources, if any. This is illustrated by a simple problem. For further details, readers are advised to refer to Operations Research book.

Example 4.1 : A manufacturer produces two products X and Y in two steps on two machines A and B. The process times for each product on two machines are X takes 4 hours on machine A and 5 hours on machine B. Y takes 5 hours on machine A and 2 hours on machine B. A has got 80 hours and B has got 120 hours available for production in the coming planning period. The profit contribution of product Y is Rs.5/- per unit and that of X is Rs.10/- per unit. The demand for both products is not restricted. Determine the optimal product mix.

Solution: When we have two products (variables) in the problem, it can be solved by graphical method. In case the problem has more than two variables, Simplex method is used to solve the problem.

First we shall discuss the **Simplex method.**

Machines	*Products (time in hours)*		*Availability (in hours)*
	X	*Y*	
A	4	5	80
B	5	2	120

(*i*) As we have to maximize the profit, the objective function of the problem is:
Maximize $Z = 10x + 5y$

(*ii*) Structural constrains are: $4x + 5y \leq 80$ for machine A
$5x + 2y \leq 120$ for machine B

(*iii*) As the production of units cannot be negative, the non-negativity constraint is:
Both x and y should be ≥ 0.

Therefore the problem may be written as:

Maximize $Z = 10x + 5y$ subject to a condition,

$4x + 5y \leq 80$

$5x + 2y \leq 120$ and

Both x and y are ≥ 0

The above inequalities are to be converted into equations to enable us to use simplex method.

To convert an inequality into an equation we consider here a variable known as *slack variable.* The slack variable generally represented by a letter S. As far machine A is concerned S_1 is the slack variable. If we want physical interpretation of S_1 it is an imaginary product, which requires processing on machine A only and requires one hour (or one unit of time) for each unit.

Now if the company does not manufacture product X or Y and want to manufacture only S_1, it can manufacture 80 units. The profit contribution of S_1 is taken as zero. Hence by manufacturing S_1

the company will not make any profit. That means to say that the machine A is idle. In simple words the slack variable S indicates the idle capacity of the facility. Similarly S_2 is the slack variable for machine B. By introducing S_1 and S_2 in the problem the inequalities becomes equations. Now the equations are written as:

$$\text{Max } \underline{Z} = 0x + 5y + 0S_1 + 0S_2 \text{ s.t}$$
$$4x + 5y + 1S_1 = 80$$
$$5x + 2y + 1S_2 = 120 \text{ and}$$
$$x, y, S_1 \text{ and } S_2 \text{ all are} \geq 0$$

First let us consider that company manufactures the imaginary products S_1 and S_2 only and earns a profit of zero rupees. This is shown in Simplex table I. If the company wants to make profit, it must utilize its idle capacity $S_1 = 80$ and $S_2 = 120$ to manufacture products X and Y. Which one to manufacture? To find this we use the concept of *opportunity cost.*

Simplex Table I:

Product	*Profit*	*Capa-city*	*10* *X*	*5* *Y*	*0* S_1	*0* S_2	*Replacement Ratio.*
S_1	0	80	4	5	1	0	$\frac{80}{4} = 20$
S_2	0	120	5	2	0	1	$\frac{120}{5} = 24$
Net evaluation	—	—	10↑	5	0	0	—

At present the company is manufacturing the products S_1 and S_2. Therefore the solution at this stage is $S_1 = 80$, $S_2 = 120$ and the profit is $Z = 0 \times 80 + 0 \times 120 =$ Rs. 00.00

Instead of manufacturing S_1 and S_2, if it manufactures x and y the company will get a profit of Rs. 10/- for each unit of x and Rs. 5/- for each unit of y. To manufacture x, for each unit of x , 4 units of S_1 and 5 units of $S_2$are to be sacrificed (or utilized). Similarly for each unit of y, 5 units of S_1 and 2 units of S_2 are to be sacrificed. Hence opportunity cost of not manufacturing x and y is:

For each unit of x, $(10 \times 1) - (4 \times 0 + 5 \times 0) =$ Rs.10/-

For each unit of y, $(5 \times 1) - (5 \times 0 + 2 \times 0) =$ Rs .5/-

This means to say that if the company does not manufacture x at this stage, it looses Rs.10/-per each unit of x not manufactured. Similarly the opportunity cost of not manufacturing y is Rs.5/-. This we can see in net evaluation row. We select the highest opportunity cost and put an arrow mark (↑) there. So product x is to be manufactured. The column under x is known as *key-column,* and is enclosed in a rectangle. The variable x is known as incoming variable.

The procedure for finding the out going variable is dividing the capacity column element by key column element. This is entered in replacement ratio column. To identify the outgoing variable, select the lowest of the replacement ratios and put a tick (√) mark against it. Enclose the elements of marked row in a rectangle as shown in the stand. This row is known as *key row.* The element at the intersection of key row and key column is known as *key number.* To get the second simplex table the steps shown below are followed.

(*i*) To transfer key row, divide all the elements of key row by key number.

(*ii*) To transfer the non key row: New row number = Old row number –Corresponding key row number × (key column number/ key number)

Simplex table II.

Z= Rs. 200/-, $S_1 = 0$, S_2=20, $x = 20$ and $y = 0$.

Product	*Profit*	*Capacity*	*10* *x*	5 *y*	*0* *S_1*	S_2 *0*
X	10	20	1	5/4	¼	0
S_2	0	20	0	−17/4	−5/4	1
N.E. Row			0	−15/2	−5/2	0

As all the elements in the net evaluation row are negative the solution is optimal. That is company will get an optimal profit if it manufactures 20 units of X. It will have idle capacity of 20 hours on machine B. Hence the solution is:

$X = 20$, $Y = 0$, $S_1 = 0$, $S_2 = 20$ and Z = Rs. 20 × 10 = Rs. 200/-

The same problem can be solved graphically, as there are two variables.

Graphical method:

Maximize $Z = 10x + 5y$ s.t

$4x + 5y \leq 80$

$5x + 2y \leq 120$ and

Both x and y are ≥ 0.

In graphical solutions we assume above inequalities as equations. Now they can be written as

Max $Z = 10x + 5y$ s.t

$4x + 5y = 80$

$5x + 2y = 120$ and both x and $y \geq 0$.

In first equation, if $x = 0$, then $y = 16$ and if $y = 0$ then $x = 20$, similarly

In second equation, if $x = 0$ $y = 60$ and if $y = 0$, $x = 24$. Plotting this on the graph, we get the graph shown below:

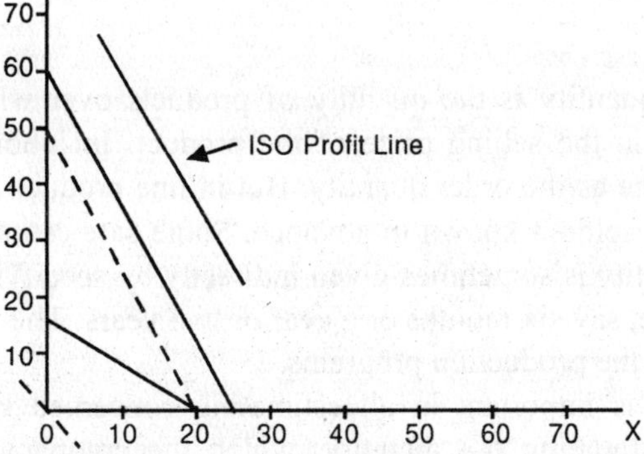

Assume a profit and find the boundary values of x and y. The mark these points on the graph and draw a line joining these points. This line is known an *iso-profit line*. Draw a parallel line to iso-profit line at origin. Then draw parallel lines to the line drawn at origin to show various iso-profit lines. While doing so, one line passes through the extreme corner (or line). This is the line, which indicates the maximum profit that the company can earn. The point through the line passes will give us the values of x and y, which are the solutions of the problem. In case the iso-profit line passes through a point, the problem has unique solution. In case the line coincides with a line on the graph, then all the points on that line are optimal solutions to the problem. We can say that the problem has got alternative solutions

This is how the production manager has to allocate the available resources to various products his company has to manufacture.

Once the resources are allocated, i.e. in the above case the capacities to machine A and B are allocated to manufacture X and Y to get a profit of Rs.200/-, the next decision is to be taken is planning of quantities for which the plans are to be prepared. This is particularly true in multi product manufacturing companies. The planning quantity standards are to be specified, so that production manager will have an idea about for what quantity of each product he has to prepare schedules.

4.4. THE PLANNING QUANTITY STANDARDS

All planning decisions are vitally concerned with quantity and before the planner can start the work, he must have at least a rough idea of the quantities for which he is to plan. Ideally, he needs four items of information about future production plans. These are known as *Planning Quantity Standards,* and are set out as discussed below.

4.4.1. Requirement Quantity

In jobbing production, the requirement quantity is simply found from the quantity specified on the order, and the period of time over which delivery is to be effected does not greatly influence the production planning decisions. In all forms of continuous production, however, the requirement quantity has little meaning unless it is related to some specific period of time. For this reason it is normally specified as so many items per annum, or per convenient planning period. In batch production it is very difficult task to work out the requirement quantity. Batch quantity for different products is to be worked out depending on the demand and other factors.

4.4.2. Write-off Quantity

The tooling write-off quantity is the quantity of products over which the cost of any special tooling must be recovered in the selling price of the product. In jobbing production the write-off quantity is normally the same as the order quantity. But in line production and batch production, the total quantity to be made is seldom known in advance. Some safe estimate of the probable quantity has to be chosen. This quantity is sometimes given indirectly by specifying that all tooling cost must be recovered in a given time, say six months or a year or two years. The write-off quantity concerned can then be calculated from the production programs.

The write-off quantity is important in all estimating concerned with the choice of planning methods. It is fixed by estimating the quantity, which the company can confidently expect to produce and sell before a design change is necessary. This particularly true when company is dealing with a product which has high rate of competition. The company has to race against competition. As the opponent companies goes on changing the aesthetic shape/design of the product, the manufacturer has to go for a change in his product also to remain in the competitive market. It is the policy decision, which should normally receive higher management approval. If you just look at the consumer products available in the market, say for example, Detergent cake or powder. First they start with Detergent cake or powder and goes on changing it a cake with extra whitening power. Then in next change they say cake with " Super Shakti" and so on. This is inevitable in a competitive market.

In general, it is sufficient for competitive purpose in production planning to compare the direct costs plus the tooling costs for alternative methods, basing the comparison in all cusses on the write-off quantity. A small error may be introduced by simplification due to variations in the direct expenses, but in general run of engineering planning this error is unlikely to be large. Consider the example in table 4.1. Here three alternatives are compared for an operation. From the information given in the table, we can calculate the write-off quantity.

TABLE 4.1 COST COMPAARISION- WRITE – OFF QUANTITY BASIS

	Particulars	*Method I*	*Method II*	*Method III*
1.	Write-off quantity (Nos)	10,000	10,000	10,000
2.	Tooling cost (Rs.)	200	4400	800
3.	Direct material cost for 10000 numbers in Rs.	2500	3000	2000
4.	Direct labour cost for 10000 units in Rs.	600	500	200
5.	Direct cost for write-off quantity in Rs.	3,300	3,900	3,000

As the method III has lowest cost for write-off quantity it is selected for production.

4.4.3. THE SANCTION QUANTITY

The sanction quantity is the quantity of products for which authority has been given to cover the purchase of materials. It represents the maximum quantity of products to which the top management is prepared to commit the company in advance as far as expenses are concerned. The sanction quantity is of particular importance in purchasing; as it is the index, which controls the quantity, specified in all purchase orders, which largely controls the cost of production. The sanction quantity is not necessarily the same as the "order quantity", nor generally same as the "batch quantity" in which deliveries are to be made.

In practice, it is usual for the long term program to be used as the basis for forward planning in its broadest sense, but this program is then confirmed periodically, the issue of sanction, authorizing the placing of purchase orders for next quantity of production. Each sanction has to be given some time in advance of the date on which the previous one will become exhausted, to allow for continuity of production. The purchase orders placed as a result of the sanction may not necessarily be for the whole sanction quantity, as there may be adjustments necessary to use up stocks and surplus purchase commitments which have arisen due to design or program changes in the previous period. The sanction given mostly depends on the financial position and credibility of the company.

Like the write-off quantity, the sanction quantity is sometimes given indirectly, by authorizing that order may be issued to cover a given period of time – say six months or a year. The sanction quantity for different parts can then be calculated from the program.

4.4.4. Rate of stock turn over and order quantity

One further piece of information, which is of vital interest to the production planner, is the quantity, which will be used for parts manufacture in the works and for purchase deliveries. The most satisfactory way of specifying this quantity is to fix a standard, or at least a minimum rate of stock turn over. There is a close linear relationship between the rate of stock turn over and the order frequency or the number of order per annum, and knowing the required rate of stock turn over, it is simply to specify a minimum order frequency. If the annual requirement of any product/material/ component is known, the order quantities for production of the parts can be worked out. This is shown in table 4.2. A simple case is given in the table. The annual requirement is 2000 units of the component.

TABLE: 4.2. TABLE SHOWING THE RELATIONSHIP BETRWEEN BATCH FREEQUENCY AND BATCH QUANTITY.

Order frequency (Orders per year)	1	2	3	4	5	6	7	8	9	10
Order quantity	2000	1000	667	500	400	334	286	250	223	200

Requirement quantity = 2000 units per year

It should be remembered that there is a limit to the amount of circulating capital available in the company, and that the quantity of output which can be obtained without risking failure is mainly limited by the rate of stock turn over, and therefore by the batch quantity. But it is very difficult in practice to obtain the required stock turn over.

4.4.5. Planning specification

A document used for showing the quantity standards and production plan is known as *planning specification.* This is shown in figure 4.1 on page number 77.

The planning specification gives us the four quantities discussed above and method of introducing and the target cost. This is a basic policy document and is to be approved by higher management.

4.5. ROUTING DECISIONS

When choosing the method of production for an item to be used in assembled product, it will be found generally that for each item there are seven decisions to be made. The seven *routing decisions* are:

(*i*) Whether the product/component is to be made or buy? (Make or Buy decision),
(*ii*) Material form and shape to be used,
(*iii*) The division of work to be done into operations,
(*iv*) The choice of machine /facility or work center, on which each operation is to be done,
(*v*) The sequence in which each operation is to be done,
(*vi*) The division of each operation into elements, and
(*vii*) The choice of special tooling.

Generally, to take decisions a committee of managers of the concerned department is arranged to discuss the matter. In fact the first decision, to make or buy, all managers such as production manager, design manager, purchase manager are consulted. As far as material form and shape are concerned, materials manager, design and production managers are the key persons. The other decisions from iii to vii, industrial engineering manager and production manager have to take decisions. Each of the above mentioned decisions are dealt in detail below:

PLANNING SPECIFICATION

Product :- **Specification :-**

A. Output Required

1. Estimated sales requirement.

Year	1995	1996	1997	1998	1999	2000	2001
Demand	12000	12000	12500	12500	12500	New model	Probable.

Program of production :

(*i*) Proto type : Already under test.

(*ii*) Pre-production batch : 200 sets by January 1995.

(*iii*) Complete tooling : 15th March 1995.

(*iv*) Start production : 20th March 1995.

B. Order Quantity or Cycle :

1. Class 'A' material (high value) : 26 batches per year.
2. Class 'B' material (medium value) : 12 batches per year.
3. Class 'C' material (common parts) : 3 batches per year.

C. Sanction Quantity :

1. Up to completion of 2100 products : 2100 sets.
2. After completion of 2100 products : Review at every 1500 sets.

D. Tooling cost :

1. Budgeted :
   - (*a*) Special tooling (Rs.) — Rs. 30,000
   - (*b*) Write-off quantity : (No.) — 13,000 sets.
2. Budgeted :
   - (*a*) Non-standard tooling (Rs.) — Rs. 15,000
   - (*b*) Write-off quantity : (No.) — 20,000 sets.

E. Target production Cost :

		Each Rs.
1. Direct material cost :	(*a*) Component products :	4
	(*b*) Assembly	1
2. Indirect Materials :	(*a*) Special materials :	7
	(*b*) General Materials :	1
	(*c*) Components :	12
	Total :	25

Issued By : Date :

Figure. 4.1 : Planning specifications

4.5.1. Make or buy decision

Every Company is faced with the problem of deciding whether to make all the components required for the product or to purchase from outside and assemble. In fact almost every company purchases some of the components required for its product and rest of them are manufactured. In case one company has to manufacture all the components required by the product, then the company will become unmanageable. Consider the manufacture of an automobile vehicle. One company will not manufacture all the components required to manufacture the vehicle. They purchase engine block, piston, tyres, bolts, nuts and glass parts required for the vehicle from various suppliers and assemble the vehicle with their brand name. There are several implications in make or buy decision, and in fact it has many aspects of policy and management involved in it. The purchase manager is usually a participant in decisions of this nature and it is he who can give expert advice on the availability and price of such materials and components to be purchased by the organizations.

Every component can be provided by two means: Procure it from outside or make it yourself in your factory. Which is more economical and practicable? The comparative merits and demerits of each of these two alternatives will have to be evaluated. There are several; parameters on which such evaluation has to make. They are shown below in table 4.3

Some times when investment is a problem, the management look for idle capacity available in other factories (specially new, small/medium sized industries) and take that capacity on lease or hire and produce the component with their own materials on the facilities available in the leased units. This will help the new entrepreneurs to get accustomed with manufacturing activities and slowly they start manufacturing the product for which they have started the venture. This act of taking the capacity on lease and helping the new entrepreneurs is known as *wet-nursing*.

Example. 4.2. If a company invests Rs. 5000/- on a new machine it will be able to make the product at a cost of Rs.2/- per unit in variable costs. If it buys the product it would cost Rs.3/- per unit for quantities up to 10,000 units. Calculate Break-Even-Point for make or buy decision.

Solution:

$3 \times N = 5000 + 2N$, where N = Break-even quantity.

By simplifying we get $N = 5000$ units,

Buying is advisable up to 5000 units and thereafter making is considered.

TABLE 4.3: FACTORS TO BE CONSIDERED TO DECIDE WHETEHR TO MAKE OR BUY A COMPONENT.

To make the component	To buy the component.
I. If the cost study shows that it is cheaper to manufacture, then make it. The cost study should not merely an estimate. It should be accurate.	1. If the cost studies shows it cheaper to buy, then buy the product.
2. If the company's product requires close *quality control*, and if the company stand in the market for its quality brand, irrespective of the cost, make the component.	2. In case the company does not insist on close quality control, then buy it.
3. If the company is already making similar components, and the *know how* of the of the component under question suits the available technology, tradition and facilities, then make it.	3. In case the technology required for making the component does not suits the available know how and facilities, buy the component.
4. When *idle capacity* is available to absorb overheads, make the component.	4. When the idle capacity is not available, by the product.

5. When the item required needs *extensive investment* in facilities that are not available at suppliers end and suppliers does not show any interest in investing and supplying you, then make the component.	5. If the investment on facilities is not high and the suppliers are interested in investing and supplying, then buy the component.
6. In case *the return on investment* is attractive, invest on assets and make the product,	6. If the return on investment is not attractive, then buy the product.
7. The *quantity* required by you is too small and no suppliers are interested in supplying that small quantity to you, then make the component.	7. If the quantity require by you is not a problem for the suppliers, then buy the component.
8. If the component demands *direct supervision* to maintain the quality, then makes the component.	8. If the direct supervision is not required and the supplier can give you the required quality, buy the component.
9. If making facilitates your *control of part changes, inventories and delivery dates*, then make the component.	9. If buying does not disturb your control of part changes, inventory problems and delivery dates, then buy the component.
10. If the *transport* of the component/product from supplier's end to your unit is a problem, then make the component/product.	10. If transport of the product/component is not a problem, the buy it.
11. When you do not want depend on a *single outside supplier,* for your requirement, then make the component.	11. If the outside sources satisfy your requirement, buy the component.
12. If the *design of the component or formula used is confidential,* then make the component.	12. If secrecy of design/formula is not a problem, then buy the component.
13. If *Tax considerations* prefers making, make the component.	13. Tax considerations prefers buying, by the component.
14. If you have a registered *patent* to make the product/ component, then make it.	14. If the patent and other legal barriers prevent you from making it, then buy the component.
15. If the *demand* for the product is steady and continuously increasing then invest in making.	15. If the demand for the component is not stable and seasonal, then better to buy it.
16. When your executives have time to divert their attention to make the product and facilities are available, then make the component.	16. When you want your executives to concentrate their effort on your specialty, then buy the component.

4.5.2. Material form and shape and quantity

When a product is designed, the designer specifies the materials to be used to make the product and shows the finished shapes of the component Now it is the duty of production planner to decide (*i*) Material form, (*ii*) Material shape and (*iii*) Quantity of materials.

The choice of material form concerns with the type of material that shall be used. Say if you want to manufacture a gear blank with mild steel, it might be possible to start with mild steel bar, mild steel casting and mild steel drop stamping. Each of the above said material has different mechanical properties depending on the process used to get a bar, casting or stamping. Selection of the material to be used depends on the function of the component, quantity required and facilities available. Depending on the function and the quantity required the production planner might prefer one of the above-said material forms.

Material shape concerns with the provisions of machining allowances and of special features in the material design, to assist the production. Providing lugs on the sides of the product can reduce often production costs, so that it will be easy to hold in the machine while machining. After the completion of production process, the lugs may be removed.

Finally, although the designer will show on the drawing the finished sizes of the component, in the case of general materials, it is necessary to work out how much material will be wasted in processing and thus determine the total quantity required to make the given number of components. The whole of the above information is provided in a document known a *material schedule,* so as to help production control department to indent the required quantity of material.

***(i)* MATERIAL FORM :** The choice of the material is mainly depends on the output. A gear wheel for a machine, of which only 50 a year were to be produced, would probably made from a bar. If the same gear wheel, the demand per year were 50,000 per year, it would be advisable to go for drop stamping. The choice is a simple and straight forward as far economics is concerned. It is not possible simply to state that the material must have a certain chemical composition and that any form of material can be used if it has that composition. The method of manufacture (drawing, casting and forging) will affect the nature and physical properties of the material and must be taken into account. This is because material structure is mostly depends on the method of manufacture. Say for example the designer might be quite satisfied with a simple mild steel for a part made from a drop stamping, but he insist on a higher alloy specification if the same part were made from a bar, because in the later case the grain flow would not have the ideal configuration. For this reason *material form* is one of the decisions, which have to be made jointly by close cooperation between design and production, planning departmental heads. The fact, however, that there is a choice must never be forgotten. The choice of most economical form of material for a given output does have a very important effect on product cost.

***(ii)* MATERIAL SHAPE :** Providing special lugs or projections or sometime holes on a casting is a common practice to ease the production. Some times this principle is applied to all types of material. (For example, *special materials* such as castings, forgings etc, and *general materials* such as bars, plates and sheets etc). Although material shape, which mainly concerns the production planner, it is necessary that they should again, cooperate with design, so that the decision concerning material shape is added to the details of product drawing.

***(iii)* MATERIAL QUANTITY :** When we use *general type of materials* the calculation of quantity required, and preparation of material schedule is essential. Whereas in case of special materials, such as castings or forgings, the quantity of material required per unit of finished product is equal to the number of units used in product. This calculation is very much similar to that of quantity of components used in the product. For example, four components are required per unit and the company plans to manufacture 100 units, the quantity of components is $4 \times 100 = 400$. Generally part list will gives us the quantity required.

In case of *general materials* such as bars, sheets, pipes etc, the finished length of or diameter or size of a part on its detailed drawing gives only a first clue. Before starting production one has to calculate the quantity of material required for a given output. The following example will explain how material quantity is calculated.

Consider the product given in the figure 4.3. This shaft is made of mild steel bar of dimension diameter '*d*'.

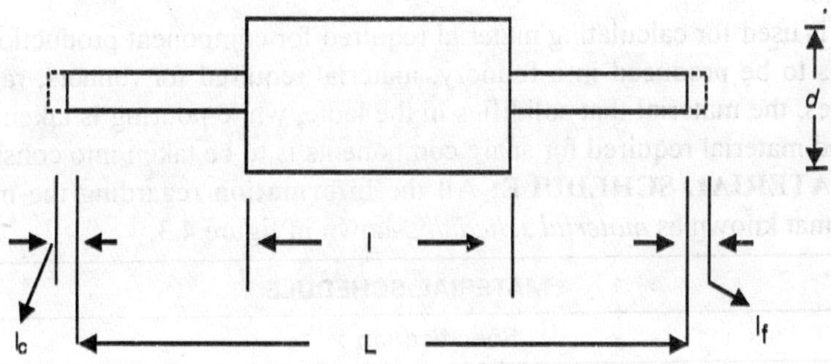

Figure 4.2 : Calculation of material required manufacuturing a shaft from mild steel bar.

In the figure L = length of the finished part, l_c = Cut-off length (allowance), l_f = facing length (allowance), l_b = batch loss.

If the company wants to manufacture 1000 pieces of the part shown in figure 4.3, the following method is used.

(*i*) Finished length of the job = $l \times 1000 = 1000\ l$

(*ii*) For every job cut of and facing operation is necessary hence these allowances are to be provided. i.e., $(2 \times l_c + 2 \times l_b) \times 1000$, this is taken as *unit loss* as this loss is involved in each unit.

(*iii*) In general the rods are available in standard lengths, say 3-meter length or 5 meter length. Loading of such a lengthy bar on the machine is not possible. Hence they are to be cut to a convenient length, say l meter or 1.5 meters. While holding the bar in a fixture fitted on the machine a short piece of bar say 10 to 15 cm length is wasted for holding purpose. This piece is common to all the pieces prepared from that length (say a batch). Hence this length is known as *batch loss.* Let us take for example that 100 finished parts can be had from one length of the bar. So, this l_b is added to the material required for 100 pieces.

Now the quantity of material required is equals to:

Finished length = $l \times 1000 = 1000\ l$

Unit loss = $(2l_c + 2l_f) \times 1000 = 2000\ (l_c + l_f)$

As 100 units are produced from one length, 10 lengths are required for 1000 pieces, hence

Batch loss = $10 \times l_b$

Total amount of material required = $1000 \times 1 + 2000\ (l_c + l_f) + 10 \times lb.$

In addition to the above, scrap loss is to be taken into consideration. But the question how much scrap to be allowed is not so simple. If the management gives higher percentage say 10% of scrap is allowed, the tendency is labor will work carelessly and produce 10% of scarp. In case, the management says only 1% of scrap is allowed, then the labor works slowly to keep the scrap; at minimum and productivity will be reduced. So it is a question of morale. Hence while calculating material required, we can take 2 to 3 % scrap allowance. So when we need material for 1000 pieces, we have to take material for 1020 or 1030 pieces, so that 1000 good pieces are available for use.

We have to consider one more point, while manufacturing components for assembly line. Suppose the company is manufacturing 1000 products on the assembly line in the planning period, 1000 pieces are required for the assembly line and the company may have to supply some units say 5 to 10% as spares to the market. So when planning for material the following factor is to be considered.

Total material required = Finished length + unit loss + Batch loss + Scrap loss + Material required for spares.

This method is used for calculating material required for component production.

If a casting is to be produced in a foundry, material required for runners, raisers and gates are taken as unit losses, the material that solidifies in the ladle, while pouring is taken as batch loss, here also scrap loss and material required for spare components is to be taken into consideration.

***(iv)* THE MATERIAL SCHEDULE:** All the **information** regarding the material required is produced in a format known as *material schedule*, shown in figure 4.3.

MATERIAL SCHEDULE					
Product :		Specification :			Reference :
Class of material :					
Part number	Description	Standard material forms	Length in mm Finished Unit loss Length	Batch loss	Issue per piece
Issued by :		R.L. : Running length :		date :	

Fig. 4.3 : Material schedule.

In general, as a policy matter, scrap loss and spares required is not shown separately. While ordering for production, these are considered and order issued.

4.5.3. PLANNING THE OPERATIONS

Once the above two decisions regarding, make or buy and Material shape, form and quantity are over, the next phase is to plan for operations. Here we consider planning the series of operations necessary to make the component, to choose appropriate work centers (facilities – a work center is a place, where the work is done, i.e., the operations are performed to make a component), where the operation is to be carried out and plan the sequence of operations to see that production is carried out without any interruption.

For doing this, first examine the work to be done and note down all changes in the material that occur during production. Here even minute changes that occur are important. Then the planner, with his knowledge of facilities available in the production shop, has to select the work center/facility on which the operation is to be done. This is very important, because, depending on the quality and quantity required, and material used, working on one particular work center will be economical. By this he decides what are the operations needed and on which facilities they have to be done. Next he has to decide the sequence of operations in which they are to be done so as to minimize throughput time. While planning, the planner must show interest in reducing/combining operations, reduce material movement, so that the plan prepared is optimal one. He has to specify: (*i*) The requirement of any special tooling necessary, (*ii*) Special information if any, and (*iii*) Special care to be taken if any in his planning documents.

4.5.4. ROUTING OR OPERATION LAYOUT

All the above information is to be presented in a format known as *route sheet* or *operation layout.* This is a very important document during production. The most important information to be presented in route sheet is:

(*i*) Every transfer of material to be shown,

(*ii*) Every work center and the operation to be done on that work center, tools used, speed, depth of cut to be used and the time to be taken should be shown

(*iii*) Any inspection to be done separately (not during operation), should be clearly shown.

In general, in large production shops where the same products are manufacture on and on, *standard route sheets* are printed and released with each production order. In case of any important information is to be given to worker that is separately marked with different colour ink on the standard route sheet to draw the attention of the worker.

4.5.5. OPERATION PLANNING

Here details of each operation are planned. That means each operation is divided into work elements. This is the lowest level in planning that is operation level planning. Here the planner has to think of the posture in which the worker works at the work center, worker's hand movements are to be considered and instructions are to be given to worker to follow the same, so that labour productivity is maintained at optimal level. For this the production planner can use his knowledge of *method study* or can take the help of Industrial Engineering department.

4.5.6. PLANNING OF AN ASSEMBLY

Planning of an assembly follows lines similar to those described above for component or part. Again the planner has to recognize all the elements involved, combine them into operations, decide the 'work stations ' to be used and choose the ideal sequence of operations.

In most of the component production tasks, considered so far, there are three principal physical entities involved. They are material, labor and plant/machinery. The most common arrangement of these entities in component production is one in which the labor and plant are placed at fixed position and the material will flow through the system to under go desired changes. Assembly planning differs from component production in that the assembly it self, as it passes from one operation to another, forms the fourth physical entity, and one of the assembly planner's main job is to decide, which these four item should move and which is given fixed position to complete the product. What ever may be the method, the planner use, important thing he has to see that the assembly line is perfectly *balanced.* Otherwise incomplete jobs will come out of the assembly line. In the following passage let us consider the methods used for *assembly line balancing.* The balanced assembly line is shown on a drawing, generally known as **line of balance (LOB).**

4.6. LINE OF BALANCE (LOB) (OR LINE BALANCING)

The term Assembly line balancing is associated with the schedule of production line jobs that balances the work load of each work station so that each of the worker on the production line has to carry out more or less equal amount of work The output of assembly line is dictated by the largest *station time* which becomes invariably *cycle time* of the line. The first step is to divide the whole work into elements and list them sequentially along with the time required to complete the element and group the tasks/elements, which have to be performed into balanced work assignments. The objective is to group the tasks so that the output rate of each work station meets, as closely as possible without exceeding, the time available for working on each unit, this procedure minimizes that workers and equipment needed to operate the line at the desired rate. This process of grouping the tasks' /elements is known as *line balancing.*

All work must be identified and broken down into elemental tasks. These later are the minimal units of work, which cannot be further divided without the resulting division requiring significantly longer time to perform than the whole. Drilling a hole, for example, would be considered an elemental task here. If the hole were started on one drill press and completed on another, additional time would be required to withdraw the first drill and remove the part from the press, to position the part on the second press, and to advanced this drill to where it makes contact with the part – all the unnecessary activities, could be avoided if the task were completed on one machine.

Once all the elemental tasks are identified, the precedence table and precedence diagram are to be drawn. When writing precedence table, the factor to be remembered is, the restrictions involved in doing a task also to be presented against the task. Now by means of some illustrated examples, let us discuss the methods used for balancing the line.

4.6.1. Heuristic Method

Heuristic means *searching to find out.* That is to find out (discover) things for one self. Heuristic describes a particular approach to problem solving, decision-making and control. Heuristic are often simple, *thumb rule* that are used to solve complex problems. They help to provide ways to solve problems while at the same time beginning of an investigation, avoid rigorous logical analysis. Heuristic models utilize common sense, logic, and more than all experience and commonsense to tackle new problems. Heuristic methods, though, have little, if any, theoretical, yet they provide most likely (though not optimal) solutions, which are good enough from a practical point of view. Though we have many methods, we use Heuristic method for intermittent flow production system.

Steps to be followed in Heuristic Method:

(*a*) Identify the work (job/task).

(*b*) Break down the work into elemental tasks or steps.

(*c*) List the various elements along with their precedence relationship or logical relationships and the time required.

(*d*) Sketch the precedence diagram.

(*e*) Consider the highest time element in the table. This time will become *cycle time.*

(*f*) Add up all the elemental times and find the *total time.*

(*g*) Divide the total time by cycle time to get the number of work stations required.

(*h*) Assign task to stations or group the elements, so that each group is considered as a station. Here, we must take care to see that the precedence relationship is not violated. Also total time of all the elements in a group does not exceed cycle time.

Problem 4.3 : There are nine elements in completing a job. The precedence relationship and the time required (in minutes) to complete each element is given in the table. Draw LOB.

Steps or elemental tasks	*Immediate predecessor*	*Duration of the element in minutes*
1	—	3
2	—	4
3	1	2
4	2	5
5	3	4
6	5	8
7	4	2
8	6	4
9	8	6
—	**Total :**	**38 minutes**

Solution : Total time = 38 minutes.

Highest time in the table = 8 minutes. Hence cycle time = 8 min. (*Note :* you can consider any higher number than highest time element as cycle time. But cycle time cannot be less than the greatest time element in the table). This is because, as the element takes 8 minutes, unless this element is completed, the job cannot be finished. If you consider any other number grater than highest element, we can proceed for a solution. But how much to take and what are the consequences, if we select very large number will be explained after the solution of the problem.

$$\text{Number of workstations} = \frac{\text{Total time}}{\text{cycle time}} = \frac{38}{8} = 4.75, \text{ say approximately 5 stations.}$$

(*a*) First we shall consider what happens if we take cycle time = total time. The line diagram will be as shown I figure 4.4 for the given problem.

Idle time Compared to Total time in Minutes	35	34	36	33	34	30	36	34	32	
	① →	② →	③ →	④ →	⑤ →	⑥ →	⑦ →	⑧ →	⑨ →	Output
Time in Min	3	4	2	5	4	8	2	4	6	
Idle time in Min. compared to cycle time 8 Minutes.	5	4	6	3	4	0	6	4	2	

Figure 4.4 : Line diagram for the problem.

There are nine persons on the line, one for each station. Worker on station number 6 works for 8 min., compared to this the idle time for other workers are shown in the figure. Now for every 38 minutes one job is completed. Compared to the total time, idle time of each worker is also shown in the figure. If we consider that the span of working day as 8 hours,

$$\text{Productivity for the day} = \frac{(8\times60)}{38} = \frac{480}{38} = 12.6 \text{ jobs.}$$

This is to say that 12.6 jobs will be completed per day with nine workers on the line.

We see that most of the time the workers are idle and the organization has o pay for the idle time. Hence the labour productivity is very low and the product cost is high.

Suppose, we group the elements in such a way that the total time of the group does not exceed cycle time (grouping should be done without violating the precedence relationship given), we will get a better-balanced line. Figure 4.5 shows the precedence diagram.

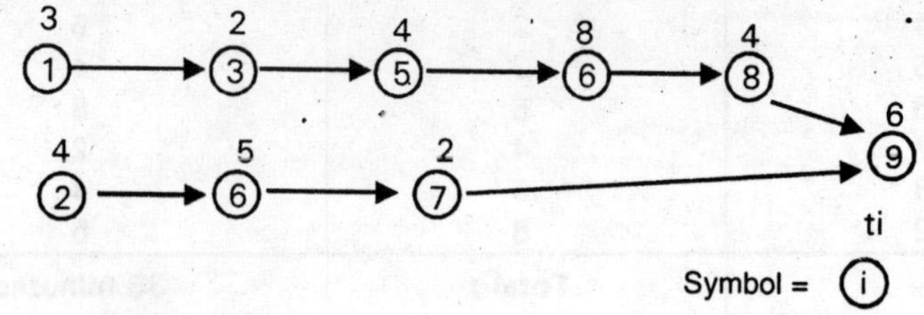

i = element number

ti = element time

Figure 4.5 : Precedence diagram

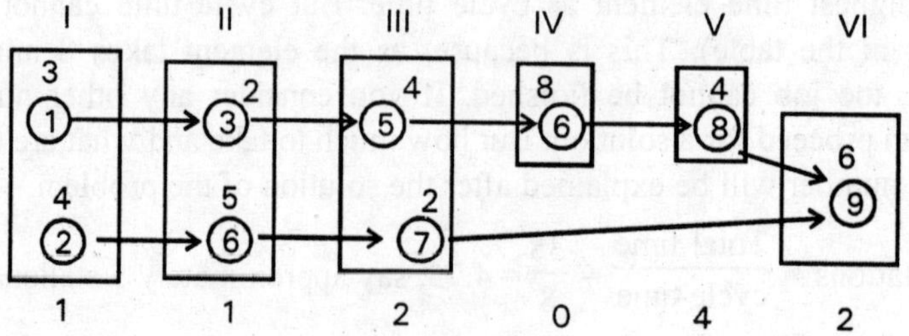

Figure 4.6 : Grouping of elements so that the total time of each group does not exceed 8 min.

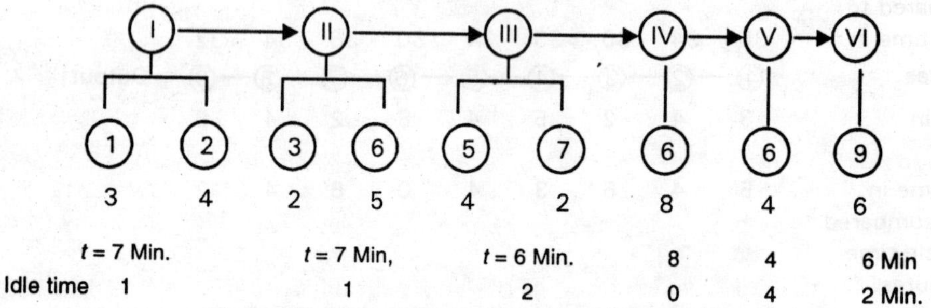

Figure 4.7 : Line of balance for cycle time = 8 minutes.

The figure 4.7 shows the line of balance for cycle time = 8 minutes. Here we have 6 stations. Station V has idle time of 4 minutes and station VI has2 minutes of idle time. Stations II and I have idle time of 1 minute each. Station III has idle time of 2 minutes. Idle time of station IV is zero minutes.

Daily productivity = (8 × 60)/8 = 60 units per day (with 6 workers only). As we see uneven idle time, the line is not perfectly balanced. The uneven idle time may lead to number of labor problems.

Solution ii. We shall try to write a LOB with a cycle time = 10 minutes. Figures 4.8 and 4.9 shows the grouping of elements and the line of balance respectively.

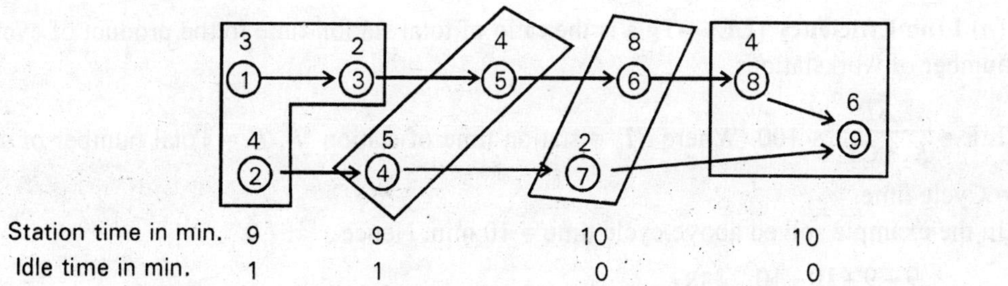

Figgure 4.8 : Grouping of elements for cycle time = 10 minutes.

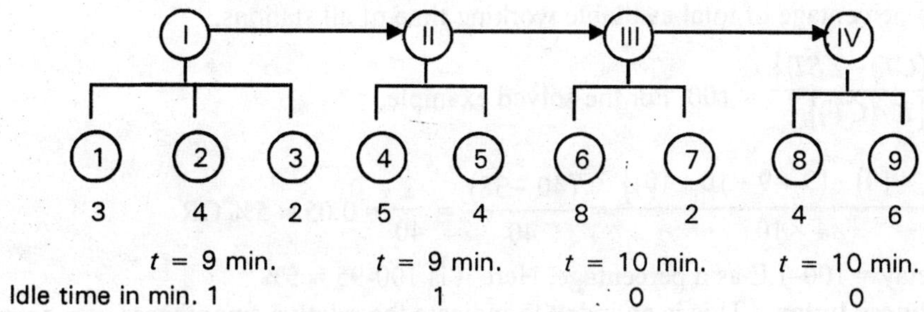

Figure 4.9 : Line of balance to cycled time = 10 minutes

Total time = 38 min.

Cycle time 10 min.

$$\text{Number of stations} = \frac{38}{10} = 3.8, \text{ say approximately 4 stations.}$$

$$\text{Taking 8 hour working day, daily productivity} = \frac{(60 \times 8)}{10} = 48 \text{ jobs per day.}$$

There are four stations and idle times at station II and I are 1 minute each. Hence the line is better balanced

In case we try the same problem with cycle time as 12 minutes, then also we get an unbalanced line, with too much of variation in station idle times. While selecting cycle time and grouping of items, the following points are to be remembered. (Reader may try the same problem with cycle time as 13 minutes and see what is the results).

Depending upon the desired production rate of the line, the cycle time (CT) or the time between the completions of two successive assemblies can be determined. This dictates the conveyor speed in the assembly line or the time allocated to each operator to complete his share of work on a manual line. The individual work elements or tasks are then grouped into work stations such that:

(*i*) The station time (ST), which is the sum of the times of work elements performed at the station and should not exceed the cycle time (CT).

(*ii*) The procedure restrictions implied by the precedence diagram are not violated.

There are many possible ways to group these tasks keeping the above restrictions in mind, we can use line efficiency (LE), Balance delay (BD), and smoothness index (SI) to measure how good or bad a particular grouping is. This is explained below:

(*a*) **Line Efficiency (LE)**—This is the ratio of total station time to the product of cycle time and the number of workstations.

$$\text{L.E} = \frac{\Sigma ST_i}{K \times CT} \times 100.$$ Where ST_j = station time of station '*j*', K = Total number of stations and CT = Cycle time.

In the example solved above cycle time = 10 min. Hence

$$\text{L.E.} = \frac{9+9+10+10}{4 \times 10} = \frac{38}{40} = 0.95, \text{ hence line efficiency} = 95\%$$

(*b*) **Balance Delay (BD)**—This is the measure of the time efficiency and is the total idle time of all stations as a percentage of total available working time of all stations.

$$\text{B.D} = \frac{\{K(CT) - \Sigma ST_i\}}{\{K \times (CT)\}} \times 100,$$ For the solved example,

$$\text{B.D} = \frac{\{(4 \times 10) - (9+9+10+10)\}}{4 \times 10} = \frac{(40-38)}{40} = \frac{2}{40} = 0.05 = 5\% \text{ OR}$$

Balance delay = 100–LE as a percentage, Here it is 100-95 = 5%

(*c*) **Smoothness Index**—This is an index to indicate the relative smoothness of a given assembly line balance. A smoothness indeed of zero (=0) indicates perfect balance. This is given by:

$$\text{SI} = \sqrt{\Sigma(ST_{max} - ST_i)^2}$$ Where ST_{max} = Maximum station time, ST_i = Station time of station '*i*', –K = Total number of stations.

For the solved example,

$$\text{SI} = \sqrt{\{(10-9)^2 + (10-9)^2 + (10-10)^2 + (10-10)^2\}} = \sqrt{1+1+0+0} = \sqrt{2} = 1.4$$

It may be noted that in designing an assembly line the number of work stations, K cannot exceed the total number of elements, N. (In fact K is an integer such that $1 \le K \le N$). Also the cycle time is greater than or equal to the maximum time of any work element and less than the total of work element times at that station. That is $T_{max} \le CT \le \Sigma T_i$, where

Where, T_i = Time of work element '*i*', N = Total number of work elements, T_{max} = Maximum work element time and CT = Cycle time.

There is yet no satisfactory methodology, which guarantees an optimal solution for all assembly line balancing problem. The emphasis has been on the use of heuristic method that can obtain a fairly good line balanced for the given problem.

4.6.2. Kilbridge and Wester Method of Balancing Assembly Line

Kilbridge and Wester propose this method. Here numbers are assigned to each operation describing how many predecessors it has. Operations with the lowest predecessor number are assigned first to the workstations. The steps to be followed in this method are explained by means of an example.

Example 4.4: A task having 12 work elements and their logical relationship and time (in seconds) taken is given in the table below. Draw the line of balance.

Element No.	*Predecessor element*	*Time in seconds*
1	—	5
2	1	3
3	2	4
4	1	3
5	4	6
6	3, 5	5
7	6	2
8	7	6
9	6	1
10	6	4
11	10	4
12	8,9,11	7
—	**Total time**	**50 seconds**

Solution:

Step.1. Construct the precedence diagram (4.9) where, i = element number, j = time in seconds.

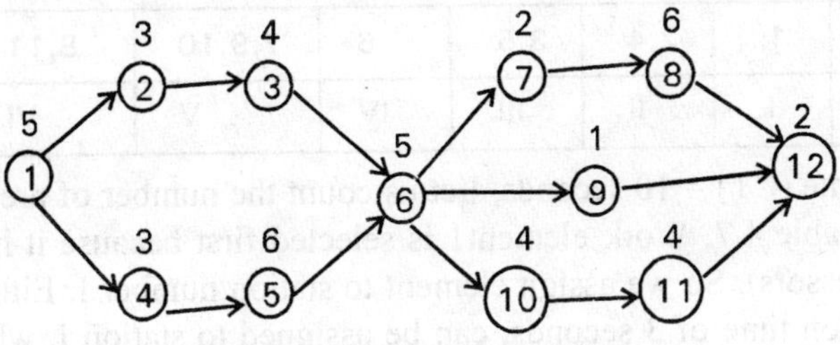

Figure 4.10 : Precedence diagram.

Step 2. In precedence diagram identify the element which do not have predecessors (does not follow other element) and enclose in a column and number that column as I. Next identify the elements those immediately follow the element in column number I and enclose them in column number II. Similarly in column number III enclose all elements that follow the elements in column number II. Continue this procedure until all elements are enclosed in columns. The element in the last column will not have any more elements to follow. By so constructing the columns, the elements with in a column can be assigned to works stations in any order, provided all the elements of the previous column have been assigned. At the same time we should not violate precedence order.

Step 3. Select a feasible cycle time (CT). By a feasible time mean one for which $T_{\max} \leq CT \leq \sum T_i$

Step 4. Assign work elements to the station, such that the sum of elemental times at a station does not exceed the cycle time, CT. This assignment preceeds from column I to II and so on, braking intra column ties using the criterion of minimum number of predecessors.

Step 5. Delete the assigned elements from the total number of work elements and repeat the above step until all the elements are assigned.

Step 6. If the station time exceeds the cycle time, due to the inclusion of a certain work element, this work element should be assigned to the next station.

Repeat steps 4 to 6 until all elements are assigned to work stations.

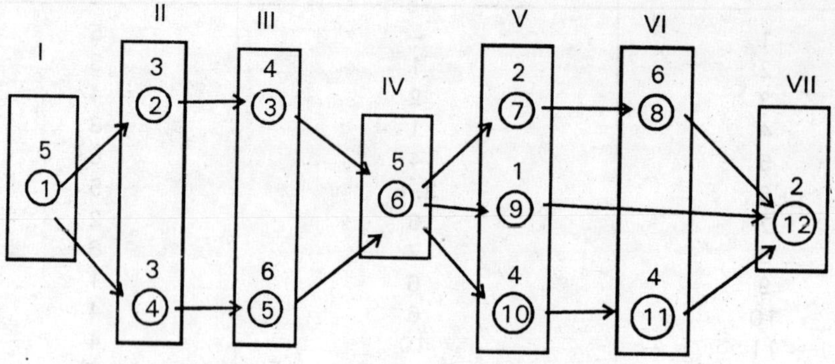

Figure 4.11 Precedence diagram with columns.

In the given problem there are 12 elements. They are arranged to columns as shown in figure 4.6. The same is given in the table 4.6 given below.

Table 4.6 : Showing arrangement of elements in the columns

Elements	1	2,4	3,5	6	7,9,10	8,11	12
Columns.	I	II	III	IV	V	VI	VII

Let us take cycle time (CT) = 10 seconds. Let us count the number of predecessor for each work element and record in table 4.7. Work element1 is selected first because it has no predecessors (or least number of predecessors). So we assign element to station number I. Either element 2 or 4 each of which has an operation time of 3 seconds, can be assigned to station I, which results in a station time of 8 seconds, which is less than cycle time (= 10 seconds). If we allocate element 2 to station I, element 4 cannot be allocated to station I, as station time will be greater than cycle time. Allocating the element 4 to station II and we continue on the same logic, until all elements are allocated, the allocation will be as shown in Table 4.7 and Figure 4.11.

Table 4.7 Number of predecessors for each element.

Work element (i)	*Number of Predecessors.*	*Time (T) in seconds.*
1	0	5
2	1	3
3	2	4
4	1	3
5	2	5
6	5	5
7	7	1
8	7	6
9	6	1
10	6	4
11	7	4
12	11	7

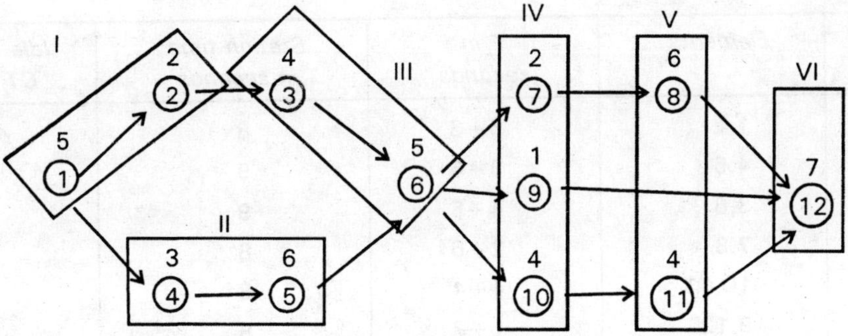

Figure 4.12 : Allocation of elements to stations.

Table 4.8 Assignment of Work element to stations.

Station number	*Element (i)*	*Time T_i in seconds*	*Station time in seconds*	*Idle time in seconds (Cycle Time = 10 sec.)*
I	1,2	5 + 3	8	2
II	4,5	3 + 6	9	1
III	3,6	4 + 5	9	1
IV	7,9,10	2 + 1 + 4	7	3
V	8,11	6 + 4	10	0
VI	12	7	7	3

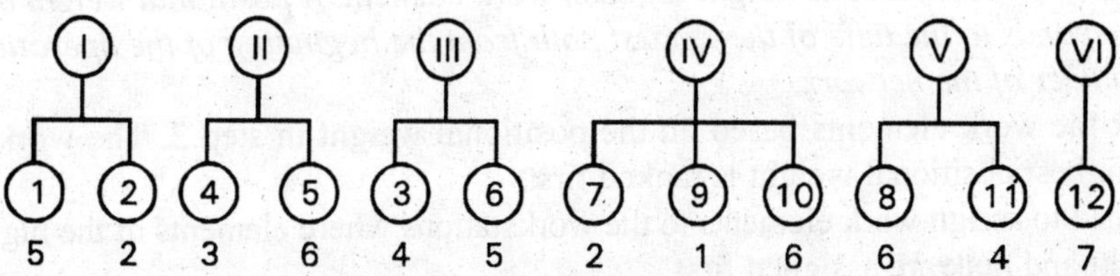

Figure 4.13 Line of Balance

$$\text{Line efficiency} = \text{LE} = \left\{\frac{50}{(6\times10)}\right\} \times 100 = 83.3\%$$

$$\text{Balance delay} = \text{BD} = 100 - 83.3 = 16.7\%$$

$$\text{Smoothening index} = \text{SI} = \sqrt{(4+1+1+9+9)} = \sqrt{24} = 4.89.$$

As the solution obtained above is not an optimal because smoothening index is 4.89. Now let use take cycle time = 9 seconds and balance the line. The allocation will be as shown in table 4.9.

Table 4.9. Allocations of elements to stations with cycle time = 9 seconds.

Station	Elements	T_i in seconds	Station time in seconds	Idle time when CT = 9 sec.
I	1,2	5 + 3	8	1
II	4,5	3 + 6	9	0
III	3,6	4 + 5	9	0
IV	7,8	2 + 6	8	1
V	10,11	4 + 4	8	1
VI	9,12	1 + 7	8	1

$$\text{Line efficiency} = \text{LE} = \frac{50}{(6 \times 9)} \times 100 = 92.6\%$$

$$\text{Smoothening Index} = \text{SI} = \sqrt{(1+1+1+1)} = \sqrt{4} = 2$$

This should cause no concern, for the Kilbridge and Waster method. As the method is heuristic method, which gives us a good working solution, with little computational effort.

4.7. HELGESON AND BIRNIE METHOD

This method is also known as *ranked positional weight technique.* The procedure of this method is as follows:

STEPS:

(1) Develop a precedence diagram.

(2) Determine the positional weight for each work element. *A positional weight of an operation corresponds to the time of the longest path from the beginning of the operation through the remainder of the network.*

(3) Rank the work elements based on the positional weight in step 2. The work element with the highest positional weight is ranked first.

(4) Proceed to assign work elements to the workstations where elements of the highest positional weight and rank are assigned first.

(5) If at any workstation additional time remains after assignment of an operation, assign the next succeeding ranked operation to the workstation, as long as the operation does not violate the precedence relationship and the station time does not exceed the cycle time.

(6) Repeat steps 4 and 5 until all elements are assigned to the workstations.

Solution to problem No. 4.4 by Helgeson and Birnie Method:

Let us have cycle times 10 seconds. The precedence diagram is shown in figure 4.8. Let us construct a table of positional weights of elements. This is shown in table 4.10.

Table 4.10.Positional weights of elements.

Table 4.7. Positional weight of elements.

Element	1	2	3	4	5	6	7	8	9	10	11	12
Positional weight (PW)	34	27	24	29	26	20	15	13	8	15	11	7

For example, the positional weight of operation number 6 equals to the maximum of (5+2+6+7), (5+1+7) and (5+ 4+4+7), that is 20. Since there are three paths, namely 6-7-8-12, 6-9-12 and 6-10-11-12, from the concerned operation to the end of the network.

If we take the element number 1, there are four paths. They are:
12-8-7-6-3-2-1, 12-11-10-6-5-4-1, 12-9-6-3-2-1 and 12-9-6-5-4-1.

The times for these paths are 32, 25, 27 and 34 seconds. Hence 34 is taken as the positional weight. In this way the positional weights of other elements are calculated and tabulated. Table 4.11 shows the allocation of elements to workstations.

Table 4.11 : Allocation of element to workstations

Station Number	*Element (i)*	*Time (T_i) (In seconds)*	*Station Time (In seconds)*	*Idle time in (Seconds)*
I	1,4	5 + 3	8	2
II	2,5	3 + 6	9	1
III	3,6	4 = 5	9	1
IV	7,10	2 + 4	6	4
V	8,11	6 + 4	10	0
VI	9,12	1 = 7	8	2

$$\text{Line efficiency} = \text{LE} = \left\{\frac{50}{(6\times10)}\right\} \times 100 = 83.3\%$$

$$\text{Balance delay} = \text{BD} = 100 - 83.3 = 16.7\%$$

$$\text{Smoothnes index} = \text{SI} = \sqrt{(4+1+1+16+4)} = \sqrt{26} = 5.09$$

Because of higher smoothness index the solution is not optimal. Reader can try to draw LOB with cycle time = 9 seconds. (We will get a better solution).

4.8. SOME PROBLEMS ONE WILL COME ACROSS IN MASS PRODUCTION AND ASSEMBLY LINES

4.8.1. Variable Work Element Times

While dealing with line of balance, it was assumed if the work element times are constant. In practice these times may be varying randomly due to factors like human variability, fatigue or carelessness on the operator's part. Even in case of machine operations, the set up time or positioning time of the part or components could lead to random variations in the individual work element times. Since the assembly line is balanced for a given fixed set of work element times, the effect of these variability are of two fold.

(*i*) Greater idle time at some workstations, and (*ii*) Reduction of the average production rate of the line.

In designing lines for random work element times with given means and variances, some modification of the deterministic line balancing methods are adopted utilizing the additional criterion, that the probability of the station time exceeding the cycle time would be kept as low as possible. Elsayed and Boucher discuss some methods of probabilistic assembly line balancing.

4.8.2. Breakdowns at work stations

The mass production system consists of a number of stages in series at which some operations are being performed. A failure (or) breakdown of one stage or workstations will results in failure of the entire production system until repairs are completed. The result of this is decreased production rate. This can be conveniently handled by providing:

(*a*) Efficient maintenance service so that the breakdown units are repaired and put into service as soon as possible.

(*b*) Buffer storage of semi finished goods between each pair of stages, so that entire line does not stop due to failure of one or more units.

The question of how much buffer storage to allocate between stages is of great practical importance, because, a higher buffer stock means greater tied up capital and a lower risk of run out and subsequent line stoppage due to break downs. A lower buffer stock leads to high probability of line shut downs.

The decision to estimate the size of the buffer can be governed by one or more of the following criteria, which consider as to what is the buffer size that:

(*a*) Maximize the production rate of the system,

(*b*) Minimize the total production cost and

(*c*) Maximizes the availability of the production system.

The problem could in general be viewed as a *Multistage waiting line system* as shown in the Figure 4.11. For details refer to Elsayed and Boucher.

Figure 4.14 : Assembly line with buffers.

4.8.3. Multi Product Lines

One of the major disadvantages with assembly lines is their relative inflexibility. A line is usually designed for one product and changes in design of the product are often difficult to accommodate on the line, unless suitable adjustments are made at workstations. But when similar products, in which a large percentage of the tasks are common, have to be manufactured, the possibility of the same production facility for the products can be explored. Since tasks are fixed with in stations, one balanced, it should e apparent that the station times and line efficiencies will vary with the products being produced. A great variety in these efficiencies might dictate that separate lines be utilized. In case a multi-product line is to be assigned for which a common precedence diagram must be developed. For example precedence diagram for two products is shown in figure 4.12. For a cycle time of 10 units of time (say seconds or minutes) the optimum solution is shown in figure 4.13. Here the line efficiencies are 73% and 100% for products 1 and 2 respectively. A computer assisted approach for multi-product and Bedworth and Bailey deals stochastic line balancing. Loss of efficiency over single product line but gain in equipment efficiencies is the trade off that must be evaluated in the mixed product line balancing problems. Figures 4.13a, 4.13b and 4.13c and 4.14 show the examples of LOB for multi-product lines.

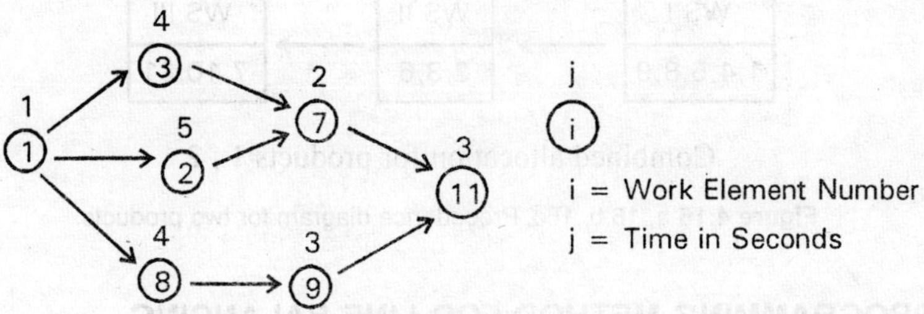

Figure 4.14a

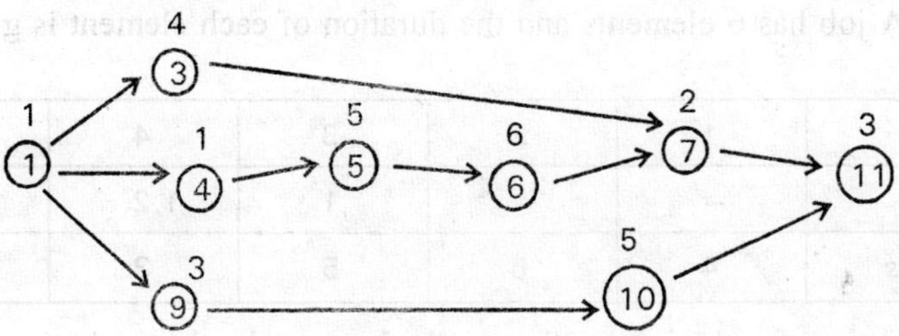

Fig. 4.14b

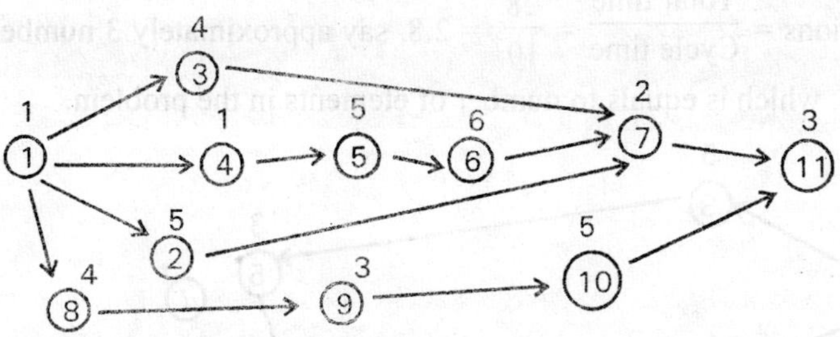

Fig. 4.14c

Figure 4.15 a,b,c Precedence diagram for two products.

(*a*)

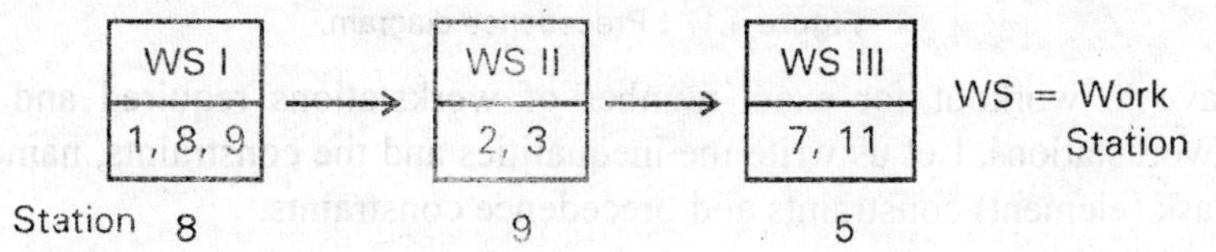

For Product 1

(*b*)

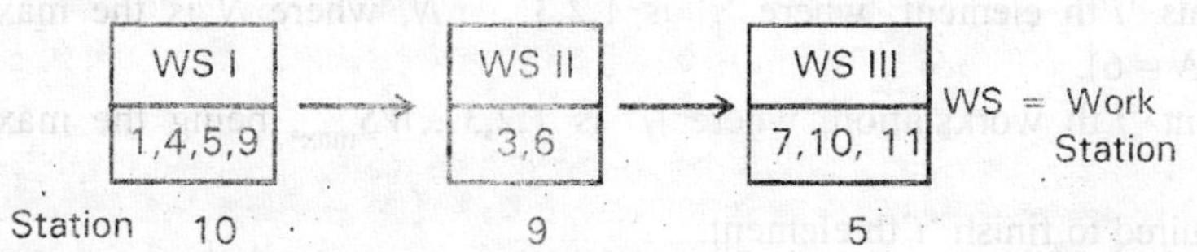

For Product 2

(*c*)

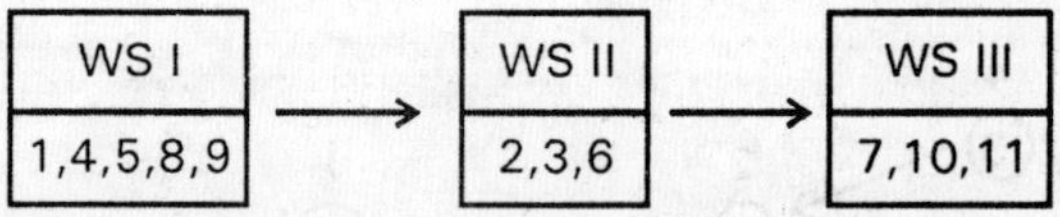

Combined allocation for products 1 , 2.

Figure 4.16 a, 16,b, 16c. Precedence diagram for two products.

4.9. LINEAR PROGRAMMING METHOD FOR LINE BALANCING

linear Programming method can be used for balancing the line. This is explained by means of an example.

Example 4.5: A job has 6 elements and the duration of each element is given below. Draw the line of balance.

Element	1	2	3	4	5	6
Predecessor	—	—	1	1,2	3	4,5
Time in seconds	4	6	5	3	3	7

Solution : Total time for the job is 28 seconds. Let us take the cycle time as 10 seconds. Then the number of stations required is given by:

Number of stations $= \dfrac{\text{Total time}}{\text{Cycle time}} = \dfrac{28}{10} = 2.8$, say approximately 3 numbers. Maximum number of workstations = 6, which is equals to number of elements in the problem.

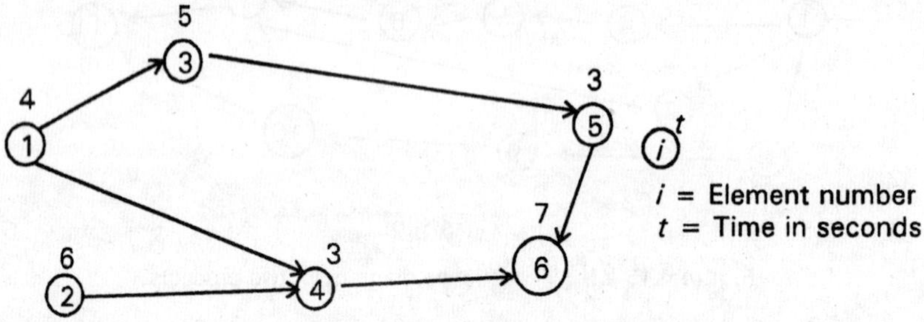

Figure 4.17 : Precedence diagram.

Now we have to workout for exact number of workstations required and the allocation of elements to the workstations. Let us write the inequalities and the constraints, namely constraints for the cycle time, task (element) constraints and precedence constraints.

ASSUMPTIONS:

i = represents 'i'th element, where 'i' is 1,2,3......N, where N is the maximum number of elements. (Here $N = 6$).

j = Represent 'j'th workstation, where 'j' is 1,2,3...WS_{max}, being the maximum number of workstations.

t_i = time required to finish 'i'th element.

Decision variables X_{ij} is equals to 1, if the element '*i*' is assigned to station *j* and is equals to zero, if the element '*i*' is assigned to the workstation other than *j*.

(i) **Cycle time constraint :** Cycle time constraint restricts the number of elements which can be assigned to a work station, such that the total station time should not exceed cycle time. $\Sigma t_i X_{ij} \leq C$, where C = cycle time assumed. And $j = 1,2,3....WS_{\max}$ for the given example,

$$4X_{11} + 6X_{21} + 5X_{31} + 3X_{41} + 3X_{51} + 7X_{61} \leq 10$$
$$4X_{12} + 6X_{22} + 5X_{32} + 3X_{42} + 3X_{52} + 7X_{62} \leq 10$$
$$4X_{13} + 6X_{23} + 5X_{33} + 3X_{43} + 3X_{53} + 7X_{63} \leq 10$$
$$4X_{14} + 6X_{24} + 5X_{34} + 6X_{44} + 3X_{54} + 7X_{64} \leq 10$$
$$4X_{15} + 6X_{25} + 5X_{35} + 6X_{45} + 3X_{55} + 5X_{65} \leq 10$$
$$4X_{16} + 6X_{26} + 5X_{36} + 6X_{46} + 3X_{56} + 7X_{66} \leq 10$$

(*ii*) **Element (task) constraint:** Element constraint makes certain that an element is assigned to one station only.

$\Sigma X_{ij} = 1$ where '*i*' is 1,2,3.... N (N = 6) for the given example.

$$X_{11} + X_{12} + X_{13} + X_{14} + X_{15} + X_{16} = 1 \text{ (for task 1 is assigned to on station)}$$
$$X_{21} + X_{22} + X_{23} + X_{24} + X_{25} + X_{26} = 1$$
$$X_{31} + X_{32} + X_{33} + X_{34} + X_{35} + X_{36} = 1$$
$$X_{41} + X_{42} + X_{43} + X_{44} + X_{45} + X_{46} = 1$$
$$X_{51} + X_{52} + X_{53} + X_{54} + X_{55} + X_{56} = 1$$
$$X_{61} + X_{62} + X_{63} + X_{64} + X_{65} + X_{66} = 1$$

(*iii*) **Precedence constraint:** Referring to the precedence diagram 4.15 the element number 3 follows the element 1, thus $X_{31} \leq X_{11}$. If element 1 is assigned to work station 1, then the decision variable X_{11} =1 and if element 3 is not assigned to workstation 1, then $X_{31} = 0$, since $0 \leq 1$, $X_{31} \leq X_{11}$ is permitted. Other precedence relationships can be written as:

$$X_{32} \leq X_{11} + X_{12}$$

This indicates that element 3 can be allocated to station 2 only after the predecessor element 1 has been assigned to either station 1 or to station 2. Similarly,

$$X_{33} \leq X_{11} + X_{12} + X_{13}$$

....

....

$$X_{56} \leq X_{31} + X_{32} + X_{33} + X_{34} + X_{35} + X_{36}$$

....

....

$$X_{66} \leq X_{41} + X_{42} + X_{43} + X_{44} + X_{45} + X_{46}$$

Objective Function : The objective is to push the last element into earlier workstations in order to reduce the number of workstations from 6 to 3 (as calculated earlier). This can be achieved by specifying the objective function as:

Minimize $Z = 1\,(X_{54} + X_{64}) + 10\,(X_{55} + X_{65}) + 100\,(X_{56} + X_{66})$

Where the assignment of final elements i.e., element 5 and 6 to last few stations has been made much more costly than their assignment to earlier stations. Elements 5 and 6 are pushed into comparatively earlier workstations and last three workstations (i.e. 4,5, and 6) have been considered for the purpose.

Our objective function is

Minimize $Z = 1\ (X_{54} + X_{64}) + 10\ (X_{55} + X_{65}) + 100\ (X_{56} + X_{66})$

X_{54} means, element 5 has been kept at workstation 4

X_{55} means, element 5 has been kept at workstation 5

X_{56} means, element 5 has been kept at workstation 6.

It can be inferred from objective function that the cost of keeping element 5 at workstation 6 is 10 times the cost of keeping the same at workstation 5 and 100 times the cost of keeping the same element 5 at workstation 4, and similar is the case for element 6.

Integer programming can be used to solve the problem for perfect balance

4.10. MODULAR PRODUCTION AND GROUP TECHNOLOGY

One criticism of manually operated assembly lines has been that they reduce the worker to mere cog in a machine. In spite of specialization, he becomes more mechanical and get bored due to monotony and will get tired as time elapses. It has been found valuable to enlarge the scope of the work of the worker, so that he assembles a complete *module*, which in turn may be used on an assembly line to assemble a product or a number of different products sharing that particular module. This job enrichment results in greater job satisfaction for the operator by reducing the monotony of the job and giving the operator a sense of accomplishment for assembling a complete module. In modular production as we tend to specialize in the production of a particular parts or activities that can then be included as components of more than one product or service. The reason for wanting to achieve such commonality is that one part or operation, if used in several products or services, can accumulate sufficient demand volume to warrant investment in a flow shop.

Group Technology provides another aspect of the same basic idea. It refers to specialization in families of similar parts. Hence components requiring primarily turning operation, such as shafts are collected in one group. Components requiring surface grinding and drilling operations such as plates are assigned to a different group. These groups become the basis on which a traditional plant layout can be arranged into a group technology plant layout in which machines are arranged in such away that, each machine is assigned to the production of only one group of parts. Group Technology (GT) typically affects only component manufacture, not the assembly stage production.

4.11. AUTOMATION AND ROBATICS

Mass production has been assisted to a large extent by automation and robotics in recent years. Automation refers generally to the bringing together of three basic items of production i.e., machine tools, materials handling and controls. Often a considerable amount of time is spent to load machine and unload work and to convey it between the single operation machines. This restriction has been partly relived by development of the multi spindle machines. With these machines, a single motor driving several spindles through a gear train allows multiple operations to be performed by one machine. Machining time cycles does not change, but more machinery operations can be performed with in each cycle. And a single operator can perform several machining operations on one machine. This considerably reduces the set up time and materials handling time and results in reduction of production cost.

Another trend with automation has been the use of industrial robots to perform some of the functions that were earlier done by manual operators.

An industrial robot is a programmable, multifunction manipulator designed to move material, parts, tools or specialized devices through variable programmed motions for the performance of variety of tasks. What separates an industrial robot from other types of automation is the fact that it can be reprogrammed for different applications; hence a robot falls under the title of *'flexible automation'*, as opposed to "hard" or "dedicated" automation.

Industrial robot composes three basic components. They are:

(*a*) *The manipulator* (*or arm*), which has a series of mechanical linkages and joints capable of movement in various directions to perform the work task.

(*b*) *The controller,* which actually directs the movements and operations performed by manipulator. The controller may be an integral part of the manipulator or may be housed in a separate cabinet.

(*c*) *The power source,* which provides energy to the actuators on the arm. The power source may be electrical or a combination.

Major reasons for the use of robot in industry are: (*a*) Increased productivity, (*b*) Adoptability (*c*) Safety, (*d*) Ease of Training, (*e*) Good return on investment and (*f*) Greater reliability. Robots are used in industry in following operations: Welding, Drilling, Assembly, Inspection, Materials handling, Machine loading, Die-casting and many more.

5

SCHEDULING, LOADING, DESPATCHING AND EXPEDITING

- Introduction.
- Scheduling and Loading
- Definition.
- Assignment Model and Solution methods
- Sequencing model –Types – Solution methods.
- Waiting line model – Solution methods.
- Types of Scheduling and Loading
- Aims of Scheduling and Loading
- Principles of Scheduling
- Forms of Scheduling.
- Scheduling Systems
- Basic Scheduling Problems
- Aggregate Planning
- The Master Production Schedule

5.1. INTRODUCTION

Scheduling is the final stage of production planning. This is the stage at which all the production activities are co-coordinated and projected on a time scale. It is a timetable that tells us which resource should do which job, and when it should do. It also shows daily activities in such a manner, so that all the work can be finished as desired.

Take for example, your class timetable, which is nothing but a schedule provided on a time scale. Your timetable is prepared with an objective, that syllabus of all the subjects are completed before the examination, so that a student can face the examination confidently. To prepare this timetable factors to be considered are:

(*i*) Volume of each subject content (syllabus),

(*ii*) Number of subjects,

(*iii*) Time required completing the syllabus of each subject,

(*iv*) Available number of working days,

(*v*) Probable number of working days that will be lost due to strikes, unscheduled holidays…etc, and

(*vi*) Availability of resources like staff members, class rooms etc.

Taking all these factors into consideration a timetable (schedule) is prepared to fulfill the objective.

Consider another example of Railway timetable. This is a schedule showing the arrival time and departure time of trains.

In production shops and service centers, schedules are prepared, which are some time known as *schedule charts or load charts,* with which the organization tries to match the requirements set out in the production order (Quantity, delivery dates) with the available resources or facilities. A man in charge of scheduling may have many ways of routing the material, many ways of sequencing the jobs, many processes to get the required shape/surface of the product and have many options of expanding or contracting the available capacity of facilities. After evaluating all the possible ways, a method, which is found to be more competitive, is selected as a production schedule. While preparing schedules, one must remember the available facilities and available capacity of each facility, so that they can be allotted with load to utilize the capacity efficiently to meet the delivery date promises. Both scheduling and loading assist in efficient and systematic planning of work sequence. Scheduling and loading are very often discussed as specific and special parts of production control.

5.2 DEFINITION

Scheduling can be defined as :

(*i*) Prescribing of when and where each operation necessary to produce a product is to be performed

(*ii*) Fixing up starting and finishing times of each operation comprising a procedure.

Loading : Loading can be defined as the study of the relationship between load and capacity of work centers or production/service facilities.

There is a certain amount of overlap between these two processes. In sscheduling fixing of where and when each operation shall be performed, also at the same time 'loads' of the work centers concerned, and often it will be found difficult to distinguish these two jobs.

Of course, the main difference between these two is the intention. When engaged in planning the order and sequence of work, with a view to completing it by a given due date, the operation being done is termed as *'scheduling'*. When thinking to compare load and capacity with a view, for example, to fixing out if there is sufficient capacity for a given production plan or program or if there is some spare capacity, which can be used for other work, can be described as *'loading'*.

Scheduling and loading deals with the following aspects:

(*a*) Which work center will do which job? Or which job is to be assigned to which work center?

(*b*) When should one operation/job be started? When should it end?

(*c*) On which equipment should it be done, and by whom?

(*d*) What is the sequence in which jobs/operations need to be handled in a facility or on an equipment?

The production planner must be well versed with Operation Research techniques, which will help; in finding the optimal sequence of doing job and optimal assignment of jobs to machines. Before we proceed to types/forms of scheduling let us discuss about some of the techniques which are helpful to production planner. Those who would like to have a detailed discussion on the models discussed below are advised to refer to a book on Operations Research. In this chapter required models are discussed briefly.

5.2.1. Assignment Model

This model is used to assign available number of jobs to available resources. Let us take a problem and solve to understand the technique.

Problem 5.1. Four jobs J_1, J_2, J_3 and J_4 are to be assigned to four machines M_1, M_2, M_3 and M_4. The time (in hours) matrix is given below. Solve the problem

	M_1	M_2	M_3	M_4
J_1	5	7	11	6
J_2	8	5	9	6
J_3	4	7	10	10
J_4	10	4	8	3

Solution: (1) **BY INDEX METHOD :** Dividing all the elements of a row (or a column) by the smallest element in the row, (or column), we get the indices. Start allocating first to the lowest index and then to the next higher and so on. Complete the assignment. This may not be an optimal solution, but very nearer to the optimal solution.

	M_1	M_2	M_3	M_4
J_1	1.0	1.4	2.2	1.2
J_2	1.6	1.0	1.8	1.2
J_3	1.0	1.75	2.5	1.75
J_4	3.33	1.36	2.6	1.0

(An index number is got by dividing all the elements in the row by the smallest element in that row)

Here in each row the smallest index is 1.0. First we allocate all ones. While doing so only one assignment is to be made in each row and in each column. In case there are more ones in a row or column, except the element of the allocated cell all other ones to be crossed. Allocation is indicated by a square as shown. After finishing all ones, next we have to move to immediate higher index. In the first step J_1 is allocated to M_1, J_2 to M_2 and J_4 to M_4. Now to allocate J_3 in the corresponding row 1.75 is the next higher index. But column M_2 and M_4 all ready allocated to J_2 and J_4. Hence 1.75 cannot be allocated. The alternate cell for allocation is J_3M_3.

Hence the allocation is J_1 to M_1, J_2 to M_2, J_3 to M_3 and J_4 to M_4. And the time required for finishing all the jobs is 5 + 5 + 10 + 3 = 23 hours.

In case capacity of machines (available capacity) is given in the problem, then before allocation, required time and the available time are to be compared. In case the required time is less than the available time, the job can be allocated, otherwise we have to move for next index number.

(ii) **SOLUTION BY HUNGARIAN METHOD OR FLOOD'S TECHNIQUE :** In this method we use the concept of opportunity cost.

Step.1. Balance the matrix. (Assignment matrix is a square matrix. To balance the matrix open a dummy column or a dummy row with cost or time elements as zero.

Step 2. Subtract the lowest element in each row (or column) from all other elements of the row (or column), which gives the *row opportunity cost matrix*. (or *column opportunity cost matrix*). The property of row opportunity cost matrix (or column opportunity matrix) is it will have at least one zero in each row (or column).

Step 3. Now you do column operation (or row operation) in the same way, i.e., subtract lowest element in each column (or row) from all other element of the column or (row). This will give total *opportunity matrix*. The property of this matrix is that it will have at least one zero in every row and column.

Step 4. Cover all the zeros in the total opportunity cost matrix by minimum number of horizontal and vertical lines. In case the number of lines thus got is equal to the number of rows or columns (remember that assignment matrix is a square matrix), assignment can be made.

Step 5. If the number of lines are not equal to the number of rows or columns, and then follow the method explained below:

(*a*) All the cells covered by lines are known as *covered cells.* The other cells are *uncovered cells.*

(*b*) Identify the smallest element in the uncovered cells.

(*c*) Subtract the above said smallest element from the elements in the uncovered cells and add this element to the elements at the intersection of horizontal and vertical lines. Do not alter the elements in the covered cells.

Step 6. Repeat the step 4 and step 5 until you get the number of horizontal and vertical lines equal to the number of rows or columns.

Step 7. Make allocations as mentioned below:

(*a*) Start row-wise or column-wise to identify a row or column having single zero and allocate that cell and cancel all other zeros in that row and column containing the allocated cell. Repeat this operation until allocations are over.

(*b*) In case of a tie (all rows and columns containing more than one zero), select any one cell and proceed as said above.

	M_1	M_2	M_3	M_4
J_1	5	7	11	6
J_2	8	5	9	6
J_3	4	7	10	7
J_4	10	4	8	3

R.O.C.M. & T.O.C.M. Number of lines = 3

Modified matrix.

M_1	M_2	M_3	M_4	
J_1	0	2	6	1
J_2	3	0	4	1
J_3	0	3	6	3
J_4	7	1	5	0

Smallest element in uncovered cells = 1, subtract one from all elements in uncovered cells and add one to the elements in the cells at the intersection of vertical and horizontal line and do not alter the elements on the lines.

	M_1	M_2	M_3	M_4
J_1	0	2	2	1
J_2	3	0	0	1
J_3	0	3	2	3
J_4	7	1	1	0

	M_1	M_2	M_3	M_4
J_1	0	1	1	0
J_2	4	0	0	1
J_3	0	2	1	2
J_4	8	1	1	0

	M_1	M_2	M_3	M_4
J_1	[0]	0	0	0
J_2	5	[0]	0	2
J_3	0	1	[0]	2
J_4	8	0	0	[0]

(Number of lines = 4)

(Each row and column has more number of zeros. Hence to break the tie by allocating any one zero and canceling all other zeros (row and column containing the allocated cell). Improved matrix is given below:

ALLOCATION: J_1 to M_1, J_2 to M_2, J_3 to M_3 and J_4 to M_4. Total time required is 23 hours.

5.2.2. Sequencing Model

This model is used for sequencing the jobs on the machines so as to minimize the total processing time. We have different sequencing models. They are:

(*i*) Sequencing '*n*' jobs on 2 machines,
(*ii*) Sequencing '*n*' jobs on 3 machines,
(*iii*) Sequencing '*n*' jobs on '*m*' machines and
(*iv*) Sequencing 2 jobs on '*m*' machines

(*i*) Sequencing of 'n' jobs on two machines:

Problem 5.2 : Five jobs are to be processed on two machines, Machine I and Machine II in the order first on machine I and then on Machine II. The matrix gives the processing time in hours. Find the optimal sequence and the total time elapsed.

Job No.	*Time in hours.*	
	Machine I	*Machine II*
I	1	9
II	7	4
III	3	8
IV	5	6
V	10	2

Solution : We use Johnson and Bellman principle to solve the problem. It states that identify the smallest element in the matrix. If it falls under machine I (first column), then do that job corresponding to the smallest element first. In case it falls under machine II (column II) do that job last. In case of tie, select any one job and then consider the other. If we have same number more than once in the same column, then the problem will have alternate solutions.

The smallest element, 1, falls in first column; hence do the job 1 first. Next smallest element, 2 falls in column II, hence do that job last. Next element, 3, falls in first column; hence do that job first (leaving the position already allotted). In the same manner complete the sequencing of all jobs. Now the sequence in which the jobs are to be processed is: I III IV II V Total time elapsed may be found as shown below:

Sequence	*Machine I*		*Machine II*		*Job*	*Machine*	*Idle*
	In	*out*	*in*	*out*	*Idle*		
I	0	1	1	10	—	—	1
III	1	4	10	18	6	—	—
Iv	4	9	18	24	9	—	—
II	9	16	24	28	8	—	—
V	16	26	28	30	2	4	—

Optimal time = $T^* = 30$ hours.

(*b*) **Sequencing of '*n*' jobs on 3- machines :** First we have to convert a 3-machine problem to a two-machine problem. While converting, the following rules are to be satisfied.

(*i*) Only three machines are involved.

(*ii*) Each job is processed in the prescribed order. Say for example first on Machine *A*, second on Machine *B* and then on machine *C*.

(*iii*) No passing of jobs is permitted. That is the same order over each machine is maintained.

(*iv*) The minimum time element on Machine *A* (column I of the matrix) should be greater than or equal to the maximum time element in Second machine column (column II of the matrix).

OR

(*v*) The minimum time element in column under machine *C* (third column of the matrix) must be greater than or equal to the maximum time element of the second machine (Machine *B*). That is ***the minimum** time on machine A **or** on machine C or both should be **greater than or equal** to the **maximum time element** of the second machine (Machine B).*

(*vi*) If the above conditions are satisfied then we assume two hypothetical machines – Machine *G* and Machine *H*, where:
Machine *G* = Time in first column + Time in second column.
Machine *H* = Time in second column + Time in third column.

(*vii*) Now the problem becomes a 2-machine and '*n*' job problem. This can be solved by Johnson and Bellman method as discussed earlier.

Example 5.3. Find the optimal sequence. Machining order is *ABC*. Time given in hours.

Job	Machine A	Machine B	Machine C
1	3	8	13
2	12	6	14
3	5	4	9
4	2	6	12
5	9	3	8
6	11	1	13

Solution : Min $A_i = 2$ and Min $C_i = 8$ and Max $B_i = 8$. Now Min C_i = Max B_i. Hence convert the problem to a 2-machine problem.

Job	Machine G = A + B	Machine H = B + C
1	11	21
2	18	20
3	9	13
4	8	18
5	12	11
6	12	14

Sequence = 4 3 1 6 2 5

Sequence	Machine A		Machine B		Machine C		Job	Machine Idle		
	In	Out	In	Out	In	Out	idle	A	B	C
4	0	2	2	8	8	20	—		2	8
3	2	7	8	12	20	29	1 + 8	—	—	—
1	7	10	12	20	29	42	2 + 9	—	—	—
6	10	21	21	22	42	55	20	—	—	—
2	21	33	33	39	55	69	16	—	—	—
5	33	42	42	45	69	77	24	35	32	—

T^* = Optimal time = 77 hours.

(*c*) **'*n*' Jobs and '*m*' Machine Problem :** Here also, we have to convert 'm' machine problem to a 2- machine problem and use Johnson and Bellman method.

(*i*) Consider machine *A* as first machine an machine *M* as the last machine.

(*ii*) All the machines between *A* and *M* are considered as machine *B* (second machine). Now Min. A_i or Min M_i or both must be greater than Max B_i (that is maximum element given under all the middle machines).

(*iii*) Then the hypothetical machine G = A + sum of all the elements of middle machine except the last machine, and H = Sum of all elements of the middle machines + element of the last machine.

(*iv*) By considering machine G and H, we can find the optimal sequence. For calculating total time elapsed consider all the machines in the given order.

(*d*) **Sequencing 2-Jobs and '*m*' Machines :** Graphical method is used in solving this type of problem.

Problem 4.4: Find the total time elapsed for the optimal sequence for the problem given below:

Job I	Order of Machining:	*A*	*B*	*C*	*D*	*E*
	Time in hours:	1	2	3	5	1
Job II	Order of Machining:	C	A	D	E	B
	Time in hours:	3	4	2	1	5

Step 1. Calculate the total of processing times of job I and Job II.

Step 2. Represent the order of machining of job I on *X*-axis and Job II on *Y*-axis.

Step 3. Draw a horizontal line from the extreme point on *Y*-axis and a vertical line from the extreme point on the *X*-axis. These two lines meets at a point *Z*.

Step 4. By drawing verticals and horizontals from each machine points on the layout construct the blocks on graph and hatch these blocks.

Step 5. Starting from the origin '*O*' and move to point *Z* in such a way that the path traveled is the minimal path. See that the line does not passes through the hatched blocks.

Any horizontal travel indicates, processing time for Job I and idle time for Job II. Any vertical line on the path indicates processing time for Job II and idle time for Job I. Any inclined line will indicate that both jobs are being processed. Select a line at 45° to reach *Z* from *O*. This line should not pass through the machine blocks constructed in step 5.

Step 6. Finally calculate the length of the path. Remember that processing time of job I + idle time of job I (vertical distance) and Processing time of Job II and idle time of job II (horizontal distance) must be equal. The figure 5.1 shows the graph for the problem given.

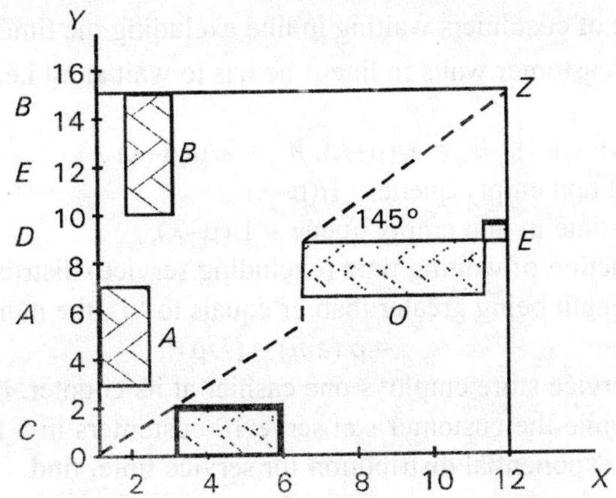

Figure 5.1 : Graphical solution for the problem.

Job I Processing time (= 12 hours) + idle time (=3 hours) = 15 hours.

Job II Processing time (= 15 hours) + idle time (= 0 hours) = 15 hours.

Following 45° line Job I is first done one Machines *A* and *B*, Job II first on machines *C*, *D* and *E*.

5.2.3. Waiting Line Model

When job arrivals/order arrivals is random in nature and when we have limited facilities to process jobs or orders, the jobs or orders pile up in the form of a queue or a waiting line. This is particularly true in service organizations or in job production shops. The production in charge has to use waiting line model to reduce the waiting time of jobs and to see that machines are optimally loaded.

5.2.3. (*a*) Waiting Line Model

Here the arrivals are represented by λ arrivals per time period and service rate is represented by μ items per time period. Then

$1/\lambda$ = Inter arrival time in time units,

$1/\mu$ = Inter service time in time units.

$\lambda/\mu = \rho$ = Utility factor.

Arrivals are considered to follow Poisson distribution and service to follow exponential distribution. The order of service is first in first out (FIFO).

The model for:

(*i*) *Single channel Poisson Arrival, Exponential Service with infinite population and FIFO is:*

n = Number of customers in the system (waiting + one at the service facility at time 't',

λ = Mean arrival time (number of arrivals per unit of time)

μ = Mean service rate per busy server (number of customers served per unit of time),

L_q = Average (expected) number of customers in the queue,

L_s = Expected number of customers in the system,

W_q = Expected waiting time per customer in the queue,

W_s = Expected time a customer spends in the system,

L_n = Expected number of customers waiting in line excluding the time when the line is empty,

W_n = Expected time a customer waits in line if he has to wait at all i.e. expected time in the queue for non empty queue.

$L_s = \lambda/(\mu-\lambda)$, $L_q = \lambda^2/\mu(\mu-l)$, $W_s = 1/(\mu-\lambda)$, $W_q = \lambda/\mu(\mu-\lambda)$,

L_n = Average length of non empty queue = $1/(\mu-\lambda)$,

W_n = Average waiting time in non empty queue = $1/(\mu-\lambda)$,

Probability density function of waiting time (excluding service) distribution = $\lambda(1-\lambda/\mu)\,e^{-(\mu-\lambda)t}$

Probability of queue length being greater than or equals to 'n', the number of customers

$$= \rho\,(\geq n) = (\lambda/\mu)^n.$$

Problem 5.5. A self-service store employs one cashier at its counter. Nine customers arrive on an average every 5 minutes while the customer can serve 10 customers in 5 minutes. Assuming Poisson distribution for arrival and exponential distribution for service time, find

(*a*) Average number of customers in the system,

(*b*) Average number of customers in queue or average queue length,

(*c*) Average time a customer spends in the system, and

(*d*) Average time a customer waits before being served.

Solution: Arrival rate $= \lambda = \dfrac{9}{5} = 1.8$ customers per minute.

Service rate $= \mu = \dfrac{10}{5} = 2$ customers per minute.

(*a*) Average number of customers in the system $= \dfrac{\lambda}{(\mu-\lambda)} = \dfrac{1.8}{(2-1.8)} = 9$ persons.

(*b*) Average number of customers in the queue $= \dfrac{\lambda^2}{\mu(\mu-\lambda)} = (\lambda/\mu)\ \lambda/(\mu-\lambda) = (1.8/2)$

$\times\ 1.8/(2-1.8) = 8.1$ persons.

(*c*) Average time the customer spends in the system $= \dfrac{1}{(\mu-\lambda)} = \dfrac{1}{(2-1.8)} = 5$ minutes.

(*d*) Average time the customer spends in the queue $= \left(\dfrac{\lambda}{\mu}\right)\left[\dfrac{1}{(\mu-\lambda)}\right] = \left(\dfrac{1.8}{2}\right)\left[\dfrac{1}{(2-1.8)}\right]$

$= 0.9 \times \dfrac{1}{0.2} = 4.5$ minutes.

5.3. TYPES OF SCHEDULING

The table given below shows principle types of scheduling and loading. (Table 5.1).

TABLE 5.1: TYPES OF SCHEDULING AND LOADING

Scheduling		*Loading*		
Task unit	*Name of the chart*	*Task unit*	*Work centre units*	*Name of the chart.*
1. Product	Program	Product	Factories/ Divisions	Product load chart
2. Orders	Order	Orders schedule	Functional departments	Order load chart
3. Operations	Operation	Operations schedule	Machine tools or work centres	Operation load chart

The above mentioned types of scheduling and loading shows that these are used in three levels of planning, that is Factory planning, Departmental planning and Work-center planning.

5.4. AIMS OF SCHEDULING AND LOADING

It is necessary to discuss why scheduling and loading are carried out and what gain it is hoped to get from them.

The principle aim of scheduling is a simple and straight forward one, that is, to plan the sequence of work, so that production can be systematically arrange towards the end of completion of all products by due date.

Aims of loading, on the other hand, are more diverse and are listed below:

(*i*) To keep *operator idle time* at a minimum,
(*ii*) To keep *machine idle time* at a minimum,
(*iii*) To keep *machine ancillary time* at minimum,
(*iv*) To keep *material waiting time* at minimum,
(*v*) To assist in *planning new work*, so that an *even balance of load* is obtained,
(*vi*) To assist in *balancing the plant and labor force* to the load,
(*vii*) To show where *additional sales effort* is needed and
(*viii*) To provide the information on which to base *reliable delivery promises.*

We have seen that the objective of production management or production planning and control is to utilize the available capacity optimally to produce the desired product. The first four aims, which mention that to keep all sorts of idle time at minimum, advocates the efficient use of available capacity. This is to say that through put time is to be reduced and inventory of stocks or work in process is kept at minimum. The next three aims, concentrates to load the available facilities to the capacity and avoid uneven loading of facilities. Some times if a section of plant is lightly loaded, to provide sufficient load to the plant, additional sales effort is to be made to procure orders. They also say about, when a new order is to be loaded, keeping in view of existing load and delivery dates. Once the loadings of new orders are finished, delivery dates can be promised. Good and efficient loading can make the best use of available resources.

5.5. PRINCIPLES OF SCHEDULING

After considering the aims of scheduling and loading, it is necessary to study the principles of scheduling to be followed to achieve the desired goals. By following these principles, we can concentrate on considering the operating conditions in a manufacturing unit, which are likely to achieve the optimum or most efficient schedules. By experience it is known that these aims of scheduling are almost nearly reached in the case of balanced line production. This is because the operations are all of same length on all the work centers or work stations on the line, there is no idle time or waiting time, and the through put time is minimum. As the machines are permanently set up for a particular operation, there is no setup time. This condition is witnessed on perfectly balanced production line. In case of imperfectly balanced lines, there will be some waiting/idle time of operator. The principles of scheduling are:

(*a*) **The principle of optimum task size:** Scheduling tends to achieve its maximum efficiency when the task sizes are small and all tasks are of the same order of magnitude.

(*b*) **The principle of the optimum Production plan:** Scheduling tends to achieve its maximum efficiency when the work is planned, so that it imposes an equal/even load on all the plant.

(*c*) **The principle of the optimum operation sequence:** Scheduling tends to achieve its maximum efficiency when the work is planned so that the work centers are normally used in the same sequence.

The first principle has a tendency when applied, not only give good results but also to be self-correcting if it is ignored. For example, if in a functional batch production machine shop the loads imposed by different operations vary greatly in length it is possible that it will be necessary to *break* many of the long operations into one or more small batches, in order to get the other orders completed by due date. In effect, this principle only repeats the known advantage of maintaining a high rate of stock turn over, and of single phase ordering. The second principle merely states that the obvious fact that there will be less idle time and waiting time, if all the plant is evenly loaded by the production planners, then if some of the machines are over loaded perhaps because direct labor cost on them are lower and others are idle for part of the time due to shortage of work. The third principle says about principle of flow. Some times it is also true if we sequence some jobs, which need the same machine set up, at a time, this avoids machine ancillary time needed, in case, the jobs of the above type are done at different times. For example, consider drilling a 10 mm hole in five different jobs may be done at a time so that the set up time required for five jobs independently at different times are avoided.

5.6. FORMS OF SCHEDULES

Here we shall discuss the presentation of production schedules. Depending on the need and use, the schedules can be prepared in different forms.

5.6.1. A Production Flow Program

If a number of components or assemblies have to be manufactured for the final assembly line and those components are to be made concurrently, the *production master flow program* is prepared taking into account the sequence of operations and the time of starting and ending each component in order to comply with the required date of completion of the product. The necessary document for this is *Operation Process Chart and the Sequence of Operation.* This is shown in figure 5.2.

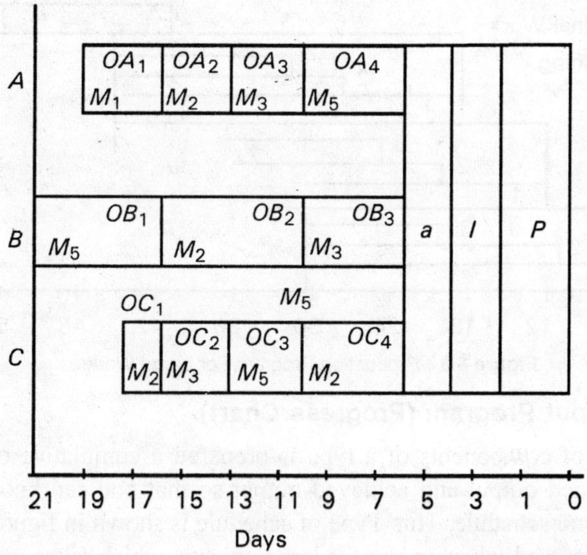

Figure 5.2 : A Production Master Program (Production Flow Diagram)

Component A has four operations: OA_1, OA_2, OA_3 and OA_4. These are to be done on machines M_1, M_2, M_3 and M_5 and takes 3,3,3, and 4 days respectively.

Component *B* has three operations OB_1, OB_2, and OB_3 to be done on machines M_5, M_2 and M_3 and takes 5,6 and 4 days respectively.

Component *C* has four operations OC_1, OC_2, OC_3 and OC_4 to be done on machines M_2, M_3, M_5 and M_2 and takes 1,3,3, and 4 days respectively.

In figure '*a*' represents assembly of *A*, *B* and *C*, takes one day and '*I*' represents Inspection, takes 2 days, similarly '*P* 'represents packing and takes 2 days.

Taking finishing of packing as the reference time *back-ward scheduling* is done to find, when to start manufacturing of parts *A*, *B* and *C* and when to start inspection of each component and so on

While doing so, we must see whether the machine is available for production of a particular component. As shown in the figure, manufacturing of component B starts 21 days before to the date of delivery. Component A should be started 19 days before the delivery date and component *C* is to be started 16 days before the delivery date. All components must be ready to assemble 6 days before the due date of delivery. This type of scheduling is known as *backward scheduling.* In backward scheduling the delivery date is fixed and the starting time is worked out. In case if we prepare a schedule starting from the beginning of producing a component and work for finding the delivery date, then it is known as *forward scheduling.*

5.6.2. Production Master Program for Integrating Work On Large Objects

This type of program is useful in planning the production of large objects such as Ships, Aero planes, Railway Coach building and Automobile body building...etc, where static layouts are used. This program is useful in long term planning. Figure 5.2 shows this type of program.

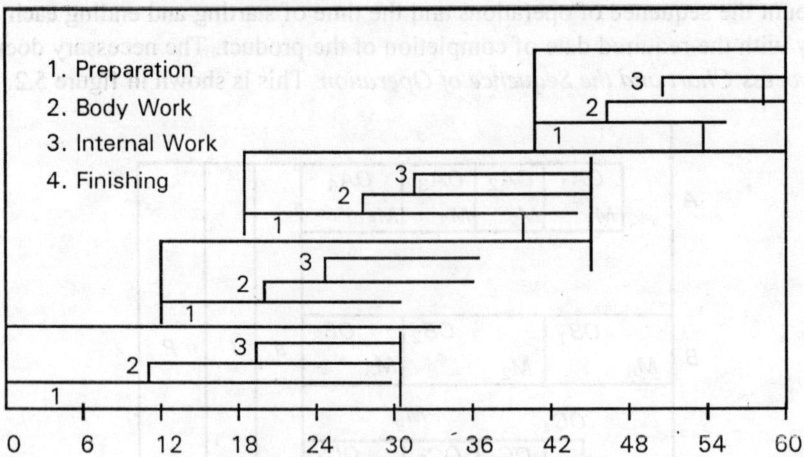

Figure 5.3 : Production Program For Large Works.

5.6.3. Cumulative Output Program (Progress Chart)

When large number of components of a type is prepared a cumulative output program may be used. We can show planned output and achieved output so that one can know whether the work is ahead of schedule or behind schedule. This Type of schedule is shown in figure 5.4

This chart can also be used when orders for large objects, which takes months or years, to show the progress of the work.

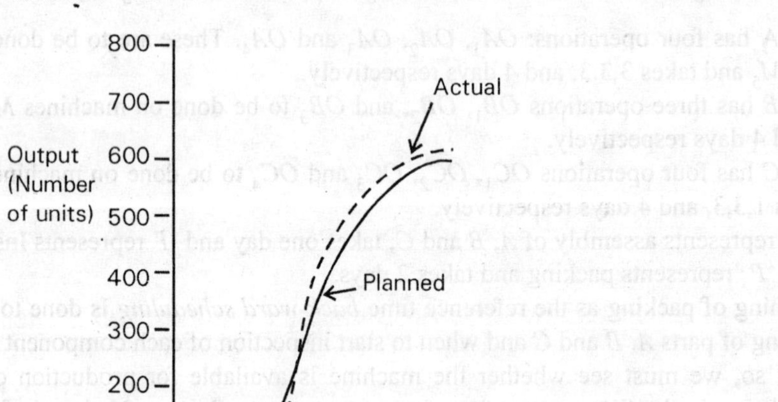

Figure 5.4 : Cumulative Output Program.

5.6.4. Out Line Master Program

In this type of program, the forecast by sales department is translated in terms of production activities. Basing on this each department will prepare a detailed program. In most of the cases *Gantt chart* (discussed later), will be used. Figure 5.5 shows an outline master program.

Orde No.	*Pro-duct.*	*Quan-tity.*	*Weeks* 1	2	3	4	5	6	7	8	9	10	11
201	*X*-23	100		*P*	*R*		*I*						
202	*Y*-43	120			*P*	*I*	*R*		*I*				
203	*Z*-21	70											
204	*A*-40	180											
205	*B*-60	75											
206	*C*-10	120											

Production Programme No. :
Date of Issue :
Week 1 starts on :
Week 11 ends on :
Programmer :

P = Preperation
R = Production
I = Inspection & Packing

Figure 5.5 : Master Production Program.

5.6.5. A Schedule For Breakdown Of Orders

This chart is used to show the rate at which work should progress; it specifies the quantities and the date on which that quantity should be completed. Here the production targets are indicated. The production department must plan the way of achieving the specified product. Figure 5.6 shows this type of schedule.

Department | *Date* | *Number:*
copies to : | *Issued by :*

Order No.	*Descrip-tion*	*Total Qnty.*	*Required from week ending on* 1 (7/6)	2 (14/6)	3 (21/6)	4 (28/6)	5 (5/7)	6 (12/7)	7 (19/7)	8 (26/7)	9 (2/8)	10 (9/8)	11 (16/8)	*To Next*
100	Part *A*-2	500	100		100		100		100			100		
101	Part *A*-5	500			200						200			100
102	Part *A*-6	800		200			300			100			100	100

Remarks :

Figure 5.6 : Breakdown Order Schedule.

5.6.6. A Cycle Schedule

This type of program is useful when the plant is engaged in batch production. This schedule shows how cycle time is distributed to products. Figure 5.7 shows a Cycle Schedule.

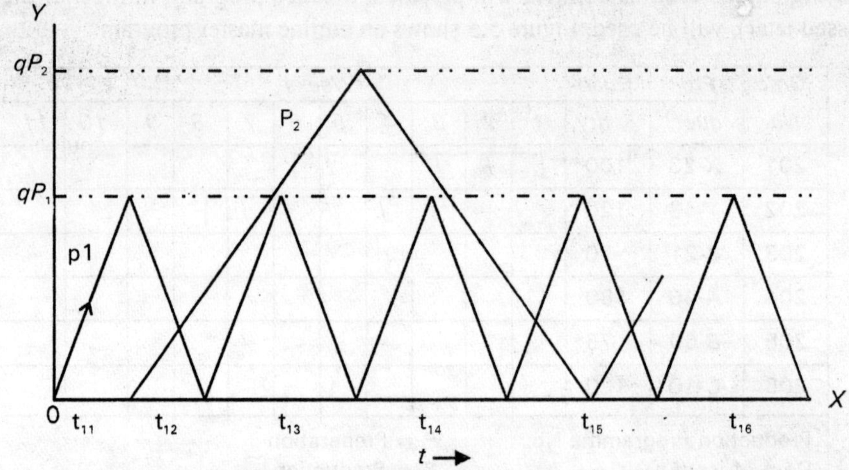

P_1 = Product 1, P_2 = Product 2, qP_1 = Quantity of product P_1, qP_2 = Quantity of Product = 2

Figure 5.7 : A Cycle Schedule for Two Products.

5.6.7. Detailed Schedule

This program is represented on a Gantt chart showing all the activities in detail. Figure 5.8 shows the Detailed Schedule.

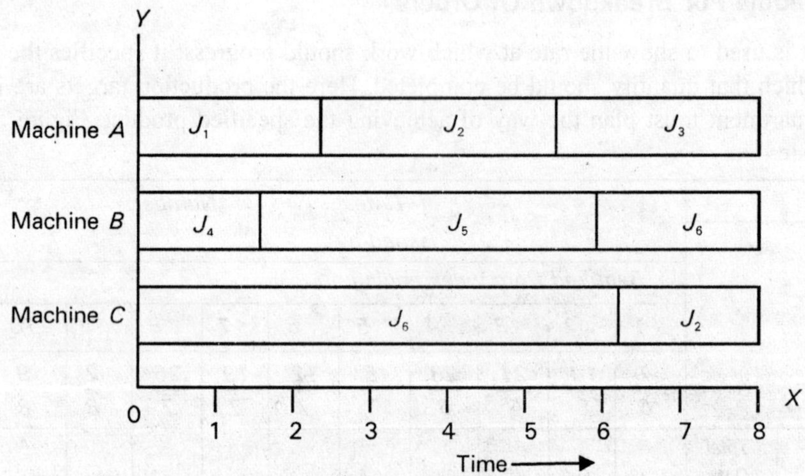

Figure 5.8 : Detailed Schedule.

5.7. SCHEDULING SYSTEMS

Scheduling Systems may be classified into four groups as shown below:

(*i*) **Unit Scheduling system:** This is used for scheduling when jobs are produced one by one and are of different types, that is for job production.

(*ii*) Batch scheduling system: When jobs are produced to order, in batches, this is used.
(*iii*) Mass scheduling system: When large number of items of similar type are produced that is in mass production, this is used.

5.7.1. Unit Scheduling System

Here we have two types of scheduling, one is Project scheduling and the other is Job Scheduling.

Project Scheduling : Generally, a project consists of number of activities managed by deferent departments or individual supervisors. It can also be said as a complex output made up of many interdependent jobs. Examples are: Railway coach building, Shipbuilding etc. The scheduling methods used are:

(*i*) Project Evaluation and Review Technique (PERT),
(*ii*) Critical Path Method (CPM),
(*iii*) Graphical Evaluation and Review Technique (GERT).

We can also use Bar charts, GANTT charts, Milestone chart, but these are less superior to the above.

Job Shop Scheduling : In Job shop scheduling, we come across verities of jobs to be processed on different types of machines. Separate records are to be maintained for each order. Only after receiving the order, one has to plan for production of the job. The routing is to be specified only after taking the order. Scheduling is done to see that the available resources are used optimally. The following are some of the methods used for scheduling.

(*i*) Arrival pattern of the job,
(*ii*) Processing pattern of the job,
(*iii*) Depending on the type of machine used,
(*iv*) Number of workers available in the shop,
(*v*) Order of sequencing.

Arrival pattern of the job : This is done in two ways. Firstly, as and when the order is received, it is processed on the principle First in First Out (FIFO). Otherwise, if the orders are received from single customer at different point of time in a week/month, then the production manager pile up all orders and starts production depending on the delivery date and convenience (This situation is generally known as *static situation*).

Processing Pattern of the Job : As the layout of Job shops of Process type and there may be duplication of certain machines, the production planner, after receiving the order thinks of the various methods of converting the requirement of customer / order in to a production plan to suit the available facilities. Depending on the process required, there may be backtracking, which is unavoidable. When facilities are busily engaged, in process inventory may be a common problem.

Machine verities available : Facilities available in the production shop will affect the scheduling. Here the size, capacity, precession and other factors of machines will have their influence on the scheduling.

Number if Men in the production shop : Many a time we see that the number of workers available in the job shops are very much limited, that is sometimes they are less in number than the machines in the shop (these shops are known as labour limited shop). Depending the availability of labour, the scheduling is to be done. In case the machines available are limited and have more men (known as machine limited shops), then availability of machine dictates the scheduling.

Sequencing rules for single facility : When we have a single facility, and the orders are in queue, then they are processed depending on the rules mentioned below:

(a) **First in first served or first in first out (FIFS/FIFO):** Here the jobs are processed as they come in. This is commonly observed queue discipline.

(b) **Shortest processing time (SPT):** The jobs having shortest processing time is processed first. This is just to avoid formation of queue. For example, when you go for Xeroxing a document, and other person comes for Xeroxing a book, then document is Xeroxed and then the book is taken for Xeroxing.

(c) **Minimum due date (MDD):** Here jobs are processed in ascending order of their available time before delivery date. By doing so, we can keep up the delivery promises. To meet the delivery promises, if necessary, overtime, sub contracting etc., may be used.

(d) **Last come first served or Last in first out (LCFS/LIFO):** This generally happens in case of inventory stocking and using. When material piles up, the material at the top i.e., material last arrived is used first.

(e) **Static slack for remaining operations (SSRO):** Static slack is given by: (Due date – Remaining processing time/number of remaining operations). Here jobs are processed in ascending order of the operations.

(f) **Dynamic slack for remaining operations (DSRO):** Dynamic slack is given by: (Due date – expected time of remaining operations / number of remaining operations). Here the jobs are done in ascending order of the ratio dynamic slack.

5.7.2. Scheduling in Batch Production Shops

Scheduling in this case depend upon the type of industry. One thing the production planner has to consider is to find the *batch quantity*. Discussed below is the method used for finding the batch quantity. The assumptions made are : (*i*) Known demand, instant supply of material, no back ordering, inventory carrying charges = C_1, Set up cost is C_3. Figure 5.9 shows the diagram for the model.

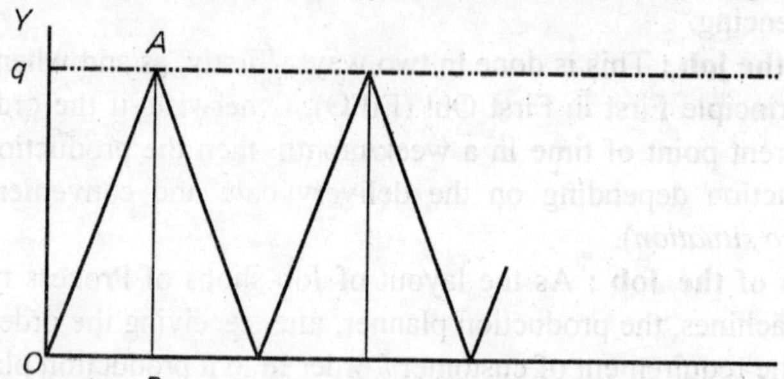

Figure 5.9 : Inventory model to find optimal batch quantity.

Suppose after every time '*t*', the quantity '*q*' is produced, throughout the period, *T*. We are to find the optimal values of *q* and *t* that is q_o and t_o, which minimize the total cost per unit of time.

In figure the total inventory in one cycle i.e. for *t* unit of time = Area of triangle $OAB = \frac{1}{2}(qt)$

As the carrying cost for *t* units of time = $\frac{1}{2}(qtC_1)$,

Also the set up cost for one cycle i.e. for *t* units of time = C_3,

Total cost in *t* units of time = $\frac{1}{2}(qtC_1) + C_3$,

Therefore, the total cost for one unit of time = $\{1/2\,(qtC_1) + C_3\}/\,t = \frac{1}{2}\,qC_1 + C_3/t$,

But $q = rt$ or $t = q/r$, substituting the same in the above equation,

$C_{(q)} = \frac{1}{2}(qC_1) + (C_3 r)/q$ this is known as *cost equation.*

The optimum value of q which minimizes $C_{(q)}$ is obtained by equating the first derivative of C_q with respect to q to zero.

Now $dC_{(q)}/dq = \frac{1}{2}C_1 - (C_3 r)/q^2$, Simplifying we get,

$$q_o = \sqrt{\frac{(2C_3 r)}{C_1}} \text{ and } t_o = \frac{q_o}{r} = \sqrt{\frac{(2C_3)}{C_1 r}}$$

The above equation is also known as *Square root formula or Harry's formula.*

Depending on the facilities available in the production workshop and the number of machines required to process the job and order of machining, sequencing may be done as discussed in the article 4.2.2

Table 5.2

ITEM	Inventory on hand (1)	Machine hour per unit (2)	Forecasted weekly demand (3)	Equivalent Machine hour for column 1 (1 × 2) (4)	Equivalent machine hour for forecasted demand (3 × 2) (5)
A	160	0.1	60	16	6
B	300	0.12	145	36	17.4
C	200	0.08	80	16	6.4
D	125	0.25	70	31.25	17.5
E	80	0.15	40	12	6.0
			Total	111.25	53.3

(*a*) **Batch scheduling by Run out method :** When a group of items are being produced by using the same facilities for scheduling we can use *Scheduling by run out method.* By this method we can find the *run out time* and inventory on hand to satisfy future demands for an item. The objective of this method is to balance the utilization of production capacity, so that run out time for all the items to be same. Production schedule is drawn in such a manner as to give equal impotence to all the items and the production efforts are truly balanced. Let us take for example that the company has to produce five items: A, B, C, D and E. The other particulars are given in the tables given below:

Aggregate Run out time in Week. = [Equivalent Machine Hours for Inventory (Col 4) + Weekly available machine — Equivalent machine hour for total forecasted demand (Col 5)] / [Equivalent Machine hour for total forecasted demand (Col. 5)]

$$= \frac{(11.25 + 88 - 53.3)}{53.3 \text{ weeks}}$$

Table 5.2 (continued)

Item	Ending inventory demand (6)	Total items required (7)	Items to be scheduled (8)	Machine hour Requirement (9)
Column	3 × 2.74	(Col 3 + Col 6)	(Col 7 – Col 1)	(Col 8 × Col 2)
A	164	224	64	6.4
B	397	542	242	29.04
C	219	299	99	7.92
D	192	262	137	34.25
E	110	150	70	10.50

(*b*) **Run out time method with specified lot sizes :** When we are dealing with batch production, by finding the optimal batch quantity to minimize the cost per piece produced, run out method may be used for scheduling. In this case of problem individual run out time is termed as the ratio of inventory on hand and forecasted weekly demand.

5.8. BASIC SCHEDULING PROBLEMS

The production planner may face certain problems while preparing production plans or Schedules. Some important problems are discussed below:

(*a*) Flow production scheduling for fluctuating demand (known smoothening problem),
(*b*) Batch production scheduling, when products are manufactured consecutively,
(*c*) The assignment problem,
(*d*) Scheduling orders with random arrivals and
(*e*) Product sequencing.

Let us discuss each one of them.

(*a*) **Flow Production Scheduling for Fluctuating Demand :** Production manager may come across a situation, where he has to plan for production when the demand for the product is fluctuating in the demand. In such a case he may have to face the situation as: (*i*) Very low demand and the capacity of the plant is larger and (*ii*) Very high demand, and the capacity of the plant is too meager when compared to the demand. This situation may be tackled in the manner mentioned below:

(*i*) ***Have a static production program :*** Here the plant will produce the products having a constant production program and maintain an inventory large enough to meet the fluctuating demand. The inventory level will fluctuate depending upon the demand pattern, replenishment being provided by a constant flow from the plant. This method is acceptable by production department, since it simplifies planning and ensures optimal plant utilization. Advantages of this method are: (*i*) It ensures higher utilization of machine capacity, (*ii*) Allows better supervision, (*iii*) Better production control, (*iv*) Promotes a sense of security among the workers. The disadvantages are: (*i*) higher inventory level, hence the capital is tied up in stocks and amounts higher inventory carrying costs.

(*ii*) ***By having a fluctuating production program :*** To satisfy the fluctuating demand, and to maintain a constant inventory level the production may follow the strategy of fluctuating the production program. In this case as the production is fluctuating to satisfy the demand, the inventory will serve as a safety cushion between production and marketing. When the demand changes, it takes some time for the to supply, during this period, the inventory can be used to meet the demand and once the production flow available, used inventory is replaced. The stock level, strictly speaking will not remain constant. But the fluctuation and the average stock level are fairly low when compared to the first one discussed above

(iii) ***To have a combination of the above said methods :*** Here the production manager follows both the methods that is sometimes to have a constant production program and some times to have fluctuating production program, so that by maintains the average inventory level at a minimum, he can satisfy the market demand and also can use the plant capacity optimally.

All the three methods are graphically illustrated in figure 5.10.

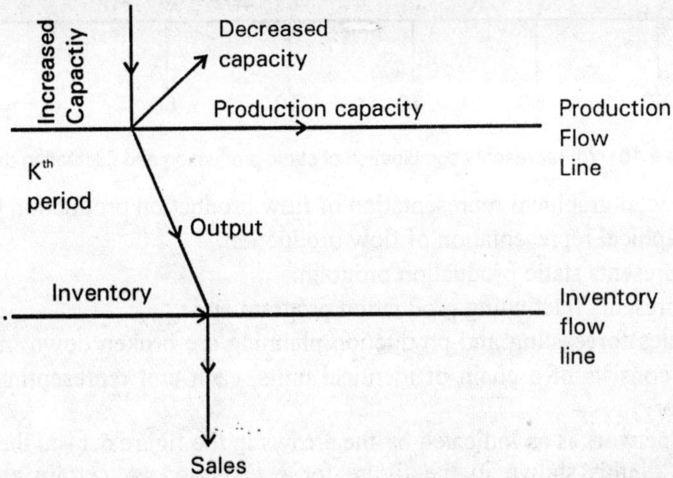

Figure 5.10 : (a) A graphical representation of flow production.

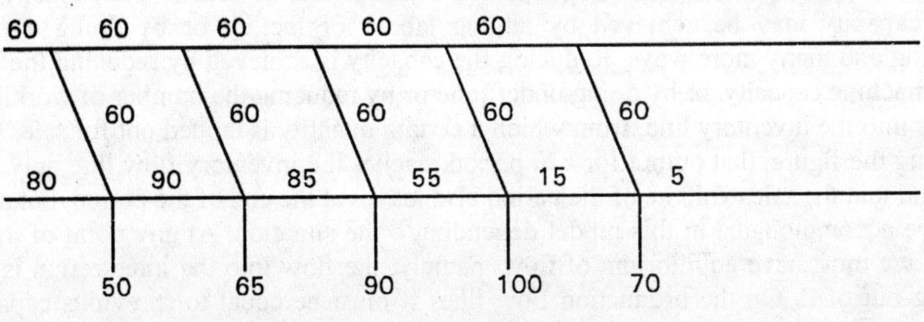

Figure 5.10 : (b) represents static production program.

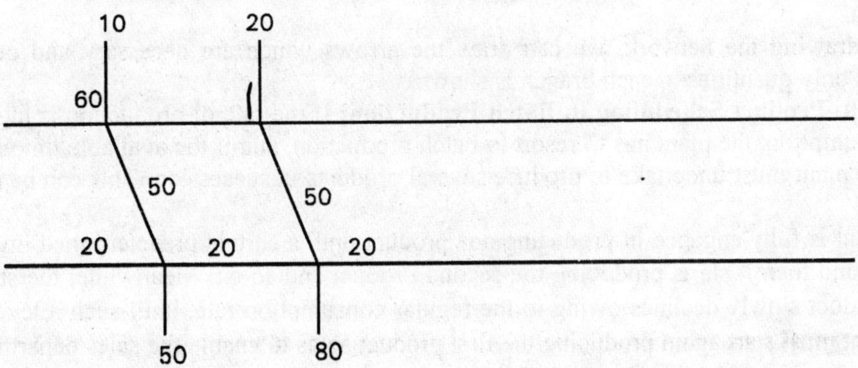

Figure 5.10 : (c) represents fluctuating production program and

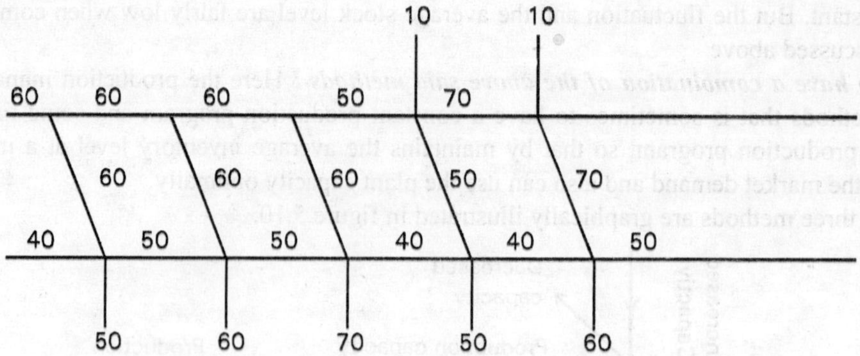

Figure 5.10 : (d) represents combination of static production and fluctuating demand.

Figure 5.10 a, b, c, d graphical representation of flow production production program.
Figure 5.10a graphical representation of flow production.
Figure 5.10b represents static production program.
Figure 5.10c represents fluctuating production program and

In the figure, sales forecasting and production planning are broken down into periods on a time scale. The network consists of a chain of identical units, each unit representing one for production and other for inventory.

The flow in the network is as indicated by the arrows in the figure 5.11 a, the flow in the network is always positive (all this shown in the figure for *k th* period. A certain amount of production capacity is carried over through the production flow line from the preceding period. At the beginning of the production manager can plan to increase the capacity or to reduce the capacity. Increase in production capacity may be achieved by adding labour or facility or by doing overtime or by subcontracting and many more ways. Reducing the capacity is achieved by reducing the labour force, renting the machine capacity, or by doing under time or by reducing the number of working days. The output flows into the inventory line, from which a certain quantity is tapped out for sale. It is assumed while drawing the figure, that output for *k th* period reaches the inventory flow line only at the end of the period and that the sales volume of the period also leaves at the end of the period, but modifications to this can be accommodated in this model depending o the situation. At any point of intersection in the network we must have equilibrium of flow; namely, the flow into the intersection is equal to the flow coming out of it. On the production flow lines it must be equal to (previous capacity) + (any increase) – (any decrease) = (Output) = (Capacity carried over to the next period).

On the inventory line: (Previous inventory) + (output) = (Sales) + (Inventory carried over to the next period).

While drawing the network, we can draw the arrows which are necessary and others can be omitted and only quantities in each branch is shown.

(*b*) **Multi Product Scheduling in Batch Production:** If the rate of production is higher than the rate of consumption, the plant has to resort to batch production, and if the available time is to be fully utilized, the plant must undertake to produce several products in succession. This can be explained as below:

The plant is fully engaged in producing one product until a certain predetermined inventory level is attained, and then it starts producing the second product and so on. Meanwhile, the stock level of the first product slowly declines owing to the regular consumption rate, until such a level is reached that the plant must start again producing the first product so as to enable the sales department to meet the demand. The figure is sown in article 5.7.2.

The other problems i.e. Assignment, Sequencing, random order scheduling are discussed in Chapter IV.

At this stage it is better to discuss about Aggregate Planning and Master schedule.

The following discussion deals with the above said topics.

5.9. AGGREGATE PLANNING

Production planning in the intermediate range of time is termed as *'Aggregate Planning'*. It is thus called because the demand on facilities and available capacities is specified in aggregate quantities. For example aggregate quantities of number of Automobile vehicles, Aggregate number of soaps etc. Here the total expected demand is specified without regard to the product mix that makes up the specified figure.

While dealing with production problems, the *planning process* is normally divided in three categories.

(*i*) ***Long range Planning*** which deals with strategic decisions such as purchase of facilities, introduction of new products, processes etc.

(*ii*) ***Short term planning*** which deals with day-to-day work, scheduling and sometimes inventory problems.

(*iii*) ***Intermediate Planning or Aggregate Planning***, which is in between long range and short term planning, which is concerned in generally acceptable planning taking the load on hand and the facilities available into considerations. In aggregate planning the management formulates a general strategy by which capacity can be made to satisfy demand in a most economical way during a specific moderate time period, say for one year. The aggregate planning is made operational through a *master schedule* that gives the manufacturing schedule (Products and dates of manufacture). Generally, day-to-day schedules are prepared from master schedule. Facility planning and scheduling has got very close relationship with aggregate planning. Figures 5.12. and 5.13. shows aggregate planning and its relation ship with other planning.

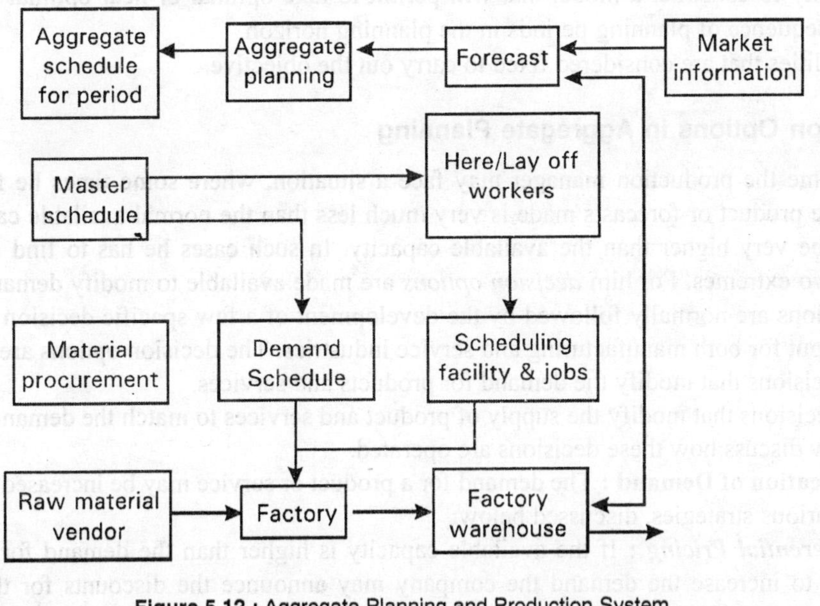

Figure 5.12 : Aggregate Planning and Production System.

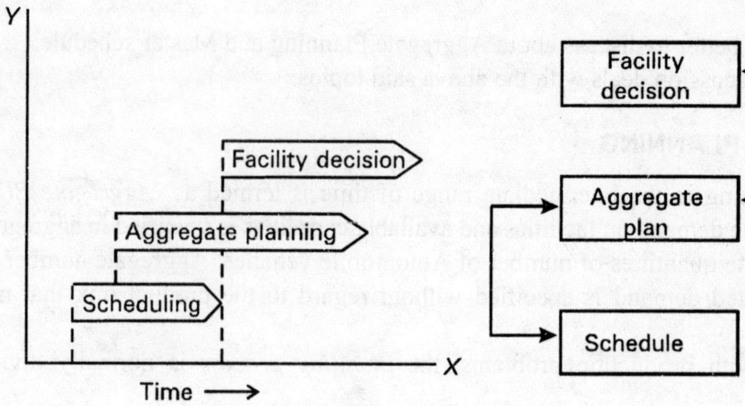

Figure 5.13 : Relationship between Facilities planning, Aggregate planning and Scheduling.

Properties of Aggregate Planning : To facilitate the production manager the aggregate planning must have the following characteristics:

(*i*) Both out put and sales should be expressed in a logical overall unit of measuring. For example, an automobile manufacturing can say 1000 vehicles per year, without giving the number of each verity of vehicle. Similarly a paint industry can say 10,000 liters of paint and does not mention the quantities of each colour.

(*ii*) Acceptable forecast for some reasonable planning period, say one year.

(*iii*) A method of identification and fixing the relevant costs associated with the plant.

(*iv*) Availability of alternatives fo. meeting the objective of the organization.

(*v*) Ability to construct a model that will permit to take optimal or near optimal decisions for the sequence of planning periods in the planning horizon.

(*vi*) Facilities that are considered fixed to carry out the objective.

5.9.1. Decision Options in Aggregate Planning

Many a time the production manager may face a situation, where some times he finds that the demand for the product or forecasts made is very much less than the normal available capacity or the forecast may be very higher than the available capacity. In such cases he has to find a way out to match these two extremes. For him *decision options* are made available to modify demand or supply. The modifications are normally followed by the development of a few specific decision rules to plan aggregate out put for both manufacturing and service industries. The decision options are:

(i) The decisions that modify the demand for products and services.

(ii) The decisions that modify the supply of product and services to match the demand.

Let us now discuss how these decisions are operated.

(*i*) Modification of Demand : The demand for a product or service may be increased or decreased by adopting various strategies, discussed below:

(*a*) ***Differential Pricing*** : If the available capacity is higher than the demand for the product, then to increase the demand the company may announce the discounts for the purchases made during certain period. You might have heard about off-season rates, which are much lesser than that of seasonal rates, like this we can get good number of examples to increase the demand. Similarly, if the demand is higher than the available capacity during a period, to reduce the demand for the product/service differential prices are fixed for the product so that the consumers may postpone their desire to purchase the product, when the price is reduced i.e during off-season.

(*b*) ***Advertising and Sales Promotion :*** To smoothen the demand to match the supply the advertisement is so timed to see that demand is increased in slack period or to shift the demand from peak period to slack period. By this the production manager is able to match the demand with the production capacity.

(*c*) ***Backlogs :*** To shift the demand from peak period to slack period, manufacturer can create backlogs and request the customer to wait for delivery.

(*d*) ***Development of complimentary products :*** Manufacturers of products, which are highly seasonal in nature, can adopt this strategy. Here a complimentary product is manufactured by using the available facility and skill so that the plant is kept engaged in manufacturing activity. By doing so they can discontinue the manufacture of the regular product to avoid building up of inventory.

(*ii*) Modification of Supply : Some of the methods by which we can modify the supply to match the demand are:

(*a*) ***Hiring and lay-off of employees :*** As this policy deals with the employees, one must be careful enough while selecting this strategy. It is because by hiring labors on temporary basis, the hiring charges may go high or some times the workers may not available in time when needed. Or, if the manager goes for lay-off strategy, he is going to invite the trouble from the labor unions, at the same time the employee morale may go down. Sometimes the company may have to face legal problems due to lay-off. Before taking decision one has to weigh both positive and negative aspects so that the decision taken will not hurt anybody.

(*b*) ***Overtime and Under time :*** When the changes in supply are meager and temporary, overtime and under time are most commonly used. By adopting overtime, we increase the production but overtime costs are to be added to the normal costs. By under time the production may be reduced and under time costs are to be considered here.

(*c*) ***Use of part-time or temporary labor :*** When the manager has to increase the supply, he has to increase the capacity. By employing the temporary or part-time labor the manager can do this. . Depending on the type of labour the cost may be slightly higher or lower than the normal labour cost.

(*d*) ***Subcontracting:*** In case the other company has some spare capacity and is ready to hire the capacity, the manager can give a part of production as subcontract to that firm.
The parent company always can send its workers to have a close control over the quality of the product produced. Depending on the hire charges, the costs of products produced under subcontracting may slightly higher than the normal cost.

(*e*) ***Carrying inventory:*** Many companies prefer this strategy. But the consequences have been already discussed in article 5.8.

To summarize the above:

When preparing aggregate planning, the production manager can select any of the above-discussed strategies, but a combination, rather than a single strategy, will result in the most economical plan. A few mathematical methods are available to select the optimal combination of the strategies, such as Linear Programming mode Transportation model; Non-linear programming model may be used.

As we know, aggregate planning involves adjusting controllable variables to respond to forecast and order fluctuations in a rational manner. The controllable variables include available manpower, overtime, idle time, inventories, subcontracting, backorders and plant capacities. The strategies that can be opted are:

(a) Level the size of the workforce and, b) Chase the demand with the workforce.

With a perfect levelinr when the work force is kept constant over a time, the rate of regular time output will be constant. In such situations, to match the fluctuating demand, the management can adopt: inventories, subcontracting, overtime. In case of second strategy mentioned above, chasing the demand, labour force is continuously changed to meet the fluctuating demand. But in real world, a production manager would like to go for combination of the above two to face the situation optimally.

5.10. AGGREGATE PLANNING METHODS

No aggregate planning methods yield truly *optimal* rates of production. For example graphic and charting technique basically works with few variables at a time on a trial and error basis. Some mathematical methods also follow this pattern, whereas others begin with limiting or unrealistic assumptions and achieve a theoretical optimality. The problem then remains to reconcile this with real-world problem. In fact charting technique is simplest one and preferred by many managers. In the following paragraph let us discuss some of the methods.

5.10.1. Graphical and charting technique

Here we construct simple tables and graphs that enable the management to compare and contrast forecasted demand with existing capacity. First thing one has to do is to construct a cumulative production requirement chart for the planning period. Then the production manager has available capacity on one hand and the fluctuating demand on the other. He tries to fulfill the demand by various combinations of workforce, overtime/under time, subcontracting and inventory maintenance and so on.

Problem 5.6. M/S XYZ Company has made the forecast given below and now it has to plan its production so as to satisfy the demand. Required safety stock and the number of production days in a month are given below. In addition the following assumptions are made as far as the resources available with the company and other production alternatives to go for aggregate planning.

(*i*) Normal production capacity is 700 units per day

(*ii*) At most 900 units may be produced per day by allowing over time at an extra cost of Rs.15/- per unit.

(*iii*) In case the production requirement is greater than 900 then subcontracting can be used at an extra cost of Rs. 20/- per unit.

(*iv*) Cost of hiring a person is Rs. 1000/- an cost of lay-of is Rs. 2000/-.

(*v*) Production rate per person is 100 units per day.

(*vi*) Number of persons working is in production shop is 5 and average salary per month is Rs.800 per month.

(*vii*) Cost of carrying inventory is Rs. 20 per unit per year.

(*viii*) Opening stock is 5000 units.

Now to use graphical method, first we have to construct cumulative production requirement. We can get Cumulative production requirement = (Cumulative demand + Safety stock requirement for the month – Opening stock at the beginning of the planning period).

In the graph (figure number 5.14.), the line A represents the cumulative production requirement line. Line *B* and *C* represents two alternative production plan to meet the production requirement. The third alternative is same with the line *A* that is the production plan is same as actual production requirement. These three alternatives are as under.

Table 5.3 : Forecast of sales and safety stock of M/S XYZ Company

Month	*Expected demand*	*Required safety stock*	*Productive days*
Jan.	9000	4000	21
Feb.	6000	2600	19
March	5000	2500	25
April	6000	2800	22
May	12000	5000	22
June	16000	7000	23
July	18000	8000	20
August	20000	9000	20
Sept.	16000	8000	22
Oct.	18000	8000	22
Nov.	14000	6000	16
Dec.	16000	7000	20
Total	**156000**	**69900**	**252**

Table 5.4 : Cumulative production requirement

Months	*Cumulative demand*	*Cumulative production requirement*	*Cumulative production days*
January	9000	8000	21
February	15000	12600	40
March	20000	17500	65
April	26000	23800	87
May	38000	38000	109
June	54000	56000	132
July	72000	75000	152
August	92000	96000	172
September	108000	111000	194
October	126000	129000	216
November	140000	141000	232
December	156000	158000	252

(Closing stock is 5000 units)

1. The production rate is 627 unit average per day with six people working throughout the year. The workers with an extra cost of Rs. 400/- per day may complete extra 27 per day. (158000/252 App.= 627) and (27×15/- = Rs. 405/-).

2. **Production for first five months is at the rate of 459 units per day with five persons and the production rate for next seen moths is at a rate of 755 units per day with 7 people working and earning of over time is considered. Hiring of two persons at the beginning of six months is considered.**
3. **Production rate is taken on actual requirement per month.**

We can consider many more alternatives to reach the desired goal. But to explain the procedure, the above three plans are given.

Table 5.5 : Cost calculations for three possible plans

Plan 1 :

Month	*Production plan*		*Cumu lative production plan*	*Cumulative production requirement*	*End of mohth seasonal inventory*
	Per day	*Per month*			
January	627	13167	13167	8000	5167
February	627	11913	25080	12800	12280
March	627	15675	40755	17500	23255
April	627	13794	54549	23800	30749
May	727	13794	68343	38000	30343
June	627	14421	82761	56000	26761
July	627	12540	95304	75000	20304
August	627	12540	107844	96000	11844
September	627	13794	121638	108000	13638
October	627	13794	135432	129000	6432
November	627	10032	145464	141000	4464
December	627	12540	158004	158000	(4)
Total					185237

Average seasonal anticipation stock = $\frac{185237}{12} = 15436$

Average safety stock = $\frac{69900}{12} = 5825$

Cost of carrying seasonal inventory = 15436 × Rs.20/- = Rs. 308720/-

Wages = 6 × 800 × 12 = Rs. 57600/-

Incentive for producing extra 27 units = 400 × 252 = Rs. 100800/-

Hiring charges for one person = 1 × 1000 = Rs. 1000/- (six persons employed in planning period)

Total cost for the plan number one = Rs. 308720 + Rs. 57600 + Rs.100800 + Rs.1000 = Rs. 468120/-

(2) Production for first five months is at a rate of 459 units per day with five workers and production rate for next seven months is at a rate of 755 units per day with 7 people working and earning of overtime is considered. Hiring two persons only at the beginning of six month is considered.

MonthProduction plan per dayProduction plan per monthCumulative Production Plan Cumulative Production Requirement.

Table 5.6 : Cost calculations for three possible plans

Plan 2 :

Month	*Production plan*		*Cumulative production plan*	*Cumulative production requirement*	*End of month inventory*
	Per day	*Per month*			
January	459	9639	9639	8000	1639
February	459	8721	18360	12800	5860
March	459	11475	29835	17500	12335
April	459	10098	39933	23800	16133
May	459	10098	40031	38000	12031
June	755	17365	67396	56000	11396
July	755	15100	82496	75000	7496
August	755	15100	97596	96000	1596
September	755	16610	114206	108000	6206
October	755	16610	130816	129000	1816
November	755	12080	142896	141000	1896
December	755	15100	157996	158000	(-4)
Total					**78104**

Average seasonal anticipation stock = $\frac{78104}{12}$ = 6509 units.

Average safety stock = $\frac{69900}{12}$ = 5825

Cost of carrying seasonal inventory = 6509 × Rs. 20 = Rs. 130180/-

Wages = (5 × 5 + 7 × 7) × 800 = Rs. 59200/-

Overtime = (55 Nos. × 143 days × Rs.15/- per unit) = Rs. 117975/-

Hiring charges = Rs. 2000/- (Hiring two persons more at the beginning of June)

Total = Rs. 130180 + 59200 + 117975 + 2000 = Rs. 309355/-

(3) Production rate is taken on actual requirement per month.

Table 5.7 : Cost Calculations for Three Possible Plans

Plan 3 :

Month	*Average production per/day*	*Number of workers required.*	*Wage*	*Number of persons hired*	*Number of persons layed off*	*Cost of hiring and laying off*	*Cost of over time*	*Cost of subcont-racting*
January	381	4	3200	–	1	2000	–	–
February	253	3	2400	–	1	2000	–	–
March	188	2	1600	–	1	2000	–	–
April	286	3	2400	1	–	1000	–	–
May	675	7	5600	4	–	4000	–	–
June	783	7	5600	–	–	–	28635	–
July	950	7	5600	–	–	–	60000	20000
August	1050	7	5600	–	–	–	60000	60000
September	636	7	5600	–	–	–	–	–
October	864	7	5600	–	–	–	54120	–
November	750	7	5600	–	–	–	12000	–
December	850	7	5600	–	–	–	45000	–
Total			**54400**			**11000**	**259755**	**80000**

Average seasonal anticipation stock = 0

Average safety stock = 5758

Wages = Rs. 54400/-

Cost of hiring and laying off = Rs. 11000

Cost of overtime = Rs. 259755/-

Cost of subcontracting = Rs. 80000/-

Total cost = Rs. 54400 + 11000 + 259755 + 80000 = Rs. 405155/-

Before drawing a graph, let us compare the costs of all the three plans. Table 5.6 shows the cost comparison of the entire three plans.

Tables 5.8 : Cost Comparison of three plans

Item	*Plan No. 1*	*Plan No. 2*	*Plan No. 3*
Seasonal inventory	308720	130180	0
Wages	158400	59200	54400
Hiring and lay-off charges	1000	2000	11000
Overtime	–	117975	259755
Sub contracting	–	–	80000
Total Rs.	**468120**	**309355**	**405155**

Note : The cost of safety stock (Rs. 20/- × 5758 = Rs. 115160/-) is same for all the plans and hence not shown in the table. Depending on the need and available alternatives different combination plans can be prepared and the best one is selected. In the above table, we can see that plan No.2 is best one.

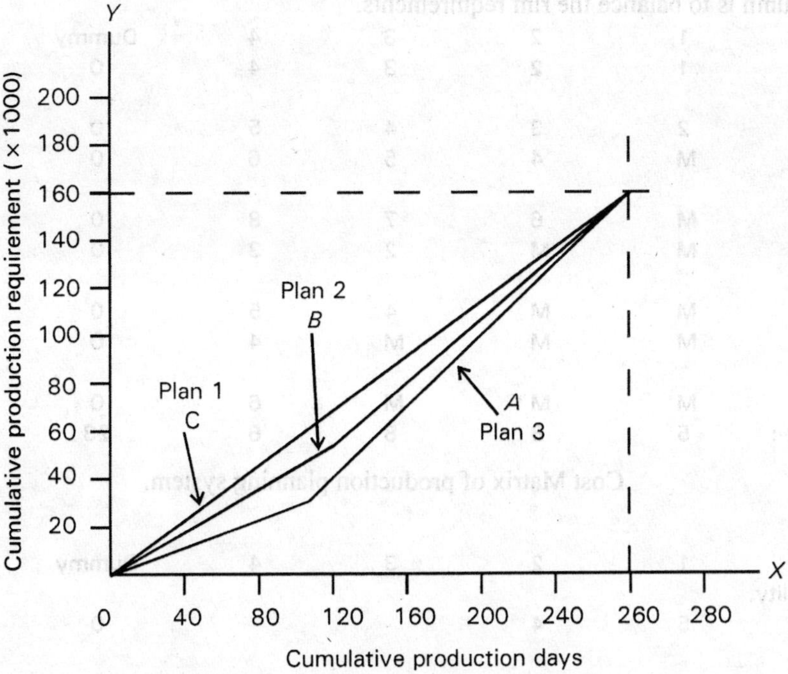

Figure 5.14 : Cumulative Demand and Production.

5.11. AGGREGATE PLANNING BY MATHEMATICAL TECHNIQUES

Operations Research Models may be used for solving Aggregate Planning problems. In addition some scholars have developed their own methods for solving aggregate planning problems

5.11.1. Aggregate Planning by Linear Programming

Vajda (Planning by Mathematics, 1973) has dealt with simple linear programming model based on transportation problem to solve aggregate planning problem. He has taken a problem of a producer who is required to supply a product of specified number of customers for future period. Cost of overtime and regular production are given and capacities of production by Regular and overtime are specified. The problem is to make optimal allocation.

Example 5.7. A manufacturer can produce 9 units in regular hours and 3 units by over time. Production requirement for four months are:

Month 1	Month 2	Month 3	Month 4
5	6	8	6

Cost of production during regular and overtime production is:

Regular Production:	Rs.	1	4	2	4
Overtime Production	Rs.	2	6	4	6

Shortage cost is assumed to be in unit cost per unit per month. The cost matrix is given below:
Symbols used in the matrix: R = Regular Production, O = Overtime production,
M = **High cost factor, so that the cell having M as the cost should not be allocated,**

Dummy column is to balance the rim requirements.

Month		1	2	3	4	Dummy	Capacity
1	R	1	2	3	4	0	9
	O	2	3	4	5	0	3
2	R	M	4	5	6	0	9
	O	M	6	7	8	0	3
3	R	M	M	2	3	0	9
	O	M	M	4	5	0	3
4	R	M	M	M	4	0	9
	O	M	M	M	6	0	3
Requirement :		5	6	8	6	23	

Cost Matrix of production planning system.

Solution :

Month		1	2	3	4	Dummy	Availability.
1	R	5	4	-	-	0	9
	O	-	2	-	-	1	3
2	R	-	-	-	-	9	9
	O	-	-	-	-	3	3
3	R	-	-	8	1	0	9
	O	-	-	-	-	3	3
4	R	-	-	-	5	4	9
	O	-	-	-	-	3	3
Requirement :		5	6	8	6	23	

The production plan is as follows:

(*i*) In the first month, the production quantities in regular time and in overtime are 9 and 2 respectively. The production requirement of first month is completely catered and five units of inventory is carried over to the second month.

(*ii*) In the second month, no production is made and the demand of the second month is met with the inventory carried over for the first month.

(*iii*) In the third month, the production of 9 units is made in regular time only. With this, production requirement of third month is fully met and one unit of production is carried for the fourth month.

(*iv*) In the fourth month, 5 units are produced in regular time to satisfy the demand of fourth month.

5.11.2 Linear Decision Rule (LDR)

Mr. Holt, Mr. Modigliani, and Mr. Muth ***of Carnegie Institute of Technology*** have developed a special type of mathematical technique know as Linear Decisions rule to solve Production Planning Problem. This technique deals with quadratic cost function for the organization with cost components such as *Regular payroll, Hiring and Layoff costs, Overtime cost and Inventory carrying cost.*

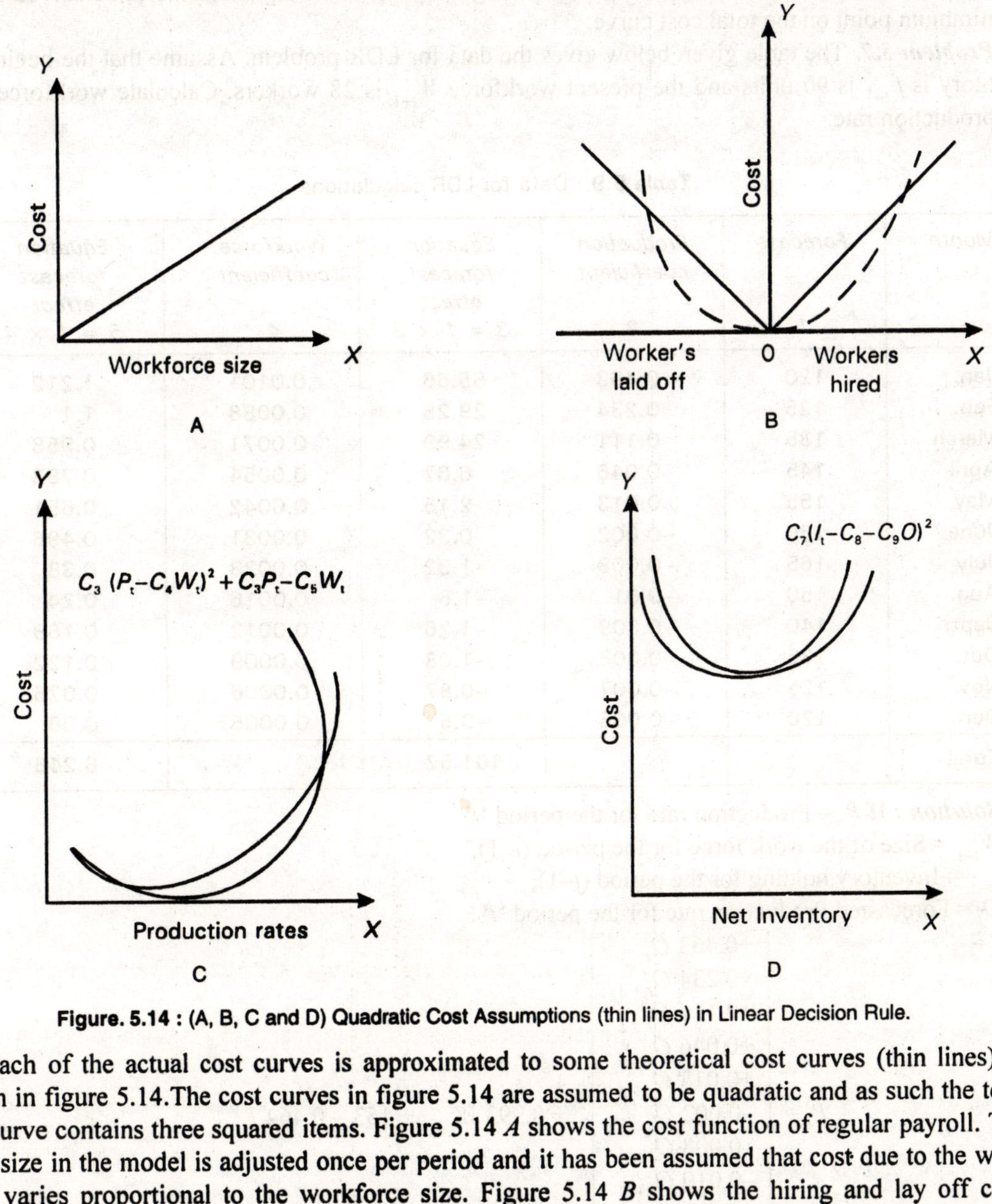

Figure. 5.14 : (A, B, C and D) Quadratic Cost Assumptions (thin lines) in Linear Decision Rule.

Each of the actual cost curves is approximated to some theoretical cost curves (thin lines) as shown in figure 5.14.The cost curves in figure 5.14 are assumed to be quadratic and as such the total cost curve contains three squared items. Figure 5.14 *A* shows the cost function of regular payroll. The work size in the model is adjusted once per period and it has been assumed that cost due to the work force varies proportional to the workforce size. Figure 5.14 *B* shows the hiring and lay off cost. Figure 5.14 *C* shows the cost of overtime and under time for various production rates, keeping workforce size as constant. If the production rate varies, the management may opt for overtime or under time or else they may hire or lay off workers. As the management will be interested in minimizing the cost of production, its decision depends on the combination of options, which minimizes the total production cost. Cost of holding inventory is shown in figure 5.14 *D*. The model is:

Minimize the total cost, C_t = Regular payroll cost + Hiring and Lay off costs + Overtime cost + Inventory costs.

This expression is quadratic and if it is differentiated with respect to workforce size and also with respect to production rate, two linear equations are generated. These equations are to be solved to get the minimum point on the total cost curve.

Problem 5.7. The table given below gives the data for LDR problem. Assume that the beginning inventory is f_{t-1} is 90 units and the present workforce W_{t-1} is 28 workers. Calculate workforce size and production rate.

Table 5.9 : Data for LDR calculations

Month	*Forecast* 1	*Production coefficient* 2	*Equation forecast effect* 3 = 1 × 2	*Workforce coefficient* 4	*Equation forecast effect* 5 = 1 × 4
Jan.	120	0.463	55.56	0.0101	1.212
Feb.	125	0.234	29.25	0.0088	1.1
March	135	0.111	24.99	0.0071	0.958
April	145	0.046	6.67	0.0054	0.783
May	155	0.013	2.15	0.0042	0.651
June	160	–0.002	–0.32	0.0031	0.496
July	165	–0.008	–1.32	0.0023	0.38
Aug.	150	–0.01	–1.5	0.0016	0.24
Sept.	140	–0.809	–1.26	0.0012	0.168
Oct.	135	–0.008	–1.08	0.0009	0.122
Nov.	125	–0.007	–0.87	0.0006	0.075
Dec.	120	–0.005	–0.6	0.0005	0.06
Total			**101.57**		**6.245**

Solution : If P_t = Production rate for the period 't'

W_{t-1} = Size of the work force for the period (t–1),

I_{t-1} = Inventory holding for the period (t–1),

O_t = Forecasted Production rate for the period 't'

$$P_t = \begin{bmatrix} +0.463\ O_t \\ +0.234\ O_{t+1} \\ +0.111\ O_{t+2} \\ +0.046\ O_{t+3} \\ +0.013\ O_{t+4} \\ -0.002\ O_{t+5} \\ -0.008\ O_{t+6} \\ -0.010\ O_{t+7} \\ -0.009\ O_{t+8} \\ -0.008\ O_{t+9} \\ -0.007\ O_{t+10} \\ -0.005\ O_{t+11} \end{bmatrix} + 0.993\ W_{t-1} + 153 - 0.464\ I_{t-1} \qquad \text{..........5.1}$$

$$W_t = 0.743\, W_{t-1} + 2.09 - 0.010\, I_{t-1} + \begin{bmatrix} +0.0101\, O_t \\ +0.0088\, O_{t+1} \\ +0.0071\, O_{t+2} \\ +0.0054\, O_{t+3} \\ +0.0042\, O_{t+4} \\ +0.0031\, O_{t+5} \\ +0.0023\, O_{t+6} \\ +0.0016\, O_{t+7} \\ +0.0012\, O_{t+8} \\ +0.0009\, O_{t+9} \\ +0.0006\, O_{t+10} \\ +0.0005\, O_{t+11} \end{bmatrix} \quad \text{.............5.2}$$

In the above equation first part of the right hand side of first equation and last part of the right hand side of second equation is the forecasted effect of the planning period were planning period is taken as twelve months.

Substituting the values in the first equation and simplifying we get,

$P_t = 101.57 + 0.993\ (28) + 153 - 0.464\ (90) = 240.61.$

Substituting the values in equation 2, we have,

$W_t = 0.743\ (28) + 2.09 - 0.01\ (90) + 6.245 = 20.139.$

The coefficient and constant values of the equation are dependent on the interrelationships of various cost parameters. It is needless to say that these coefficients vary with the condition and the type of industry where this model is applied.

5.11.3. Heuristic Method

These methods are thumb rule methods. They do not give optimal solution but generally provide a workable solution for planning the production. We have 1. Management coefficient method and 2. Search decision rule.

1. *Management coefficient method :* Models discussed above attempts to capture the important trade-offs required by complex analytical structures. Difficulties arise, however, when we estimate the esoteric costs required for complex mathematical models. As an alternative, *Bowman* developed the management coefficient model on the premise that management's past decisions can be incorporated into a system for improving present decision. This involves rigorous statistical analysis of management's past decisions. This method assumes that management is quite aware of the sensitive to the criteria of the system. Managers then make a decision through a process of natural screening with a sense and intuition that may relate to the system variables even if the decision is more erratic than biased. It has been seen that many a times even the manager is not able to explain the reason for taking such a decision. Possibly the decision is taken by him subconsciously after seeing and experiencing a number of small occurrences.

Bowman's theory states that the management's performance can considerably improved upon by applying these rules consistently. One of the reasons that a set of decision rules will yield better results is due to the fact that most of the cost functions are shallow and dish shaped at the bottom and any decision that is slightly deviated from the optimum decision does not change the cost criteria drastically from the value that corresponds to the optimum solution.

Bowman in his model developed a procedure in which a multiple regression analysis of management's past behavior on a particular decision set is performed. The coefficient so derived can be used to indicate any future decision of such type. The decision, it is expected, will still have some amount of biasness but the variance can be minimized.

2. *Search decision rule (SDR)* : Search decision rule (SDR) is another type of the heuristic model that can be used for solving production-planning problems.

This model takes into account two linear feed back decision rules. The first one is work force size, which includes two parameters: a) work-force changes and b) over time. The second one is production rate, which includes two more parameters: a) Back orders and b) Inventory. These four parameters in various combinations generate numerous alternatives for planning purpose. A heuristic search procedure may then be applied to get the values of four parameters that can result the minimum cost of operation.

There are other SDR models developed by *Jones and Tauberi.* Jones model is *parametric production planning model* in which the parameters for four cost functions are assumed to be quadratic in nature. Tauberi's SDR model assumes cost functions either quadratic or other mathematical expressions. In this model, cost functions are taken as best estimates of actuals. Another model developed by *virgin* uses simulation approach, where cost functions can be taken as linear, quadratic or step functions.

5.12. THE MASTER PRODUCTION SCHEDULE

A master Production Schedule (MPS) represents a plan for manufacturing. When a firm uses Material Requirement Planning System (MRP), the MPS provides the top-level input requirements. It develops the quantities and dates to be exploded for generating per period requirement, for subassemblies, piece parts, and raw materials. The MPS is not a sales forecast, but it is a feasible manufacturing plan. It also serves as a customer order backlog system. It considers changes in capacity or loads, changes in finished goods inventory, and fluctuations in demand. A detailed MPS also determines the economics of production by grouping various demands and making lot sizes. Thus MPS maintains the integrity of the total system backlogs, anticipated backlogs, and lower- level component requirements. This is to say that master schedule or master production schedule formalizes the production plan to converts it into specific material and capacity requirements.

The MPS should consistent with the aggregate production plan (APP) from which it is derived. It should consider, in detail, the unit measure, such as tons of steel or number of units of a component required per period, the efficiency, and the utilization factor of the system. There are different time horizons, aggregation levels, and time brackets in MPS and APP. The relationship of MPS to other manufacturing and control activities is given in figure number 5.15. The output of the aggregate planning process is set of parameters indicating aggregate inventory or backlog levels, the number of shifts to be operated, the number of employees to be hired or laid off, the anticipated amount of sub-contracting, and the aggregate amount to be produced with in a certain time periods. The APP provides a basis for decision making regarding specific production dates, available capacity, total demand, lead-time, or inventory constraints that cannot be reconciled within the company policy objectives. Although this information is necessary, it is not sufficient for the smooth functioning of a firm. What is necessary is a plan stated in terms of specific products that are to be produced in certain quantities by certain dates. The process of deriving such an MPS that is consistent with the overall APP is called *desegregation.*

It is important to recognize that the MPS is not a control technique or a system.

Rather, it is a logical representation of information for decision-making. The MPS highlights conflicts that can be solved only by people. If the MPS is done properly, the rest of the system can be harnessed to reach the desired objectives of management.

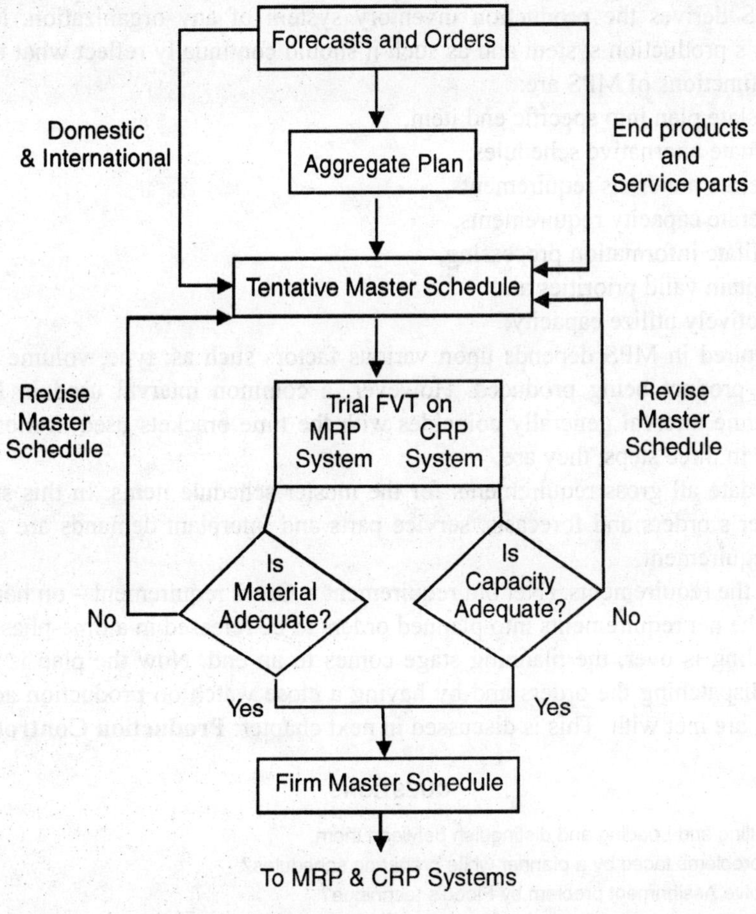

Figure 5.15 : Relationship of MPS to other manufacturing and Control activities.

Figure 5.15 relationship between MPS and other systems.

5.12.1. The Effect of Capacity on the MPS

The importance of an accurate and feasible schedule cannot be overemphasized. The MPS is an important input in deriving rough-cut capacity planning, as exhibited in figure 5.15. The existing capacity and changes to it over the planning horizon become a major constraint. Considerations to capacity should include actual number of shifts scheduled, number of days scheduled in a week, overtime policy, available equipment, and workforce levels. The capacity should be expressed in terms of what is feasible, rather than in theoretical possibility estimates. In addition to scheduling hours, factors such as efficiency and utilization should be included.

When the total requirement specified by the inputs exceeds available capacity, the MPS should indicate a need for corrective action. The alternative decision may involve extending the delivery date, changing capacity, finding ways to divert parts from other activities, and so forth that may need critical inputs from management, especially when policy guidelines are inadequate.

Inputs such as labour, material machinery, and equipment needed for each job must be computed and as such MPS derives the production inventory system of any organization. MPS is the key element of a firm's production system and as such it should continually reflect what the firm can and will do. The key functions of MPS are:

(*i*) To translate plan into specific end item,
(*ii*) To evaluate alternative schedules,
(*iii*) To generate materials requirements,
(*iv*) To generate capacity requirements,
(*v*) To facilitate information processing,
(*vi*) To maintain valid priorities and
(*vii*) To effectively utilize capacity.

The time required in MPS depends upon various factors such as: type, volume and component lead time of the product being produced. However, a common interval used in MPS is weekly schedule as this time interval generally coincides with the time brackets used in most MRP system. MPS can be done in three steps, they are:

1. Consolidate all gross requirements for the master schedule items. In this stage along with customer's orders and forecasts, service parts and interplant demands are also included in gross requirement.
2. Net out the requirements. (Net out requirement = Gross requirement – on hand inventory)
3. Group the net requirements into planned orders to be released in a time-phased schedule.

Once Scheduling is over, the planning stage comes to an end. Now the plan is to be executed. This is done by dispatching the orders and by having a close watch on production activities, so that delivery promises are met with. This is discussed in next chapter: **Production Control**

QUESTIONS

1. Define Scheduling and Loading and distinguish between them.
2. What are the problems faced by a planner while preparing schedules?
3. How do you solve Assignment problem by Flood's technique?
4. Explain the method of sequencing the jobs by Johnson's rule.
5. What is Aggregate Planning? What are the techniques available to prepare Aggregate Planning?
6. What do you mean by LDR and SDR? Explain them briefly.
7. What is Master Schedule? How it is prepared?
8. What priority rules are observed while preparing schedules in industries?
9. What is backward scheduling and forward scheduling? When will you use them?

6

PRODUCTION CONTROL

PART – A : DISPATCHING

- Introduction
- Stages and Activities of Control.
- Duties of Dispatcher.
- Complexity of Dispatching.
- Aims of Dispatching
- Dispatching Systems
- Documents maintained by Dispatching Department.
- Operation Route Card or Technological Route Card.
- Job Card.
- Move card.
- Inspection card.

PART – B: EXPEDITING OR FOLLOW-UP OR PROGRESSING.

- Types of Follow – up
- Program Control.
- Gantt Chart
- Z Chart
- Tabulated charts.
- Control Boards.

PART – A: DISPATCHING

6.1. INTRODUCTION

It is customary for any company to know the efficiency at which their unit is working. If we want to measure the efficiency of a machine, it is easy to measure because the ratio of output to input will give it. Similarly, if we want to measure the efficiency of a production organization, by knowing the output and by summing up the inputs of all sorts and if we take the ratio, we can get the efficiency with which the organization has worked. The input includes all the resources and potential capabilities of the plant, men, materials and machines, as well as organizational abilities; the output is simply the results realized with in a certain period of time, generally planning period. But it is not obvious that 'input' and 'output' are rather difficult to define in accurate terms in this case, especially if we are to measure them quantitatively in so many units. Hence the only way in which we can assess the efficiency of the production plant is by comparing actual performance with targets specified in the specified program, provided this program is planned in good faith and provided the plant is capable of coping with it.

The production control not only concerned with passive assessment of the plant performance but is an active function; which operate like an automatic self regulating mechanism that registers events and reacts to them by adjusting relevant parameters in the production centers, also the production controller can learn lessons from the mistake committed while planning and control and rectify himself not to commit the same in future.

6.2. STAGES AND ACTIVITIES OF CONTROL

Control begins as soon as the production operations begin; in fact slightly earlier, by the actual issues of the production orders to the shop floor. The four stages of production control are:

1. Triggering off production operations; observing progress and recording it.
2. Analyzing the data by comparing progress with the plans and with achievements of competitors.
3. Taking immediate action to modify plans and redirect activities in order to attain the target.
4. Post-operation evaluation, feeding back information and conclusions to the planning section in order to improve future planning.

Each of these stages is important, each is a link in the control procedure, but each is worthless and indeed pointless without the others. There is no need to make observations and collect data if they are not being used for analysis. Any analysis is equally pointless if its results are disregarded, and when corrective action is undertaken but confined to immediate patching up, the control procedure lacks the vital feedback that is possible only after evaluation, and without which the system is deprived of the opportunity of learning from mistakes and experience.

The function of program planning is concerned with the planning of what the factory shall make in terms of products and times. This broad plan is broken down at the ordering stage into instructions to departments in terms of batches of components and is concerned with the planning of work operations on individual work centers.

This activity of disseminating information is known as *dispatching.*

Table 6.1 : Elements of control procedure

Particulars	*Proces*	*Inventory*	*Inspection*	*Cost*
Observation	1. Active Process : output vs Time, 2. Idle Process : Machine idle time; break downs	Records of stock level	Process control charts.	Collect cost data
Analysis	Compare progress with plans	Distribution of demand, trend, seasonal fluctuations	Process capabilities, trends	Compute cost and compare with estimates
Immediate action	Expedite	Issue pro- duction and	Initiate 100% inspection.	Adjust sales price,

		procurement orders	adjust processes	if posible
Evaluation	Process capacity, maintenance schedules.	Replenish-ment policies, inventory systems	Reassessment of specifi-cations, process improvement inspection procedure	Economic evaluation of processes preparing better data for future estimates.

The function of program planning is concerned with the planning of what the factory shall make in terms of products and time. This broad plan is broken down at the ordering stage into instructions to departments in terms of batches of components and time. Dispatching is the final process in this analysis of the program and is concerned with the planning of work operations at individual work centers.

This activity of disseminating information to the production department to start production is known as *Dispatching.* This stage where scheduling or planning ends and production starts. Once the production activities are started, control starts. In small departments dispatching is done by foreman or other line manager concerned normally carries out as a function, which as a part-time job. In large departments, particularly, if they are equipped with general purpose machinery, if they are laid out on a process (functional) layout, and if they carry out large number of different operations, there is too much detailed clerical work involved in controlling the orders for it to be done as a part-time job by the foreman, and a specialist *dispatcher* is usually appointed for this purpose.

6.3. DUTIES OF A DISPATCHER

Dispatching has been defined as a general control of shop orders in Production shops; the different parts of the job can be listed as follows:

(*i*) The receipt and filling of all of Shop Orders and associated documents.

(*ii*) The selection of job for issues, in the most favorable sequence.

(*iii*) The issue of Job Cards or other forms of instruction to the operatives.

(*iv*) The issue of instructions to the setup workers, concerning what machines are to be set-up-, for which jobs.

(*v*) The issue of instructions concerning the movement of materials between work centers.

(*vi*) The issue of instructions concerning the issue and return to stores of special tooling.

(*vii*) Maintenance of records of production.

All these different jobs are normally controlled from a Dispatcher's office, located near that of the foreman and equipped with a desk at a window or hatch, at which the operatives report to receive instructions concerning which job they are to do next.

Occasionally the dispatching duties are split between a number of different people. For example, a time clerk dealing with the actual issue of Job Cards and the maintenance of time and quantity records, without any responsibility for scheduling the order of work, or for material and tool movement.

The dispatcher, in this case, is a member of the Foreman's staff. In many organizations the dispatcher in each shop are part of Production control staff and report directly to the Production controller.

6.4 THE COMPLEXITY OF DISPATCHING

The dispatching jobs listed in the above section are required only in the complex cases of jobbing and batch production, on general-purpose machinery, which are laid out as per process layout. In the line production dispatching is very simple, because the operator normally do the same jobs all the time, and there are no special component shop orders, material movement, set ups or tool moves to be organized. In line production it is only in the assembly shops that dispatching can be complicated. In case of Group lay outs, where jobbing and batch production is carried out the dispatching tends to be simple. It is because in-group layout a group of machines are set in as a group and they are tooled to do specific similar of jobs (family of products) by using special tooling designed for minimum set up. Using *period batch control or standard batch control* and a group of incentive scheme with this type of layout, dispatching paper work can be reduced to the absolute minimum. The complexity of dispatching is mainly a function of layout, and of organization. Figure 6.1 gives the duties and documents of dispatching.

Various documents to be prepared by dispatcher in batch production (on functional layout) are:

(*i*) A Shop Order for each component,
(*ii*) A copy order known as Due-date copy,
(*iii*) A Material Requisition,
(*iv*) A Follow card,
(*v*) A Progress record card,
(*vi*) A Job card, one for each operation,
(*vii*) A Material Move Order for each operation,
(*viii*) Tool Move Order for each operation.

If the product is made of several parts, the production order is broken down accordingly, and for each operation there is a material and tool issue, a job card that details the task and the methods to be used, an inspection order and information about the next destination of the component. Finally the dispatching function is responsible for keeping records of actual operation times, idle man and machine times, length and causes of breakdowns, and any other relevant information about reality keeping within schedule or deviating from it. These records can be used for:

(*i*) *Calculating wages,* if the wage scheme in the plant is dependent on output,
(*ii*) *Examining the cost* of the job and the product and comparing with the planned budget and the initial cost estimates,
(*iii*) *Comparing operation times* with the estimated times and verifying whether the discrepancies are consistent with past experience, so that future estimates can be made more accurate,
(*iv*) *Locating weak points in the production line,* so that work-study can be undertaken to explore ways of alleviating the difficulties,
(*v*) *Studying how much idle time was caused* because of schedule interference i.e. overlap in operation times due to uncontrollable delays or too tight a production schedule,
(*vi*) *Studying how much delay was caused* by machine breakdown and whether the maintenance and emergency repair facilities were compatible with the requirements of the situation, (to find optimal number of repair men required to install preventive maintenance scheme),
(*vii*) *Analyzing the delays* caused by tool breakdown, regrinding and resetting, to ensure that the specified speeds are compatible with reasonable amount of tool wear,
(*viii*) *Analyzing* to what extent both queues and delays are cause by inadequate materials handling systems.

One thing we have to remember is that the exercising the dispatching function depends very much on the type of production and on the size of the plant. The dispatching effort, after releasing the orders, would then be mainly devoted to maintaining the records, and this can be done effectively by dispatching stations located along the production line, each being responsible for recording progress at production centers.

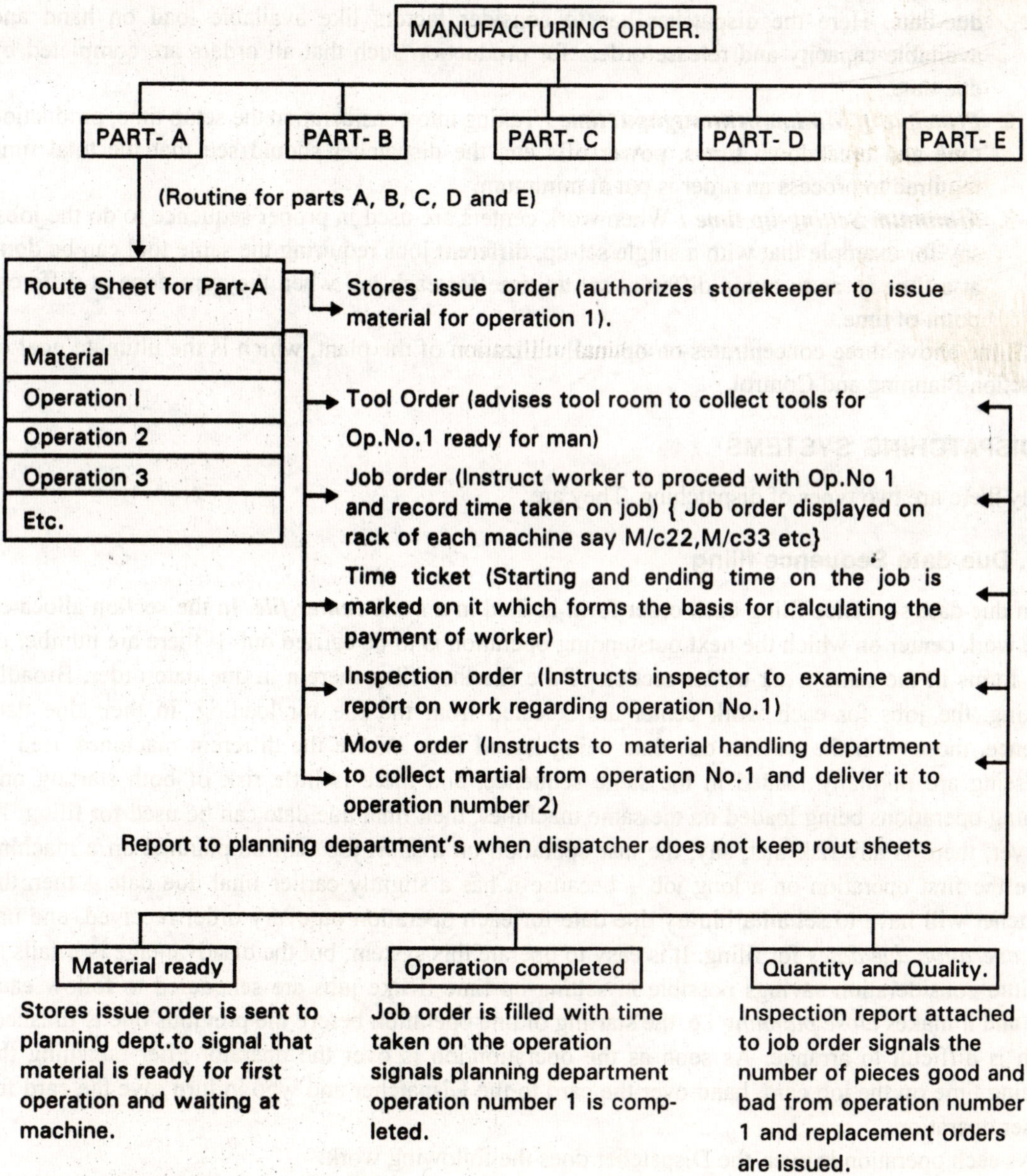

Figure 6.1 : Sequence of dispatching activities.

6.5. AIMS OF DISPATCHING

Earlier it is mentioned that the dispatcher should select a *most favorable sequence* of jobs while issuing for production. That is the sequence, which takes less through put time. For this the dispatcher has to follow three principles, they are:

1. ***Principle of completion: by due date :*** This aim states that all jobs are to be completed by due-date. Here the dispatcher has to consider factors like available load on hand and available capacity and release orders for production such that all orders are completed by due date.
2. ***Principle of Minimum throughput time :*** Taking into consideration the setup time, production time and breakdown times, power offs etc, the dispatcher should see that the total time required to process an order is put at minimum.
3. ***Minimum Setting-up time :*** When work centers are used in proper sequence to do the jobs, say for example that with a single set-up, different jobs requiring the same tool can be done at a time so as to avoid different set up time for each job when they are done at different point of time.

All the above three concentrates on optimal utilization of the plant, which is the ultimate goal of Production Planning and Control.

6.6 DISPATCHING SYSTEMS

Mainly there are two types of dispatching. They are:

6.6.1. Due date Sequence filing

In due date sequence filing each order form is filed in a ***work center file,*** In the section allocated to the work center on which the next outstanding operation is to be carried out. If there are number of order forms in the same work center section of the file they filed therein in due date order. Broadly speaking, the jobs for each work center are selected from the file for loading, in their due date sequence, those with the earliest due date being issued first. Where the different machines used in processing are normally loaded in the same sequence, and there is little risk of both starting and finishing operations being loaded on the same machines, then final due date can be used for filing. If, however, there is any risk that, say, the last operation on a short job will be planned on a machine before the first operation on a long job – because it has a slightly earlier final due date – then the dispatcher will have to set an arbitrary due date for each operation on every order received, and use these *operation due dates* for filing. It is easy to operate this system, but the disadvantage is it fails to take into consideration savings possible in setting-up time if like jobs are scheduled to follow each other and it makes *close planning* i.e. the starting of one operation before the previous one is finished, which is difficult to arrange. As soon as the operation/job is over the operator after punching the finishing time on the job card, hand over the card to the Dispatcher and who in turn give the card for another operation.

As each operation is over, the Dispatcher does the following work:

(*i*) Moves the order in the work center file to the section reserved for the work center for the following operation.

(*ii*) Issue a move ticket for the movement of the materials to the next machine.

(*iii*) Enters particulars on the progress copy and on the daily plan of the quantity completed.

6.6.2. Dispatching With Operation Scheduling

On receipt of the order and associated documents the first work done by the dispatcher is to load the different operations on the chart against the appropriate work center. The advantage of this method is it gives a good visual indication of the load ahead and of progress achieved and that it enables *close scheduling* to be practiced, thus giving higher throughput rates than are possible by due date sequence filing.

6.7. DOCUMENTS MAINTAINED BY DISPATCHING DEPARTMENT

Let us discuss here regarding the various documents that are maintained by the Dispatching department. The documents mentioned below are important among many more, we find in real world situations. Some times we find that few of the documents discussed below may be used in production shops. Some times more details are involved in the proforma given in this section depending on the need of the company, which uses the document. Some times some of the information given in the documents given here might have been eliminated. The proformas discussed in this section has academic orientation rather than practical approach.

OPERATION / ROUTE SHEET

No. / .

Part No..................
Name:...............................
Material with Specification:............................

Drawing No...........
Part Drawing:

Quantity:..........................
Issue date:.......................

Routing. Dept. Machine	Ope-ration	Description	Material handling	Tools	Jigs & fixtures	Time	
						Set up	Operation

Prepared by: Checked by: Date: Head of P.P.C dept.

TECHNOLOGICAL ROUTE CARD.

No...../.....

Department/Shop.................... Order No........ Assembly/Machine No.......
Job No.

Material:.....................Quantity:................... Weight per piece:.......Kg. Drawing No.:.............

Date of issue:.......................... Standard time:...............................Hrs................................Mins.

Operat-tion total No.	Description of operation	Machine & its No.	Special Instrum-ments &	Feed cut/mm	Speed m/min	Depth of cut mm	Finish size mm.	Tools & Jigs	Time	
									Set up	Opern. time

Technologist Checked by : Date.................

JOB CARD (SIDE : A) No. : ....../.....

Company : .... Job Card No. .... Part No. : ....
Shop : .... Drawing No. : ....

Name of the Job : .... Quantity/sets : .... Total Sets : ....
Material type : ....(Cast/Forged/Rolled/Machined)
Gross Weight/piece : kg.
Net Weight/piece..... Total
Quantity : ....

Operation Number	Descrip-tion of operation	Set up time in sec	Operation time in sec	Scheduled time				Actual time			
				Start		Finish		Start		Finish	
				Date	Time	Date	Time	Date	Time	Date	Time

Machine No. ...... Incentive Group No. : .... Total time allowed for quantity......Hours.
Card location : .... Previous operation........ Next operation .....
Rate setter : .... Date.......... Checked by............ Planner.........

(Job Card : Side 1)

JOB CARD : SIDE - B								
Delay greater than 30 mins.						Inspection.		
From	To	Lost hours	Code	Delays	Code	Quantity Passed	Quantity Rejected	Signature of Inspector.
				1. No. Drawing	D			
				2. No. Material	M			
				3. Breakdown	B			
				4. No. Crane	C			
				5. No. Tool	T			
				6. No. gage	G	Rejection due to		
				7. Operator Idle	I	Man	Material	Drawing
				8.				
				9.				
				10.				
Inspection Report :								
Remarks :								
....								

(Job Card : Side 2)

MOVE CARD			No. : ...../.....
Move Card No : .... Part No.	Order No. :	Quantity :	Date : ....
Moving facility : Loco/Truck/Fork lifter/Trolley/Crane/Man			
Origin Department :	Machine No.	Bay No. :	
Destination Department :	Machine No. :	Bay No. :	
Moving facility Number :	Moved By :		
Foreman :	Date :	Time :	

MOVE CARD

INSPECTION CARD				No. : ..../..........
Inspection Branch :		Order No. :		Part No. : ....
Type of Inspection :		Charged to :		Date : ....
Quantity	Material	Number passed	Number rejected	Number scrapped
Causes of rejection :				
Description :				
Inspector :				Date : ....

INPECTION CARD

6.7.1. Route Card

This document has many names, such as Technological Route Sheet, Route card etc., These cards are prepared by process engineers, who have a knowledge of processes and facility available and physical changes required in the material to get the final shape. This card indicates the details of operations that are to be carried out in the production shop in order to prepare the product. This will help the operator to decide the sequence of operations that have to be carried out, tools he has to use, cutting speeds, feed and depth of cut (for the parts to be machined), next machines to be used and also materials being used and how they are handled. Technological card differ with shops and are prepared in the way they feel it convenient and useful, some times, some sketches are also made for explaining the operator about the job. For routine jobs, printed route cards are prepared and will be supplied to the production shop, when a fresh batch is started. In case due to the demand in the market, any small change is made on the product, this is indicated on the printed route sheet by different color ink to draw the attention of the worker. When the component is one, which is purchased and supplied for assembly, then an entry is made in the route sheet, that the component is *purchased component*, which indicates that it is to be indented from stores. Present day mass production shops and batch production shops uses computerized route sheets.

6.7.2. Job Card

Job card is prepared by dispatching section with an idea to book the labour involved in each operation. The idea is to fill in the time spent by an operator on each operation. Number of job cards is equal to the number of operations to be performed in a shop. The information includes part details, operator number, and quantity to produce, time allowed, inspection report and destination of the component after the last operation.

Some of the features of a job card may be given in other cards, if used, for example: Time ticket, Work ticket, Inspection card and move card etc. In such a case, only the required information is filled in. Before release of work card or job card, it is date stamped. If it is used as an authority to withdraw tools, jigs etc., When order is finished, it is again date stamped and other passing through the planning department, to signal the completion of operation, it is available for costs and pay roll work.

6.7.3. Inspection Card

In this card the details of inspection are noted. Out of total produced quantity, how many are rejected, how many are passed, reasons for rejecting, precautions to be taken in future to reduce/avoid defective components are noted in this card. This will give information to the quality control department. If a separate inspection card is used, it is sent to planning department to signal the completion of the job and time or work card is sent directly to the pay roll department. Inspection card helps planning department to help the department to take decisions regarding replacement or repair of faulty components.

6.7.4. Move Card

Move cards are often used, where he transport problem/handling problem justifies their use: For example, Steel Plants, Power Plants and Automobile Units uses move card for handling the components. In case, a check on material handling person's time is desired to calculate his pay, provision is made on the move card to note the time taken to move the materials. In small units, this card is combined with inspection card or job card.

Generally five sets are prepared each set containing a job card, a route card, a move card and an inspection card. The first set is retained by the dispatching department, second copy is tied to the first material entering the production shop (or to the container/trolley/or a material handling equipment carrying the material), third copy is given to the follow-up engineer, fourth copy individually given to concerned departments, and the final copy is given to costing department.

PART: B – EXPEDITING OR FOLLOW UP OR PROGRESSING

Follow-up is that part of the production control function which go round the production shop and compares the actual performance with the production plan and prepares a report, which will be submitted to the line managers, who in turn will see that the variations mentioned in the report are corrected and will not repeat in future. The main purpose of this progressing is to see that a feed back is sent to the production shop and to the production planning department to give warning regarding deviations from the production plans. The activities of expediting are:

(*i*) The recording of the actual production,

(*ii*) The comparison of actual production with planned production,

(*iii*) Measurement of the deviation and identify the causes of deviation

(*iv*) Make arrangements of correcting the small deviations by taking the help of shop floor manager,

(*v*) Reporting of all excessive deviations to the authorities responsible for executing the plans, as planned.

6.8. TYPES OF FOLLOW-UP

There are five types of important follow-up procedures, they are:

1. *Program control:* Here the actual production output is compared with the production program, in case of sales, compare actual sales with the sales program and report the deviations to the line managers to take necessary steps in order to avoid such deviations in future.

2. *Order Progressing:* Here the due dates of production orders and purchase orders are compared with their actual completion dates or material received date. In case any over due is noticed, it is immediately reported to the line managers to see that thee corrective action is taken.

3. *Shortage Chasing:* Here actual available materials at workstations are compared with the required quantity of martial. In case any shortages are found, to report and make immediate arrangements to supply the required material in order to avoid stoppage of production. While sending feedback, a detailed report is made regarding this shortage of material to the line managers so as to enable them to take corrective actions.

4. *Daily plan progressing:* This is the control used at the third level of production control, to see that the daily plans made during dispatching are achieved or not. In case the plans are not achieved to the required extent, the reasons are noted and sent in feedback to the management.

5. *Departmental progress control:* Here the departmental performance is measured with the targeted production plans with actual achievement by the department and a report is prepared regarding the efficiency of the department, in order to help line managers to take corrective action.

6.8.1. Program control

There are many different ways in which production output can be recorded and compared with production plan. Three different types of methods are discussed below:

1. *Gantt charts:* Gantt chart used in scheduling and loading also in expediting the progress of production. The American engineer, Henry L. Gantt, originates this chart, and consists of a simple rectangular grid, divided by a series of parallel horizontal and vertical lines, as shown in the figure number 6.1

Plant		*Monday*	*Tuesday*	*Wednesday*	*Thursday*	*Friday*	*Saturday*
No.	*Description*						
1.	Turning on lathe (No. L 201)						
2.	Rough drilling (No. D 108)						
3.	Reaming (No. R 105)						
4.	Tap						

Figure 6.1: Gantt Chart.

The vertical lines always divide the horizontal lines into units of time. The scale units can be years, months, weeks, days, hours or minutes according to the need for which the chart is used. The horizontal line divides the chart into sections, which can be used to represent either work tasks (in work schedules) or work centers (in load charts). When chart shows only work tasks i.e. products, orders, or operations to be completed, it is known as Work Schedule. When it shows these tasks opposite to work centers at which they are to be produced say for example factories, departments, workshops, machine tools or man, then the chart is known as Load Chart.

The units scheduled or loaded on these charts are always the same; they are work tasks, which generally have a known standard time, so that the time from start to finish of each is known. These tasks may be products or parts, to be made, or work operations to be carried out in the course of manufacture.

6.8.2. Symbols Used in Gantt Chart

Either numbers or special symbols can represent the work task on the chart. When numbers are used in the production and sales program, the number shown in the space represents the number of units to be produced in that particular time intervals. But, most of the times, in scheduling and loading charts special symbols used to indicate the job to be completed in the planned time interval. The symbols used to represent work task on the chart vary from company to company. Here the symbols discussed are academic in nature and most commonly used. One of the important features of Gantt chart is that it can be used to schedule the tasks and also can be used to record the progress of the work. Progress is recorded by drawing a thick line on the legs in the table. Provisions are made to show set up time, time saved and time lost. One draw back of the chart is that, in case the job is not

Table showing the symbols used in Gantt chart

Symbols used in Gantt chart	Description
┌	Start the task
┐	Finisth the task
┌ ┐	The time required for the job
┌ ┐ S ┌ ┐	Set-up time
┌ ┐ (thick line over first part)	Progress of the job (25% of the job is completed)
┌ ┐ S	Time gained against plan. Next job is shown above the line at correct tarting time.
┌ J5(100) ┐	Number of jobs to be completed
┌ MIOS(100) ┐	Identification symbol shown

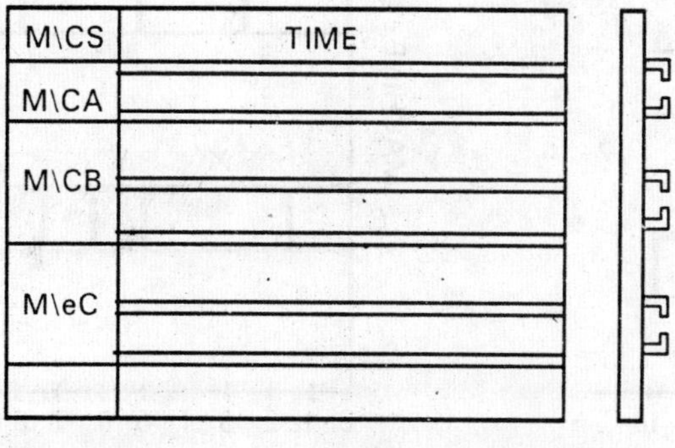

Figure 6.2 : Control Boards.

completed in the prescribed time due to some trouble, to reschedule it else where when the facility is idle is very difficult. For this, whole chart is to be redrawn. To overcome this defect, control boards have been devised. These control boards are provided with slots than the lines on the chart. In these slots, a card cut to size of the time interval and with job details drawn on it is inserted. When we look at the board, we see number of cards inserted on the chart. As and when one particular job is over, that card is removed and another job in sequence is allocated to the facility. To know the progress, a thread is fixed on the frames of the board and this thread is pulled to the required time and the progress of each job is noted along the thread and recorded. When the job is half the way and due to some difficulty it could not be continued, then the card is removed and inserted again when the facility becomes idle. Control boards are very useful and convenient for scheduling and loading. It is very common that one can see a control board in a modern production shops. Advantages gained in control boards are: Sliding of the cards is very easy and quick when compared to redrawing a chart. When there is a change in the plan it is a relatively simple job to reposition the cards in the sliding holder. If there in any gain or loss of time in plan for any particular work center can be resynchronized, by sliding the holder itself to the right or left, without moving the cards themselves in the holder.

Another type of control board is also available, where the cards are fitted into overlapping card pockets, with transparent lips. Each card is cut to the length representing the standard time of the job concerned. When all the job pockets are hanging down the board has the appearance of a Gantt chart. If details are required about any scheduled item, turning back the top cardholder and reading the information from the card in the pocket concerned can find them. Some of the symbols mostly used on Gantt chart are given above:

Example 6.1. Draw a schedule chart and load chart for the following problem by using Gantt chart, and find the optimal sequence.

Jobs	Machines (time in hours), Machining order : *AB*	
	A	*B*
X	2	4
Y	3	1
Z	3	2

Solution :

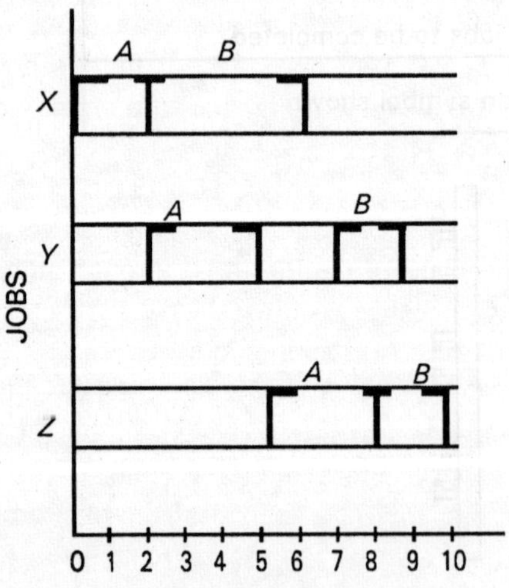

(*a*) Gantt chart for job scheduling.
Optimal sequence = 10 Hrs

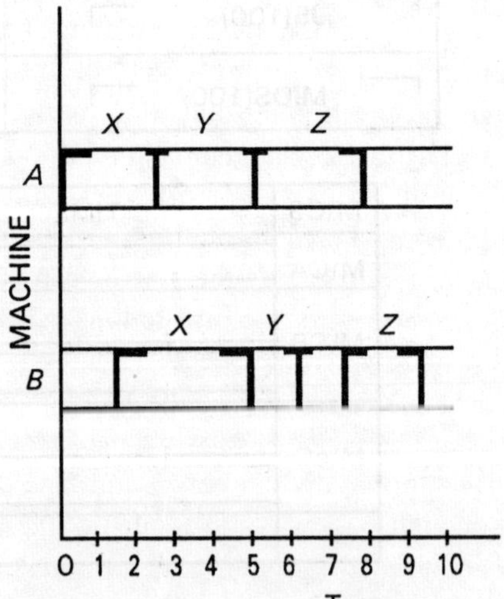

(*b*) Gantt chart for machine loading.
Optimal time = 10 hours

6.8.3. 'Z' Chart

Another method of program control is by the use of *Z Charts*. These charts show actual output at a required period of time (at the end of a week or at the end of a month. Etc.,) along with cumulative output from the beginning of the year or period and moving totals at the same time interval. (Figure 6.4). Z charts can be used to show both the plan and the performance, and deviation from the plan by blocking in the gap between two curves

6.8.4. Tabulated Records

The plan, performance and deviation can be neatly tabulated instead of chart symbols, so that every one can understand clearly. This is shown in figure 6.5.

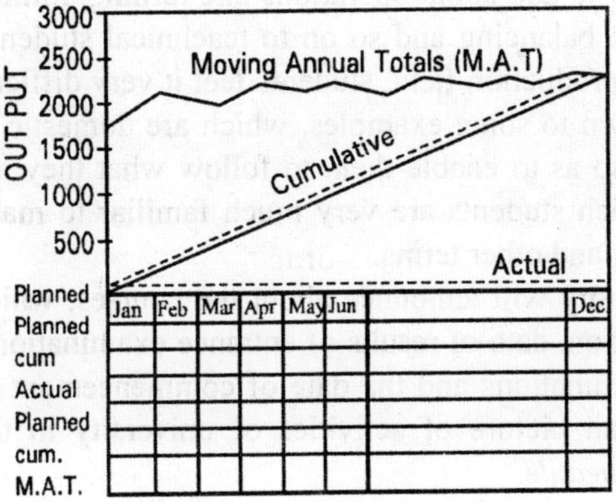

Figure 6.4 : Z chart.

Week no.	Product A					Product B				
	Plan	Actual	Cumulative	Up (+)	Plan	Down (–)	Actual	Cumulative	Up (+)	Down (–)
1										
2										
3										
4										
5										
6										

Figure 6.5 : Tabulated records

To conclude, follow up or expediting procedure requires recognition of delays, evaluation of its consequents and action to remove its causes or at least minimize their effects. Expediting function consists in keeping a watch on the flow of material and whenever any trouble occurs expediter locate the source of trouble and take action to remove it. A more advanced form of expediting attempts to prevent trouble by setting up check points along the way to start expediting if the job does not get through the check point operation on the scheduled date. A common practice is to employ persons to trace work through the plant and to report on its progress.

Suppose an expeditor observes or learns from the progress charts that a batch of components have failed to arrive at a certain production center on the date scheduled, he proceeds to investigate the cause, and to decide the way he can put things right. If the difficulties arise through ambiguities or misunderstanding of the instructions in the production order, the expeditor should clarify the points. If he is unable to solve the problem on his own, he turns to planning department for assistance. Expeditors are concerned only with keeping up of schedules and with flow of materials; they are also given responsibility of moving the semi-finished components to the next workstation. They are not asked to do lengthy studies of intricate cause and effect systems. They are neither trained nor they have enough patience and requisite qualification required for such analysis. They can contribute to such analysis by providing up to date facts, they should also be told of any conclusions, after the study is completed.

The basic problem of follow up is that of how much follow up on goods in process is necessary. Theoretically, if routing, scheduling and dispatching have been properly done, no follow up is necessary. The reporting of progressing may be done periodically (daily, weekly or monthly). Some times, in routing work, when the assistance is needed from the control department and, if necessary, reporting may be done of progress to the higher ups, This type of reporting may be done by interdepartmental telephones or in person or in writing etc.

It is difficult to know where dispatching ends and where expediting starts. But each one is told about their respective duties by planning section. In general dispatching records events, expediting tries to adjust them wherever necessary.

For a teacher, who teachers Production Operations Management, to management students, it will be difficult to make the students to understand the subject matter with technical examples. This is because; the management class will have heterogeneous mix of students from various disciplines, which does not have any technical background. It is easy to talk about operations like turning, milling and drilling etc., and routing, scheduling, assembly line balancing and so on to teachnical students. But in a management class, when examples given from production field, students feel it very difficult to follow. Hence many a time the teacher has to go down to some examples, which are domestic in nature, or examples, with which the students familiar, so as to enable them to follow what they are learning. Hence, I am discussing an example, with which students are very much familiar to make them to understand what are routing, scheduling, loading and other terms.

Take the example of education system. The University will announce about the courses, which are offered and announces the date of entrance examination, date of results of entrance examinations, date of commencement of courses and date of end examinations and the date of commencement of next semester. This announcement will give the overall picture of activities of university in the academic year and is known as *master plan or master schedule.*

Master Schedule of a university for the year 2000-2001

S. No.	*Course*	*Date of entrance exam*	*Date of EE resu-lts*	*Date of admi-ssions*	*Date of comme-ncement*	*Date of I semes-ter exam*	*Date of results of I Sem results*	*Date of comme-II Sem.*
1.	B.A.	10, May	2, June	10, June	1, July	4, Dec.	26, Dec.	1 Jan. 2001
2.	B.Com	08, May	26, May	06, June	1, July	4, Dec.	26, Dec.	1, Jan. 2001
3.	B.Sc.	06, May	24, May	06, June	1, July	4, Dec.	26, Dec.	1, Jan. 2001
......	......	......	......	......	......	......	......	......
						etc.		

Once the above master schedule is released, the examination department, affiliated colleges will start planning their work. The examination department will prepare detailed schedule showing when the question papers of the entrance examinations to be prepared, when the applications are to be received and when the examination schedule to be informed to the candidates, when the evaluation of papers are to be started and completed and see that the results are announced on the specified date.

Similarly affiliated colleges will prepare the timetables and allocate loads to the staff members. Here the subject is a job and the contents of the syllabus of the subject are the load (hours required to complete the syllabus). Teacher is the facility. Depending one the available hours of a staff member he is loaded with one or two subjects, by taking into consideration the available number of working days (here loss of working days due to public holidays, and other reasons are taken into consideration). Here a time table is a schedule when it is prepared to show which subject will be taught in which period of the day. When the same is prepared with respect to a teacher, it will be known a load sheet. The head of the institution or a department will see that the classes are going on smoothly and the syllabus of the subjects are being completed uniformly is considered as the control. The head of institution may go round the classes to see that no class is left idle and this is follow up. Considering the subjects prescribed for first semester and second semester and so on, care is taken to see that the student who completes the first semester, will be in a position to follow the second semester subjects and those who pass the second semester will follow third semester subjects. This can be considered a routing.

QUESTIONS

1. Discuss in brief the elements of control.
2. Explain the duties of a dispatcher.
3. Give the names of various documents maintained by dispatching department and give the specimen of the document, which shows how, the material move during manufacture.
4. Write a short notes on Gantt chart.
5. Explain the symbols used in Gantt chart.
6. What are control boards, discuss how they are used.
7. What is expediting? Why is it necessary in production control?

7

CAPACITY MANAGEMENT

- Introduction
- Definition of Capacity
- Definition of Capacity Management.
- Forms of Capacity.
- Determining the Capacity Requirement.
- Design Capacity.
- System Capacity
- Determination of Equipment Requirement.
- Capacity Planning.
    - Long term Capacity Strategies.
    - Phase in Capacity
    - Phase out Capacity
- Short term Capacity Planning

7.1. INTRODUCTION

During the last decade tremendous changes have taken place in the field of Production Management because of changes in manufacturing processes and in management approach to solve the problems. Fundamental changes have taken place and are taking place; in the way manufacturing companies plan and control their resources. The increased knowledge of Production Planning and Control has grown in parallel with the development of faster and more sophisticated computer hardware and increased availability of software. Inspite of all the development in Production Planning and Control, one can find the problem of *Capacity Management* is not tackled properly and is the least developed one. One reason for this might be that the companies usually install their manufacturing information systems module by module. This may be due to the fact that the required information about technology required may not completely available at the time of installation or there may be financial constraint at the time of installation. One more point we have to consider is that the technology is developing at a very fast rate and due to competition in the market, the companies have to upgrade their technology. In such situations, the company cannot change over to the new technology overnight. The company has to consider this problem, in piece meal. Many companies do not consider the capacity problem as a critical one because, capacity can be increased or contracted in various ways with some related cost element.

The importance of good Capacity Management cannot be overestimated. This is because; two factors must be present to produce the goods or the products. They are material and productive resources, like men and machines. When we speak of men and machines we have to consider in terms of capacity of men and machines. When there is no material, the productive resources will remain idle, similarly when there are no productive resources, material is of little use. Hence, all manufacturing firms deal with capacity management in one way or the other in most informal way or through a loosely structured formal planning system. It is possible to get by with reactive instead of proactive capacity planning and control if the productive resources are easily and inexpensively controllable. Today because of rapidity of flow of information and various ways of procuring industrial finance and involvement of professional management in the coming days capacity management will take an increased importance.

7.2. DEFINITION OF CAPACITY

Capacity can be defined as products or productive resources per a particular unit of measure. Thus, capacity is *rate* that can be measured at either the input side or the output side of a productive system, as seen in figure 7.1.

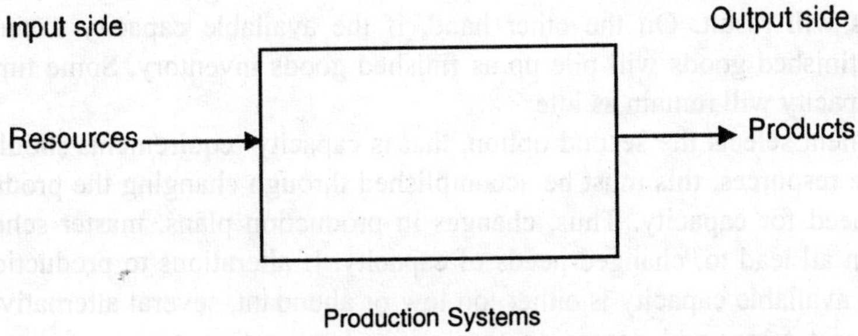

Figure 7.1 : Productive Systems.

For a manufacturing firm, the productive resources usually consists of material, labor, and equipment, while for a service- oriented firm, the customers themselves can be considered key resources together with labor and equipment. For example a service station can state its capacity as 10 four wheelers per day. A transport company can state as 60 seats per trip.

Consider a company manufacturing a single product X, and its resources can produce 1000 units per day, we can quote the capacity of plant is to produce 1000 units of product per day. In case of multi product companies it is difficult to mention in terms of products, as all the products share the same productive resources. In such cases, the capacity is stated in aggregate units per time periods disregard of product mix. But in Capacity Management perspective, however, these are not always useful measures. Thus, manufactures of discrete items must often resort to measuring capacity at the input side, in terms of resources that are used in the manufacturing process. Available capacity can, then, be stated in labor or machine hours per unit of time. Similarly, required capacity can be stated in labour or machine hours per manufactured units. A production schedule will convert required capacity per unit into required capacity per unit of time, in order to make it comparable to the available capacity. Hence, Capacity can be defined as a measure of the ability to produce, or serve that is having enough worker or equipment time to do the jobs. More informally, capacity is often referred to as a rate of output. A less acceptable measure is in monetary terms, say products worth Rs.10, 000 manufactured per day. This is less acceptable because the price changes will not affect volume changes. Regardless of measure, capacity expresses some bounds on the organization's ability to produce. In our discussion, we concentrate on maximum capacity, but the minimum capacity is also important, because any organization cannot operate below certain capacity in order to reach the break-even.

7.3. DEFINITION OF CAPACITY MANAGEMENT

Two basic factors are needed in order to execute a production schedule and they are *material and capacity*. Assuming that material is available, a potential problem area is the relationship between the needed resources per unit of time, derived from the production schedule, and the currently available resources per unit of time. Many a time the production manager will come across a situation that the available and required capacity do not balance and he has to take certain action to balance the two. The three options at his disposal are: (*a*) Do nothing, (*b*) Change Capacity requirements and (*c*) Change available capacity.

In case the management selects the first one, i.e. to do nothing about the imbalance between the available and required capacity, we have two situations.

(*i*) if capacity is not sufficient to meet the requirements, a waiting line of jobs or orders may build up and late orders will result. On the other hand, if the available capacity exceeds the required capacity, then the finished goods will pile up as finished goods inventory. Some times we may find that some of the capacity will remain as idle.

If the management selects the second option, that is capacity requirements should be changed to match the available resources, this must be accomplished through changing the production schedules that generate the need for capacity. Thus, changes in production plans, master schedules and parts order schedules can all lead to, changed needs of capacity. If alterations to production schedules are not warranted, and available capacity is either too low or abundant, several alternatives exist. Each is associated with a cost factor and degree of ease of implementation. Some of them are mentioned below:

(*i*) Schedule Overtime,

(*ii*) Use alternate routings that is the work is performed by a different workstation than original specified on the route sheet.

(*iii*) Shift workforce that is move operators from an area with excess capacity to an area with capacity needs.

(*iv*) Subcontract jobs, that is buy manufacturing services from other companies or sell excess capacity to other firms.

(*v*) Re-evaluate the make and buy decision, that is decide whether purchased parts could actually be made more economically in-house or whether there are manufactured parts that could be purchased from an outside supplier at lower cost.

(*vi*) Hire casual labors or contract labors or lay-off labors depending on the situation.

(*vii*) Introduce or cancel work shifts. Additional shifts demand more personnel and intense use of existing capital equipment.

(*viii*) Invest in new equipment. In addition, replacement old machinery or proper maintenance schedules can also increase the capacity.

(*ix*) Increase efficiency that is increase productivity of all elements of production.

The alternative chosen depends on where in the planning process the decision is made and for how long the implemented change is expected to last. In the context of the above-mentioned strategies, we can say that the Capacity Management encompasses the translation of production schedules into capacity requirements, the estimation of available capacity, and the actions taken to align capacity needs with capacity availability.

7.4. FORMS OF CAPACITY

Several forms of available capacity exist. One can distinguish between *maximum, nominal, and demonstrated* capacity. As far as the time element is concerned, the first concept is of not much use. This is because; any company could work for 24 hours a day, seven days a week and any thing less than that would provide less than maximum capacity. If the company operates with a single shift, *maximum capacity* defined this way is, thus of no practical significance. The normal capacity, on the other hand, refers to the capacity that would be available under normal circumstances. Take for example, a work center operating on a single shift, the weekly nominal capacity could be 7.5 hours × 5 days × I operator or 37.5 hours per week. This is to say that the maximum capacity is equal to nominal capacity under normal working conditions.

But in real world, the production manager will have to face quite a lot of problems, which prevent him from using the nominally available capacity for productive purpose. The problems he has to face are of the type: Non-availability of material, changing schedules, machine breakdowns, scheduled breaks, absenteeism and so on. All these will have an effect on the actual usage of resources. A measurement of the historical use of productive, hours is called *demonstrated* capacity. This way of expressing capacity indicated the average attainable capacity, based on past measurements. It should be pointed out that there is a potential danger in letting the demonstrated capacity represent the planned available capacity for the future. The historical or demonstrated capacity might not have been achieved under the best conditions or the highest efficiency. Hence the demonstrated capacity is always less than that of ideal situation.

Capacity utilization is a measure that should indicate to what degree the potential capacity is used. Hence we can say that the capacity utilization can be defined as a ratio between the demonstrated and the nominal capacity, where nominal capacity reflects a situation where the plant/department/ work center is fully staffed.

Now the question arises as how to specify the capacity. As discussed earlier, capacity – available or required – will be measured in hours. However, since we are interested in the productive use of manufacturing resources, only productive hours are of interest for capacity planning purposes. This means that the hours available in a day must first of all be adjusted because of allowances for machine breakdowns, absenteeism, and other losses of time. This is generally known as utilization:

$$\text{Utilisation} = \frac{\text{Number of direct productive hours per day}}{\text{Total number of scheduled hours per day}}$$

For example, 10% of total number of available hours in a day is considered non-productive, and then the utilization factor will be 90%. Utilization is normally worked out for a plant or for a department or for a work center. Due to normal variations in skills and speed, different operators can produce a different number of units of the same item per elapsed hour (unless used facility is automatic). Also, different items require varying amounts of work per piece. Since it is of interest to know the quantity that can be produced per hour, given a certain level of capacity, and also the capacity that is needed to ensure a certain output rate, the way in which capacity and resources usage are measured must be standardized. For this the company must find out what amount of standard hours of machine and labour are required through work-study. The use of standard hours has two effects. First it provides a way of measuring output in hours instead of units. These hours represent the *normal* hours needed for manufacturing. Secondly, based on observations of past events, an *efficiency factor* that relates the actual number of direct hours used to the standard hour work content of the output can be derived as:

$$\text{Efficiency} = \frac{\text{Standard hours processed per day}}{\text{Actually used direct hours per day}}$$

The efficiency factor can be recorded for an individual operator, a work center, a department or the plant as a whole. The significance of the efficiency factor is of two fold. First of all it indicates, if observed over time, changes in productivity. That is, an increased efficiency indicates that the same output has been achieved with a lower input. Secondly, the efficiency factor helps to estimate future available capacity, measured in standard hours.

Let us take an example that a work center with two employees per shift. In an 8 hour, two-shift operation, with utilization factor of 90 % and an efficiency factor of 105 %, the total expected number of standard hours that can be produced per day is:

Total number of hours per day × utilization factor × efficiency factor.

= 2 shifts × 2 operators × 8 hours × 0.90 = Productive hours per day,

Productive hors per day × efficiency factor = total number of standard hours per day = 2 × 2 × 8 × 0.90 × 1.05 = 30.2 Standard hours per day.

The expected available capacity for a work center can, thus, be calculated and expressed with a common denominator. Likewise, the required capacity for the work center for a particular day can be found by multiplying the scheduled number of parts to be manufactured by their standard hourly content:

Required capacity per day = Scheduled number of units per day × standard hours per unit.

For accounting purposes it is common to classify work hours as either direct or indirect. A direct hour is a productive hour directly used in manufacturing and assignable to a particular job. An indirect hour is an hour considered not to be directly associated with a particular job or directly used for manufacturing. Sometimes, overtime is commonly classified as an indirect cost since the reason overtime is scheduled might demand on circumstances not related to the job in question. Supervisors salary are also classified as indirect costs, as their hours allocated for setups and changeovers of equipment. The machine setup time required for production complicate the determination of available and required capacity. Processing time, is the sum of the setup and the run time, the latter being time actually spent on the fabrication or assembly operation in question. If for example, setup time is recorded as indirect time, then actual hours earned will be related to run time only. The standard time per unit for an operation, in order to be consistent, should not include setup time either. On the other hand, if the time spent on setup can be recorded as and singled out as indirect time, then the actual hours in the efficiency factor can consider both run time and setup time. In this case, the numerator in 'efficiency', as well as the standard hours per unit for an operation, should include setup time. If using a form of moving average smoothens the efficiency factor, the effect of setup times related to varying lot sizes will be diminished. The same will hold good in case of numerator in utilization factor.

7.5. DETERMINING CAPACITY REQUIREMENTS

In order to estimate how much of a resource is needed per unit of time, a translation of production schedules into standard hours must take place. Production schedules can exist on different aggregation levels and also be stated in different units of measures as shown in table below. Another factor of interest is the level of detail at which the capacity needs are to be specified. Estimating required capacity at machine level requires more attention to detail, and is done for a different purpose, than the estimation of the required at the plant level. Obviously, if capacity requirements are known at the lowest level, the requirements can always be added to generate the aggregate needs. The opposite, however, is not as easy. Determining the capacity requirements for a particular machine from a Master Schedule stated in end items clearly requires approximate procedures, since the Master Schedule does not contain the detailed parts schedule that is needed to estimate the use of the machine. Further, an estimation of capacity requirement at the plant level based on the Production Plan can clearly be done based on historical relationships between total aggregate production levels and number of standard hours used. Breaking this information down in order to determine the capacity needed for a specific week cannot be accomplished with accuracy. Determination of capacity requirement can be done in many ways, depending on the details available in order to get required information. The purpose of capacity planning and need for detail must therefore be determined before the appropriate technique is chosen. If the planning horizon is larger, planning period also larger and the revisions are attempted very frequently to meet the required demand for capacity. The planning horizon and planning period will be determined depending on the purpose of the planning effort. In general, capacity planning is concerned with defining the long and short-term capacity needs of the organization and determining how those needs will be satisfied. Figure 7.2 gives this interaction in a conceptual sense. Note that capacity decisions must merge consumer demands with the resources, such as manpower, material, and financial resources of the organization.

Important variable in capacity planning

Schedules which form the basis for capacity requirement.	Unit of measure in which production schedules can be stated	Units for which the capacity requirements can be determined
Production plan	Aggregate units of end items	Company, plant
Mater Schedule	End items	Company, plant
Planned order, schedules for parts and assemblies	Parts and assembles	Department
		Work centre/machine.
Open order schedules for parts and assembles		

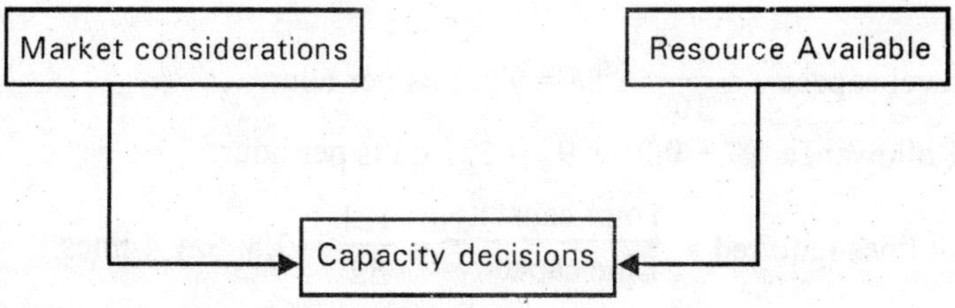

Figure 7.2 : Input to capacity decisions.

7.6. DESIGN CAPACITY

Production systems design involves planning for the inputs, transformation activities, and output of a production operation. Design decisions are far-reaching because they often entail significant investment of funds and they establish cost and productivity patterns that continue far into the future. They affect both fixed and variable costs. Preliminary estimates of capacity typically come from long-range forecasts that may project demands as much as 5 or 10 years into the future. Long-range projections help to ensure that the demand is not just temporary, and they also allow enough lead-time for constructions of major facilities. The *design capacity* of a facility is the planned rate of output of goods or services under normal conditions. (Eg: A plant manufactures 300 cars a day, A plant manufactures 100 tons of cement a day, A transport organization has a capacity to carry 200 passengers per hour and so on). Organizations do not necessarily plan for enough capacity to satisfy all their immediate demand. They first install the bare minimum (probably, some in-between, happy medium level of capacity) capacity and go on expansion scheme gradually. The design capacity should reflect management's strategy for meeting demand.

Example 7.1. A company is producing 32 units per hour on one of its production line. Now the management is planning to expand their capacity to satisfy the increasing demand. The operations manager has conducted survey and the outcome of the survey is as follows:

	Number of units per hour				
	0<40	40<80	80<120	120<160	160<200
Probability (% chance)	0.10	0.35	0.40	0.13	0.02
Cumulative probability :	0.10	0.45	0.85	0.98	1.00

The operations manager is considering two alternatives for deciding how much capacity to install. What capacity is required to (*a*) meet 85 percent of the estimated *peak* hourly demand, and (*b*) accommodate 110 percent of the estimated *average* demand plus a 25 percent for growth?

Solution :

(*a*) From the cumulative probability given in the problem, 85 percent of the estimated demand is less than 120 units per hour. Therefore,

$$\text{Number of production lines required} = \frac{\text{Total capacity}}{\text{Line capacity}} = \frac{120}{32} = 3.75.$$

Say approximately 4 lines.

(*b*) Average demand can be found by $E(X) = \Sigma\{XP(X)\}$, where X is mid point of each class interval given in the problem. Now $E(X) = 20\ (0.10) + 60\ (0.35) + 100\ (0.40) + 140\ ((0.15) + 180\ (0.02) = 88$ units.

$$\text{Therefore base-level capacity} = \frac{110}{100} \times 88 = 97 \text{ units per hour.}$$

Add to this 25 % allowance: $97 + 0.25 \times 97 = 121$ units per hour.

$$\text{Hence, number of lines required} = \frac{\text{Total capacity}}{\text{Line capacity}} = \frac{121}{32} = 3.8. \text{ Say 4 lines.}$$

By installing 4 lines the production manager can satisfy both the requirements.

Example 7.2. A hotel, which maintains both boarding and lodging sections in a summer resort place, is planning to increase its lodging facilities for the coming summer period. The manager has collected the following data. Find what would be the new capacity?

(*i*) Management wants to increase its capacity to accommodate 10% customers more than the average summer demand.

(*ii*) Composite demand (X) 0 – 10 10 – 20 20 – 50 50 – 80 80 – 100
Percentage of time: $P(X)$ 5 30 50 10 5

Solution : The data colleted has an unequal demand class size distribution and overlapping class limits. That is it is difficult to say in which class 20 and 50 and 80 falls. Hence we have to take midpoints for our calculation.

Mid-point (*X*)	*F* (*X*)	*X.P* (*X*)
5	0.05	0.25
15	0.30	4.50
35	0.50	17.50
65	0.10	6.50
90	0.05	4.50
Total		**33.25**

Expected demand = $E(D) = \Sigma\{XP(X)\}$ = 33.25 customers. Add 10 % to it as per the management's decision.

= 33.25 + 0.10 × 33.25 = 36.57 customers.

The manager has to provide accommodation for 37 customers.

7.7. SYSTEM CAPACITY

The system capacity can be explained as the maximum output of a specific product or product mix that the system of workers and machines is capable of producing as an integrated whole. As the output of a system may be limited by the product mix / quality specifications/ current balance of equipment and labour, the system capacity, many a time less than the designed capacity. But the actual output may be less than the system capacity, because it is affected by short-range factors such as actual demand, equipment breakdowns and personnel absences or productivity. Figure 7.3 shows the relationship between Design Capacity, System Capacity and Actual Capacity.

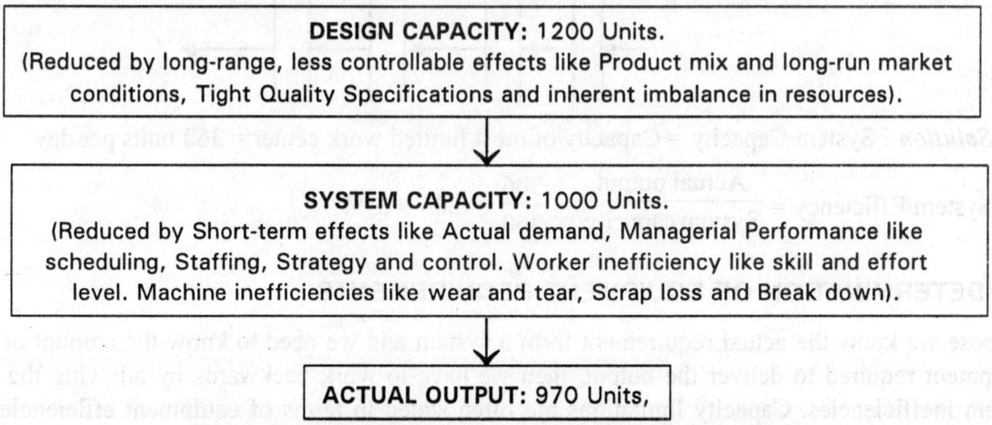

Figure 7.3 : Relationship between Capacities and outputs.

$$\text{System Efficiency} = \frac{\text{Actual Output}}{\text{System Capacity}}$$

The ratio of Actual measured output of goods or a service to the system capacity is referred as *System efficiency.*

Example 7.3. A chemical processor has been making a white plastic compound for dish wear on a continuous basis by processing it through a series of four tanks namely, mixing tank, heating tank, molding tank and cooling tank, at a rate of 40 Kg of chemical per minute. The firm now plans to produce different colored plastic compounds on the same equipment. However, the individual capacities of the tank will then be limited because of the time needed for cleaning, maintain different temperatures for different compounds and other changes required. If the individual capacities in Kg/min and actual output for new operations are as shown in figure below, find a) The system capacity and b) The system efficiency.

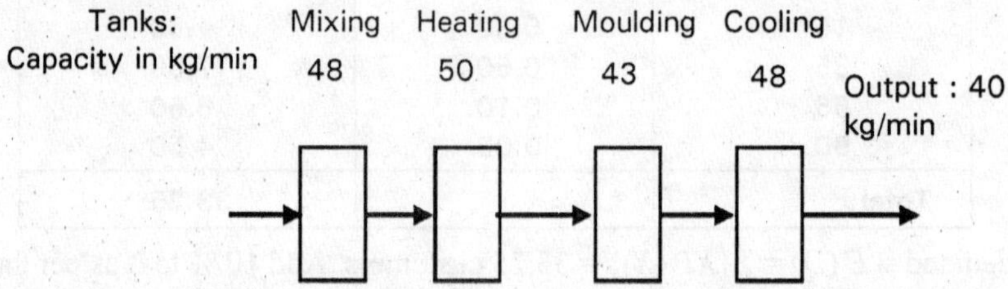

Solution : (a) System capacity = The limiting capacity in the given system is 43 Kg./Min. Therefore the system capacity is 43 Kg/min.

$$(b)\ \text{System Efficiency} = \frac{\text{Actual output}}{\text{System capacity}} = \frac{40}{43} = 0.93 = 93\%.$$

Example 7.4. A manufacturing firm has four work stations: *A, B, C* and *D* in series with individual capacities of 450, 390, 360 and 400 units per day and the actual out put is 306 units per day. Find System capacity and System Efficiency.

Solution :

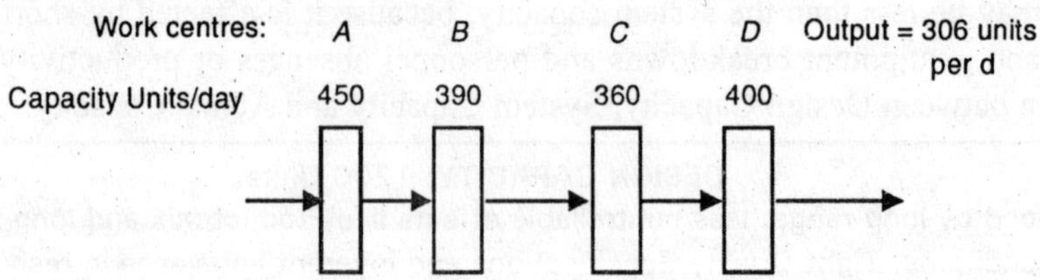

Solution : System Capacity = Capacity of most limited work center = 360 units per day.

$$\text{System Efficiency} = \frac{\text{Actual output}}{\text{System capacity}} = \frac{306}{360} = 0.85 = 85\%.$$

7.8. DETERMINATION OF EQUIPMENT REQUIREMENTS

Suppose we know the actual requirement form a system and we need to know the amount or size of equipment required to deliver the output, then we have to work backwards by allowing the normal system inefficiencies. Capacity limitations are often stated in terms of equipment efficiencies or an amount of scrap loss. Say for example the scrap loss is 5 percent, and then the system efficiency is only 95 %. And the required system capacity is determined by dividing 0.95 into the actual output required. By dividing this system capacity by the individual machine capacity gives us the number of machines required.

Example 7.5. A turning department wants to install enough Semi automatic lathes to produce 2,50,000 good components per year. The turning operation takes 1.5 minutes per component. But it is observed that the output of lathes will have 3 percent defectives. How many lathes will be required, if each one is available for 2,000 hours of capacity per year?

Solution : Required system capacity $= \dfrac{\text{Actual good components required}}{\text{System efficiency}}$

$$= \frac{2{,}50{,}000}{0.97} = 2{,}57{,}732 \text{ components per year.}$$

$$= \frac{2{,}57{,}000 \text{ components per year}}{2000 \text{ hours per year}} = 129 \text{ units/hr.}$$

$$\text{Individual lathe capacity} = \frac{60 \text{ minutes per hour}}{1.5 \text{ minutes per component}}$$

$$= 40 \text{ components per machine hour.}$$

$$\text{Number of lathes required} = \frac{129 \text{ units per hour}}{40 \text{ units per machine hour}}$$

$$= 3.2 \text{ machines}$$

Now the firm can go for 3 or 4 lathes. If it installs three machines, it may have to carefully manage the capacity by proper scheduling or using overtime or by over loading of lathes. If it installs 4 machines, the firm will have some excess capacity. This idle capacity may be utilized by accepting orders, which need the services of lathes, or it can lease the capacity to the firms, which needs the capacity.

Example 7.6. A manufacturing company is considering the expansion of one of its product line by adding additional capacity. The capacity of the new line is 1 ton. The process consists of loading and processing and unloading. Putting all together, the processing time for one tone is 30 minutes to produce 1 ton. The line can work 80 % of the shift due to power restrictions and availability of materials handling equipment. The expected output of the new layout is to be 16 tons per shift of 8 hours. Plant (system) efficiency is 50 % of the system capacity. Find the number of lines required and estimate the percentage of time the line will be idle.

Solution : Required system capacity $= \dfrac{\text{Actual output}}{\text{System efficiency}}$

$$= \frac{16 \text{ tonne per shift}}{\text{System efficiency}} = \frac{16}{0.50} = 32 \text{ tonne per shift.}$$

$$= \frac{32 \text{ tonne per shift}}{0.8 \times 8 \text{ hour shift}} = 5 \text{ tonne per hour}$$

$$\text{Individual line capacity required} = \frac{1 \text{ ton}}{0.5 \text{ hour}} = 2 \text{ tonne hour per Line.}$$

$$\text{Number of line required} = \frac{\text{5 tonne per hour}}{\text{2 tonne per hour per line}}$$

= 2.5 lines say approximately 3 lines.

Percentage of idle time:

Total hours available per shift = 3 lines at 8 hours each = 24 hours.

Total hours of actual use per shift = (16 tons) × (0.5 hours per ton) = 8 hours

Idle time = Available time – Time actually used = 24 – 8 = 16 hours.

$$\text{Percentage of idle time} = \text{idle hours / total time available} = \frac{16}{24} = 0.67 \text{ idle time} = 67\%$$

Example 7.7: A film developing shop must determine how many photo enlarger cubicles are required to maintain an output of 200 god prints per hour. The setup and exposure time can theoretically be done in 2 minutes per print, but operators are on the average only 90 percent efficient and, in addition, 5 percent of the prints must be scrapped and redone. Also, the cubicles can be utilized for enlarging only 70 percent of the time.

(*a*) What is the required system capacity in prints per hour?

(*b*) What average output per hour can be expected from each cubicle, taking its use factor and efficiency into account?

(*c*) How many enlarger cubicles are required?

Solution:

(*a*) $\text{Required system capacity} = \dfrac{\text{Good output}}{\text{System efficiency}}$

$\dfrac{200}{0.95} = 200 / 0.95 = 210.50$ prints per hour.

(*b*) $\text{Output per hour} = \dfrac{\text{Unit capacity}}{\text{Utilisation }\%} \times (\text{efficiency})$

$\text{Unit capacity} = \dfrac{\text{60 minutes per hour}}{\text{2 minutes per print}} = 30 \text{ prints /Hr.}$

Out put per hour = (30 prints per hour) (0.70) (0.90) = 18.9 prints per hour.

(*c*) $\text{Number of cubicles required} = \dfrac{\text{210.5 prints per hour required}}{\text{18.9 prints per hour}}$

= 11.14 cubicles (required cubicles = 11 or 12)

7.9. CAPACITY PLANNING

In previous discussion, we have seen the definition of Capacity. It is the measure of ability to produce or serve that is, having enough workers to equipment time to do the job. It can also be referred as rate of output. It can also be expressed in monetary terms. When we talk of capacities, we sometimes refer to maximum and minimum capacity. Maximum capacity concentrates on how best to utilize the available resources to produce the maximum required and the minimum capacity indicates that, to produce below this capacity is not economical to the company as it has to meet the breakeven point. Capacity planning is concerned with defining the long-term and short-term capacity needs of the organization and determining how those needs will be satisfied. Capacity decisions consider consumer demands and the available resources and coordinate both to decide to estimate the required capacity.

7.9.1. Long-term capacity Strategies

When an organization wants to develop a new product or plan for expanding the existing facilities, or construct or phase out production plants, the capacity problem bothers the management. As the long-range capacity decisions take more time (more than an year), these decisions deal with accommodating major changes that affect the overall level of output in the longer term. Here management must assess the market demand and implement the long range decisions in an orderly and effective way, so as to benefit the organization.

When the firm is manufacturing more than one product, it can enjoy certain benefits.(*i*)It can have an optimal product mix to optimize their returns and at the same time they can plan for better utilization of capacity. Not only this, when some products show declining demand, they can divert to produce such a product which is showing increasing demand. It also helps them when planning for a new product, by suspending the available non-profit product (which needs some initiation time) to produce a profitable product so that best utilization of capacity is achieved.

(i) *Phase in Capacity:* Some firms, which have high-technology face a unique capacity-planning problem. The pace of new developments forces them to get products onto the market very quickly, before they become obsolete. In some cases the time required to construct a factory may be longer than the technological window or time frame within which their production decisions must be implemented. Some firms convert their old warehouses or take existing convenient building on lease or on rent into production shops. Some established firms, commit capital and they phase in portion of the capacity on a modular (or partial) basis as new products become available. This can be an effective way of capitalizing on technological break troughs without tying up excessive amount of capital at an early stage.

(ii) *Phase Out Capacity:* Old companies, which have installed capacities and which have become outdated now, and as the companies has to face competitions, has to face a peculiar capacity problem. In the past, capacity planners have concerned themselves primarily with having the equipment installed and train personnel ready to start up plants when they scheduled to go online. Today, as firms face more intense domestic an international competitions, planers must know how to phase out operations that are no longer competitive. This is too severing problem in high technology firms, where one has to decide very quickly to phase out operations that are no longer competitive. Closing of capacity or lay off employees leads to many socio-economic problems. Hence these problems have to be solved in a most humanistic way. In some cases, companies even assist employees to assume ownership of the plant if the takeover has prospects of success, either because the new owners will accept lower wage costs or productivity improvements can be made which were previously unacceptable to the labour unions.

7.9.2. Short-term Capacity Planning

Short-term capacity planning deals with fluctuations in demand due to seasonal and economic factors and to match the available capacity with demand or adjusting the demand to the available capacity. Manufacturing firms with sufficient equipment capacity may use overtime or a second and third shift to meet a temporary raise in demand. This may also be satisfied by routing the work to alternate processes or subcontracting a part of order to the outsiders, or some times the firms accumulate the inventory by stocking the products manufactured during the period when the demand is lean. Service industries tend to rely more heavily on work scheduling and strategies aimed at shifting demand to suit their capacity, such as using flexible work hours, hiring part-time employees and overtime work scheduling to meet peak demand. Professional service, such as medical, legal offices use an appointment system to smooth out demand. Capital service systems, such as transport system or airways accomplish the same thing by adopting a fixed service schedule. This arrangement forces the customers to adapt to the system's capacity. Service units such as repair shops simply use queues and delay the delivery of the service until they can produce it with their regular work force. It is up to the planning manger to use suitable combinations of the above-mentioned strategies to achieve the desired goal of the organization.

QUESTIONS

1. Define Capacity. Explain what do you mean by:
   (*a*) System capacity, (*b*) System efficiency, (*c*) Actual capacity and (*d*) Designed Capacity.
2. Explain the various methods of increasing and decreasing the existing capacity to meet the demand.
3. Explain what is meant by phasing in and phasing out capacity with examples.
4. Explain what factors you consider while long range capacity planning.
5. What factors affect the short-range capacity planning?

8

PLANT LOCATION AND LAYOUT

- Introduction
- Location for units dealing with goods and services.
- Steps in selecting Plant site.
- Weber's theory.
- Factors of Location.
  - Primary Factors.
  - Secondary Factors.
- Rural Vs Urban Location.
- Location Analysis.
  - Cost Analysis
  - Comparative Analysis.
- Plant Layout.
  - Objectives of a Good Plant layout.
  - Principles of Good Plant Layout.
  - Types of layout.
  - Process Layout.
  - Product Layout.
  - Fixed Position Layout.
  - Combination of Process and Product Layout
  - Group Layout.
- Effect of Layout on Production Control.
- Symptoms of Bad Layout.
- Flow Line or Flow System.
- Determining the space required for a facility.
- Work Place Design.
- Methods of Preparing a Layout.
  - Templates
  - Two and Three Dimensional Models.
  - Flow or Process Chart.
  - Methods of Flow Pattern
  - Layout Analogues.
- Evaluation of a Layout.
- Computerized Facility Layout Design.
- Physical Distribution System.

8.1. INTRODUCTION

A plant is a place, where men, materials, money, machinery and equipment, etc. are brought together for manufacturing products. Plant location decisions are crucial because they commit organizations to long lasting financial, employment, a distribution patterns. As such, they deserve the careful attention of finance, personnel, marketing, and other managers, as well as that of the operations managers who manage the facilities. But location decisions need not always be 'cast in concrete'. Relocation opportunities arise as firms alter their product lines, as labour and material requirements change, or as market conditions change. So the management should always be alert to the advantages of expanding or closing the existing facilities, or of developing new ones. Plant location is not a static decision that can be made and forgotten. Plant layout or Facility layout choices follow the location decisions. They influence the type of equipment and level of technology employed, the flow of work and design of jobs, inventory levels, and other operating characteristics of the firm. Layout can be changed more easily than locations. However, so they represent more of a continuing concern. In addition, they fall more directly within the responsibility of operations manger because they deal with the physical arrangement of productive facilities.

8.2. LOCATION PLANNING FOR UNITS DEALING WITH GOODS AND SERVICE

No method of analysis assures a firm that it has selected an optimal location. Some firms will have high *potentially satisfactory* locations. On the other hand, some, locations would be exceptionally poor. When a firm opts for a poor location, it will have to face many problems like: non-availability of required raw materials easily, power supply problems, problems from local people, problems of waste disposal and many. In order to avoid a bad location, it is better to have a systematic method and followed to evaluate the location.

1. Define the location objectives and related *constraints.*
2. Identify the relevant decision *criteria.* (*a*) Quantitative factors like economic factors. (*b*) Qualitative factors (less tangible).
3. Relate the objectives to the criteria using appropriate *mathematical models /economic models* such as Break-even analysis, economic cost models, Linear Programming and qualitative factor analysis.
4. Do field research to generate relevant data and use the models to *evaluate alternate locations.*
5. Select the location that best satisfies the criteria.

Location and layout are matters of basic importance in business. In fact, it should be noted that location and layout are inter-dependent. If the situation of a new establishment is satisfactory, it will not be difficult to arrange internal facilities; but it will provide space to satisfy the current and future needs of a concern. We should see, therefore, that the location determines the best housing of equipments and activities. It should, however be the aim of the planners to see that the site is chosen to fit the requisites of plant construction and processes. Plant location requires the analysis and weighing of many factors. Particularly, over long periods of time, the economy, markets, technology and other factors may so change as to dictate an eventual move by a firm which might have been well-situated for many years previously. The problem of location may also arise in the case of expanding companies, which may have to consider the suitable locations for their branch plants and also on the existing site for the purpose of expanding facilities. However, it can be emphasized here that factors in plant location vary among industries with changing technical and economic conditions. Thus some industries follow markets, while others, such as textile industry may find its location around the source of power and Steel and iron industries may find a location nearer to raw material. *Hence the optimum location is the outcome of proper reconciliation of various considerations relevant to the question on hand.*

8.2.1. Steps in Selecting the Plant Site

The decision regarding the location of an industrial plant may be studied in three parts: a) Determination of the region where the plant is to be located; b) Choice of the city or suburbs and community where the plant is to be constructed; and c) Choice of a particular site for the plant. Theories of industrial location have been concerned with the reasons for the concentration of localization of industrial plants in certain regions. These theories provide a good basis to a systematic analysis of factors affecting plant location and are discussed below.

(*a*) **Weber's Theory of Location of Industries :** This theory divides the factors of industrial location into two groups. They are:

(*i*) Those, which influence the distribution of industrial units over the different regions, i.e., *primary factors* and

(*ii*) Those, which cause either the concentration of industries in certain regions or their dispersal from the original regions, i.e. *Secondary factors.*

Weber analyzed the factors responsible for the location of industry by referring to those of the costs of production, which vary with different regions. For this purpose, he excluded such costs as depreciation, interest, cost of land and rent, etc., for they exert little or no influence on the geographical location of industrial plants as between various regions. In his theory he stressed the influence of raw material cost and labour cost as the important factors, which differ from region to region and cause an industry to be concentrated in one region in preference to another. He identified that regional distribution of industries is governed by the cost of transportation raw material to the plant or products to the market from the plant. Robinson also states that all commodities must have at least two points of attachment to the earth's surface, a place of consumption of the finished product, and a place of origin of a raw material. The place of production will be either at the source of material or at the place of consumption, according as the material or the finished goods is the more expensive to carry. In other words, if the cost of carrying the raw material from the place of its origin to the plant is more than the cost of transporting the finished product to the market, the industrial unit will be located nearer to the source of raw material, and vice versa. Weber further examined the problem and concluded that the nature of raw material used will have its influence on the cost of transportation. According to him, the raw material may be classified as: a) *Localized, i.e.,* those which are confined to certain regions (Source or place of supply), such as iron ore, cotton, coal, oil etc., and b) *Ubiquitous,* i.e., those which are found every where, such as water, clay, etc. Obviously, only localized materials can have any bearing on the original distribution of industries over various regions.

Localized materials have been further sub-divided into two classes by Weber: a) *Gross raw materials or Weight losing* materials are those which get consumed in the process of manufacture. These materials add little or no part of their weight to the finished goods. b) *Pure raw materials or Non-weight losing* materials are those which do not lose their weight in the process of manufacture and impart the whole or much of their weight to the finished gods. If an industry uses pure material, the weight of the end product will be much the same as that of the input raw material. Industries using gross raw materials are located nearer to the source of raw material because cost of transporting raw martial will be less. Industries, using pure raw materials are attracted more towards the market for the end product. The mathematical model given by Weber in this connection is:

$$\text{Material Index} = \frac{\text{Weight of the localised materials}}{\text{Weight of the finished product}}$$

If the material index is greater than one, the industry concerned will be attracted more towards the source of raw materials. If the index is less than unity, the industry will be localized more probably near the markets than the material deposits. Every promoter will have a *location figure*, which will represent as an index to select the location, and this figure represents the minimum transport cost of material to the plant or the products to the market.

As per Weber's theory one more factor which has influence in selecting a right choice of location for an industrial unit is *labor cost.* He assumes that there are certain centers of cheap and skilled labor. If the unit proposed to establish is labor intensive and the labour cost forms the major portion of the production cost, then the industry will tend to localize at the labor center.

There are some more factors, which influence the location of the plant, they are facilities like banking, credit and insurance and better communication attracts the industries to concentrate at these places, where the above-mentioned facilities are easily available. Weber calls these factors as *Agglomerative factors.* Weber names factors, which encourage dispersal of industrial units as *Deglomerative factors.* Because of influential fetors, some times an industry may be located at more than one place and is known as *split location.*

8.3. FACTORS OF LOCATION

Decision regarding location requires a careful balancing of several factors. Some of them are more important and are known as *primary factors*, while the less important one are known as *secondary factors.* Some times in real problem secondary factors may show greater influence in selecting the location.

8.3.1. Primary Factors

1. Availability of Raw Material : In order to minimize the transport cost of raw material to the industrial plant, the nature of raw material is of great importance. A good deal of economy in transport costs can be achieved if the industries, which use weight-losing materials, are located nearer to the source of raw materials. In case industries uses ubiquities material, the material transport cost factor do not influence the location much. In addition to the cost factor, other factors related to material to be considered, while taking a decision regarding the location is: (*i*) Whether the material available indigenously or to be imported? (*ii*) Any financial linkage to the supply of raw material, so that the material is available below market price, (*iii*) Reliability and continuity of the source of supply and (*iv*) The security factor of transport. When two locations are equally suitable, then promoter should think of other materials required for processing and availability of market for by-products.

2. Nearness of Market for the finished product : Industries, using pure raw materials, are generally located nearer to the market for the product produced. By locating the unit nearer to the market, the transportation cost of finished goods will be minimum. In addition to this factor, the chances of finished goods getting damaged or spoiled during transport can be reduced. As the industry is nearer to the market, it can catch a big share of the market and can render quick service to the customers.

3. Availability of Fuel and Power : The problem of fuel and power can also be solved with reference to the nature of raw materials. Industries, which use coal as the source of power for their industries, are located nearer to the coal bed. Because coal loses substantial weight during processes. Now a day as the electricity is generally used as power source, this factor is losing its importance.

4. Transport facilities : A lot of money is spent both in transporting the raw material and the finished goods. Depending on the size of raw material or finished goods, a suitable method of transportation like roads, rail, water or air is selected and accordingly the plant location is decided. The point to be considered here is that the cost of transport must be kept at a minimum. This is because, the movement of material will simply add to the cost and nothing to the use / economic value of the material or product.

5. Availability of Labour : Another important factor influencing the location of industries is availability of suitable and adequate number of labour at a reasonable labour wages. This particularly true in case of plants like, tobacco companies, and tea estates etc., However, labour will not attract industry by itself, it is mobile. Any labour intensive companies have to select a location nearer to the source of labour. In case industry needs skilled labour, it has to select a location nearer to the source of skilled labors.

6. Availability of Water : In case water is used for processing, as in paper and chemical industries, and is also required for drinking and sanitary purposes. Depending on the nature of plant, water should be in adequate quantity and should be of desired quality.

8.3.2. Secondary Factors

1. Soil and Climate : The question of soil and climate is really an influencing factor for an units processing agricultural products like tea, coffee and rubber etc., With the development in the field of heating, ventilating and air-conditioning climate of the region is not a problem these days.

2. Industrial Atmosphere : The industrial atmosphere cannot be measured in tangible terms, but it has a very important advantage in selecting a location for a plant. Industrial atmosphere may said to exist where people living at a place think instinctively of industry and learn the intricacies of machines without much effort. This is an added advantage for the growth of industries in a particular area.

3. Financial And Other Aids : The plant should be located in an area where financial institutions are available to get a part of capital as loan and getting working capital and for other financial aids.

4. Availability of facilities like housing, schools and hospitals and recreation clubs : The site should be nearer to infrastructure facilities, so that the labour will have housing facility at a reasonable cost and they will take advantage of educational institutions to educate their children. For health problems, they can use hospitals. They can relax during off periods in recreation clubs. All the above said facilities will help in motivating the labour to stick to the job, i.e. labour turnover will be at low rate.

5. Momentum of an early start : There are number of places where, to begin with, only one or two factories were started. With the passage of time these places gained importance and attract industries. As the number of industrial units increase, certain facilities are developed in that area. Some of the facilities are banking facility; maintenance units and other service related units will come up. With these, availability of skilled labour also increases.

6. Special advantages of the place ; Some times certain facilities are offered by the state, in case the particular region is selected. Facilities like providing subsides, tax holidays etc., in this way state tries to develop the underdeveloped areas.

7. Personal factors : Some times, promoters, irrespective of economic factors, prefer to start their unit in their place of origin to develop the area and help the fellow community. A good example for this is Ford Company at Detroit.

8. Historical Factors : Factors like personal fancies of entrepreneurs or historical incidents may in many cases lead to the development of a place as the center of an industry. Example is development of Kanpur as textile industrial center.

9. Political Stability : The lack of political stability in a state makes for uncertainty in the attitude of State Governments to industries. In locating industrial plant, it must be seen as to whether the State has a record of political and economic stability.

The above-discussed points are mostly economic in character. They however, ignore the broader national interest and lead to concentration of industries in a few places. This is an undesirable factor as far as national defense is concerned. If there is a balanced development in all the regions, many industrial problems can be reduced. In this connection both Central and State Governments are encouraging entrepreneurs to start their units in underdeveloped areas by giving many incentives. The location pattern of an industry can be measured by the formula:

(Number of workers employed in the industry in a certain area) / Total number of workers employed in the industry all over the country).

This formula gives us an idea about the degree of concentration of industries in one particular area. If we work out the ratio of number of workers in a particular industry and the total number of industrial workers in an area, it will show us how far that particular place depends on that industry.

8.4. RURAL VS URBAN LOCATION

After considering the economic factors and working out which particular site among the proposed sites, next thing is to think of whether the site should be in rural area or in urban area? No doubt each one has its own advantages and disadvantages. In view of developing rural areas and underdeveloped areas, now a days state is encouraging the entrepreneurs to start their units in rural and underdeveloped areas by giving certain incentives. Let us now discuss the advantages and disadvantages of rural and urban sites.

8.4.1. Selecting the site in Urban areas

The advantages of selecting the site in urban areas are:

ADVANTAGES :

1. Urban places will generally have good transport facilities such as rail, road and airways. It will help the entrepreneurs to save time in getting the raw material from source or sending the product to the market point. Also, it provides transport to the employees.
2. Urban places are good market for products manufactured. Hence the producer can avail this opportunity to sell his goods in the local market.
3. A good mix of labour: skilled / semiskilled / trained / experienced is available in urban areas. This is an added advantage for an entrepreneur. He can get suitable labor without any difficulty.
4. Power is easily available. Corporations at a reasonable rate supply water to a certain extent.
5. Good medical facilities, good schools and colleges, banks and financial institutions are available in urban areas.

6. Some times for small units, which do not use heavy machines, readily built building are available for rent to start the unit with out delay before getting a proper site.
7. Training facilities are available to the workers, foremen and other staff.
8. Services of professional people are available with least difficulty.
9. Many related industries, Maintenance units and other facilities are available in plenty in urban areas. Sometimes small units working around may serve as ancillary units.

DISADVANTAGES :

1. Land cost is very high, and the area one can get may be very small and limited. Hence future expansion may become a problem.
2. Cost of building construction is generally high.
3. Expansion in the same area may be a problem.
4. Local taxes and labour charges comparatively will be high.
5. Labour union problems may exist, which will strain the employee – employer relationship.

8.4.2 Selecting a Site in Rural/Sub-Urban Areas

ADVANTAGES:

1. Plenty of land available at reasonable price. For future expansion of the unit it will be very convenient.
2. Unskilled labors are available in plenty at reasonable wages. If the unit is operating on seasonal basis, then seasonal labors are also available in rural areas.
3. As the labor union strength is meager, labour problems are less and employee and employer relations will be good.
4. Municipal and other regulations and taxes are seldom burdensome.
5. Government will give subsides, incentives and tax holidays.

DISADVANTAGES :

1. It is difficult to get skilled labor and managers.
2. Transport facilities may not be that good compared to urban areas.
3. Availability of continuous power may be problem.
4. Good hospitals, schools, financial institutions and banks may not be available.
5. It is difficult to get ancillary service units.

It is better for an entrepreneur to select a site in a place, which is not purely urban or purely rural. That is it is better to have a location in sub-urban area.

8.5. LOCATION ANALYSIS

Analysis of location alternatives should consider both *objective factors* such as availability of proper transport facilities, availability of suitable labour, tax considerations, material cost and market potentialities and *subjective factors* like civic amenities, Labour union activities, weather conditions etc. However, the analysis for the choice of appropriate location / site is based on certain methodology commonly adopted by professionals in the field. The below mentioned analysis is generally carried out.

(*a*) Cost analysis, (*b*) Quantitative methods, (*c*) Weight method and (*d*) Ranking method.

An ideal plant location is one, which results in lowest production cost and least distribution and procurement cost per unit. These costs are influence by a number of factors as discussed above. The various costs which decides the location economy are those of: Land, Building or rent of the premises,

Equipment and machinery, Labour charges, Water, Fuel, Power, Freight (both incoming and out going), Raw material cost and taxes etc., Besides these costs, community attitude, Community facilities and housing facilities are also worth considering. The economic aspect of locations are considered or an economic survey or economic analysis is carried out to decide as to which of the possible two or three preliminary selected locations, is the overall best location.

8.5.1. Cost Analysis

A cost study is made regarding all the alternative sites, to work out what would be the expected production cost per unit of product or what is the rate of return on investment expected and they are compared to select the optimal site. Cost analysis can be done in three ways. They are:

(*i*) Comparative cost analysis, (*ii*) Rate of return analysis and (*iii*) Break-even analysis.

(*i*) Comparative Cost Analysis : In this method all the costs involved in establishing and operating the plant at the site is listed and total cost is worked out the total cost involved. Basing on the total cost plant site is selected. The problems given below will demonstrate the method.

Example 8.1. An entrepreneur wants to select a location for his enterprise and he has conducted economic survey of two locations. The following is the details of his survey. Suggest him which location he has to select.

Factors	*Location 1*	*Location 2*
Cost of	Rs.	Rs.
Land	1,00,000	90,000
Building	1,200,000	1,300,000
Water	5,000	6,000
Power	15,000	17,000
Labour	1,40,000	1,20,000
Incoming freight	1,20,000	1,10,000
Out going freight	1,60,000	1,50,000
Fuel	40,000	35,000
Raw material and other supplies	1,40,000	1,30,000
Taxes	4,000	2,000
Total cost	**1,924,000**	**1,960,000**
Community facilities	good	Excellent
Community attitude	All right	Encouraging
Housing facility	Very good	Good
Cost of living	High	Normal
Community size	Small	Medium

(Community shows that area is rural, sub-urban or urban – which gives a rough idea about, land cost, labour cost, housing and other factors).

When we consider the total cost, we find that the location 1 is better. But other factors indicates location 2 is better, As the cost difference is not much and the plot 2 is having good characteristics, we can suggest to the entrepreneur, that the he can chose plot 2.

Example 8.2. In a survey to find out the optimal location for a plant, the entrepreneur has collected the following data. Suggest the appropriate location.

Particulars	*Location A* Rs.	*Location B* Rs.	*Location C* Rs.
Operating costs per year :			
Transportation cost	180,000	185,000	190,000
Labour	200,000	225,000	250,000
Power	50,000	55,000	60,000
Water	28,000	30,000	32,000
Fuel	50,000	60,000	70,000
Rent	50,000	55,000	60,000
Taxes	10,000	12,000	15,000
Insurance	6,000	6,000	6,000
Miscellaneous	5,000	10,000	8,000
TOTAL OPERATING COST	**584,000**	**638,000**	**691,000**
CONSTRUCTION COSTS			
Land	150,000	100,000	75,000
Building	200,000	180,000	170,000
Other requirements	50,000	40,000	30,000
TOTAL CONSTRUCTION COST	**400,000**	**320,000**	**275,000**
GRAND TOTAL COST :	**984,000**	**958,000**	**966,000**

On the basis of total costs involved, site B appears to be most appropriate site for the plant proposed.

Some times, cost comparative chart is represented by graphical means. All cost factors are shown to scale on a bar chart, (one bar for each plant). Comparing the heights of the bars, the decision is taken to opt for a particular site. The bar, whose height is smaller, is selected. Figure 8.1 shows one such chart.

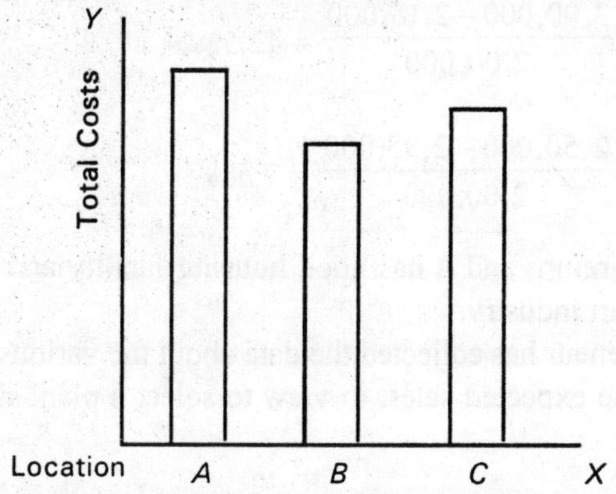

Figure 8.1 : Graphical representation of Costs to select a site for a plant.

(*ii*) **Rate of Return (ROR) Analysis :** This analysis is based on the rate of return on the total investment. Any person who invests money in any business is more interested in knowing what rate of return he is going to get by investing the money? He compares the alternatives and selects the business that yield higher rate of return.

Example 8.3. From the following data, select the most advantageous location for setting up a plant to manufacture electric and electronic products.

Particulars	*Site X*	*Site Y*	*Site Z*
(*i*) Total initial investment	2,00,000	2,00,000	2,00,000
(*ii*) Total expected sales for the period	2,50,000	3,00,000	2,50,000
(*iii*) Distribution expenses	40,000	40,000	75,000
(*iv*) Raw material expenses	70,000	80,000	90,000
(*v*) Power and water supply expenses	40,000	30,000	20,000
(*vi*) Wages and salaries	20,000	25,000	20,000
(*vii*) Other expenses	25,000	40,000	30,000
(*viii*) Community attitude	Indifferent	Wants business	Indifferent
(*ix*) Employee housing facilities	Poor	Excellent	Good

Solution :

Particulars	*Site X* *Rs.*	*Site Y* *Rs.*	*Site Z* *Rs.*
Total expenses : Add (*iii*) to (*vii*)	195,000	215,000	235,000
Rate of Return (R.O.R.) $= \dfrac{\text{Total Sales} - \text{Total Expenses}}{\text{Total Investment}} \times 100$	27.5%	42.5%	7.5%

$$\text{Rate of return of site } X = \frac{2,50,000 - 1,95,000}{2,00,000} = 27.5\%$$

$$\text{Rate of return of site } Y = \frac{3,00,000 - 2,15,000}{2,00,000} = 42.5\%$$

$$\text{Rate of return of site } Z = \frac{2,50,000 - 2,35,000}{2,00,000} = 7.5\%$$

Site *Y* has higher rate of return and it has good housing facility and community wants business. Hence it is the ideal site to start industry.

Example 8.4. **An entrepreneur has collected the data about the various costs involved in producing a Product and worked out the expected sales, in view to select a plant site. Advise him which is the best site.**

Solution :

Sales and distribution cost	*Location A* Rs.	*Location B* Rs.	*Location C* Rs.
Total initial investment	200,000	200,000	200,000
Expected sales in the year	225,000	300,000	225,000
Distribution Expenses	50,000	40,000	60,000
Raw material and other supplies	80,000	75,000	60,000
Power and Water	20,000	30,000	25,000
Wages and salaries	20,000	20,000	25,000
Miscellaneous expenses	40,000	25,000	30,000
Total expenses	210,000	190,000	200,000
Rate of Return = $\frac{(\text{Total sales} - \text{Total expenses}) \times 100}{\text{Total investment}}$	7.5%	55%	12.5%

Site B is the best compared to A and C.

***(iii)* Break-even analysis :** using the break-even analysis concept one may compare Objective cost factors. For this one has to identify the fixed and variable expenses for each alternative location and the total cost is worked out. These total cost curves are plotted on a single graph. The location with the lowest cost is selected.

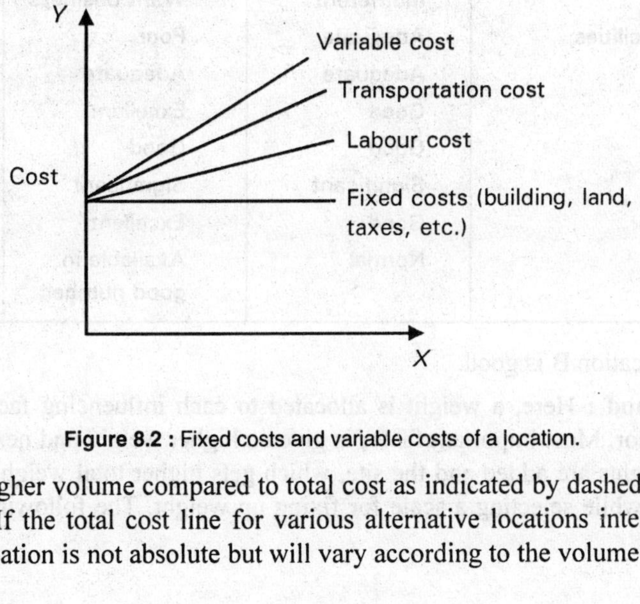

Figure 8.2 : Fixed costs and variable costs of a location.

With expected higher volume compared to total cost as indicated by dashed line in figure 8.3 i.e., location is selected. If the total cost line for various alternative locations intersect, it indicates that advantage of each location is not absolute but will vary according to the volume of output.

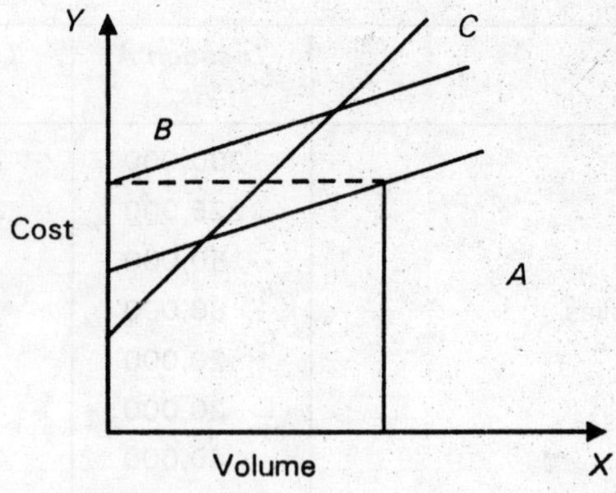

Figure 8.3 : Total cost of alterative sites A, B, C

(iv) Qualitative methods : The entrepreneur, who is making a choice between different sites, has to consider intangible factors in addition to the cost factors. Intangible factors, which cannot be measured quantitatively, can be expressed as *significant, good, excellent, bad etc.,* Such factors are: housing facility, Community attitude, education facilities and medical facilities etc., The total contribution of intangible factors for each location can be evaluated by the comparative chart as shown below:

Comparative Chart for Qualitative Factors

Factors	*Location A*	*Location B*	*Location C*
Community attitude	Indifferent	Want business	Indifferent
Employee housing facilities	Adequate	Poor	Excellent
Labour supply	Adequate	Adequate	Adequate
Education facilities	Good	Excellent	Insignificant
Recreation	Good	Good	Bad
Union activity	Significant	Significant	Poor
Hospitals	Good	Excellent	Good
Financial institutions	Normal	Available in good number	Normal

Comparatively location B is good.

(v) Weight Method : Here, a weight is allocated to each influencing factor depending on the importance of the factor. Most important factor is given a higher weight and next one is lesser weight and so on. These weights are added and the site, which gets higher total weight, is given preference. One must be careful while selecting a scale for fixing up weight. The following table illustrates the method.

Rating Chart for Alternative Location

Factors	*Maximum weights in units*	*Location A*	*Location B*	*Location C*
Labour cost	250	225	200	150
Nearness to market	200	175	150	125
Nearness to raw materials	400	300	250	200
Water supply	200	100	150	100
Taxes and laws	50	40	45	30
TOTAL WEIGHTS	**1100**	**840**	**795**	**605**

Location A has got higher weight and this may be recommended. In case two sites are having more or less same weights factor, then other important factors are selected and weights are allocated to select the location.

***(vi)* Ranking Method :** In Ranking method, each factor is allocated a rank or a rate according to its importance. Important factor is given a rank of one and all other factors are expressed in whole numbers as multiple of the least number as shown in the table below. Each rank is then multiplied by the appropriate weighting factors, to get the score for each location. The scores are totaled and the site, which has higher score, is selected.

Relative Ranking for Different Factors

Factors	*Location A*	*Location B*	*Location C*
Labour cost	3	3	4
Nearest to market	2	5	3
Nearness to raw materials	5	1	4
Water supply	4	4	2
Taxes and laws	3	2	1

Total Score for Each Location

Factors	*Weightage*	*Location A*	*Location B*	*Location C*
Labour cost	20	60	60	80
Nearnes to market	30	60	150	90
Nearness to raw materials	40	200	40	160
Water supply	10	40	40	20
Taxes are laws	5	15	10	5
Total score	105	375	300	355

As the location A has higher score, it is recommended.

Transportation Model and Linear Programming models are used sometimes to find out mathematically which is the optimal site for the plant. This is particularly true when company is dealing with multiplant location problem.

Procedure for qualitative factors evaluation:

(*i*) Develop a list of relevant factors (use a check list),

(*ii*) Assign a weight to each factor to indicate its relative importance (Weights may total 1.00),

(*iii*) Assign a common scale to each factor (0 – 100) points, and designate any minimum,

(*iv*) Score each potential location according to the designated scale, and multiply the scores by the weights,

(*v*) Total the points for each location, and choose the location with the maximum points.

An entrepreneur is evaluating four locations for new plant and has weighted the relevant factors as shown below. Scores have been assigned with higher values indicative of preferred conditions. Using these scores, develop a qualitative factor comparison for the four locations.

Weights and Acores for four locations

		Site I	*Site I*	*Site II*	*Site II*	*Site III*	*Site III*	*Site IV*	*Site IV*
Relative Factors	*Assigned Weight*	*Score*	*Weighted Score*	*Score*	*Weighted Score*	*Score*	*Weighted Score*	*Score*	*Weighted Score*
Land cost	0.33	50	16.50	40	13.20	35	11.35	30	9.90
Nearness to raw material	0.25	70	17.50	80	20.00	75	18.75	80	20.00
Labour availability	0.20	55	11.00	70	14.00	60	12.00	45	09.00
Cost of living	0.05	80	04.00	70	03.50	40	02.00	50	02.50
Environment	0.02	60	01.20	60	01.20	60	01.20	90	01.20
Others	0.15	80	12.00	90	13.50	85	12.75	50	07.50
Total location score	1.00		62.60		65.40		58.25		50.70

Weighted scores are computed by multiplying the score times the assigned weight (for example, 50 × 0.33 = 16.50) and summing those products. Based on the above table Site II is better than all others.

8.6. PLANT LAYOUT

Layout decisions are concerned with arrangement of production, support, customer service, and other facilities used in operation. The flow patterns for future work activities affect the efficiency of handling materials, the utilization of capital equipment, inventory storage levels, the number and productivity of workers, and even behavioral characteristics such as group communications and employee morale.

Plant facility layout is a companion problem to facility location. The word *layout* is here used to indicate the physical arrangement of the plant and of the various parts of the plant. The layout will therefore encompass both the location of equipment within a department or shop and arrangement of departments upon a site, which include offices, warehouses, rest rooms and other facilities associated with the total system. Thus facility layout is the overall arrangement of machines, men materials, martial handling and service facilities and passage required to facilitate efficient operation of the production system. It integrates all aspects of production.

8.6.1. Determination of Layout

Whether you are preparing the layout for a new plant or want to change the existing layout of an unit for some reason or the other the below mentioned points will generally help the operations manager. The type of layout is generally determined by:

(*a*) ***Type of Product :*** This concerns whether the product is a article or a service, the product design and quality standards, and whether the product is produced for stock or for order.

(*b*) ***Type of Production Process :*** This relates to the technology used, the type of materials handled, and / or the means of providing service.

(*c*) ***Volume of Production :*** Volume affects the present facility design and capacity utilization, plus provisions for expansion or change.

8.6.2. Factors Affecting the Plant Layout

While preparing a layout, the layout engineer has to remember the factors, which influence the type of layout and the location of machinery or facilities in the layout. Some of the factors, which are important in nature, are discussed below:

(*a*) ***Product and Material Specification :*** The form of material, weight of material, physical and chemical characteristics of material used has great influence in locating a facility. These factors influence all parameters of the layout. Products requiring hazardous and dangerous operations call for isolation of the facility instead of integration on a line basis.

(*b*) ***Location and Site of the Plant :*** The site, which has been selected, has great influence while preparing layout. A plant has to get raw martial from source and send the products to the market. Hence the receiving department and the shipping department must be properly located so that the receiving and shipping will not become a problem. The attitude of the community, availability of power supply and water has influence in locating the departments appropriately.

(*c*) ***Manufacturing Process :*** This is a very important factor to be considered while preparing a layout. The manufacturing process decides the flow of material, type of machines required and the material handling facilities required. Depending on the size and weight of the machine and raw material, the working area required and additional space required to store in process inventory has to be decided. In case this problem is not given due consideration at the layout design stage, the management has to face lot of problems afterwards.

(*d*) ***Material Handling :*** In any manufacturing process, material handling is inevitable. Not only inevitable, but also material handling adds to cost and nothing to value. Hence we have to keep handling of material as low as possible, so that the production cost will be under control. This point applies to all aspects of manufacturing, i.e., raw material handling, handling of in process inventory, handling of scrap and waste and finished product. Material handling and plant layout are closely related, hence the layout engineer should integrate these two, while preparing the layout.

(*e*) ***Storage of In-Process inventory :*** While preparing layout, the material waiting time should be kept at minimum, as it adds to the cost. Hence, the layout should be designed in such a way, as far as possible material do not wait in-between two processes. If possible thought should be given to integrate movement of material while it is being processed (for example, process like, drying, painting, cleaning etc.,)

(*f*) ***Plant Personnel and Employee Facilities :*** Facilities like rest rooms, cloak rooms, vehicle parking facilities, canteen, emergency medical aids and safety guards for machines should be considered while preparing layout.

(g) Service Facilities : Service facilities related to personnel, material, machinery and equipment, and operations should be given due considerations while preparing layout, because, they play a significant role in cost reduction and in increasing productivity.

(h) Design of Building : The building should be designed in such away that ample of natural ventilation and lighting is obtained. Also care should be taken to see that in case of expansion or modification there should not be much headache.

(i) Flexibility : At the time of starting, the entrepreneur might have selected best available machinery and process, but as the time passes, the method may become absolute. In such cases, the plant needs a change. Because of change in the product design or change in the material used or change in the process used, the layout may need to be changed. In such cases, these changes must be accommodated with least difficulty. Hence while preparing the layout, one should incorporate the factor of flexibility.

(j) Work Areas and Equipment : Work areas are properly designed, so that workers can move without much difficulty and material can be handled with least difficulty. Sufficient place should be provided for maintenance personnel to attend to the repairs or maintenance of the machines.

(k) Working Conditions : If this fact is given due consideration, it will maximize human data sensing, processing and transmitting abilities. The work area should have sufficient light intensity and quality without direct or indirect glare. Provisions should be provided to reduce the noise due to process, control of temperature and humidity, so that the personal can work comfortably.

(l) Disposal of waste and dangerous gasses : Proper waste disposal facilities should be provided at appropriate places, so that they are disposed to a remote place, so that they will not be harmful to the workers or to the community living around the plant.

8.7. OBJECTIVES OF A GOOD PLANT LAYOUT

The primary goal of plant layout is to arrange all the factors of production in a most optimal way so that the production cost is kept at minimum and returns are increased and employee moral is boosted up. To fulfill the above goal, the plant engineer must remember certain objectives, while preparing the layout. The objectives of a good plant layout are:

1. Material handling and transport is minimized and efficiently controlled, so that the handling cost is minimized.
2. Bottlenecks and points of congestions are eliminated by using the line balancing techniques, so that raw material and semi finished goods will move fast from one work station to the other.
3. Work stations are designed and located suitably, so that there will be least resistance to the smooth flow of material and movement of men.
4. Sufficient space and proper location should be allocated to production centers and service centers.
5. Waiting line of semi-finished goods should be minimized.
6. Safe and proper working conditions are provided to avoid accidents and causalities.
7. Designed layout should be provided with sufficient flexibility to accommodate future minute changes in product design or change in the material specification.
8. Care should be taken to see that the space available is used optimally. Not only length and breadth of the building but the height of the building also to be used.
9. The layout should make the plant maintenance simple and easy.

10. Plant layout should be designed in such a way that the productivity and quality of product is increased.
11. The layout should promote the effective utilization of manpower,
12. A good layout should maintain high turnover of work in process.

8.8. PRINCIPLES OF A GOOD PLANT LAYOUT

Plant layout engineer has to follow certain principles to design a good layout. There are certain principles to guide him; still the commonsense is a must to get optimal result. Important principles are discussed below:

8.8.1. Integration

The first principle is the integration of production centers and other facilities and means of production in a logical and balanced manner. While preparing layout we have to think of all factors of production to achieve the objectives of a good plant layout.

8.8.2. Minimum movement and material handling

The movement of material and men should be minimized. Because the movement will add only to the cost and consume time unproductively. There are instances where plant managers after recognizing the defect in the layout and after careful work study, changing the layout, have saved quite a good amount of money per year.

8.8.3. Smooth and continuous flow of Material

Bottlenecks, congestion points and back tracking should be removed by proper line balancing techniques so that productivity is increased.

8.8.4. Cubic Space Utilization

Besides using the floor space of a shop, if the ceiling height is also utilized, more materials can be accommodated in the same shop. The vertical space may be used to stock raw material, semi finished goods or finished goods or some times tools. When the unit is dealing with continuous production, it is better to use the vertical space for movement of material.

8.8.5. Safe and Improved Environment

Working places should be free from noise, dust, odors and other hazardous conditions so that the workers can concentrate on their work. Work places should have safety when work is being done and they are well ventilated so that the workers will work happily. This will improve the operating efficiency of workers and boost their morale. All these lead to satisfaction amongst the workers and thus better employer – employee relations.

8.8.5. Flexibility

In automotive and other industries where models of products change after some time, it is better to permit all possible flexibility in layout to accommodate the changes required to meet the demand of the market. The machinery is arranged in such a way that the changes of the production process can be achieved at the least cost or disturbance.

8.9. ADVANTAGES OF GOOD PLANT LAYOUT

A good layout provides many advantages to workers and to the management.

A. Advantages to Workers :

1. Lesser number of martial handling and lesser operations.
2. Reduction of length of hauls and motions between operations minimizes thoughput time and activities of workers.
3. Improved labour productivity and hence the higher wages.
4. More safety and security because of reduced accidents and severity of accidents.
5. Better working conditions and improved efficiency.

B. Manufacturing Costs:

1. Reduced Maintenance and replacement costs.
2. Minimized cost due to reduced waste and spoilage of work
3. Improved quality of the product and reduced handling cost.
4. Better Cost control.

C Advantages to Production Control:

1. More space for production operations.
2. Better storage facility for in-process inventory.
3. Scope for better supervision.
4. Better utilization of machinery and labour.

8.10. TYPES OF PLANT LAYOUT

Although if is convenient to classify layouts into two or three basic types, in reality there is a continuum of different types of layouts which can be combined in a verity of ways. Classified on the basis of volume of identical products, these layouts range from fixed position facilities assembled to produce just one product, to continuous-flow facilities that produce millions of identical units. The table given below gives the characteristics of different types of layouts. In the chart, the fixed position layout is shown in a separate row, because of its unique characteristics. But Job Production, Batch Production and Continuous Production are in one row and an arrow is shown extending between Job and Continuous Production. This is because, depending on the type of product and the demand for the product, and frequency of production, job production slowly converts into Batch Production and Batch Production slowly converts into Continuous Production. This aspect is discussed in Chapter I, while discussing the characteristics of different systems of production and the graph shown (Figure No. 1.4) clearly demonstrates this aspect.

8.10.1. Process Layout

This layout is also known as Functional layout and is characterized by keeping similar machines or similar operations at one location or place. In other word all turning machines are placed in turning department and all drilling machines are arranged in drilling department and so on. The machines are arranged according to their functions. This type of layout is generally employed for industries engaged in job order production and non-repetitive kind of manufacturing and maintenance activities. The batch production shops prefer process layout.

Advantages :

1. Flexibility in equipment or manpower allotment for specific tasks. Thus load distribution can be controlled, and this is particularly of importance in case of breakdowns, for maintenance schedules and for multi products manufacture.
2. Better utilization of machine available time, consequently fewer machines are required.
3. Comparatively low investment in machines is required.
4. Each section can be benefited form specialized supervision.

Table 8.1. Characteristics of different types of layouts.

Type of layout	*Type of product*	*Type of process*	*Volume of production*
Fixed position (Shipbuilding, Railway Coach building, etc.,)	Customised (Influenced by Location)	Individual Projects (Unique or tailored Specifications)	Very Low (Possibly only once)
JOB SHOP (e.g. : Machine shop, Repair shop, Hospital)	Customised ↑	Flexible process ↑	Relatively low (Short runs) ↑
	Many different Products ↑	Materials and labour Requirements less Certain ↑	More work in process Inventory ↑
	Compete via features and service ↕	Labour is higher percentage of total costs ↕	Planning horizon is relatively short ↕
BATCH PROCESSING (Batch production of components)			
LINE PRODUCTION (Automobile, assembly line)			
	Compete via distribution and price ↓	Labour is lower percentage of total costs ↓	Planning horizon is relatively long ↓
	Fewer new products ↓	Material and labour requirement more certain ↓	More finished goods inventory ↓
CONTINUOUS FLOW (Oil, Cement, Sugar plants)	More standardised	Standardised process	Relatively high (long runs)

5. The diversity of tasks offers a more interesting and satisfying occupation for the operator.
6. Better product quality because of effective supervision.
7. Workers in one section are not affected by the nature of operations carried out in another section.

Limitations or Disadvantages:

1. Long flow lines; hence more expensive handling.
2. Comparatively large amounts of work in process, waiting for the next operation.
3. Space and capital are tied up by work in process.
4. Production, planning, and control systems are more involved.
5. Total production time is longer, owing to time consumed in materials handling and to waiting times.
6. Because of the diversity of the jobs in specialized departments, higher grades of skill are required.
7. For the same amount of production, process layout needs more space.
8. Automatic martial handling is extremely difficult.

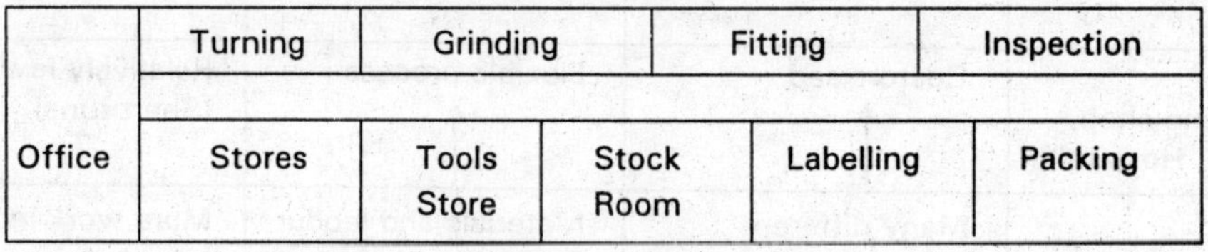

Figure 8.4 : Process layout.

Characteristics : This layout is used when

1. Volume is low
2. Variety of products is many.
3. The demand for the product is small or intermittent.
4. General purpose, low cost machines are desirable.
5. Machines or processing produces unbearable noise, vibration, fumes or heat can be located in isolated area.

8.10.2. Product Layout or Line Layout

In Product layout, in which machines and auxiliary services are located along the product flow line. The layout is suitable for continuous types of production and can employ one of the basic horizontal flow lines or their combinations. The raw material enters at one side and gets processed along the line and finished product leaves the system at the other end. The various operations on the product are performed in a sequence and the machines are placed along the product flow line, that is the machines are arranged in the sequence in which a given product will be processed upon.

Advantages :

1. Layout corresponds to sequence of operations, resulting in smooth and logical flow lines.
2. Reduced materials handling, since the machines are so located as to minimize distances between consecutive operations.
3. Small amounts of work in process, as the work from one process is directly fed into the next.

4. Less space is occupied by work in transit and for temporary storage.
5. Total throughput time per unit is short.
6. Simple Production planning and control system and simplified supervision.
7. Little skill is usually required by operators at the production line; hence training is simple, short, and inexpensive.
8. Automatic materials handling is quite common and materials handling cost per unit is less.

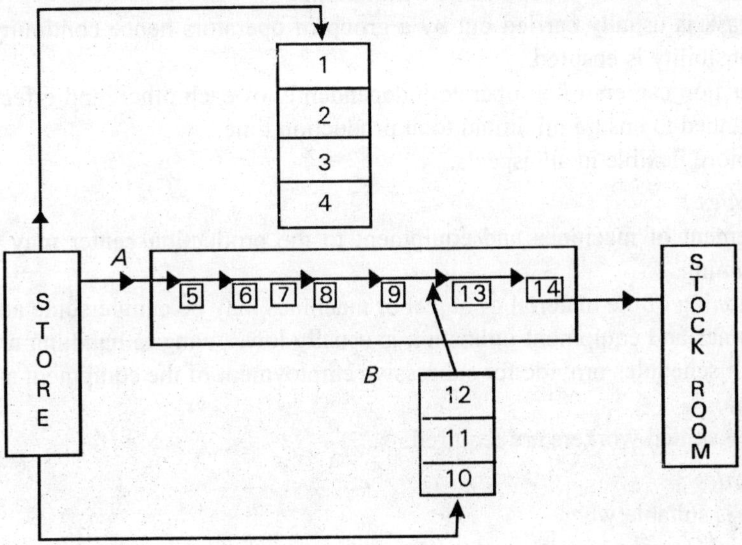

Figure 8.6 : Product Layout.

Disadvantages :

1. Layout is determined by the product and leaves little room for flexibility. A change in product design may need major alterations in layout.
2. The pace is determined by the slowest machine; hence speed of machines is deliberately reduced or machine has excessive idle time.
3. A breakdown of one machine may lead to a complete stoppage of the line that follows that machine.
4. Comparatively high investments are required, as identical machines (a few not fully utilized) are sometimes distributed along the line; also, machines may be required to stand by in case of breakdowns.
5. Supervision is general but not specialized.
6. It is difficult to increase production beyond the capacity of production line.

Characteristics :

This type of layout is used where:

1. The number of end products is small.
2. The products are highly standardized and interchangeable.
3. The volume of production for any item is high or large.
4. The demand of the product is fairly steady
5. The continuity of material flow can be maintained.

8.10.3. Static Product Layout or Layout By Fixed Position

When the product is very big or too heavy and very difficult to move it from one process to the other this type of layout is used. Here product is fixed in one position and machine, equipment, components and men are brought to the product to do the required operations. This layout is typical of job production in constructional work, such as Ship building, Railway coach building etc.,

Advantages :

1. Material movement is reduced to a minimum.
2. The task is usually carried out by a group of operators hence continuity of operations and responsibility is ensured.
3. Production centers often operate independently of each other, and effective scheduling can be planned to ensure minimum total production time.
4. It is more flexible in all aspects.

Disadvantages :

1. Movement of machines and equipment to the production center may be costly and time consuming.
2. Positioning of the material or object or machines may be cumbersome and costly.
3. Machines and equipment utilization is usually low, owing to handling and positioning time, even if schedules provide for successive employment of the equipment at several production centers.
4. Highly skilled workers are required.

Characteristics :

This layout is suitable when

1. Material forming or treating operation requires only tools or simple portable machines.
2. Only one of the few pieces of an item is to be manufactured.
3. The cost of moving the major piece of material is very high.
4. Skill of the workmanship lies in the abilities of the workers or when it is desired to fix the responsibility of product quality on the workmen or a group of workers.

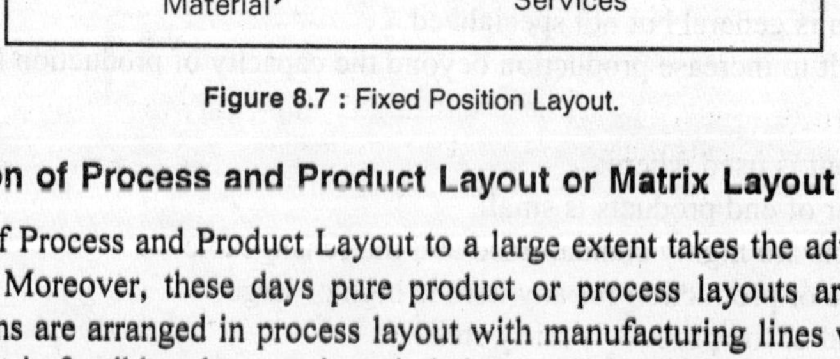

Figure 8.7 : Fixed Position Layout.

8.10.4. Combination of Process and Product Layout or Matrix Layout

A combination of Process and Product Layout to a large extent takes the advantages of both the layout into account. Moreover, these days pure product or process layouts are rare. Most of the manufacturing sections are arranged in process layout with manufacturing lines whenever necessary. A combination layout is feasible where an item is being made in different types and sizes. In such cases machinery is arranged in a process layout but process grouping (a group of number of similar machines) is then arranged in a sequence to manufacture various types and sizes of products. The point to note that, no matter the product varies in size and type; the sequence of operations remains same or similar. Figure 8.8 shows one such layout.

The extension of this is the *Group layout or Group Technology,* which is very common in present days.

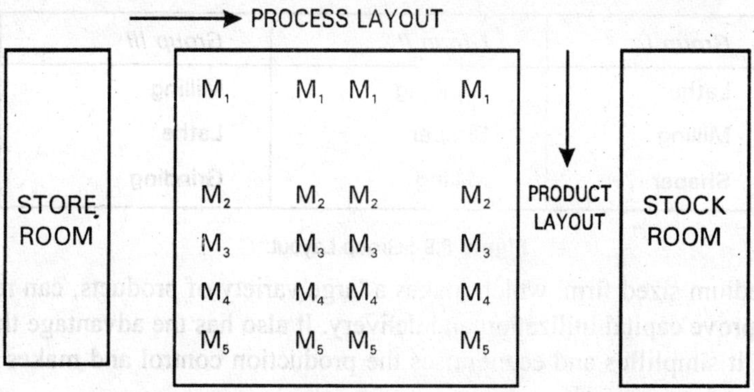

Figure 8.8 : Combinations of Process and Product Layout.

A combination layout is also useful when a number of items are produced in same sequence but none of the items are to be produced in bulk and thus no item justifies for an individual and independent production line. (Example: files, hacksaws, circular metal saws, woods saws etc. are manufactured by using this type of layout).

8.10.5. Group Layout

Group layout is the type of plant layout in which the plant is divided into groups, each of which contains all the Plants necessary to carry out all the operations applied to a given *family* of parts. The parts in the *group family* are generally similar in form, but the essential criterion is that they can all be completed in the special plant group, laid out for that purpose. It will be noted that a change from *functional layout or process layout* to *group layout* changes the emphasis from *process specialization* to *product specialization.* Each group consists of a set of machines, which can process a wide range of products of different sizes, each requiring processing on the same group of machines, may be in same sequence or different sequence. Figure 8.9 shows a group layout.

8.11. THE EFFECT OF LAYOUT ON PRODUCTION CONTROL

Differences in layout have an important effect on the efficiency of production control. In line layout the controlling of production can be done more effectively and cheaply than in process layout. Line layout will give better utilization of labour, plant and capital. Even in the small to medium-sized concern, where the mathematics of the subject will sometimes seem to show that the line layout would give poor machine and labour utilization, the simplicity of control and the psychological effect of flow and of the *pace line,* will often make nonsense of the mathematics.

Considering the case of *group layout,* in both *line layout and group layout* each section is arranged to deal with a particular family of parts. The essential difference between the two is that with a *line family* all components in the family use the plant in the same sequence, but with a *group family,* this restriction does not apply. Group layout is, in a sense, a transitional state in the change from *functional (process) layout* to *line (product) layout.* Any viable *line family*, which exists, will normally exist inside the group family. If the group families are found first, this greatly simplifies the next step of fining the line families and rearranging the plant into lines.

Group layout comes some way between line and functional layout when considering its effect on the efficiency of production control. Its particular advantage is that it offers an alternative method by which

Group I	*Group II*	*Group III*
Lathe	Grinding	Milling
Milling	Shaper	Lathe
Shaper	Milling	Grinding

Figure 8.9 : Group Layout.

The small or medium sized firm, which makes a large variety of products, can reduce throughput time and thereby improve capital utilization and delivery. It also has the advantage that in comparison with process layout, it simplifies and economises the production control and makes it more effective and efficient.

8.12. SYMPTOMS OF A BAD LAYOUT

A plant layout usually grows and develops. Not every minor change in the production program or additions of machines or sections justify redesign of the plant layout, but these changes accumulate and gradually alter the basic pattern of flow lines in the plant, until re- planning of the layout becomes inevitable. The symptoms of a layout in need of redesign are:

1. Congestion of materials, components, and assemblies.
2. Excessive amounts of work in process.
3. Poor utilization of available space.
4. Long transportation lines.
5. Production bottlenecks at certain machines while similar or identical machines have idle time.
6. Excessive handling by skilled operators.
7. Long production cycles and delay in delivery.
8. Mental or physical strain on operators.
9. Difficulties in maintaining effective supervision and control.

8.13. FLOW LINES OR FLOW SYSTEM

The flow of material though the plant is one of the major factors that determines the type of layout. The flow of material governs the cost of material handling, the amount of work in process, the capital and space tied up by work in process, and the length of the total production time. All these are important factors and each one is to be analyzed individually and collectively to justify the flow system selected to prepare the layout. Furthermore, the rate of performance and coordination of operations my have to be related to the rate of flow, and line production in particular may impose considerable physical and mental strain on the operators. Supervision and control mechanism may also be affected. Simple flow lines are ideal for control purposes, and visual supervision is often possible. A complicated flow system usually implies complicated control system. Quite often a plant layout design starts with the flow system, around which services and other facilities are added to building designed or modified accordingly, but some times the flow must be adapted to existing buildings. Many a time available space will dictates the flow line. The principle of minimum movements forms the basis of selecting the best flow line. This principle reduces the material handling cost, in process inventory and space required for processing. While designing the layout for a new plant, generally the flow patterns are decided earlier and then a system of facilities and building are designed and built around the flow pattern. As far as possible the flow line should be simple in order to have easy supervision and control. Various flow patterns, one come across, while preparing a plant layout are discussed below.

Flow Pattern	*Characteristics of flow and where it is used*
1. Line Flow : 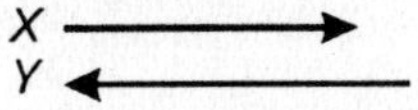	Simplest in nature. Material enters at one end (*X*) and leaves the system at other end (*Y*). It is preferred when the building is having long lengths and small widths.
2. L Flow pattern : 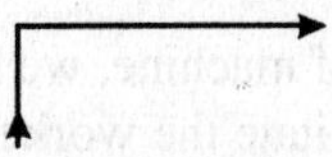	Resembles line flow and is used where buildings are more wide but less long as compared to line flow type of building.
3. Circular flow : 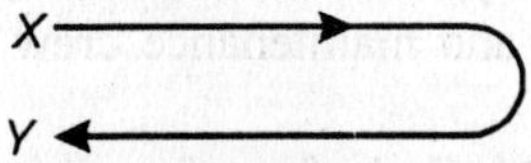	Preferred for rotary handling systems. Different workstations are located along the circular path. Raw material enters at *X* and leaves at *Y*. Preferable for square-shaped building.
4. U-Type flow : 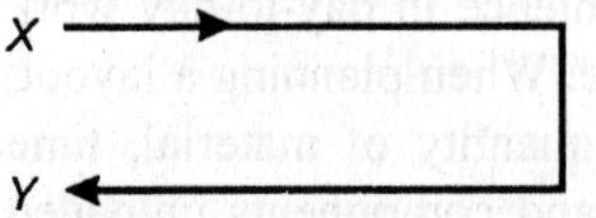	Supervision is simpler when compared to 1 and 2 above. Preferable for square-shaped building. Raw material enters at *X* and finished goods leaves at *Y*.
5. S or l Inverted S Flow : 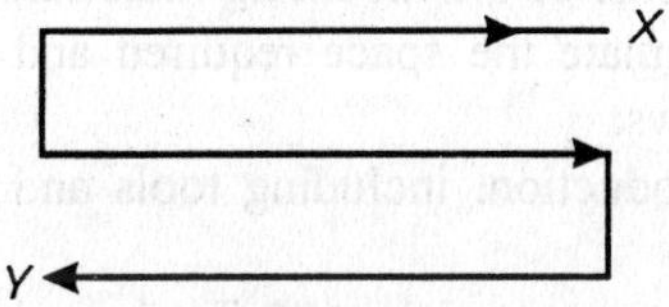	Preferred when production lines are longer than 4 above and the building is wider and less long. Supervision is better.
6. Combination of U and line, S and line Circular and line. 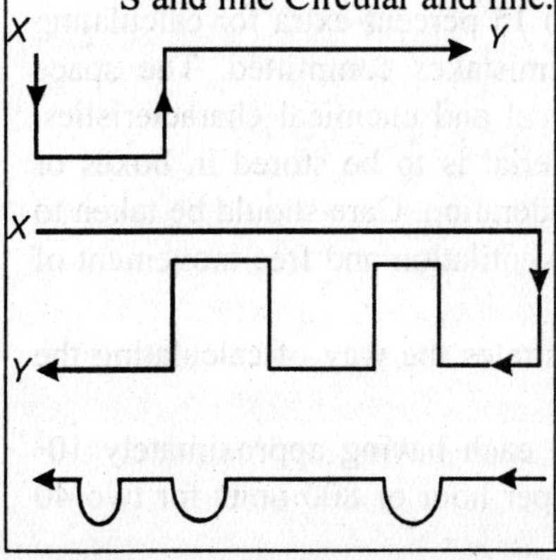	These are useful in square type of building and when production lines are long.

Flow Pattern	*Characteristics of flow and where it is used*
7. Flow lines for multi-storied buildings. 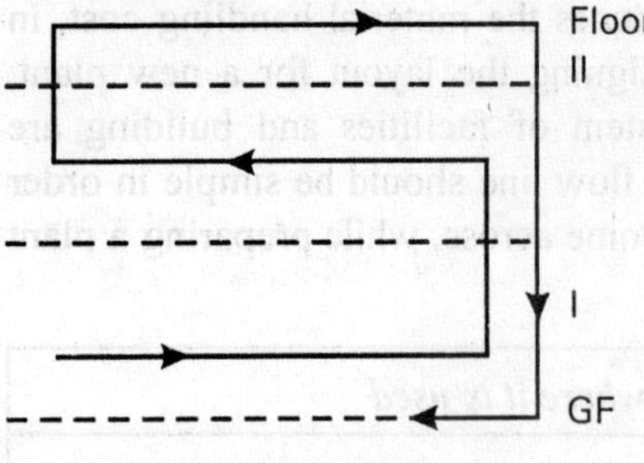	These flow lines vary depending upon the dimensions of each floor. May use any combination of flows shown at 1, 2, 3 and 4 above. Material is processed while in motion either upward or downward. Gravity helps for downward movement.

Fig. 8.10 : Flow lines.

8.14. DETERMINING THE SPACE REQUIRED FOR A FACILITY

When we fix up a position for a facility may be a Machine tool or any other type of machine, we have to bear in mind that sufficient space around the machine must be provided to facilitate the workers to move around the machine for loading and unloading, to provide space for in process material waiting at the machine, for material handling people to handle the material safely and maintenance crew to attend the maintenance when needed.

Sufficient space for different materials and supplies is badly needed particularly for safe and easy keeping and delivery of materials. Insufficient storage may cause inconvenience in day-to-day work causing congestion and also in long run, when need arises for larger storage. When planning a layout, the designer must have in his mind about the size of the material and quantity of material, time required for processing and expected waiting time of incoming material and components unloaded from the facility before moved for next workstation. Depending on the size of the incoming material, tools required, in process material and finished goods, he has to calculate the space required and provide space around the facility. The step-by-step procedure is as follows:

1. Listing of all the items which need storage space during production, including tools and spares.
   Materials to be listed are (*i*) Incoming materials, (*ii*) In-process materials, (*iii*) Tools and other supplies and (*iv*) Finished parts. After listing the items depending the production plans and demand pattern, it is always better to add about 10 to 15 percent extra for calculating the cubic space required in order to take care of any mistakes committed. The space required depends on the size and weight, quantity, physical and chemical characteristics, frequency of use and handling methods. In case the material is to be stored in boxes or barrels, the size of the container also to be taken into consideration. Care should be taken to see that stored material should no way an obstruction for ventilation and free movement of men.
2. Calculate the space required: The following example illustrates the way of calculating the space required:
   Assume storage of two weeks supply of certain material each having approximately 10^3 cubic centimeter size, and the production rate is 10 units per hour or 800 units for two 40

hour-week (considering 5 days in a week and 8 hour per day). Consider 4 units and it will occupy 4×10^3 cubic centimeter space. A $10^2 \times 10^2 \times 10^2$ container will hold $(10^6/4)^3 \times 10$ or 250 units. Therefore 800 units will require 800/250 = approximately 3 containers. In case the floor load or ceiling height is a limitation or a constraint, the Containers can be stacked only three high, then 3/3 or one stack will be required. This will require 10^4 square centimeters of floor space to store a two-week supply of the material in question. By doing such calculations, one can find out the approximate space required storing the material. Many a time, the layout engineers will be able to workout the floor area required by their experience. Any way it is better to provide 10 to 20 percent of excess area to accommodate future requirements or changes. One has to workout the space required for each work center. While doing so, the planner has to consider the space required for handling materials, movement of worker around the work center and space required for movement of other related persons near the work center. Another important point to consider is the location and width of aisle. A thumb rule for providing aisle is for every 0.10 square meters of manufacturing and storage area, 0.12 square meters of aisle is to be provided. Actual machinery may occupy only 25 percent of floor area and rest 75 percent of the floor area is for storage and aisle.

8.15. WORK PLACE DESIGN

A work place or workstation is a place where the production activities are carried out. A work place will have the workbench or a machine tool or equipment or a group of similar machines and worker or a group of workers. (Some times the worker standing and working on an assembly line is also considered as workstation). While designing the work place the following points are to be considered.

1. Providing more economical method of doing work to reduce the fatigue of the worker and create interest in him to work (to increase labour productivity).
2. Standardizing the method.
3. Training of workers to follow the standard method of doing the work.

Workstation design is not an easy matter to solve. Generally each workstation is considered as a small factory having its required facilities and designed, so as to enable to avoid future problems of congestion and backtracking and bottlenecks. After designing each workstation they are fitted into the floor space available for production with sufficient aisles. The main interest is to see that material and men will have a smooth flow during production to have maximum utility of the space available. Some principles are followed to ease the design of workstation. They are:

1. Determine the general direction of flow and flow pattern of material and men during production in each department and in plant as a whole. Also consider in detail the movement of material at the machine and the storage space, the location of the storage place, the movement pattern of worker while doing work and estimate the space required to accommodate all these.
2. After finding the space required, prepare a rough sketch of the place and check, whether all the necessary precautions are taken to avoid inconvenience. It is always better to draw flow chart or flow diagram and plan the workplace accordingly to have a better workstation.
3. See that safety provisions are easily accessible in case of emergency. Also in case of necessity, inspection/ maintenance should be carried out easily. Another point is to provide ample of lighting and ventilation (preferably natural).

8.16. METHODS OF PREPARING PLANT OR FACTORY LAYOUT

A layout furnishes details of the building to accommodate various facilities (production facilities, material and workers etc.). In addition it integrates various aspects of design of production system. The information required for plant layout includes, dimension of work place, sequence of operations, flow pattern of materials, storage space desired near workplace for raw materials and in process inventory and finished goods, space and location of office, aisles; toilets etc. As such there is no single universal technique leading to best layout, hence depending on the requirement, a combination of methods are used to get a better layout, which aims at best utilization of the available resources. Different methods that are used while preparing the layout are: -

8.16.1. Process Flow Chart

A flow chart is drawn using the method study techniques to show the flow of material during production, the operations used. This will also show sequence of operations. Basing on the flow chart, a flow diagram is prepared to scale to show how actually material and men move during production.

8.16.2. Material Flow Pattern

The flow pattern of materials are drawn with usual symbols used in method study and the enclosing line is drawn by providing place for aisles and movement of workers, which will give the proposed layout. This is generally termed as Flow diagram.

8.16.3. Layout Analogues

This consists of two dimensional templates or cutouts and three-dimensional scale models.

(*a*) ***Templates :*** Templates are most commonly used while preparing layouts. Templates are two-dimensional or block templates made up of cardboard, colored paper or celluloid. They are made to scale (generally 1:50) and are placed on the scaled outline plan of the building. Templates show the plan of the various facilities and the building. They show the actual floor space utilization. The templates can be placed and attached with a tape either on a board or on a crosshatched surface or on a graph paper and thus being known as *graphic technique*. These templates have flexibility in use and can be moved on the graph paper from place to place in order to evaluate various feasible positions for different machines. It is better to photograph a layout before shifting the templates to try another layout of facilities. Otherwise, with number sets of templates different feasible layouts are prepared on different graph paper for comparison and evaluation purpose and the best one is selected. Templates save lot of time and labour which otherwise would be spent in making drawings for each alternative plant layout arrangement. They visually present various characteristics, advantages and limitations of a layout. Coloured templates have still better vision effect. A two dimensional template gives machine outline and its details where as a block template shows the boundary of the maximum projected area of the machine. Templates, though simple and inexpensive, do not give real situation effect, which is obtained through the use of three-dimensional models or block models. The advantages of two-dimensional templates are: (*i*) They are inexpensive, (*ii*) They can be readily interpreted and followed by technical people, (*iii*) Duplicate copies can be made. (*iv*) One can show different machines or departments by using different colors. The disadvantages or limitations are (*i*) It is very difficult to understand by non-technical people, (*ii*)Third dimensional place utilization cannot be shown.

(*b*) ***Three Dimensional Models :*** These are scale models of a facility and more nearer to the real situation as, besides length and width they show height of the facility also. Models are especially suitable for persons who are not familiar with plant layout practice. Models are made up of wood or die cast plastic or thermo coal. They show minor details and can be mounted on a thick plastic sheet representing the floor plan. Models are used mainly to develop floor plans and elevations. Models of production facilities, men, materials handling equipment or any other facility can be made. Models are much more effective and fast as compared to drawings or templates especially when multistoried plant layout is to be designed. Multistoried models can be made of Lucite (a clear plastic). Models though expensive have resulted in substantial saving in laying out of chemical factories and refineries. The advantages of three-dimensional models are: (*i*) Layouts made of models are easier to understand by laymen. (*ii*) It is easy to explain to the management, (*iii*) Models can be shifted easily and quickly to study operational arrangements, (*iv*) Overhead structures can easily be checked, (*v*) They convey more or less a real situation. It provides means for installation of overhead equipment, structures and clearances required for the same.

The disadvantages are: (*i*) They require more storage area, (*ii*) They are comparatively expensive than templates, (*iii*) It is difficult to take them to shop floor for referenced purposes. (*iv*) It involves the additional cost of making a two dimensional model layout to make it more effective.

8.16.4. Quantitative Layout Analysis

Once a layout is prepared, before accepting it should be evaluated quantitatively and compared with other alternative layouts to have a better layout. There are various methods of evaluating a layout. Some of them are discussed below:

(*a*) ***Travel Chart :*** A basic tool that is primarily used to analyze the material handling cost or in certain cases number of moves in a process layout is the travel chart. A travel chart, as the name suggests, is a chart of record of the amount of travel by the material in process while going from machine to machine or from one department to another. This chart some times known as a *From to chart* or *Trip Frequency Chart* or *a Cross Chart*, which is actually an adoption of the form of a mileage chart commonly found on a road map. Travel charts are extensively used in solving various production management problems such as (*i*) To analyze and plan departmental location, (*ii*) To analyze material movement, (*iii*) To reduce work-in-process, (*iv*) To reduce labour cost, and to make appropriate use of floor space etc. From a travel chart, management can easily determine the optimum relative arrangement of various departments. This is found by computing the magnitude of the material handling cost for all possible arrangements of the departments and finally selecting the layout for which the magnitude is minimum. The layout analyst frequently locates the receiving and shipping department first depending upon the existing locational condition. He may then follow a procedure, similar to that, as shown below. A travel chart also helps in improving the existing layout. The use of travel chart is explained through an example below.

Problem 8.5 : A manufacturing unit has six departments A, B, C, D, E and F. They are located as shown in figure 8.6. The daily expected load transactions in tons also given. Check whether the given arrangement of departments is optimal or not. If not suggest a better layout.

Existing arrangement of departments:

A	B	C
D	E	F

Fig. 8.11

The load transaction between departments is given below:

From *A* to *B* 20 tons, From *B* to *A* 10 tons, from *B* to *C* 15 tons, from *A* to *F* 25 tons, from *C* to *D* 30 tons, from *D* to *F* 40 tons, from *D* to *C* 50 tons from *E* to *F* 10 tons and from *E* to *F* 15 tons.

Solution :

Step 1: Summarize the load transactions between departments (already given in the problem),

Step 2. Draw the existing layout (already given in the problem)

Step 3. Construct a square grid (matrix) showing the load transaction between departments.

Load matrix

From → / To ↓	A	B	C	D	E	F
A		10				
B	20					
C		15		20		
D			30			15
E	25					
F			40	10		

Step 4. As the load transaction from *A* to *B* and *B* to *A* covers the same distance, they may be added and shown at one place in the matrix. Similarly for other departments also. Another matrix is drawn to consolidate the load transaction.

Consolidated load matrix:

From → / To ↓	A	B	C	D	E	F
A						
B	20					
C		15				
D			80			
E						
F	25			40	25	

Step 5. Arrange the departments, which are having highest load transactions, should be side by side so that the material handling costs can be reduced. Hence arrange the departments having highest load transaction side by side.

Now from the consolidated load matrix the transaction between departments is:

Between *A* and *B* = 30 tons, between *B* and *C* = 15, between *C* and *D* = 80 tons, between *A* and *F* = 25 tons, between *D* and *F* = 40 tons and between *E* and *F* = 25 tons. Depending on the information available departments *D* and *C* should be side by side, next preference to departments *D* and *F* and then to *A* and *B*, then *A* and *F* and finally to *B* and *C*.

The new layout will be as shown :

C	*D*	*A*
E	*F*	*B*

The travel chart is advantageous because it brings out the relative importance of having different pairs of departments close to each other but it gives an optimum linear arrangement, which may not be always preferred.

(*b*) *Load Distance Matrix or Load Path Matrix Method* : This method aims at reducing the movement of in-process inventory from section to section. Line travel chart it also helps deciding the position of the department in relation to the other. The ultimate purpose is to modify the existing layout or the preliminary plant layout made by other techniques. The departments having higher tractions or the movement of material are kept closer to each other. This is explained by means of an example.

Problem 8.6. Departments *A, B, C, D, E* and *F* are located as shown in the figure. The number on the arrows connecting two departments is the amount of material moving from one department to the other in the direction of arrow given. Check is the existing layout is good or not.

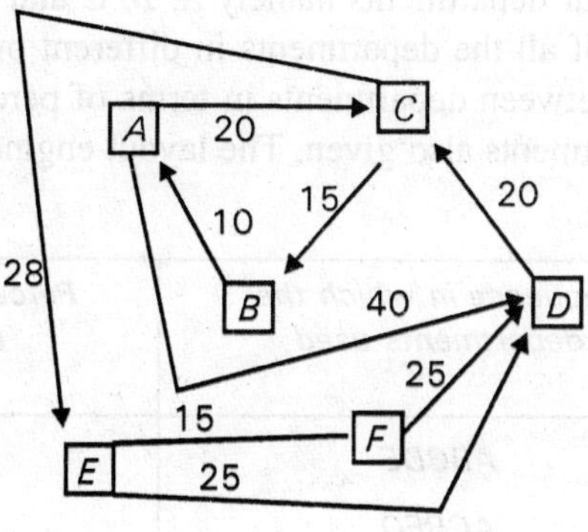

Figure 8.11

Solution : From the given diagram, prepare a travel chart and enter the material moving from one department to the other.

From

	A	B	C	D	E	F
A		10				
B			15			
C	20			20		
D	40				25	5
E			28			
F					15	

Load matrix showing tons of material moved per day.

From the load matrix let us identify the departments, which are having larger movement of material between them. Here for example *A* to *C* or *C* to *A* is considered as same. We are having more transaction between *A* to ***C*** (= 40). Then comes *E* and *C*, next will be *D* and *E* and so on. Now the improved layout is given below.

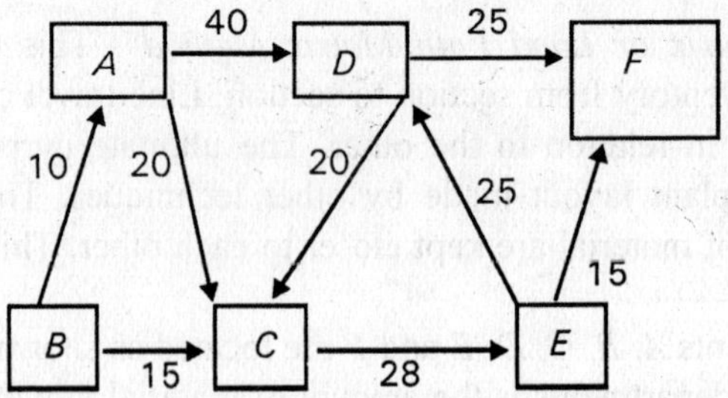

Figure 8.12 : Modified layout

Problem 8.7 : There are four departments namely *A, B, C* and *D*. The products manufactured by the factory needs the services of all the departments in different proportion. The volume of material for the products that move in between departments in terms of percentage of volume is given below. The distance between the departments also given. The layout engineer has prepared two layouts. Find which lay out is better.

Product Group	*Sequence in which the departments used*	*Percentage of volume of material moves from department to department*
I	*ABCDE*	30
II	*ACBED*	35
III	*ACDBC*	20
IV	*AEDC*	15

Distance between departments in meters in each layout is given below :

From	*To*	*Layout I*	*Layout II*	*From*	*To*	*Layout I*	*Layout II*
A	*B*	20	25	*C*	*B*	10	15
A	*C*	15	10	*C*	*D*	30	35
A	*E*	40	35	*D*	*B*	25	30
B	*C*	10	15	*D*	*C*	30	40
B	*E*	25	25	*E*	*D*	15	10

Solution : First let us write the load matrix and distance matrix from the data given.

Load Matrix or Volume Matrix

To

		A	*B*	*C*	*D*	*E*
F	*A*	—	30	55	—	15
R	*B*	—	—	50	—	35
O	*C*	—	35	—	50	—
M	*D*	—	20	15	—	30
	E	—	—	—	50	—

Distance matrix for layout I

To (distance in meters)

		A	*B*	*C*	*D*	E
F	*A*	—	20	15	—	40
R	*B*	—	—	10	—	25
O	*C*	—	10	—	30	—
M	*D*	—	25	30	—	15
	E	—	—	—	15	—

Next step is to multiply both volume matrix and distance matrix and workout volume-distance matrix. The row elements of this matrix are added and then these totals are added to get the grand total. The layout, which gives smaller total, will be the preferable layout.

The distance matrix of the second layout is:

To (distance in meters)

		A	*B*	*C*	*D*	*E*
	A	—	25	10	—	35
	B	—	—	15	—	25
From	*C*	—	15	—	35	—
	D	—	30	40	—	20
	E	—	—	—	10	—

Distance – Volume Matrix (L_1 for Layout I and L_2 for layout II)

From

		A	*B*	*C*	*D*	*E*	*Total for Layout I*	*Total for Layout II*
A	L_1	—	600	825	—	600	2025	
	L_2	—	650	550	—	525		172
B	L_1	—	—	500	—	875	1375	
	L_2	—	—	750	—	900		1650
C	L_1	—	350	—	1500	—	1850	
	L_2	—	540	—	1750	—		2290
D	L_1	—	500	450	—	450	1400	
	L_2	—	600	600	—	600		1800
E	L_1	—	—	—	750	—	750	
	L_2	—	—	—	500	—		500
		Grand total for layout I =					7400	
		Grand total for layout II =						6250

As layout II is having lesser grand total i.e. weighted distance for layout II is smaller, it is preferable. When number of layouts is prepared, weighted distance for all is calculated and the smaller is selected.

(c) *Trial and Error Method : Here* we use simple travel chart and graphical approach to reduce to minimize nonadjacent flows by centrally locating the active departments.

Example 8.8. A company wants to establish plant with six production areas as shown in the facility outline below. The firm proposes to locate six departments, A, B, C, D and E which have the number of moves a day between departments as shown in the travel chart given below. Develop a layout of the facility out line location.

1	2	3
4	5	6

Travel Chart

	Number of moves to					
From	*A*	*B*	*C*	*D*	*E*	*F*
A	-	7				5
B	-	-	-	4	10	-
C		7	-	-	2	-
D	-	-	8	-	-	-
E	4	-	-	-	-	3
F	-	6	-	-	10	-

Six departments, which minimizes the non-adjacent flows.

Solution :

1. Identify the departments having most frequent links with other departments. This is done by totaling the number of entries in each row and column. For example A has two row entries and one column entry that is total links is three.

Department :	A	B	C	D	E	F
Number of links :	3	5	3	2	5	4

2. Try to locate the most active departments in central positions. In this problem department B and E are in location 2 and 5.
3. Use trial and error to locate the other departments so that nonadjacent flows will be minimized.
4. If all nonadjacent flows are eliminated, the solution is complete. If non-adjacent flows still exist, try to minimize the number of units flowing to nonadjacent areas as weighted by the distance away.

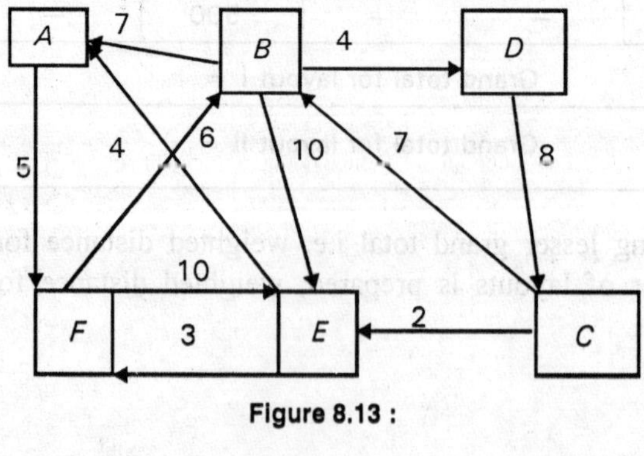

Figure 8.13 :

(*d*) ***The Correlation Chart:*** In this technique, we draw a grid with rows presenting alternative solutions. Plant item can be a ground floor (G.F), First floor (FF) or second floor (SF), or other floors like TF, FF, FTF an so on.

After the grid is drawn, the next step involves identifying the objectives and constraints of the layout and apply the same to find out the better layout. For example the constraints may be:

1. Product *X* cannot be done on ground floor (GF).
2. Operation *Y* cannot be performed on first floor (FF), similarly the objectives may be
3. Product *W* should be done on second floor (SF) like this first list out the constraints and objectives and give certain codes them.

These constraints objectives are then filled in the squares of the grid. The way in which we have to apply these codes is—when a constraint stops an item going in to a square, the number of that constraint is marked. After that the objectives or preferences are applied and the number of that preference or objective is filled in the corresponding square. Suppose the given objective is product *W* is restricted to second floor (SF), it cannot be done on other floors. Hence the identification number of this objective i.e. 3 is written in all squares except SF. Similarly other objectives are marked on the grid. *A* line *PQ* gives a feasible solution of the layout problem. This line is traced along the grid rows from the first plant item to the last item by joining open squares (Where no number is entered). The possible solution is:

$$W_{FF} - X_{SF} - Z_{GF} - Y_{SF}$$

Correlation chart is a very useful technique and shows the visual presentation. But it takes some time to draw the same

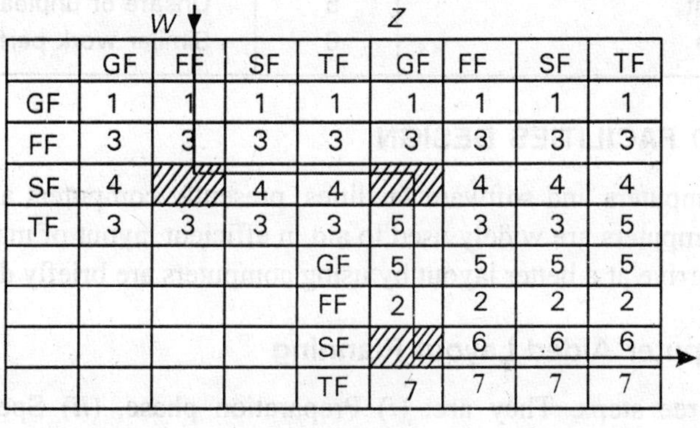

Correlation chart

(*e*) ***Activity Relationship Chart or Relationship chart or REL Chart :*** This is known as relationship chart or simply REL chart which indicates the relationship between pair of departments in terms of closeness depending upon the activities of the department as:

A = Absolutely Essential, *I* = Important, *O* = Ordinary, *U* = Unimportant, and *X* = Undesirable.

This chart is devised by Muther and it helps to assist in layout design with the help of a special format namely Activity Relationship Chart. Relationship between two departments shown in a diamond shaped cell, which contains one letter and a numeric digit. The letter which shown on the upper portion of the cell indicates the degree of closeness of the relationship and the numeric digit below represents the reasons for the relationship. Sometimes it simply shows the letters and no numbers giving only the degree or closeness. Figures 8.14 shows REL charts.

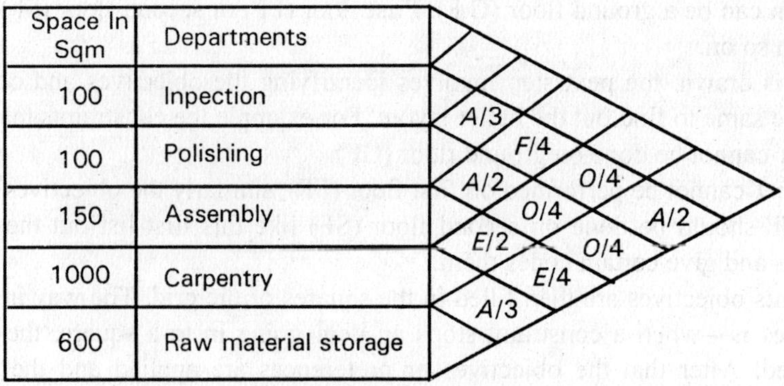

Figure 8.14 : REL Chart

Code description of REL chart

Code	*Importance of closeness*	*Code*	*Typical reasons for closeness*
A	Absolutely necessary	1	Use same equipment or facilities
E	Especially Important	2	Share same personnel or records
I	Important.	3	Sequence of workflow
O	Ordinary importance/OK	4	Ease of communication
U	Unimportant	5	Unsafe or unpleasant condition
X	Undesirable	6	Similar work performed

8.17. COMPUTERIZED FACILITIES DESIGN

Due to the advent of computers and software facilities, presently computers are used to design the facility layout. Digital computers are widely used to aid in efficient layout of manufacturing facilities. Some of the methods to arrive at a better layout by using computers are briefly discussed below.

8.17.1. CALP Or Computer Aided Layout Planning

This method has three steps. They are: (*i*) Preparation phase, (*ii*) Specification phase and (*iii*) Analysis phase.

In the preparation phase, planning objectives are defined and the information necessary for decision-making is identified. This phase specifies the input required for computer. Structuring of different computer disc files are also defined.

In the specification phase one has to decide how relevant planning details are to be fed to the computer.

In the third phase, i.e., analysis phase, model building and analysis of output is considered. The CALP system should be flexible to date change and error corrections. With an appropriate computer model major summaries and output reports are generated, which give a good documentation to measure the effectiveness of various alternatives.

8.17.2. Automated Layout Design Programme Or ALDEP

Here the closeness relationship between two departments is used to build up layout. Computer selects randomly the first facility and locates. Subsequent facilities selected on the basis of closeness relationship factor given in the preference matrix. When no further high relationship facility is found the other facilities are located at random. The preference matrix provides the relative facility location preferences denoted by letters ranging from *A* (absolutely essential) to *F* (Undesirable). Various arrangements of facilities can be generated in the same way for further analysis. The effectiveness of each of the layout is measured by performance score, which says how well the wanted relationships are fulfilled. This program requires the inputs: (*i*) Size of each facility, (*ii*) Description of building specifying features (aisles etc.) if any, (*iii*) Preference matrix and (*iv*) Number of layouts to be generated.

The layouts so generated are plotted using a plotter, which gives the layouts with preference scores to help to select the best layout. This ALDEP program can also handle layout problems of multistory buildings (up to three floors). This program is more suitable for re layout problems where one or more than one departments can be kept in fixed locations and other departments may be shifted from the present location.

8.17.3. Computerized Relative Allocation Of Facilities Technique (CRAFT)

This is the earliest method used on computers to assist inlaying out plant facilities. The objective of this method is to determine desirable arrangements of various facilities in an attempt to minimize total material handling cost incurred between all the facilities.

The following inputs are necessary for CRAFT program.

(*i*) Initial block layout giving exterior shape of the layout.

(*ii*) Inter departmental flow matrix or load matrix.

(*iii*) Material handling cost matrix giving handling cost per unit distance per unit load between departments.

CRAFT considers exchanges between locations repeatedly untill no further cost reduction can be found. The out put of CRAFT program is a block layout, shaped to confirm to building dimensions and the material handling cost to each layout.

In CRAFT cretin areas can be fixed in specific locations, for example, the location of an elevator or location of receiving or shipping departments. This can be done by giving instruction to the computer that the department / departments are not candidates for exchange, so that the existing layout need not be changed completely. At a time CRAFT can handle 40 departments.

The improved versions of CRAFT are PLOP-2 (*Plant Layout Optimization Procedure –2 way swap*), which improves an initial layout by first calculating the change in total cost caused by exchanging the location of all pairs of facilities. It then exchanges the location of the part of activities the maximum amount in the total cost. It continues with the procedure till no further reduction in cost is possible. In PLOP-2 two departments are exchanged at a tie. In modified version PLOP – 3 and PLOP – 4, 3 – way swap and 4 – way swap are used respectively. That is exchange of 3 departments and 4 departments at a time is considered. Further modifications of PLOP is a new series namely, QUAINT –3 (*Quadratic Assignment implicit N –Level Technique*). *QUAINT-3* adopts the same type procedure to that of PLOP –2 for two way swap but when no two-way swap can give any further reduction in total layout cost, PLOP –3 is used to find possible reduction through 3 – way swap is used to find possible solution through 3 – way swap. When three-way swap gives the solution with reduced cost, the program returns back to PLOP-2 algorithm.

Computer-Aided Facility Layout (CAFL), devised by *Choudhrui and Manivannan* uses a similar methodology of interchanging two departments at a time like CRAFT. But unlike to CRAFT it gives little importance to cost of handling between any two departments. This method can be well utilized by an organization where materials moved from one to another department are lightweight and not bulky in size. The input data for this program is:

(*i*) Number of departments and their dimensions, i.e. designation and length and breadth of the department.

(*ii*) Numeral values for placement rating.

(*iii*) Initial layout.

(*iv*) Relationship chart giving the desirability of closeness factor of any two departments.

The objective function of CAFL is to minimize the total sum of the products of the relationship between two department and the centeroid distances between them. This system evaluates the initial layout and then considers the effect of interchanges between two departments. The interchange of each pair of activities continues so long some improvement can be made.

8.18. PHYSICAL DISTRIBUTION MANAGEMENT (PDM)

Some times it becomes a problem for the management to find a location for its product distribution warehouse or distribution shop. The customers are served by: (*i*) Manufacturing the product, which satisfies the needs of the customers, (*ii*) Identifying the potential customers and locating the distribution center nearer to him and create awareness through advertisement and publicity, so that the product is available to the customer at right place, right time and right price. The second alternative is possible by a proper arrangement of the movements and local storages of the product. The technique used for solving the problems of identifying suitable distribution center is given the name ***Logistics.*** This is also known as ***Physical Distribution System Or PDM.*** As far the industries are concerned the PDM helps them to find a suitable location for their factory, so that the required raw material may be transported at least cost and finished products may be distributed to the deserving customers in time at least cost. It provides time and place utility to the customer.

The major decisions to be taken in PDM are:

(*i*) Identifying a suitable location for distribution of product or service to the potential customers in time at reasonable price so that the customers will have maximum satisfaction. The size and number of supply centers or depots or warehouses etc. are to be decided.

(*ii*) The method of meeting the demand of different customers from different supply centers.

(*iii*) Inventory requirement and control at the supply depots.

(*iv*) Means and combination of different transport means to transport the products from the factory to warehouses / depots and to customers (Rail, Road, Water transport or a combination of them)

(*v*) Packing method.

All the above decisions are made in the light of serving customer economically that is the total cost of serving customer is at minimum.

If D = Total cost of Distribution, TF = Total fixed cost of transport, TV = total variable cost of transport, SF = Fixed cost of service centers, SV = variable cost of service centers, I = inventory costs and P = Packaging cost then the total cost of distribution which should be kept at minimum is

$$D = TF + TV + SF + SV + I + P$$

The manager in charge of PDM has to consider customer satisfaction factor, all the costs in totality and competition, so that he can meet the organizational goals to a great extent. The three important problems the manager has to solve are:

(*i*) Finding a suitable location for Warehouse or distribution center

(*ii*) Finding the warehouse or distribution center capacities allocate a center to a group of customers,

(*iii*) Route for transporting the product from factory to ware house and warehouse to customer.

Good examples of such problems are:

(*i*) Location of warehouses of State Food Corporation.

(*ii*) Location of Fair price shops by the state government.

(*iii*) Location of public utility systems by the government. Etc.

8.18.1 Optimum Location of Distribution Center or Warehouse

There are analytical methods available for deciding upon warehouse location, with the objective of minimizing the total costs. This cost depends upon the distanced between the warehouse and the customer served by the respective warehouse and the loads of product supplied to him (quantity and number of loads). An analog model may be prepared to represent the warehouse location problem. Here number of strings is tied to ring and different weights are attached to the strings representing the demand of the customer. These are all placed on a tabletop to which number of holes are drilled and string passed through these holes. The holes through which the string passes represent the customer's location. Now the ring represents the warehouse, the holes through which the string passes represents the customer's location and the weight attached to the string represents the demand of the customer / consumer. Due to the different weights pulling the ring, it experiences pull in different directions and will stabilize at one particular point. This is the point of minimum potential energy, which analogous to optimal warehouse location. This is shown in figure 8.15. Mathematically also the location of warehouse can be found. The formula is:

X = x-co-ordinate of the warehouse, Y = y-co-ordinate of the ware house, d_i = Linear distance between the customer and the warehouse location, x_i and y_i are x and y coordinate of i *th* customer and w_i = Weightage given to each of the customer, then:

$$X = \sum_{i=1}^{n}\left(\frac{w_i x_i}{d_i}\right) \div \Sigma\left(\frac{w_i}{d_i}\right) \quad \text{and} \quad Y = \sum_{i=1}^{n}\left(\frac{w_i y_i}{d_i}\right) \div \Sigma\left(\frac{w_i}{d_i}\right)$$

By simplification the denominator d_i cancels and the equation will have weightage factor in denominator. Hence the formula is :

$$X = \Sigma(w_i x_i) \div \Sigma w_i \quad \text{and} \quad Y = \frac{\Sigma w_i y_i}{\Sigma w_i}$$

In the formula d_i is the distance between the depot and the customer. Hence, the initial distance between the depot and the customer must be known. Afterwards, finding the optimal location can modify it.

Initial depot location can be found out by means of another simple method known as Center of Gravity Method. The coordinates of the depot location are found by means of the following expression.

$$X = \sum_{i=1}^{n}(w_i x_i) \div \sum_{i=1}^{n} w_i; \text{ Similarly } Y = \sum_{i=1}^{n}(w_i y_i) \div \sum_{i=1}^{n} w_i$$

And $d_i = \sqrt{\{(X - x_i)^2 + (Y - y_i)^2\}}$

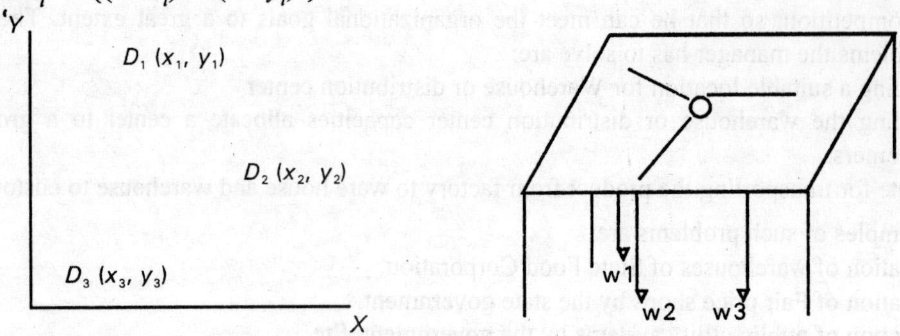

Figure 8. 15 : String and weights method of location.

Example 8.9. **A distributor wants to locate a warehouse to distribute goods to three of his customers whose locations are given. Find the optimal location for his warehouse. Particulars are given in the table given below.**

S.No.	*Customer*	*Coordinates*	*Load to be transported*
1	*A*	(10,15)	40 units
2	*B*	(30,25)	60 units
3	*C*	(20,25)	50 units

By using the formula :

$$X = \frac{40 \times 10 + 60 \times 30 + 20 \times 50}{40 + 60 + 50} = \frac{3200}{150} = 21.33 \text{ Approximately} = 21$$

$$Y = \frac{15 \times 40 + 25 \times 60 + 25 \times 50}{40 + 60 + 50} = \frac{3350}{150} = 22.33 \text{ Approximately} = 22$$

Warehouse co-ordinates = (21.22).

For routing problem refer to transportation problem discussed in earlier chapters.

QUESTIONS

1. Explain the importance of Layout with reference to Production control.
2. What factors you consider while selecting a location for a plant – Discuss with respect to a plant to manufacture Cement.
3. Discuss Weber's theory of selecting a location.
4. Mention different types of Layout. Discuss any two of them in detail, giving a neat sketch and their advantages and limitations.
5. What do you mean by a Group Layout?
6. What type of Layout you prefer to a unit engaged in Bus bodybuilding? Give reasons and give a neat sketch of the layout of unit.
7. What are the Characteristics of Good Plant Layout?
8. Discuss the advantages of Rural and Urban Locations for a Plant.
9. What do you mean by a Material flow line? In what way it will be helpful to prepare a plant layout?
10. How do you determine the space required for a facility?
11. What methods you use to prepare a Plant layout? Give the advantages and disadvantages of each.
12. How do you evaluate a layout?
13. Write short notes on CRAFT, CAFL.

9

MATERIALS HANDLING

- Introduction
- Importance of Materials Handling.
- Benefits of Materials Handling.
- Definition of Materials Handling.
- Scope of Materials Handling.
- Who solves the Materials Handling Problem.
- Selection of Materials Handling Equipment.
- Handling Functions.
- Categories of Materials Handling Equipment.
- Classification of Equipment by Function.
- Materials Handling Principles.
- Materials Handling Equipment.

9.1. INTRODUCTION

Industrial production involves considerable movement of one or more of the basic elements of production i.e. *materials, men, and machine.* In mass production by the assembly line method, or in the product or process layout of machines, men and machines do not have to move, but materials are moved to them. Only in case of static product layout for large and heavy jobs (such as construction of ships, airplanes, railway coaches etc.) men and equipment have to be moved to the job. Whatever may be the form of production, movement of men and materials becomes essential. As men being self-moveable and materials are more widely moved than machines in most industrial processes, this whole operation is termed as *materials handling.*

One of the basic functions of management is to employ capital efficiently so as to yield the maximum results. This can be done in either of two ways: (*i*) By maximizing the margin of profit or (*ii*) By maximizing the production with the given amount of capital that is by increasing the productivity. This means that management should try to make its capital to work as hard as possible. However, this is all too often forgotten and much time and ingenuity are devoted to make only labour to work harder. In the process, the capital turn over and hence the productivity of capital is often totally neglected. Several new techniques have been developed and employed by the modern managers to remedy this deficiency. Among them *materials management* has become one of the most effective. Materials handling is one aspect of materials management. Materials handling is the means by which the good of greater efficiency may be attained not only in industry but wherever materials are moved. One has to plan to reduce handling of materials as far as possible to reduce the production costs. This is because, materials handling consumes time and labor and add to the cost of production and add nothing to value of the product. It offers greatest opportunity to reduce the production costs.

9.2. IMPORTANCE OF MATERIALS HANDLING

The importance of materials handling arises from the fact that the cost of handling operation is of the order of 40 percent of the wage bill in many industrial organizations. Sometimes it will be as much as 50 to 60 percent of the product cost. This means it takes a considerable share in the variable cost. In the total production time too, materials handling take about 50 percent. When we consider material handling as an operation, it adds only *cost* to the materials but not any *value* to it and takes so much of valuable *production time* in the process. Importance of materials handling study is in reducing both the cost and time of materials handling, which fully appreciated.

9.3. BENEFITS OF MATERIALS HANDLING

Materials handling offers a wide scope for reducing costs, improving productivity and increasing profit margin. It will be easier to reduce materials cost and handling cost than to reduce labor costs or overheads; as mentioned earlier, handling costs predominate the total cost of the product, and saving in handling cost is substantial. By careful financial analysis, it can be shown that a 2 percent reduction in materials handling costs will results in increased profits equivalent to a 25 percent increase in sales. This is shown by means of a break even chart shown in figure 9.1 The chart shows that the profit starts accumulating much earlier as the break even point is shifted backwards with the with the same total production of 100 percent. The importance of materials handling function is greater in those industries where there is a high ratio of handling cost to the total processing cost than in those activities where the ratio is considerably smaller.

From the standpoint the national economy, the cost involved in the movement of materials or handling of materials assumes gigantic proportions. Within industry, the cost of moving materials from one workstation to another is often more than the processing cost itself. When the cost of transportation of raw materials or partially finished components / assemblies and of the finished product is added, the result is one of the largest single item of expense in the total economy.

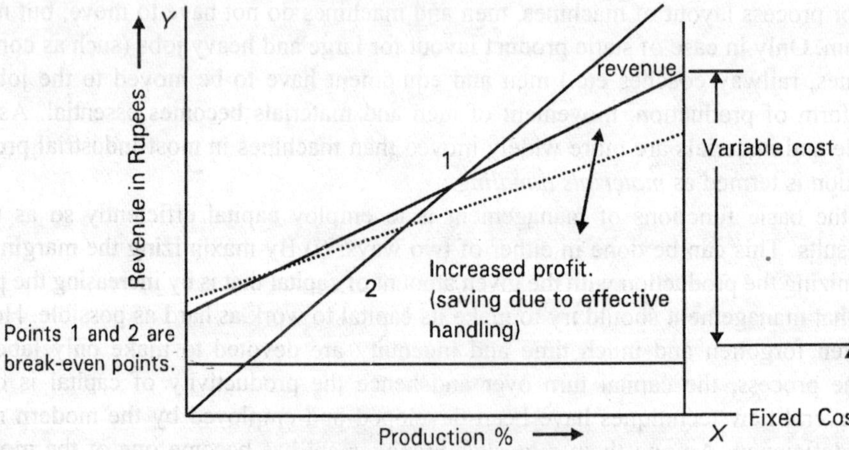

Figure 9.1 : Break-even point.

From the standpoint of individual company, materials handling can be a milestone that plunges the firm into bankruptcy or push it to a second place position in the competitive industrial scenario. On the other hand, efficient materials handling may be the means of launching a new business or the sole means of co~~inuing corporate existence in the face of restricted price levels and raising costs.

From the standpoint of labour, improved methods of materials handling offer a greatest prospects for higher wages and better working conditions. Since wages are dependent on productivity, it is to the interest of labour to assist management in lowering production costs and increasing the output. At the same time decreases in heavy lifting and *manual handling* of materials has removed a large part of hazard, and fatigue from many production jobs. The efficient plant is the safe plant, and efficient movement of materials is the best and safe for the worker's welfare.

All the above can be summarized as, that the reduction of prices in goods manufactured could only be effected by (*i*) Improved manufacturing methods giving higher productivity for man-hour at the same time lower unit cost of the product. (*ii*) Reduction in cost of servicing the manufacturing and processing departments.

9.4. DEFINITION OF MATERIALS HANDLING

Materials handling is defined as *Art and science involving movement, packaging and storing of materials in any form, by means of gravity, manual effort or power actuated machinery.* It is the preparation, placing and positioning of materials to facilitate their movement or storage. It includes every consideration of the product, except the actual processing operation and, in many instances, is included in this as an integral part of the process.

If for no other reason, this broad interpretation of the subject is dictated by the fact that maximum, economy in materials handling is achieved only by the consideration of what happens to the product from its very first movement as a raw material to its final place of consumption. Any other interpretation of materials handling will result in a restricted outlook and will prevent a company from obtaining the maximum benefits and savings, which the efficient movement of material can provide. The movement of materials should be minimized and handling should be avoided as far as possible or handling be integrated with processing. Materials have to received and stored, moved to processing departments, moved from workstation to another workstation and in process inventory are moved from department to department, then moved to the assembly section and then to inspection and testing department and finally to the shipping section – all the above said movements within the units is known as materials handling. All other movement of materials outside the unit is generally termed as *transportation.*

9.5. SCOPE OF MATERIALS HANDLING

Materials handling activity is integrated with all types of industrial activities. The problem of moving materials at a lowest expenditure of time and effort is definitely not restricted to any industrial unit. Most of the developments in the materials handling field and large share of the techniques and methods of analysis have come from industrial activity. But we can have the applications of the above in any field of activity.

9.5.1. Manufacturing Industry

The movement of material with in the manufacturing units and the volume of movement and the need for reducing the manufacturing cost in view of growing competition made the management of manufacturing units to set up a coordinating committee to think of reducing the handling of materials. Another important point is to see that material have uninterrupted flow during process of production. Some industries uses weight loosing materials, which looses their weight, during process and unless tries to reduce handling cost it cannot stand in the competitive market. Hence materials handling is very important aspect in manufacturing units.

9.5.2. Transportation Industries

In the transportation industries the movement of materials is the primary problem. Here they have equipment and overhead expenses, terminal loading and unloading and deals with rolling stock. Materials are moved from source to the manufacturing units and finished products from factories to the marketing points. In these industries the handling charges are as high as 60 to 65% of the operating costs. Any attempt in reducing the handling cost will give raise to substantial savings to the management.

9.5.3. Extractive Industries

In these industries the materials handling function is integrated with the operations involved in extracting the material. Most of the extracted materials are of weight loosing nature. Hence units, using such materials are located nearer to mines to reduce the handling costs. This shows the importance of material handling.

9.5.4. Process Industries

The handling function as such, has long been recognized in the process industries as one of the most important aspect. Especially in these industries, materials handling is the supporting function and not an end by itself. It is a means of supporting and simplifying production processes and it has therefore to be integrated with plant layout. Material handling problem has to be considered with the layout problem. Hence the layout is drawn by first drawing the material flow lines. For this, while preparing the layout, the concerned person has to study the flow of material from raw stage to the finished stage. Draw flow lines, flow charts, and flow diagrams, study the problem carefully before finalizing the layout. This sort of care and exercise will avoid future material flow problems.

9.6. WHO SOLVES THE MATERIALS HANDLING PROBLEM

The solution to any handling problem lies in getting the necessary information together and ascertaining from that the basic relationships involved. There is no substitute for plain commonsense. The accumulated experience in solving handling problems of various industrial processes, serves as an invaluable guide in accomplishing this rational analysis. In present day industrial scenario, every man concerned with production must have basic fundamental knowledge of materials handling, so as to solve problem as they arise, individually, without depending the specialist. In general Industrial Engineer or Layout Engineer is the better persons to solve complicated material handling problems. Important qualities of an engineer who deals with materials handling problems are :

(*i*) He must familiar with techniques and methods of industrial engineering.

(*ii*) He must keep in mind that materials handling is one special aspect of broader field *materials management.*

(*iii*) He must have thorough knowledge about Work-study, Production, Materials control and Industrial Processes.

(*iv*) He must be familiar with all the aspects of making layouts.

(*v*) He must have trained in understanding the functions and organization of materials handling and analysis of material handling problems, which will have effect on other processes, and functions of the organization.

(*vi*) He must be in position to understanding of fundamental relationships, which affect the movement, storage, and handling of materials.

(*vii*) He must have the knowledge of techniques and methods by which these relationships may be analyzed.

(*viii*) He must be acquainted with the various types of movement involved and the equipment, which may be used to accomplish each type.

(*ix*) He must grasp the relationship of materials handling to management, labour and the public.

(*x*) He must be familiar with the operational and managerial problems involved in materials handling.

(*xi*) He must have working knowledge of the different ways by which different handling problems are tackled and have a determination to obtain a feasible solution.

(*xii*) He must have technical training in technical aspects of the equipment used.

9.7. SELECTION OF MATERIAL HANDLING EQUIPMENT

The materials handling engineer must be careful in selecting the appropriate equipment to handle the materials during production, so that the production cost are kept under control. For this he has to bear in mind certain points while selecting the desired equipment.

9.7.1. Basic Factors To Be Integrated

Whatever may be the project – to plan a materials handling program for a new location or for an existing facility or to extend a partially completed installation – certain conditions are compelling in their influence on a decision that which are known as *basic or controlling factors*. They are : (1) THE PRODUCT, (2) THE ENVIRONMENT, (3) THE INDUSTRIAL OPERATION, (5) THE HANDLING CUNCTION, (6) THE HANDLING EQUIPMENT, and (7) THE WORK METHOD.

(1) The Product : The product handled is of very important point to consider while selecting materials handling equipment. Each of materials characteristics such as state (solid, liquid or semisolid), size, weight, surface features and attributes like rigidity, temperature and fragility and chemical properties – all these have their particular effects with regards to the equipment best suited to handle it and method of handling to be employed. Closely associated with the product are its activity, the quantities involved, and the frequency with which they are handled. Liquid handling is a separate specialized aspect.

(2) The Work Area : The work area covers in a broad way the locality, where the product is to be stored or handled. The work may have to be done in wide-open space, in a yard, along a high way, in a building (single or multistoried), or in other places each with unique characteristics.

(3) The Environment : The environment refers to atmospheric temperature and similar conditions in which the handling operations are to be performed. An important aspect of this factor occurs when industry deals with dangerous explosive gasses or chemicals and which dictates the modification of equipment in order to see that the desired operation is done safely.

(4) The Industrial Operations : The industrial operations which materials handling operation performs or with which the frequently must be co-coordinated, fall into two groups. Firstly the materials handling is a service function. In some instances, such as, receiving, storing, and shipping, the techniques are the means to an end. Such activities are generally classified as indirect operations. In contrast, direct operations, such as assembling, heat-treating, spraying and producing leave their imprint on the product involved. Many of these activities impose sever conditions, such as extremes of heat or moisture which call for modification of handling equipment.

(5) **Handling Functions :** The handling function cover the six basic functional operations which materials handling machine performs. They are: Transporting, Elevating, Conveying, Transforming, Self-loading and bulk handling.

(6) **Handling Equipment and The Work Method :** These two are interrelated. It is very difficult to say which is to be considered first – the equipment or the method. In some instances as where machines are already on hand and the problem is to extend the technique to other facilities or to include new products, which is usually logical to make use of the available machines. On the other hand, it may be possible to justify the purchase of new equipment or equipment recently brought on the market, which in all likelihood will affect the work method to be employed.

9.8. HANDLING FUNCTIONS

The primary objective of materials handling is to move articles or materials from one place to the other. The handling elements, which when combined together in various ways, make up the characteristics of the various categories of handling. The elements of handling movements are:

9.8.1. The Path Traveled

The path traveled must be viewed from the side or in profile and from the above (its projection on the horizontal plane) in order to have a complete picture of the situation. The names of different paths indicate, to some extent, their inclination. Horizontal means zero inclination, vertical refers to 90^0 inclinations, and incline and decline indicates plus and minus, respectively, but less than 90^0 inclination. Thus, we may refer to roadways as being *horizontal,* when it has but very slight pitch and *vertical* may be applied to paths, which deviate a small amount from being perfectly upright. *Straight* and *curved* ways are shown in figure 9.1.

9.8.2. The Course Followed

The course followed indicates, to a certain extent, the freedom of movement, which can be exercised. For example, consider industrial railroad, where the trolleys are used to move material. This has a fixed route i.e. the material moved must follow the direction of rails. Again consider a industrial four wheel truck or two wheel hand trucks, the materials moved on these may follow almost any route desired i.e. along aisles or other places where obstructions are not there.

9.8.3. The Kind Of Motion

The kind of motion refers to the motions of the actuating medium. It may be continuous motion such as we get by means of a belt conveyors. Intermittent motion is characterized by stop and go and it need not necessarily be along any particular kind of path or course. In contrast, reciprocating motion is a to and fro over same fixed path of travel (for example lifts).

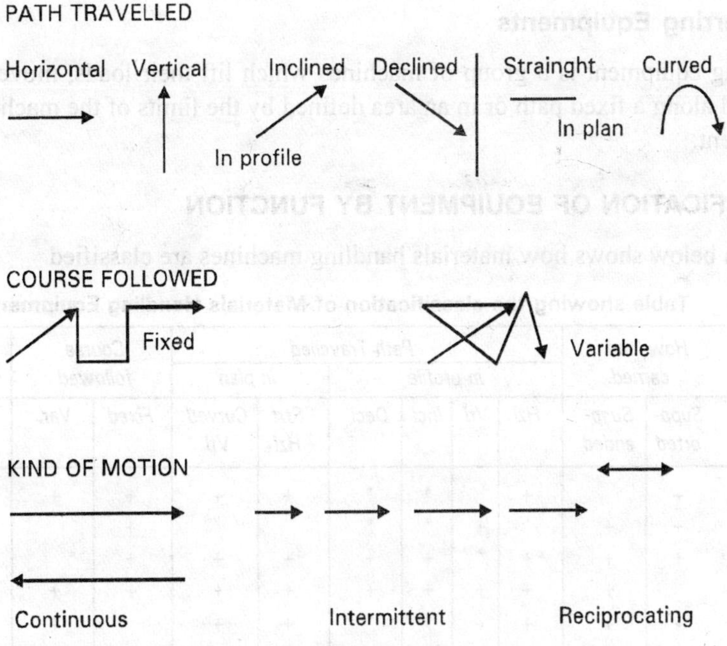

Figure 9.2 : The Elements of Handling Movement.

9.9. CATEGORIES OF MATERIALS HANDLING MACHINES

Machines are designed by combining the above said elements into handling functions. All types of materials handling equipment are machines which incorporate certain elements in such away that they can be grouped into broad categories for the purpose of ready identification. When we examine the different kinds of equipment in detail, we shall find that some of their characteristics are important, but for the present let us deal with the elements, which they incorporate. By means of functions they perform, we have four groups of equipments. They are:

9.9.1. Transporting Equipments

Transporting equipment comprises carriers equipped with running gear for moving loads over normally horizontal, straight, or curved paths along fixed or variable routes.

9.9.2. Elevating Equipments

Elevating equipment includes mechanism for raising and lowering materials, vertically or at steep inclined path, with continuous, intermittent or reciprocating motion.

9.9.3. Conveying Equipment

Conveying equipment defines gravity and power-driven machines for moving materials over horizontal, inclined, or inclined paths which, though fixed, may be straight or curved, with continuous and some times reciprocating motion.

9.9.4. Transferring Equipments

Transferring equipment is a group of machines which lift their loads, move the load in air, and deposit the load along a fixed path or in an area defined by the limits of the machine itself; the motion being intermittent.

9.10. CLASSIFICATION OF EQUIPMENT BY FUNCTION

The table given below shows how materials handling machines are classified.

Table showing the classification of Materials Handling Equipment.

Functional handling equipment	*How load is carried.*		*Path Travelled*						*Course followed*		*Kind of motion*		
			in profile				*in plan*						
	Supp-orted	*Susp-ended*	*Hzl*	*Vtl*	*Incl*	*Decl*	*Strt Hzl*	*Curved Vtl*	*Fixed*	*Var.*	*Cont.*	*Inter-mitten.*	*Recipro-cating*
Transporting	+		+		*	*	+	+	+	+		+	
Elevating	+	+		+	*	*			+		+	*	+
Conveying	+	+	+	*	+	+	+	+	+		+		
Transferring		+	+	+	+	+	+	+	+	+		+	
Self-loading	+	+	+	+	*	*	+	+		+		+	

How a machine carries its load in a characteristic distinct from the elements of motion it is capable of imparting. The two possibilities of load carrying characters are some machines support the load such as platform of a truck or arms of a truck or on a belt conveyor and others carry their load suspended below the actuating mechanism, or example cranes, hoists etc. Since loading is a term use to designate the action of mechanisms which are capable of picking up, transporting, and setting down their burden, without breaking the bulk or without any additional handling. Some of the machines lifts the load and transfer it to the desired location. In addition to basic factors and handling functions mentioned above, other point to be considered while selecting the materials handling equipments are:

(*i*) Permanency of operation,
(*ii*) Sequence of Operation,
(*iii*) Volume of handling operation,
(*iv*) Continuous or Intermittent flow,
(*v*) Nature and extent of movement,
(*vi*) Plant facilities available,
(*vii*) Plant building characteristics
(*ix*) Existing Materials Handling Equipment,
(*x*) Safety to workmen, while materials being moved,
(*xi*) Noise of the machine and fumes or exhaust gasses of the machine if any,
(*xii*) Flexibility and Reliability of the equipment,
(*xiii*) Initial and Operating Costs of the equipment and
(*xiv*) Rate of depreciation and obsolescence

9.11. MATERIALS HANDLING PRINCIPLES

Let us now discuss about the guiding principles of materials handling, which are essential to understand materials handling clearly. There are four principles of materials handling. They are :

1. Planning Principle, 2. Operating Principle, 3. Equipment Principle and 4. Costing Principle.

In addition to these, there are numerous fundamental relationships both in the movement of materials and in the installation and operation of equipment.

9.11.1. Importance of Principles

From the point of view of students, they provide a convenient framework to get information, examples, techniques and methods. They also serve as a test of the values of these examples and methods of realizing in a practical form why and how the methods illustrated are so effective.

From the point of view of the public these principles help to explain the phenomenal and often fantastic savings reported as a result of new handling methods. For experienced materials handling engineer topics like – How overhead handling saved warehousing cost? How productivity increased many fold by adopting effective materials handling? Etc will help to solve his problems.

For a business executive, these principles provide a valuable guide in decision-making regarding materials handling. The principles will help him in solving his materials handling problems. Materials handling is one of the promising area in increasing productivity and reducing costs.

9.11.2. Planning Principles

Efficient handling of materials is the outcome of efficient planning. Planning involves recognition of the fundamental relationship of materials movement and storage. An understanding of their effects of cost on production and knowledge of method of achieving the most efficient relationship of these cost factors is essential for a planer. For this certain principles are followed:

(*a*) Plan handling for over-all economy.
(*b*) Sell the philosophy of handling to the organization.
(*c*) Revise the layout for reducing handling of materials.
(*d*) Delegate planning responsibility of handling to one person.
(*e*) Utilize the third dimension for handling (over-head handling).
(*f*) Utilize live storage (storage on the move).

9.11.3. Operating Principles

Due to mechanization of materials handling and invention of new type of machines and techniques to handle materials, we see change in the scenario of handling operations. From these and from the case studies of materials handling, some operating principles have been evolved. They are:

(*a*) Efficient handling is the safe handling.
(*b*) Avoid re-handling.
(*c*) Move the material in unit loads.
(*d*) Use gravity for moving materials wherever possible.
(*e*) Where gravity will not suffice, use mechanical handling means, it practical.
(*f*) Establish schedules and procedures for maintenance of handling equipments.

9.11.4. Equipment Principles

With the many verities of equipment available today for the handling and movement of materials, it is sometimes difficult to see any hard and fast rules in the relationships of their use and operation. Because of this number there is an even greater need for definite principles to guide both the beginners and experienced materials handling engineer.

(*a*) Select proper equipment for the job.
(*b*) Integrate the equipment into the plant handling system.
(*c*) Co-ordinate the operations of materials handling equipment.
(*d*) Reduce the terminal time for power units.
(e) Standardize equipment and method of handling.
(*f*) Select equipment for flexibility.

9.11.5. Costing Principles

(*a*) Know your handling costs.
(*b*) Select Equipment for lowest over-all handling cost.
(*c*) Amortize the equipment within a reasonable length of time.

9.12. MATERIALS HANDLING EQUIPMENTS

Now let us discuss certain important materials handling equipment.

9.12.1. Two wheeled trucks and Four wheeled trucks

These trucks are very common in industrial units. These carry material in unit loads. Sometimes they are used to carry bulk materials also. These can move in any direction desired. They will have a platform with two or four wheels with a handle hold and push the platform. Materials are loaded manually and unloaded manually. Depending on the need, different sized trucks are available.

(*a*) Two-Wheeled Truck (*b*) Four-Wheeled Truck.

9.12.2. Forklift truck

This truck is power driven. It will have two arms in the front of the truck. These arms are used as lifting means. They are actuated by hydraulic drive or mechanical drive. When the load is kept on a pallet (pallet is a wooden platform with two supports below at the ends, so that there will be hollow space through which the arms of the fork lift truck are inserted and lifted), the truck inserts its arms below the pallet and lift the load and moves to the desired designation, keeps the pallet on the floor and take back the arms. Generally, the truck is operated by battery power or diesel power.

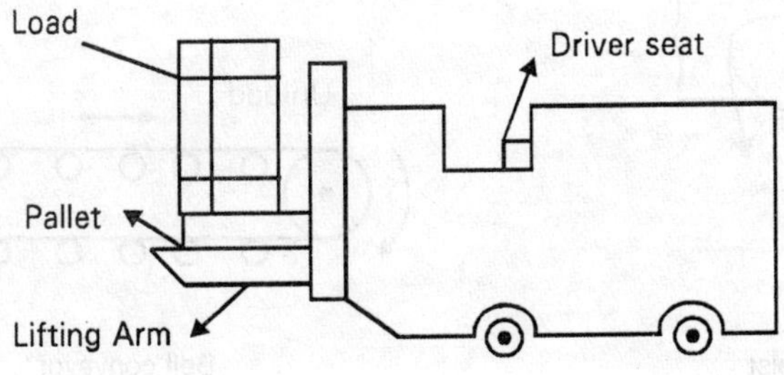

(c) Fork lift truck

9.12.3. Overhead Bridge Crane

This is used for Overhead handling. This is power driven. The operator operates either operates it from a remote point on the floor or it can also be operated by a driver in the cabin of the crane. It will have horizontal rail or beam, which runs on wheels on the rails supported by walls of the building. It can move load horizontally or move up and down. The load is suspended by the arrangement provided.

9.12.4. Jib Crane and Gantry Crane

Jib crane consists of a cantilever of 'I' section on which the load carrying trolley with hoist will move. It is power operated. For small type of crane it may be hand operated. It is preferred where the building features do not suitable for installation of overhead bridge crane. Gantry crane acts as an auxiliary to bridge crane. This may be installed in open space by means of fabricated framework.

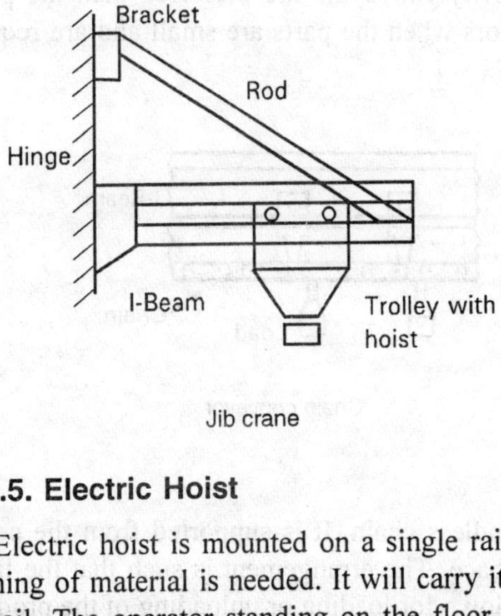

Jib crane

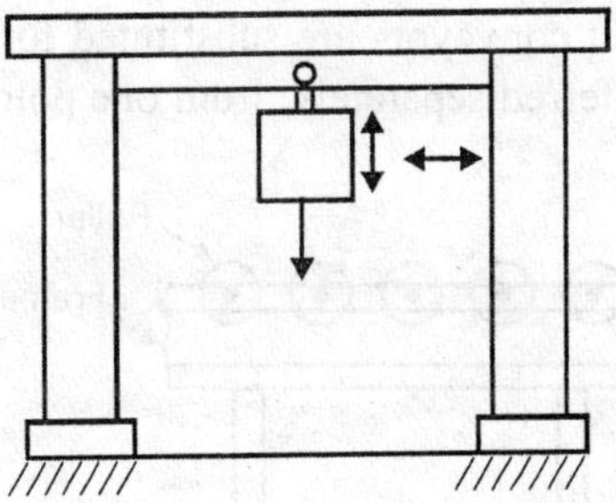

Gantry crane

9.12.5. Electric Hoist

Electric hoist is mounted on a single rail. It finds its applications in processes where chemical cleaning of material is needed. It will carry its load suspended from a hook and is moved parallel to the rail. The operator standing on the floor can control it. Where heavy weights are to be moved across the shop floor, this is very useful.

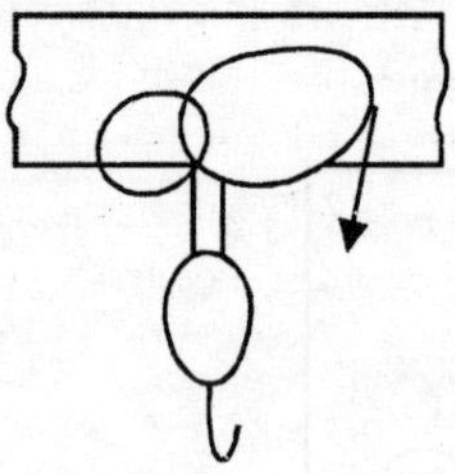

Electric hoist

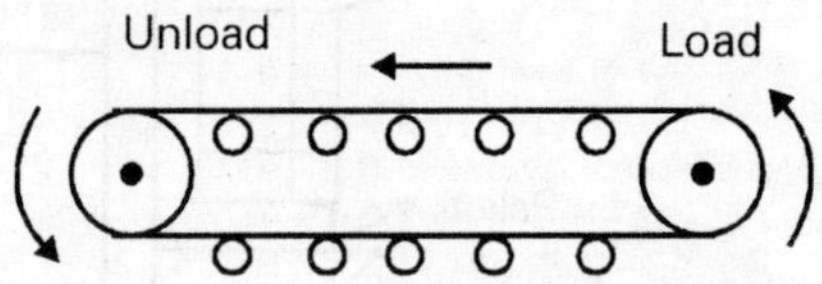

Belt conveyor

9.12.6. Belt Conveyor

Conveyors are employed to transport materials, over a fixed path, which may be horizontal or inclined (up or down), to different locations in a factory. They are economical, when the flow of material is continuous and may be used for bulk material or unit loads. In a belt conveyor, the belt may be flat or of trough shape to hold (granular materials which may tend to fall from the belt) materials. The belt material may be rubber covered canvas/ steel / plain fabric / woven wire (for high temperature material). A fixed conveyor is used on the mass production shop floor whereas portable conveyors are preferred for intermittent jobs like unloading of a freight car, etc. Use of belt conveyor is used versatile in handling of materials (bulk and unit loads) in industrial world.

9.12.7. Roller Conveyor

Roller conveyors consist of a series of rollers fixed in bearing fixed in bracts. When load is kept on the roller conveyor, it will move when the rollers rotates either due to the weight of the load and gravity or they may be power driven to move the load. They are generally used to transport flat-based unit loads either in a straight path or curved path. Gravity conveyors are preferred than the power driven. Belt conveyors are substituted for roller conveyors when the parts are small and are required to be transferred separately, from one point to the other.

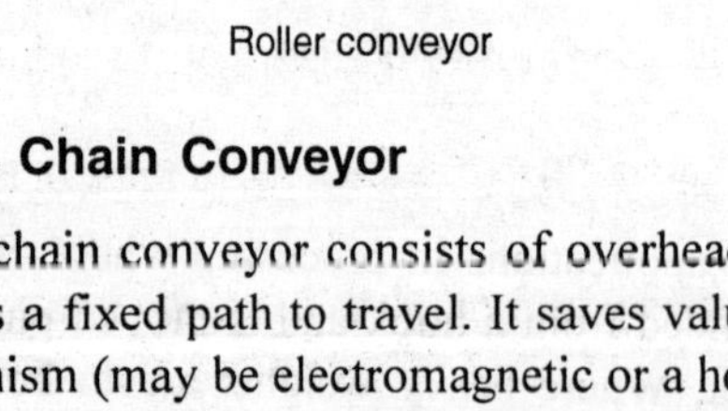

Roller conveyor

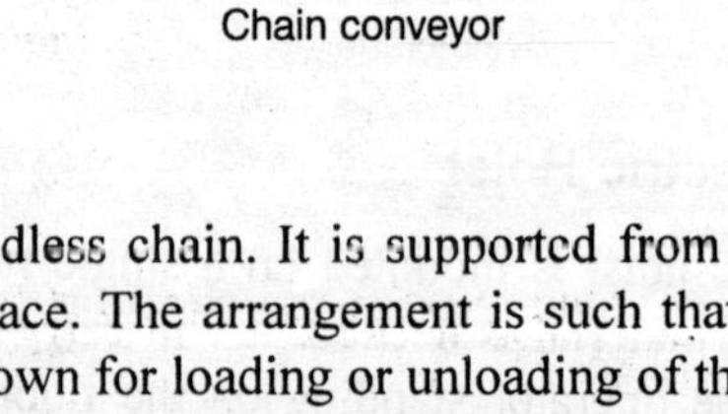

Chain conveyor

9.12.8. Chain Conveyor

A chain conveyor consists of overhead mounted endless chain. It is supported from the ceiling and has a fixed path to travel. It saves valuable floor space. The arrangement is such that the lifting mechanism (may be electromagnetic or a hook) lowers down for loading or unloading of the products. Chain conveyors are used in refrigeration industries for painting or plating the refrigerator shells. It is also used in some assembly lines.

Readers are advised to refer to the book on Materials Handling for more information.

QUESTIONS

1. Explain the factors to be considered while selecting a materials handling equipment.
2. Explain the Principles of Materials Handling.
3. Give a neat sketch of a Belt Conveyor and explain how it works.
4. Explain the benefits of materials handling.
5. Define handling functions.
6. How materials handling equipments are categorized.
7. Give the classification of materials handling equipment.
8. Why materials handling is considered as an important function? Explain.

10

STATISTICAL QUALITY CONTROL

- Introduction.
- Meaning of Quality.
- Quality Control
- Aims and Objectives of Quality Control.
- Quality Characteristics.
- Quality Control And Inspection.
- Quality Policy
- Statistical Quality Control.
- The Purpose of Statistical Control
- Development of SQC
- Advantages of SQC
- Theory And Techniques Of SQC
- Types Of Control : Process Control
  Acceptance Inspection
- Control Charts And Their Application.
- Definition And Concept.
- Control Chart Purpose And Advantages.
- Types of Control Charts.
- Variable Process Control Mean Chart
  σ – Chart
  Range Chart
- Attributes Process Control P – Chart
  np – chart
  C – chart
- Sampling Inspection
- Acceptance Sampling By Inspection
- Acceptance Sampling By Variables.
- Sampling Plans: Single Sampling Plan
  Double Sampling Plan
  Multiple Sampling Plan
  Sequential Sampling Plan.
- Reliability and Reliability Prediction.
  Reliability Calculations.
  Reliability Increasing Technique

10.1. INTRODUCTION

Quality Control is as old as industry itself. It started with the time the man started to manufacture articles / products because he is interested to see that the customer purchases his product.

The interest on quality control techniques increased as the number of manufacturing units are increased and due to the competition in the market. Every manufacturer is concerned with the quality of his product at the same time he is interested in supplying the needs of the market and optimal utilization of the resources available. The manufacturer is interested in customer satisfaction through the supply of desired quality and quantity of the product at the right time and at right price. Stiff competition in national and international market and consumer awareness of the quality of the product made it a mandatory to the manufacturer to mention the desired level of quality of his product or service. To run the business at desired economic level and to satisfy the customer, the management has to integrate quality development, quality maintenance and quality improvement of the product, which is possible through a sound quality control system.

10.1.1. Meaning of Quality

Quality is a relative term and it is generally used with reference to the end use of the product. Any product when it meets the desired specifications, we say it is of good quality. The quality is thus defined as the fitness for use / purpose at the most economic level. The quality depends on the perception of a person in a given situation. The situation may be user- oriented, cost oriented or supplier oriented. Since the customer manufactures the product for the use, the requirement (specifications) of the customer decides the quality of the product. Quality is to be planned, achieved, controlled and achieved continuously. The word *quality* has quite a good number of meanings. Some of them are:

(*a*) ***Fitness for purpose:*** The component is said to be of good quality, if it works or functions properly to give the service needed by the customer, when needed. Hence quality can be defined as **fitness for purpose.**

(*b*) ***Conformance to the requirement or Specifications :*** Quality is the ability of material or component or product to perform satisfactorily in an application for which it is intended by the user. Quality of the product thus means **conformance to requirement.** Customer needs have to be assessed and translated into specifications, and these specifications will be the yardsticks to assess the quality.

Other terms, which are used in reference to the quality and to assess the quality, are: Grade, Degree of Performance, Degree of Excellence and measure of fulfillment of promises.

10.1.2. Quality Control

Quality control is the process through which we measure the actual quality performance and compare it with the standards and take corrective action. It is systematic control of various factors such as Material, Tools, Labour used during production, that affects the quality of the product. It is effective system for integrating the quality development, quality maintenance and quality improvement efforts of the various groups in an organization, so as to enable production and services at the most commercial levels which allow full customer satisfactions.

10.1.3. Aims And Objectives Of Quality Control

1. To make the company's product more acceptable by the customer and thereby increase the sales of the company.
2. To reduce the cost of production by proper control of outgoing product by reducing the defects.
3. To achieve interchangeability.
4. To develop quality consciousness in the organization.

10.1.4. Quality Characteristics

Physical or Chemical property of a product or dimension, temperature or pressure or taste or smell or any other requirement used to define the nature of the product or service

(Which contributes the quality aspects of the product) may be termed as quality characteristic. They may be classified as:

(*i*) Technical: Length, frequency, Diameter, Viscosity etc.,
(*ii*) Psychological: Sensory qualities such as taste, odour, and beauty,
(*iii*) Time based items such as Reliability, Maintainability, life etc.,
(*iv*) Contractual such as guarantee, safety, and
(*v*) Ethical such as Honesty, Integrity etc.

10.2. QUALITY CONTROL AND INSPECTION

Quality control should not be confused with inspection. Inspection means checking of material, product or component of a product at various stages, with reference to certain *pre-determined factors* and detecting and sorting out the faulty or defective items. In inspection activity, the emphasis is placed on the quality of the past production or products already produced. Here inspector is concerned with, whether the product conforms to the quality characteristics or not. On the other hand *quality control* is a broad term, it involves inspection at particular stage but mere inspection does not mean quality control. As opposed to the inspection, in the quality control more emphasis is placed on the future production. The most effective way of controlling quality is to use statistical means to controls the incoming material, process, so that if anything found incorrect, immediate steps are taken to rectify the mistake and continue the production. This will help to a great extent that only good products will leave the manufacturing unit. The lesson learnt from the inspection of the sample is used as a basis to ascertain whether the quality of the product is as per specifications or not. In short, in inspection quality of past production is ascertained, and in quality control quality of future production is regulated. Also, Inspection is merely an act of checking and sorting out the defective items, whereas quality control is a broad term which includes number of activities in order to provide quality product / service to the customer.

DIFFERENCES BETWEEN INSPECTION AND QUALITY CONTROL

S. No.	*Para-meters*	*Inspection*	*Quality control*
1.	Scope	Inspection is a part of quality control.	Quality control is a broad term, it involves inspection at particular stages, but mere inspection does not mean quality control.
2.	Definition	Inspection is an act of checking materials, parts, components or products at various stages in manufacturing and sorting out the faulty or defective items from good items.	Quality control is an effective system for integrating quality development, quality maintenance and quality improvement efforts of various groups in an organisations to enable the production to be carried out at most economical level and to achieve satisfaction of customers.
3.	Devices used	Inspection uses precision measuring instruments such as vernier calipers, micrometer, etc., and devices such as toolmaker's microscope and flaw detector.	Quality control uses devices such as statistics, control charts, acceptance sampling, process capability study, and quality audit and field complaints.
4.	Applica-bility	Inspection is concerned with quality of past production to judge conformance with specifications and sorting out defective items from good items.	Quality control is concerned with the quality of future production. For example, take a sample, inspect it, and if it is defective find out the reasons and take corrective action so that such type of defects will not occur in the future. What is learnt from inspection is used as basis of ascertaing whether the quality of product to be produced will meet the specifications or it is necessary to make changes in production process.
5.	Concern	Inspection is mainly the responsibility of the inspector.	Everybody working in an organisation is responsible of quality of products produced.

10.2.1. Quality Policy

Quality policy refers to the basic principles, which are used to guide the actions of the company, in order to meet the quality objectives. However, economy may be the additional factor while determining the quality policy. Quite logically, the cost of production will increase as the level of accuracy or quality of product is raised. Thus functional use of the product and cost should be considered simultaneously while formulating the quality requirement or policy. While formulating quality policy the effect of policy on manufacturing process, Effect on sales, Customer profile, cost of inspection and optimal utilization of available resources should be considered.

10.3. Statistical Quality Control (S.Q.C.)

A quality control system performs inspection, testing and analysis to ensure that the quality of the products produced is as per the laid down quality standards (or specifications) is known as *Statistical Quality Control,* when statistical methods are used for control of quality. SQC, controls, improve and maintains quality or solves problems related with quality. Statistics is the collection, organization, analysis, interpretation and presentation of the data. It is based on the law of large numbers and mathematical theory of probability. It is just one of the many tools necessary to solve the quality related problems. It takes into account the existence of variation. It is in this sense that the adjective *statistical* is used in the expression Statistical Quality Control. Building an information system to satisfy the concept of *'prevention'* and *'control'* and improvement of product quality requires the use of statistical methods.

Statistical quality control is systematic as compared to guesswork of haphazard process inspection and the mathematical or statistical approach neutralizes personal bias and uncovers poor judgment. SQC consists of the following activities.

(*i*) Systematic collection and graphic recording of accurate data.

(*ii*) Analysis of the data and

(*iii*) Practical Engineering or Management action, if the information obtained indicates significant deviation from the specified limits.

10.3.1. Causes of Variation in Quality

The departure from specified or standard quality is due to *'chance'* factors or due to *'assignable'* causes. So long as only the chance factors are in operation, the manufacturing process is deemed to be under control. It means that all departures from the standard or specification do not indicate lack of control, but only those departures, which are due to assignable causes, show that the production process is not under control. Quality would be deemed to be under control even when goods produced are not of an exactly identical nature, up to the standard or specification so long as the deficiency is due to causes that are natural and inherent in the process of manufacture and, therefore, termed as chance factors. These causes being natural or inherent are neither preventable nor assignable, nor is it necessary to prevent them; for they are within limits, known as tolerance limits. These variations may due to the variation in skill of the worker, wear and tear of the tool and variations in the quality of material. To accommodate all these variations, the designers will provide upper limit and lower limit to various characteristics of the product, so that as far as the characteristic does not cross these limits, we say the product is within the limit and the error is due to chance and not of an assignable cause. For example take a dimension of the product is given limits as $10.00^{+0.001}_{-0.001}$. When the product is getting processed, the dimension may lie between 10.00 + 0.001 and 10.00 – 0.001. As far as the dimension is with in this limit, we say the product is satisfying the specification. Once the dimension crosses this limit, then we have to find out the cause of the variation as it is out of limit. The cause may be wear in tool or miss alignment of machine or any other reason. This mistake is to be rectified and process is to be re-started.

10.3.2. The Purpose of Statistical Quality Control

When Statistical Quality Control Techniques are not in use; the defects in quality were detected by inspection after the finished goods were available. Obviously, there was very little that could be done to improve the quality. SQC techniques, which permit constant inspection during the process of manufacture and enable the SQC man to know almost immediately as soon as the process of manufacture goes out of control. They are a sort of *'in-manufacture'* techniques. The managements can then take remedial measure, restore control and redeem the quality of the product. SQC techniques involve the application of the theory of probability and theory of sampling, the study of mean and variations. By the application of above methods and theories, it is possible to isolate the chance factors from those of the assignable causes and take appropriate measures. Thus SQC is a collection of specialized techniques used to improve the technical efficiency of production.

10.3.3. Development of S.Q.C.

The movement for quality control dates back to the period of Second World War (1939-1945), when the needs of modern warfare required turning out highly standardized machine parts and other goods according to strict specifications. Before the growth of SQC, the practice was of post-manufacture inspection, which led to waste of large amounts of scarce resources and man-hours. Further, a cent percent manual inspection besides being costly is also no guarantee against defective manufacture of some pieces passing undetected.

10.3.4. Advantages of SQC

The chief advantages of SQC are therefore:

(*i*) It saves precious and scarce resources in terms of men and material and enables the goods of a *standard and uniform quality* being supplied from the manufacturing unit.

(*ii*) This inspection is much more *economical* as compared to hundred percent manual inspection.

(*iii*) From the technical point of view the greatest advantage is – since the control is exercised through carefully selected sample, *it is possible to apply the technique to such cases, where an inspection is of destructive nature.* Also it can be applied to such cases where *a margin of error* can be specified in advance.

(*iv*) The SQC techniques enable to find out the extent to which a change in production techniques would result in an improvement in quality, and whether the cost would be justified.

(*v*) SQC technique enables to distinguish the good worker from the bad worker on the basis of the quality of the products produced by them.

10.3.5. Theory and Techniques of SQC

In the technique of quality control the first thing is the determination of a standard quality or laying down the specification. This is done with reference to the production techniques and other considerations such as cost of production, selling price, skill of the worker, specification of raw materials and the function of the product. One must be careful while laying down the specification, which has its effect on the cost of the product. If we fix up very close limits, the cost of meeting that specification will be very high, because of the technology and skill to be used. If the specifications are very coarse, the product may not function properly, though the cost of production is low. Hence the specifications must be specified appropriately. Figure 10.1 illustrates the cost of quality.

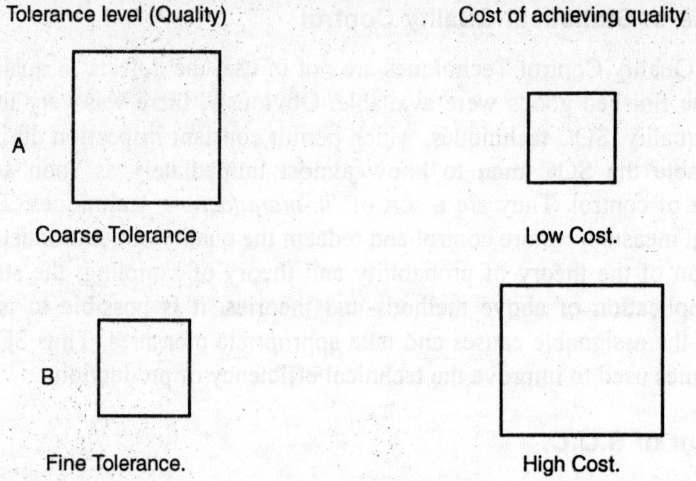

Figure 10.1 : Cost of Quality.

Consider an example of a bolt of 20 mm diameter and 50 mm. length. When this bolt is to be used in the assembly of an Aero engine, because of the operating conditions of the engine, finer tolerances are provided, and hence the cost of this bolt will be considerably high. In case the same sized bolt is to be used in the assembly of a tractor engine, the bolt need not be given fine tolerances, as the operating conditions of the engine totally different. In this case the cost of the bolt is much less than the above.

How to know that the quality of outturn has varied beyond limit, is a vital question. It involves the consideration of the theoretical distribution under a normal curve. It is known on *a priori* basis that 99.73 percent of the items would lie between the mean $\bar{x}$ and 3σ on either side of mean as illustrated in figure 10.2.

Figure 10.2 : Normal Distribution.

Thus $\bar{x} \pm 3\sigma$ gives limits, which are referred to as *empirical control limits.* A constant watch would be kept on the process by taking out samples of the product from the production line occasionally and finding out their standard deviations. If the 3σ limit on either side of $\bar{x}$ is beyond the limit of variation pre-determined by the manufacturing or quality control departments it would indicate that the process has strayed out of control. If a really satisfactory SQC system were in vogue, the fault would be detected at once. Causes of variation in quality would be investigated. These would be known as *assignable causes.* If variations are nominal these are attributed to *chance factors* and do not call for any action.

10.4. TYPES OF CONTROL

Control of quality may be exercised either *in the process of manufacture or after the goods has been produced.* In the first case it is known as ***process control,*** and in the second it is known as ***product or lot control.*** The process control is exercised through *control charts,* while sampling inspection, also known as Acceptance Inspection, does the product or lot control.

10.4.1. Process Control

Process control is a method of exercising control to determine whether the process of manufacture is within control or not. It is a constant system of control exercised *during* the process of manufacture to maintain and to preserve the standards of quality by detecting assignable causes. In this method standard of goods is inherent in the system of manufacture and in the plant that is used for manufacturing. Here continuous vigil is maintained on the process of manufacture by drawing and examining samples from the production line to ensure that the process of manufacture has not gone out of control.

10.4.2. Acceptance Inspection

In acceptance inspection a decision has to be taken to determine whether the goods *already manufactured* are up to the specified standards or not and should be accepted or rejected. Here the standard is determined on the basis of specification and requirements. In acceptance inspection sampling is resorted to for the purpose of ensuring the acceptance of lots of a specified quality standard determined on the basis of sampling plan.

10.5. PROCESS CONTROL

Quality is measurable in one of the following two ways: (*i*) *Quantitatively* and (*ii*) Qualitatively.

When quality is measured in the form of *quantity,* and expressed as variables is referred to as a quantitative type of quality measure for example, the length of an article in mm, or strength in Kg. When quality is measured in the form of *attributes,* it is referred to as a qualitative type of quality measure, for example soap cakes containing a larger than the standard proportion of soda etc.

Some times we come across a situation where both qualitative and quantitative measures can be employed to express the quality of the product. When we are dealing with the length of an object, when expressed that it is 10 mm shorter or greater than the required, it is quantitative measure. When we say it is larger or shorter and reject the then it is qualitative measure of quality.

10.5.1. Control Charts And Their Applications

Control charts are base on statistical sampling theory, according to which an adequate sized sample drawn, at random, from a lot represents the lot. All processes, whether semi-automatic or automatic are susceptible to variations, which in turn result in changes the dimension of the products. These variations occur due to either chance causes or assignable causes. Variation in the diameter of spindle, being manufactured on lathe may be either due to tool wear, non-homogeneity of bar stock or changes in machine setting, etc. The purpose of control chart is to detect these changes in dimensions and indicate if the component parts being manufactured are within the specified tolerance or not.

10.5.2. Definition And Concept

Control chart is a (day-to-day) graphical representation of the collected information. The information pertains to the measured or otherwise judged quality characteristics of the item or the samples. A control chart detects variations in the processing and warns if there is any departure from the specified tolerance limits. A control chart primarily is a diagnostic technique. It is dynamic in nature, i.e. it is kept current and up-to-date as per the changes in processing conditions. It depicts whether there is any change in the characteristics of items in the start of the production run. Successively revised and plotted control chart immediately tells the undesired variations and it helps a lot in exploring the cause and eliminating manufacturing troubles.

Let us take an example of producing a shaft of diameter of 20.00 mm. After manufacturing the required number of shafts say, 1000 numbers, and their dimensions are measured and plotted on a graph. The graphs appear like figure 10.3. Certain measured diameter values lie quiet close to the desired dimension i.e. 20.00 mm. This diameter is known as *mean diameter* or *mean value*, whereas other diameter values are quite far from the mean value. Because of the fact that variations are inherent in all processes and therefore in product dimensions, it becomes necessary to accept all those pieces which fall under a set of specified tolerance limits or control limits; otherwise, if we stick to the mean dimension of 20.00 mm only, then there will be more rejected shafts. As soon as the control limits are incorporated, which are shown as *upper limit* and *lower limit,* the graph becomes a control chart. These limits can be 1σ, 2σ, or 3σ, depending upon whether the confidence level is 68.27%, 95.45% or 99.73%. Normally 3σ limits are taken for plotting control charts, and (3σ + 3σ) i.e., 6σ is spread is known as *basic spread.* Besides 3ó control limits certain control charts also show *warning limits* spaced at 4σ spread. Warning limits inform the manufacturer that the items in the sample are approaching the danger level so that he can take an action before the process goes out of control.

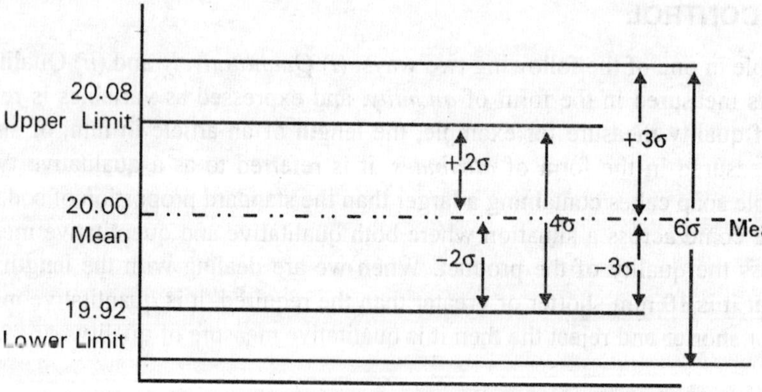

Figure 10.3 : Control Chart.

10.5.3. Control Chart Purpose And Advantages

The advantages of control chart are :

(*i*) A control chart indicates whether the process is in control or out of control.

(*ii*) It determines the process variability and detects unusual variations taking place in a process.

(*iii*) It ensures product quality level.

(*iv*) It warns in time, and if the process is rectified at that time, scrap or percentage of rejections can be reduced.

(*v*) It provides information about the selection of process and setting of tolerance limits.

(*vi*) Control charts build up the reputation of the organization through customer's satisfaction.

10.5.4. Types Of Control Charts

All the control charts are based on *Attributes* and *variables.* In other words, quality can be controlled either through actual measurements of dimensions, weights, strength etc. or through attributes as *yes* or *no* criteria. A good example for this is the use of Limit gages used in mass production to see whether the manufactured article is within limits or not. The gage will not reveal the actual dimension, but one can judge, whether the dimension under examination is under control or not. The properties of variable chart and attributes charts are:

1. Variable chart involve the measurement of the job dimensions and an item is accepted or rejected if its dimensions are within or beyond the fixed tolerance limit. Variable chart are more detailed and contain more information compared to attribute chart. Variable charts are relatively expensive because of greater cost of collecting measured data.
2. Attributes charts only differentiate between a defective item and a non-defective item without going into the measurement of its dimensions. These charts contain less information. Attribute chart being based upon go and no go data requires relatively bigger samples and they are less expensive. Attribute charts are only way to control quality in those cases where measurement of quality characteristics is either not possible or it is very complicated and costly to do so as in the case of checking color or finish of product, or determining whether a casting contains cracks or not, where the answer is yes or no.

There are several types of control charts in use, depending upon the type of quality measure relevant to a particular purpose.

Variable Process Control or Quantitative Measure of Quality : In case of quantitative measure of quality the following types of control charts are used: -

(*i*) *Standard deviation Chart or σ chart, (ii) Mean or $\bar{x}$ Chart, (iii) Range or* $\bar{R}$ *Chart.*

Attribute Process Control Or Qualitative Measure Of Quality : When qualities are expressed as attributes, the following types of control charts are used: -

(*i*) Fraction or p-defective chart, (*ii*) Number defective or np–Chart, (*iii*) Number Defective Per Unit Chart or *C* chart.

(*a*) **Standard Deviation or σ Chart :** When standards of manufacture and allowable or tolerance limits are not specified, a σ chart is prepared to determine whether the process is under control or not. The method consists of finding out a mean quantity and the standard deviation by taking a large number of items. This is necessary to determine the standards as none have been specified in advance. The standard error of σ would give us the control limits, depending upon the degree of accuracy required. Having determined the control limits we will be applying quality control to samples, which we will be taking off the run with regular frequency.

Example 10.1. It is required to determine whether an automatic device for cutting candies is in order or not and remain so or not throughout the process of manufacture or not. For this, a sample of 4 candies is taken soon after the cutting device is fixed to cut the candies. The average of the sample is found to be 20 mm with a standard deviation of 0.01 mm. Find the control limits and draw the graph.

Solution : Suppose it is decided that every time it is desired to test the control of process, a sample of 4 candies will be taken. The standard error of the mean would be $\bar{x} = \sigma / \sqrt{n} = 0.01 / \sqrt{4} =$ 0.005 mm. The $3\sigma \pm \bar{x}$? distance on either side of the mean 20 mm would determine the limits i.e. $20.00 \pm 3 \times 0.005 = 19.985$ and 20.015, within which the size of candies can vary to enable the manufacturing department to claim that the process is under control. For this purpose subsequent samples of size 4 would be taken at regular intervals, and plotted on chart known as control chart which is a graphical method of representing the size characters of a sequence of samples and showing the Upper Control Limit (UCL) and the Lower Control Limits (LCL) with in which the item sizes can vary in order to regard the process under control. Figure 10.4 shows the chart.

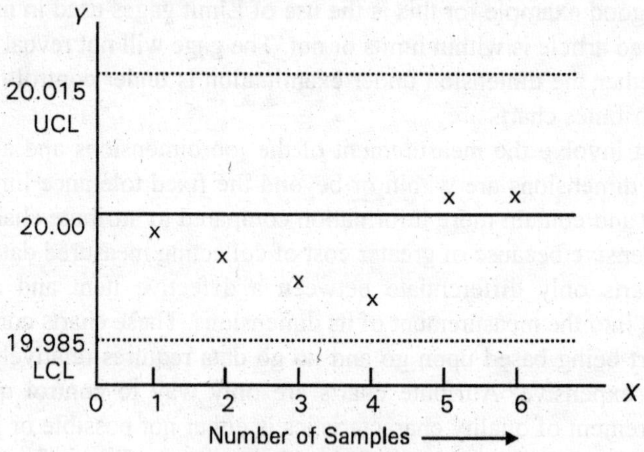

Figure 10.4 : Control Chart.

Procedure: Find the mean $\bar{x}$, Find Standard deviation (σ), Find Standard error of mean, Find 3σ and then workout the limits and then draw the charts and mark the samples.

(*b*) ***Mean or $\bar{x}$ chart :*** This shows changes in process average and is affected by change in process variability. This chart is used for measuring central tendency. It shows erratic or cyclic shifts in the process, it also detects steady progress changes, like tool wear. It is most commonly used chart in quality control. When used with R chart, it tells when to leave the process alone and when to chase and go for the causes leading variations, it secures information in establishing or modifying process, specification or inspection procedures. It can be used along with R chart to control the incoming materials.

(*c*) ***$\bar{R}$–Chart :*** It controls general variability of the process and is affected by changes in process variability. It also measures spread. It is generally used along with $\bar{x}$ chart.

The main disadvantage of these charts is that they require the use of tables of *Factors useful in the construction of Control Chart.*

(*d*) ***Plotting of $\bar{x}$ and $\bar{R}$ charts :*** A good number of samples of items coming-out of the machine are collected at random at different intervals of time and their quality characteristics (diameter or length or any other) are measured. For each sample the mean value and range is found out. For example if you have five diameters, the mean is given by sum of the diameters divided by the number of items. And the range is given by the difference between maximum diameter and the minimum diameter. Then the averages and ranges are tabulated. The procedure to draw the chart is explained by means of an example.

Example 10.2. In the following table the length of 10 samples of 5 rods are shown. Construct $\bar{x}$ and R charts.

Sample	*Length in cm*					*Total*	*Mean*	*Range*
	1	2	3	4	5	6	7	8
1.	6.2	6.8	7.2	6.0	5.8	32.00	6.4	1.4
2.	5.8	6.0	7.4	6.8	6.6	32.6	6.5	1.6
3.	4.8	5.2	5.8	6.4	6.8	29.0	5.8	2.0
4.	6.6	6.8	6.4	6.2	6.0	32.0	6.4	0.8
5.	6.6	6.2	7.2	7.4	7.2	34.6	6.9	1.2
6.	6.8	6.6	4.2	4.8	4.0	26.4	5.3	2.8
7.	8.8	7.2	7.8	3.8	5.6	33.2	6.6	5.0
8.	4.6	4.8	6.6	6.8	6.0	28.8	5.7	2.2
9.	6.8	7.2	6.6	6.4	6.0	33.0	6.4	1.2
10.	6.6	4.4	5.2	6.2	6.6	29.0	5.8	2.2
	TOTAL					309.6		20.4

Note : Columns 1 to 5 are the problem part and columns 6 to 9 are calculated as a part of solution.

$$\text{Mean of Samples} = \overline{X} = \frac{309.6}{(10 \times 5)} = 6.182 = \text{approximately } 6.2 \text{ cm.}$$

$$\text{Mean of Range} = \overline{R} = \frac{20.4}{10} = 2.04$$

To construct $\overline{X}$ chart and $\overline{R}$ chart, we have to refer to factors table. The formulae used for finding the limits are:

For Mean Chart Lower Control Limit = LCL = $\overline{X} - A_2\,\overline{R}$, where A_2 is the value taken from the table for the sample size (= n).

Upper Control Limit = $\overline{X} + A_2\,\overline{R}$

For Range Chart (R chart) , LCL = $D_3\,\overline{R}$ and UCL = $D_4\,\overline{R}$, where D_3 and D_4 are the values taken from table for sample size n.

Table 10.1 Factors for Estimating 3-σ Control Limits for $\overline{X}$ and $\overline{R}$ charts from $\overline{R}$

($\overline{R}$ = Average range of subgroups for samples)

Lower Control Limit for $\overline{X}$ Chart = $\overline{X} - A_2\,\overline{R}$, Lower Control Limit for R = $D_2\,\overline{R}$

Upper Control Limit for $\overline{X}$ = $\overline{X} + A_2\,\overline{R}$, Upper Control Limit for R = $D_4\,\overline{R}$.

Where $\overline{X}$ is the average of arithmetic mean of samples.

Number of observations in subgroup (n)	Factor for $\overline{X}$ chart A_2	Factor for R chart LCL D_2	UCL D_4
2.	1.88	0	3.27
3.	1.02	0	2.57
4.	0.73	0	2.28
5.	0.58	0	2.11
6.	0.48	0	2.00
7.	0.42	0.08	1.92
8.	0.37	0.14	1.86
9.	0.34	0.18	1.82
10.	0.31	0.22	1.78
11.	0.29	0.22	1.74
12.	0.27	0.28	1.72
13.	0.25	0.31	1.69
14.	0.24	0.33	1.67
15.	0.22	0.35	1.65
16.	0.21	0.36	1.64
17.	0.20	0.38	1.62
18.	0.19	0.39	1.61
19.	0.19	0.40	1.60
20.	0.18	0.41	1.50

For the given problem $n = 5$. From Chart, $A_2 = 0.58$, $D_2 = 0$ and $D_4 = 2.11$. Substituting

For $\overline{X}$ chart LCL $= \overline{X} - A_2\overline{R} = 6.2 - 0.58 \times 2.04 = 5.0$ Approximately.

UCL $= \overline{X} + A_2 \overline{R} = 6.2 + 0.58 \times 2.04 = 7.4$ Approximately.

For R chart, LCL $= D_2\overline{R} = 0 \times 2.04 = 0$ and UCL $= D_4\overline{R} = 2.11 \times 2.04 = 4.31$ Approximately.

Example 10.3 : Draw $\overline{X}$ chart and $\overline{R}$ chart for the given data.

Sample No. Size n = 5	$\overline{X}$	R
1.	7.0	2
2.	7.5	3
3.	8.0	2
4.	10.0	2
5.	9.5	3
6.	11.0	4
7.	11.5	3
8.	4.0	2
9.	3.5	3
10.	4.0	2
	$\Sigma X = 76$	$\Sigma R = 26$

$$\overline{X} = \frac{\Sigma X}{n} = \frac{76}{10} = 7.6 \text{ and } \overline{R} = \frac{\Sigma R}{n} = \frac{26}{10} = 2.6$$

For $\overline{X}$ chart LCL = $\overline{X} - A_2\overline{R} = 7.6 - 0.58 \times 2.6 = 6.092$ and UCL = $7.6 + 0.58 \times 2.6 = 8.658$.

For $\overline{R}$ chart, LCL = $D_2\overline{R} = 0 \times 2.6 = 0$ and UCL = $D_4\overline{R} = 2.11 \times 2.6 = 5.486$.

(*d*) **Fraction Defective Chart or p- defective chart :** Quality control is also exercised through the construction of Fraction Defective or p- defective charts; the object being to control the proportion of defective according to specified attributes. If attribute standard is not specified, it is inferred by fining the average of fraction defectives. It can be a fraction defective chart or % defective chart (percent defective chart or 100 p chart). Each item is classified as good (non-defective) or bad (defective). This chart is used to control the general quality of the component parts and it checks if the fluctuations in product quality (level) are due to chance causes alone. It can be used even if sample size is variable (i.e. different for all samples), but calculating control limits for each samples is rather cumbersome. p- chart is plotted by calculating, first, the fraction defective and then the control limits. The process is said to be in control if fraction defective values fall within the control limits. In case the process is out of control an investigation to hunt for the cause becomes necessary.

Example 10.4. A quality controller examines a sample of 1000 items each and finds the number of defectives as follows: (Note: Column Number 1 and two in the example constitutes the question and column 3 is calculated for construction the fraction defective chart).

Solution :

On the p-defective chart, the control line is given by the average of fraction defectives, i.e. 0.2367 and the UCL and LCL is calculated by using the formula:

$\overline{P} \pm 3\sqrt{(pq)}/n$, Where p = Average of fraction defectives, q = Average of fraction not defectives and n is number of items in each sample.

Sample number	*Number of defectives*	*Fraction defectives*	*Sample number*	*Number of defectives*	*Fraction defectives*
1.	215	0.215	11.	285	0.285
2.	227	0.227	12.	287	0.287
3.	220	0.220	13.	312	0.312
4.	180	0.180	14.	195	0.195
5.	320	0.320	15.	180	0.180
6.	240	0.240	16.	190	0.190
7.	218	0.218	17.	215	0.215
8.	195	0.195	18.	210	0.210
9.	280	0.280	19.	215	0.215
10.	310	0.310	20.	240	0.240
Total				4734	4.734
Average				236.7	0.2367

$$\text{Now } \frac{3\sqrt{pq}}{n} = \frac{3\sqrt{[0.2367(1-0.2367)]}}{1000} = 0.0402.$$

UCL = 0.2367 + 0.0402 = 0.2769 and LCL = 0.2367 – 0.0402 = 0.1965 and central line on graph = 0.2367. The fraction defectives for each sample is calculated (column Number 3) and plotted on the graph. The points outside the limits would indicate that the process of manufacture was out of control.

Example 10.5. Draw p – chart for the following problem.

Date	Number of pieces inspected (a)	Number of defective pieces found (b)	Fraction defectives p = b/a	% defective 100 p
November 4	300	25	0.0834	8.34
November 5	300	30	0.1000	10.00
November 6	300	35	0.1167	11.67
November 7	300	40	0.1333	13.33
November 8	300	45	0.1500	15.00
November 10	300	35	0.1167	11.67
November 11	300	40	0.1333	13.33
November 12	300	30	0.1000	10.00
November 13	300	20	0.0666	6.66
November 14	300	50	0.1666	16.66
Total days = 10	3000	350		

$$\text{Upper Control Limit} = \text{UCL} = \frac{\bar{p} + 3\sqrt{[\bar{p}(1-\bar{p})]}}{n} \text{ and}$$

$$\text{Lower Control Limit} = \text{LCL} = \frac{\bar{p} - 3\sqrt{[\bar{p}(1-\bar{p})]}}{n} \text{ where}$$

$$\bar{p} = \frac{\text{Total number of defective parts found}}{\text{Total number of pieces inspected}} = \bar{p} = \frac{350}{3000},$$

i.e., $\bar{p} = 0.1167$ and n = number of pieces inspected everyday = 300. Therefore $1 - \bar{p} = 1 - 0.1167 = 0.8833$, therefore,

$$\frac{\sqrt{\bar{p}(1-\bar{p})}}{n} = \frac{\sqrt{0.1167 \times 0.8833}}{300} = 0.01852 \text{ and } \frac{3\sqrt{\bar{p}(1-\bar{p})}}{n}$$

$= 3 \times 0.01852 = 0.05556$

Therefore LCL = 0.1167 – ± 0.05556 = 0.06114 = 0.0611 approximately.

UCL = 0.1167 + 0.05556 = 0.17226 = 0.1723 approximately.

***(e)* Number Defective or np- defective chart :** Some times it is simpler to prepare a number defective chart. This chart dispenses with the necessity of calculating the proportion or fraction of defectives in each sample. Consider the example 10.4. In this example, the sample taken is 1000; hence it was easy to calculate the fraction defectives. Instead, if we have taken any other number say, for example the sample size is 879; the calculation of fractions would have been a tremendous task by itself. In such cases, number defective chart is easier for construction.

The limits are found by the formula = $n\overline{p} \pm 3\sqrt{n\overline{p}\,(1-\overline{p})}$

Example 10.6. In a manufacturing process, the number of defectives found in the inspection of 15 lots of 400 items each is given below

Lot number	Number of defectives (np)	Lot number	Number of defectives (np)
1.	2	9.	18
2.	5	10.	8
3.	0	11.	6
4.	14	12.	0
5.	3	13.	3
6.	0	14.	0
7.	1	15.	6
8.	0		

Determine the trial control limits for *np*-chart and state whether the process is in control or not. What will be new value of mean fraction defective if some obvious pints outside control limits are eliminated? What will be the corresponding upper and lower control limits and examine whether the process is still in control or not.

Solution: Σnp = Total number of defective = 66

Σn = Total number inspected = 400 × 15 = 6000 = $\overline{p} = \dfrac{\Sigma np}{\Sigma n} = \dfrac{66}{6000} = 0.011$

$n\overline{p}$ = 400 × 0.011 = 4.4, therefore UCL = $np + 3\sqrt{n\overline{p}(1-\overline{p})}$

= $4.4 + 3\sqrt{4.4 \times 0.989}$ = 10.65.

LCL = 4.4 – 6.25 = a negative value, hence the lower limit is = 0

If you plot the curve you will observe that the lot numbers 4 and9 falls out of control. Therefore, the process is not in statistical control.

For new value of fraction defective eliminating lot numbers 4 and 9 we have,

Σnp = 66 – (14 + 18) = 34 and Σn = Total number inspected = 400 × 13 = 5200.

$\overline{p} = \dfrac{34}{5200}$ = 0.00654 and $n\overline{p}$ 400 × 0.00654 = 2.616. Therefore,

UCL = $n\overline{p} + 3\sqrt{n\overline{p}\,(1-\overline{p})} = 2.616 + 3\sqrt{2.616\,(1-0.00654)} = 2.616 + 4.826 = 7.452$ and

LCL = 2.616 – 4.836 = a negative value hence is equals to 0.

The process is still out of control, as the number of defectives for lot number 10 goes out of control.

(*f*) Number Defective Per Unit Chart or C- Chart : Sometimes, it is more convenient to make a per unit number defective chart. In *p*-chart and we have seen that the number of items in each sample was uniform. If, however, the sample consists of no uniform number of items, the limits on the control chart cannot be laid out, as '*n*' would vary. In such a case, a fraction or a number defective chart cannot be used and a Number Defective per Unit chart has to be constructed.

It is the control chart in which number of defects in a piece or a sample is plotted. It controls the number of defects observed per unit or per sample. Here sample size is uniform. The chart is used where average number of defects is much less than the number of defects, which would occur otherwise if everything possible goes wrong. Whereas *p*–chart considers the number of defective pieces in a given sample, C-chart takes into account the number of defects in each defective piece or in a given sample. A defective piece may contain more than one defect. For example cast part may have blowholes and surface cracks at the same time. The C–chart is preferred for large and complex parts. Such parts being few and limited however restrict the field of use for C–chart as compared to p-chart. This chart is plotted in the same manner as p-chart except that the control limits are based on Poisson distribution, which descries more approximately the distribution of defects.

Example 10.7. The following figures show the number of defective items discovered in 10 samples taken on 10 consecutive days in a month.

Date : (Month January)	1	2	3	4	5	6	7	8	9	10
Number of defectives per unit of sample	1	2	4	16	4	3	5	20	16	4

Construct a control chart for the number of defectives per unit from the above data.

Solution : The total number of defectives = 75.

Average number of defectives per day = 7.5

The control limits are given by $\overline{C} \pm 3\sqrt{\overline{C}}$, hence

The Upper Control Limit = UCL = $\overline{C} + 3\sqrt{\overline{C}} = 7.5 + 3 \times 2.7 = 7.5 + 8.1 = 15.6$

The Central Line = 7.5 and

Lower Control Limit = LCL = 7.5 – 8.1 = Negative value hence it is equals to 0.

When a chart is drawn, it shows that the process is out of control on January 4th, 8th and on 9th.

Problem 10.8. Ten castings were inspected in order to locate defects in them. Every casting was found to contain certain number of defects as given below. It is required to plot a C-chart and draw the conclusion.

Castings :	1	2	3	4	5	6	7	8	9	10	Total = 10
Number of defects found on inspection	2	4	1	5	5	6	3	4	0	7	Total = 37

$\overline{C} = \dfrac{37}{10} = 3.7$, UCL = $\overline{C} + \sqrt{\overline{C}} = 3.7 + 3\ \sqrt{3.7} = 9.472$ and LCL = $\overline{C} - 3\sqrt{\overline{C}} = 3.7 - \sqrt{3.7}$

= -2.972 = 0

When the values are plotted on the graph paper, we see that all the values are with in control limits and hence the process is under control.

(g) Where charts are used : (*i*) Final assemblies use attribute charts. (*ii*) Manufactured components such as shafts, spindles, balls, pins, and holes and slots use Variable charts. (*iii*) Bullets and Shells: use Attribute chars. (*iv*) Soldered joints: use Attribute chart. (*v*) Castings and cloth lengths: use Attribute and C-charts. (*vi*) Defects in components made of glass: use C-charts. (*vii*) For studying tool wear: Use variables chart. (*viii*) Punch press works, forming, spot welding works: Use Attribute charts. (*ix*) Incoming materials: Use Attribute charts and variables chart. (*x*) Large and complex products like Power plant engines and turbines: Use C-charts.

(h) Care to be taken while using Control Chart : So far we have discussed about the control charts. It is understood that the points fall outside the control limits, we would say that the process is out of control. It does not fallow from this that if the points are within control limits the process is fully under control and shows no abnormality whatsoever, so far as the process of manufacture is concerned. It is quite possible that the process may heading for trouble and assignable causes may be in existence. A careful SQC man would immediately take note of the pattern of such points. All the points falling in almost a line indicating a downward or upward trend i.e. an index of progressive deterioration in process conditions. Another pattern of points, which is regarded as unusual, is when points fall on one side of the central line near the UCL or LCL. When points are uniformly scattered within limits will indicate the usual pattern. Any departure from this will call for attention of the SQC person.

10.6. ACCEPTANCE INSPECTION.

Acceptance inspection consists in judging the quality of the goods which have already been manufactured. The goods thus subjected to test is known as a *lot* and the action of judging is known as *inspection,* after which inspected goods are *accepted* or *rejected. Acceptance inspection is done only after the goods have been produced and not during the process of manufacture, as* in the case of process control.

Acceptance inspection is done on the basis of samples and it is that area of quality control, which determines whether a particular lot should be accepted or rejected, on the basis of a specified quality standard. In connection with the application of acceptance inspection techniques certain expressions are used, the implications of which may be understood at the outset.

10.6.1. Inspection

Any item or component or product, which is manufactured, is required to perform certain functions. The act of checking whether a component actually does so or not is called *inspection.* In other words, inspection means checking the acceptability of the manufactured product. The act of inspection serves two purposes. First, it separates defective components from non-defective ones and thus ensures the adequate quality of the product. Secondly, inspection locates defects in raw materials and flaws in processes which otherwise cause problems at the final stage. For example, detecting the parts, not having proper tolerances during processing itself will minimize the troubles arising at the time of assembly. To check some products, sampling inspection is only the way. For example, the agricultural products cannot be tested until they are harvested.

10.6.2. Sampling

Sampling is an act of drawing samples from a batch on random basis. Sampling depends upon statistical probability and therefore samples must be collected from all sides and from different depths of box or heap containing the lot or batch (of component parts) so that every part has an equal chance of being selected. The samples should be collected at regular intervals from the entire production run. The purpose is to obtain a sample truly representative of the lot. The sample size normally increases with the lot size and depends upon the degree of quality to be assured. The *sample size* can be found from the reformulated statistical tables. The following relation also serves as a good guide for calculating sample size. If N is the batch or lot size, then the sample size equals to $\sqrt{2N}$.

10.6.3. Producer's Risk

When items are inspected, there is the risk of sometimes rejecting satisfactory items, i.e. those items that are satisfactory according to the standard of the *producer*. This is known as *producer's process average or AQL* or (*Acceptance Quality Level*) as adopted by him at the level of fraction defective (indicated by p in process control fraction defective chart). Such a situation is described as *producer's Risk,* indicated by P_p.

10.6.4. Consumer's Risk

Compared to above, when opposite is the situation i.e. that there is a risk of some times accepting unsatisfactory items, such as those items which are not satisfactory according to *lot tolerance fraction defective level* showing the maximum allowable fraction defective, then it is known as *consumer's risk* and is indicated by P_c. Often the allowable *fraction defective* is indicated as *percent defectives,* in which case lot tolerance per cent defective (P_t or LTPD) or *rejectable quality level* (*RQL*) is the standard on the basis of which the items are accepted.

10.6.5. Acceptable Quality Level (AQL)

It indicates a small proportion of bad components in a lot such that the lots having less than this proportion of bad components have a high probability of getting accepted.

10.6.6. Lot Tolerance Percent Defective (LTPD) or Limiting Quality (LQ)

It indicates a small proportion of bad components somewhat larger than Acceptable Quality Level in a lot such that the lots having more than this proportion of defective components have a small probability of getting accepted.

10.7. SAMPLING INSPECTION

Sampling Inspection is a technique to determine whether a lot or population should be rejected or accepted on the basis of the number of defective parts found in a random sample drawn from the lot. If the number of defective parts exceeds a predefined level, the lot is rejected. As compared to 100 percent inspection, the sampling inspection claims the following advantages.

Advantages of Sampling Inspection:

(*i*) It involves less amount of inspection to achieve a predefined degree of certainty about the quality.

(*ii*) It takes less time and is less expensive.

(*iii*) Fatigue and boredom incurred by the inspectors is much less, hence their operating efficiency remains high.

(*iv*) It is more accurate because in 100 percent inspection, errors get introduced because of the fatigue and boredom incurred by the inspectors due to large inspection work of repetitive nature.

(*v*) Since fewer pieces are inspected, no damage is done to the remaining pieces of the lot as they are not handled.

(*vi*) In certain cases, where the components are to be inspected by destructive testing or where a powder is to be chemically analyzed, 100 percent inspection can never be employed.

(*vii*) Rejection of a complete batch on the basis of sample decidedly pressurizes for improvement in quality.

10.7.1. Classification of Sampling Inspection

Sampling Inspection and sampling plans may be classified as follows:

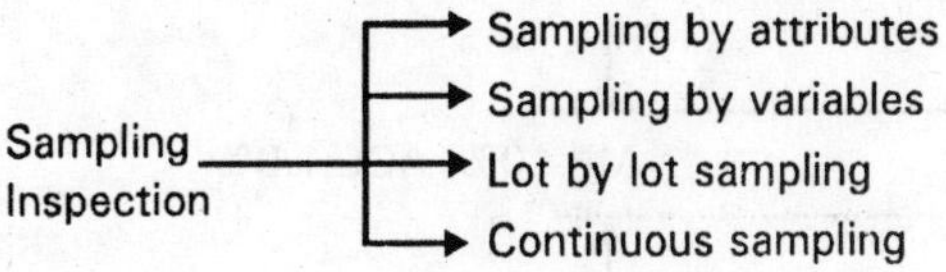

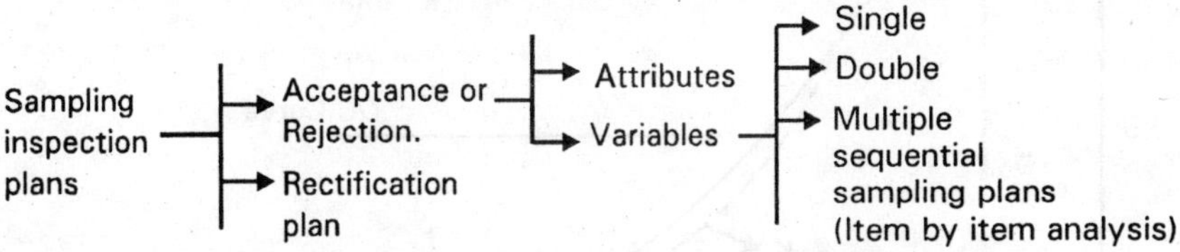

10.7.2. Acceptance Sampling Inspection By Attributes

Attributes (Yes or No) inspection is used to differentiate between a defective and a non-defective part and the part is rejected or accepted without using quantitative measure. For example, if out of a sample taken from a lot a predefined number of bullets fire, the lot is accepted otherwise rejected. Attribute inspection is very important and also very common. The parts can be inspected at an isolated calm, place away from the production floor. Firstly, *attribute inspection* is used where components are obviously defective and non-defective. Secondly, where it is very difficult and costly to measure the quality characteristics of a product (for example, paints, refrigerator). Thirdly, attribute inspection finds application where the manufacturer does not see any need to measure the exact job dimensions and he feels that go and no go type of inspection can serve his purpose. Large part of sampling inspection is done by attributes.

Suppose, a manufactured lot contains N components, and the purchaser would like that the lot should contain no defective components but the manufacturer know that under normal conditions the defective parts are not likely to be eliminated completely, then both the manufacturer and purchaser have to strike a balance and come to an agreement that if the lot contains more than, say X number of defective components, the lot will be rejected. One way of finding the number of defective parts is 100 percent inspection, which is costly, and this cost again in one way or the other is recovered from the purchaser. Considering the above, both parties bring sampling inspection into picture.

By going into the details, one finds that there is always some probability or doubt associated with the sampling inspection. A sample not necessarily always represent the true condition of the lot as it gets biased due to the human element involved in drawing the sample from the lot. It is quite possible that by chance the sample may contain all good components, but the remaining pieces in the lot may have a big number of defective components or all the sample pieces may turn out to be defective but otherwise the lot may be excellent. So it involves a risk to both of the purchaser as well as the manufacturer. But, certain risk will have to be borne by two parties if they go for sampling inspection. These risks are plotted on a graph and the result is *Operating Characteristic Curve* (*OCC*).

10.7.3. Steps Involved In Inspection By Attributes

(*i*) **Select a Sampling Plan :** First we have to fix the proportion defective which will decide whether to accept a lot or to reject it. A purchaser always thinks about the cost of making a wrong decision, i.e. the loss he will have to bear in case he accepts a bad lot on the basis of a good sample. By changing the parameters of an *O.C.* Curve he can easily choose the most appropriate curve for him, the one which involvers minimum purchaser's risk. Figure 10.5 shows *O.C.* Curve.

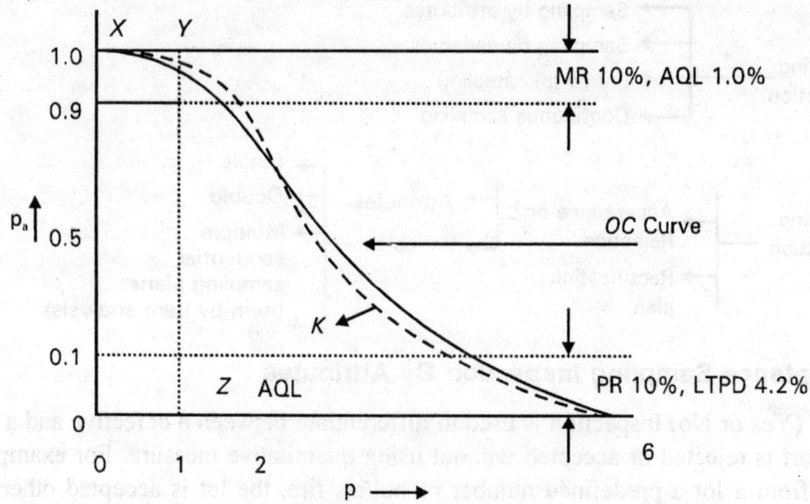

Manufacturer's risk = 10%, AQL = 1.0%

MR = Manufacturer's risk, P_a = Probability of batch getting accepted, *p* = Per cent defective, *AQL* = acceptance quality level, *LTPD* = Lot tolerance per cent defective, *PR* = purchaser's risk,

Figure 10.5 : Operating Characteristic Curve.

If a batch contains *N* pieces and a sample containing *n* of them is taken out, the batch will be accepted if the number of defective pieces (*d*) does not exceed the acceptance number (*a*). Both '*a*' and '*n*' are the parameters of *O.C.*Curve. If the batch size is large as compared to lot size, which is commonly the situation in industrial applications, the operating characteristic curve is independent of the batch size. However *n* and '*a*' influence the shape of an *O.C.* curve. As *n* and '*a*' both increase, the *O.C.* curve shifts inside towards *K* as in figure 10.5. The dotted inner curve is for a greater value of *n* as compared to that of the outer *O.C.*Curve.

(*ii*) **Determine The Operating Characteristic Curve For The Chosen Sampling Plan** : As described above, a single sampling plan involves tow parameters, *n*–the sample size and *a*–the acceptance number; and a batch is rejected or accepted depending upon the criteria whether the number of defective components *d* in a sample of *n* components is more than the acceptance number a or not.

The shape of the operating characteristic curve depends upon the value of '*a*' and *n* and accordingly it defines the risk involved or the probabilities of a good lot being rejected and a bad lot being accepted. A balance has to be struck regarding the value of *n*. A large sample size raises the cost of selecting, handling and inspection. A small size does not truly represent the lot; the *O.C* Curve shifts away from the ideal curve (*OABD*) and the chance of error increases. The concept of ideal *O.C.* Curve having rectangular operating characteristics (*OABD*) is that the lots having not more than 1 % defective components will definitely be accepted and others with more than 1 % defectives will certainly be rejected. The method of calculating the probability of a lot being accepted or rejected.

Example 10.9. Find the probability of a lot being accepted if it has a coming quality 5 % defective, a sample size of 40 and an acceptance number 1.

Solution : Given that $p = 0.05$, $n = 40$ and $a = 1$ and since for being accepted d should not exceed a, therefore, $a = d = 1$.

Now by statistics, $p = \sum_{r=o}^{r=a} C_d\, q^{n-r} .p^r$ Now $d\, r = d$ and $q = 1-p$ hence

$p = \sum_{d=0}^{1} {}^{40}C_4 \,(0.05)^4\, (0.95)^{40-d}$ By simplifying we get $p = 0.39905$

The probability can also be found from the statistical tables of cumulative Binomial Probabilities.

10.7.4. Sampling By Variables

When inspection is carried out by measuring the quality characteristics of a product, for example, by measuring length, diameter or weight etc., it called Inspection by variables.

Variables involve the averages of measurements whereas attributes deal with percentages of parts rejected. Inspections using variables is mostly done on the shop floor and is important for the control of operations. Inspection using variables is more detailed, contains more information, but involves higher inspection and other costs, per unit, as compared to attribute inspection. The manufacturer has to decide at some stage, which inspection to use, of course depending upon the requirements of his product.

10.8. SAMPLING PLANS

Sampling plans using attribute or variables are:

10.8.1. Single Sampling Plan

In this plan, a lot is accepted or rejected on the basis of a *single* sample drawn from the lot. The procedure is:

(*a*) Draw a single sample of size '*n*' i.e. take out '*n*' components, which may be calculated or taken from statistical tables.

(*b*) Inspect the sample and find the number of defective components.

(*c*) If defective pieces exceed the acceptance number '*c*,' the lot is rejected. In case the defective pieces are less than '*c*,' the lot is accepted by replacing the defective components by non-defective components.

(*d*) In case the lot is rejected, inspect each and every component (100% inspection) of the lot and replace the defective parts and salvage or correct the defective parts by processing them.

Calculation of Sample Size :

Given AQL or p_1 = 2 % and LTPD = 9.2 %, Therefore Operating Ratio $= \frac{\text{LTPD}}{\text{AQL}}$

$= \frac{9.2}{2} = 4.6 = R_0$

Referring to the tables for $R_0 = 4.6$, acceptance number $c = 4$ and $np_1 = 1.97$, Thus Sample Size $= \frac{Np_1}{p_1} = \frac{1.97}{0.02} = 99.$

TABLE : 10.1. Showing R_0, c, np_1.

R_0	C	Np_1
4.6	4	1.97
4.0	5	2.61
3.6	6	3.29

TABLE. 10.2. Sample Size for given lot size.

Lot size	*Sample size*	*Allowable per cent defectives*				
		1	2	3	4	5
		C	*C*	*C*	*C*	*C*
Up to 499	75	1	2	3	4	5
500-799	115	2	3	4	6	8
800-1299	150	3	4	5	8	10
1300-3199	225	4	5	8	11	14
3200-7999	300	5	7	10	14	18
8000-21999	450	6	9	14	20	26

For lot size of 850 and allowable percent defective of 3%, the sample size is 150 and acceptance number is 5. This means from the lot containing 850 parts, a random sample of 150 parts is picked up and inspected to find out the number of defective pieces. If the defective pieces are up to 5, accept the lot; if their number is > than 5, reject the lot or do 100 percent inspection. The characteristics of single sampling plan are:

(*i*) A single sampling plan is easy to design, explain and administer.

(*ii*) It is the only practical type of sampling plan under conveyorised production conditions when only one sample can be selected.

(*iii*) It involves lower cost of training and supervising employees, transporting and sorting samples.

(*iv*) It very accurately estimates lot quality.

(*v*) It is more economical than double sampling plan when lots have their percent defectives close to the AQL.

(*vi*) It involves a bigger sample size than the double sampling plan.

(*vii*) It involves record keeping less than that of double and multiple sampling plans.

(*viii*) A single sampling plan provides maximum information concerning the lot quality because each sample can be plotted on the control chart.

10.8.2. Double Sampling Plan

Some times it will be very difficult to decide the fate of a lot on the basis of the first sample, a second sample is drawn out of the same lot and the decision whether to accept or reject the lot is taken on the basis of the combined results of the first and second samples. The procedure is as follows:

Given C_1 and C_2 as acceptance numbers; $C_2 > C_1$.

Take a sample of n_1 items and inspect them. Count the defective units in sample of n_1. Let it be K_1. If K_1 is greater than C_2 Reject the lot. If K_1 is less than or equals to C_1 Accept the lot.

If C_1 is < than K_1 and less than or equals to C_2, then draw another samples of size n_2. Now total sample size is $n_1 + n_2$. Inspect the defective parts now. Let it be $K_1 + K_2$. If $K_1 + K_2$ is greater than C_2 Reject the lot. In case $K_1 + K_2$ is less than or equals to C_2, then accept the lot, and replace the defective items with good items. Characteristics of double sampling plan are as follows:

(*i*) A double sampling plan is more expensive to administer compared to single sampling plan.

(*ii*) Double sampling plan is easer to sell to the personnel because psychologically the idea of giving a second chance to a lot before rejecting it exercises popular appeal.

(*iii*) It involves less inspection than that required for a single sampling plan.

(*iv*) It permits a smaller first sample than is called for by the samples size of the corresponding single sampling plan.

(*v*) A double sampling plan involves more overheads than a single sampling plan.

(*vi*) It involves more record keeping than a single sampling plan.

(*vii*) It does not give as accurate estimation of lot quality as is provided by a single sampling plan.

10.8.3. Sequential Sampling Plan

This consists of (*a*) Multiple Sampling plan and (*b*) Item by Item analysis.

(*a*) **Multiple Sampling Plan :** A multiple sample plan accepts or rejects lot depending on the results obtained from several samples drawn from the lot. Consider a lot size *N*. Take a random sample n_1 from it and inspect the sample. If the number of defectives is greater than C_1 reject the lot, otherwise accept the lot and replace the defective components. In case reject the lot, draw a second sample n_2 from lot and inspect the same. In case the number of defectives, say $K_1 + K_2$ put together is greater than $C_1 + C_2$ reject the lot. If it is less than the sum of C_1 and C_2 accept the lot. If you reject the lot, take a third sample n_3 from the lot. Find the number of defectives. In case all the defectives put together $(K_1 + K_2 + K_3)$ is greater than $C_1 + C_2 + C_3$ reject the lot other wise accept the lot and replace the defectives. Like this we can draw any number of samples and decide the quality of the lot.

Characteristics of Multiple Sampling Plan :

(*i*) A multiple sampling plan involves smaller first samples than single or double sampling plans.

(*ii*) A multiple sampling plan is comparatively difficult to design and explain, and expensive to administer.

(*iii*) It involves higher overhead costs as compared to single and double sampling plan.

(*iv*) It involves more record keeping.

(*v*) In theory, multiple sampling may often permit lower total inspection than double sampling for a given degree of protection because of smaller sample sizes required.

(*vi*) New Methods, which simplify multiple sampling, such as automatic sampling boxes may result in greatly improved efficiency in administering multiple sampling plans.

10.8.4. Sequential Sampling Plan (Item By Item Analysis)

It is a plan in which sample size is increased by one piece (or component) at a time till the sample becomes large enough and contain sufficient number of defective pieces to decide intelligently whether to accept the lot or to reject it. It is easy to design, but more expensive to administer than a comparable multiple sampling plans, since more steps are needed to take a decision. Since sample size is increased by one at a time, sample results are analyzed much faster than single or double sampling plan. Sampling and overhead costs are minimum. It is seldom used in lot acceptance control but is important because multiple sampling is based on it.

10.9. RELIABILITY AND RELIABILITY PREDICTION

Definition and Concept : The study of reliability is important because it is related to the quality of a product. Generally, components having low reliability are of poor quality but extra high quality does not always make a product of higher reliability. A poorly designed component even having very good material, surface finish and dimensional tolerances may have low reliability.

The reliability of a product is the Mathematical Probability that the product will perform its mission successfully and function for the required duration of time satisfactorily under prerecorded operating conditions.

In manufacturing almost all products and especially those, involving human lives like aircrafts, submarines, nuclear plants, it is highly essential to know and to be sure about the reliability of the individual parts and of the whole structure as a single entity. The reliability prediction involves a quantitative evaluation of the existing and proposed product design. It leads to a much better end product. The reliability for a given time T and M (Mean Time Between Failures: MTBF) is given by:

$R_T = e^{-T/M}$ for an individual part............(1)

And for the system $R_S = R_{a(T)} \times R_{b(T)} \times R_{c(T)} \times \ldots\ldots\ldots \times R_{z(T)}$ .... (2) Where $R_a, R_b \ldots R_z$ are reliabilities of parts *A*, *B*......*Z*.

10.9.1. Reliability Calculation

Step. 1. Find form the previous use of the product the number of parts and part failure rates.

Step 2. Design overall reliability of the product considering stress levels and information of step 1.

Step. 3. Finally design and evaluate overall reliability using information of first two steps and environmental conditions, cycling effects, special maintenance, system complexity, etc.,

Step 4. Obtain the test results of the system. Calculate MTBF by using formula 1 / failure rate. = $1/n\lambda$, where n = number of units used, λ = Failure rate per part.

Example 10.10 : To test the design of a typical circuitry of a weapon system, Mean Time Between Failures = 1600 hours.

Name of the part	*Number used (n)*	*Failure rate (λ) % per 1000 hrs.*	*Total part failure rate (nλ) % per 1000 hours*
V	30	0.40	12.0
W	20	0.35	07.0
X	40	0.35	09.6
Y	50	0.12	06.0
Z	70	0,20	14.0
		Total :	48.6

$$\text{Mean time between failures} = \frac{1}{\text{Failure rate}} = \frac{1}{\lambda n}$$

$$= \frac{1 \times 100 \times 10000}{48.6} = 2058 \text{ hours.}$$

Against the requirement of only 1600 hours. Thus the modified design is perfectly reliable and hence acceptable.

10.9.2. Reliability Increasing Techniques

Using following techniques one can increase Product reliability.

(*a*) **Through simplification of design,** that is by decreasing the number of component parts for a system and believing in *Vital Few.* It is clear from equation 2 in article 10.9.1. that the reliability of a system is obtained multiplying the reliabilities of the various components or parts. If a product has 5 parts, each with reliability of 0.9, then the total probability if 0.9 × 0.9 × 0.9 × 0.9 × 0.9 = 0.59. Where as if there would have been only three pats the probability of the system would be 0.9 × 0.9 × 0.9 = 0.73.

(*b*) **By having redundancy built into the system :** Redundant components are provided in the system to take over, as soon as the actual component stops functioning. For example consider using a four engine aircraft which otherwise flies on three engines; the fourth engine being redundant.

(*c*) **Principle of differential screening :** From a batch, screen, select and separate those components which exhibit high reliability, medium reliability and low reliability and see these component in products requiring only that much reliability. For example, highly reliable components may be used in military signaling devises and those of medium reliability in commercial applications.

(*d*) **Principle of truncation of distribution tails :** Referring to figure 10.3 the components which fall under 1σ limits are not likely to fail easily as those under 3σ limits, hence try to adjust the distribution pattern.

(*e*) Reliability can be increased by avoiding those component parts, which cannot stand maximum, strength and stress requirements in their intended applications.

(*f*) **Principle of burn in screening :** It involvers short-term environmental tests which are conducted under sever stress conditions for eliminating parts having low reliability.

10.10. TOTAL QUALITY MANAGEMENT

The job of quality management is not just advising a sampling plan for the acceptance or rejection of the incoming material and controlling manufacturing process conditions; it is in fact *a job at every step of the company's activities.*

Quality management is a company-wide activity and various functional departments contribute to its success. The Marketing department, especially Market research, have information about what quality characteristics the customers desire and to what extent? This is a valuable input for planning quality. Also the information regarding the quality of the manufactured product needs to be presented to the customers. The marketing department also does this. Product design write the specifications from the product, raw materials, bought out components and the contracts with the customers. The purchasing department makes contracts with the supplies of raw material, components and selects the vendors, develops the vendors, keeps track of the vendors. Product design and purchasing have much to contribute to the quality of the final product. Production Engineers select the processes, methods, and equipment for the manufacture of the product and can provide valuable information regarding the anticipated difficulties in implementing a certain product quality specification. The contribution of manufacturing line is obvious. They are responsible for the actual production, and therefore the final product quality depends much upon their skills, motivation to work, and their interpretation of the specifications. Since the finished product may take as much as one year before it reaches the final consumer, the product quality depends upon the design of the packaging and the method of storage in the warehouse. The quality depends also on how the product is shipped. The purpose of good product quality is to create a good image of the company and this image should be maintained. Therefore the company has to attend complaints from the customer and provide periodic services to the customers.

The quality control laboratory/department, which inspects a batch of raw materials, coming inside the company or semi finished goods or finished product and approves or rejects them has much to contribute to quality desired. Many a time, the quality control job is misunderstood because of this last function alone., The product quality has inputs from various angles and a total quality control programme should consider all the different aspects contributing to quality. It is stated by many "quality is everybody's job in a business". When we take a look at the organizations whose products are of top quality, we always notice that in such organizations all the company employees at all levels and in all functions are motivated to contribute to the total quality establishment effort.

Since each functional department has a contribution to make towards quality, it is imperative that the *total quality management effort be properly organized to coordinate the various contributing aspect to quality.* Without such coordination, there may be chaotic situation, and although the quality is everybody' concern, it may become nobody's concern. Therefore, quality management should be a separate function headed by a person quite high in the organizational hierarchy so as to facilitate the coordination of the various contributing functions to quality. And, not only should the Quality Management belong to the top management, but the entire top management should be committed to quality.

10.10.1. Quality Planning

Just as any management process, quality management also, has three main components. They are: (*a*) Planning for implementation, (*b*) Implementation, and (*c*) monitoring and control. The planning part of quality management, i.e. *quality planning* should deal with the following aspects:

(*i*) To set quality objectives and targets and take into account customer's wants and marketability of the products, etc.,

(*ii*) To carry out pre-production process capability or quality deliverability studies (to assess whether the company is capable of producing and marketing the products of desired quality).

(*iii*) To establish the relative importance of the quality characteristics and specifications, and communicate it to the production line people as well as to the vendors supplying the raw materials. Specifications and drawings can never communicate what that particular specification stands for and why.

(*iv*) To look after various *vendor quality control* aspects such as examining new vendor facilities, their procedures and systems, setting up of the vendor rating scales and periodic performance evaluation of the vendors.

(*vi*) To establish training programs for various personnel in the company so that quality consciousness gains a firm ground in the organization.

In short, designing the desired and deliverable quality standards is the job of quality planning.

10.10.2. Quality Implementation

The implementation part of quality management deals with:

(*i*) Performing laboratory tests and analysis on the raw materials, finished products, and the semi-finished products for acceptance or rejection for process control.

(*ii*) Maintaining quality control equipment (Processes, laboratory and Inspection).

(*iii*) Advising and providing assistance for the clarification and solution of quality management problem in manufacture.

10.10.3. Quality Monitoring And Control

The monitoring and control function deals with:

(*i*) Apprising the quality plan *vis-a-vis* the problems of production and the problems of vendor quality, so that the appropriate action is taken tc correct the initial planning errors.

(*ii*) Apprising quality planning *vis-a-vis* the actual quality which has reached the customer and what the latter's reaction is regarding the product quality; how such reactions can be set right by modifications to the original quality plan.

(*iii*) In addition to performing quality audits, monitoring the costs of quality and providing such information to the quality planners so that they take appropriate action for the future.

10.10.4. Integration of Planning, Implementation and Control Feedback

The organization for quality should ensure that the planning, implementation. monitoring and control feedback cycle is properly facilitated. This is very important, because, quality control is everybody's concern, the organization for quality should be so structured that in making the quality everybody's concern it does not lead to a chaotic situation. In spite of the fact that many functional departments are involved in the maintenance of quality, the integrity of the management feedback cycle should be maintained for effective total quality management. One may delegate certain of the quality management tasks to certain departments. For instance, one may assign the urgent in-process testing and inspection work to the shop floor people. But certain important considerations must predominate to make this decentralization effective enough, e.g.

(*a*) The quality management personnel should periodically check the degree or strictness to which the in-plant quality control procedures are being followed; (*b*) They should also check periodically or continuously the finished product quality; (*c*) The quality management department should provide competent technical support to the shop floor people in helping them to solve day-to-day quality problems; and (*d*) The inspectors on the shop floor should have been trained sufficiently well to perform their jobs properly. These are some of the precautions, which need to be taken for the decentralization of the quality management effort. Whenever there is such delegation, a tight control by quality management is necessary.

10.10.5. Organization

The organization of quality management should be such that it is not a combination of bits and pieces of responsibilities assigned to different departments; rather, quality management should be responsibility which is properly organized and which can be properly located. This leads us to the maintenance of separate functional department for quality management, with its top man ranking high in the organizational hierarchy. The next in the hierarchy to the top man for Quality Management should subdivide the work along the specialized skills required in carrying out the jobs. Therefore, if it is the work of looking after different production lines or if it is the specialized work of looking after different functional specialists within the organization, these special tasks should be assigned to specialist personnel. The organization for quality management should, therefore, as far as possible comprise a large span of control and few levels of hierarchy. This is necessary to maintain quick feedback of information. The wider span of control is necessary; sine a high degree of specialization is very desirable in quality management.

The following points are important to consider in organizing for quality.

(*i*) To ensure that the integrity of the planning, implementing and control feedback cycle is maintained in the total organization for quality.

(*ii*) Whatever the responsibility of quality management is to be delegated to different departments, it should be done with many precautionary measures whereby the monitoring and control is in the hands of the quality management people.

(*iii*) To maintain high quality standards, it is necessary that quality management should have top-management support. Therefore the highest person in quality management should be of the same rank or a level below that of the top-most management of the company.

(*iv*) The hierarchy structure of quality management should be kept to as few levels as possible. The span of control should be as broad as possible. The division of responsibility at the second or third level of quality management organization should be based on the needs of specialized skills, either product-wise, function- wise or technique-wise. Figure 10.6 shows a typical organizational chart for quality management.

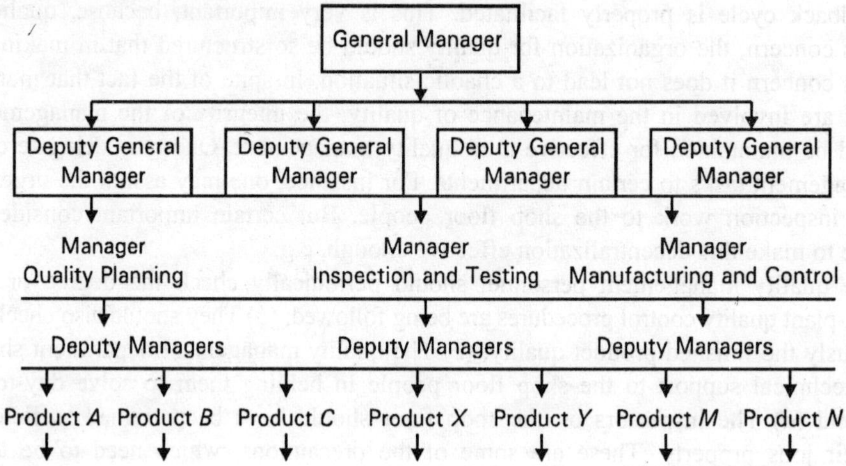

Figure 10.6 : Organizational Chart for Quality Management.

10.10.6. Costs Of Quality

Quality Management is not only concerned with maintaining the quality characteristics of a product but also with doing the same at least cost. What is the cost to improve quality? What will it cost to not improve quality? These are basic questions that manager needs to ask as they focus on the bottom line and company strategic decision. These questions about the cost of quality have served to draws attention to the quality movement. No one will deny the importance of quality, but it is the confusion surrounding the payoff and the trade-off between cost and quality that is unclear to many decision makers.

(*a*) **Cost Of Quality Defined :** The cost of quality has been defined in a number of ways, some of which are:

(*i*) Quality cost equals actual cost minus no failure cost. That is, the cost of quality is the difference between the actual cost of making and selling products and services and the cost if there were no failures during manufacture or use and no possibility of failure.

(*ii*) Quality costs usually are defined as costs incurred because poor quality may or does exist.

(*iii*) The cost of not meeting the customer's requirements i.e. cost of doing wrong things.

(*iv*) All activities that are carried out that are not needed directly to support departmental (quality) objectives are considered the cost of quality.

These definitions leave unanswered the question – How much quality is enough? In theory, the answer is analogous to a principle of economics i.e. basic marginal cost equals marginal revenue ($MC = MR$). That is, spend on quality improvement until the added profit equal the cost of achieving it. This is not so easy in practice. The cost of quality or, more specifically, "non – quality is a major concern to both national policymakers as well as individual firms. Today's quality managers seem to think in the following way.

(*i*) **Higher or Finer quality means higher cost** : Quality attributes such as performance and features cost more in terms of labor, martial, design and other costly resources. The additional benefits from improved quality do not compensate for the additional expenses.

(*ii*) **The cost of improving quality is less than the resulting savings.** This view was originally promoted by Deming and is widely held among Japanese manufacturers. The savings result from less rework, scrap, and other direct expenses related to defects. This is said to account for focus on continuous improvement of processes in Japanese firms.

(*iii*) **Quality costs are those incurred in excess of those that could have been incurred if the product were built or the service performed exactly right the first time.** Adherents of the Total Quality Management (TQM) philosophy hold this view. Costs include not only those that are direct, but also those resulting from lost customers, lost market share, and the many hidden costs and foregone opportunities not identified by modern cost accounting systems.

The attention now being given to the more comprehensive view of the cost of poor quality is a new development. But still many managers ignore or downplay this opportunity because of a continuing focus on production volume or frustration with the problem of computing the trade-off between volume and quality.

One more difficulty is that accounting system does not recognize the expenses as manageable. There are three categories of costs of quality.

(*i*) **Cost of Appraisal :** There are costs of inspection, testing, and such checking operations as are necessary to maintain the product quality. This includes the cost of implementation of quality, as also the cost of monitoring and control.

(*ii*) **Costs of Prevention :** These are costs to prevent the production of bad quality output. This include cost of activity such as quality planning which tries to ensure that proper precautions have been taken to avoid wrong sampling plans being made or bad quality of raw material entering into plant or improper methods and processing being followed in the plant, etc. all of which may lead to bad quality of the finished product.

(*iii*) **Costs of Failure :** In spite of prevention and appraisal, there will still be losses due to rejects, rework, spoilage, etc. to some extent. These, as well as costs of attending to customer complaints and providing product service, are included under the category of costs of failures.

The costs of quality can be analyzed in two different ways :

(*i*) **Category-to-Category Comparison :** Comparing the relative amounts spent on each of the above-mentioned cost categories, i.e. how much is spent on planning? How much on appraisal? And how much on failure?

(*ii*) **Time to Time Comparison :** For instance, comparing one quarter's operation with the previous quarter's operation.

(*b*) ***Analysis of Quality Costs :*** When the latter type of analysis is to be performed, care should be taken to relate the total quality costs to the levels of organizational activity in that period. For example, if the manufacturing activity is increased considerably in the present quarter, it is meaningless to compare straightaway the present quality costs with the previous quarter's quality costs. Therefore, it is suggested that quality costs should be related to a base. The base could be (*a*) number of units produced in a time period, or, (*b*) the net sales for that period, or, (*c*) The total direct labor cost for that period, or (*d*) the value added (net sales minus the direct material cost). Unless the base is selected, the comparison of quality costs from one time-period to the other will be meaningless or baseless. The selection of the base to be used depends upon the particular product characteristics of the organization. For example, *'value added'* is preferred to the net sales when the material cost is a larger part of the sales volume and where the price fluctuations of the materials would distort the 'net sales' base. Also, when there are a number of end products, the basis of 'number of units produced in a period' does not make much sense, because a change in the product-mix would distort the comparison of the quality costs in two different periods. Similarly, the sales have to be properly related to the quality costs. The sales in one period may not have any relation to the costs of quality in that period. The sales lag the production, and therefore, the base of 'net sales' is to be used with a lot of care. After having selected the base, a comparison of the different products or product-lines could be made with respect to the components of the cost of quality. These comparisons for instance, may reveal that the company is spending a considerable amount on failure and on appraisal, and is spending very little on quality planning. In such a case, spending more on planning aspect might bring down the cost of failure as well as that of appraisal.

10.11. MOTIVATION IN QUALITY MANAGEMENT

10.11.1. Zero Defect Programme

The best example of the motivational aspect of quality management could be given by means of the relatively novel ideas generated by the *Zero Defect Program and quality circles*. The philosophy behind Zero Defect is to negate the commonly held views that "to err is human". Instead, Zero Defect philosophy believes in total perfection or *"to do the job right the first time"*. This idea first originated in 1961 in the Orlando Division of the Martin Company in U.S.A, which manufactured Missiles Systems. It was noticed in this company that failures in the Missile System were caused, many a time, by small items costing as $ 1.50. The Zero Defect Program reportedly paid rich dividends to this company. Errors or defects are caused by two factors, i.e. (*i*) Lack of knowledge and (*ii*) Lack of attention. While the former factor can be taken care of by imparting more knowledge, the latter is an attitudinal problem.

10.11.2. Modern Worker Vs Traditional Worker

The main theme behind Zero Defects is that the worker should be positively motivated to achieve as much perfection in his job as possible. The modern worker, as opposed to the traditional worker, is alienated with the product, i.e. he has little pride in his work. The mass production of goods may one of the causes responsible for this. Also achievement, enjoyment and responsibility is lacking significantly in modern workers. Thus, the modern worker resorts to complaints regarding his working environment, wages, and other things.

Motivating the worker to take pride in his job and to do his job as perfectly as possible the first time itself is the heart of the Zero Defects Program.

(*a*) **Means of Motivation :** Motivation is achieved thorough various means, such as posters, publicity, voluntary pledges by workers, visits of customers to the plant, etc. The thrust is on each worker fixing his own defectives reduction goal by himself, not by the supervisor, although the supervisor may help him on his work. Before such pledges and other motivational techniques, it is necessary to generate a good awareness about the product amongst workers, such as, what is the product, where is it used, etc. It is also necessary to generate an awareness of the performance of the product quality in the past. Such an awareness campaign should precede the actual implementation of the Zero Defects Program.

(*b*) **Organization of the Zero Defects Program :** The Zero Defects Program should be a separate activity coordinated probably by an administrator with the help of a number of Zero Defects representatives working in various functional areas and manufacturing departments of the company. The Zero Defects Administrator may report to the Quality Manager of the organization. The top management support is absolutely essential for implementing a radical program such as Zero Defects Program.

(*c*) **Removal of Errors :** For the actual implementation of the Zero Defects Program, in addition to the positive motivation of the worker to do a better job, it is also essential to probe by various means the causes of defects or errors. One such vital component of the Zero Defects Program is the Error Cause Removal campaign. Suggestions are invited from all, in writing, as to how the errors are caused in his/her won work as well as in other areas of work in the company. Of course, not all the causes could be genuine. But the idea here is to encourage all suggestions, because some small things may cause large errors. The Zero Defects administrator, with the help of others might scan these suggestions and implement only a few, but it is necessary that he give positive recognition to all the workers who have shown interest in the company's magazine, or it may simply be a pat on the back. But such feedback to the workers is important to keep up the tempo of Zero Defects Program.

(*d*) **Criticism of the Zero Defects Program :** The Zero Defects Program is, therefore, basically motivational program, where the workers are made more responsible, more achievement-oriented and more proud of their work. It cannot be short-term program; it has to be a long-term program. Because of this, some think that interest in Zero Defects Program may be lost in the long-term. Such apprehensions are not warranted, provided (*a*) the management, including top management itself noted-motivated towards the program, and (*b*) provided that all the important precautions regarding implementing the Zero Defects Program are properly taken care of. To explain the latter, if a company has a large component of bought-out parts in its final assembly, it goes without saying that the Zero Defects Program should be applicable and operating in the vendor organization also. Although many feel that it is conceptually impossible to have zero defects, nevertheless, benefits from Zero Defects in terms of improved quality are substantial in the light of costs associated with the Zero Defects

Program. In many organizations abroad, the benefits-to-cost ratio has been said to be as high as 70 to 1. In addition to the benefits in terms of better quality of product, there are many indirect benefits such as improved industrial relations, better plant utilization, etc. On the whole, the Zero Defects Program, if properly applied, can product results on a long-term basis. In fact, if the management can inculcate the concept/idea of Zero Defects ideology in the minds of its employees from the day of their induction into the organization, and orient their minds through proper training, it is not so difficult to achieve the goals of Zero Defects Program.

10.12. Quality Circle

Whereas Zero Defects Promoters motivation individually, *quality circle* is a collative effort, where 3 to 15 volunteers from the workers form a group and meet regularly, may be weekly or bi-weekly for about an hour, in order to identify, analyze and search for solutions to work-related problems and the ways of implementing the solutions. The meetings, which are generally supervised (usually by a Foreman), address themselves to technical problems and follow a strict problem-solving approach (workers and management are trained in it) so that the meetings do not fritter the time away and become forums to handle grievances. The problem addressed can have its Quality Circles and this should depend largely on the initiative of the workers themselves, with the support and encouragement from the management. Quality Circles should encourage participation by all members and should foster creativity. The idea is to *develop the talents* of the workers and to *develop leadership* besides getting a bunch of good ideas to solve problems by tapping the collective intellect and creative genius of the working staff.

10.12.1. Philosophy Behind Quality Circles

Quality Circle is a Philosophy of *worker's direct involvement* in solving problem, that affect their work, their work output and their work place. It is also a philosophy of *Human Resources Development,* of nurturing and bringing out the human potential. The results of Quality Circle could therefore, only be measured in the long-term although many organizations here and abroad have claimed significant benefits within a short prod of time.

The successes of Quality Circles in Japan are striking and it is sometimes referred to as a Japanese Management Technique. The Circles can be effective here or elsewhere also, if the management commitment to the basic philosophies underlying the concept of Quality Circles is there. This philosophy and commitment takes time to permeate all levels of the organization. Of course this depends upon the already existing organizational climate and culture, and upon the social culture within which a organization has to function. In India, BHEL started its first Quality Circle at its Hyderabad unit in 1980-81. The idea caught on the entire corporation and in two years there were more than 200 circles with about 1800 members. Other companies also followed suit. Some of these are Jyothi, Shriram Refrigeration, Kirloskars, Sundaram Fasteners, Crompton Greaves, Madurai Coats, Bharat Fritz Werner, Essae Industries and Mangalore Chemicals and Fertilizers. The results of the experiment of Quality Circles in Indian Industries are encouraging. The reasons for this, it has seen in the firm commitment and continual supportive guidance by the top and senior managers to the Quality Circles Program. Quality Circle concept may be extended to Production Circle, Design Circle etc. so that the persons in the circles can discuss the problem of a particular activity and come out with a suitable solution. In the present day trend, we can see this concept is used Police Department to solve the problems of law and order, traffic control. This we can witness from the 'Sadbhavana

Meetings" conducted, to involve public in general to solve the social problems. It clearly advocates, involvement of the concerned people for solving a problem will save lot of time and also get a good solution, which is amicable to all.

10.12.2. Indian Experience

It should be noted that, Quality Circles couldn't immediately be imposed on any unit and expect to yield results. Mutual trust, mutual concern for development, and cooperation, if not already exist in sufficient measure take time to build. Circles can help accelerate this building process but the introduction of this potent concept in any organization has to be gradual. Or else, with few initial failures the zeal may not be sustained in the long term.

10.12.3. Factors Influencing The Success Of Quality Circles

Quality Circle is a case where the leadership in bringing about change is taken by workers themselves leaving the management with the new role of an advisor, a catalyst, a facilitator. The labour unions also have to change their traditional concept of leadership style. This change in attitude and in the style of leadership takes time. The management has to get over its phobia of losing the management prerogative of decision-making, and likewise unions have to get rid of the fear that management are trying to undercut their power through this new gimmick. These fears may be far-fetched, because Quality Circles address themselves only to technical problems. But it is also true that Quality Circles are not just a modified version of the old *'suggestion box'*; and is far from it.

For the good work done by such circles, some organizations believe in giving tangible recognition such as monetary incentives. Although recognition is essential, monetary incentive pose tricky problems such as: How much of incentive and how to distribute it amongst the workers? Moreover, monetary incentives may be unnecessary. As a worker from BHEL has pointed out, in Quality Circles the work itself is a reward besides having a safer and improved work environment.

The Concept of Quality Circles is also, reportedly, being experimented in various non-industrial sectors such as hospitals, banks, educational institutions, etc. in India. Professional bodies such as the National Institution for Quality Awareness and the Indian Association for Quality and Reliability have been helpful. The Quality Circle Forum of India has be active in the propagation of knowledge, gained from experience, about the methodology for starting and establishing Quality Circles in the Indian Environment.

Finally, Quality Management is a *total organizational* activity. One has to be quality-conscious at every step of the functioning of an organization, if the organization desires to ensure the quality of its products or services. Quality management is neither an activity involving any of functional area nor is it an activity which ends with the control of the process an the proper selection of raw materials. It is a process encompassing the total management effort of the company. Unless the latter is understood and imbibed, ensuring product quality may not be possible.

10.13. ISO 9000: SERIES OF QUALITY SYSTEM OR ISO 9000 UNIVERSAL STANDARDS OF QUALITY

ISO 9000 is a set of five World- wide standards that establish requirements for the management of quality. Unlike *Product Standards,* these standards are for *Quality Management System*. They are being used by twelve- nation European Economic Community to provide a universal framework for quality assurance – primarily through a system of internal and external audits. The purpose is to ensure that a certified company has a quality system in place that will enable it to meet its published quality standards. The ISO standards are generic in that they supply to all functions and all industries, from banking to chemical manufacturing. They have been described as the *"one size fits all standards"*.

History of ISO : ISO 9000 series of standards on quality system was formulated by International Organization for Standards in order to meet the requirements of internationally uniform quality system. The European Nation trade has reached an understanding that the post 1992 trade transaction would be dealt only with those companies who have registered ISO: 9000 quality system.

The developed countries started producing their own standards for specifying the variety of products manufactured. In 1972, British Standards Institution, United Kingdom published BS 4891 – a guide to quality assurance. This standard was used as basic guidance for companies willing to set up quality systems. It covered the following:

(*i*) Management involvement and objective.
(*ii*) Programming and planning,
(*iii*) Principles of Quality control,
(*iv*) Design and specification Control,
(*v*) Purchasing control and vendor appraisal,
(*vi*) Production Control,
(*vii*) Marketing and service quality function,
(*viii*) Documentation,
(*ix*) Defects and failure analysis and
(*x*) Non-conformance Control.

MIL standards were introduced in 1974. In 1975 BSI published BS 5179 in thee parts drawn from the contents of Defiance Standard 05-21 series. This standard was not written in mandatory term but used by major purchasers for evaluation and selection of their vendors. To met growing awareness of quality in the industries BS 5750 standard was developed by BSI in 1979. Further in 1981, the guides were published for the usage of BS 5750.

International Organization for Standards (ISO) revised and issued BS: 5750 in 1987 as ISO 9000 series of standards on quality system. Since then, many countries have produced their own standards in exact replica of ISO: 9000 series. More than forty countries have adopted them as EN 29000. In India BIS (Bureau of Indian Standards) published IS: 14000 series as quality system standard.

10.13.1. 9000 Series Standards In General

International Organization for Standardization has developed the following standards on quality systems, the corresponding Indian Standards are given in the brackets in chart 10.1.

ISO: 9000 quality standards stipulate certain management practices as guidelines and minimum requirements for making quality of products and services confirming to the needs of customers. These are developed for facilitating international exchange of goods and services. All these systems are essentially self-disciplined standards based on the principles of harmonization of specification and continuous surveillance of the third party.

Chart 10.1 : Structure of quality control standards.

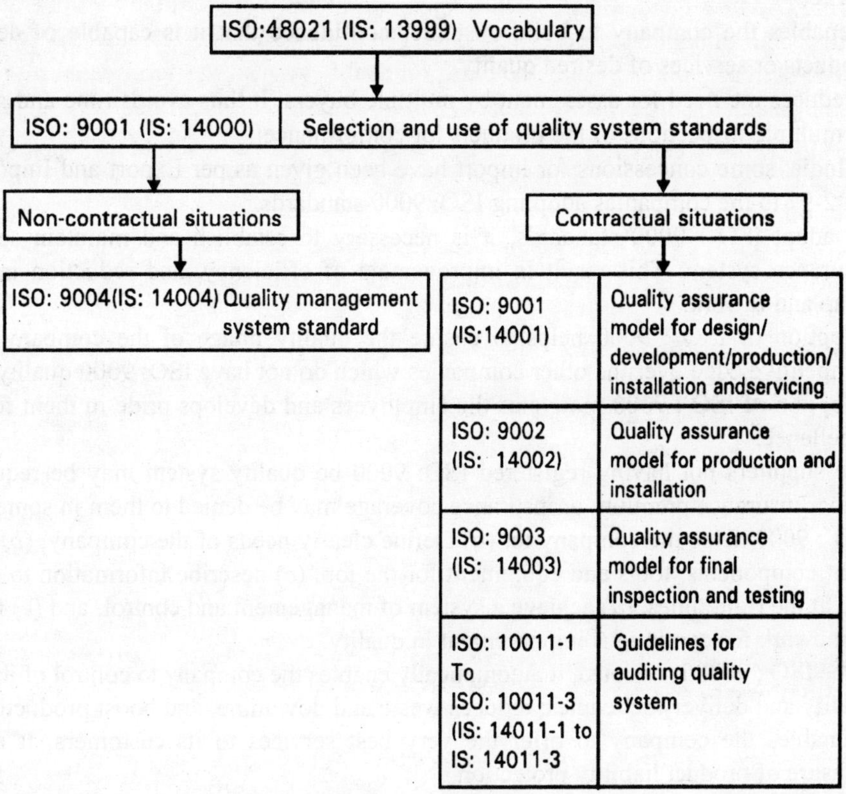

10.13.2. ISO: 9002: 1982 (IS: 14002: 1988): Model For Quality Assurance In Production And Installation

Some products require quality assurance only during production and till they are delivered to the customer / or installed in his premises. ISO: 9002 gives a model quality assurance for such products. In such cases the manufacturer gives his own design to meet the customer requirement and has to only prove the production processes is capable of producing the product / equipment as per the requirements of the customer; and that the supplier can install the product / equipment at the customer's premises satisfactorily. Civil structures, construction of bridge etc. are the examples. So, this model is applicable where the assurance on quality is required only during production and up to satisfactory installation.

10.13.3. Benefits By Becoming An ISO: 9000 Company

(*i*) ISO : 9000 series of standards enable to meet the requirements of an internationally uniform quality system. Countries affiliated to European Free Trade Association (EFTA), have reached an agreement that the post-1992 trade transactions would be dealt with only those companies, who have registered ISO: 9000 quality system. ISO: 9000 is thus recognized internationally as a benchmark for measuring quality.

(*ii*) If Indian Industries adopts the ISO: 9000 standards, it would enhance foreign exchange. So, it is important for the Indian Industries to adopt ISO: 9000 to compete in the international market.

(*iii*) It enables the company to build customer confidence that it is capable of delivering the products or services of desired quality.

(*iv*) It reduces the need for assessment by multiple buyers. It thus avoids time and money spent on multiple inspections of the products for conformance.

(*v*) In India, some concessions for import have been given as per Export and Import Policy of 1992-97 to the companies adopting ISO: 9000 standards.

(*vi*) To adopt ISO : 9000 standards, it is necessary to establish and maintain sound quality assurance system. This result in improvement of efficiency, and reduction in inspection, scrap and rework.

(*vii*) Adoption of ISO : 9000 helps to ensure the quality image of the company and give a competitive edge over the other companies which do not have ISO: 9000 quality system.

(*viii*) Adoption of ISO : 9000 motivates the employees and develops pride in them for achieving excellence.

(*ix*) The suppliers not having registered ISO: 9000 be quality system may be required to pay higher insurance premium or insurance coverage may be denied to them in some countries.

(*x*) ISO : 9000 helps the company to: (*a*) Define clearly needs of the company, (*b*) Specify the right components, tools and equipment for the job, (*c*) describe information to right people and at the right times, (*d*) achieve a system of management and control, and (*e*) It provides a framework for continuous improvement in quality.

(*xi*) Once ISO : 9000 is adopted, it automatically enables the company to control of its production quality and delivery schedules, reduces waste and downtime, and boost productivity.

(*xii*) It enables the company to offer the very best services to its customers. It also gives a measure of product liability protection.

(*xiii*) In business-to-business relationships the organization that applies ISO : 9000 to itself can create confidence about their quality assurance system among its business partners.

10.13.4. Disadvantages (or limitations)

There are few disadvantages of ISO : 9000 series of standards. They are:

(*i*) The implementation of ISO : 9000 series of standards is very much demanding of resources. The formulating and documenting of system is time consuming, and may involve considerable clerical expenses.

(*ii*) Assessment and registration are also expensive.

(*iii*) Unless carefully interpreted and planned, the system can become burdensome and expensive, quite often impending normal operations.

(*iv*) The need to change the attitudes and accept new working practice may strain the management capability of the company beyond its ability to cope.

10.14. INDIA AND ISO : 9000

Indian company is progressively developing towards a free market oriented economy. Indian Industry has recognized the importance of the aspects like productivity, efficiency, quality and competitiveness for long-term survival and entry into the global market. India has launched a vigorous program for implementation of ISO: 9000 in Indian Organization, both in industrial and service sector. As a first step it adopted ISO: 9000 series in 1988 (Initially as IS : 14000 series).

All agencies concerned with quality such as the National Standards Body, Industry association, Government Agencies, Training Institutes, Quality Promotion Agencies and Consultancy Organizations started a nation wide movement to prepare the industry in the application of ISO: 9000. These promotional efforts included quality system orientation programmes, quality surveys, and consultancies services by industry association (like CII) etc.

During the last decade a considerable progress has been made, over 550 organizations in the field of Engineering, Chemical, Textile, Food Processing Industries, Testing Laboratories, Service Organizations and Financial Institutions have already obtained ISO: 9000 certification. The Import and Export Policy 1992-1997 announced by government of India focuses on building international competitiveness in our goods and services. The government initiative to support and promote the quality program and encourage manufactures and exporters to attain internationally accepted standards of quality for their products includes :

10.14.1. Quality Assurance Campaign

The Government is assisting Trade and Industry Association to conduct a nationwide programme on quality awareness and to promote the concept of Total Quality Management and application of ISO: 9000. Most of State Governments have also initiatives and launched sate level programs for propagation of quality management in industry.

10.14.2. Rewards and Benefits

The manufacturers who have acquired the IS / ISO: 9000 or any other internationally recognized equivalent certification on quality system are eligible for special Import license in proportion to the value of their exports.

10.14.3. Incentives For Small Scale Industries

The Government of India has introduced in 1993-1994 a scheme to encourage Small Industries to go for ISO: 9000 certification. The scheme provides a monitory incentive of Rs. 75,000/- for Small Scale Industries for getting ISO : 9000 certification. This includes reimbursement towards certification fee and counseling and training charges. Different State governments are also introducing similar Incentive Schemes.

10.14.4. Up gradation Of Testing Facilities

The Central Government assists the laboratories in their modernization to bring them up to international standards and to adopt ISO : 9000 certification. To ensure that laboratories follow internationally accepted criteria in their operation, a National Accreditation Board has been established for accreditation of testing and calibration laboratories in the country.

In India, the following standard bodies provide guidance and consultancy in connection with adoption ISO: 9000 series standards. They are: (*i*) Bureau of Indian Standards (BIS), (*ii*) Confederation of Indian Industry (CII), (*iii*) National Productivity Council (NPC) and (*iv*) National Center for Quality Management (NCQM).

QUESTIONS

1. Define the term quality and state the various factors which affect the product quality.
2. Distinguish between Quality Control and Inspection.
3. Define the term Quality Control and explain its objectives.
4. Define Total Quality Control and state its functions.
5. Explain TQM operations in brief.
6. What are control charts? Classify them. Explain the difficulties in constructing the charts. What are the limitations of the chart?
7. Explain the Sampling System w.r.t to Quality Acceptance.
8. What is ISO : 9000? Briefly give a note on it?

11

PLANT MAINTENANCE AND MAINTENANCE MANAGEMENT

- Introduction
- Objectives of Maintenance.
- Importance of Maintenance.
- Economic Factors of Maintenance.
- Bath Tub Curve.
- Down time Cost.
- Optimum degree of Maintenance Efforts.
- Duties, Functions and Responsibilities of Maintenance Department.
  Inspection
  Maintenance
  Clerical Work.
- Organization of Maintenance Department.
- Scope of Plant Maintenance.
- Advantages of Good Maintenance.
- Requirement of Good Maintenance.
- Maintenance, Maintainability and Reliability.
- Basic Types of Maintenance.
  Capital Replacement.
  Stand by Capacity.
  Breakdown Maintenance.
  Scheduled Maintenance.
  Planned Maintenance.
  Preventive Maintenance.
  Predictive Maintenance.
- Type of Planed And Preventive Maintenance
- Organizing of Maintenance Work.
- Terotechnology.
- Total Productive Maintenance (TPM)
- Overall Equipment Effectiveness.
- Standard Data For Maintenance.

11.1. INTRODUCTION

A Plant is a place, where men, materials, money, equipment, machinery, etc. are brought together for manufacturing products. In any manufacturing unit, equipment and machinery are very important part of the total productive requirement and the quality of the product depends much on the performance of these things. In modern industrial scene, the presence of highly sophisticated machinery in manufacturing system will bother the manager, when any one of them goes out of order or breakdown. Because of the breakdown of one equipment, may bring the entire system to stand still position. The loss of production hours is a more expensive factor for the unit. Hence, the management must take interest in maintaining the production facilities properly, so that their available time will be more than the downtime. All the production facilities are subject to deterioration due to their use and exposure to the environmental condition. The process of deterioration, if unchecked and unattended, culminates and brings the facilities useless. Hence the management must see that these facilities are checked periodically, repair them or recondition them, so that their useful life is extended. In this context maintenance assumes importance as an *engineering function.* It is made responsible for provision of a condition of these facilities and serve that will permit uninterrupted implementation of plans requiring their use.

11.1.1 Objectives of Maintenance

The objectives of maintenance are :

(*i*) To keep all the production facilities and other allied facilities such as building and premises, power supply system, etc .in an optimum working condition.

(*ii*) To ensure specified accuracy to products and time schedule of delivery to customers.

(*iii*) To keep the down time of the machine at minimum, so that the production program is not disturbed.

(*iv*) To keep the production cycle with in the stipulated range.

(*v*) To modify the machine tools to meet the augmented need for production.

(*vi*) To improve productivity of existing machine tools and to avoid sinking of additional capital.

(*vii*) To keep the maintenance cost at a minimum as far as possible, there by keeping the factory Overheads at minimum.

(*viii*) To extend the useful life of plant and machinery, without sacrificing the level of performance.

11.1.2. Importance of Maintenance

The maintenance act is very important, because the breakdown of any production equipment leads to wastage of production hours to the management and production schedules are disturbed and delivery promises cannot be met with. This is particularly true that in line production, if a piece of equipment in line goes out of order, the whole line will have to remain idle. This leads to diminished productivity. Not only this, in case machines are not properly maintained, and their performance efficiency is low, we get low quality output, which spoils the image of the company. If plant and machinery maintenance is neglected or postponed, sooner or later it requires expensive repair or frequent repairs. Plant maintenance plays a prominent role in production management because the neglected maintenance involves: (*i*) Loss of Production time. (*ii*) Rescheduling of Production. (*iii*) Spoiled material, (*iv*) Failure to recover overheads. (*v*) Need for overtime, subcontracting of work and temporary shortages of work.

11.1.3. Economic Factors Of Maintenance

In cost accounting, maintenance cost is also an element of costs. While calculating the production cost, the cost of maintenance is also considered. Though it does not directly contribute to the cost of production, it can help in increasing the productivity, by keeping the down time of machines at minimum, i.e. available time of productive machines are increased. In fact, Maintenance management is one of the most neglected aspects of management in India. In many Indian industries, (Public or Private), maintenance is given less importance, when compared to the other aspects of management. We can see the working of our Thermal Plants; they are working almost at 50 to 60 percent of operating efficiency. Similarly, we can examine the capacity for which it is installed and the actual production coming out, which shows that the plant is not operating at its full efficiency. If we go though the reports given by national committee, which examined the performance of public sectors, we can understand that even rudimentary preventive maintenance is not followed in may units, which have resulted in large downtime and a loss to national economy. The reasons quoted for the neglected maintenance are:

(*i*) Machine failures are random in nature and cannot be predictable with accuracy.

(*ii*) Maintenance of each failure is different from other failure and hence there is no standard procedure of maintenance.

(*iii*) Any plant or manufacturing unit will not purchase all its production facilities at a time and purchase them as and when necessary. Many a time there will be machines of different makes, which results in a heterogeneous stock of equipment. Hence it will be difficult to have trained manpower and stock of necessary spare parts, which delays the maintenance. In case, if the equipment is imported from some other country, arranging for a spare part is a difficult task, as the quantity required is small or the design of the machine is out dated. It is difficult to apply management principles and generate economies in such cases.

As discussed in the objective of management, above, it is primary duty of maintenance management to see that the availability of machine is increased. One of the basic definitions of *availability* is:

Let T_a = Availability over a specified Period, T_r = Total time of operating in the normal operating state, T_d = Total time for which the plant or equipment is out of operation due to breakdown and being under maintenance or waiting for maintenance, then

$T_a = T_r / (T_r + T_d)$

The availability of the plant can be improved by:

(*i*) Diagnosing the faults and attending them as early as possible, to avoid future loss of time and cost.

(*ii*) To avoid major breakdowns, apply the principles of *preventive maintenance*.

(*iii*) By increasing the reliability of the plant and machinery by proper design of the system.

(*iv*) By adopting proper replacement policy and see that the spares are available when needed.

(*v*) Though it is difficult, try to practice standard procedures in maintenance.

(*a*) **Bath Tub Curve :** If one carefully analyses the failures of an equipment, he finds that the failures in the early stages of installation are many, this is because the equipment has to set itself to the system and the operating characteristics of the worker. A good example for this is suppose you purchase a new two wheeler, you find that you have to visit the mechanic very often in the early stages, because the vehicle may give trouble as it has to accustom to your driving habits. So also, any production equipment. Once the vehicle or the equipment is set to the operating characteristics of the operator, it gives trouble free service for a long period. For Production equipments, the operating efficiency will be around 85 to 95 percent during this period. Due to usage, there will be wear and tear and the equipment or vehicle shows the symptoms of failure. In case they are not attended, it fails and the cost of maintenance after failure will be high. When the machine or vehicle becomes old, the operating efficiency will be around 50 to 60 percent. At this level of efficiency, the productivity will be very less (for vehicles, consumption of fuel is very high); hence it is better to replace the same. This phenomenon is very much similar to the life pattern of human being. During infantry stage, as the baby has to accustom to the external environment, it will cry and proper medical care is necessary. In case care is not taken, the baby may loose its life. Once it gets accustomed to the environment, it will live happily during its youth. As the man grows, due to old age, his working efficiency will fall down and becomes weak and some day ends life. This is shown in the form of a curve known as *Bath Tub Curve* in figure 11.1.

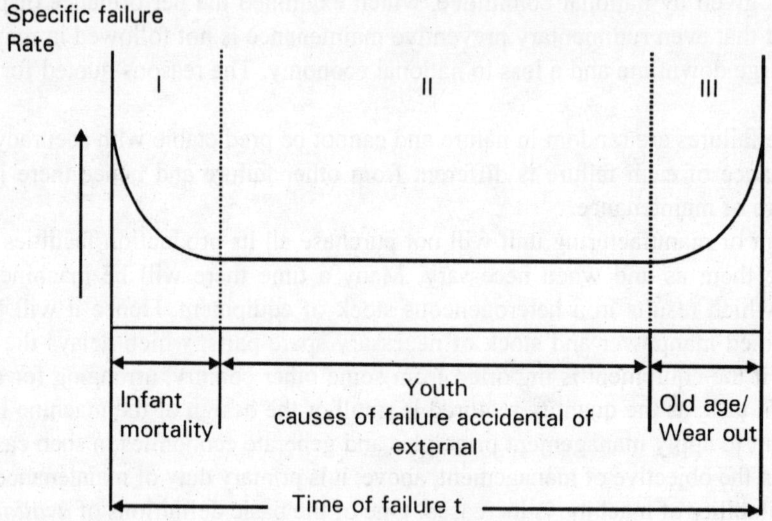

Figure 11.1 : Bathtub curve.

(*b*) **Down Time Cost :** When the machine breakdown and waiting for maintenance, we say the time between breakdown and reset as down time. The cost of down time includes : (*a*) Loss of profit for the period that the machine remains stopped for attention by maintenance, (*b*) Wages paid to the direct workers while they remain idle, (*c*) Depreciation of the machine for the same period of time, (*d*) Overheads proportioned for the period of machine idleness as per the company system of allocating these costs and (*e*) Loss due to scrapping or reworking of material that may be spoiled due to machine breakdown. (*f*) The cost of spares and other materials used for repairs, (*g*) Cost of maintenance labour and overheads of maintenance department, (*h*) losses due to inefficient operation and production (as the machine is not given due care when it has shown symptoms of failure) (*i*) Capital expenditure required for replacement of machine.

Analysis of cost of breakdown and maintenance is important while taking decisions regarding the strength of maintenance staff required, level of spare parts inventory to be maintained, to decide the maintenance scheduled and so on.

Example 11.1. An electro chemical plant uses a catalyst pad made of 10 layers of platinum. The catalyst pad costs Rs. 15,000/-. This pad requires to be reactivated every 4 weeks. The plant remains stopped because of reactivation for a total of 3 hours. The loss of income during this period works out as Rs. 600/- @ Rs. 200/- per hour. There is a proposal to buy a spare set of pad, which would be replaced in the plant, and the pad thus removed would be reactivated while the plant is in operation. This would reduce down time of the plant to 45 minutes. The spare pad would tie up Rs.15, 000/- which represents as annual cost of Rs. 3750/- made up of loss on return from investment in another venture, spoilage and insurance. Should this proposal be adopted?

Solution : Here savings arising from purchase of spare pad = 2.25 × 200 × 13 weeks = Rs. 5,850/-

Annual savings = (5,850 – 3,750) = Rs. 2,100/-

It is economical to buy a spare catalyst pad.

Example 11.2. M/S XYZ Company uses a reciprocating compressor in its plant to boost the air pressure. Air required for the process carries with it oil from this compressor into the pipe where gases are mixed. This oil in combination with oxygen forms carbon deposits which settle in the pipe Carbon deposits constitute an explosion hazard. Consequently the pipe has to be cleaned once in two weeks. The time required for cleaning consists of cooling of the plant, disconnecting instruments, removal of pipe, cleaning, refitting of the pipe and instruments and warming up the unit. The total time required for this is 4 hours and 45 minutes. The plant produces at the rate of 1.5 ton per hour. The product fetches a profit of Rs. 100/- per ton. The cost of labour and overheads of maintenance department, amounts to Rs. 5/- pr hour. A new compressor is available which would cost Rs. 10.000/-. It will reduce the frequency of cleaning to once in 4 weeks. The old compressor can be sold for Rs. 2,000/-. The company works out the cost of equipment @ 25% per annum which consists of depreciation, maintenance and interest. At present, annual capital costs is calculated to be Rs. 500/-. The decision to change the compressor is to be taken. Suppose you are the person concerned, what would be your decision?

Solution : Loss of output each fortnight = 4.75 hrs. × 1.5 tons = 7.125 tons.

Loss of profit each fortnight = 7.125 tons × 100 = 712.50 Rupees.

Cost of labour and overhead each fortnight = 5 × 4.75 = Rs. 23.75.

Total cost per fortnight = (Rs. 712.50 + Rs. 23.75) = Rs. 736.25

Present cost per year = Rs. 736.25 × 26 = Rs. 19,142.50.

Additional capital expenses = Rs. 10,000 – Rs. 2,000 = Rs. 8000/-

Capital cost per year = Rs. 8,000 × 0.25 = Rs. 2000/-

Present capital cost per year = Rs. 500/-

Additional annual capita cost = Rs. 1500/-ds

Annual cost of cleaning after change of compressor = 736.25 × 13 = Rs. 9,571.25

Annual Savings = 19,142.50 – 9,571.25 = Rs. 9,571.25

Net annual savings = 9,571.25 – 1,500 = Rs. 8,071.25/-

Therefore, it is economical to change the compressor.

(c) **Optimum Degree of Maintenance Efforts :** The objective of maintenance is to increase the availability of machine for productive activity. This objective is to analyze economically. That is the maintenance personnel should determine the optimal degree of maintenance effort for each equipment. Figure number 11.2 shows the relationship between cost and degree of maintenance. Low degree of maintenance is referred to extremely haphazard state and high degree of maintenance to a situation where no breakdowns occur.

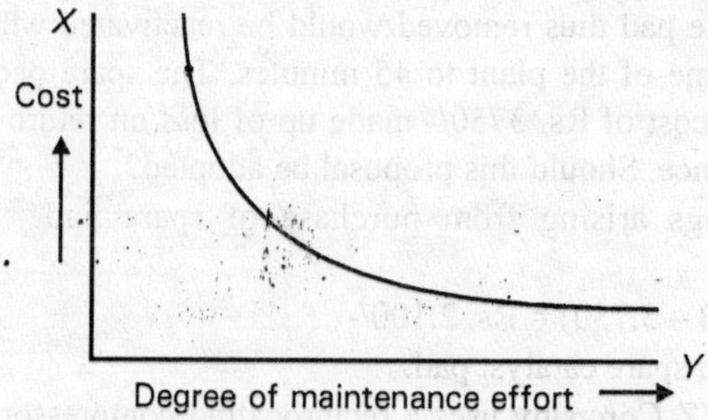

Figure 11.2 : Degree of Maintenance Vs Cost.

11.2. DUTIES, FUNCTIONS AND RESPONSIBILITIES OF PLANT MAINTENANCE DEPARTMENT

Depending on the size of the maintenance department, it has wide range of activities to perform. Plant Engineer or Maintenance Engineer will lead maintenance work and they directly report to the Works Manager. In general the department carries out the following duties.

11.2.1. Inspection

Inspection is concerned with routine scheduled checks of the plant facilities. This includes daily checking of the production facilities and other allied facilities to find out whether they are in good condition or not. In case the situation warns, arrangements may be made for repairs. Inspection also concerned with checking the disassembled components and to find out the extent of repairs and causes of failure. A report is prepared regarding this and submitted to the management, so that management may think in the direction of avoiding failures. Inspection also concerned with inspecting the incoming spare parts.

11.2.2. Maintenance

Maintenance of existing plant, production machines, building, and other service facilities is the duty of this department. It must adopt the proper type of maintenance such as Repair Maintenance, Scheduled Maintenance, Predictive Maintenance and Preventive maintenance depending on the need. This department takes up overhauling jobs also. In some cases it looks to construction also. This department in some cases also does salvaging and disposing of scrap or surplus materials.

11.2.3. Clerical work

Maintenance department will keep the records of stock, maintenance attended, special features of the different types of maintenance and standard maintenance procedures. It also maintains the record of cost incurred in attending a repair. Good house keeping is also the duty of maintenance department.

11.3. ORGANIZATION OF MAINTENANCE DEPARTMENT

At least 50 to 60 percent of investment of any organization is spent on Building and Production facilities. Hence, it is worthwhile to give due consideration for effective maintenance of these items. The maintenance department will looks after the upkeep of equipments, buildings and other facilities.

For effective contribution of its work, the maintenance department must have proper place in the organization and it must also have a good organizational structure. Figure 11.3 shows a typical organization chart for the maintenance department.

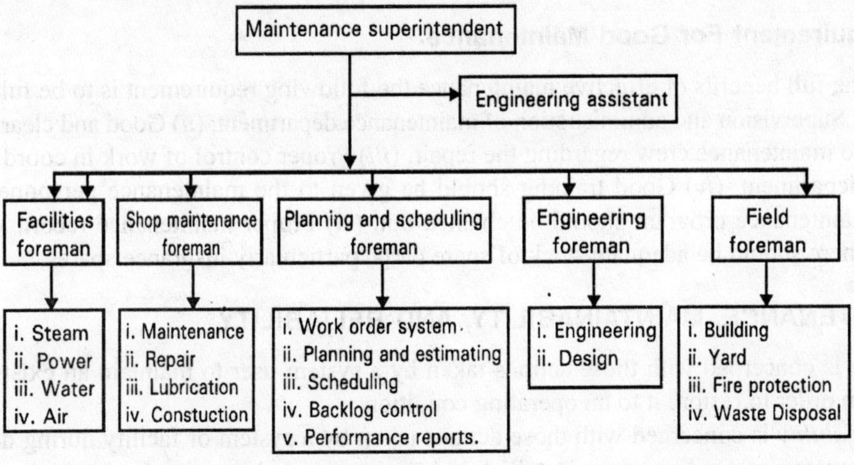

Figure 11.3 : Organization Structure of Maintenance Department.

While organizing a maintenance department one must remember that there should be clear division of authority with little or no overlap. Vertical lines of authority and responsibility must be kept as short as possible. Keep the span of control to an extent of 3 to 6 for a manager. The organizational structure should be flexible. The structure should be designed to suit the types of maintenance work involved. Depending on the need, the maintenance activity may be centralized or decentralized.

11.4. Scope Of Plant Maintenance

The plant maintenance services are a lop sided attention for the maintenance of machines and equipment due to their frequency of use and strategic position in the entire production function. A machine is a mechanism consisting of the services of sequential components, each performing its specific function, which is a part of the whole mechanism. Some parts of the machine are fixed and some are replaceable. Such mechanical devices and their parts need the constant and continuous service like cleaning, lubricating, repairing, replacing, etc, so that their operational efficiency can be maintained. It should be noted that the plant maintenance service is not confined only to the machines and equipments. Under the wide spectrum of the plant maintenance service, the maintenance of the ground, building, power plant, materials handling equipments, transport services, water supply, steam, and gas pipeline, fire fighting facilit8es are also covered. The frontiers of the plant maintenance service also extend to include the provision of maintenance equipments and stocking up of the repair spares and maintenance materials. Thus, it is a broad and exhaustive function, which covers the wide range of production facilities contributing to the production either directly or indirectly.

11.5. ADVANTAGES OF GOOD MAINTENANCE

Following are some of the advantages of efficiently planned and well-executed maintenance program: (*i*) It reduces the down time of production facilities. (*ii*) Reduces overtime bill of maintenance department. (*iii*) Less number of standby equipment are needed. (*iv*) It reduces repair expenditure. (*v*) Due to planned maintenance, lesser inventory of spare parts are required. (*vi*) Safety factor is increased.

11.5.1. Requirement For Good Maintenance

To get the full benefits of effective maintenance the following requirement is to be fulfilled.

(*i*) Good Supervision and administration of maintenance department, (*ii*) Good and clear instructions to be given to maintenance crew regarding the repair, (*iii*) Proper control of work in coordination with production department, (*iv*) Good training should be given to the maintenance personnel, (*v*) Good scheduled maintenance program should be chalked out, (*vi*) Proper maintenance record keeping is a must, (*vii*) There should be adequate stock of spare parts, particularly insurance spares.

11.6. MAINTENANCE, MAINTAINABILITY, AND RELIABILITY

Maintenance is concerned with those actions taken by a system user to maintain an existing systems or facilities in order to restore it to an operating condition.

Maintainability is concerned with those actions taken by a system or facility during development so that the system or facility when installed and operated can be maintained with eases. That is maintainability means design for ease of maintenance. It is a characteristic of system design that determines the ability of a system to be retained in (preventive maintenance) or restored to (corrective maintenance) an effective operational condition. Here the manufacturer of a facility has to take care while designing the equipment or facility, so that the parts/components susceptible to breakdown are easily accessible for inspection and repair during maintenance. This is generally termed as *design for maintenance*.

Reliability is the capability of a system to achieve a standard performance and to maintain that standard for a period of time intended under the operating conditions encountered during the system's up *time*. Maintainability, on the other hand is concerned with the system's *down time*. So, reliability and maintainability are different but complementary engineering disciplines, which determine the system's operational readiness, often called *availability*.

11.7. BASIC TYPES OF MAINTENANCE

Maintenance can be classified as :

(*i*) Capital Replacement,
(*ii*) Provision of stand-by facility,
(*iii*) Break down maintenance,
(*iv*) Scheduled maintenance,
(*v*) Predictive maintenance,
(*vi*) Planned maintenance, and
(*vii*) Preventive maintenance.

11.7.1. Capital Replacement

When an equipment or a facility is installed and start working on it, due to wear and tear, some of its component may loose their operating efficiency and productivity of the facility will reduce. More over the percentage of scrap or rework will also increase. This leads to increase in production cost and affects the quality of the products produced. At that time the maintenance department attends to suitable maintenance of the facility and bring back the operating efficiency of the facility. The efficiency thus obtained may be somewhat less than the previous efficiency. After a considerable period and after several maintenance, a situation will arise, that the maintenance cost will increase and it will be found that efficiency of the machine deteriorate and it will be better to replace the machine by similar or a better machine. Maintenance department must workout an appropriate replacement time for each and every equipment. The reader may refer to a textbook on *Operations Research*, where one can find various replacement models.

11.7.2. Stand-by Capacity

Stand- by capacity is often provided for the items of equipment that critical in production/service system. It is often considered as an economical maintenance practice to install, such spare capacity to be put into operation, while the original unit is under repair or is over-hauled. Production; in this situation, is held up only for the period of time required to switch over from one machine to the other machine. A standby, however, ties up capital. But here criticality of production is more important than the capital tied up. This is particularly true in line production system.

11.7.3. Break Down Maintenance

Here the production facility is run without much routine maintenance until it breakdown. Once the machine breakdown it is taken for repair and inspected to find out the defects. After identifying the defect, the required repair is planned and the spares are procured to repair the machine. As the breakdowns are random in nature and the machine cannot be used during the repair period, production hours are lost hence the productivity is reduced. Repair maintenance is not a recommended practice, in general, but many a time many organizations prefer this, because they do not want to keep the machine idle for maintenance. But they ignore the fact that the break down repair costs more than the regular maintenance practice. It is however, an economical way of maintaining certain non-critical items whose repair and down time costs are less this way than with any other system of maintenance.

11.7.4. Scheduled Maintenance

Scheduled maintenance is a *stitch-in-time* procedure aimed at avoiding breakdown. Breakdowns increase the production costs, by reducing the productivity and are not desirable by management. Sometimes they are dangerous to the life of labour also. Scheduled maintenance practice incorporates inspection, lubrication, repair and overhaul of certain equipments, which if neglected can result in breakdown. Scheduled maintenance practice is generally followed for overhauling of machine, cleaning of water tanks and other tanks, whitewashing of buildings and regular lubricating of movable parts of machinery. This type of maintenance is practiced to a certain extent even in those companies, where breakdown maintenance is otherwise a rule. Pre-determination of dates of commencement of work ensures comparatively better allocation of man-power keeping in view the requirements of production and other activities of the maintenance crew. Mere scheduling however, is not sufficient. It cannot ensure completion of work in time because the nature and details of work required to be done remains unknown., It consequently leads to an increased down time due to non availability of requisite skills and material. In such situations, manpower may also remain idle.

11.7.5. Planned Maintenance

Planned Maintenance is an extension to scheduled maintenance practice. Briefly stated, planned maintenance visualizes the work contained in a future job; determines the best method to be adopted and skills required for its execution; estimates the time, material and costs involved and assign the jobs to individuals or a group of people; programs the work to specific time periods on the basis of priority and after ascertaining production requirements; and arranges for availability of material, tools and man-power and for release of machine in time. Planned maintenance also provides for a system of feed back of information for necessary changes in the original plan.

11.7.6. Preventive Maintenance

A system of scheduled, planned or preventive maintenance tries to minimize the problems of breakdown maintenance. It locates weak parts in all equipments, provides them regular inspection and minor repairs thereby reducing the danger of unanticipated breakdowns. The underlying principle of preventive maintenance is that *prevention is better than cure.* It involves periodic inspection of equipment and machinery to uncover conditions that lead to production breakdown and harmful depreciation. The system of preventive maintenance varies from plant to plant depending on the requirement of the plant. Any company, adopting the preventive maintenance should keep the record of failure of various components and equipment, which help the maintenance department to statistically analyze the failure pattern and replace the item before it fails, so that the breakdown can be eliminated. This reduces the unanticipated breakdowns, increases the availability of the equipment, maintain optimum productive efficiency of equipment and machinery reduces the work content of maintenance job, increases productivity and safety of life of worker.

Production department or maintenance department depending on the size of the plant generally takes up preventive maintenance work. As the preventive maintenance is a costly affair, it is better to maintain records of cost (both labour, materials used and spares used) and a valuation of the work done by the department will show us what benefits are derived from preventive maintenance. The analytical approach to evaluate the work done by preventive maintenance is

(*i*) (Inspections incomplete) / (Inspections scheduled) × 100 should be less than 10%

(*ii*) (Hours worked for maintenance) / (Scheduled hours) × 100 = Performance of the department.

(*iii*) Down time to be given as a ratio of the available hours and to be compared against a standard to be worked out for each company or against a figure of the past. The ratio is given as:
= (Down time in hours) / Available hours (= working days × hours per day × number of machines). Here down time is the total time of stoppage of the machine for scheduled and unscheduled maintenance work.

(*iv*) Frequency of break downs = (Number of break downs) / (Available machine hours)

(*v*) Effectiveness of planning = (Labour hours on scheduled maintenance) / (Total labour hours spent on maintenance). OR
(Down time due to scheduled maintenance) / (Down time due to total maintenance work).

Advantages of preventive maintenance are (*i*) Reduced breakdowns and downtime, (*ii*) Greater safety to workers, (*iii*) Fewer large scale repairs, (*iv*) Less standby or reserve equipment or spares, (*v*) Lower unit cost of the product manufactured, (*vi*) Better product quality, (*vii*) Increased equipment life and (*viii*) Better industrial relations.

11.7.7. Predictive Maintenance

In predictive maintenance, the user of the equipment senses that the equipment is going to give some trouble by hearing to the noise made by the equipment while in operation. For example, consider a two-wheeler. Whenever it gives some uneasy sound, the user immediately stops the vehicle and examines where from the sound is coming. If he can locate it, he takes it to a mechanic and gets it repaired. In case, he neglects it, he may have to face a major repair work. Predictive maintenance makes use of human senses or other sensitive instrument such as: Audio gages, Vibration analyzers, Amplitude meters, Strain gages to predict troubles before the equipment fail. Predictive maintenance extends the service life of equipment.

A best example of all the above said maintenance is our body. We take care of our body by washing our teeth everyday, taking bath every day, drink clear water and eat healthy and good food, so that our availability to day-to-day work is more. This we can call as preventive maintenance. We take oil bath once in a week or a fortnight to keep ourselves healthy and have regular health checkups, which may be taken as scheduled maintenance. Some times we feel uneasy in breathing and slight body pains, we predict that there will be some trouble in near future and hence consult a doctor and get treatment. This we may consider as predictive maintenance. If we neglect all the above, some day, we will be on bed and major medical treatment is necessary to bring us back to normal condition.

11.8. TYPES OF PLANNED AND PREVENTIVE MAINTENANCE

These types of maintenance are carried out either when the plant is running (on line) or when it is taken down as per an agreed schedule when no production is possible. These may be classified as:

11.8.1. Time Based

It means doing maintenance work at regular time intervals – herein the deterioration is linked to time rather than usage. For example, undertaking monthly, quarterly, six-monthly or yearly maintenance work as per the time calendar. Such schedules are easy to monitor. A best example of this may be quoted from maintenance schedules followed in A.P.R.T.C., where we have schedule1, Schedule2, Schedule 3 and so on which are based on time as daily, weekly, monthly etc.

11.8.2. Work based

In this, maintenance work is undertaken after a set number of hours of plant working or processing of certain volume of products on the machine. It is more difficult to monitor. We have to use some kind of auto-counter. For example, servicing a vehicle every 2000 kilometers.

11.8.3. Opportunity Based

This implies doing maintenance work when the equipment is available. For example, doing maintenance work on Sunday or weekly-off days or doing maintenance work outside the normal working shifts.

11.8.4. Condition – based

When condition of the machine is such that if we do not maintain it, it may lead to costly breakdown or equipment failure.

Often, all these types of maintenance operate together, overlap or coincide.

11.9. ORGANIZING MAINTENANCE WORK

In order to facilitate proper control of maintenance work; we must enforce three rules as below.

11.9.1 Maintenance Request

This must be made in writing to a central point in the organization. No work should be carried out without the knowledge and approval of maintenance supervision – if this discipline is not followed by the organization, it leads to wastage of skilled manpower and inability of the maintenance personnel to schedule essential maintenance work.

11.9.2. Maintenance Stores

Non-availability of vital spare parts when required to meet an emergency like breakdown, may lead to excessive shutdown of the plant and equipment. A large number of items or materials are required to be stored and it involves investing valuable funds from the working capital. A proper stores management is essential as a backup service of good maintenance.

11.9.2. Records Of Maintenance Work Done

Paper work for maintenance is crucial for establishing a good maintenance organization and is often neglected. The records of maintenance work carried out from time to time have to be kept equipment wise. History cards or logbooks of all the plants and equipment must be compiled meticulously giving details of materials used, components replaced and time spent by the workforce. Creation and maintaining this database is essential for proper planning and control, which alone will lead to effective and efficient maintenance management.

11.10. TEROTECHNOLOGY

Like most management functions, maintenance work also enjoins a data based management orientation. This has given birth to a new branch of science called *terotechnology,* which is the application of managerial, financial, engineering and other practice to physical assets of the organization in pursuit of total maintenance for total life cycle economy. It encompasses the concept of *'design to discard'* and focuses on improving reliability and maintainability of all physical assets so as to achieve minimum cost per unit of output and may be considered as the precursor to the modern concept of total productive maintenance system.

11.11. TOTAL PRODUCTIVE MAINTENANCE

This is a fresh way to look at our total attitude to maintenance and maintenance management. To be successful with Total Productive Management (TPM), we have to have a complete re-orientation of the roles. Just like *Zero Defects Program in Quality Control,* we can have *Minimum Breakdown Program (MBP).* This may be done by *Safety Circles or Maintenance Circles,* which consists of people from operator and supervisor level to the concerned managers, who meet periodically and chalk out programs to achieve the MBP goal.

11.11.1. Role Of Operator

Workplace is a man-machine-environment system. The operator must take over the complete responsibility of correct operations, changing gears, making adjustments, cleaning, maintenance etc.

of the machine. Roles of worker and equipment are to be combined in such a manner as to produce quality products at reduced costs. Equipment has to be operated as specified in order to maintain accuracy. Operators, maintenance and production personnel have to work together as a team to (*i*) Make efforts to maintain machines in the best condition. (*ii*) Maintain machines in such a way that they perform consistently over a long period of time (to achieve MBP).

11.11.2. Equipment Must Change

When the introduction of TPM, equipment becomes an area of focus. We must clean it properly because when we inspect it, we uncover problems and when we solve problems, it leads to improvement in the machines. Only when we are able to eliminate the problem, we achieve satisfaction, which also imparts confidence. Once the team has succeeded in making changes in the equipment, it changes their attitude to work in general.

11.11.3. People Must Change

The above step-by-step approach is easy to follow and invariably, it leads to recognizing the problems in the equipment and need to solve them. After we correct the trouble in the machine, it implies changes in the equipment to obtain good results. People change only when the equipment is changed – those who cannot or are unable to change the equipment, cannot change their way of thinking. Successful changes brought about in the machines impart confidence among the operators and this sows the seed in them for rethinking about themselves.

11.11.4. Workplace Must Change

Once the equipment is changed, problems in the surrounding areas also start getting noticed – people look more closely at the jigs and fixtures, processes, conditions and management systems etc. Once the workers start noticing problems in their respective areas, it unleashes creative thinking and leads to change in their workplace. The most important aspect of this phenomenon is that the workers start to think and find solutions to problems.

TPM is therefore, a basic concept and style of management. In essence, it is a three-step approach: First change the equipment, then change the views of the people and then change the workplace. When all these are done in a regular pattern we lead to achieve MBP.

10.12. OVERALL EQUIPMENT EFFECTIVENESS

TPM is closely linked to quality and productivity of the equipment and is computed as below:

(*i*) $$\text{Availability} = \frac{\text{Loading time} - \text{Downtime}}{\text{Loading time}} \times 100$$

(*ii*) $$\text{Performance} = \frac{\text{Theoretical cycle time} \times \text{Processed quantity}}{\text{Operating time}} \times 100$$

(*iii*) $$\text{Rate of Quality Products} = \frac{\text{Passed quantity} - \text{Defective quantity}}{\text{Processed quantity}} \times 100$$

As per TPM, the Overall Equipment Effectiveness (OEE) is the product of above three parameters.

OEE = Availability in % × Performance Efficiency in % × Rate of quality products in %

11.13. STANDARD DATA FOR MAINTENANCE

In fact maintenance repairs breakdowns vary from machine to machine and breakdown to breakdown, depending on the severity of breakdown. Hence it is very difficult to build up a standard procedure for maintenance and fix up time standards and work standards for maintenance. Still attempts are made to build up time standards and procedure standards for some type of maintenance work. Time standards indicate the time required to complete a maintenance job. Certain maintenance works like lubrication, can be standardized by time and interval between lubrications. In case maintenance standards are available, they will help the department in planning and scheduling maintenances work and to workout optimal number of workmen required to carryout the job and the incentives to be payable to them.

Owing to the variable and non-repetitive nature of maintenance work, a great deal of technical study is required before the standard data collected and assembled presents sufficient coverage of the work to be effective planning. Standard data derived from *time studies* is probably the most widely used system for applying sophisticated labour control to maintenance departments. For an individual firm, it will be a laborious task to fabricate standard data. But any organization, wants to develop maintenance as standard requirement to support production system, may start maintaining proper records from the beginning and workout standards for certain maintenance work. The best way is to divide entire maintenance job into convenient elements, which are easy to standardize and can build up data. When need arises they can assemble the necessary elements to find the standard time required to complete the job.

However, there are management consulting firms who have assembled standard data banks for maintenance and established programs that are available to clients for installation of maintenance planning and controls. Advantages of using standard data are: (*i*) Consistent estimating of maintenance jobs, (*ii*) Eliminating of delays through efficient scheduling, (*iii*) Improved supervisory controls, (*iv*) Comparison of alternate methods of maintenance, (*v*) Determination of optimal labour requirement, (*vi*) Eases the evaluation of maintenance work.

Use of Network Planning (PERT, CPM), Operations Research models (Replacement Model) and by using computers in record keeping and scheduling the maintenance work will help to carry out maintenance problems more effectively and without errors.

QUESTIONS

1. Define Plant Maintenance. What is involved in Maintenance Management?
2. What are the objectives of Plant Maintenance?
3. What Economic Factors influence Maintenance?
4. What are the advantages of good maintenance?
5. Explain the scope of Maintenance.
6. What are the duties and responsibilities of Maintenance department?
7. How do you distinguish between Maintenance, Maintainability and Reliability?
8. List out the basic types of Maintenance and explain what is Breakdown Maintenance.
9. Explain in detail what do you mean by Breakdown Maintenance.
10. What is Predictive Maintenance?
11. Bring out the significance of maintenance management in the efficient and effective running of operations.
12. Write a note on Terotechnology, and TPM.
13. Describe the parameters of overall equipment effectiveness and what does it measure?

12

VALUE ANALYSIS AND VALUE ENGINEERING

- Introduction.
- Types of Values.
- Value Analysis.
- Value Approach.
- Value Analysis Procedure.
- Causes of Unnecessary Costs.
- Benefits of Value Analysis.
- Difference between Value Analysis, Value Engineering and Value Control.

12.1. INTRODUCTION

Value analysis aims at identification and elimination of unnecessary costs resulting in the increased use of alternative, less expansive material, design, process to provide the same performance, quality and efficiency with decrease of overall unit cost and consequently generate higher profits. Value Analysis is, in essence, a study of function i.e. the function of a component or a material or a service. Everyone has his own definition of value depending on time, place, need or other circumstances. What is valuable to one may be of no value to another. As an individual, one assigns a value to the commodities or services he supply or purchase at a point of time. When he needs the same service or commodity next time the value he assigns may be different. Take for example a fountain pen.

When we have a pen in our pocket and we are going to enjoy an entertainment show, the value we attach to fountain pen may be negligible, as we may not need the use of the pen at that time. But for the same man, when he is attending an examination, the value he attaches to pen is very high. Here value in the sense, what is the *worth* of the object. The money value (price), we pay for purchasing the pen and worth is totally different. Here worth necessarily refers to *use value.* Basically *value analysis* is a cost reduction technique.

During the Second World War, one of the most serious problems faced by manufacturers engaged in the War effort was the shortage of raw materials. This led to experimenting with substitutes, quite often in very unorthodox way. In many cases, the experiment clicked and surprisingly there were a large number of instances where the substitute material was much cheaper and offered more effective service than the original material. After the war, Harry Erlicher, the Vice President of Purchasing Department of General Electric Company (U.S.A.) felt that this problem of finding out substitute could be done in a more scientific and systematic way and as a deliberate approach, rather than by an ad-hoc crisis approach. He entrusted the job to a team of engineers headed by *Lawrence Miles.* In fact, it was Miles who coined the term *value Analysis* and its synonym, *value engineering.* But in the present day context, the term value analysis is applied for analyzing the value of an existing product to reduce the cost and give more use value to the user. Value engineering is applied for the technique applied for increasing the use value and reducing the cost at the design stage of the product. In United States, this technique is very widely used and is given a great deal of importance. In U.S.A Defiance Department insists that Value Analysis should be applied in all contracts in excess of $ 100,000. In India, value engineering is slowly winning the hearts of industrialists and engineers.

12.2. TYPES OF VALUES

Value is both real and imaginary. There are different types of values. They are:

(*i*) *Esteem Value:* It is the desire to secure or own a certain article for status or prestige. OR It is the association of an article with certain people, place or thing.

(*ii*) *Exchange Value* : It is the value that makes the object possible of being traded for other items.

(*iii*) *Use Value:* It is property, which accomplish a use, or a work, or a service.

(*iv*) *Cost Value:* It is the sum of all the costs involved in manufacturing the product (material, labour, overheads etc.).

We can list out other values, such as Moral value, Esthetic Value, Social Value, Political Value, Religious Value. But in this chapter, we are more concerned with *Use value and Cost Value.*

12.2.1. Value Analysis

Value differs from both price and cost in the sense that it is the cost proportionate to the function. This can be written as:

Value or Worth = (Function or Utility) / Cost (i.e. price we pay)

If we want increase the worth or value, either we have to increase the utility or functions of the product with the same cost or by decreasing the cost for the same function. Another way is increase function by a disproportionately low increase in costs. Here function specifies the purpose of the product or what the product does, what is its utility, etc. Function may be classifies as:

(*i*) Primary Function, (*ii*) Secondary function, and (*iii*) Tertiary function.

Take the example of R.T.C. Buses, they are painted with Red color and at the top Cream color. The primary function of the color is to protect the body of the bus from getting corroded from atmospheric conditions. The secondary function is recognition. That is any body can say the bus belongs to R.T.C. The third function is say whether it is express or ordinary.

12.3. VALUE APPROACH

It is an organized system dedicated to every effective means of identifying and eliminating the unnecessary costs. An unnecessary cost is one, which neither adds to quality nor to life or to appearance of the product. Value approach has two elements, namely *value analysis* and *value engineering.*

12.3.1. Value Analysis Procedure

Value analysis discovers new tactical alternatives. It is special type of cost reduction technique, which unlike other methods does not blindly accept the product design. Rather, it critically investigates and analyses the different aspects of materials, design and production of each and every component of the product. A component, to be a part of the product must perform some function and serve some purpose. Value analysis examines the design, function and cost of each and every component in order to produce it economically without decreasing its utility, function or reliability. Value analysis is applied to existing product rather than a new product.

Aims of Value Analysis : The main aim of value analysis is to generate promising and novel ideas of reducing the cost or increasing the utility of a product. This includes (*i*) Simplifying the product, (*ii*) Use alternate cheaper material for manufacturing (without sacrificing the function of the product), (*iii*) Use of efficient and easier methods of manufacture, (*iv*) Reduction of product cost, (*v*) Increase the utility of the product and (*vi*) Save money or increase the profits.

The value analyses team should include personals, from different sections such as: R & D, Purchases, Materials control, Design, Manufacture, Inspection, Packaging, Marketing and Finance departments.

Value Analysis Technique : *Mr. Miles,* G.E.C and his team have framed to conduct value analysis. Each and every component is analyzed in the light of these questions until a satisfactory answer is reached. The questions are:

(*i*) Does the component (or material, or process etc. depending upon the subject of the analysis) contribute value (use value) to the end product?

(*ii*) Does its cost proportionate to its function?

(*iii*) Can some of its features be combined or eliminated?

(*iv*) Would there be a better product or component?

(*v*) Can the component be produced by less costly process?

(*vi*) Can one go for an available standard product or component?

(*vii*) Taking into account the quantity required, is the component being manufactured by using proper Tools?

(*viii*) Does the product have reasonable selling price?

(*ix*) Can the product or component be procured at a lesser price from elsewhere?

(*x*) Is anybody purchasing the product or component at a lower rates?

Value analysis seeks answers to the following questions also which may be asked about a complete product, a component or a process.

(*i*) What must this item or process do? What is the function? The answer may be expressed in one or two words (for example " the paint protect the surface").

(*ii*) What else does the item do? (If the item performs functions that are not needed, then it may be a symptom worth investigating to find out if there is a waste?).

(*iii*) What does it cost?

(*iv*) What else could perform the same function?

(*v*) What will be possible substitute's cost?

It is usually said that one of the most important reasons for the success of Japanese business is the word *"WHY'?* Having a constructive discontent of everything around them it is said is a part of Japanese character. The result is that they want a change. This is exactly the philosophy of Value Analysis. This is well quoted by a poem: "*ours is not to do or die, ours is to question WHY.* Add to this we can add the sequence of questions to be asked: What? When? How? Why? Where? And Who?

Value Analysis Procedure : The basic steps in conducting value analysis are:

A. Blast : → 1. Identify the Product.
→ 2. Collect relevant information.
→ 3. Define different functions.

B. Create : → 4. Create different alternatives.
→ 5. Critically evaluate the alternatives.

C. Refine: → 6. Develop the best alternative.
→ 7. Implement the alternative.

Step 1. The first step is to identify the product for which the value analysis is to be carried out. The product should be one which if redesigned can add to the sales income and would not become obsolete in near future. Value analyses may be applied to the product as a whole or to only some of its component parts.

Step 2. The information relevant to the product may be as follows:(*i*)Technical specifications with drawing,(*ii*)Manufacturing processes, machine layout and instruction sheets,(*iii*)Time study details and manufacturing capacity,(*iv*)Complete cost data and marketing details,(*v*)Latest developments in related products.

Step. 3. Identifying the primary, secondary, and tertiary functions of the product. Specify value content of each function and identify the high cost areas.

Step 4. Knowing the functions of each component part and its manufacturing details, generate the ideas and create different alternatives so as to increase the value of the product. The value analysis team can hold *brainstorming* sessions. All suggestions feasible or non-feasible are recorded without any criticism; rather, persons are encouraged to express their views freely.

Step 5. The different ideas recorded above are compared, evaluated and critically examined, assessed for their virtues, validity and feasibility with regards to their financial and technical requirements. Ideas technically sound and involving lower costs are further developed.

Step 6. Detailed development plans are made for those ideas that appear most suitable and promising during the critical examination (step 5). Development plans comprise of drawings, building of models and conducting discussions with related departments.

Step 7. The best-found idea in step 6 is converted into a prototype manufacture, which ultimately goes into operation, and its results are recorded. The product cost and functional analysis is carried out to assess the net savings as the result of the value analysis.

12.4. CAUSES OF UNNECESSARY COSTS

Value analysis attacks unnecessary costs. It would therefore, be very much necessary to find out how unnecessary costs arise that we may overcome or minimize costs. The reasons for unnecessary costs are:

12.4.1. Lack of Information

Many a time, it so happens that the designers are not so sure of the real needs of the user and over design the product with features that are not used by the user. Another reason is that most of the managers do not have the information regarding the cost involved in manufacturing the product.

Some may say that they have rough idea but they do not know how much rough it is. World is advancing at a fast rate and new technologies, new products, new materials and new processes are coming up at a fast rate and makes the existing one obsolete and hence the costs which were considered satisfactory yesterday are becoming unnecessary today. Because of the fact that there is gap between the advancement taking outside and the flow of information to the manufacturing firm, if value analysis is made on the product in light of new information, in the present cost structure some of the items of cost (material cost and labour charges) may appear to be excess.

12.4.2. Lack of Ideas

A survey conducted in USA has revealed that most of the mangers use less than 5% of their creative ability and say that " We have hardly any time to think". Many people likes to go with the already available tailor made designs, materials, processes, thinking that they need not take any risk and do not bother about new methods and new changes. This is also one of the reasons of over design and unnecessary cost.

12.4.3. Wrong Beliefs, Habits And Attitudes

Most of the people use their judgment more than it is valid and takes all types of wrong decisions. Most of these decisions will not stand a moment's scrutiny, if tested on the anvil of facts, but still we believe them as if they were taken out of the holey book. Some of typical statements very often made by such people are:

(*i*) "It will not set a nasty precedent".
(*ii*) "It won't work".
(*iii*) "Costs too much".
(*iv*) "The public won't touch it".
(*v*) "It is impracticable".
(*vi*) "The production department will have none of these".
(*vii*) "Why change it? It works".
(*viii*) "There is no other source of supply".
(*ix*) "That is not our responsibility".
(*x*) "The management will not accept it".
(*xi*) "It is company's policy".

Wrong beliefs, such as above stated statements, suppress the cost reduction idea before they are tested and installed and unnecessary costs will continue to be incurred.

12.4.4. Changed Circumstances

Everyone likes progress but hardly anyone wants change, especially of that change that affects him or his work. Circumstances might have changed, yet one likes to be conservative and continue the same features of previous years. As an example of this, we can see in our post office, very old methods of record keeping is still followed, in spite of advent of computers. We can find many such examples in our day-to-day life.

12.4.5. Resistance to Change

In any organization or group of people, we can find people who resist any change in the work. These individuals, knowingly or unknowingly, will use every means at their command to resist change. It is important to be able to recognize roadblocks and then take steps to overcome them. Some typical restrictions and possible ways of tackling them are s follows:

(*i*) "We tried this a couple of years ago but it was not successful". (Conditions change. Why not try again now?)

(*ii*) "It can't be done". (If it has not been tried how does one know?)

(*iii*) "The customer is satisfied with the price as it is". (If this is so, he will be more satisfied and so will many others if the prices are reduced.)

(*iv*) "Sampling is not as accurate as 100% inspection". (This is not always true, but in any case, does it need to be that accurate?)

(*v*) "This way processing would produce too many rejects to the specifications" (Then, are the design limits too tight?)

(*vi*) "There is no other technique". (Have you looked for one?)

People have a natural resistance to change, which may be further conditioned by experience, but favorable experience will help to reduce the resistance.

12.5. BENEFITS FROM VALUE ANALYSIS OR ADVANTAGES OF VALUE ANALYSIS

There are several direct and indirect benefits which accrue from the introduction and practice of Value Analysis. Some of these are:

(*i*) A reduction of cost of existing products or systems.

(*ii*) Prevention of unnecessary cost in new products or systems. These two are quantifiable and can be easily measured.

(*iii*) The introduction of Value Analysis leads to overall cost consciousness and a general attitude change towards costs.

(*iv*) Product value gets improved and the quest for new materials and processes gets encourage, it provides a great boost for import substitution.

(*v*) Systems relating to cost and estimating usually benefit from reorganization necessitated by wider use of cost information.

(*vi*) A greater return on investment results (Greater profits).

(*vii*) Value analysis is a much faster cost reduction technique.

(*viii*) It requires little expenditure because the value analysis team can be formulated out of the staff available in different sections.

12.6. DIFFERENCE BETWEEN VALUE ANALYSIS, VALUE ENGINEERING AND VALUE CONTROL

12.6.1. Value Analysis

Value Analysis is a technique that is used to avoid unnecessary cost and improve the utility of the existing product.

12.6.2. Value Engineering

Value Engineering is the application of the concepts of value analysis at the design or pre-manufacture stage of the component part with a view to cut down the unnecessary costs, without impairing the function or utility of the product.

12.6.3. Value Control

Value control means controlling the value of a product; either by reducing its cost for the given function or by increasing its utility for the given cost.

QUESTIONS

1. Define Value Analyses. Distinguish between Value Engineering and Value Analysis.
2. Explain the steps of Value Analysis.
3. What are the advantages derived from Value Analysis.
4. What are the causes of unnecessary cost?
5. Conduct Value Analysis on the toothbrush you use every day.
6. Explain the different types of values.

13

MATERIALS MANAGEMENT AND INVENTORY CONTROL

13.1. INTRODUCTION

One of the basic functions of management is to employ capital efficiently so as to yield the maximum results. This can be done in two ways or by both : 1) By maximizing the margin of profit; or 2) by maximizing the productivity i.e. maximizing the production with a given amount of capital. That is management has to utilize its capital optimally. However, this is all too often forgotten and much time is ingenuity is devoted to make only labour work harder. In the process, the capital turnover and hence the productivity of capital is often totally neglected. Several new techniques have been developed and employed by modern managers to remedy this deficiency. Among these, *Materials Management* had become one of the most attractive.

Materials management is a body of knowledge, which helps the manager to improve the productivity of capital by reducing material costs, preventing large amounts of capital being locked up for long periods, and improving the capital- turnover ratio. The techniques of materials management were evolved and developed during and after the Second World War and have helped the more industrially developed countries to make spectacular progress in improving productivity.

Materials management is a comparatively new concept in our country. In early sixties, managers in India changed their attention towards the materials management. Until early sixties, they were concentrating on items such as purchasing, transporting, storekeeping. Since two decades, that an increasing understanding of the importance of materials management is slowly finding its way among management circles in India. Since last five years, materials management has been recognized as a major functional area of management. In western advanced counties this field of management has been recognized as most powerful area in increasing capital productivity and increasing the profit margin.

Materials management covers all aspects of material costs, materials supply and utilization. It covers the whole range of functions involved in converting raw materials and ancillary supplies into finished products. It is concerned with the planning and programming of material and equipment; market research for purchases; pre-design value analysis; procurement of all materials including capital goods, raw materials, components and assemblies, finished goods, packaging and packing, stores control and inventory control; transportation of materials; materials handling; value analysis; disposal of scrap and surplus; salvage; and operations research for materials. Many managers many a time refer materials management to inventory control or materials handling or material control. But materials management covers a wider area regarding materials. Though materials management is a widely accepted term, some organizations use 'supply management' and specially, defense organizations use logistic management, which is concerned with the functions of materials management.

While the field of materials management covers all aspects of material costs, supple and utilization, opinion is divided as to what function should be included under the unified direction of the materials manager. The question here is what should be the scope of materials management? And what functions should be included under the duties of materials manager. It is up to an organization to allocate the functions to the materials manager. Some companies, can allocate even production Control also under material manager, because of entire production is involved with utilization of materials and materials cost play a major role in the cost of production.

The importance of materials management arises from the fact that materials account for 60 to 65 percent of the sales value of a product, that is to say, from every rupee of the sales revenue, 65 paise are spent on materials. Hence, small changes in material costs can result in large sums of money saved or lost. Materials management should, therefore, be considered as a function of prime importance for our industrial economy. Materials costs form the bulk of the total cost of a manufactured product. A survey in India revealed that in major industries the materials cost on an average works out to 64 paise per rupee, the balance of 36 paise being accounted for by wages and salaries, overheads and profits. In material intensive production industries, the share of materials cost may be still higher. If we take material carrying charges, procurement charges into consideration, the percentage may be still higher. Materials management provides tools and techniques, most of which are very simple, to reduce material costs substantially. As a large chunk of the revenue i.e. 64% is exposed to these techniques, correspondingly larger savings result when they are applied than when attempts are made to save on other items of expenditure like wages and salaries, which are about 16%, or overheads which may be around 20%. As the resultant savings are of a recurring nature, the advantages gained are enormous and lasting. In addition to this savings, efficient materials management also brings a substantial reduction foreign exchange or reduced value of imports. Industrial managers have been slow in appreciating the importance of materials management as they have been preoccupied with other maters such as finding news markets, labour problems and so on. Materials management brings about increased profits without any trouble from labour or any other source. It results in increased productivity of capital by preventing large amounts of capital being locked up for long periods in inventories.

13.1.1. Objectives of Materials Management

Materials management function is a staff function and it has to support the objectives of the undertaking as a whole they are: (*i*)Survival and Growth, (*ii*) Maximum satisfaction to customers, (*iii*) Good working conditions to employees, (*iv*) Technological lead over competitors. In addition objectives of materials management are:

(*i*) Maintaining continuity of productive operations by ensuring a uniform flow of materials,
(*ii*) Reducing materials cost by using systematic inventory control techniques,
(*iii*) Releasing working capital for productive purposes, by efficient control of inventories.
(*iv*) Increasing the competitiveness of end products by ensuring right quality at right price in both national and international markets.
(*v*) Saving foreign exchange through economic use of foreign purchases and import substitutes.
(*vi*) Establishing good buyer and seller relations.
(*vii*) Ensuring low departmental costs and high efficiency, and
(*viii*) Setting high ethical standards.

By careful financial analysis, it can be shown that a 5% reduction in material costs will result in increased profits equivalent to a 36% increase in sales. Reduction of materials cost is more preferable by a manager than achieving an increase in sales. To increase sales, lot of efforts are to be made and as it deals with external environment and uncertainties, it will be easier to tackle the problem of reducing the materials cost.

13.2. METHODS OF INVENTORY CONTROL

After considering the importance of materials management, now it is worthwhile to consider some of the important methods of controlling inventory. They are discussed below:

13.2.1. A-B-C Analysis

A-B-C analysis is a basic technique of materials management and is recognized as the starting point of materials management. The applicability of this technique extends over almost all aspects of material management, such as purchasing, receiving and inspection of materials. In fact, this technique can be applied to any aspects of a business or individual problems to control the cost. The origin of ABC analysis is PARETO'S 80 – 20 rule. This rule says that 80 percent of county's economy is controlled by 20 percent of people. If we apply this rule to verify its correctness, the results say that it is correct. Let us consider some examples.

(*i*) List out all the expenses we do over a period of time and arrange them in the order from highest to the lowest. Find the total of expenses and workout percentage of each with respect to the total. We see that only 20 percent of items consume 80 percent of our expenses.
(*ii*) We have 24 hours in a day. List out the times you have spent on each activity and arrange them in descending order, workout the percentage, we find that 20% of items covers 80% of time.

(*iii*) Take the example of any office and conduct ABC analysis on the salary bill of the office, we find that 80% of the bill refers to 20% of the staff and rest 20% to others. Like this, we can apply the principles of ABC analysis to any aspects of business or life.

ABC analysis, VED analysis, FSN analysis and periodic revision classification comes under *Selective Management control.* The principle of Management by Exception is a better term under which we can classify ABC analysis. Items of Inventory are classified into A-B-C, or other class for *Selective Management Control.* Controls applied *selectively* to contribute to a better management, in most cases avoiding wastages of precious management time and, importantly avoiding the confusion resulting from excessive controls. The degree and characteristics of controls to be exercised by the management should depend upon: (*i*) The necessity of control, (*ii*) The relative necessity of the martial to be placed under control, and (*iii*) The particular characteristics of the maternal.

Materials may be divided into three categories or three classes for selective management control. More grades than this may not give fruitful results. These three grades in which materials are classified is known as A-Class materials, B-Class Materials and C- Class materials. In fact any items under classification may be classified like this. In reality A, B, C stands for three different classes. But many a time this classification is known as Always Best Control._ABC Analysis is based on the relative importance of the materials. Therefore there are various bases for ABC classification. They are *material price, material's criticality, Availability status of materials, Material's physical characteristics such as size and weight, frequency of material's usage etc.* Depending on the situation and importance of above said characteristics, classification is made. Conventionally, however, the basis for ABC analysis is the basis is '*Annual consumption value*' of the material. Here one should understand clearly, that annual consumption value does not refers to the unit price of the material and it refers to the annual consumption value. For example, consider the firm is using a component whose unit cost is Rs. 1000/-. It uses 3 units in a year. Hence the annual consumption value is Rs. 1000 × 3 = Rs. 3000/-. Consider another item the firm is using is a bolt, whose unit price is Re.1/-. The quantity used in a year is 10,000 units. Hence the annual consumption cost works out to Rs. 10,000/-. Here the bolt is considered to be high consumption value item. It has been found in many industries, that a small number of items account for a large proportion of the annual turnover (money) of the inventory. These items should attract the Materials Manager's attention immediately. Such items are known a 'A' Class items. It is also observed in industries that very large number of items of inventory accounts for a small portion of the annual turnover or annual consumption value of the materials. *There are many items contributing very little to the ultimate problem of managing the working capital investment.* Naturally, materials manager should turn his attention to those items only after he has *taken care of* high annual *turnover* items i.e. 'A' class items. *Such items are classified as 'C' class items.* Class 'B' items belong to the in-between categories; neither their total consumption value high nor the total numbers is high. The above-discussed phenomenon occurs in almost all industries, and therefore, the conventional ABC classification can be applied in most of the industries.

Procedure for ABC analysis : (*i*) List out all the materials used in the company. (All types of materials are to be considered, whether they are used for manufacturing product or they may indirect material). (*ii*) Work out their annual consumption value, which is given by: Number of units used in a year × Unit price. iii, Arrange all of the items in the descending order of their annual consumption value. (*iv*) Add all the consumption costs and get the total annual inventory cost. (*v*) Write the cumulative consumption value and find the percentage of this cumulated consumption value to total inventory value. Note down this percentage against the item. (*vi*) Write a was line at 70 % and 90%. (*vii*) All the items, which falls under 70%, are 'A' class items, items those falls between 70% and

90% are 'B' class items and others, which are between 90% and 100%, are 'C' class items. Figure 13.1 shows graphical representation of ABC analysis

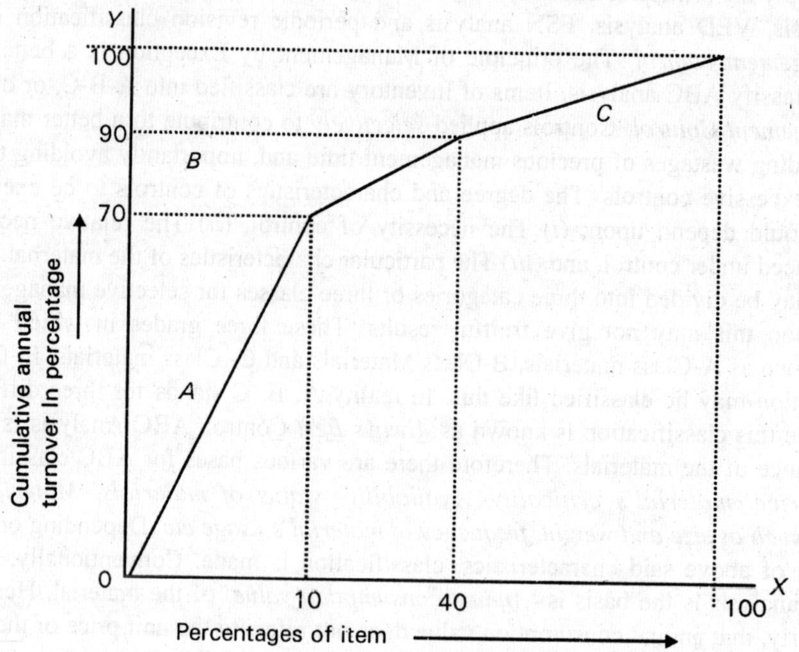

Figure 13.1 : A-B-C analysis.

Problem 13.1. 20 items stocked in a firm is given below. Other particulars such as annual consumption value etc are given in descending order. Draw ABC curve.

Item No.	*Cumulative % of items %*	*Annual consumption units*	*Unit price in Rs.*	*Annual consumption value in Rs.*	*Cumulative percentage %*
1	*2*	*3*	*4*	*5*	*6*
1	5	100	400	40,000	40.00
2	10	500	60	30,000	70.00
3	15	200	75	14,000	84.00
4	20	25	200	5,000	89.00
5	25	25	100	2,500	91.50
6	30	65	20	1,300	92.80
7	35	50	25	1,250	94.05
8	40	50	20	1,000	95.05
9	45	30	30	900	95.95
10	50	50	14	700	96.65
11	55	20	30	600	97.25
12	60	90	05	450	97.70
13	65	40	10	400	98.10
14	70	35	10	350	98.45

Contd.

15	75	20	17.50	350	98.80
16	80	50	6	300	99.10
17	85	100	3	300	99.40
18	90	25	10	250	99.65
19	95	20	10	200	99.85
20	100	25	6	150	100.00
			Total :	**1,00,000**	

In the above table second column shows cumulative percentage of total items and column number 6 shows cumulative percentage of percentage of annual consumption cost with respect to total cost of inventory. In the table **10 percent** of the items (Column Number 2) consumes **70 percent** of annual consumption cost. Item number 3 to 5 i.e. another **15% of the items** cover **20 percent** of annual consumption cost. From item number **6 to 20 i.e. 75% of items** consume only **10 percent** of the annual consumption value. First 10% of items are known as A class items, second 20% of items are known as B class of items and the last 75% of items are C class items. It shows that by exercising control over first two items, we are exercising the control over 70% of inventory cost. Even if you save 10% of the value, it is substantially handsome savings. Hence top level managers are involved, while purchasing A class items, middle level managers are involved, while purchasing the B class items and C class items are purchased in bulk by lower level personnel, like store keeper.

Problem 13.2. Management of a company has the following information about its inventory stock. Find the percentage of items management should place in each class according to the ABC classification method.

Item number	*Annual usage (number of pieces)*	*Unit price in rupees*
1	600	20
2	5,600	30
3	60	20
4	2,200	10
5	80	10
6	4,400	20
7	300	10
8	1,600	10
9	1,200	30
10	160	20

Solution : First step is to calculate annual consumption value and rank them. Afterwards they are arranged in descending order and cumulative percentages are worked out. This is shown in the following two tables.

We see that only two items will be A class items and 6 are B class items and rest will be C class items.

Item number (1)	*Cumulative percentage (2) (number of pieces)*	*Unit price in Rs. (3)*	*Usage value in Rs. (4) 2 × 3 = 4*	*Ranking (5)*
1	600	20	12,000	6
2	5,600	30	1,68,000	1
3	60	20	1,200	9
4	2,200	10	22,000	4
5	80	10	800	10
6	4,400	20	8,800	2
7	300	10	3,000	8
8	1,600	10	16,000	5
9	1,200	30	36,000	3
10	160	20	3,200	7

Item number	*Cumulative percentage of items*	*Cumulative usage value in Rs.*	*Cumulative percentage of usage values*	*Category*
2	10	1,68,000	47.97	
6	20	2,56,000	73.10	A
9	30	2,92,000	83.38	
4	40	3,14,000	89.66	
8	50	3,30,000	94.23	B
1	60	3,42,000	97.66	
10	70	3,45,200	98.57	
7	80	3,48,200	99.43	
3	90	3,49,400	99.77	
5	100	3,50,200	100.00	C

13.2.2. Periodic Revision Of Classification

ABC classification depends not only on the value of unit, but also on the number of units consumed over the year. Because, in this classification, we are dealing with the annual consumption value. Therefore, if the value of item were to increase or if the amount of annual consumption of the item were to increase, the annual consumption value of the item would increase. Hence the classification of an item may change from one class to other. This is to say that ABC classification is not done once and for all time, the classification needs to be monitored periodically and any change need to be incorporated accordingly. A proper ABC analysis will lead to better control over materials and consequent reduction in costs associated with inventories.

13.2.3. VED Analysis

In addition to the intrinsic or market value of materials, which is invested in the materials, there is sometimes a *nuisance* value to the materials. In ABC analysis, we have seen that annual consumption value; quantity of material consumed and the unit cost plays a vital role. This is to say that *ABC Analysis deals with the annual consumption value of the item due to their presence and not any other aspect such as the criticality of the martial or the nuisance value.* The nuisance value is the cost associated with materials due to their absence. Some of the materials are important by their absence and not merely by their presence. In case they are not available, the whole production system may come to standstill and involve high cost of loss of production. Here the cost of the item is not the question, but the availability is the matter. The investment in these materials may be small but for non-availability of the item the costs or losses that the company going to involve will be very high. These are critical items, which are required in adequate quantity.

With the above discussion, we can understand that materials may be classified depending upon their criticality, i.e. on functional basis. The degree of criticality can be stated as whether the material is **vital** to the process of production, or **essential** to the process of production or **desirable** for the process of production This classification is known as **VED** analysis, **V** stands for *vital,* **E** stands for *essential* and **D** stands for Desirable items. In addition to the conventional ABC analysis, VED analysis also plays an important role in materials management. VED ranking may be done on the basis of the shortage costs of materials, which can be either quantified or qualitatively expressed.

(*a*) **Combination of ABC and VED Analysis :** ABC and VED analysis, used for classification, one depending on the consumption value and the other on the criticality of the item both are important. In case we combine the both and classify the materials depending both on the consumption value and the criticality, it will give us a fruitful result. This can be made in nine ways, which is shown in the matrix given below:

	V	E	D
A	AV	AE	AD
B	BV	BE	BD
C	CV	CE	CD

ABC – VED classification Matrix.

	V	E	D
A	90%	80%	70%
B	95%	85%	75%
C	99%	90%	80%

ABC-VED Matrix showing service Levels.

This type of classification helps the management to decide the materials policy and what service levels are expected to see that no difficulty is faced. An item belongs to both V class and A class, is costlier (more annual consumption), at the same time of higher criticality, the management should see that it should be available any time the need arises and the stock levels to be controlled properly to see that inventory carrying costs are kept under control. The service levels to be maintained are shown in the matrix for various combinations.

(*b*) **Fast Moving, Slow Moving And Non-Moving Analysis : (FSN Analysis)** This analysis relates to the demand for the materials and stock-moving pattern. Fast moving materials are to be stocked nearer to the store keeper and slow moving materials are stocked at a considerable distance and the non-moving materials are stocked in a place without causing inconvenience to day-to-day movement of men and materials. Similarly, Fast moving materials must be kept in a place easily reached by the storekeeper. Non-moving materials are kept in a remote place, as they are required for use. This analysis will help for optimal utilization of space available and materials handling time of the storekeeper.

In addition to the above analysis, we can also use some of the characteristics of material for classification. For example, *perishable or obsolescence.* These characteristics are particularly helpful for chemicals and drugs, which have low shelf life. Here classification is made on the basis of shelf life as long shelf life, medium shelf life and short shelf life. This classification is known as **PQR** classification. Sometimes the bulk versus weight of the materials is of importance in terms of providing space for the materials in the stores, and therefore another classification i.e. **XYZ** classification is used. Here the classification is bulky, medium bulky and not bulky materials.

13.3. QUANTITTIVE METHODS FOR INVENTORY CONTROL

In this section, we shall see types of inventories, necessity of maintaining inventory, costs associated with inventory, and certain inventory models used to maintain inventory costs at minimum. In addition, let us also discuss, spare parts management, Material requirement planning and certain latest concepts with regards to inventory. For more details, readers are advised to refer to a book on Operations Research.

13.3.1. Types of Inventory

Inventory consists of usable but idle resources, such as men, machines and materials and money. When resource involved is material, the inventory is also called stock. When we talk of men, we call it is Human resource. When we deal with living being, other than men, we call it live stock inventory and when it is money, we deal with management of funds. In this chapter, we are much concerned with the materials only. An inventory problem is said to exist if either the resources are subjected to control or if there is at least one such costs that decreases as inventory increases. The objective is to minimize total (actual or expected) cost. However, in situation where inventory affects demand, the objective may also be to maximize the profit.

Inventory may be classified as :

(*i*) ***Raw material inventory :*** which is used in manufacturing. When the demand arises, they are drawn from stores and processed or use value is added during the process and finally finished product comes out.

(*ii*) ***Semi finished goods :*** When the material being processed, it may have to wait between two process, such material are known as semi finished goods or semi finished material or Work in process inventory.

(*iii*) ***Components :*** The parts used in assembly of product, are known as components. When these components are purchased from outside, it is known as bought out components or bought out material.

(*iv*) ***Spare Parts Inventory :*** When a manufacturing or servicing facility breakdown, it is to be repaired. In such case, the defective or worn-out parts of the machine are to be replaced by new one. These new parts of the machine are known as spares or spare parts.

(*v*) ***Obsolete inventory :*** When any facility becomes unserviceable, and it is to be replaced by a new one, after replacing, the old machine/facility is to disposed. Such machines, which have become useless, are termed as obsolete inventory.

(*vi*) ***Waste, Scrap and rejects :*** This type of inventory occurs in manufacturing firms or in service organizations. While processing material, chips are produced and it is of no use for the organization and it is to be disposed. Similarly, defective components, which cannot be reprocessed (rejects) and materials which cannot be used in any way in the organization (waste), all these are to be disposed. They may not be having any use value for the organization, but they may be reprocessed by some other organizations to produce a useful product.

13.4. NECESSITY FOR MAINTAINING INVENTORY

Though inventory of materials is an idle resource (as they are not used immediately and stocked for future use), almost every business must maintain it for efficient and smooth running of its operations. If an enterprise has no inventory of material at all, on receiving a manufacturing order, it will have to place order for purchase of raw material, wait for arrival and receive of material and then start production. The customer will have to wait for a long period for the delivery of his product and may get frustrated and turn to another manufacturer. Maintaining of inventory becomes necessary for the following reasons :

(*i*) It helps in smooth and efficient running of the production system and the enterprise. It decouples the production from the customers and vendors and simplifies the otherwise complex organization for manufacture and reduces the co-ordination effort.

(*ii*) It provides services to the customers at a short notice. Timely deliveries may increase the goodwill of the company.

(*iii*) In the absence of inventory, the enterprise may have to pay very high prices because of piecemeal purchasing. Maintaining inventory may earn price discounts on bulk purchases. It also takes advantage of favorable market.

(*iv*) It reduces the product cost, since there is an added advantage of batch production and mass production runs.

(*v*) It acts as a buffer stock when raw materials are received late and shop rejects are too many.

(*vi*) Process and movement inventories (also known as pipeline inventories) are quite necessary in big enterprises where significant amounts of time are required to tranship items from one location to another.

(*vii*) Bulk purchases reduce the number of orders and hence less clerical work.

(*viii*) As many of customers and vendors are away from the organization, it is better to have stock of inventory to continue production during the lead period.

(*ix*) It helps in maintaining economy by absorbing some of the fluctuations when the demand for an item fluctuates or is seasonal.

However, too often inventories are wrongly used as a substitute for management. For example, if there are large finished goods inventories, inaccurate sales forecasting by marketing department, may never be apparent. Similarly, a production Forman who has large in process inventories may be able to hide his poor planning since there is always something to manufacture. Furthermore, inventory means unproductive and *tied up* capital of the enterprise. The capital could be usefully utilized in other venture as well. With large inventories there is always likelihood of obsolescence too. Also maintenance of inventory costs additional money to be spent on personnel, equipment, insurance, etc. Thus excess inventories are not desirable. This necessitates controlling the inventories in the most useful way.

13.5. CAUSES OF POOR INVENTORY CONTROL

There are certain instances, which leads to poor inventory control. They are:

(*i*) Over buying without regard to the forecast or proper estimate of demand to take advantage of favorable market.

(*ii*) Over production or production of goods much before the customer requires them.

(*iii*) Over stocking may also result from the desire to provide better service to the customers. Bulk production or purchase to cut down production costs also will result In large inventories.

(*iv*) Cancellation of orders and minimum quantity stipulations by the suppliers may also give rise to large inventories.

13.6. COSTS ASSOCIATED WITH INVENTORIES

The three important costs considered in controlling inventory costs are:

13.6.1. Inventory Carrying Costs or Stock Holding Costs (C_1)

They arise on account of maintaining the stocks and the intrest paid on the capital tied up with the stocks They vary directly with the size of the inventory as well as the time the item is held in stock. Various components of the stockholding cost are:

(*a*) ***Costs of money or Capital tied up in inventories :*** This is, by far, the most important component. Money borrowed from the bank may cost of about 18 to 20%. But usually the problem is viewed in a slightly different way, i.e. how much the organization would have earned, had the capital been invested in an alternative project such as developing a new product, etc. It is generally taken somewhere around 15 to 20% of the value of the inventories.

(*b*) ***Cost of Storage Space :*** This consists of rent for the space occupied by the inventory. Besides space expenses, this will also include heating lighting and other atmospheric control expenses. Typical value may be from 1 to 3%.

(*c*) ***Depreciation and deterioration :*** They are especially important for fashion items or items undergoing chemical changes during storage. Fragile items such as crockery which are liable to damage, breakage, etc. This may range form 0.2 to 1.0% of the inventory cost.

(*d*) ***Pilferage Cost :*** It depends upon the nature of the item. Valuable items may be more tempting, while there is hardly any possibility of heavy casting or forging being stolen. This may be around 1.0% of the inventory value.

(*e*) ***Obsolescence Cost :*** It depends upon the nature of the item in stock. Electronic and computer components are likely to be fast outdated. Changes in design also led to obsolescence. It may be possible to quantify the percentage loss due to obsolescence and it may be taken at 5% of the stock value.

(*f*) ***Handling Cost :*** These include all costs associated with movement of stock, such as cost of labour, overhead cranes, gantries and other machinery used for this purpose.

(*g*) ***Record Keeping and Administrative Costs :*** Various records are maintained by the storekeeper to have a proper account of the inventories on hand and inventories issued, all the costs involved in keeping these records will be included in carrying cost. This may amounts to 0.05 to 1.0%.

(*h*) ***Taxes and Insurance :*** Taxes paid on inventories and insurance cover for the inventory in stock is taken into account. This may amounts to 1 to 2% of the inventory cost.

As it is very difficult to calculate the inventory carrying costs day to day, the average inventory concept is used in calculating the inventory carrying costs. This is to say that in a cycle if the initial inventory is 'q' and at the end of the cycle is '*zero*' the average inventory is $(0 + q)/2 = q/2$. The inventory carrying cost is calculated for the average inventory.

13.6.2. Procurement Cost Or Setup Cost (C_3)

They include the fixed and variable costs associated with placing of an order. In case of purchase models it is known as ordering cost. In case of manufacturing model, it is known as setup cost. To place an order certain paper work is to be done. The cost of this paper work is taken as cost of ordering. In case of manufacturing, before starting production, the machine is to be set up. Only on setting of machine, the material is loaded and the production is started. The ordering cost is distributed over the items purchased in that order. Similarly, the setup cost is distributed equally over the products manufactured in that setup. This cost is also known as *replenishment cost.*

13.6.3 Shortage Cost or Stock-out Cost (C_2)

These costs are associated with either a delay in meeting demands or the inability to meet it at all. Therefore, shortage costs are usually interpreted in two ways. In case the unfilled demand can be filled at a later stage (backlog case), these costs are proportional to quantity that is short as well as the delay time. They represent loss of goodwill and cost of idle equipment. In case the unfilled demand is lost (no backlog case), these costs become proportional to only the quantity that is short. These results in cancelled orders, lost sales, profit and even the business itself.

13.7. INVENTORY CONTROL PROBLEMS

Two basic factors, which we have to answer when dealing with inventory problems, are (*i*) When to order (produce or purchase)? *(ii)* How much to order or purchase?

13.7.1. When to Order?

This is related to the lead-time of an item. Lead-time may be defined as the time interval between the placing an order and to receipt of material. It may be replenishment order on an outside firm or within the works. There should be enough stock for each item so that customer's order can be reasonably met from this stock until replenishment. This stock level, known as *reorder level,* has, therefore, to be determined for each item. It is determined by compromising the cost of maintaining these stocks and the disservice to the customer if his orders are not filled in time.

13.7.2. How Much To Order

Each order is associated with it the ordering cost or acquiring cost. To keep it low, the number of orders should be as few as possible i.e. the order size should be large. But larger the size of the order, higher will be the inventory carrying costs. These two are contradictory to each other. Hence a balance is achieved by selecting the right quantity for each order. This quantity is known as '*Economic order quantity*' when dealing with purchase models and *'Economic batch quantity'*, when dealing with manufacturing models. Next section deals with some important inventory models. These models depend on the nature of demand. Whether the demand is *deterministic* or *probabilistic* in nature. They are known as deterministic models or probabilistic models respectively. Before discussing the models, let us try to understand what are *Fixed Quantity System* and *Fixed Period System.* They are generally known as *p – System and q – System.* These two are also inventory control methods.

(i) p – System or Fixed Period System : Here orders for materials are placed every time at a fixed period, say on every first of the month or once in every 15 days and so on. But the quantity for which order is placed will differ from order to order depending on the demand or rate of consumption. That is the period of order is fixed but the quantity varies.

(ii) q – System or Fixed Quantity System : In this system, the order quantity remains same with all orders placed for a material but the period of placing order for the material will differ. This period once again depends on the demand or the rate of consumption. This is also known as *'two – bin' system.* Both are shown in figure 13.2.

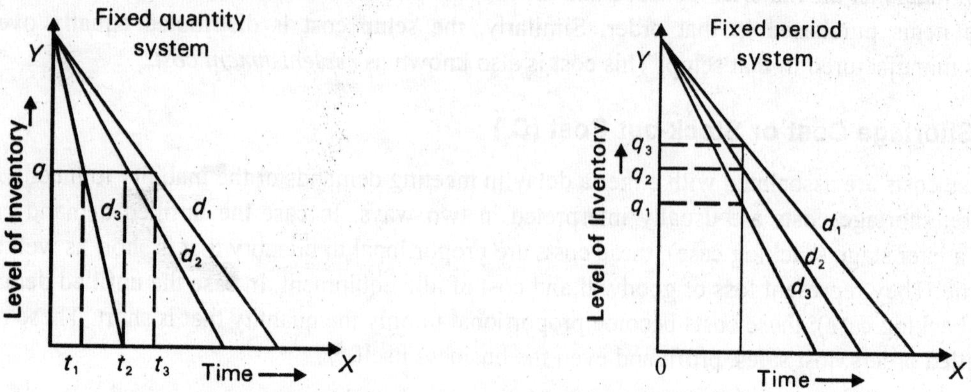

Figure 13.2 : Fixed period system and Fixed Quantity System.

13.8. INVENTORY CONTROL MODELS

In the below discussed models, the following symbols are used.

C_1 = Inventory Carrying Cost in Rupees of the average inventory cost.
C_2 = Stock out cost or shortage cost in Rupees.
C_3 = Ordering cost per order in rupees.
i = Rate of carrying charges, as a percentage of average inventory costs
p = Unit cost of the materials in rupees per unit.
t = Time period
r = Rate of demand or rate of consumption in units per time period.
λ = Demand per year in units per year.
q_0 = Optimal order quantity in units (EOQ or EBQ).
t_0 = Optimal time for placing the order.
τ = Lead Time.

(i) Deterministic Demand or Infinite production rate, Ordering Cost is C_3, Inventory carrying cost is C_1 and instantaneous replenishment i.e. lead time is zero and shortage cost C_2 is also zero.

If the production run is made at intervals t, a quantity $q = rt$ must be produced (or in purchase models, purchased) in each run (or by each order).

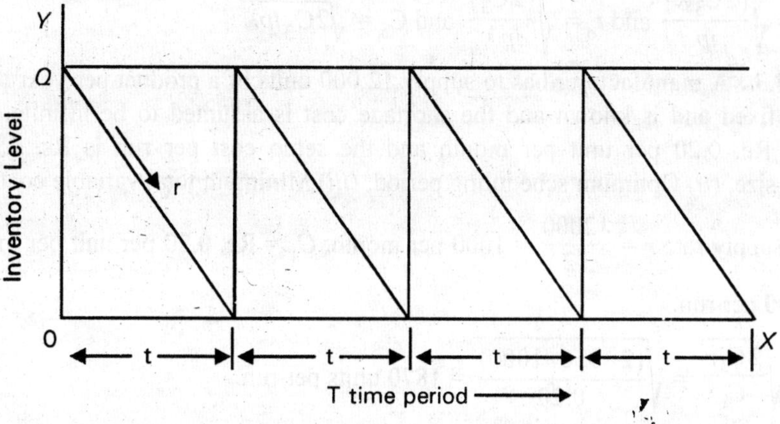

The average inventory in the period = quantity × $\frac{\text{period}}{2} = \frac{qt}{2}$ or it may be worked out as the area of the traingle $AOB = \frac{1}{2}$ × base × altitude = $q \times \frac{t}{2} = \frac{qt}{2}$.

Inventory carrying cost = $\frac{qt}{2} \times C_1$

Ordering cost per order = C_3

Total cost = Inventory carrying cost + Ordering cost = $(qt/2)\,C_1 + C_3$

Total inventory cost per unit of time = $C_q = \{(qt/2)\,C_1 + C_3\}/t$

$= (q/2)\,C_1 + C_3/t$

We know that $q = rt$ or $t = q/r$, substituting this in the above equation, we get

$C_q = (qC_1)/2 + (C_3 r/q)$ ....(1) This is kown as *cost equation*.

This should be minimum, which we get by equating the first derivative of C_q to zero.

The first derivative = $\frac{dC_q}{dq} = \frac{C_1}{2} - \frac{C_3 r}{q^2}$, Simplifying the same, we get

$q_o = \sqrt{\frac{2C_3 r}{C_1}}$ *This is known as Square root formula or Harry' formula or Wilson formula or Economic Order Quantity formula (for manufacturing models it is known as Economic Batch Quantity formula).*

If we substitute this in $q = rt$ formula, we get that optimal time for placing an order is :

$T_o = \sqrt{\frac{2C_3}{C_1 r}}$ and if we substitue the value of q_o in total cost equation we get optimal cost of inventory = $C_o = \sqrt{2C_1 C_3 r}$

In case we are dealing with purchase models, taking unit price as 'p' and inventory carrying charges as 'i', and the yearly demand as λ the above model can be written as :

$$EOQ = q_o = \sqrt{\frac{(2C_3\lambda)}{ip}} \text{ and } t_o = \sqrt{\frac{(2C_3)}{ip\lambda}} \text{ and } C_o = \sqrt{2C_3 ip\lambda}$$

Example 13.3 : A manufacturer has to supply 12,000 units of a product per year to his customer. The demand is fixed and is known and the shortage cost is assumed to be infinite. The inventory holding cost is Re. 0.20 per unit per month and the setup cost per run is Rs. 350/- Determine (*i*) Optimum lot size, (*ii*) Optimum scheduling period, (*iii*) Minimum total variable cost pr year.

Solution : Supply rate $r = \frac{12000}{12} = 1000$ per month, C_1 = Re. 0.20 per unit per month, C_3 = set-up cost = Rs. 350 per run.

$$q_o = \sqrt{\frac{2C_3 r}{C_1}} = \sqrt{\frac{(2\times350\times1000)}{0.20}} = 1870 \text{ units per run.}$$

$$t_o = \sqrt{\frac{2C_3}{C_1 r}} = \sqrt{\frac{(2\times350)}{0.20\times1000}} = 1.87 \text{ months} = 8.1 \text{ weeks between runs.}$$

$$C_o = \sqrt{2C_1 C_3 r} = \sqrt{2 \times 0.20 \times 12 \times 350 \times (1000 \times 12)}$$

$$= \text{Rs. } 4490 \text{ per year.}$$

(For further discussion on the inventory models students are advised to refer any book on OPERATIONS RESEARCH).

13.9. MATERIALS REQUIREMENT PLANNING (MRP)

Material Requirement Planning or MRP as it is called, is a special technique to plan the requirement of materials for production. This is different from EOQ model discussed above. In spite of safety stock maintained to meet the uncertainties in delivery times of inventory, some times, production requirements are not met with. Many production managers come across a problem, where raw materials required for production are purchased as per EOQ and still they do not have the availability of material required at the time when demand arises. This is particularly true when the product requires many raw materials or components. Out of many components or materials even one of them is not available when needed the production cannot be continued. It is because the service levels of each stock of materials are not taken into account.

Let us consider an example that a product requires 10 different components for assembly. The manager fixed 95 % service level for the stock of each component. This means that only 5% of the time there may a stock out position and 95% of the time the stock available for production. But the manager experiences more stock out positions than his expectations. The manager needs 10 components all at one point of time. Each material is stored with 95% service level. The probability that each material is separately available over a long length of time is 0.95. But, the probability that all the ten materials are available simultaneously is equals to $(0.95)^{10}$ = approximately 0.60. This means to say that actual availability is only 60% of the time. That is 40% of the time he experience shortage of components. Hence the statistical methods must be understood properly and applied to the situations to avoid difficulty. EOQ and Safety stock calculations are made for individual components and not for *bunched* requirement of components. In such cases, instead of adopting statistical safety calculations, better we go for *Materials Requirement Planning.*

Material requirement planning deals with the requirement of raw materials or components, which directly depend upon the requirement of production. It seems, it would be better if we know the production plan or production schedule for the assembly of the finished product and accordingly arrange for all the raw materials that go into the finished products, rather than depending upon the statistics and probabilities and EOQ and safety stock. This is exactly what we do in Materials Requirement Planning (MRP). It is simple system of calculating arithmetically the requirement of the input materials at different point of time based on the actual production plan. In fact it is a good old method. When the factory system was in infant state, the artisan, who has to produce a product, use to calculate the requirement of material arithmetically depending on the number of products he has to produce and use to purchase that amount and never felt shortage of materials during production.

There are no probabilities involved anywhere, only the derivation of the requirement of input materials based on the requirement or plan for production of the final product. Such a system will work well for materials that have no direct demand of their own, but have only a derived demand. These materials can be called as *dependent demand items.* Finished assembly has the direct demand of its won and therefore it is an *independent demand item.* In EOQ model the order quantity is calculated by using a formula, which has been worked out by averaging the demand (or the stock of material). The problem of shortage of dependent materials arises because of averaging the consumption of materials. Present day industrial scene shows that industries use hundreds of materials for their product and hence computerized packages are used for calculating the requirement of materials. The success of MRP depends on the pre-requisites of the system. The requisites are:

(*i*) This system is suitable for *dependent demand materials.*
(*ii*) The demand for dependent material is derived from the master-schedule for the final finished goods and the requirement should take lead-time into consideration.
(*iii*) A firm delivery schedule should be available.
(*iv*) MRP should incorporate flexibility.
(*v*) MRP should incorporate self-correcting mechanism depending on the changes in demand.

Better results may be obtained by using MRP and EOQ together.

13.10. JUST-IN-TIME PRODUCTION

Just-in-time production/inventory system is a revolutionary concept becoming very popular in industrial world. Think of a situation that a company produces the required goods *only at the time when they are needed* and *in the quantity that is needed* (it applies equally to finished goods or components). Now, the company makes an agreement with its vendors or suppliers of raw materials that they should supply the materials and components only at the time and in the quantities needed, and then almost inventories are eliminated. The raw materials and components are supplied to the point, where they are needed and when they are needed (at point of time). This is known as ***Just-In-Time*** or ***J.I.T. production system.*** This system is seeded by *Taiichi Ohono*, Vice–President of *Toyota Motor Company of Japan.* JIT uses a peculiar material withdrawal and work ordering system, known as *KANBAN or MARKER* system.

Another way of adopting the same concept is consider for example an Industrial Estate having number of industrial units, manufacturing different type of products using different type of materials. An entrepreneur can take the responsibility of supplying the materials for these industrial units. He can collect the information regarding the requirement of materials from every unit and prepare list of various materials required by the units and purchase them in bulk and maintain a centralized stores.

Every unit will indent their requirement daily / weekly / monthly and draw the material from this centralized stores. This will help the industrialists in two ways.

(*i*) They can get rid of all the records, stock registers and the workers of stores.

(*ii*) As the material is available locally, they need not go in search of vendors. Payment for the materials may be made at the agreed period. As there may be many common materials required by many industries, the entrepreneur, managing the stores, can purchase them in bulk quantity and get the advantages of bulk purchase.

13.11. SPARE PARTS MANAGEMENT

Spare parts management is different from the regular inventory management. It is because the regular inventory is maintained for manufacturing purpose, but the spare parts inventory is maintained to replace the worn-out parts of machinery. These are special independent demand items deriving their demand from the failure characteristics of the component of a machine and deals with a specialized supply situation. A survey shows that, the extent of obsolete and surplus spare parts maintained in India is to an extent of more than Rs. 3000 crores. Moreover, the spare parts requirement has got special characteristics and depends on the type of maintenance practiced in the industry. In addition to this, the machine for which spare parts are required may be out dated or the equipment may be imported from other countries, or supply of spares for the old machines might have been stopped. More over the breakdowns are random in nature. All these add to the problem of spare parts inventory management.

One of the good ways of dealing with spare parts inventory management is to classify them by VED and ABC analysis to arrive at the level of inventory to be maintained. VED analysis, which depends on the criticality of the items, is the best one compared to ABC analysis, this is because the purpose of spares is to avoid production stoppages. Vital items need to be stocked at a much higher level than the essential items, which in term stocked at a higher level than the desirable ones, as criticality decreases from vital to desirable. When we take cost factor also into consideration with VED analysis, we get a good result. The following matrix gives the service levels of spares, with respect to their importance (criticality and cost).

	V	E	D
A	90%	80%	70%
B	95%	85%	75%
C	99%	90%	80%

Another method, which gives better results, is *codification* of spare parts materials. Codification is generally used for identification of the material. The codification used to identify the spares must particularly suit the need and purposes of the organization. In addition proper classification of spares for stocking may also help the management to see that the desired spares is available at the time of need. Spares are classified as:

13.11.1. Breakdown or Maintenance Spares

These are the spares required in large quantities at more or less frequent periodic intervals as and when the breakdowns occur. These resemble, somewhat, the regular inventory items in their consumption patterns. The policies of regular inventory management may be applied to these items. Maintenance record of equipment may reveal the active life of components of spares and one can study the life pattern of these spares from historical data collected by examining the failure distribution. The service level of a spare part is given by :

Opportunity cost of under stock of one unit / (opportunity cost of under stock of one unit + opportunity cost of over stock of one unit) = $\frac{OC_u}{OC_u + OC_o}$.

Example 13.4 : A company using fixed order quantity system for ordering the inventory. The average rate of consumption is 16 units per quarter and follows Poisson distribution. Service level is 95% and lead-time for procurement is one quarter, the cost of ordering is Rs. 500/- per order and cost of carrying inventory is Rs. 18/- per unit pre year. Find the average level of inventory.

Solution : Mean consumption rate, $r = 14$ units per quarter,

Standard deviation = $\sqrt{r}$ = $\sqrt{16}$ = 4, From the Poisson distribution tables $z = 23$ (height of the ordinate)

As the lead-time is one quarter, buffer stock = 23 – 16 = 7 units.

EOQ = $\sqrt{\frac{(2 \times 500 \times 64)}{18}}$ = 60 approximately. As the EOQ is very nearer to the annual requirement, order is placed once in a year.

Therefore average inventory = $\frac{64}{2} + 7 = 39$ units.

13.11.2. Insurance Spares

The purpose of insurance spares is to provide an insurance against the relatively remotely possible breakdown of failure of an equipment or component. The probability that such a component or equipment will survive the lifetime of the machinery or plant is quite high. The reliability of such spares has been observed to be as high a 95 to 99% over the life span of the machinery. Requirement of these spare is very rare. In case they are not available, when the need arises, the production system will come to standstill. These items may be high value items. Generally, requirement of these spares are ordered along with the machine. This is because, when purchased along with the machine the cost of them may be less. In case they are ordered separately, the cost may be high or some times it may not be available with the manufacturer because of the changes in the design of the machine. In general the decision to purchase the insurance spare along with the machine is either to purchase no spare part or purchase one only.

13.11.3. Capital Spares

These are also high reliability spares, but not as high as the insurance spares. Also the reliability is not as low as that of the maintenance spares. Moreover, these spares have relatively higher purchase cost than the breakdown spares. Generally, 6 to 7 items are purchased along with the machine.

13.11.4. Rotable Spares (or Re-usable spares)

These are re-usable spare parts, which after their breakdown can be reconditioned and re-used. As they have re-life (may be little bit less than the original life), judicious decision is taken while purchasing these items for stock. Waiting line models may be used to find out how much items to be ordered.

To have further information regarding the other aspects of materials management such as Stores Management, Purchase Management, Materials Handling and Physical Distribution Management, readers are advised to refer a book on Materials Management.

QUESTIONS

1. What do you mean by the term inventory? Give classification of inventories.
2. Write a brief notes on costs associated with inventory.
3. Explain the concept of ABC analysis.
4. Briefly describe how do you conduct ABC Analysis.
5. What is VED Analysis? Briefly explain.
6. Distinguish between ABC and VED Analysis.
7. What do you mean by FSN analysis?
8. Briefly explain p-system and q-system of inventory control.
9. Derive EOQ Formula.
10. What are the causes of poor inventory control?
11. What factors you consider in the management of spare parts? How does it differ from inventory control?
12. Explain JIT System of production.

14

WORK STUDY

PART–A : METHOD STUDY.

- Introduction.
- Productivity and Work-study.
- Definition of Work-Study, Method study and Work measurement.
- Introduction to Work-study.
- Introduction to Method Study.
- Steps in Method Study.
- Points to be remembered while drawing charts and diagrams.
- Charts and Diagrams.
  - Flow Process Chart.
  - Two hand process chart.
  - Multiple Activity Chart or Man Machine chart.
  - SIMO Chart.
  - Flow Diagram.
  - Two and Three-dimensional models.
  - Cyclegraphs and Chronocyclegraphs.
- Examine or Critical Examination or Brainstorming.
- Examination Procedure.
- Develop the new method and submit.
- Principles of Motion Economy.
- Submit the proposed method to top management.
- Install and Maintain.

PART–B WORK MEASUREMENT OR TIME STUDY.

Work measurement.

- Introduction.
- Definition of Work Measurement.
- Work measurement techniques.
- Rate of Working.
- The unit of work
- Steps in Work measurement or Procedure for conducting Work measurement.
- Stopwatch Time study principles and procedures.
- Time scale and stopwatches.
- Standard rate of working.
- To break the task into elements.

- Rating and Basic Times.
- Factors affecting rating.
- Time study Procedure.
- Relaxation and Contingency Allowances.
- Calculation of Standard Time.
- Synthesis from Elemental Data.
- Pre determined Motion Time Systems (PMTS)
- Analytical Estimating.
- Comparative Estimating.
- Activity Sampling
- Tail Note and Questions.

PART : A. METHOD STUDY

14.1. INTRODUCTION

Man for some reason or the other always try to simplify his work. For example a person wants to reach a destination B from his place A. He always leaves the main road joining the two places A and B and follows a across path which saves his *energy and time.* In fact every man is a good expert in the techniques of simplifying his work. But it is very difficult for us to tell where and when exactly the science of simplifying the work has begin. But in the interest of knowing much about the subject, we can identify some of the pioneers, who contributed to spread the knowledge of science of simplifying the work and measuring the work in terms of time units. While there is nothing essentially new in work-study the novelty is apparent in the intensity of the analytical approach. It has always been practiced as an unconscious art, an attribute of individuals, gained through experience and lost in the same way.

To understand the history of work-study, let us discuss some of the persons who have done remarkable work in the area.

(*i*) *Frederick W. Taylor* (1856 – 1915) : He is the first man who evolved the principle of breaking a job down into detailed elements to determine by time study a time to be allowed for the job. He is rather a remarkable man. He joined Midvale Steel Works as an apprentice and reached the position of Chief Engineer at the age of 31 years. He his given a Scientific base in analyzing the work. The objectives of his Scientific Management are:

(*a*) The development of science for each element of a man's work, thereby replacing the old rule of thumb method.

(*b*) The selection of right worker of each particular task and give training and develop him as skilled worker, rather than allowing man to select his work and learn the work by himself.

(*c*) To develop hearty cooperation between workers and management.

(*d*) Dividing the work into almost equal shares between management and the workers and each department is allocated the work for which it is best suited.

Taylor undertook his famous studies of shovelling at Bethlehem Steel Works during 1898 and designed optimal size for the shovels, which increased the productivity of workers.

He is the man who devised functional management also initiated the method of measuring work in terms of time units, by breaking down the work into measurable elements. He also invented high-speed steel, which has a longer life than the conventional tool material.

(*ii*) Another pioneer was Henry L. Gantt (1861 – 1919), who is famous for his work known as Gantt chart, widely used in work-study and scheduling of works. He has developed incentive schemes and planning and control systems.

(*iii*) *Frank and Lillian Gilbreth* : Mr. Gilbreth is the founder of Motion Study (or Method Study) (1869 – 1924). He eschewed his education at the age of 17 and learnt bricklayer's work. He studied various hand motions adopted by workers while laying the bricks and found the best pattern of movement of hands for laying the brick. Later he became a contractor and industrial consultant. His wife, Dr. Lillian Gilbreth, a trained Psychologist, helped in his work. The knowledge of Psychology and scientific thinking of work given a wonderful contribution to the industrial world, which is Method Study. He developed laws of human motion and principles of motion economy.

14.2. PRODUCTIVITY AND WORK STUDY

Productivity is the relationship between inputs used and output produced. As far the inputs are concerned, we have to take all the resources that go into production, such as material, man-hours, machine hours, money, etc. Therefore, when we talk about productivity, the question arises whether it is material productivity or machine productivity or labour productivity? Hence while calculating, it we take one particular resource, then we say it is the productivity of that particular resource. For example, if we consider the total man-hours used to produce the goods, we say that it is the *labour productivity* and so on. If we consider all the resources put together and calculate productivity, it is *Total Productivity*. Therefore, we can say that the *factors* affecting productivity are:

(*i*) Nature and quality of raw materials,
(*ii*) Basic nature of process employed,
(*iii*) Amount and plant and equipment employed,
(*iv*) Efficiency of plant and equipment employed,
(*v*) Volume, quantity, continuity and uniformity of production, and
(*vi*) Utilization of manpower.

Productivity can be improved by any of the following.

(*a*) Either by improving the basic process by research and development or by providing more and improved physical means of production. These needs lot of time to implement and they are considered long term strategies.

(*b*) It can also be improved by simplifying and improving the product and reducing the variety, Which enable us to save scarce resources and improve the use value of the product also reduce the cost of the product.

This though not takes that much of time as (*a*) above, but needs considerable time and hence considered as medium term strategy.

(*c*) Productivity can also be improved by improving the methods of operation and by increasing manpower efficiency at all levels and practicing effective planning and organization. This can be achieved by following scientific management in day-to-day work; hence this is considered as short-term strategy. One of the technique used for improving manpower utilization and improve the methods of production is the application of *Work Study Techniques*.

14.3. DEFINITION OF WORK STUDY, METHOD STUDY AND TIME STUDY OR WORK MEASUREMENT

Work study can be considered as the study of work in all its context with utmost honest and commitment to achieve the desired goal. It is defied in British Standards Institute (3138 – 1969) as ***A management service based on those techniques, particularly Method Study and Work Measurement, which are used in the examination of human work in all its contexts, and which lead to the systematic investigation of all the resources and factors which affect the efficiently and economy of the situation being reviewed in order to effect improvement.***

As pef the definition work-study is the combination of Method study and Work measurement that means on one hand we have to examine the method of doing the work and on the other hand, we have to find the time required to do the work. Studying the method is to improve the method of production, which results in more effective use of material, manpower and equipment. Work measurement on the other hand assess the human effectiveness and gives guidelines to improve the planning and control methods also serves as the basis of sound incentive scheme. These two techniques are used for optimal utilization of available resources and to improve productivity.

Method Study is defined in British Standard (3138 – 1969) as The systematic recording and critical examination of the factors and resources involved in existing and proposed ways of doing work as a means of developing and applying easier and more effective methods of reducing costs.

Work Measurement is defined in British standard as the application of techniques designed to establish the time for a qualified worker to carry out a specified job at a desired level of performance.

The purpose or objective of work-study is to use the resources required for production in the best possible way to improve the productivity. That is available manpower, equipment and machinery (plant) and material are to be used optimally.

14.4. INTRODUCTION OF WORK STUDY IN THE ORGANIZATION

As work-study mostly deals with improvement of productivity, when the question of labour productivity is considered, the general tendency of labour is to oppose the work study thinking that the management is trying to exploit them. Not only the labour class, sometimes the senior managers may also think that when they are managing the organization effectively, what is the necessity of work-study, and may think that it is to reveal their inefficiency. Hence, the management must be careful enough while introducing the work-study in the organization. First it must create awareness in senior managers regarding the benefits of work-study. For this purpose, the organization may send some its senior managers for sandwich courses in Work-study, so as to enable him to realize the advantages of work-study and guide their juniors in the direction. Management may also invite Work-study consultants and arrange training classes to the lower level managers and make them fully aware of the advantages of work-study. The consultants may show some films on work-study and show how some of the organizations are benefited from work-study. Work-study team may meet the lower operation level workers and slowly acqualnt wlth them and explaln to the workers and foremen about the work the team wants to carryout in the organization. Meanwhile, the management may circulate a note on work-study in the local language to make the workers to cooperate with the work- study team and ease their work. The work-study team must concentrate on the following points in their orientation classes: (*i*) The economic necessity of reducing the production cost. (*ii*) The advantages of systematic method study and work measurement. (*iii*) Regarding wages and incentives.

Once confirmed that all are willing to cooperate and considering the work-study as a friend and not an enemy, work-study team may fix up schedules for conducting work-study in various departments.

14.5. INTRODUCTION OF METHOD STUDY

Method study can be applied to any type of work. But to get the best advantages, it is better we apply method study to repetitive type of work. The method study man must be in a position to understand the human factors of method study and must have desire, determination and ability to produce the best results by taking economic and technical considerations of the work.

Method study is basically concerned with finding the better way of doing work. Hence its objectives are to:

(*i*) Improve layout and design of factory, plant and work place,

(*ii*) Improve working procedures,

(*iii*) Optimal utilization of material, manpower and plant and equipment,

(*iv*) Improve the working environment,

(*v*) Improve the design or specifications of end product.

In Method Study, we analyze the true facts concerning the situation and examine those facts critically and develop the best methods of doing the work.

14.6. STEPS IN METHOD STUDY

There is a step-by-step procedure to conduct Method Study. The first step is to ***select the job*** or ***work*** which needs method study. When a job is examined, if it shows the following defects, we can select the job for conducting method study.

The work study man may find that there may be unnecessary movement of material and men and bottlenecks due to bad layout and bad operation planning, or the quality of the work may be low and the products may require re-processing or he my notice that unnecessary overtime working of workmen, or employees may complain about their work and their uneasiness while doing work or of fatigue. Any one of the above reasons or a combination of the above may indicate that the application of method study may results in improved situation. To decide whether to conduct method study or not, the benefits gained from the application of method study are weighed in the light of cost of method study. If the benefits are really worthwhile, the job is selected for method study. The benefits may include, (*i*) Increased productivity, (*ii*) Savings in materials, (*iii*) Improvement of quality, (*iv*) Improved safety to workers and equipment, (*v*) Reduction in scrap and (*vi*) Improved housekeeping.

The second step is to ***record_the_facts_*** Recording of the facts regarding the job selected for analysis is very mush essential because it helps in critical examination of the facts and to compare the conditions before and after improvement. Also, the record will serve as guidelines to train the employees in method study. There are many ways of recording the facts. The selection of a particular method depends on the purpose for which the record is prepared and cost of recording. The recording methods are classified into two categories. (a) Charts (for process and time records), (b) Diagrams and Models (for path of movement records). Depending on the need and the purpose, sometimes more than one method is to be used for recording. In order to make recording easy certain symbols are used for recording the facts. The symbols are:

Sl. No.	Symbol	Activity	For which it is used
(i)	○	Operation	Showing the operations, for example : pressing, opening, etc.
(ii)	→	Transport	Movement, travelling, etc.
(iii)	∇	Storage	Holding, stocking, storing or retaining, etc.
(iv)	D	Delay	Waiting for transport, waiting for operation, etc.
(v)	□	Inspection	Verifying, inspection or Quality checking the dimension, etc.,

14.6.1. Charts

There are different types of charts, depending on the need and purpose. Principle types are:

(i) ***Outline Process Chart :*** This chart is used for recording operations and inspection. .This chart is mainly used in the initial state, to know the overall position of the problem and to assess the problem to know whether method study is necessary or not. (This chart will only record ○ and □.)

(ii) ***Flow Process Chart :*** This chart uses all the symbols mentioned above and record the movements of men, material and equipment.

(iii) ***Two Hand Process Chart :*** This chart records activities of both hands of the worker. Here the symbol ∇ is used for indicating, "hold", i.e. holding a job in hand.

(iv) ***Multiple Activity Chart :*** Multiple Activity chart records the activities of men, Machine or both on a common time scale in the form of a bar chart. This chart is generally drawn on a graph sheet.

(v) ***Simultaneous Motion Cycle (SIMO) Chart :*** On SIMO Chart, the activities of worker's hands, legs, and other body movements are recorded on a common time scale.

14.6.2. Diagrams and Models

Some times, it will be necessary to study the problem by using the diagrams and models, which will give enough scope to study the movement of men and materials.

(i) ***Flow Diagram :*** Same symbols are used in charting is used in preparing the diagram. These diagrams are prepared on a paper to scale by indicating flow lines. This diagram will be helpful to study the quality of layout.

(ii) ***String Diagram :*** This diagram is also used for studying a layout. The difference between the string diagram and flow diagram, on flow diagram we draw different colored lines to indicate the movements of different subject. In string diagram, we use different colored threads to indicate the movements of different subject.

(iii) ***Two and Three Dimensional Models :*** These are models prepared to study the problem in detail. Two Dimensional models uses templates and three dimensional models use actual working model, for example, we can construct the model of the plant to scale, so that it will be easy for one to study the movement of men and material in all directions.

(*iv*) ***Cyclegraphs and Chrono-cylegraphs :*** This diagram is used for recording high speed, short-cycle operations. Generally a camera is used to record the movements. In cyclegraph, a bulb is tied to one of the fingers of worker's hand, which receives power from a battery with the worker and the whole movement is photographed. The movement of worker's hand will appear as a white line on the film. In this case it is very difficult to know the direction of movement of the hand. In Chrono-cylcegraph, the bulb is arranged to off and on mode, so that on the picture of an oval shaped dots appears, which shows the direction of movement of hand. Figure 14.1 shows all the above-discussed charts and diagrams.

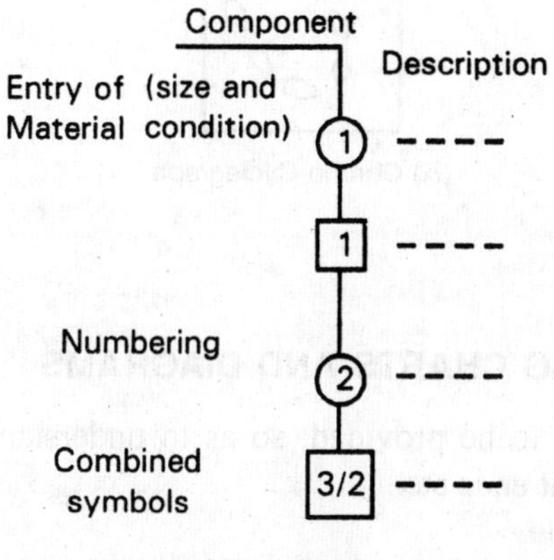

(*i*) Outline Process Chart

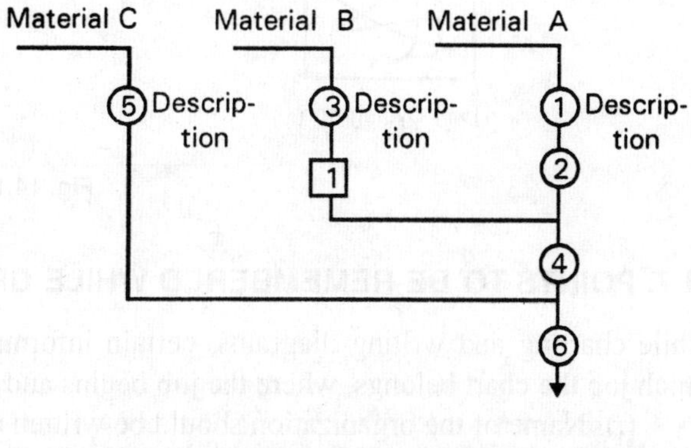

(*ii*) Flow Process Chart

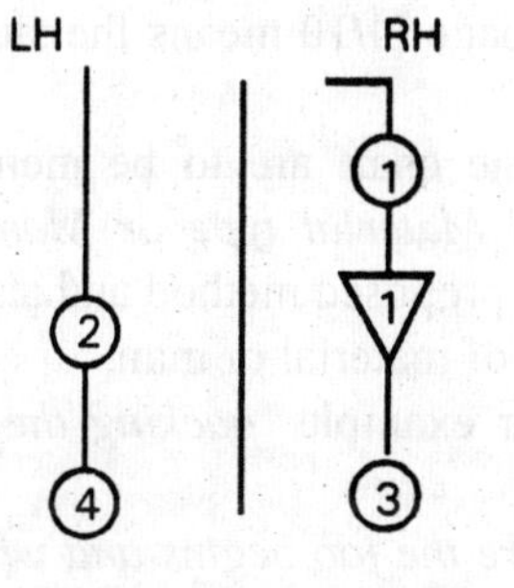

(*iii*) Two Hand Process Chart

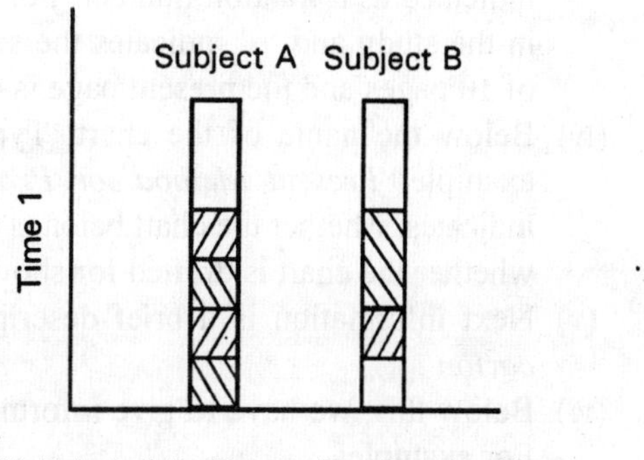

(*iv*) Multiple Activity Chart or Man Machine Chart

LH				*RH*		
Description	*Time*	*Therblig*	*Frame No.*	*Therbig*	*Time*	*Description*

(*v*) Simultaneous Motion (SIMO) Chart

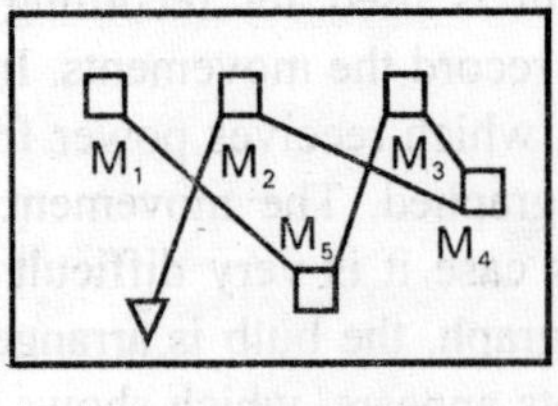

(*vi*) Flow Diagram

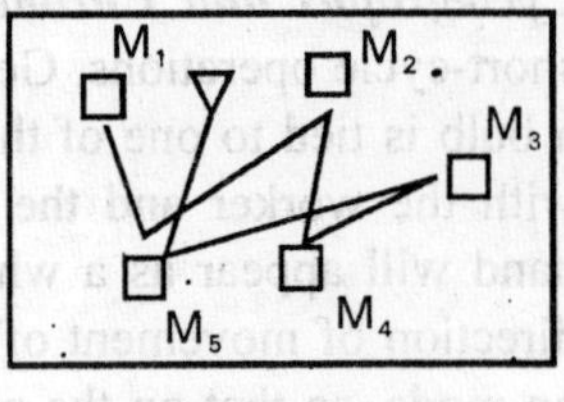

(*vii*) String Diagram

(*viii*) Cyclegraph

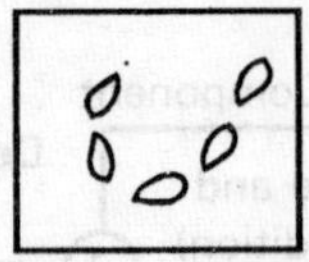
(*ix*) Chrono-Cyclegraph

Fig. 14.1

14.7. POINTS TO BE REMEMBERED WHILE DRAWING CHARTS AND DIAGRAMS

While charting and writing diagrams, certain information is to be provided, so as to understand to which job the chart belongs, where the job begins and where it ends etc.

(*i*) Name of the organization should be written at the top.

(*ii*) Title of the chart should be written below the name of the company.

(*iii*) On the right hand top corner against to the name of the chart page number should be indicated as a fraction number. For example, a/b, where '*b*' indicates total number of pages in the study and '*a*' indicates the serial number of the page (4/10 means the study consists of 10 pages and the present page is 4 th page).

(*iv*) Below the name of the chart, Type and Subject of the chart are to be mentioned. For example *'Present Method' or Proposed Method' and Material type or Man type.* This indicates, whether the chart belongs to present method or proposed method and also indicates, whether the chart is drafted for showing the movements of material or man.

(*v*) Next information is a brief description of the job. For example '*packing the bottle in a carton'*.

(*vi*) Below this, we have to give information regarding *where the job begins and where it ends.* For example:

Job begins : Operator loads the material on the machine.

Job Ends : Operator switch off the machine.

The above statements tells us that the study is conducted between the above two events.

(*vii*) Just below the ' job end' statement, it is better; we present the layout of the workstation.

(*viii*) Then comes the actual chart or diagram.

(*ix*) At the end of the chart a summary of the study along with date of study and name of the person who conducted the study is to be presented.

Figure 14.2 shows a typical format of the chart.

While constructing the chart, an arrow is to be shown at the top indicating the entry of first material and a brief description of material is to be given with the arrow. Then the other particulars are entered say operation, transport, storage etc. as they occur by means of symbols and the description of the event and for movement the distance if any is to be entered on the right side. When we are showing the assembly of a component, the first material is entered on the left side with particulars as mentioned above and the next component to the right of the first component and so on. The following figures show the various means of showing assembly, disassembly, repetition of operations etc. All facts, which are entered, should be numbered in the order they exist.

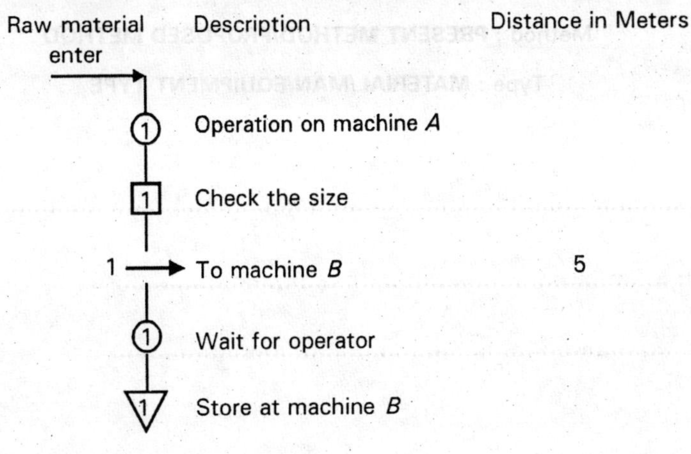

Method of writing a chart.

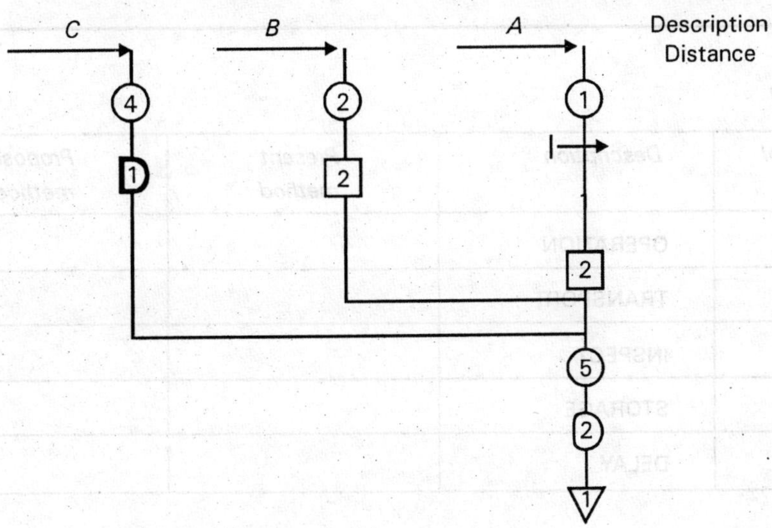

Method of Showing an Assembly.

XYZ COMPANY, ABC CITY

Name of the chart : **FLOW PROCESS CHART** No. 1/5

Method : **PRESENT METHOD/PROPOSED METHOD**

Type : **MATERIAL/MAN/EQUIPMENT TYPE**

Job : ....

Chart begins : ....

Chart ends : ....

Workstation layout

THE CHART OR DIAGRAM

SUMMARY

Symbol	*Description*	*Present method*	*Proposed method*
○	OPERATION		
→	TRANSPORT		
□	INSPECT		
∇	STORAGE		
D	DELAY		

Date : **Charted by :** .... **Checked by :** ....

Figure 14.2 : The format for charting.

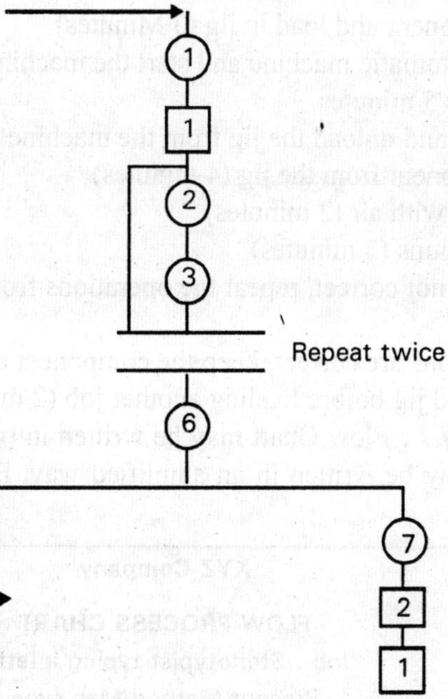

Process chart for showing the division of process.

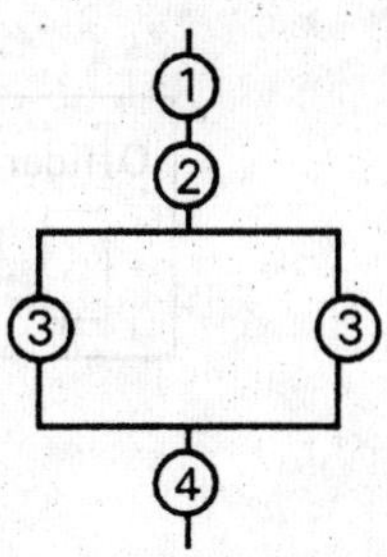

Showing duplicated operation.

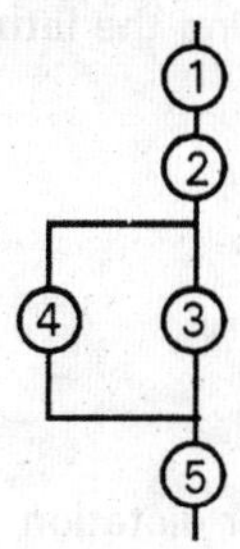

Showing dismantling and reassembling.

14.7.1. Flow Process Chart

Problem 14.1 : Prepare a man type of flow process chart for the details given below.

A steno typist waiting for dictation from his officer leaves to his officer's room, which is 5 meters away in 2 minutes, takes dictation for 3 minutes, returns to his seat in 2 minutes. He prepares typing set in 2 minutes and inserts it in the machine in two minutes and types the letter for 10 minutes, removes the typed set from the machine in 1 minute, separate the copies in 2 minutes, checks for 3 minutes and places the set on the pad in 1 minute. Takes the pad to the officer for signature in 2 minutes, waits for the signature for 3 minutes, returns to his seat with the pad in two minutes. Inserts the original copy in the envelope in one minute and close it and put it in out tray in ½ a minute.

Problem 14.2 : The activities of an operator in machining a component are as follows. Draw a flow process chart.

(*i*) Pick up the component and load in jig (3 Minutes)
(*ii*) Load Jig on an automatic machine and start the machine. (3 minutes).
(*iii*) Machining time is 5 minutes.
(*iv*) Stop the machine and unload the jig from the machine (4 minutes)
(*v*) Unload the component from the jig (4 minutes)
(*vi*) Clean component with air (2 minutes)
(*vii*) Check the dimensions (5 minutes)
(*viii*) If dimensions are not correct, repeat the operations from (*i*) To vii (this happens only 5% of the time)
(*ix*) Once the dimensions are correct, keep the component aside in a tray (1 minute).
(*x*) Clean machine and jig before loading another job (2 minutes).

Solution to Problem 14.1 : Flow Chart may be written in two ways. First we can write the chart as explained above or it may be written in an amplified way. Both are shown in the solution to the problem 14.1.

XYZ Company

FLOW PROCESS CHART

Job : Stenotypist typing a letter

Present Method/Man type

Chart begins : Stenotypist waiting for officer's dictation.

Chart ends : Keeping the letter in the tray.

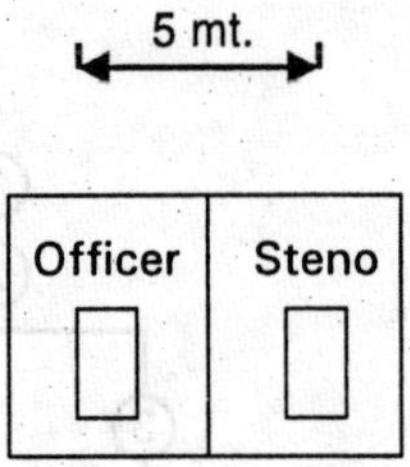

THE CHART

Steno waiting for dictation

Symbol	No.	*Description*	*Distance*	*Time in minutes*
→	1	To officer's room	5	2
○	1	Take dictation		3
←	2	To his room	5	2
○	2	Prepare typing set		2
○	3	Insert in machine		2
○	4	Type letter		10
○	5	Remove set		1
○	6	Separate copies		2
□	1	Check the letter for correction		3

Symbol	Description	Distance	Time
○ 7	Place set in pad		1
→ 3	To officer's room	5	2
D 1	Wait for Signature		3
← 4	To his room	5	2
○ 5	Insert original in envelop		1
○ 9	Put the letter in out tray		$\frac{1}{2}$

SUMMARY

S. No.	*Symbol*	*Description*	*Present method*	*Proposed method*	*Savings*
1	○	Operation	9		
2	→	Transport	4		
3	□	Inspect	1		
4	D	Delay	1		
5	∇	Storage	—		

1/1

ABC COMPANY

FLOW PROCESS CHART/MAN TYPE

Job : Machining a component

Chart Begins : Load the job on the jig

Chart ends : Clean machine for loading the jig

Layout

THE CHART

Picking up product →

Symbol	Description	Time in Minutes
○ 1	Pick up component and load on jig	3
○ 2	Load jig on machine	3
□ 1	Machining (automatic)	5
○ 3	Stop machine and unload jig	4
○ 4	Unload component	4
○ 5	Clean component	2
□ 1	Check dimensions	5
○ 6	Keep component in tray	1
○ 7	Clean machine to load jig	2

Reprocess component (5% of time)

SUMMARY

S. No.	Symbol	Description	Present method	Proposed method	Savings
1	○	Operation	7		
2	→	Transport	—		
3	□	Inspection	1		
4	D	Delay	—		
5	∇	Storage	—		

The solution for Problem Number 14.1 may also be presented in Material type style, as shown below.

Solution for 14.1 in Material type. Here material is contents of letter.

1/1

XYZ Company

Flow Process Chart/Material type/present method

Job : Writing a letter using a stenotypist

Chart begins : Contents awaiting dictation by author

Chart ends : Contents of letter to out tray

Layout

The Chart

Symbol	Activity	*Distance mt.*	*Time (min.)*
○ 1	Dictation		3
→ 1	To typist	5	2
○ 2	Type		10
□ 1	Check		3
← 2	To typist	5	2
○ 3	Signature		3
→ 3	To typist	5	2
○ 4	In envelop		1
○ 5	Aside in tray		½

SUMMARY

S. No.	*Symbol*	*Description*	*Present method*	*Proposed method*	*Savings*
1	○	Operation	5		
2	→	Transport	3		
3	□	Inspect	1		
4	D	Delay	—		
5	∇	Storage	—		

14.7.2. Two Hand Process Chart

When work is confined to a single place, such as assembly work done by a worker on a table, clerical work done at a table etc., where two hands are used to do work, *two-hand process chart* is used to record the facts. It gives graphical representation of the movement of hands. The symbols used for flow process chart are used for recording. But here the storage symbol (triangle) is used to represent to holding the work in hand; hence *'hold'* is written against the symbol. Inspection symbol (Square) is omitted, because the inspection is done when the job is in the hand. But for these changes, rest everything is same. Recording may be made on a chart in which we have all the symbols are printed as shown in the figure 14.3, or it may be drawn on a plain paper with all details as in the case of a flow process cart, showing the movements of right hand on right hand side and the movement of left hand on the left hand side. If needed, two more columns, representing left leg and right leg, can also accommodate the movements of two legs. Before conducting a detailed study, to check whether the problem needs a detailed study, two-hand process chart is written with operation symbol only to get the overall picture.

XYZ Company Two-Hand Process Chart Present/Proposed Method Job : Chart begins : Chart ends : Workplace layout			a/b
Left hand	The Chart		Right Hand
Description	Symbol	Symbol	Description
	○ → ∇ D	○ → ∇ D	
	○ → ∇ D	○ → ∇ D	
	○ → ∇ D	○ → ∇ D	
	○ → ∇ D	○ → ∇ D	

	○ → ∇ D	○ → ∇ D	
	○ → ∇ D	○ → ∇ D	
	○ → ∇ D	○ → ∇ D	
	○ → ∇ D	○ → ∇ D	
	○ → ∇ D	○ → ∇ D	
	○ → ∇ D	○ → ∇ D	
	○ → ∇ D	○ → ∇ D	

SUMMARY

S. No.	*Symbol*	*Description*	*Present method*		*Proposed method*		*Savings*	
			L.H.	*R.H.*	*L.H.*	*R.H.*	*L.H.*	*R.H.*
1	○	Operation						
2	→	Transport						
3	∇	Hold and						
	–	Inspect						
4	D	Storage						

Figure 14.3.a : Two- Hand Process Chart.

a/b

XYZ COMPANY

TWO HAND PROCESS CHART

Method: Present / Proposed.

Job:

Chart Begins:

Chart Ends.

Work Place Layout

The Chart.

Left Hand		Right Hand.	
Description	Symbols.	Symbols	Description

SUMMARY

S. No.	Symbol	Description	Present method		Proposed method		Savings	
			L.H.	R.H.	L.H.	R.H.	L.H.	R.H.
1	○	Operation						
2	→	Transport						
3	D	Delay						
4	∇	Hold and Inspect						

Figure 14.3.b : Two-hand process chart printed type.

Problem 14.3. Write a two hand process chart for two washers kept on the right hand side of the table and nut which is kept at the center to a bolt which is on the left hand side of the table as shown in the layout.

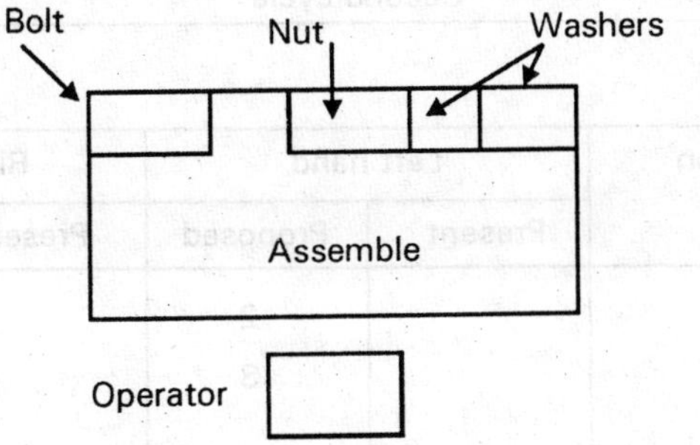

Solution :

TWO HAND PROCESS CHART - PRESENT TYPE 1/1

Job : Assemble two washers and nut to bolt

Chart begins : Hand empty material in boxes

Chart ends : Completed assemble aside in tray

Layout

The Chart

Left Hand		Right Hand	
Description	Symbol	Symbol	Description
To Bolt	←1	→1	To first washer
Pick up bolt	○ 1	○1	Pick up washer
To position	→2	←2	To position

Contd.→

Left hand description	Left hand symbol	Right hand symbol	Right hand description
Hold	∇1	O2	Assemble to bolt.
		→3	To second washer.
		O3	Pick up washer
		←4	To position
		O4	Assmble to bolt
		→5	To nut
		O5	Pick up nut
		←6	To position
		O6	Assemble to bolt
To box	→3	D1	Delay
Aside to box	O2		

Second cycle

SUMMARY

S. No.	Symbol	Description	Left hand Present	Left hand Proposed	Right hand Present	Right hand Proposed	Savings
1	○	Operation		2		6	
2	→	Transport		3		6	
3	D	Delay		—		1	
4	∇	Storage		1		—	

14.7.3. Multiple Activity Chart Or Man Machine Chart

This chart is used when one want to record the activities of a group of persons or activities of men and machine on a same time scale and compare and analyze them in order to improve the method. Reducing the idle time of men or machine or both can do this chart. Activities of each subject are represented on a bar. An example of a bar chart is shown in figure 14.4.

XYZ Company

Multiple Activity Chart Present Method a/b

MAN MACHINE TYPE

Job :

Chart begins :

Chart ends :

Contd.→

THE CHART

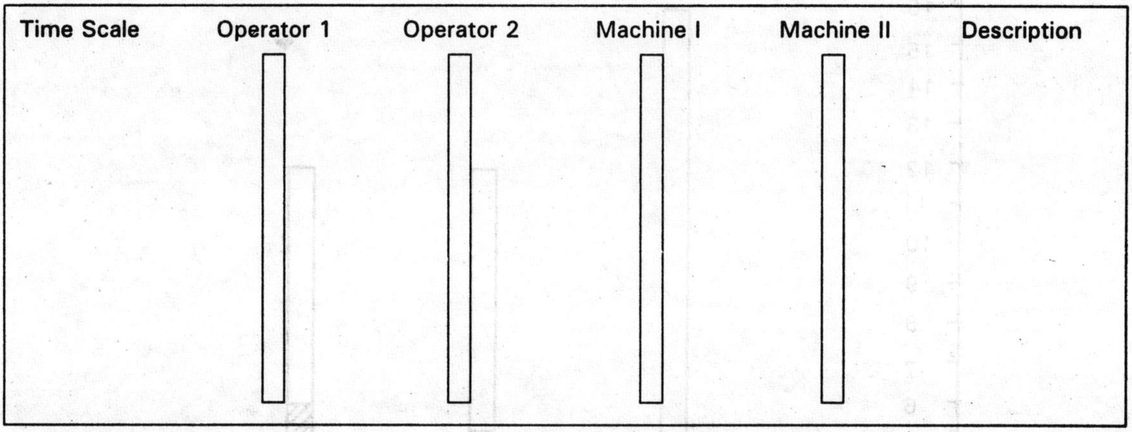

SUMMARY

Particulars	*Present Metod*			*Proposed Metod*			*Difference*		
	Sub I	*Sub II*	*Sub III*	*Sub I*	*Sub II*	*Sub III*	*Sub I*	*Sub II*	*Sub III*
WORK									
IDLE									

While representing the activity and idle times on the bar different colors or different marking may be used. This is shown by taking a problem.

Problem 14.4 : **Draw a man machine chart showing one operator operating two semi automatic lathes. The cycle consists of load machine ½ a minute, machining the part 1 minute. The machine stops automatically at the end of the cut. Unload the machine ½ a minute. The two machines are alike and each completes the machining operation and stops automatically. The man and machine chart is to show the operator starting in the morning, with both machines empty and continues till it has made two pieces.**

Solution :

XYZ COMPANY

MAN MACHINE CHART — PRESENT METHOD 1/1.

Job : Machining components on two semi-automatic lathes

Chart begins : Two machines empty in the morning

Chart ends : Two components are prepared on both machines

Layout

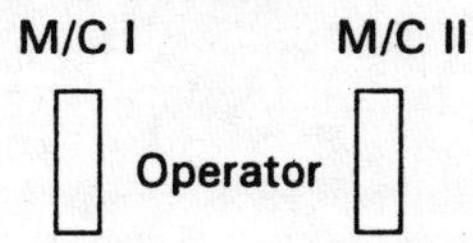

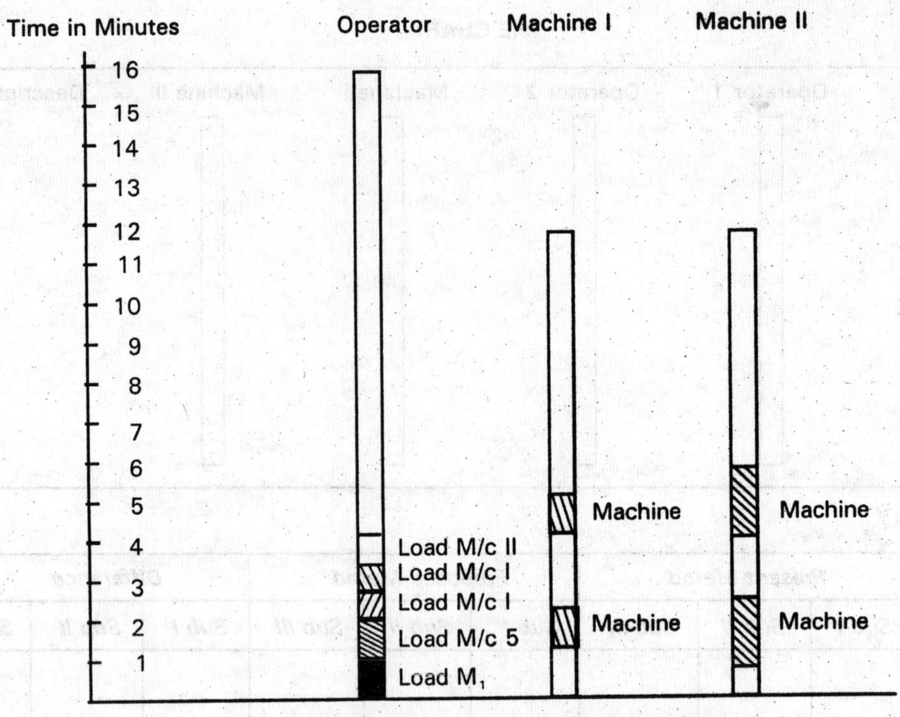

Man-Machine chart for one operator and two machines.

Problem 14.5 : An operation consists the following elements:

Load the machine	1 minute (manual)
Machine component	4.5 minutes (automatic)
Inspect component	0.5 minutes (manual
Unload machine	0.5 minute (manual)

Draw a man machine chart and find out the time per component under the following conditions: (*a*) One machine per operator, (*b*) Two machines per operator and (*c*) 3 machines per operator.

Solution :

ABC Company 1/1

Man-Machine Chart present method.

Job : Machining a component on a machine
(one operator and one machine)

Chart begins : Machine idle and man loads the machine

Chart ends : Man unloads the machine

Layout

Machine : ▭

Operator ○

The Chart

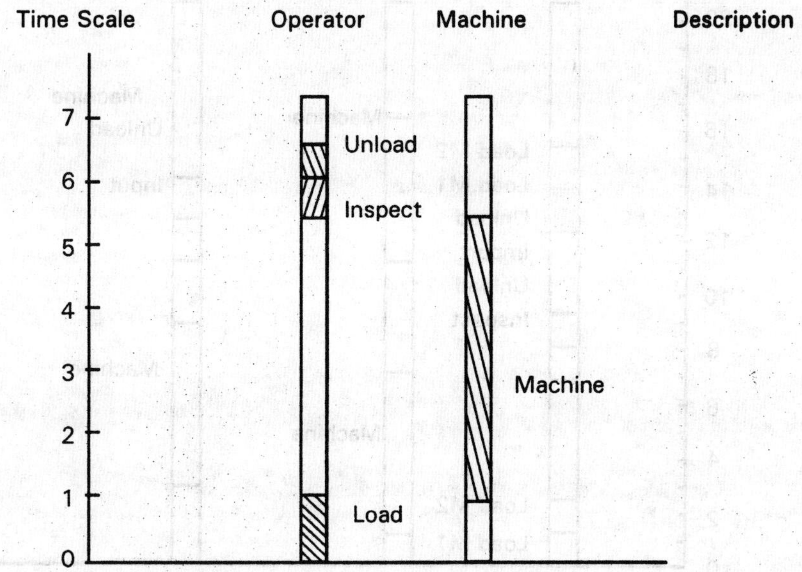

SUMMARY

Particulars	*Present method*		*Propoed method*		*Difference*	
	Man	*Machine*	*Man*	*Machine*	*Man*	*Machine*
Idle (min.)	1	1.5 2.5.				
Working (min.)	3	2 2				

Man Machine Chart (One machine and one operator)

Total Time: 6.5 Minutes. **Machine Working: 4.5 Minutes.** **Man working: 2.0 Minutes.**
Machine Idle: 2.0 Minutes. **Man idle: 4.5 Minutes.** **Time per component: 6.5 Minutes.**

XYZ Company 1/1

Man-Machine Chart Present type

(one operator and two machines)

Job : Machining component on two machines by one operator

Chart begins : Man loading the first machine

Chart ends : Man unloading the second machine

Layout

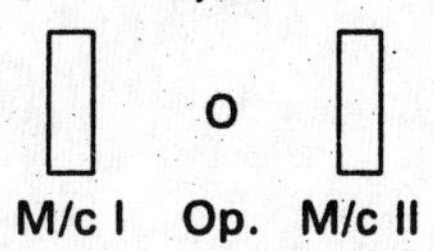

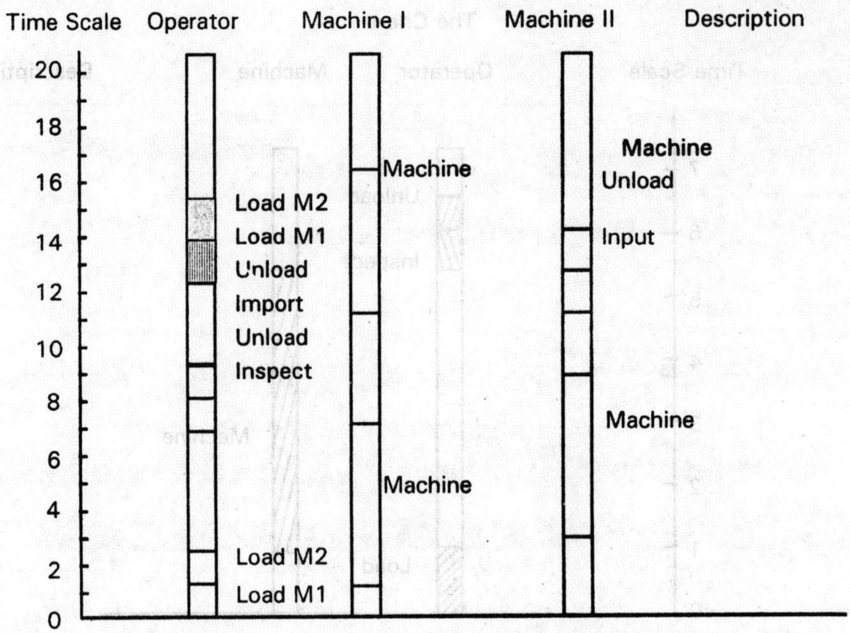

SUMMARY

Particulars	*Present Method*			*Proposed Method*			*Difference*		
	M/C I	*M/C II*	*Man*	*M/C I*	*M/C II*	*Man*	*M/C I*	*M/C II*	*Man*
Idle	3	4	3.5						
Working	6	9	9						

Man–Machine chart–2 machines and 1 operator.

Idle time of: Machine I	3 Min.	Machine II	4 Min	Man: 3.5 Min.
Working of: Machine I	6 Min	Machine II.	9 Min.	Man: 6 Min.

Total Time: 14 Min. Number of components Produced: 4.

Time per component = 14/4 = 3.5 min.

XYZ Company 1/1

Man Machine Chart (Present Type)

Job : Machining a component on three machines by one operator

Chart Begins : Operator loading first machine

Chart ends : Operator unloading the third machine

Layout

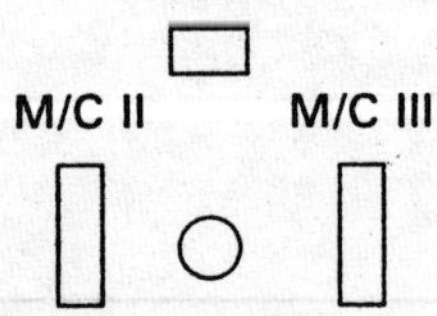

The Chart

op.

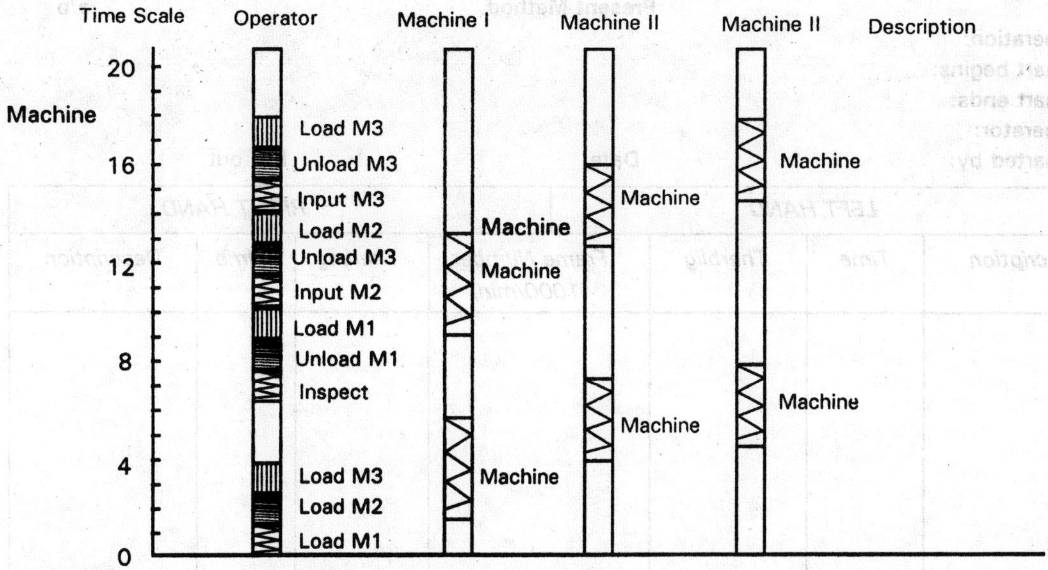

SUMMARY

Partures	*Present Method*				*Proposed Method*				*Difference*			
	M/C I	*M/C II*	*M/C II*	*Man*	*M/C I*	*M/C II*	*M/C II*	*Man*	*M/C I*	*M/C II*	*M/C II*	*Man*
Idle	6	6	6	6.5								
Working	9	9	9	9								

Three machines and one operator (Man machine chart).

Total Time in Min: 16 minutes
Working Time: M/C I 9.0 Min M/c II 9.0 Min M/c III 9.0 min.
Total idle time: M/c I 6.0 Min. M/c II 6.0 Min M/c III 6.0 Min.

Time per piece = Total time / Number of pieces $= \frac{16}{6} =$ **2.6 Min.**

14.7.4. Simultaneous Motion Cycle Chart Or SIMO Chart

The Simultaneous Motion Cycle Chart is used to record simultaneously on a common time scale the activities of the two hands, or other parts of the worker's boy during the performance of a single cycle of the operation under study. This chart is used to record short cycle operations, which requires a fraction of a second. Generally for recording short cycle operations, motion pictures are used. After taking the motion picture, the roll of the film is recorded in the laboratory frame by frame, by using *'THERBLIGS'*. Therbligs is a simple anagram of the name *Gilbreth.* In the beginning, Gilbretrh identified seventeen elementary movements or group of movements into which he divided all types of human activity. He has given symbols, letter codes and color codes for these therbligs. Figure 14.4 shows a specimen of SIMO chart.

SIMO Chart

Present Method. a/b

Operation:
Chart begins:
Chart ends:
Operator:
Charted by: **Date:** **Lay out.**

LEFT HAND				*RIGHT HAND.*		
Description	*Time*	*Therblig*	*Frame Number (1000/min)*	*Therblig*	*Time*	*Description*

14.7.5. Flow Diagrams

When one wants to study the layout or the flow of materials in the plant or movement of men in the plant, the best tool is *Flow diagrams and /or String diagrams.* The work area or the lay out is drawn to scale and the flow lines are marked on the layout to show the movement of the subject under question. After recording is over, the distance traveled by the subject under study is noted and by rearranging the positions of the equipment and machines on the layout, flow lines are drawn for the improved method. By comparing the distances moved in both the cases, will give us the idea about the improved layout's advantage. When different subjects are under study and want to use the same layout, different colored lines are drawn one for each subject. In String diagram, instead of lines, we use different colored threads to represents the path traveled by each subject. One pin is pressed near each work place and the string is tied to the first pin and as the movements are made it is taken round each pin until the study is over. At the end of the study, the length of the string gives the distance traveled by the subject. For recording, the symbols used in the flow chart are used. Figure 14.5 shows a typical

String / flow diagram.

XYZ Company. **a / b**
Flow Diagram (or String Diagram)
Method: Present / Proposed.
Type: Man / Material / Equipment
Job:

SUMMARY

S.No.	*Symbol*	*Description*	*Present Method*	*Proposed method*	*Difference*
1	○	Operation			
2	→	Transport.			
3	□	Inspect			
4	D	Delay			
5	∇	Storage			

Figure 14.5 : String / Flow Diagram.

Example 14.6. The layout of the reference section of a technical library is shown in the figure 14.6. The books kept in the reference section are meant for reference in the library itself and can be borrowed only for the overnight duration and are issued just before closing of the library. The procedure for issue of reference book is as follows: (figures within parentheses indicate average time in minutes for the particular activity). The cycle starts with the appearance of a student on the counter. The library assistant gets up from workplace and comes to the counter (0.032) and enquires about the title and author(s) of the book (0.020). The she walks over to the box containing reservation slips (0.024) and checks if some other student has already reserved that particular book (0.250). If there is no reservation, she walks to the box containing Issued Books Cards of the books already issued for the night (0.016) and checks if the particular book has already been issued for the night (0.300). If not, she walks she walks over to the reference book stalk (0.030), selects and picks up the required book (0.320) and walks back to the counter (0.400). She gets a borrower's ticket from the student (0.030), opens the back cover of the book and takes out an Issued Book Card from the flap (0.048), writes the number of the borrower's ticket on the card (0.060), hands over the book to the borrower (0.016). Then she walks to the box containing issued book cards (0.032) and deposits the card along with borrower's ticket in the box (0.040) and moves back to her workplace (0.046) and starts her original activity. If there is a prior reservation or the book has already been issued, she informs the person accordingly.

Record the existing method using suitable recording technique. Examine the present method critically and develop an improved method. You can suggest a new layout if necessary. Record the improved method I appropriate form and evaluate it in terms of percentage reduction in cycle time as compared to the existing method.

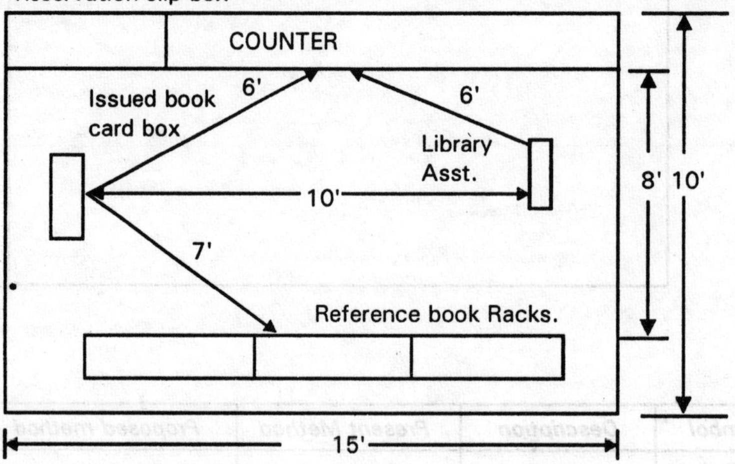

Present layout of the reference library.(not to scale). All dimensions are in feet.

Solution :

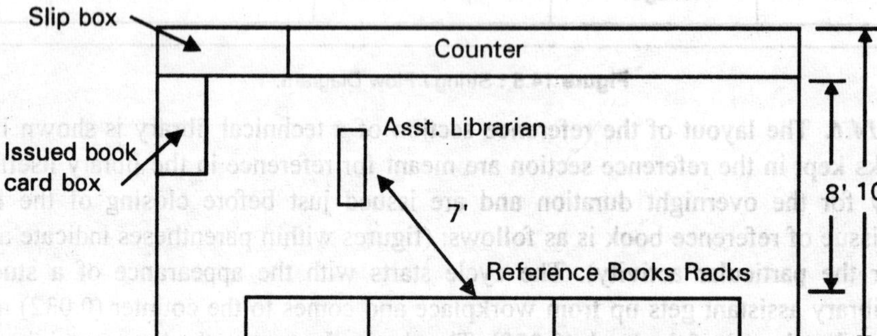

Improved Layout of the library (not to scale)

Summary of string and flow diagrams.

Method	*Movements time*			*Loading and unloading time*		*Total savings as % of clocked time*	*Savings in distance travelled*
	Distance	*Min.*	*%*	*Min.*	*%*		
Present	35 mt	1.544					
Proposed	20 mt	1.00					

14.7.6. Two Dimensional Models and Three Dimensional Models

Two-dimensional models are generally prepared by using templates and the layout is drawn to scale. This is useful for studying the flow of material and men in a more clear way. Three-dimensional models are prepared by using wood or thermo coal. This will be useful to study when movement of material uses third dimension. When the processing of material takes place in different floors, this type of model us more useful. The improved and final layout may be photographed as a means of record. Though, three-dimensional and two-dimensional models are costlier than other recording techniques discussed, they will be very useful in explaining to non-technical personnel.

14.7.7. Photographic Aids

In the above-discussed recording techniques, the recordings made by the observer by seeing the operations or activities with naked eye. When it is necessary to have a more detailed study of the workplace, where work is being carried out at a fast rate, it is necessary to use motion picture cameras (short duration operations performed at high speed). This type of recording is also used when we want to record simultaneously large number of activities. Both still and cine photography are employed for this work. The advantages of Photographic recording are:

(*i*) It will be a permanent record of the activity and its storage is easy.
(*ii*) The record may be referred by any number of people at any place and any number of times.
(*iii*) It is an excellent method used for demonstrating and for giving training to the workers to show how improved method is helpful to the worker.
(*iv*) Useful for repeated studies of the method.
(*v*) If cine films are used they can be projected at any required speed and can be stopped at any convenient point.
(*vi*) They can be moved backwards to study clumsy and awkward movements in detail.

14.7.8 Micro motion

The therbligs can often be determined only from a frame-by-frame analysis of a cine film record. For this purpose, the film is exposed at a speed of 1000 frames per minute. Recording may be done at 1000 frames and while analyzing it is projected at the desired speed to study the operations carefully. In case, if the camera is coupled with timing device and the films are exposed at predetermined timings, then the recording technique is known as ***Memomotion recording.***

14.7.9. Cyclegraphs and Chronocyclegraphs

When we want to record the movements of hand or finger of a worker, this type of recording technique is used. This method is originated by Gilbreth to enable comparatively short motion patterns to be recorded on a photograph of the work place itself. The record can be made as a continuous or dotted white line, known as a ***cyclegrah or chronocyclegraph*** respectively.

A cyclegraph is a record of path of movement, usually traced by a continuous source of light on a photograph. It is produced by attaching a small bulb to the worker's wrist or wherever the work study man desired to observe, and making a time exposure, while a single cycle or portion of a cycle is performed. The camera shutter is then closed after which a normal instantaneous exposure is made on the same film.

A similar photographic procedure is used to make a chronocyclegraph in which the light source is suitably interrupted so that the path appears as a series of pear-shaped spots. This enables both the direction of movement and the speed at any point along the path to be recorded. If the speed of interruption is known, then the speed of movement can be calculated. The figure 14.6 shows how a cyclegraph and chronocycle graph appears.

Figure 14.6 : Cyclegraph and Chroncyclegraph

14.8. EXAMINE OR CRITICAL EXAMINATION OR BRAIN STORMING

Critical examination stage is a very important stage in method study. During critical examination, all the recorded facts are critically examined by asking a set of questions to develop an improved method of doing work. A group of work-study people sit together, and subject each event of the record to a set of *primary and* a set of *secondary* questions to find alternative ways of doing the subject under question. While doing so, they must avoid any hasty judgment. Any hint for improvement must be committed in writing for future investigation. And new method should not even be considered until all the undesirable features of the existing method have been exposed by systematic examination. The objective of critical examination is to determine the true reasons underlying each event and to draw up a systematic list of all possible improvement for later development into a new and improved method.

14.8.1. Examination Procedure

Two sets of questions are asked. First the *primary set of questions* to indicate the facts and reasons underlying the subject examined, and the *secondary questions* to indicate alternatives and consequently the means of improvement. The questions are asked under five headings, which examines the purpose of operation or event, place where it is done, person by whom it is done and the sequence in which it is carried out and the means by which the operation is carried out.

(*a*) **Primary Questions :**

(*i*) **Purpose :** The question *What is achieved?* And *is it necessary?* And *Why?* Is asked to challenge the existence of the action. The answer will guide us to remove this operation or to improve the operation or to include this as it is in the proposed method or to combine the operation with any other event.

(*ii*) **Place :** The questions are *Where is it done?* And *Why there?* These questions help us to find alternate place for the work to have a better environment or to have a better layout.

(*iii*) **Sequence :** *When it is done?* And *Why then?* Questions asked regarding the sequence of operation with reference to other operations would enable us to develop a better sequence of carrying out the operation or combining the operation with some other operation.

(*iv*) **Person :** This question refers to the person performing the activity. *Who does it?* And *Why that person?* This question will help us to know why a particular person is doing the work.

(v) Means : Finally the means of carrying out the activity is challenged by asking *How is it done?* And *why that way?*

Secondary Questions : The secondary questions seek to establish suitable alternatives to existing or previously proposed method. While doing so, we may get many numbers of alternatives. To select one particular alternative once again a third question is asked. The questions are shown below:

Purpose: *What else could be done?* And *What should be done?*

Place: *Where else could it be done?* And *Where should it be done?*

Sequence: *When else could it be done?* And *When it should it be done?*

Person: *Who else could do it?* And *Who should do it?*

Means: *How else could it be done?* And *How should it be done?*

The answers to these questions indicate the lines along which a new method for the overall process should be developed. A further examination of proposed alternative may give us a better way of doing work. These questions may be tabulated as under for better understanding.

Description of the element:..

The present facts (Primary Questions)	*Alternatives (Secondary questions)*
1. PURPOSE; What is achieved? Is it necessary? Yes/No.	What else could be done? What?
2. PLACE: Where is it done? Why there?	Where else could it be done? Where?
3. SEQEUCNE: When is it done? Why then?	When else could it be done? When?
4. PERSON; Who does it? Why that person?	Who else could do it? Who?
5. MEANS: How is it done? Why that way?	How else could it be done? How?

14.9. DEVELOP THE NEW METHOD AND SUBMIT

During critical examination, some of the operations or events might have been eliminated / combined or improved. These form the basis of proposed method. Before finalizing the proposed method, certain factors regarding working environment and working conditions of workers are be given due consideration to have a comfortable and economical working conditions. Present day trend is to adopt man's working environment to his needs and capabilities. This led to the study of man at work and his needs at workstation for comfortable working, and is given the name – *Human Engineering* or *Ergonomics*. Ergonomics is study of relation between man and his occupation, equipment and environment and, particularly, the application of anatomical, physiological and psychological knowledge to the problem arising the reform. Other factors considered to design the comfortable workstation are Sight and Lighting, Color contrast, Ventilation and heating, Noise, Seating and Amenities.

As far the sight and lighting are concerned, the workplace must be provided with suitable lighting, preferably natural lighting and the work should not cause strain to the eyes of the person working. The actual place of working should be within the normal visual range. When man is working with the material get within the normal visual range, the eyes will at rest when looking, otherwise eye muscles strained. Color is generally used to improve or increase contrast or can be used as codes to indicate different items. Color can also be used to give a sense of pleasure and well being to the employees of a particular department.

Health and comfort of employees are directly affected by the ventilation and heating of the building in which they work. Therefore proper care should be taken to see that good ventilation and temperature are maintained so that the workers are self-motivated to work. Good ventilation will also minimize the risk of infection among the people working together. Any production process producing heavy noise should be isolated, so that it will not cause damage to the ears of other workers. The workers working on machines, producing noise should be provided with earplugs or provision may be provided to damp the noise. Properly designed seating is also an important factor in increasing the efficiency of the worker. Amenities like: safety of personal belongings, good toilet facility, and canteen, drinking water, and transport facility must be provided.

Improvement of plant and workplace layout, material used, design specifications of end product, process used, materials handling, work environment should be given due consideration while working for an improved method. Another factor to be considered is the motions of hand at the workplace. This enables us one to design a better workstation layout. It is recognized that there are certain basic movement of hand, which will ease the working procedure. These are known as *Characteristics of Easy Movement* or *Principles of Motion Economy*.

Before discussing the principles of motion economy, let us see how the movement of body is classified. Gilbreth gives these classifications. They are:

Class of movement.	*Movement.*
I	Fingers only
II	Fingers and Wrist.
III	Fingers, Wrist and Lower Arm.
IV	Fingers, Wrist, Lower and Upper Arm.
V	Fingers, Wrist, Lower Arm, Upper Arm and Shoulder.

There are six basic principles of motion economy. They are:

1. Principele of Minimum Movement : This principle states that, tools, materials and equipment should be positioned so that they can be used with minimum movement by the worker, and at the same time ensure that the movement classification used is to the lowest practicable group in the circumstances. If distances moved are to be kept to a minimum, knowledge of working areas is required. When worker is seated at a work place there is an area in front of him, which can be called his normal working area. The normal working area in the horizontal plane is bonded by the arcs drawn by the right and left hands with the lower arms pivoted from the elbows which are held naturally by the side of the body. If the tools used by worker are kept in the normal working area then least movement is required to reach the tools by the worker. Where all the tools used by worker cannot be located in normal working area, and then they should be placed in maximum working area. The maximum working area is the area covered by the arcs drawn by the right and left hands, with the arms pivoting from the shoulders. Objects placed in the normal working area may require class I type of movement and those placed in maximum normal working area, requires class III and IV movements. Application of this principle of minimum movement has resulted in the use of semicircular work places. When considering layouts of work place, it is obvious that movements will be kept at a minimum if the most frequently used equipment/tool is nearest to hand. In vertical plane, the minimum and maximum working areas can be found by the arcs drawn with hand hinged at the elbows and at the shoulder.

2 and 3. Principle of Simultaneous Movements and Symmetrical Movements : These two principles are considered together, which suggest that the movement of the arm and hands should be balanced by being simultaneous and / or symmetrical. The anatomy of human beings is such that if movements are unbalanced, excessive fatigue is caused. Perhaps you might have experienced that it is very difficult to walk with different loads in two hands than with equal load in both hands. Also, it is very easy to move hand in the form of an arc than in the form of a right angle. Example for symmetrical movement is one feels it difficult to write a square with right hand, while describing a circle with left hand. It is very easy to move both hands simultaneously in the form of the movement of one hand is the mirror image of the other.

4. Natural Movements : This principle requires that the movements used should be those, which can be performed most naturally by the body. The application of the principle includes the use of other limbs, fingers etc. so that the workload is spread over those parts of the body best fitted to the work. This Principle also concerned with the correct use of muscles and posture when weight lifting.

5. Rhythmical Movements : This principle states that *rhythm* should be present in movements. Rhythm may be described as the regular repetition of a movement pattern. When rhythm is established, hesitations are eliminated and movements are carried out at higher speeds with less fatigue.

6. Habitual Movements : This principle states that the movement pattern should be arranged so that it becomes habitual. Human beings possess a natural ability to form habits. When a set of movements performed habitually, less fatigue is caused and the movements are carried out almost in a relaxed mood.

7. Continuous Movements : Always smooth and continuous movements are preferable, as they cause less fatigue and inconvenience to the worker than movements involving sharp changes in direction. This is because, before hand changes its direction it must slow down and stop and subsequently accelerate again to its normal pace. Smooth and continuous movements employ natural momentum of does not involve muscular strain.

In considering the characteristics of easy movements, the field of visions an important factor, which is all too frequently ignored. Where inspection work is involved it must take place within the field of vision of the worker, which is relatively limited area.

Once, the improved method is decided with all the changes and improvements, the chart is constructed and now is ready to submit it to the management with report.

14.10. SUBMIT THE PROPOSED METHOD TO THE TOP MANAGEMENT

Once, the improved method has been developed with the help of specialists in the department and other technical personnel, the method is to be submitted to the top management. The report must consist of the following headings in its summary. (*i*) Recommendations, (*ii*) Reasons for recommendations, and (*iii*) Results expected from recommendations.

The detailed report must consist the following titles.

1. Summary, 2. Summary of recommendations, 3. Introduction, 4. Acknowledgements, 5. Description of the existing situations, 6. The work-study approach to the existing situation, 7. Extraction and evaluation of relevant factors, 8. Recommendations, 9. Implication for Management.

14.11. INSTALL AND MAINTAIN

To install the new method, first thing is to get cooperation of every person concerned with the job and then educate them about the benefits of the improved method and train them to accustom to new movements (better to have as many as rehearsal desired). Once it is evident that every body is following the new method, it is put into practice.

PART – B. WORK MEASUREMENT

14.12. INTRODUCTION

In order to keep up the delivery dates, the plans and schedules prepared for human work must be perfect. The usual practice is to prepare plans by previous experience. But some times planning by previous experience may put the manager in difficulty. In case the manager has an idea about the amount of work involved and time required to complete the job, his plans are workable and he will be in a better position to meet the delivery promises. Work measurement or time study is a technique or a tool by which a manager can set times required to carry out the required work and set time targets by taking into account all the allowances required by the worker while doing work. By definition ***work measurement is the application of techniques designed to establish the time for a qualified worker to carryout a specified job at a defined level of performance.*** In fact work measurement is a prerequisite to method study. It is because, Without knowing the time required to do the work, there is no meaning in saying a particular method is a right method of doing work.

14.13 OBJECTIVES OF WORK MEASUREMENT

The objectives of fixing the target times for work by the application of work measurement (at defined level of performance by a qualified worker) are:

It assist in :

(*i*) Compare the methods devised by method studies of doing a particular work and select the best method.

(*ii*) To allocate the labour to the jobs in proportion to the work involved having a proper balance the labour on the job.

(*iii*) In the preparation of realistic incentive scheme.

(*iv*) In the organization of labour by comparing the actual time taken and the targeted time for doing the work.

(*v*) In preparing the labour budget and control.

(*vi*) In preparing the estimates for present and future work.

14.14. WORK MEASUREMENT TECHNIQUES

The work under question may be repetitive type or non-repetitive type. In repetitive operations, the elements of operations will repeat many times during the study. In non-repetitive works, work cycle is hardly repeated; the examples of such work are maintenance work and construction work. Depending on the type of work, i.e. repetitive or non-repetitive proper method of work measurement is selected.

Basically, there are eight methods of work measurement. They are:

1. Stop watch time study, 2. Synthesis, 3. Predetermined Motion Time Systems (PMTS), 4. Analytical Estimating, 5. Comparative Estimating. 6. Estimating, 7. Activity Sampling, and 8. Rated Activity Sampling.

Before going to deal with the actual methods of work measurement, let us try to understand some of the terms we come across very frequently during the study.

14.15. RATE OF WORKING

If you observe a worker doing a work, you notice that sometimes he work faster and sometimes he work very slowly or if you observe a group of workers, doing same work, you see that some of them working faster and some of them very slowly. This may be due to various reasons. But our interest here is *the actual time taken to do a job depends on the rate of working maintained by the individual concerned.* To facilitate the calculation, work measurement values, unless otherwise stated, are always related to what is termed as ***standard performance.*** Standard performance means optimum rate of output that can be achieved by a *qualified worker* as an average for the shift or working day, due allowances being made for the necessary time required for rest. A qualified worker is one who is Physically and mentally suited to the job given to him and having necessary qualification, skill and knowledge to carry out the work satisfactorily.

14.16. THE UNIT OF WORK

In order to represent human work content of various jobs of different types on a common time scale the unit of work is used. In this unit of work is provision is made both for the effort required to do work and the allowances required related to the concept of *standard rate of working.* When expressed in units of work the work content of any job should be related to its most suitable characteristic for planning, control, costing, payment and other purposes and in this form it may be compared with other job on a quantitative basis (for example time per part or per ton processed etc.). Let us consider for example, three persons working on three different jobs. Mr. A is sitting in air-conditioned office and involved in decision-making work. Mr. B, is involved in some clerical work and sitting in a room with moderate comfort. Mr. C, a mason, who is working in hot sun, whose work needs physical exercise. If we consider one unit of work of all the above three persons they appear as shown in figure 14.7.

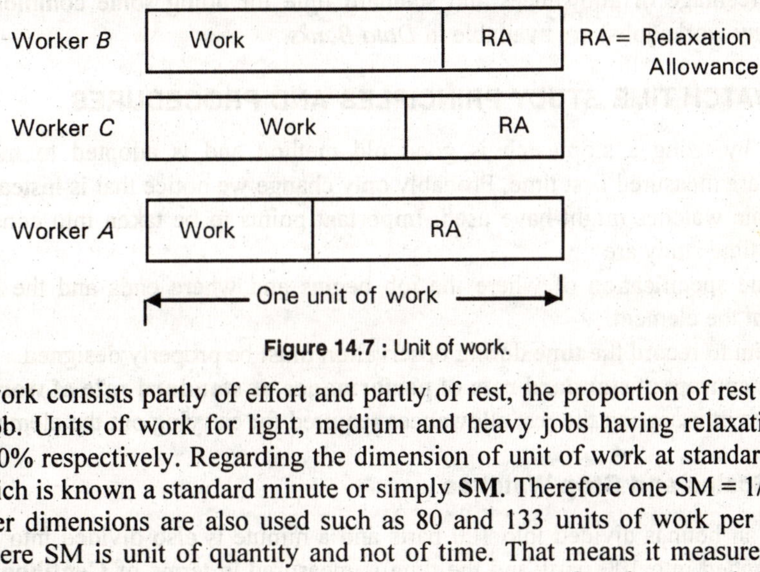

Figure 14.7 : Unit of work.

A unit of work consists partly of effort and partly of rest, the proportion of rest varying with the nature of the job. Units of work for light, medium and heavy jobs having relaxation allowance of 10%, 20% ad 30% respectively. Regarding the dimension of unit of work at standard performance is One minute, which is known a standard minute or simply **SM.** Therefore one SM = 1/60 th of an hour. In addition other dimensions are also used such as 80 and 133 units of work per hour at standard performance. Here SM is unit of quantity and not of time. That means it measures the quantity of human work in a job. SM may be converted into time if the rate of performance is known. This will be discussed latter.

14.17. STEPS IN WORK MEASUREMENT (TIME STUDY) OR PROCEDURE FOR CONDUCTING WORK MEASUREMENT

1. Break the job into recognizable pieces, known as **element**, whose size should be convenient to measure the time by the method selected.

2. The time required to carry out these elements at the standard rate of performance is measured by some means and this time is known as ***Basic time for the element.***
3. Percentage of basic time is added to the basic time individually or for the work as a whole to allow for recovery from the effort induced by doing the work. This is the quantity of human work in the job expressed in terms of standard minutes.

Many a time the work measurement team may find it is not appropriate to use the same method of time measurement to all the elements and also they may notice that there may be some common elements, whose work content may be same. In such cases, they may build up time from various techniques available. In practice the following steps are followed.

(*a*) The job is broken down into its measurable and recognizable elements.

(*b*) For elements involving human work, the records of basic time are consulted for this times for each element.

(*c*) For those elements for which there is no basic time already available, the time is measured by appropriate technique (for example: stopwatch time measurement, PMTS etc.).

(*d*) In case it is seen that the element, whose time is measured, reoccurs in some other job, the element's time is added to the records of basic time for future reference.

(*e*) The rest allowances are taken from the table and the required percentage of time is added to the time calculated in (*c*) above, to arrive at the time for doing the work at standard rate of performance.

(*f*) In addition, any relaxation allowances are deserved; the same may be added as a percentage to this time.

Required percentage of allowances and standard time for doing some common elements of a work (in fact many works/jobs) are available in *Data Banks.*

14.18. STOP WATCH TIME STUDY PRINCIPLES AND PROCEDURES

Measuring time by using a stopwatch is good old method and is adopted to measure time for elements, which are measured first time. Probably only change we notice that is instead of mechanical watches, electronic watches might have used. Important points to be taken into consideration while doing stopwatch time study are :

(*i*) Accurate specification of where the job begins and where ends and the method used to carryout the element.

(*ii*) A system to record the time during observation must be properly designed.

(*iii*) A clear concept of **standard rate of performance or standard rate of working.**

(*iv*) A means of assessing the rest allowances required for carrying out the element.

14.18.1. Time Scales and Stop Watches

In common, an hour is divided into 100 parts and a minute is also divided into 100 parts and a second is also divided into 100 parts and the time is measured in terms of **Centihour, Centiminute and Centiseconds (CH, CM, CS respectively).** The stopwatch dial is also divided into 100 parts to enable the observer to note down the time in centiminutes. These watches are known as decimal minute watches.

In decimal hour stop watches, the sweep hand makes 100 revolutions per hour or one every 36 seconds. One hundredth of an hour can be described as a decimal hour unit and abbreviated as CH. Figure 14.8 shows decimal hour stopwatch.

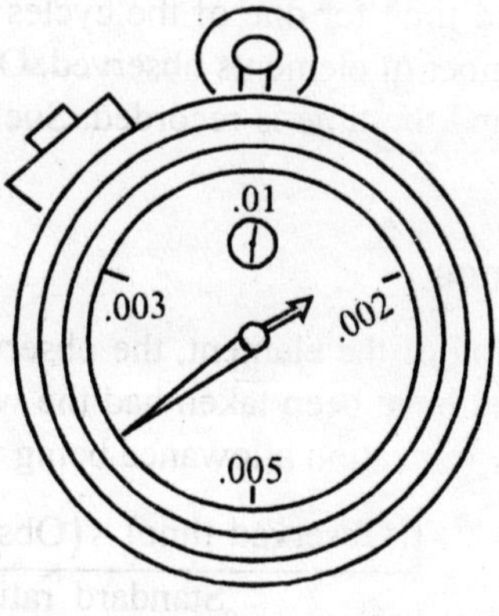

Figure 14.8 : Decimal hour stopwatch.

14.18.2. Standard Rate Of Working

The time observed and noted is known as **observed time.** The time study man must assess the rate at which the worker is working. He must have enough experience to assess the rate of working. Generally, he compares the work of the worker with a man walking at a speed of 6 miles per hour. A man can walk six miles per hour without much strain and effort. Suppose, he rates the speed of a man walking at 6 miles per hour as 100 and compare the speed of the worker and rates 80, it means that the worker's speed is below the standard performance. In case he rates it as 120, then the rate of performance of the worker is above the normal performance. Generally rating scale of 0-100 is used. The observer must note the time as well as rate at which worker is performing the element / job simultaneously. There are different rate of scales are available, such as 0 to 100, 0 to 80, 0 to 133 and 0.00 to 1.00. But 0 to 100 scales are commonly used.

14.18.3. To Break The Task Into Elements

The work measurement man may notice that the rate of working of a worker will be varying for the same element in each cycle. Hence it will be very difficult for him to find the time required to perform the element. Generally, while dividing any job into elements, it is customary to see that the element is of short time and may be of the range 10 to 50 centiminutes (6 to 30 seconds). The following principle is observed to divide the job into elements.

(*i*) Element should be clearly distinguishable and it should be of the size that it takes not more than 10 to 50 centiminutes.

(*ii*) Separate elements, which are identical from those, which are variable in the work they comprise.

(*iii*) Separate heavy work from the light work

(*iv*) When convenient, use audible points in the work, such as the snap of a switch or the sound of an article dropping into a container, as element break point.

When we have some elements taking more than ½ a minute or longer than 50 centiminutes, and no break points are available, then break points are arbitrarily made every ½ minute and the rating recorded. The rating for the whole element will be the weighted average value of the rating for the portions of the element. Such elements are known as long-cycle repetitive elements. In some cases, we may come across certain elements, whose total time may be less than 10 centiminutes. In such cases time of a number of cycles of exactly similar elements occurring succession is taken and an overall rating is made. The observed time for one of the cycles or elements can then be obtained by dividing this overall time by the number of elements observed. Or the element is observed in isolation, without including it in main study and the time is recorded. Such elements are known as Short Cycle repetitive work.

14.18.4. Ratings And Basic Times

Once the observer does the rating of the element, the observed time can be converted into **Basic time.** Basic time is one which would have been taken had the work been done at the standard rate of performance, i.e. at 100 without any relaxation allowance being taken.

$$\text{Basic Time} = \frac{[(\text{Observed time}) \times (\text{Observed rating})]}{\text{Standard rating}}$$

(Here standard rating is taken as 100)

For example if the observed time is 10 centiminutes and observed rating is 80, then the basic time is given by (10 x 80) / 100 = 8 centiminutes.

If the observed time is 10 centiminutes and the observed rating is 120, then the basic time is given by $= \frac{(10 \times 20)}{100} = 12$ centiminutes.

In the first case the worker has taken 10 centiminutes for an element, which needs only 8 centiminutes, i.e. the rate of performance is slow. In the second case the worker has taken 10 centiminutes for an element, which needs 12 centiminutes, that is his rate of performance is fast. It is appropriate to fix up most desirable motion pattern and train worker in that pattern and observe the time and rate the performance. For satisfactory rating the following conditions must satisfy. (*i*) There must be ample supply of work must be available. (*ii*) Rating should not be influenced by restrictions imposed by the nature of the work, (*iii*) While rating, one must see that the required quality specifications are met with. However, there are certain factors, which affect the rating some of them may be outside the control of the worker and some of them may be controlled.

14.18.5. Factros Affecting Ratings

The time taken to do a job depends on various factors, such as conditions of the machine, environmental conditions, attitude of the worker, quality of the material supplied, etc. Depending on the conditions stated above the performance rate may also differ. In addition to the above, effectiveness of a man's work is affected by certain controllable factors and certain uncontrollable factors. Some of them are: variations in quality or specification of the material used, changes in the operating efficiency of tools or equipment, minor changes in methods and variations in mental attention necessary for the job will influence the rate of working. These are outside the control of the worker. Factors like alteration in the quality within the specification given, Worker's skill and attitude of workers mind affects the rate of doing work. These are under the control of the worker. The speed at which the worker works will depend on the effort demanded by the job and the care requried on the part of the worker while doing the work.

14.19. TIME STUDY PROCEDURE

All the workers whose work is affected by the time study, is informed regarding the purpose of time study and the advantages of time study well in advance to get their cooperation during the study.

Permission from the management also sought. The time study man must go round the shop and have acquaintance with the worker. Better the management personnel accompany the time study man. After having introduced himself to all concerned workers, he has to plan regarding the breakdown of job into elements, Element breakdown points and establishing synthetic data both for cycle and element times.

14.19.1. Tools of Time study

(*a*) ***Stop Watch :*** There are two types of stopwatches used for time study in general. In one of the type the winding knob returns both hands to zero when pressed and immediately pressure is released, the watch restarts. It can be made to stop completely by means of a slide alongside the winder, which stops the hands at the position they were in at the moment of bringing the slide into action. This type of watch is known as *fly back stopwatch.* It must be checked now and then for its accuracy. This type of watch is always is clipped to the time study board and after the use watch is allowed to run down to pressure the spring. Another type of watch is *continuous* type. In this watch the time is recorded continuously. If we press the knob, the watch handle stops at the point where it is. The second pressing takes the handle to zero. The recording on this watch is known as *cumulative time record.*

14.19.2. Time Study Board

The study board is used to hold recording sheets and the to clip the watch. The board is designed well to size and shape, so that it is convenient to hold in the hand while taking reading. A specimen of recording sheet is given in figure 14.9.

STUDY SUMMARY RECORD. Study Ref:
Page No.

Time study: Work: Date:
Production Study: Department: Taken at:
Location: Labour Classification:

Time Check: Operation Description:
Finish Time: Started Time Elapsed Time: Total Recorded Time: Error:
Materials: Machine: Working Condition:
Number of Cycles: Average rating: Quality: Quantity:

S.No.	*Element description.*	*No. of Occasions.*	*Basic Time*	*Relaxation Allowances % Factors.* *A B C D E F G H*	*Total*

Figure 14.9 : Time Study Summary Sheet.

The Time Study record sheet is shown in figure 14.10. The basic time and average rating calculated from this sheet is entered in the summary record sheet shown in figure 14.9. Using fly back stopwatch or continuous typę of stopwatch may do the recording either. If we use cumulative type of recording, the time for each element is worked out by taking the difference between current reading and previous reading (subtraction of successive readings). The element number and rating also entered. For each element number of readings are taken and the average is calculated for getting *observed time.* Similarly average rating is also calculated. Once we get average observed time and average rating, basic time is calculated by multiplying the both and dividing the product by the standard rating (= 100).

OBSERVATION RECORD (TIME STUDY) date:			Study Ref :	Page No: /	
S.No.	*Element Description*	*ObserveTime (x)*	*Rating (y)*	*Ineffec Time (w)*	*Basic time*

Figure 14.10 : Observation record for time study.

Once the study is over the stopwatch is left running until it is compared with the clock by which it was started. The procedure of calculating the basic time from the recorded time and recorded rating is known as *extension.*

$$\text{Basic Time} = \frac{\left[(\text{Observed time}) \times (\text{Observed rating})\right]}{\text{Standard rating}}$$

When time for an element is observed many times and rating is also recorded, if we calculate basic time for each observation, we may find the basic time will vary for each reading. In such case, we can take the average of the basic times. Best way is to take the average of observed times and observed ratings and calculate the basic time. There are many methods for finding the average, one such method is finding graphic average.

14.20. RELAXATION AND CONTINGENCY ALLOWANCES (RA)

Once the basic time is calculated, relaxation allowances and contingency allowances are to be added to basic time to get standard time. Relaxation allowance (RA) is added to for personal needs and to recover from fatigue caused during the work. The relaxation allowances depend on the nature of work, work environment, sex and age of the worker. There are charts available showing the allowance required (which have been calculated taking all factors such as nature of work, age and sex of the worker and environmental factors). Relaxation allowance is expressed as a percentage of basic time. These allowances are çlassified as:

Letter Code	*Allowance for*	*Letter code*	*Allowance for.*
A	Energy output	E	Personal needs
B	Posture	F	Thermal conditions
C	Motions	G	Atmospheric Conditions.
D	Visual Fatigue.	H	Other influence of environment.

14.21. CALCULATION OF STANDARD TIME

Once the basic time for an element is calculated, then allowances to be added are decided depending on the nature of work and workmen and tables of relaxation allowances is referred and recommended percentage of allowances are added to find the percentage of allowances required. Then that much percentage of basic time is added to find the ***standard time or the work content of the element or the job*** as the case may be. Some jobs need certain contingency allowance (also expressed as percentage of basic time). These allowances are added to take care of number of minor activities, which may be so spasmodic or infrequent that work measurement cannot be done economically. To get the standard time contingency allowance is also added to the basic time. The total sum of basic time, relaxation allowance and contingency allowance will give the standard time or the work content of the element or the job.

Therefore Standard time = {(observed time × observed rating) / standard rating} + Relaxation allowance as percentage of basic time + contingency allowance as a percentage of basic time

Problem 14.7 : The following table gives the elemental normal time established after time study for a milling operation on a casting using a vertical milling machine. The rest allowances for the elements are also given. Normal timings for element numbers 1 to 7 are per piece and that for element number 8 is per 100 pieces. Give a contingency allowance of 5 % on normal time. Compile the normal output per hour.

S.No.	*Element description*	*Normal time in minutes*	*Rest allowance %*
1	Pick up Casting, locate in fixture, lock 2 nuts, Set guard, start machine and auto feed.	0.35	13
2	Break edge of milled face, clean with Compressed air.	0.33	11
3	Gauge depth on surface plate.	0.16	11
4	Place casting in box; place new casting Beside machine.	0.25	13
5	Wait for machine to complete milling.	0.21	11
6.	Stop machine, return table, open guard, unlock fixture, remove finished casting and place on surface plate.	0.34	13
7	Clean machine table with compressed air	0.14	11
8	Help another worker to unload new casting and load Finished casting on truck (for 100 castings)	1.50	0.33

Solution :

Time required for 8th element is given for 100 pieces. Hence time required for one piece = 1.50 / 100 = 0.015. Now let us calculate standard time for each element and add them to get the work content for the job.

Element number	*Normal time In minutes*	*Rest Allowance %*	*Allowance*	*Normal time + Allowance*
1	0.35	13	0.35 x 0.13 = 0.046	0.35 + 0.046 = 0.396
2	0.33	11	0.33 x 0.11 = 0.40	0.33 + 0.40 = 0.370
3	0.16	11	0.16 x 0.11 = 0.180	0.16 + 0.180 = 0.180
4	0.25	13	0.25 x 0.13 = 0.033	0.25 + 0.033 = 0.283
5	0.21	11	0.21 x 0.11 = 0.023	0.21 + 0.023 = 0.233
6	0.34	13	0.34 x 0.13 = 0.044	0.34 + 0.044 = 0.374
7	0.14	11	0.14 x 0.11 = 0.015	0.14 + 0.015 = 0.155
8	0.015	33	0.015 x 0.33 = 0.0021	0.015 + 0.021 = 0.0171
				TOTAL 2.0081 = App. 2.01 minutes.

Add 5 % of contingent allowance: 2.01 + 0.05 × 2.01 = 2.01 + 0.1005 = 2.1105 minutes.

Hourly out put = $\dfrac{60 \text{ minutes}}{2.1105 \text{ minutes}}$ = 28.429 pieces. Say 28 pieces. (If centi hours take 100 minutes)

(*b*) If the job is performed on a piecework basis, what will be the output per shift of 480 minutes?

Time per piece = 2.1105 minutes. Hence for 480 minutes out put = $\dfrac{480}{2.1105}$ = 227.434. Say approximately 227 pieces are the output for 8-hour day.

Problem 14.8 : In one of the operations, the following elemental times were observed with corresponding rating. Give 10% relaxation and 5% contingency allowance, calculate the standard time for the operation and find out the weekly production, assuming 8 hours per day and 6 days per week.

Element Number	Element description	Average Observed Time in Minutes	Average Rating
1.	Pick up gasket and element.	0.25	120
2.	Pick up gasket and apply adhesive to it and keep on conveyor.	0.15	90
3.	Pick up element, apply adhesive to it and keep it on table.	0.15	90
4.	Drying.	1.00	—
5.	Pick up gasket and element, fix them together and place in bin.	0.10	110

Solution :

Element Number	*Average Observed Time in min.*	*Average Rating*	*Basic time = Observed time x observed rating/ standard rating.*
1	0.25	120	0.25 x 120 /100 = 0.300
2	0.15	90	0.15 x 90/100 = 0.135
3	0.15	90	0.15 x 90/100 = 0.135
4	1.00	—	1.000
5	0.10	110	0.10 x 110/100 = 0.110
		Total	1.680 min.

Relaxation allowance = 10% of basic time = 1.680 × 0.1 = 0.168

Contingency allowance = 5 % of basic time = 1.680 × 0.05 = 0.084

Total allowance = 0.168 + 0.084 = 0.252 minutes.

Therefore work content = Standard time = 1.680 + 0.252 = 1.932 minutes.

Total number of hours in a week (given) = 6 × 8 = 48 hours.

Output for 48 hours = $48 \times \frac{60}{1.932} = \frac{2880}{1.932}$ = 1490.68 units. Say approximately 1490 units.

Problem 14.9 : A summary of a time study taken by you on the assembly of three terminal blocks with two screws each to a chassis gives the following result:

Element Number	*Element*	*Normal Time in Minutes*	*Frequency*
1.	Pick up 4 kg chassis, place on table and position	0.10	1
2.	Pick up and align one terminal on chassis	0.20	3
3.	Pick up two screws and fix terminal by hand.	0.40	3
4.	Pick up and position tool on screw	0.10	1
5,	Tighten screw	0.10	6
6.	Reposition tool on next screw.	0.05	5
7.	Aside tool.	0.05	1
8.	Aside chassis (4 Kg).	0.10	1

The company works on 8-hour shift, which includes two tea breaks of 15 minutes each. Working conditions in the factory are good.

Establish the standard time for this operation giving appropriate allowances as applicable. Show the breakdown of the allowances given by you.

Solution :

Element Number	*Normal time*	*Frequency*	*Total Normal time*	*ALLWANCES Posture*	*Motion*	*Energy*	*Total %*	*Allowance*	*Standard time*
1	0.1	1	0.1	0.05	0.05	0.05	0.15	0.015	0.015
2	0.2	3	0.6	0.04	0.04	0.04	0.12	0.072	0.672
3	0.4	3	1.2	0.03	0.03	0.04	0.1	0.12	1.32
4	0.1	1	0.1	0.03	0.03	0.04	0.1	0.01	0.11
5	0.1	6	0.6	0.04	0.04	0.04	0.12	0.072	0.672
6	0.05	5	0.25	0.03	0.03	0.04	0.1	0.025	0.275
7	0.05	1	0.05	0.03	0.03	0.04	0.1	0.005	0.055
8	0.1	1	0.1	0.04	0.04	0.04	0.12	0.012	0.112
						TOTAL			3.331

Add 5% of contingency allowance = 0.05 × 3.331 = 0.16655

Total time = Standard time = 3.331 + 0.16655 = 3.49755 minutes. Say approximately 3.5 minutes.

Total time available = 8 hours – 30 minutes = 7 hours and 30 minutes. Hence Productivity = $\frac{450 \text{ minutes}}{3.5 \text{ minutes}}$ = 128.57 pieces. Say approximately 129 pieces.

Problem 14.10 : A stopwatch time study has been made of a light machining operation. The results are given in the following table. For this type of operation it is estimated taht405 minutes of the 480 minutes day are available to the operator for production purposes. Complete the computations to determine the standard time and the number of pieces per standard hour.

TIME STUDY OBSERVATION SHEET															
Operation : 11 Part No. 1074861. Date : 20.2.2001 Observer : Mr. Venkat. Operator : Mr. Ram															
Beginning time : 3.22 hours. Closing time : 3.34 hours.															
Element description and break down points.		Cycles. 1 0.00	2	3	4	5	6	7	8	9	10	Summary. ET	T	RF	NT
1. Check Part and engage	T														
feed.	R	.14	.32	.49	.62	.79	.96	.11	.28	.45	.59			.85	
2. Cut 7/8"	T														
diameter.	R	.06	.24	.40	.54	.71	.87	.03	.19	.36	.52			1.00	
3. Remove part and dispose to	T														
rack	R	.15	.33	.48	.62	.81	.96	.11	.29	.45	.62			1.05	

Solution :

Add the given timings for each element and divide by 10 to find the average observed time and multiply by rating factor (RF) to get the basic time. As the allowances are not given assume suitable allowance and add to basic time to get the standard time. Divide the available time per shift by standard time to get the number of units manufactured in a day.

Element No. 1. Total observed time = 15.8 min. Average observed time = $\frac{15.8}{10}$ = 1.58
Basic time = 1.58 × 0.85 = 1.343 minutes.

Element No. 2: Total Time = 15.1 min. Average time = $\frac{15.1}{10}$ = 1.51 Basic time = 1.51 × 1 = 1.51 min.

Element No. 3 Total time = 16.2 min. Average Time = $\frac{16.2}{10}$ = 1.62. Basic time = 1.62 × 1.05 = $\frac{16.2}{10}$ = 1.701 minutes.

Total basic time for all the three elements (Job) = 1.58 + 1.51 + 1.701 = 3.954 minutes.
Add 10% contingency allowance = 3.954 + 0.3954 = 4.3494 minutes.

Available time = 405 minutes. Hence number of units produced in 405 minutes = $\frac{405}{4.3494}$ = 93 units.

As it is 8 hour day hourly production $= \frac{93}{8} = 11.6$ units say approximately 12 units per hour.

Problem No. 14.11 : The following time study data relate to the operation of packing a set of gaskets in a carton. Determine the standard time per carton after allowing 5% for contingency work, which is found uneconomical to measure.

S.No.	Element	Frequency Per cycle	Observed Time in Min.	Rating	Relaxation Allowance.
1	Place carton in position	1	0.07	110	12%
2	Place one large gasket in carton.	2	0.08	120	10%
3	Place one medium gasket in carton.	4	0.08	120	10%
4	Place two small gaskets in carton	1	0.07	120	12%
5	Place two washer gaskets in carton	1	0.07	120	12%
6	Fold ends, seal and label the carton.	1	0.09	100	11%
7	Keep the carton aside.	1	0.05	110	15%

Solution:

Ele. No.	Frequency per cycle	Observed time in min.	Rating	Basic time In minutes 3 × 4/100	Allowance % of basic time	Allowance 5 × 6/100	Standard time 5 + 7	Total time 8 × 2
1	2	3	4	5	6	7	8	9
1	1	0.07	110	0.077	12	0.00924	0.08624	0.08624
2	2	0.08	120	0.096	10	0.00960	0.10560	0.21120
3	4	0.08	120	0.096	10	0.00960	0.10560	0.42240
4	1	0.07	120	0.084	12	0.01008	0.09408	0.09408
5	1	0.07	120	0.084	12	0.01008	0.09408	0.09408
6	1	0.09	100	0.090	11	0.00990	0.09990	0.09990
7	1	0.05	110	0.055	15	0.00825	0.06350	0.06350
							Total	1.07140

Total standard time = 1.07140 minutes for this add 5% contingency allowance. Hence the standard time for the job = 1.07140 + 0.0857 = 1.1571 minutes.

14.22. SYNTHESIS FROM ELEMENTAL DATA

In production work or in work of any nature, we may find some operations will be commonly appearing with other operations necessary for the work. Say for example, a worker picking up a bolt from a box and another worker picking up some machine component from tray. Both the operations involves picking up and the workers may use same type of motions. Though the works are different, the hand motions may be the same. It is similar to spellings of many words, where certain letters will appear in the spelling of many words. In such cases, if one have time data for repetitive or non-repetitive operations, it can be used for building up of time of an operation, which consists the element for which the *Synthesized* time data is available. In large companies large accumulated time data may be available and time for many common operations may be picked up from such accumulated data. Once the time for commonly used operations are available, other operations are subjected to time study and the total time required for the entire operation may be build up. Some organizations, may do time study on some common operations / elements and supply the basic times for the element or operation for which the necessary allowances are added depending on the situation to get the standard times. Building up of times for elements or operations in this manner is known as ***SYNTHESIS FORM ELEMENTAL DATA***. While measuring time for small elements if we isolate the element and measure the data it is known as *selective timing* and if we club the small element with some large element and measure the time and time for small element is worked out by taking the difference, then it is known as *differential timing*. But the best way for getting the time for very small element is to use *Pre determined motion times*.

14.23. PREDETERMINED MOTION TIME SYSTEM (PMTS)

In addition to synthetic data arrived at by time study of job elements, there are several systems of standards based on the elementary human motions on which all human work is based. In the year 1934 a well-known system being called *work-factor* was developed. The objective of this system is to avoid human judgment in conventional stopwatch time study. The basic time values and the means of modifying the values for different classes of motion were developed through thousands of observations involving special measuring devices. In 1941, the Methods Engineering Council at Pittsburgh made some refinements in the system hitherto made public and a parallel work was done by the *Methods-Time Measurement Association* (*MTM*). Work factor recognizes certain basic motions, which are modified by elements of difficulty, all of which tend to make movements slower. Factors which makes motions slower are weight or resistance, directional control, the need for care, change of direction and stopping a motion by manual control. Each such factor is called a "*work factor*" and modifies the basic time value. In MTM the basic motions are analyzed in greater detail and the predetermined times, therefore, need no modifications. Many companies are using this system under common label **PMTS or PREDETERMINED MOTIN TIEM SYSTEMS.** The theory behind the system is that manual work in industrial conditions can be regarded a consisting of different combinations of a relatively small number of basic motions. Since it has been demonstrated that within practical limit the time required for skilled worker to perform any one of these basic motions is constant, then by synthesis it is possible to construct patterns of basic motions for such work and to build up time values for them.

The MTM data were obtained from studies of operations working under normal industrial conditions. Accurate observations of the motions and their times were made by mans of a special type of *Synchronous cine-camera*. The data were based upon a large sample of different type of operators, of differing ages and both sexes, working in different localities. In order to bring the times for all motions to a common level, it was necessary to rate operations while the film record was being made. This was done on each occasion by at least three trained observers who rated each job as it was being filmed. By analyzing the leveled times, isolating suitable *basic motions* and determining the importance and effect of the variables, a short cut comprehensive table of data was constructed. There are 23 basic motions used in MTM. In conventional time study, normally the basic times will have a value from 0.10 to 0.50 minutes. But in PMTS the basic times fall between 0.001 to 0.04 minutes. The data are thus of the order of milliminutes and are expressed in *Time Measurement Units or TMUs*. One TMU is one hundred-thousandth part of an hour. This way of measuring time has become very successful.

In order to improve methods research work being carried out. This work has led to what is now the family of MTM techniques, each with particular characteristics and suitable for different work measurement situations. These are labeled as MTM-1, MTM-2 and MTM-3.

14.24. ANALYTICAL ESTIMATING

Analytical estimating is used for measuring non-repetitive work, when it has not been possible to compile sufficient data to enable basic times to be synthesized for all the elements involved. The same principle of breaking the job down into elements is observed as in other work measurement techniques, except that those elements for which times are to estimated are of longer duration than for elements for timing and rating. The technique serves all the basic purposes of other work measurement techniques, though it is slightly less precise owing to the greater reliance on judgment. It is being satisfactorily used in engineering maintenance as well as in engineering construction, and its use is likely to be extended to many aspects of process work and other fields. When need arises, synthetic data is used.

14.25. COMPARATIVE ESTIMATING

The development of Analytical Estimating enables Work Measurement to be applied to fields that had hitherto been considered inappropriate for the techniques. This technique requires specialist work-study personnel in the form of estimators to be attached permanently to the unit. An estimator may be attached with 10 to 20 workers for observation. Many a time it is very difficult to see that one estimator is permanently attached to the work study always. To overcome this difficulty, ***Comparative Estimating*** is in practice. The term ***Universal Maintenance Standards*** **or** ***UMS*** has been used for the idea in the United States. British standard defines comparative estimating as ***A work measurement technique in which the time for a job is evaluated by comparing the work in it with the work in a series of similar jobs-bench-marks, the work content of which has been measured.*** The arranging of jobs into broad bands of time is referred to as *slotting*, which reveals the basis of the technique. Each band will show the time in minutes and average work value. For each band there will be a representative selection of jobs whose work content falls within the range of whose work content has been measured by an appropriate technique (time study or MTM). These will be the sample jobs or benchmarks of their band.

When we want to prescribe time for a new job, it is compared with the benchmark jobs and a judgment is made as to which band of jobs it most nearly compares with. It is then judged to be of this band and the appropriate work value from the band is taken as being the work value applicable. Many a times we come across people who are professionally good in some work, and ask what time it takes to complete a particular work (which is similar with the work of the man whom we consult). He by his experience compare the work referred to a similar type of work and spell out the time.

14.26. ACTIVITY SAMPLING

In certain types of work it may not be practicable to use the work measurement techniques discussed above, either to establish work contents directly or for the purpose of building up a fund of synthetic data. The types of work of this category are: large number of people working in offices, or number of workers operating different machines in a production shop. Quite often, management wants to know what is taking place in such situations in terms of the proportion of time being devoted to each type of activity. In such cases, it is better to go for a technique similar to that of statistical quality control. In statistical quality control, by observing the result of a small sample, it is decided whether to accept the lot or reject the lot.

In ***Activity Sampling*** also the work-study man go round the office / workshop and note down what exactly happens at a particular workstation when he visits. He note down whether the worker /

machine is *working* or *idle.* He has to plan his work. First he must decide what should be the sample size. His work may take one day or number of days. Say for example he conducts study for one day of 8 hours. He found that during 8 hours, he has collected 100 samples (working or not working).

(*a*) In case he observes that the worker is idle (not working) for a period of 2 hours, the non working time as a percentage of total time is $\frac{2}{8} \times 100 = 25\%$.

(*b*) Random observations made = 100. In case he finds non-working observation record as 25, then the percentage of idle time is $\left(\frac{25}{100}\right) = 25\%$.

That is proportion of non-working time estimated, as a percentage of total time is 25%.

Accuracy of Results : It is true that the result obtained by activity sampling method differs from that of continuous study. If the sample selected by the observer were more then the result would have been very nearer to that of the time given by time study. The number of random samples selected by the observer depends on the degree of accuracy desired. ***In practice it has been found that a ninety five percent guarantee of the specified limits of accuracy (commonly known as the 'ninety five percent confidence limits') is acceptable for most purposes.*** This means, in effect, that the accuracy of the figure obtained can be guaranteed to obtain within ± *L* nineteen times out of twenty, *L* representing the limits of permitted variation stated as a percentage of total time. The number of observations (N) necessary to achieve such result is obtained by using the formula:

$$N = \frac{[4\,p(100-p)]}{L^2} \text{ OR } L = \frac{2\sqrt{\{p(100-p)\}}}{N}$$, where p is the occurrence of the specified activity expressed as a percentage of *N*.

As the technique requires only spot observations, it is possible to use it to study groups by visiting the individuals in sequence, recording in each case what activity or delay is occurring at the instant of observation. Activity sampling is a cheaper method of obtaining information about groups than continuous observation, since small number of observers can cover relatively large groups. The advantage of using activity sampling is that the required observations can be spread over a longer periods than would be economical when continuous studies are carried out. To find the required number of observations, let us consider that about 75% of the total time of a group of men or machines is devoted to various activities ($p = 75$), then if a satisfactory degree of accuracy would be ± 3 percent of the total time ($L = 3$) with 95% confidence, the required number of observations is given by:

$$N = \frac{(4\,pq)}{L^2}. \text{ Where } q = (1-p), \text{ i.e., } \frac{[4 \times 75(100-75)]}{3^2} = 833.$$ Say approximately 850 observations.

Rated Activity Sampling : As an extension of the normal uses of activity sampling, attempts have been made to modify the technique so that it may be used in determine the work content, and standard times for jobs. After recording the appropriate activates, observers have made rating assessments by watching workers for short periods of time; the assumption has then been made that such ratings are applicable to the corresponding activates recorded; the difficulties of such a procedure will be apparent. The main problem, however, is that because activity sampling recorded in general terms only what actually happens, even if workers are rated the broad context of existing methods of working must be accepted. The technique, to which the name *Rated Activity Sampling* is given, has been used successfully to establish standard times for jobs where groups of workers are employed on a wide range of activities.

Note : For solving the problems in Activity sampling, knowledge of statistics is essential. Given below are some of the formulae used from statistics while solving the problems.

In a sampling process, if there are '*n*' independent trials, with constant probability of success '*p*', then expected number of successes = *np*; and the standard deviation or standard error of the number of success is ($\sqrt{npq}$, where $q = 1 - p$). Hence mean standard deviation = $(\sqrt{npq})/n = \sqrt{\{p(1-p)/n\}}$. Where p = probability of success, q = probability of failure and n = sample size.

The theory of sampling is concerned with (*i*) Estimating the properties or parameters of the population. (*ii*) Assigning the limits with which the parameters of the population are expected to lie with a specified degree of confidence.

In normal distribution curve the area covered by normal curve covered by $\pm 1\sigma$ = 68.27 %, $\pm 2\sigma$ = 96.45% and $\pm 3\sigma$ = 99.73%. The concept of normal curve is related to assigning the limits with which the parameters of the population are expected to lie with specified degree of confidence, i.e. how much area should be covered by the chance phenomenon. Therefore, it is essential to decide the level of confidence. Generally the management as their policy matter takes this decision. Once the confidence level is decided, the number of observations can be computed. For 68 % of confidence level, the probability is 68% that the observation will present facts and 32% they will not. Hence the number of observations should be far a certain confidence level with certain degree of accuracy. Most commonly and accepted confidence of level is 95% ($\pm 2\sigma$ limits) and ± 5 % accuracy.

± 5 % accuracy can be expressed as standard error (*S*) i.e. S = ± 0.05. If '*p*' is probability of occurrence of an activity being measured expressed as a percentage of total number of observations then

$$S.p = 2 \times \sqrt{\frac{[p \times (1-p)]}{n}}. \text{ If } S = 0.05, n = \frac{[4p \times (1-p)]}{0.0025 \times p^2}$$

If the value of '*p*' is known or can be estimated with the help of past data or trial study, the number of random observations '*n*' can be computed.

Problem 14.12 : The management is interested to know the percentage of idle time of an automatic machines section. Work sampling study was conducted assuming level of confidence 95% and the accuracy of ± 5 %. Calculate the number of observations necessary to obtain the desired results. In order to estimate the value of '*p*', a trial study was conducted consisting of 1000 random observations. 250 observations showed that the machine was idle.

Solution : Obviously the percentage of idle time would be 25 % i.e. $p = 0.25$. Hence number of

$$\text{observations} = n = \frac{[4p \times (1-p)]}{0.0025 \times p^2} = \frac{(4 \times 0.25 \times 0.75)}{(0.0025 \times 0.00625)} = \text{Approximately 4800 observations.}$$

(**Note :** The number of observations can also be computed with the help of alignment charts or the tables and nomograms which are prepared for 95 % confidence level and ± 5 % accuracy).

If it is desired, 99 % confidence level with ± 2 % accuracy should be obtained; the formula will be accordingly changed. 99 % confidence level is approximately 3σ limits, hence the formula will be

$$S \times p = 3 \times \sqrt{\frac{[p \times (1-p)]}{n}} = (0.02 \times p)^2 = \left\{\frac{9 \times p(1-p)}{n}\right\}$$

$$\text{Therefore, } n = \left\{\frac{9 \times p(1-p)}{0.0004 \times p^2}\right\}.$$

Therefore, with the help of this formula, the number of observations desired can be calculated for a given confidence level and accuracy.

Suppose, we want to know whether the results are within in the desired accuracy or not, it can be done by calculating 'S' in the formula instead of 'n' as was previously done.

Assume that the final results of a study were as follows:

Number of observations machine working = 3000,

Number of machine idle = 1000,

Total number of observations = 3000 + 1000 = 4000

$$p = \left(\frac{1000}{3000}\right) \times 100 = 33.34\%, \text{ say} = 33\%$$

$$S.p = 2 \times \sqrt{\frac{p \times (1-p)}{n}} = S \times 0.33 = 2 \times \sqrt{\frac{(0.33 \times 0.67)}{(4000 \times 0.33^2)}} = 0.02 \text{ approximately}$$

$S = 4.46$ % which is less than 5 % the required accuracy.

This would mean that we are 95 % confident that the machines were idle 33 % of the total time. The accuracy of 4.46 % means that the results were correct within ± 4.46 % of 33 % (4.46 % × 33 % = ± 1.47%) or the time value will be 34.47 % to 31.53 %.

Problem 14.13 : A group of workers working 8 hours per day (one shift) on a group of lathes (excluding lunch time). During the study, it was observed that the workers were idle 15 % of the total time available and 85 % of the time they worked at an average performance of 110 %. It was recorded that they produced 420 pieces of acceptable quality. It was also assumed that the allowance for this machine group is taken from the company time study manual, which happened to be 15 % of standard time. Calculate standard time.

Solution :

Information	*Source of Data*	*Data for one day.*
Total time available to the operator	Time card	60 x 8 = 480 minutes.
Number of parts produced.	Inspection department	420 pieces.
Working time %	Work sampling	85 % = 408 minutes.
Idle time %	Work sampling	15% = 72 minutes.
Total allowance	Company time study manual	15 % of the standard time.

Assuming all the work carried out manually,

$$\text{Standard Time} = \frac{\{(\text{Total time in minutes})\times(\text{Working time in \%}) \times \text{Index}\}}{(\text{Total number of pieces produced}) + \text{Allowance}}$$

$$S.T. = \frac{(480 \times 0.85 \times 1.10)}{420} + 0.15$$

$$S.T. = \frac{(480 \times 0.85 \times 1.10)}{(420 \times 0.85)} = 1.26 \text{ minutes.}$$

Problem 14.14 : Following data relates to a work sampling study of a long cycle non-repetitive operation:

(*a*) Total Time Study = 10 days.
(*b*) Total number of observations = 1200
(*c*) Observation of Productive activity = 900
(*d*) Manually controlled elements = 600
(*e*) Machine controlled elements = 300
(*f*) Total acceptable units produced = 4000 pieces.
(*g*) Average rating index = 110 %
(*h*) Observations of unavoidable delay = 100

Calculate the standard time.

Solution :

Assumptions :

(*i*) The number of observations is sufficient to attain the desired accuracy and confidence level.
(*ii*) The process is assumed to be within control.
(*iii*) The study was conducted during working hours at the rate of 6 hours per day (of 8 hours).
(*iv*) No over time is permitted.

Total time during which the study was conducted = 60 hours.

$$\text{Productive time percentage} = \left(\frac{900}{1200}\right) \times 100 = 75\%$$

$$\text{Productive time} = 60 \times 0.75 = 45 \text{ hours} = 45 \times 60 = 2700 \text{ minutes.}$$

$$\text{Time per piece} = \frac{2700}{4000} = 0.675 \text{ minutes.}$$

$$\text{Manually controlled elements} = 600 \text{ observations.}$$

$$\text{Manually controlled time} = \frac{(0.675 \times 600)}{900} = 0.450 \text{ minutes.}$$

$$\text{Machine controlled time} = 0.675 - 0.450 = 0.225 \text{ minutes.}$$

$$\text{Basic time per unit} = (0.450 \times 1.10) + 0.225 = 0.721 \text{ minutes.}$$

$$\text{Unavoidable delay time} = \left(\frac{100}{1200}\right) \times 100 = 8.3\%$$

$$\text{Hence allowance to be provided} = (0.083 \times 0.750) \times 100 = 11\%$$

$$\text{Therefore, standard time} = 0.721 + 0.11 \times 0.721 = 0.721 + 0.07931$$

$$= 0.8 \text{ minutes approximately.}$$

Problem. 14.15 : Given the following work sampling data, determine the standard time per unit. Working Time = 60 %, Average rating = 90%, Relaxation allowance = 12.5%, Actual out put during the study = 1000 units and Study duration = 480 minutes.

Solution : Duration = 480 minutes.

Working time = 0.60 × 480 minutes = 288 minutes.

$$\text{Basic time} = \frac{288 \text{ minutes} \times \text{rating}}{100} = 288 \times 0.9 = 259.2 \text{ minutes.}$$

Standard time = Basic time + allowances = 250.2 + 12.5% of 250.2

= 259.2 + 32.4 = 291.6 minutes.

$$\text{Time per unit} = \frac{291.6}{1000} = 0.2961 \text{ minutes.}$$

Problem 14.16 : Given below are the observations of a work sampling study of a maintenance gang. Calculate (*i*) Individual utilization, (*ii*) Percent time lost for each cause by the gang, (*iii*) Overall utilization and its accuracy for 95% confidence limit.

Worker	*Round Number*									
Worker	1	2	3	4	5	6	7	8	9	10
Fitter No, 1	W	B	B	S	W	B	B	B	A	A
Fitter No. II	S	S	B	B	B	G	G	A	B	B
Welder	W	G	B	B	B	A	I	B	B	A
Electrician	W	W	S	B	B	B	I	B	B	W
Helper	I	B	B	I	B	B	A	B	B	I

B = Busy in worksite, working. *W* = Walking between Jobs. *G* = Getting materials or tools. *S* = Getting instructions. *I* = Idle. *A* = Away, not in work spot.

Solution : There are fifty observations Out of which 26 observations shows busy, 6 readings shows walking between machines, 4 readings are getting instructions, 6 readings are away, 3 readings are getting materials and 5 are idle.

(*a*) Fitter I is busy 5 times out 10 readings, hence individual utilisation is 50%.

Fitter II is busy 5 times out of 10 readings, hence individual utilisations is 50%.

Welder and electrician are also 5 times busy out of 10 readings; hence individual utilisation is 50%.

Helper is 6 times busy hence his utilisation is 60%.

(*b*) Time lost in walking is $\frac{6}{50} = 12\%$

Time lost in getting material = $\frac{3}{50} = 6\%$,

Time lost in Getting instructions = $\frac{4}{50} = 8\%$

Time lost in getting away from work spot = $\frac{6}{50} = 12\%$

Idle time = $\frac{5}{50} = 10\%$

(c) For 95% confidence limit and number of observations 50,

$$S \times p = 2 \times \sqrt{\left\{\frac{p \times (1-p)}{n}\right\}}. \text{ Here } p = \frac{26}{50} \text{ as 26 times busy out of 50 readings.} = 0.52$$

$q = 1 - p = 1 - 0.52 = 0.48$ and $n = 50$.

$$S \times 0.52 = 2 \times \sqrt{\frac{(0.52 \times 0.48)}{50}} = 2 \times \sqrt{0.005} = 2 \times 0.071 = 0.141$$

$$S = \frac{0.141}{0.52} = 0.027 \text{ say approximately } \pm 3\%.$$

Problem 14.17 : **Work sampling study is to be conducted to determine utilization of machines in a large machine shop. In a preliminary study, 200 observations were made and 50 observations showed the machine to be idle. What will be the number of random observations required to obtain a confidence level of 95 % and relative accuracy ± 5%.**

Solution : Here $p = \frac{50}{200} = 0.25$. q is $1 - p = 1.0.25 = 0.75$. $S = 0.0025$.

n, The number of observations required $= \frac{(4 \times 0.25 \times 0.75)}{0.0025 \times 0.00625} = 4800$ observations approximately.

Tail Note: THERBLIGS :

While discussing micro motion study, we have discussed about **THERBLIGS**. Now to give a clear understanding about Terabits below given is the symbols and letter codes used for some therbligs.

S.No.	*Therblig*	*Symbol*	*Letter code*
1.	Search		Sh
2.	Found		Fd.
3.	Assemble	#	A
4.	Transport Empty		TE
5.	Transport loaded or Hold		TL
6.	Unload		UL
7.	Sitting Idle		SI
8.	Thinking		T
9.	Disassemble	≠	DA

QUESTIONS

1. What role can work study play in efficient operation of an enterprise?
2. Discuss critical examination procedure with special reference to the role of creative thinking and brainstorming.
3. Manual assembly of 3-point plug used in the home. Quantity assembled per day is 300 units. Components involved are:

   (*i*) 3 pins with threaded tops(*ii*) 3-threaded housing for accommodating wire terminals and to be assembled to the pins.(*iii*)3 screws for holding wire terminals.(*iv*)2 plastic housing parts.(*v*)One screw for holding two hosing parts together.

   Draw a two-hand process chart for the above said assembly.
4. **Why study work? Explain the need and rationale for study of work. What is the scope of work-study?**

5. What is ergonomics? Discuss its relevance to method study.
6. A laundry, with five washers, one extractor, and two dryers, provides prompt cleaning service to its clients. Its equipment require the following time to complete a work cycle:
   Washer = 30 minutes, Extractor = 9 minutes, Dryer = 21 minutes/
   It takes 3 minutes to load or unload each of these three machines. One worker has been assigned to perform all the loading and unloading activities.
   (*a*) Construct a multiple activity chart to illustrate the total work process to complete one batch of washing.
   (*b*) What is the cycle time?
   (*c*) Construct a chart showing utilization of man and machine. Show a complete cycle.
7. Write short notes on: a) Critical examination, b) Man machine chart, c) Fatigue allowance, d) Flow charting. e) Work sampling.
8. What is work sampling? Of what value is it to the management?
   A work sampling study is to be used to measure the down time of a group of machines. A preliminary study showed that out of 500 observations 150 observations correspond to down time. Determine the number of observations required for this study for a 95% confidence level and a desired accuracy of ±5%. Use the standard formula for solving this problem.
9. Define Work measurement. What are its uses?
10. Mention briefly various steps in making a time study.
11. What are the various allowances given in time study? What allowances you recommend for the following activities?
   (*a*) Clerk posting a ledger in an air-conditioned office.
   (*b*) Operator doing spray-painting in a painting booth.
   (*c*) Mason plastering a compound wall.
   (*d*) Operator taking the readings of the instruments in a chemical plant.
   (*e*) Operator working on a computer.
   (*f*) Operator driving a battery operated truck on the shop floor.
   (*g*) Worker pouring molten metal in a mold in a small foundry.
   (*h*) Operator of an overhead crane traveling with load.
   (*i*) Tailor stitching garments on a sewing machine.
   (*j*) Work man carrying a cement bag on his head.
12. A work sampling study is to be conducted to determine the idleness of milling machines in the milling section of large engineering works. In a preliminary study 100 observations were made and 25 observations showed the machines to be idle. What will be the number of random observations required to be made to obtain a confidence level of 95% and an accuracy of ± 5 %.
   If after 600 observations it were found that the incidence of machines being idle is 30 % what would be the revised number of random observations to be made?

15

USE OF COMPUTERS IN PRODUCTION AND OPERATIONS MANAGEMENT

- Introduction.
- Use of Computers in Production Control.
- Sales analysis
- Schedule analysis
- Design of new procedure.
- Capacity Loading
- Advantages of using computers in P.P.C.

15.1. INTRODUCTION

Computers have become very important and essential requirement in the life of a modern man. Computer education is spreading like a wild fire and is occupying every aspect of human life. This is because, lot of information can be stored in the computer and can be made use of the same when needed. Modern business uses computers to store the business data and uses it when needed for effective decision – making. As far as production control is concerned the computers may be / are used in the following areas.

(*i*) Production control

(*ii*) Control of production process (use of Numerical controlled machine tools).

(*iii*) Forecasting and demand analysis.

(*iv*) Loading, Scheduling and Assignment of jobs to machines,

(*v*) Assembly line balancing,

(*vi*) Inventory Control,

(*vii*) In MRP

(*viii*) In management information and integrated data processing system.

15.2. USE OF COMPUTERS IN PRODCUTION CONTROL

Production control system involves large number of calculations, sorting and storage of huge amount of data and the printing of considerable volumes of information. But one thing to remember is that the computer will give us necessary information and the decision is to be taken by the concerned manager only. But if decision – making depends on a mathematical logic, then computers can be make decisions. But whether the decision is to be accepted or not depending on the prevailing conditions is the duty of the in charge manager himself. In such cases the quality of decision will depend on the information available. If the data regarding the capacity of each machine available and information about the available load is on hand, by the use of scheduling programme, loading of machines and assignment of jobs to machine can be made by using a computer.

As far as inventory management is concerned, computers are useful to calculate / estimate the quantity of materials required, to prepare purchase orders, after receiving the material, they may be used to make stock entries, when materials are issued on indent, entries can be made in stock ledger. Computers are also useful to find out the economic order quantities, re-order levels. Inventory control by *p – system* is very conveniently being done by the use of computers.

Computers çan be conveniently used to get more benefits in plants dealing with a wide variety of products, with a greater diversification of specifications of materials, products and components and with highly dynamic schedules, which has to cope with changing customer's requirements. Such situation would arise in large batch and job production plants. It would appear that the type of production in itself is not the decisive factor as to whether or not the computer be usefully employed in production control. Many flow production firms, are in fact, engaged in batch – production of components and assemblies for their final flow assembly lines; they are conscious of scheduling problems in their batch shops, as well a production smoothening problem associated with their final lines, find the computer very much useful.

15.2.1. Sales Analysis

From the previous records of sales, the organization can easily analyze the deviation in sales of various products and think of changing the design of product or diversify the product or increase the production and so on. One can design the programmes for this purpose and get the data analysed to take timely decision.

Following from the sales analysis one can study the effect of changing characteristics of past orders on the diversification of products and component's specifications, the increase in variety of required material and the extent to which material and components can be made interchangeable from product to product and model to model. These effects are compared with expected trends in future, based on the sales forecasts, in order to conclude whether any trends of past events may be reasonably expected to proceed and also decide whether it would be advantageous to arrest them and reformulate fundamental managerial policies.

15.2.2. Schedule Analysis

By analyzing the data concerned with failure of meeting delivery dates, the scheduling for future production may be done effectively to meet the delivery dates properly., The complexities involved in matching the available capacity with expected load might be handled successfully with the help of a computer. Any unexpected change in the schedule can also be dealt conveniently.

15.2.3. Design of a New Procedure

If we consider computer as an integral part of the existing system, the advent of new and advanced software enable us to redesign and update the existing system and install totally a new and advanced system, which will be help us to process the data in a short time and enable the manager to take qualitative decision in time.

15.2.4. Capacity Loasing

The details of operation and the bill of materials for the manufacture of a product can be held on a computer file. When an order for the product is obtained form the customer, the computer, if suitably programmed, can explode the product into its component parts and load each manufacturing operations into its appropriate cost centers at a time when capacity is available and in accordance with the time schedule which ensures that production can proceed with the least possible delay between manufacturing stages.

In general, we can say the computers are useful in production control in the following areas: Order analysis, Preparation of operation details and prepare bill of materials, Capacity loading and Preparation of schedules, Inventory control and stock control, Work order documentation and integration of production control and other control functions.

15.2.5. Advantages to be Expected From The Use of Computer For Production Control

The following are the advantages derived from the use of computers in production control:

(*a*) Reduction of clerical costs,
(*b*) Maximisation of machine utilistion,
(*c*) Minimisation of work – in – progress or Work – in process inventory,
(*d*) Minimisation of delays in processing of jobs,
(*e*) Minimisation of set – up time,
(*f*) Reduction of lead-time,
(*g*) Reduction of errors in forecasting and
(*h*) Reduction of inventory costs.

QUESTIONS

1. Write a short notes on the use of computes in production control.
2. What advantages are derived by the use of computers in production control?

16

PRODUCTIVITY ENGINEERING AND MANAGEMENT

- Introduction.
- Productivity and Production.
- Definition of Productivity.
    - Partial Productivity.
    - Total Factor Productivity.
    - Total Productivity
- Factors affecting productivity.
- Productivity benefit model.
- Productivity Engineering and Productivity Management.
- Productivity Measurement
    - International level.
    - National level.
    - Industrial level.
    - Company level.

16.1. INTRODUCTION

A country's effort to improve productivity must first begin with basic economic units, namely: Manufacturing units and Service organizations. To manage productivity, in its true sense, four formal phases are important. They are:

Productivity Measurement,
Productivity Evaluation,
Productivity Planning, and
Productivity Improvement.

These four phases are known as **Productivity Cycle.** Once the productivity of an organization for the current period is measured (Period may be a month, year or any time unit), it must be compared with the target level set up in the previous period. Based on the evaluation, a new productivity target or level must be planned for the next period. Finally, depending on the nature and level of the planned target of productivity, improvements must take place in the next period. To check whether the planned productivity level is achieved or not, once again the measurement of productivity in the next period must take place. The cycle repeats.

16.2. PRODUCTIVITY AND PRODUCTION

Productivity has become such a buzzword these days as every one talks of improving or increasing productivity. Productivity is defined as the **"quotient obtained by dividing the output by one of the factors of production".** In this way it is possible to speak of Productivity of capital, investment,

Productivity of raw material or Productivity of labour etc., depending on the consumption of a particular resource by the product manufactured.

The term productivity is often confused with the term production. Many may think that greater the production, greater will be the productivity. This is not necessarily true. Production is concerned with the activity of producing goods or service or both. Productivity is concerned with efficient utilization of resources available in producing the product or service. To understand it let us see the problem below:

Problem 16.1 : A company is producing a product X. It produces 10,000 units of X by employing 50 workers at 8- hour day for 25 days in a month. Suppose the company increases its production of X to 12, 000 units by hiring 10 additional workers at 8 – hour day for 25 days a month, calculate the increase in productivity.

Solution :

$$\begin{aligned} \text{Production of } X &= 10{,}000 \text{ units. Hence} \\ \text{Total man-hours utilized} &= 50 \times 25 \times 8 = 10{,}000 \text{ man} - \text{hours.} \\ \text{Productivity} &= 10{,}000 / 10{,}000 = \text{Output in units / Input in man} - \text{hours} \\ &= 1 \text{ unit of } X \text{ per man} - \text{hour.} \end{aligned}$$

When production of X is 12, 000 units,

$$\begin{aligned} \text{Labour input} &= 60 \times 25 \times 8 = 12{,}000 \text{ man hours.} \\ \text{Productivity} &= \text{output / input} = 12{,}000 / 12{,}000 = 1 \text{ unit of } X \text{ per man-hour.} \end{aligned}$$

Here we can notice that the production of X has gone up by 20 percent but the productivity remains same. Suppose the company manufactures 12,000 units of X with the same 50 workers, and then the productivity is $\frac{12{,}000}{10{,}000} = 1.2$ units of X per man-hour.

Here, the same 50 workers have been worked efficiently and the productivity is increased from 1 unit of X to 1.2 units of X per man-hour. Hence we can say labour productivity is increased by 20 percent. Another point one has to remember is some times, we see labour productivity decreases even though production increases or sometimes the labour productivity and production both will go up. This is to make clear that ***the increased production does not necessarily mean increase in productivity.*** Sometimes a decrease in man – hour is interpreted as increase in productivity. ***This is also wrong.***

Suppose in a company, the direct man- hours reduced from 1000 hours last month to 800 hours this month, the company management may hastily conclude that the labour productivity improved by 20 percent in the current month, while in fact this reduction in direct man- hours may have been accompanied a corresponding 20 percent reduction in production of units manufactured. The high absenteeism rate this month, which caused a reduction in direct man-hours, should be a symptom of concern that a false claim of productivity improvement.

Quite often the terms Productivity, Efficiency and Effectiveness are confused with each other. Efficiency is the ratio of actual output attained to standard output expected.

For example if the standard output expected per a given time is 100 units, and the worker produces 85 pieces in the time period given his efficiency is $\frac{85}{100} = 0.85$ or 85%

Effectiveness is the degree of accomplishment of the objectives. That is how well a set of results is accomplished reflects the effectiveness, whereas how well the given resources are utilized to accomplish refers to Efficiency. Productivity is a combination of effectiveness and efficiency, since effectiveness is related to performance, while efficiency is related to resource utilization.

Efficiency and Effectiveness need not go together, because efficiency implies reaching a certain level of range of results that is acceptable but not necessarily desirable. The relationship between all the three can be shown as:

$$\frac{\textit{Productivity Index} - \textit{Output obtained}}{\textit{Input expended}} = \frac{\textit{Performance achieved}}{\textit{Resource consumed}} = \frac{\textit{Effectiveness}}{\textit{efficiency}}$$

Although the fist two i.e. is output and input of the above expression are clearly consistent with the usual definition of productivity the last one is somewhat confusing for two reasons:

(*i*) Productivity index is a numerical value but efficiency is not.

(*ii*) It is not clearly defined efficiency in a technical sense as the ratio of actual output to expected or standard output. Further, the definition implies that reducing efficiency, which is not logical, can increase productivity. To avoid this confusion, productivity index can be written as:

$$\textit{Productivity index} = f\,(\textit{Effectiveness}) \,/\, f\,(\textit{Efficiency}).$$

16.3. BASIC DEFINITION OF PRODUCTIVITY

Depending on the situation or the person who defines productivity, whether it is an Economist, Accountant, Manger, Politician, Union leader or an Industrial Engineer, one can get a slightly different definition of the term productivity. We can easily recognize three basic types of productivity and they are:

16.3.1. Partial Productivity

Partial productivity is the ratio of output to one class of input among various factors of production. For example, Labour productivity, is the partial productivity measure, which measures the productivity of labour class. Similarly we can define other partial productivity as Material productivity, Capital productivity and so on.

16.3.2. Total Factor Productivity

Total factor productivity is the ratio of net output to the sum of associated labour and capital (factor) inputs. By net output mean that output minus intermediate goods and services purchased. The denominator of this ratio is made up of only the labour and capital input factors.

16.3.3. Total Productivty

Total productivity is the ratio of total output to the sum of all input factors. Thus, a total productivity measure reflects the joint impact of all the inputs in procuring the output.

In all the above definitions, both the output and input (inputs) are expressed in **real or physical terms** by being reduced to constant Rupee or any other monetary value of a reference period often referred as **basic period.** This reduction to base period is accomplished by dividing the values of output and input (inputs) by deflators or inflators, depending upon whether the prices of outputs and inputs have gone up or down respectively. This is done to avoid price variation.

Problem 16.2. The data regarding output and inputs of M/S XYZ Company is given below. Find the partial productivity and the total productivity.

Output = Rs. 1000/-

Human input = Rs. 300/-
Material input = Rs. 200/-
Capital input = Rs. 300/-
Energy input = Rs. 100/-
Other input expenses = Rs. 50/-
Assume that the values given are in constant rupees with respect to a base period.

Solution :

(*i*) $\text{Human productivity} = \frac{\text{Output}}{\text{Human input}} = \frac{1000}{300} = 3.33$

(*ii*) $\text{Material productivity} = \frac{\text{Output}}{\text{Material input}} = \frac{1000}{.200} = 5.00$

(*iii*) $\text{Capital productivity} = \frac{\text{Output}}{\text{Capital input}} = \frac{1000}{300} = 3.33$

(*iv*) $\text{Energy productivity} = \frac{\text{Output}}{\text{Energy input}} = \frac{1000}{100} = 10.00$

(*v*) $\text{Other expense productivity} = \frac{\text{Output}}{\text{Other expense input}} = \frac{1000}{20} = 20.00$

(*vi*) $\text{Total factor productivity} = \frac{\text{Net output}}{(\text{Labour} + \text{capital})\text{ input}}$

Net output = 1000 – (200 + 300 + 100 + 50) = 1000 – 650 = Rs. 350
Labour + Capital input = 300 + 300 = Rs. 600

$$\text{Therefore, total factor productivity} = \frac{350}{600} = 0.583$$

$$\text{Total productivity} = \frac{\text{Total output}}{\text{Total input}}$$

$$= \frac{1000}{(300+200+300+100+50)} = \frac{1000}{950} = 1.053$$

16.4. FACTORS AFFECTING PRODUCTIVITY

There are various factors that affect productivity, they are:

(*a*) Investment,
(*b*) Capital / labour ratio,
(*c*) Extent of research and development in the country,
(*d*) Capacity utilisation,
(*e*) Regulations imposed by the Government,
(*f*) Age of the plant and equipment,
(*g*) Energy costs,
(*h*) Workforce mix,
(*i*) Work ethic,

(*j*) Worker's fear of losing the job,

(*k*) Union influence, and

(*l*) Attitude of management.

The factors mentioned above may have individually contributed effect or combined effect on productivity.

16.5. PRODUCTIVITY BENEFIT MODEL

Whenever management talks about increasing productivity, labour unions and workers suspect that management wants to exploit them. This may be due to one reason that management many a time thinks of increasing labour productivity and do not pay not much importance for other ways of increasing productivity. But management must think of other opportunities of increasing productivity, such as material productivity or capital productivity and other resources productivity. In spite of increase in productivity, the cost per unit is not reduced and the quality of the product is not improved, and then there is no use of increasing productivity. As the price per unit is equals to cost per unit + profit margin per unit, if the price per unit could not be reduced by the techniques of increasing the productivity, management has to reduce the margin of profit, which is not advisable in the competitive market. The improvement of total productivity of a product or service results in the reduction of the total cost per unit. Therefore improving the total productivity results in two favorable management strategies. They are:

(*i*) Reduce the selling price of a product or service **without** sacrificing the present profit margin.

(*ii*) Increase profit margin **without** reducing the selling price.

The effects of first strategy are:

(*a*) The consumer will benefit from savings by purchasing the product or service at lower prices for the same quality or even better quality in some cases.

(*b*) The organization will benefit from an increase in market share and higher revenues.

(*c*) The employees get higher real wages due to increased revenues of the organization and get job security.

The second strategy help shareholders or promoters to get higher dividends. Both these help the nation to have a healthy economy. All the above shown in figure 16.1.

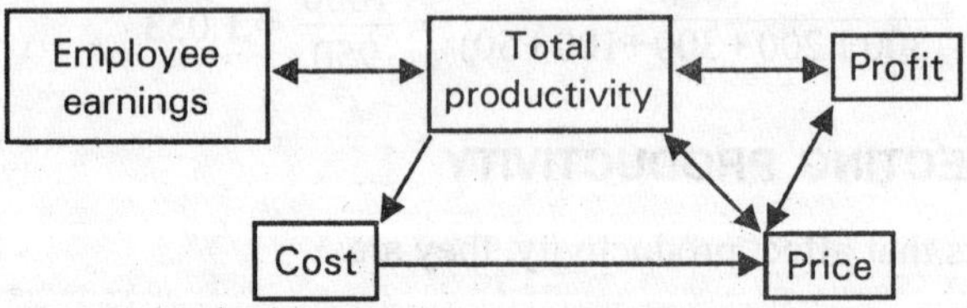

Problem. 16.3 : Productivity benefit model.

Example 16.3 : A company manufactures one of its products, say *X*, for Rs.7/- per unit last year and sold 10,000 units of product *X*. The selling price of Rs.7 /- includes Rs. 2/- per unit profit after the costs are accounted for. This year as a result of improvement in the total productivity level for the product, the company was able to reduce the total cost per unit by Re.1/-. What benefit does this company realize this year?

Solution :

Previous Year: Selling price = Rs. 7/- per unit.

Profit margin per unit = Rs.2/-

Total cost per unit = Rs.7/- – Rs. 2/- = Rs. 5/-

Total profit earned = 10,000 × Rs. 2/- = Rs. 20,000/-.

Sales revenue = 10,000 × Rs.7/- = Rs. 70,000/-

Current year: Total cost per unit = Rs.5/- – Re.1/- = Rs 4/-

(*a*) Suppose the company wants to generate the same profit as that of previous year i.e. Rs. 2/- per unit. Then the company's revenue = 10,000 × Rs.6/- = Rs. 60,000/-. Compared to previous sales revenue is reduced by Rs. 10,000/-

(*b*) In case the company wants to maintain the total cost as same as that of last year, the company will earn a revenue of Rs. 70,000/-, which includes a profit of Rs. 30,000/. This increase is due to productivity improvement.

16.6. PRODUCTIVITY CYCLE

For every organization, which is interested in introducing the productivity improvement has to follow productivity cycle. The productivity cycle includes:

(*a*) Productivity Measurement,

(*b*) Productivity Evaluation,

(*c*) Productivity Planning, and

(*d*) Productivity Improvement.

This is represented by **M.E.P.I (MEASUREMENT, EVALUATION, PLANNING AND IMROVEMENT).** An ongoing organisation may start at any one stage and a new unit has to start from the measurement and proceed further.

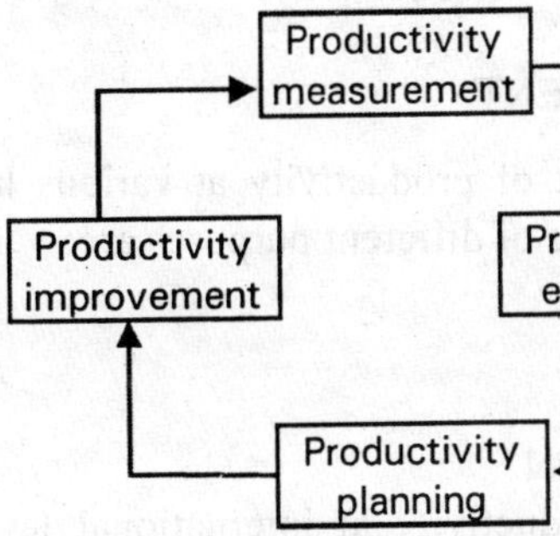

Figure 16.2 : Productivity cycle.

An organisation that begins a formal productivity programme for the first time can begin with productivity measurement. Once the productivity levels re measured, they have to be evaluated or compared against the planned targets. Based on this evaluation, target levels or productivity are planed on the both short term and long term bases. To achieve the planed targets, productivity improvement takes place in formal manner. In order to assess the degree to which the improvement will take place next period, productivity levels are to be measured again. This cycle thus continues for as long as the productivity programme operates in the organisaton.

16.7. PRODUCTIVITY ENGINEERING AND PRODUCTIVITY MANAGEMENT

To have more clear idea about Productivity Engineering and Productivity management let us first study the definition Industrial Engineering.

Industrial Engineering is concerned with the design, improvement and installation of integrated system of men, materials, and equipment. It draws upon specialised knowledge and skill in the mathematical, physical and social sciences together with the principles and methods of engineering analyses and design to specify, predict, and evaluate the results to be obtained form such system.

PRODUCTIVITY ENGIEERING : *Productivity Engineering concerned with the design, development and maintenance of productivity measurement, evaluation, planning and improvement system in manufacturing and service organisations.*

The more direct effort of productivity engineering to maintain and improve the productivity of system designed and installed by industrial engineers can be instrumental in addressing the productivity aspects of a system. The productivity engineers, who are a separate set of industrial engineers within the company is concerned with total productivity values for the various products processed in the plant.

PRODUCTIVITY MANAGEMENT: Productivity management is a *formal* management process involving all levels of *management* and *employees* with the ultimate objective of reducing the *cost* of the manufacturing, distributing and selling of a product or service through an *integration* of four phases of the productivity cycle namely productivity measurement, evaluation, planning and improvement.

This definition implies that the management of an organization sets up a formal structure to administer and control the productivity level and growth rate. Both management and employees should be actively involved by whatever approach is most appropriate in their organization, whether it is called **'participatory approach'** or **'team approach'** or **'consensus approach'.** The ultimate objective of all the concerned is to improve productivity.

16.8. PRODUCTIVITY MEASUREMENT

Let us briefly discuss the measurement of productivity at various levels. The levels at which the productivity is to be measured for the use of different purposes are:

(*a*) International level,
(*b*) National level,
(*c*) Industrial level and
(*d*) Company or organizational level.

(*a*) **International level :** The productivity at international level may be measured by four approaches:

(*i*) Comparison of the value of the gross output per unit of labour,
(*ii*) Comparison of the value of the net output per unit of labour,
(*iii*) Comparison of the physical output (gross as well as net) per unit of labour, and
(*iv*) Comparison of the physical input of materials.

(*b*) **National level :** This measurement will help us to forecast national income and compare the competitive power of various industries. The various approaches for measurement of productivity at national level are:

(*i*) Index approach such as
* Labour productivity index,

* Capital productivity index, and
* Labour and Capital productivity index.

(*c*) **Productivity measurement at the industrial level :** This type of measurement will help to use it as Economic indicators. This may also be used to analyze the manpower utilization. May be used for analyzing the company performance. Different approaches for measuring productivity at industrial level are:

(*i*) Index approach,
(*ii*) Production function approach and
(*iii*) Input – output approach.

(*d*) **Productivity measurement at Company or Organisation level :** This measurement will help to study the productivity of resources used. Higher company productivity will guarantee higher real wages. Public will realise greater social benefits. Consumer will pay lesser price from increased use value through increased productivity. The approaches are:

(*i*) Economists approach: Production function approach and input – output approach.
(*ii*) Engineer's approach: Index approach, Utility approach and Servo-system approach.
(*iii*) Manager's approach: Array approach and Financial ratio approach and
(*iv*) Accountant's approach: Capital budgeting approach and Unit cost approach.

For more detailed study, readers are advised to refer to a book on **PRODUCTIVITY ENGIEERING AND MANAGEMENT By David J. Sumanth, a McGraw Hill Book Company Publication.**

17

PERT AND CPM SCHEDULING TECHNIQUES

PERT AND CPM

- Introduction.
- PERT AND CPM
- PERT way of drawing network.
  - Optimistic time.
  - Pessimistic time.
  - Most likely time.
  - Project completion time.
- Numbering the network events.
- Slack and Probability of completion of the project.
- CPM Method of calculating Project completion time.
- Writing CPM Network.
- Time estimation in CPM
  - Earliest event time.
  - Latest allowable occurrence time.
  - Float and various types of Floats.
- Project Cost Analysis.
  - Direct Cost.
  - Indirect cost.
  - Total cost.
  - Cost slope.
- Updating the network.
- Resource leveling.
- Resource smoothening.

INTRODUCTION TO PERT AND CPM:

Net work analysis – Project management – Programme Evaluation and Review Technique (PERT) Vs Critical Path Method (CPM) – Identifying Critical Path – Probability of completing the project with in given time under PERT – Project Cost Analysis – Project Crashing.

PROGRAMME EVALUATION AND REVIEW TECHNIQUE AND CRITICAL PATH METHOD (PERT AND CPM)

17.1. INTRODUCTION

Program Evaluation and Review Technique and Critical Path Method (PERT and CPM) are two techniques that are widely used in planning and scheduling the large projects. A project is a combination of various activities. For example, Construction of house can be considered as a project. Similarly conducting a public meeting may also be considered as a project. In the above examples, construction of house includes various activities such as searching for a suitable site, arranging the finance, purchase of materials, digging the foundation, construction of superstructure etc. Conducting a meeting includes, printing of invitation cards, distribution of cards, arrangement of platform, chairs for audience etc. In planning and scheduling the activities of large sized projects, the two network techniques – PERT and CPM are used conveniently to estimate and evaluate the project completion time and control the resources to see that the project is completed within the stipulated time and at minimum possible cost. Many managers, that use of PERT and CPM techniques have claimed that these techniques drastically reduces the project completion time. But it is wrong to think that network analysis is a solution to all bad management problems. In the present chapter, let us discuss how PERT and CPM are used to schedule the projects.

Initially, bar charts and mile stone charts represented projects. But they had little use in controlling the project activities. *Bar chart* simply represents each activity by bars of length equal to the time taken on a common time scale as shown in figure 17.1 This chart does not show interrelationship between activities. It is very difficult to show the progress of work in these charts. An improvement in bar charts is *milestone chart.* In mile stone chart, key events of activities are identified and each activity is connected to its preceding and succeeding activities to show the logical relationship between activities. Here each key event is represented by a node (a circle) and arrows instead of bars represent activities, as shown in figure 17.2. The extension of milestone chart is PERT and CPM network methods.

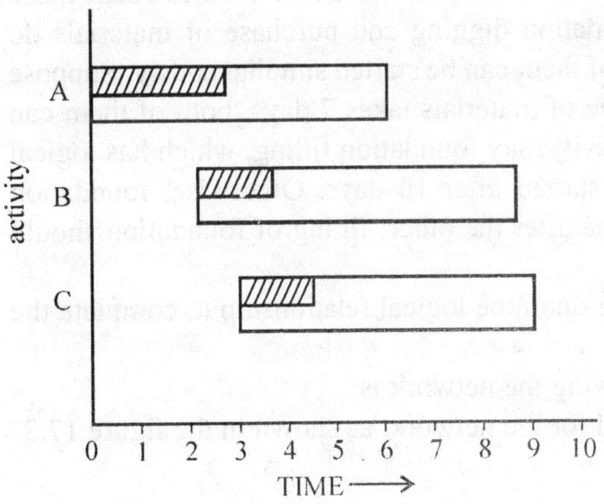

Figure 17.1 : Bar chart.

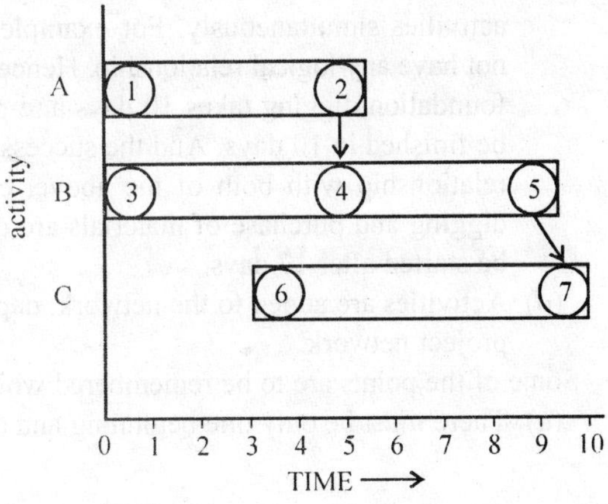

Figure 17.2 : Milestone chart.

17.2. PERT AND CPM

In PERT and CPM the milestones are represented as *events*. Event or node is either starting of an activity or ending of an activity. Activity is represented by means of an arrow, which is resource consuming. Activity consumes resources like time, money and, materials. Event will not consume any resource, but it simply represents either starting or ending of an activity. Event cam also be represented by rectangles or triangles. When all activities and events in a project are connected logically and sequentially, they form a *network*, which is the basic document in network-based management. The basic steps for writing a network are:

(*a*) List out all the activities involved in a project. Say for example, in building construction, the activities are:

(*i*) Site selection,
(*ii*) Arrangement of Finance
(*iii*) Preparation of building plan
(*iv*) Approval of plan by municipal authorities,
(*v*) Purchase of materials,
(*vi*) Digging of foundation
(*vii*) Filling up of foundation,
(*viii*) Building superstructure,
(*ix*) Fixing up of doorframes and window frames,
(*x*) Roofing
(*xi*) Plastering,
(*xii*) Flooring,
(*xiii*) Electricity and water fittings
(*xiv*) Finishing.

(*b*) Once the activities are listed, they are arranged in sequential manner and in logical order. For example, foundation digging should come before foundation filling and so on.

(*c*) After arranging the activities in a logical sequence, their time is estimated and written against each activity. For example: Foundation digging: 10 days, or 2 ½ weeks.

(d) Some of the activities do not have any logical relationship, in such cases; we can start those activities simultaneously. For example, Foundation digging and purchase of materials do not have any logical relationship. Hence both of them can be started simultaneously. Suppose foundation digging takes 10 days and purchase of materials takes 7 days, both of them can be finished in 10 days. And the successive activity, say foundation filling, which has logical relationship with both of the above, can be started after 10 days. Otherwise, foundation digging and purchase of materials are done one after the other; filling of foundation should be started after 17 days.

(*d*) Activities are added to the network, depending upon the logical relationship to complete the project network.

Some of the points are to be remembered while drawing the network is

(*a*) There must be only one beginning and one end for the network, as shown in the figure 17.3.

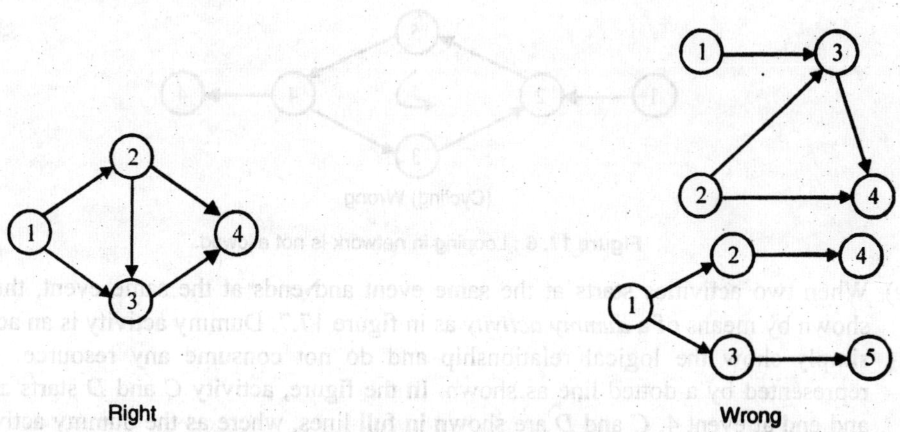

Figure 17.3 : Method of writing Network.

(*b*) Event number should be written inside the circle or node (or triangle/square/rectangle etc). Activity name should be capital alphabetical letters and would be written above the arrow. The time required for the activity should be written below the arrow as in figure 17. 4

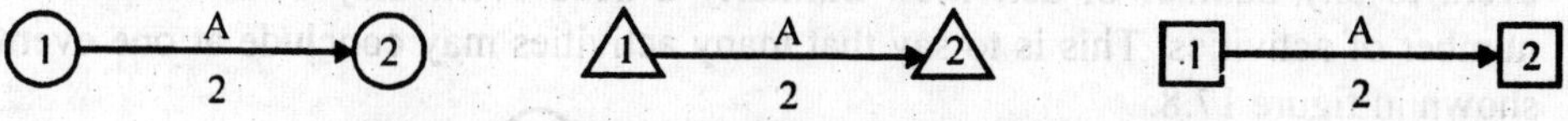

Figure. 17.4 : Numbering events and naming activities.

(*c*) While writing network, see that activities should not cross each other. And arcs or loops as in figure 17. 5 should not join Activities.

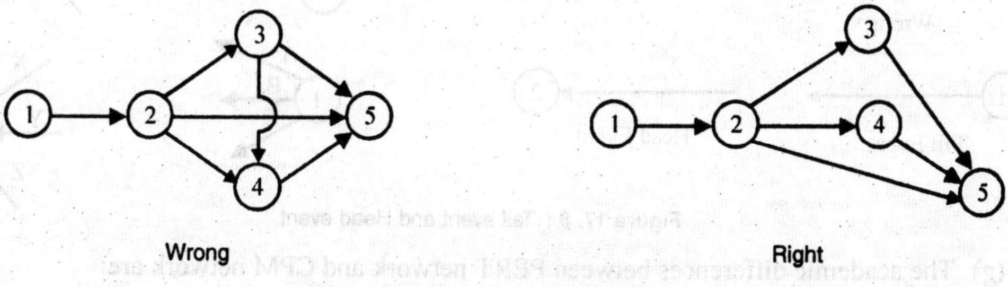

Figure 17. 5 : Crossing of Activities.

(*d*) While writing network, looping should be avoided. This is to say that, the network arrows should move in one direction, i.e. starting from the beginning should move towards the end, as in figure 17. 6.

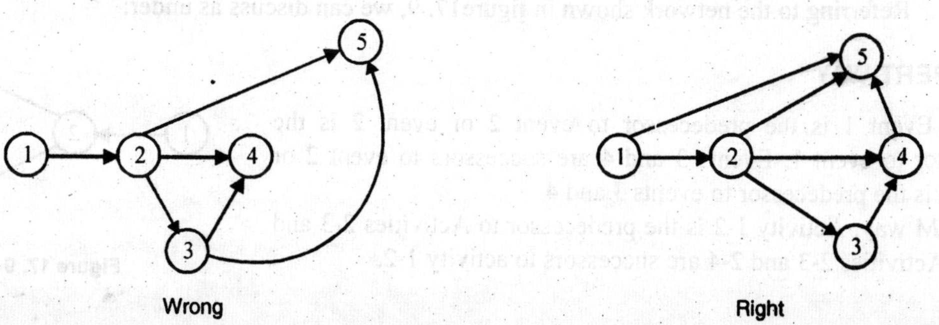

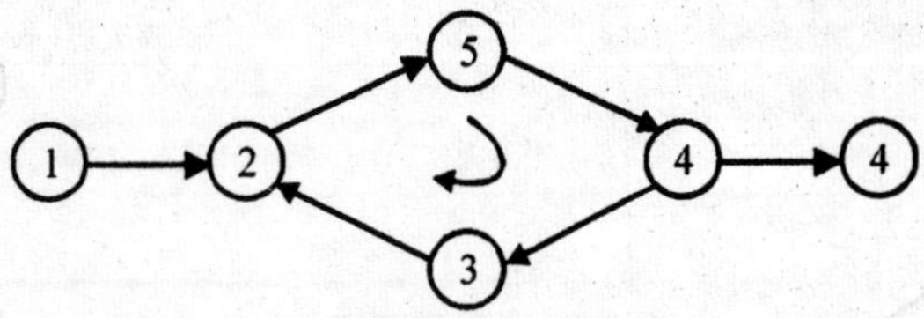

(Cycling) Wrong

Figure 17. 6 : Looping in network is not allowed.

(*e*) When two activities starts at the same event and ends at the same event, they should be shown by means of a *dummy activity* as in figure 17.7. Dummy activity is an activity, which simply show the logical relationship and do not consume any resource. It should be represented by a dotted line as shown. In the figure, activity *C* and *D* starts at the event 3 and end at event 4. *C* and *D* are shown in full lines, where as the dummy activity is shown in dotted line.

(*f*) When the event is written at the tail end of an arrow, it is known as *tail event.* If event is written on the head side of the arrow it is known as *head even t.* A tail event may have any number of arrows (activities) emerging from it. This is to say that an event may be a tail event to any number of activities. Similarly a head event may be a head event for any number of activities. This is to say that many activities may conclude at one event. This is shown in figure 17.8.

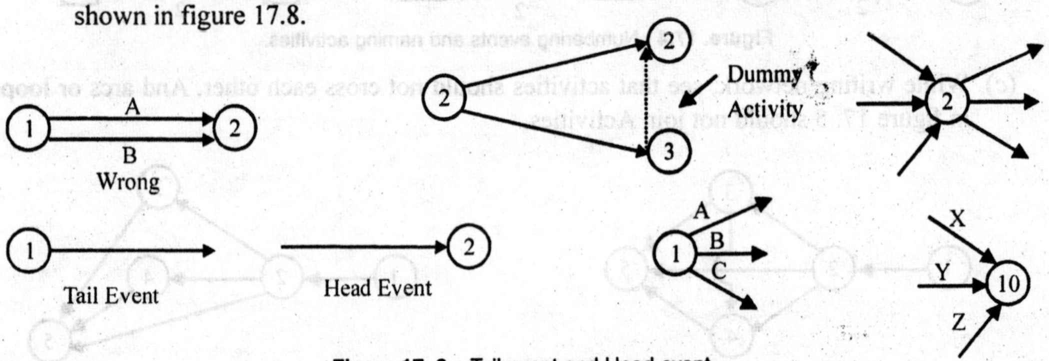

Figure 17. 8 : Tail event and Head event.

(*g*) The academic differences between PERT network and CPM network are:

(*i*) PERT is event Oriented and CPM is activity oriented. This is to say that while discussing about PERT network, we say that, Activity 1-2, Activity 2-3 and so on. Or event 2 occurs after event 1 and event 5 occurs after event 3 and so on. While discussing CPM network, we say that Activity *A* follows activity *B* and activity *C* follows activity *B* and so on. Referring to the network shown in figure17. 9, we can discuss as under:

17.3. PERT WAY

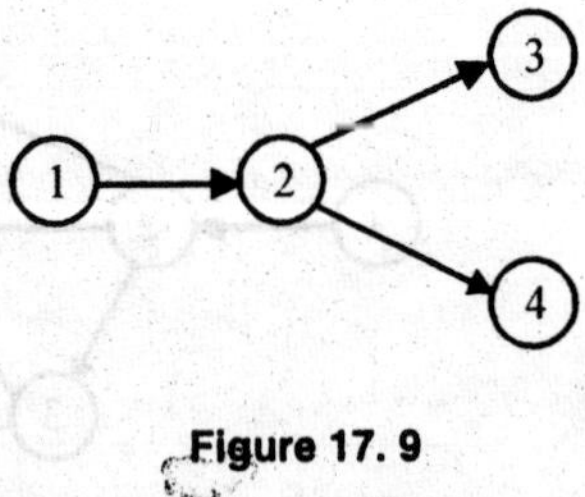

Figure 17. 9

(*i*) Event 1 is the predecessor to event 2 or event 2 is the successor to event 1. Events 3 and 4 are successors to event 2 or event 2 is the predecessor to events 3 and 4.

CPM way: Activity 1-2 is the predecessor to Activities 2-3 and 2-4 or Activities 2-3 and 2-4 are successors to activity 1-2.

(*ii*) **PERT activities are probabilistic in nature. The time required to complete the PERT activity cannot be specified correctly. Because of uncertainties in carrying out the activity, the time cannot be specified correctly. Say for example, if you ask a contractor, how much time it takes to construct the house, he may answer you that it may take 5 to 6 months. This is because of his expectation of uncertainty in carrying out each one of the activities in the construction of the house. Another example is if somebody asks you how much time you require to reach railway station from your house, you may say that it may take 1 to 1 ½ hour. This is because; you may think that you may not get a transport facility in time. Or on the way to station, you may come across certain work, which may cause delay in you journey from house to station. Hence PERT network is used when the activity times are probabilistic.**

There are three time estimates for a PERT activity. They are:

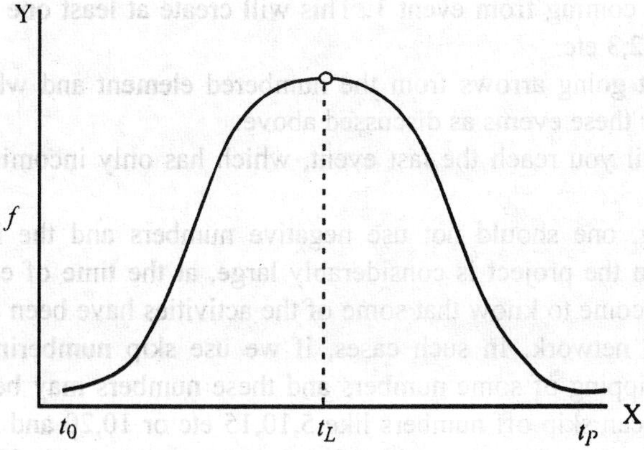

Figure 17.10 : Three Time Estimates

(*a*) ***OPTMESTIC TIME :*** **Optimistic time is represented by t_0. Here the estimator thinks that everything goes on well and he will not come across any sort of uncertainties and estimates lowest time as far as possible. He is *optimistic* in his thinking.**

(*b*) ***PESSIMESTIC TIME :*** **This is represented by t_P. Here estimator thinks that everything goes wrong and expects all sorts of uncertainties and estimates highest possible time. He is pessimistic in his thinking.**

(*c*) ***LIKELY TIME :*** **This is represented by t_L. This time is in between optimistic and pessimistic time. Here the estimator expects he may come across some sort of uncertainties and many a time the things will go right.**

So while estimating the time for a PERT activity, the estimator will give the three time estimates. When these three estimates are plotted on a graph, the probability distribution that we get is closely associated with ***Beta Distribution curve.*** For a Beta distribution curve as shown in figure 17.11, the characteristics are:

Standard deviation = $(t_P - t_O)\backslash 6 = s$, $t_P - t_O$ is known as range.

Variance = $\{(t_P - t_O)/6\}^2 = s^2$

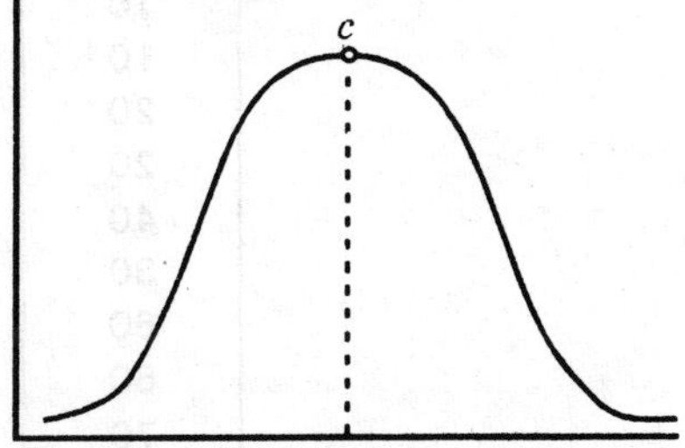

Figure 17. 11 : Beta Distribution

Expected Time or Average Time = $t_E = (t_O + 4t_L + t_P)/6$

These equations are very important in the calculation of PERT times. Hence the student has to remember these formulae.

Now let us see how to deal with the PERT problems.

17.4. NUMBERING OF EVENTS

Once the network is drawn the events are to be numbered. In PERT network, as the activities are given in terms of evens, we may not experience difficulty. But in case of CPM network, as the activities are specified by their name, we have to number the events. For numbering of events, we use D.R. Fulkerson's rule. As per this rule:

An initial event is an event, which has only outgoing arrows from it and no arrow enters it. Number that event as 1.

Delete all arrows coming from event 1. This will create at least one more initial event. Number these initial events as 2,3 etc.

Delete all the out going arrows from the numbered element and which will create some more initial events. Number these events as discussed above.

Continue this until you reach the last event, which has only incoming arrows and no outgoing arrows.

While numbering, one should not use negative numbers and the initial event should not be assigned 'zero'. When the project is considerably large, at the time of execution of the project, the project manager may come to know that some of the activities have been forgotten and they are to be shown in the current network. In such cases, if we use skip numbering, it will be helpful. Skip numbering means, skipping of some numbers and these numbers may be made use to represent the events forgotten. We can skip off numbers like 5,10,15 etc or 10,20 and 30 or 2,12, 22 etc. Another way of numbering the network is start with 10 and the second event is 20 and so on. This is a better way of numbering the events.

Let now see how to write network and find the project completion time by solving some typical problems.

Problem 17. 1: A project consists of 9 activities and the three time estimates are given below. Find the project completion time (T_E).

1. Write the network for the given project and find the project completion time?

Activities		Days		
i	*j*	t_O	t_L	t_P
10	20	5	12	17
10	30	8	10	13
10	40	9	11	12
20	30	5	8	9
20	50	9	11	13
40	60	14	18	22
30	70	21	25	30
60	70	8	13	17
60	80	14	17	21
70	80	6	9	12

Solution :

In PERT network, it is easy to write network diagram, because the successor and predecessor event relation ship can easily be identified. While calculating the project completion time, we have to calculate t_E i.e. expected completion time from three time estimation. In case, we calculate completion time by using t_o or t_l or t_p alone, we will have three completion times. Hence it is advisible to calculate t_E expected completion time for each activities and then the project completion time. Now let us work out expected project completion time.

Predecessor event	Success or event	Time in days t_o	t_L	t_P	t_E $(t_e + 4\, t_l + t_p)/6$	Range $t_p - t_o$	S.D (s) $(t_p - t_o)/6$	Variance s^2
10	20	5	12	17	11.67 (12)	12	2	4.0
10	30	8	10	13	10.17 (10)	5	0.83	0.69
10	40	9	11	12	10.83 (11)	3	0.5	0.25
20	30	5	8	9	7.67 (8)	4	0.66	0.44
20	50	9	11	13	11.00 (11)	4	0.66	0.44
40	60	14	18	22	18.00 (18)	8	1.33	1.78
30	70	21	25	30	25.18 (25)	9	1.5	2.25
60	70	8	13	17	12.83 (13)	9	1.5	2.25
50	80	14	17	21	17.17 (17)	7	1.16	1.36
70	80	6	9	12	9.00 (9)	6	1.0	1.0

For the purpose of convenience the value 't_E' got by calculation may be rounded off to nearest whole number (the same should be clearly mentioned in the table). The round off time is shown in the brackets. In this book, in the problems, the decimal, will be rounded off to nearest whole number.

To work out the network program, start from the beginning i.e. we have 10 – 20, 10 – 30 and 10 – 40. Therefore from the mode 10, three arrows emerges. They are 10 – 20, 10 – 30 and 10 – 40. Next from the mode 20, the arrows emerge and they are 20 – 30 and 20 – 50. Like this the network is constructed. The following convention is used in writing network in this book.

$T_L^{\,i} - t_E^{\,ij} = T_L$

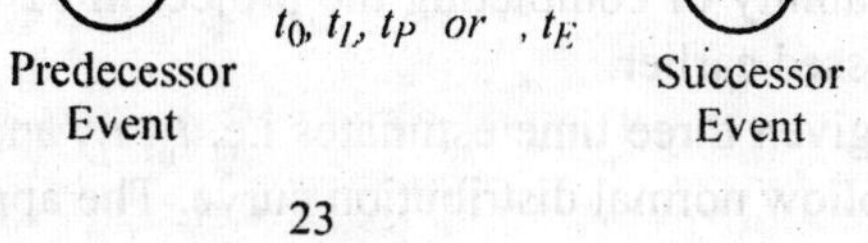

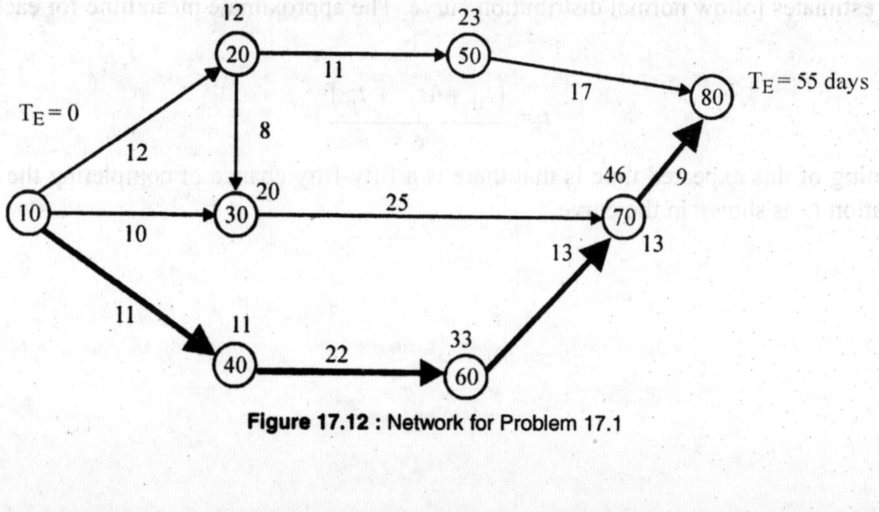

Figure 17.12 : Network for Problem 17.1

Let us start the event 10 at 0th time i.e. expected time $T_E = 0$. Hence T_E represents the occurrence time of the event 10, which has t_E, is the duration taken by the activities. T_E belongs to event, and t_E belongs to activity. Hence,

$T_E^{10} = 0$
$T_E^{20} = T_E^{10} + t_E^{10-20} = 0 + 12 = 12\text{days}$
$T_E^{30} = T_E^{10} + t_E^{10-30} = 0 + 10 = 10\text{days}$
$T_E^{30} = T_E^{20} + t_E^{20-30} = 12 + 8 = 20\text{days}$

The event 30 will occur only after completion of activities 20-30 and 10-30. There are two routes to event 30. In the forward pass i.e. when we start calculation from 1st event and proceed through last event, we have to workout the times for all routes and select the highest one and the reverse in the case of the backward pass i.e. we start from the last event and work back to the front event to find out the occurrence time.

$T_E^{40} = T_E^{10} + t_E^{10-40} = 0 + 11 = 11\text{days}$
$T_E^{50} = T_E^{20} + t_E^{20-30} = 12 + 11 = 23\text{days}$
$T_E^{60} = T_E^{40} + t_E^{40-60} = 11 + 22 = 33\text{days}$
$T_E^{70} = T_E^{30} + t_E^{30-70} = 20 + 25 = 45\text{days}$
$T_E^{70} = T_E^{60} + t_E^{60-70} = 33 + 13 = 46\text{days}$
$T_E^{80} = T_E^{70} + t_E^{70-80} = 46 + 9 = 55\text{days}$
$T_E^{80} = T_E^{50} + t_E^{50-80} = 23 + 17 = 40\text{days}$
$T_E^{80} = 55\text{days}.$

Hence the project completion time is 55 days. The path that gives us 55 days is known as critical path. Hence 10-40-60-70-80 is the critical path. Critical path may be represented by double line (⟹) or thick line (⟶) or hatched line (—///→). In this book thick line is used. All other parts i.e. 10-20-30-60-70-80, 10-20-50-80 and 10-30-70-80 are known as non-critical paths. All activities on critical path are critical activities.

The significance of critical path is delay in completion of critical activities will increase the project completion time.

Now in the above project, the project completion time is 55 days. In case every thing goes correctly the project will be completed in 55 days. Suppose the project may wants to be completed in 52 days what is the probability of completing the project in 52 days? To find the answer for this, let us recollect what is discussed earlier.

(1) Activity $i - j$ is given three time estimates i.e. t_o, t_L, and t_p and assumed that the distribution of these time estimates follow normal distribution curve. The approximate mean time for each activity given by

$$t_E = \frac{(t_0 + 4t_L + t_p)}{6}$$

The meaning of this expected time is that there is a fifty-fifty chance of completing the activities in a time duration t_E as shown in the curve.

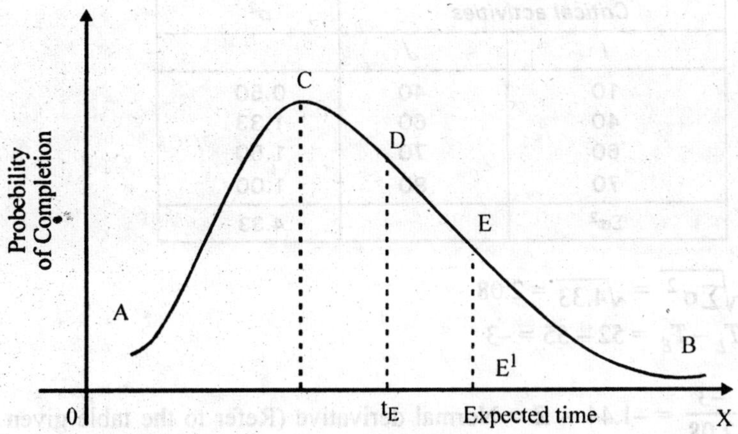

Figure 17.13 : Probability distribution

The vertical line at D represents t_E and the chance of completing activities at t_E is ½, suppose we want to find out probabilities of completing the activities at E, E_1,

The probability = Area under ACE / Area under ACB

While calculating the probability of completing the project (having number of activities), the following procedure or we apply central line theorem

Step 1 : Identify critical path and critical activities

Step 2 : find variance (s^2) for critical activities.

$$s_{ij}^2 = [(t_p^{ij} - t_o^{ij})/6]^2$$

Step 3 : List out critical activities and their σ^2

Step 4 : Find the sum of variance of critical activities i.e. $\Sigma\sigma^2$

Step 5 : Find the square root of sum of variance i.e. $\sqrt{\Sigma\sigma^2}$

Step 6 : Find the difference between calculation time (T_L) i.e. by which the project is to be completed and project completion time T_E, i.e. $T_L - T_E$

At the values of T_L, thus may be +ve or 0 as –ve number.

If $T_L = T_E$ then $T_L - T_E = 0$

If $T_L > T_E$ then $T_L - T_E$ = Positive Number

If $T_L < T_E$ then $T_L - T_E$ = Negative Number

Step 7 : Find the ratio $(TL - T_E)/\sqrt{\Sigma\sigma^2} = Z$, this is the length of coordinate at T_L on the curve.

Step 8 : Refer to the table no.1, which gives the length of Z and the probabilistic completion of the project.

If $T_L = T_E$ the probability is ½.

If $T_L > T_E$ then Z is Positive, the probability of completing the project is higher than 0.5

If $T_L < T_E$ then Z is Negative, the probability of completing the project is lower than 0.5

Table

Critical activities		σ^2
I	*J*	
10	40	0.50
40	60	1.33
60	70	1.50
70	80	1.00
$\Sigma\sigma^2$		4.33

$$\sqrt{\Sigma\sigma^2} = \sqrt{4.33} = 2.08$$

$$T_L - T_E = 52 - 55 = -3$$

$\dfrac{T_L - T_E}{\sqrt{\Sigma\sigma^2}} = \dfrac{-3}{2.08} = -1.44 = Z$ = Normal derivative (Refer to the table given at the end of the chapter).

−1.44 falls at probability.08. The probability is very low. Hence the manager should not accept to complete the project in 52 days.

Say for example given that T_L = 58 days then 58 – 55 = +3

$\dfrac{(T_L - T_E)}{\sqrt{\Sigma\sigma^2}} = \dfrac{3}{2.08} = 1.44 = Z$ = Normal derivative

1.4 falls at 91.9% probability. The probability of completing the project is high. The manager can accept the offer.

Let us continue our discussion on problem no.1

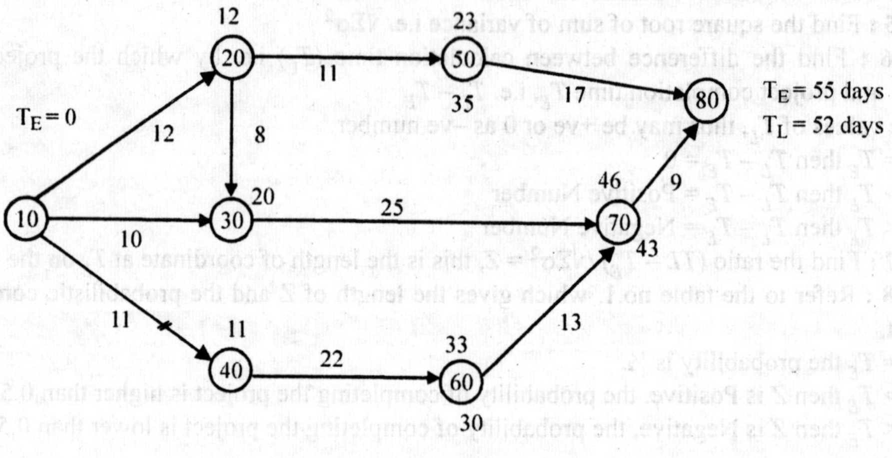

Figure 17.14.

Let us assume that the contractual time = 52 days.

This is written at the end event. Now let us work back to find out when the project should be started if the delivery time is 52 days

T_L^{80} = 52days

T_L^{70} = T_L^{80} - t_E^{70-80} = 52 - 9 = 43days thus we write below the node

T_L^{50} = T_L^{80} - t_E^{50-80} = 52 - 17 = 35days

T_L^{60} = T_L^{70} - t_E^{60-70} = 43 - 13 = 30days

T_L^{40} = T_L^{60} - t_E^{40-60} = 30 - 22 = 8days

T_L^{20} = T_L^{50} - t_E^{20-50} = 35 - 11 = 24days

T_L^{30} = T_L^{70} - t_E^{30-70} = 43 - 25 = 18days

T_L^{20} = T_L^{30} - t_E^{20-30} = 8 - 8 = 0days

T_L^{20} has two values i.e. 24 days and 0(zero) days. Here we are going back to find out when the project is to be started, take lowest of the two i.e. T_L^{20} = 10.

T_L^{10} = T_L^{20} – t_E^{10-20} = 10 – 12 = –2days

T_L^{10} = T_L^{30} – t_E^{10-30} = 8 – 10 = –2days

T_L^{10} = T_L^{40} – t_E^{10-40} = 8 – 11 = –3days

Take T_L= –3days which is lowest. Hence the project is to be started 3 days before the scheduled starting time.

Now at the critical path calculate $(T_L - T_E)$. For all critical events it is –3days.

This $(T_L - T_E)$ is known as slack and is represented by τ (tau). On the critical path remains to be same. In fact slack is the breathing time for the contractor. If $(T_L - T_E)$, slack for all critical events is zero. If $(T_L > T_E)$ it is a positive number and if it is $(T_L < T_E)$ it will be a negative number for all critical events. For non-critical activities this difference between T_L and T_E i.e. $(T_L - T_E)$ shows the breathing time. Take event 50.

For this event T_L = 35 days and T_E = 23 days i.e. 35–23 = 12 days of time available. In case of any inconvenience he can start the activity any day between 23rd day and 35th day. Now let us work out some model examples.

Example 17.2:

Steps involved in executing an order for a large engine generator set are given below in a jumbled manner. Arrange them in a logical sequence, draw a PERT network and find the shortest execution time period.

Activities	*Time in weeks*		
	t_o	t_l	t_p
Order and receive engine	1	2	3
Prepare assembly drawings	1	1	1
Receive and study order	1	2	3
Apply and receive import license for generator	3	5	7
Order and receive generator	2	3	5
Study enquiry for engine generator set	1	2	3
Fabricate switch board	2	3	5
Import engine	1	1	1
Assemble engine generator	1	2	3
Submit quotation with drawing and full specifications	1	2	3
Prepare base and bedding	2	3	4
Import generator	1	1	1
Order and receive meters, switch gears for switch board	2	3	4
Test assembly	1	1	1

Solution : As the activities given in the problem are not logical order, first we have to arrange them in a logical manner

S.No.	Activities	Time in weeks		
		t_o	t_l	t_p
A	Study enquiry for engine generator set	1	2	3
B	Prepare assembly drawings	1	1	1
C	Submit quotation with drawing and full specifications	1	2	3
D	Receive and study order	1	2	3
E	Apply and receive import license for generator	3	5	7
F	Order and receive engine	1	2	3
G	Order and receive generator	2	3	5
H	Import engine	1	1	1
I	Order and receive meters, switch gears for switch board	2	3	4
J	Prepare base and bedding	2	3	4
K	Assemble engine generator	1	2	3
L	Fabricate switch board	2	3	5
M	Test assembly	1	1	1

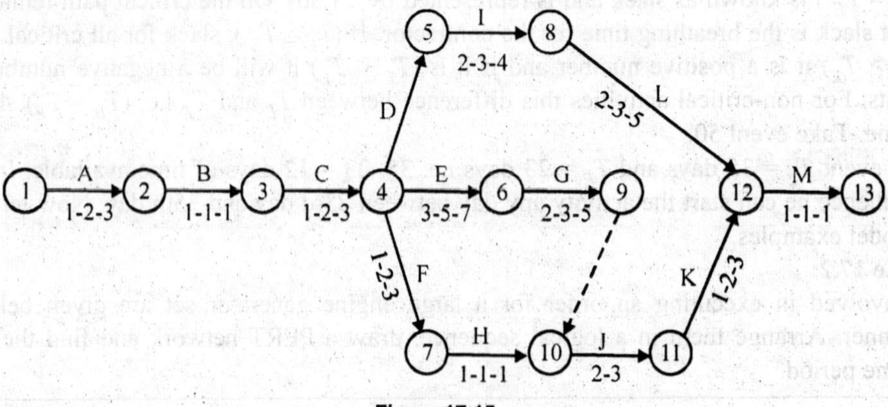

Figure 17.15

The second step is to write network and number the events

Activities	Predecessor Event	Success event	Weeks			$t_E = t_E + 4t_L + t_P/6$	$\sigma = (t_p - t_o)/6$	σ^2
			t_1	t_2	t_3			
A	1	2	1	2	3	2	1/3 = 0.33	0.102
B	2	3	1	1	1	1	0	0
C	3	4	1	2	3	2	0.33	0.102
D	4	5	1	2	3	2	0.33	0.102
E	4	6	3	5	7	5	0.66	0.44
F	4	7	1	2	3	2	0.33	0.102
G	6	9	2	3	5	3	0.5	0.25
H	7	10	1	1	1	1	0	0
I 5	8	2	3	4	3	0.33	0.102	
J	10	11	2	3	4	3	0.33	0.102
K	11	12	1	2	3	2	0.33	0.102
L	8	12	2	3	5	3	0.5	0.25
M	12	13	1	1	1	1	0	0

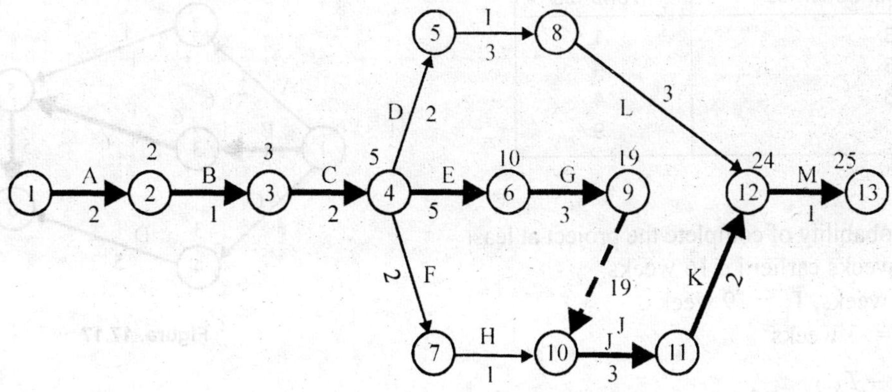

Figure 17.16

CRITRICAL PATH = 1 – 2 – 3 – 4 – 6 – 9 – 10 – 11 – 12 – 13

T_E = 25 Weeks

Example : 17.3: A small project is composed of activities as shown below.

Activities		Time in weeks		
i	*j*	t_o	t_l	t_p
1	2	1	1	7
1	3	1	4	7
1	4	2	2	8
2	5	1	1	1
3	5	2	5	14
4	6	2	5	8
5	6	3	6	15

1. Draw the network
2. Calculate the expected variances fore each
3. Find the expected project completed time
4. Calculate the probability that the project will be completed at least 3 weeks than expected
5. If the project done date is 18 weeks, what is the probability of net meeting the due date?

Solution :

Activities		Weeks			$t_E = t_E + 4t_L + t_P$	t_E	$s = (t_p - t_o)/6$	s^2
i	*j*	t_1	t_2	t_3				
1	2	1	1	7	2	6	1	1
1	3	1	4	7	6	6	1	1
1	4	2	2	8	3	6	1	1
2	5	1	1	1	1	0	0	0
3	5	2	5	14	6	12	2	4
4	6	2	5	8	5	6	1	1
5	6	3	6	15	7	12	2	4

Critical activities	*Variance*
1 - 3	1
3 - 5	4
5 - 6	4
$\Sigma\sigma^2$	9

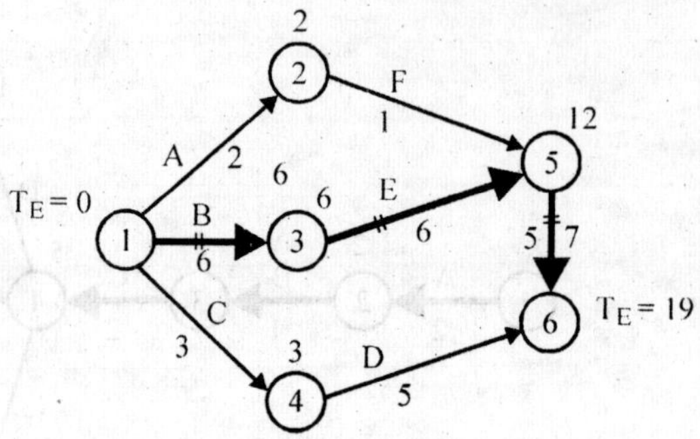

Figure. 17.17

(*d*) Probability of complete the project at least 3 weeks earlier i.e 16 weeks

$T_L = 16$ weeks, $T_E = 19$ weeks.

$T_L - T_E = -3$ weeks

$$Z = \frac{(T_L - T_E)}{\sqrt{\Sigma\sigma^2}} = \frac{-3}{3} = -1 = 15.9\%$$

From table the probability of completing the project = 15.9%

(*e*) if T_L = 18 weeks. Probability of completes in 18 weeks is (18–19) / 3 = –1/3 from table probability = 38.2%

Probability of not meeting due date = 100 – 38.2 = 61.8%

*i.*e 61.8% of the time the manager can not complete the project by due date.

Example 17.4 : There are seven activities in a project and the time estimates are as follows

Activities	*Time in weeks*		
	t_o	t_l	t_p
A	2	6	10
B	4	6	12
C	2	3	4
D	2	4	6
E	3	6	9
F	6	10	14
G	1	3	5

The logical of activities are:

1. Activity *A* and *B* starts at the beginning of the project
2. When *A* is completed *C* and *D* starts.
3. *E* can start when *B* and *D* are finished
4. *F* can start when *B,C* and *D* are completed and is the final activity.
5. *A* can start when F is finished and s final activity

(*a*) What is the expected time of the duration of the project?

(*b*) What is the net probability that project will be completed in 22 weeks

Solution :

First we use to establish predecessor / successor relationship and find their standard deviation σ, variance σ^2 and expected time of completing activities t_E.

Activities	*Predecessor Event*	*Weeks*			$t_E = t_E + 4t_L + t_P/6$	$\sigma = (t_p - t_o)/6$	σ^2
		t_1	t_2	t_3			
A	-	2	6	10	6	8/6 = 1.33	1.77
B	-	4	6	12	10	8/6 = 1.33	1.77
C	A	2	3	4	3	2/6 = 0.33	0.11
D	A	2	4	6	4	4/6 = 0.66	0.44
E	B, D	3	6	9	5	1	1
F	B, C, D	6	10	14	10	8/6 = 1.33	1.77
G	E	1	3	5	3	4/6 = 0.66	0.44

To write network the logical (predecessor) relationship is considered.

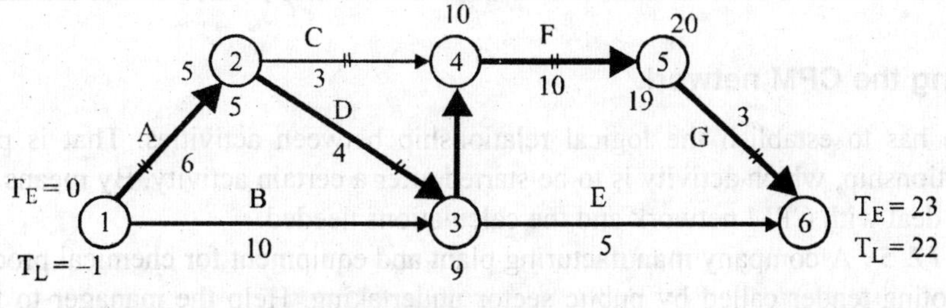

Figure 17.18

After writing the network, numbering of events and t_E is entered on the network. Next the project complete time is worked out. The project completion time T_E = 23 weeks. Then project has two critical paths i.e A-D-F-G and B-F-G.

Critical path	*Variance* σ^2
A	1.77
D	0.44
F	1.77
G	0.44
$\Sigma\sigma^2$	4.42

Critical path	*Variance* σ^2
B	1.77
F	1.77
G	0.44
$\Sigma\sigma^2$	3.98

$\sqrt{\Sigma\sigma^2} = \sqrt{4.42} = 2.1$ $\sqrt{\Sigma\sigma^2} = \sqrt{3.98} = 1.99$

In the problem T_L is given as 22 weeks. Therefore $T_L - T_E = 22 - 23 = -1$

Therefore probability of completing the project in 22 weeks

–1/2.10 or –1/1.99 = 0.502

= –0.476

The probability of completing the project is approximately 49%

17.4. CRITICAL PATH METHOD (CPM) OF CALCULATING PROJECT COMPLETION TIME

In critical path method, the time duration of an activity is deterministic in nature i.e. there will be a single time, rather than their time estimates as in PERT networks. The network is activity oriented. The ways in which the CPM type of networks differ from PERT networks are:

CPM	PERT
(a) Network is constructed on the basis of jobs (or) activities(activity oriented)	(a) Network is constructed basis on the events.
(b) CPM does not take uncertainties involved in the estimation of times. The time is deterministic and hence only one time is considered.	(b) PERT network deals with uncertainties and hence three time estimations are considered (optimistic time, most likely time and pessimistic time)
(c) CPM times are related to cost. That is by decrease in the activity duration direct cost will increase (crashing of activity duration is possible)	(c) As there is no certainty of time, activity duration cannot be reduced. Hence cost cannot be expressed correctly. We can say expected cost of completion of activity (crashing of activity duration is not possible)

17.4.1. Writing the CPM network

First, one has to establish the logical relationship between activities. That is predecessor and successor relationship, which activity is to be started after a certain activity. By means of problems let us see how to deal with CPM network and the calculations needed.

Example 17. 5 : A company manufacturing plant and equipment for chemical processing is in the process of quoting tender called by public sector undertaking. Help the manager to find the project completion time to participate in the tender.

S.No.	Activities	Predecessor	Duration in days
1	A	-	3
2	B	-	4
3	C	A	5
4	D	A	6
5	E	C	7
6	F	D	8
7	G	B	9
8	H	E,F,G	3

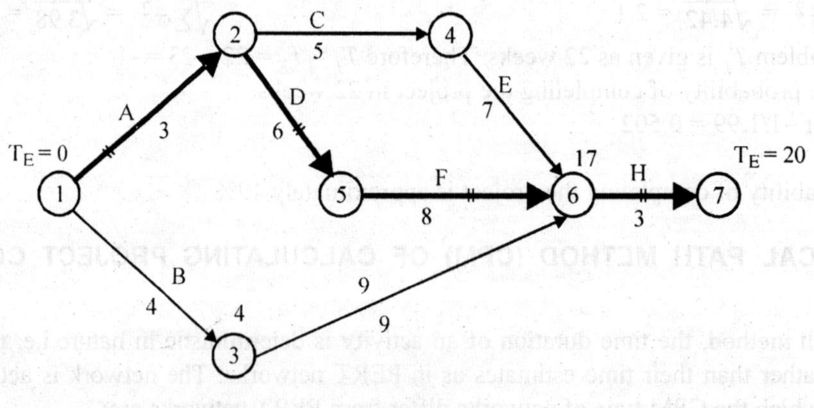

Figure 17.19

(1) Write the network referring to the data given.
(2) Number the events as discussed earlier.
(3) Calculate T_E as done in PERT network ($T'_E = (T_E^i + T_E^{ij}))_{max}$
(4) Identify the critical path

Project complete time = 20 weeks and the critical path = A – D – F – H

Example 17.5 : A small project has 7 activities and the time in days for each activity is given below

Activity	*Duration in days*
A	6
B	8
C	3
D	4
E	6
F	10
G	3

Given that activities *A* and *B* can start at the beginning of the project. When *A* is completed *C* and *D* can start. *E* can start only when *B* and *D* are finished. *F* can start when *B, C* and *D* are completed and is the final activity. *G* can start when *E* is finished and is the final activity. Draw the network and find the project completion time.

Activity	*Immediate predecessor*	*Time in days*
A	-	6
B	-	8
C	A	3
D	A	4
E	B , D	6
F	B,C or D	10
G	E	3

Solution :

Draw the network and enter the times and find T_E.

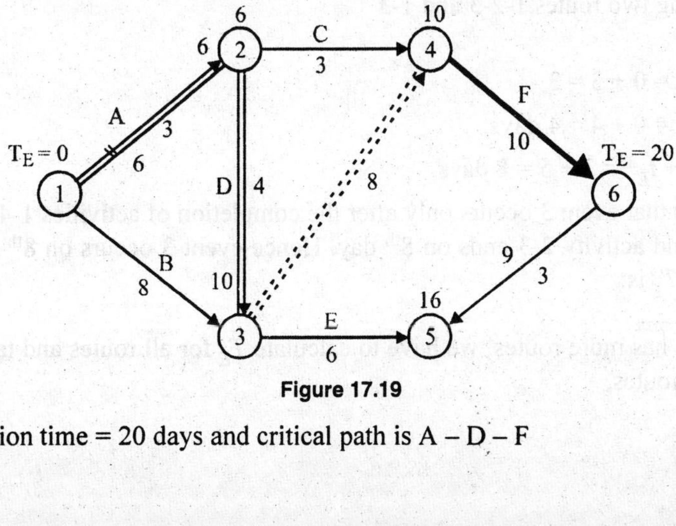

Figure 17.19

Project completion time = 20 days and critical path is A – D – F

17.5. TIME ESTIMATION IN CPM

Once the network is drawn the next work is to number the events and enter the time duration of each activity and then to calculate the project completion time. As we know, the CPM activities have single time estimates, and no uncertainties are considered, the system is deterministic in nature. While dealing with CPM networks, we come across the following times.

17.5.1. Earliest Event Time

We have defined event as either starting or ending of an activity. Earliest event time means what is the earliest time by which that event occurs. Let us consider a small example to understand this. Consider the figure 17.20.

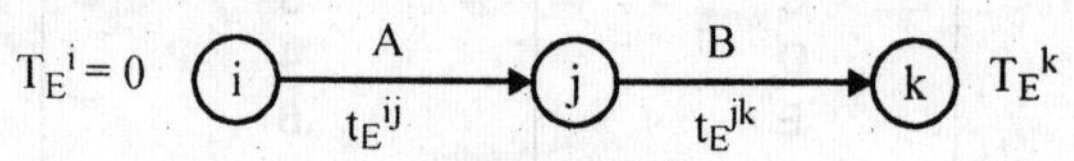

Figure 17.20

In figure 17.18 the network has two activities *A* and *B*. Activity *A* i.e. ij is predecessor to activity *B* i.e. activity *jk*. The time taken by activity *A* is t_E^{ij} and that of *B* is t_E^{jk}. If the event '*i*' occurs at time 0, then event '*j*' occurs at the earliest at $0 + t_E^{ij}$ i.e $T_E^i + t_E^{ij} = T_E^j$ and the earliest time by which event '*k*' occurs is given by $T_E^K = t_E^j + t_E^{jk}$. But when various lines, as shown in the figure 17.21 connect a node:

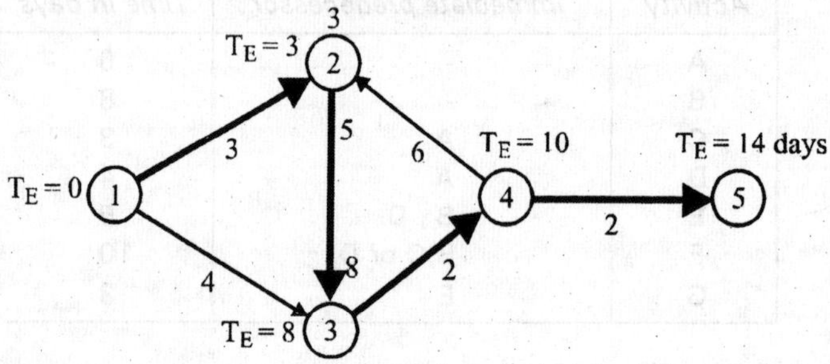

Figure 17.21

Event 3 is having two routes 1-2-3 and 1-3

$T_E^1 = 0$

$T_E^2 = T_E^1 + t_E^{12} = 0 + 3 = 3$

$T_E^3 = T_E^1 + t_E^{13} = 0 + 4 = 4$ days.

Also $T_E^3 = T_E^2 + t_E^{23} = 3 + 5 = 8$ days.

As the rule says that event 3 occurs only after the completion of activities 1-4 and 2-3. Activity 1-3 ends on 4th day and activity 2-3 ends on 8th day. Hence event 3 occurs on 8th day. This means the formula for finding T_E is:

$T_E^j = (T_E^i + t_E^{ij})_{\max}$

When the event has more routes, we have to calculate T_E for all routes and take the maximum T_E among T_E 's all the routes.

Example: 17. 6 : Find the slack of each event

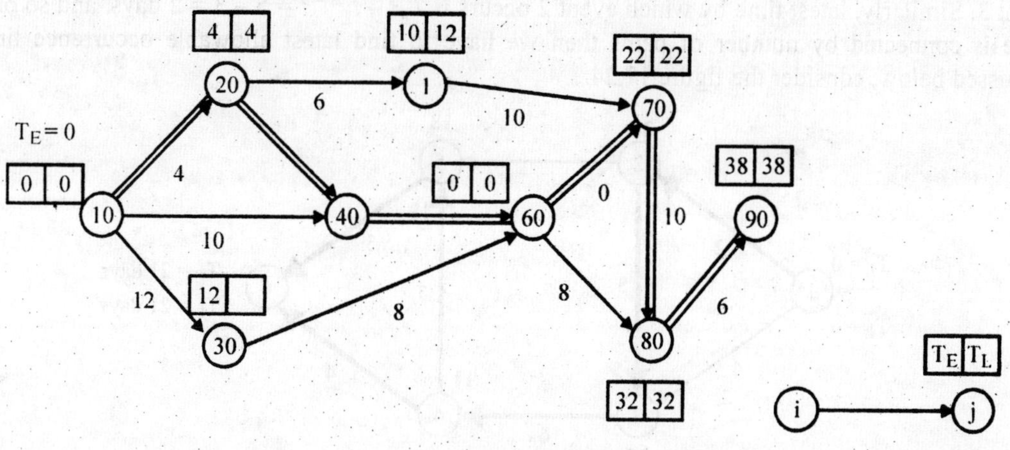

Figure 17.22

$T_E^{90} = 38$ days, $T_L^{90} = 38$ days

Critical path = 10 – 20 – 40 – 60 – 70 – 80 – 90

i	j	t_E^{ij}	T_E^i $T_E^i + t_E^{ij}$	T_E^j	T_L^i	T_L^j	T_j $T_L - T_E$
90	80	6	**38**	38	**22**	38	0
80	70	10	**32**	32	**22**	32	0
80	60	8	30	32	24	32	0
70	60	9	**22**	22	**22**	22	0
70	50	10	20	**22**	**12**	22	0
60	40	10	**22**	22	**12**	22	0
60	30	8	20	22	**14**	22	0
50	20	6	**10**	10	6	12	+2
40	20	8	**12**	12	**4**	12	0
40	10	10	10	12	2	12	0
30	10	12	12	12	2	14	+2
20	10	4	**4**	**4**	**0**	4	0

(Maximum element in 4 th column and minimum in column 6 for activities are bold numbers).

17.5.2. Latest allowable occurrence time

The next one is the latest allowable occur time represented by T_L^i. This is discussed by a simple example

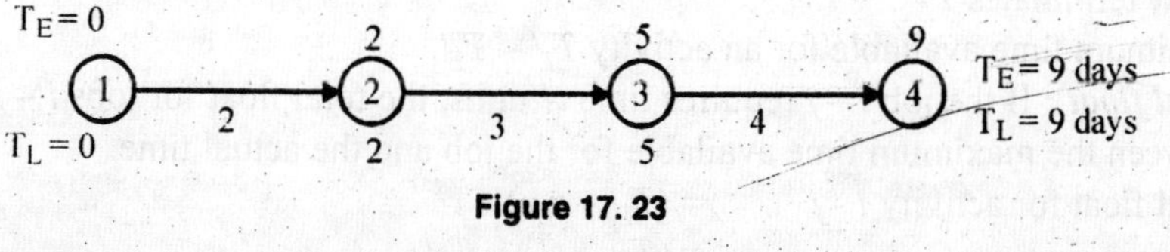

Figure 17. 23

Earliest occurrence time of event 4 = 9 days. As the activities 3 – 4 takes 4 days, the latest by which activity starts is $T_L^4 - t_E^{3-4} = 9 - 4 = 5^{th}$ day, which is also the earliest occurrence time of event 3. Similarly, latest time by which event 2 occurs is $T_E^3 - t_E^{2-3} = 5 - 3 = 2$ days, and so on. If a node is connected by number of paths then we have to find latest allowable occurrence time as discussed below, consider the figure 17.24.

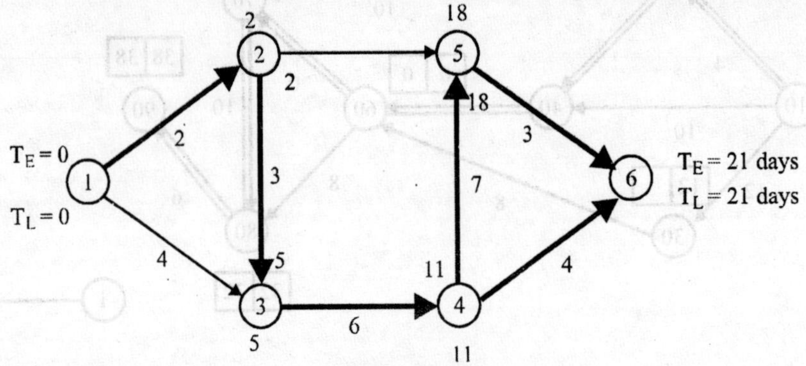

Figure 17. 24

The earliest occurrence time of event 6 is 21 days. As activities 4-6 takes 4 days the earliest occurrence time is $T_L^6 - t_E^{4\text{-}6} = 21 - 4 = 17$ days. But there is another route 6 – 5 – 4. If we consider this route $T_L^5 = T_L^6 - t_E^{5-6} = 21 - 3 = 18$ days, $T_E^4 = T_E^5 - t_E^{5-4} = 18 - 7 = 11$ th day. As the latest allowable occurrence time for event 4 is 17th day and 11 th day. The event 4 will not occur until activities 6 – 4 and 6 –5 are completed. As 11th day is the smallest, the event 4 occurrence on 11th day. Hence the formula for $T_L^i = (T_L^i - t_E^{ij})_{\text{minimum}}$.

17.5.3. Slack time

Slack time is difference between latest event and the earliest event time i.e.

$T_L^j - t_E^i = \bar{\tau}^i$ ($\bar{\tau}$ = Tou)

17.5.4. Float

Now let us define the times for activity $i - j$.

(*i*) ***Earliest start time :*** This is the earliest occurrence time for the event from which the activity arrow originates and is represented by $T_E^{\,i}$.

(*ii*) ***Earliest finish time :*** This is the earliest occurrence time of the event from which the activity arrow originates plus the duration of the activity. $T_E^i + t_E^{ij}$

(*iii*) ***Latest start time :*** This is the latest occurrence time for the node at which the activity arrow terminates minus the duration of activity i.e. $T_L^j - t_E^{ij}$.

(*iv*) ***Latest finish time :*** This is the latest occurrence time for the node at which the activity arrow terminates T_L^j.

(*v*) Maximum time available for an activity $T_L^j - T_E^i$.

(*vi*) ***Total float :*** If the job $i - j$ requires time t^{ij} units, the total float for jobs $i - j$ is the difference between the maximum time available for the job and the actual time.

Total float for activity i - j $= (T_L^j - t_E^i) - t^{ij}$

$= (T_L^j - t^{ij}) - T_E^i$

This is the latest time for the activity minus the earliest start time.

(*vii*) ***Free float:*** **- Free float for an activity is based on the possibility that all events occur at their earliest times, that means all activities starts as early as possible. If you have two activities $i-j$ and $j-k$ i.e., activity $j-k$ is a successor activity to activity $i-j$.**

Let T_E^i = Earliest occurrence time for event 'i'.

T_E^j = Earliest occurrence time for event 'j'.

This means that the earliest possible start time for activity $i-j$ is T_E^i and for the activity $j-k$ is

T_E^j. Let the activity duration be t_E^{ij}. In case T_E is greater than $T_E^i + t_E^{ij}$ activity, $j-k$ cannot start until T_E^j. The difference between $T_E^j - (T_E^i + t_E^{ij})$ is known as free float.

Therefore free float for activity $i-j = T_E^j - (T_E^i + t_E^{ij})$. But $(T_E^i + t_E^{ij})$ is earliest finish time for activity $i-j$. Hence free float = T_E^j Earliest finish time of $i-j$.

Free float for activity $i-j$ is the **difference** between its **earliest finish time** and **earliest start time** of its successor activity.

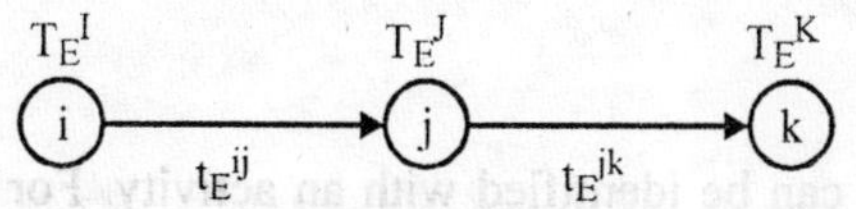

Figure 17.25

(*viii*) Another type of float is **interference float.** Interference float is the difference between total float and the free float. In fact it is head event slack.

Interference float = Total float - Free float

$$F_{IT} = F_T - F_F$$
$$F_T = (T_L^j - T_E^j) - t_E^{ij}$$
$$F_F = (T_E^j - T_E^i) - t_E^{ij}$$
$$F_{IT} = (T_L^j - T_E^i - t_E^{ij}) - (T_E^j - T_E^i - t_E^{ij})$$
$$F_{IT} = (T_L^j - T_E^j) = \text{Head event slack.}$$

Summary of float:

S.No.	*Type of float*		*Formulae*
1.	Total float (F_T)	Excess of maximum available time over the activity time.	$F_T = (T_L^j - T_E^j) - t_E^{ij}$
2.	Free float (F_F)	Excess of available time over the activity time when all jobs start as early as possible.	$F_F = (T_E^j - T_E^i) - t_E^{ij}$
3.	Independent float (F_{ID})	Excess of minimum available time over the activity time.	$F_{ID} = (T_E^j - T_L^i) - t_E^{ij}$
4.	Interfering float (F_{IT})	Difference between total float and free float	$F_{IT} = F_T - F_F$

(*ix*) Another type of float is **"Independent float"** (Refer to figure 17.26).

Consider the activity $i-j$. Activity $h-i$ is predecessor to $i-j$ and activity $j-k$ is a successor to activity $i-j$ and T_L^i is to latest finish time of activity $h-i$.

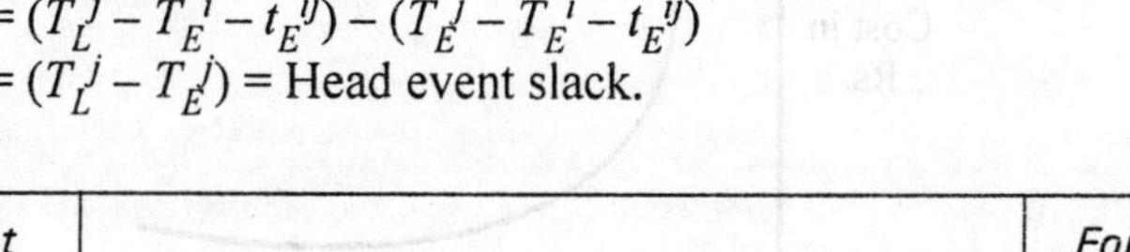

Figure 17.26

And activity $j-k$ starts at the earliest possible moment i.e. T_E^j. This means activity $i-j$ can take time duration between t_E^{ij} to $T_E^j - T_L^i$, without affecting the network. The difference between the $T_E^j - T_L^i$ and t_E^{ij} is known as **independent float.**
Independent float for $i-j = (T_E^j - T_L^i) - t_E^{ij}$

17.6. PROJECT COST ANALYSIS

So far we have dealt with how to find project completion time in PERT and CPM networks. In CPM network, when the time required by an activity is deterministic in nature, we may come across a situation that we may have to reduce the activity duration. This is not possible in PERT activity; because the activity duration is probabilistic in nature and we have three time estimates. Which time (either t_o, t_L or t_P) is to be reduced is a question. Hence activity time crashing is possible in critical path network.

Before crashing the activity duration, we must understand the costs associated with an activity.

17.6.1. Direct Cost

Direct costs are the costs that can be identified with an activity. For example, labor costs etc. When an activity whose duration is to be reduced (crashed), we have to supply extra resource, specially man power. Let us say an activity takes 7 days with 2 men. If 4 men works, it can be done in 4 days. The cost of 2 workmen increases. As we go on reducing the activity time, cost goes as increasing as shown in figure 17.27.

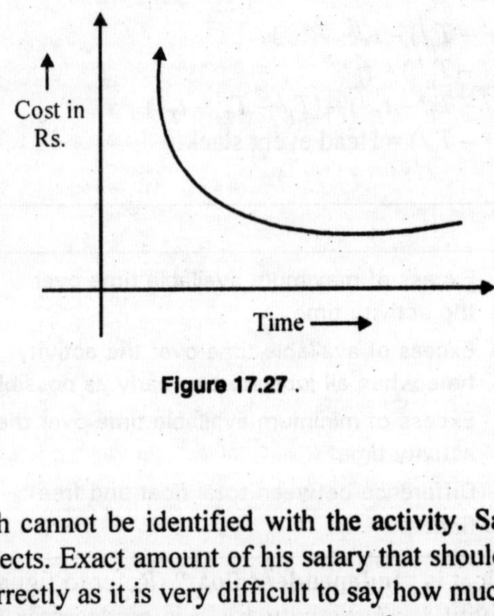

Figure 17.27.

17.6.2. Indirect cost

These are the costs, which cannot be identified with the activity. Say the salary of a manager, who is in-charge of many projects. Exact amount of his salary that should be changed to a particular project cannot be estimated correctly as it is very difficult to say how much time he has spent on each project. We can express all indirect costs put together in terms of amount per time period, for example say Rs. 100/- per day. As the indirect costs are expressed as so much of amount per time period, as the duration of project goes on reducing the indirect cost also goes on decreasing as in figure 17.28.

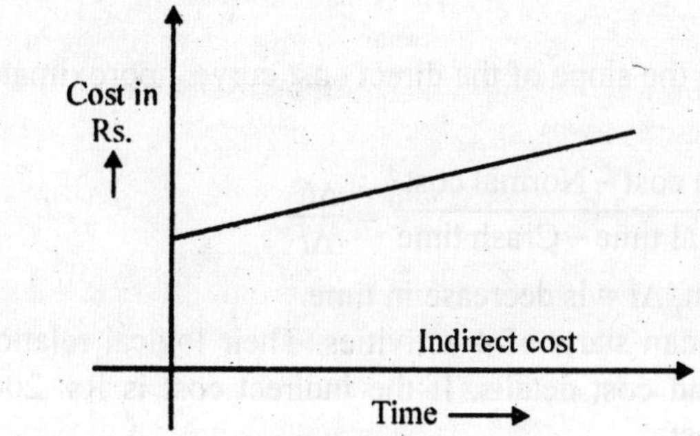

Figure 17.28

17.6.3. Total cost

The total cost which is the sum of direct cost and indirect cost is shown in the figure 17.29. As the project duration goes on reducing the total cost reduces from B to C and if duration is still crashed the total cost increases to A. Hence our problem is to find out the optimal duration of the project and optimal cost.

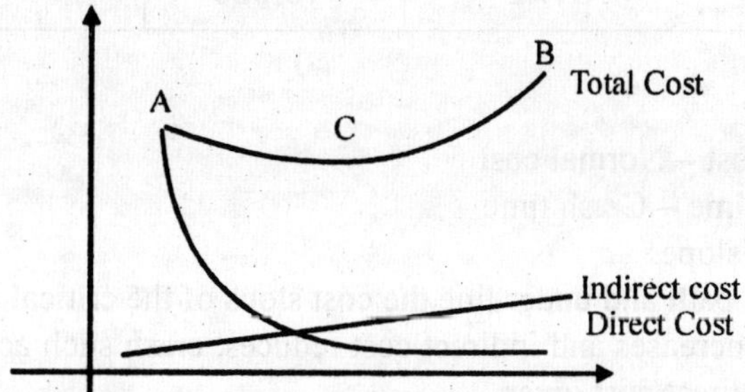

Figure 17.29 .

17.6.4. Cost slope

Consider a small portion of total cost curve and enlarge it. It appears like a straight line as shown in figure

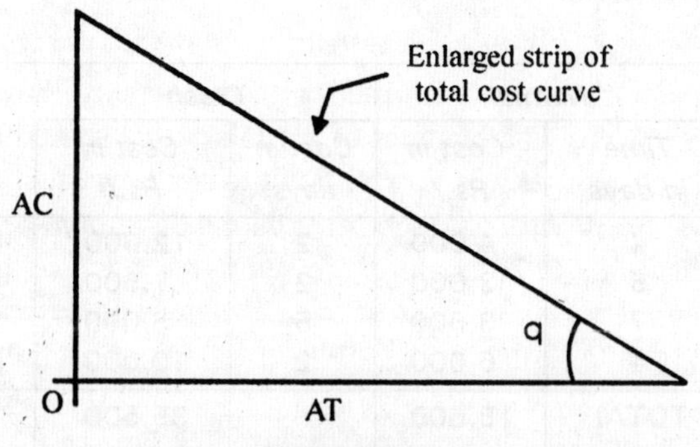

Figure 17.30 .

If θ is the inclination then $\tan \theta = \Delta C/\Delta t$. This indicates how much cost increases for crashing one unit of time period.

In other words cost slope is the slope of the direct cost curve, approximated as a straight line. It is given by

$$\text{Cost Slope} = \frac{\text{Crash cost} - \text{Normal cost}}{\text{Normal time} - \text{Crash time}} = \frac{\Delta C}{\Delta t}$$

Where ΔC = increase in cost, Δt = is decrease in time.

Problem. 17.7 : A project can starts of 4 activities. Their logical relationship and time taken is given along with crash time and cost details. If the indirect cost is Rs. 2000/- per week. Find the optimal duration and optimal cost.

Activit	*Predecessor*	*Normal*	*Crash*		
		Time in days	*Cost in Rs/-*	*Time in days*	*Cost in Rs/-*
A	–	4	4,000	2	12,000
B	A	5	3,000	2	7,500
C	A	7	3,600	5	6,000
D	B	4	5,000	2	10,000
		TOTAL	15,600		35,500

Solution Procedure :

Steps :

(1) Find ΔC = Crash cost – Normal cost
(2) Find Δt = Normal time – Crash time
(3) Find $\Delta C/\Delta t$ = Cost slope.
(4) Identify the critical path and under line the cost slops of the critical activity.
(5) As the direct cost increases and indirect cost reduces, crash such activities whose cost slops are less than the indirect cost given.
(6) Select the lowest cost slope and crash it first, then next highest and so on.
(7) Do not crash non-critical activities until they become critical activities in the process of crashing.
(8) In case, a non-critical activity becomes critical activity at the time of crashing consider the cost slopes of both the critical activities.
(9) Crashing should be continued until the cost slope becomes greater than the indirect cost.
(10) Do not crash such activities whose cost slope is greater than the indirect cost.
(11) Crashing is a done on a graph sheet with squared network drawn to scale.

Solution :

Activity	*Predecessor*	*Normal*		*Crash*				
		Time in days	*Cost in Rs./-*	*Cost in days*	*Cost in Rs./-*	ΔC	Δt	$\Delta C/\Delta t$
A	-	4	4,000	2	12,000	8,000	2	4,000
B	A	5	3,000	2	7,500	4,500	3	1,500
C	A	7	3,600	5	6,000	2,400	2	1,200
D	B	4	5,000	2	10,000	5,000	2	2,500
		TOTAL	15,600		35,500			

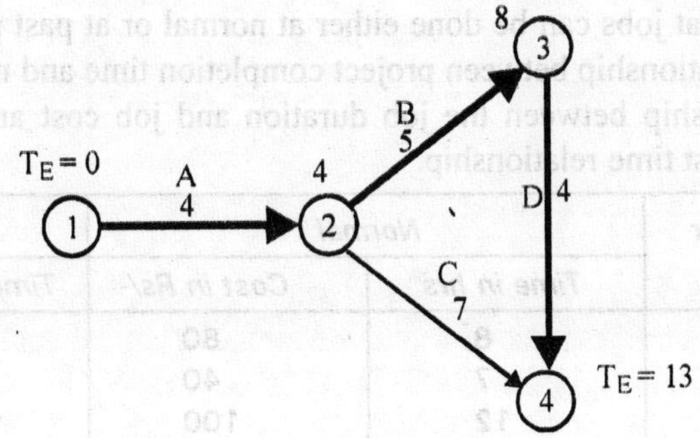

Figure 17.31

Now activities *A*, *B* and *D* are critical activities. Activity *B* is only the activity whose cost slope is less than indirect cost. Hence we can crash only activity *B*. For crashing we have to work with squared network. While writing squared network critical activities are shown as a straight line as in the figure 17.32. And non-critical activities are shown in the figure above and / or below the critical path as the case may be. That is non-critical path above critical path are sown above and vice versa.

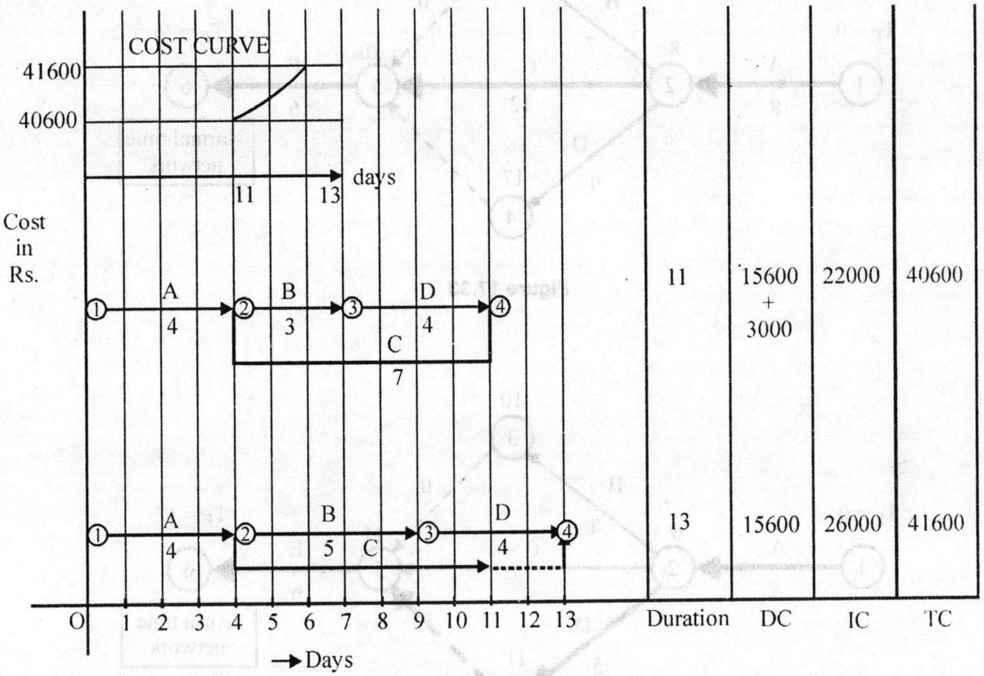

DC = Direct Cost IC = Indirect Cost TC = Total Cost

Figure 17.32

Though the activity *B* can be crashed by 3 days, only 2 days are crashed because after crushing 2 days at 11th day, activity 2-4 (*c*) also becomes critical. At this stage if we wants to crash one more day we have to crush activity 2-4 i.e *C* also along with 2 – 3. Now the cost slope of activity *B* and *C* are to be considered, which will be greater than the indirect cost. Hence no crashing can be done. 11 days is the optimal period and optimal cost is Rs. 40, 600/-.

Problem. 17.8 : A maintenance project has following estimates of times in hours and cost in rupees for jobs. Assuming that jobs can be done either at normal or at past pace, but not at any other pace in between. Plot the relationship between project completion time and minimum project cost.

(*b*) Assuming a relationship between the job duration and job cost and with overhead cost of Rs. 25/- per hour, plot the cost time relationship.

Jobs	*Predecessor*	*Normal*		*Crash*	
		Time in hrs	*Cost in Rs/-*	*Time in hrs*	*Cost in Rs/-*
A	-	8	80	6	100
B	A	7	40	4	94
C	A	12	100	5	184
D	A	9	70	5	102
E	B, C, D	6	50	6	50
		TOTAL	300		530

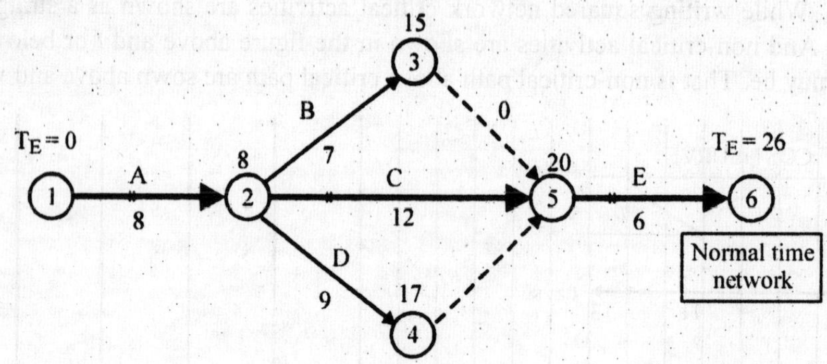

Figure 17.33

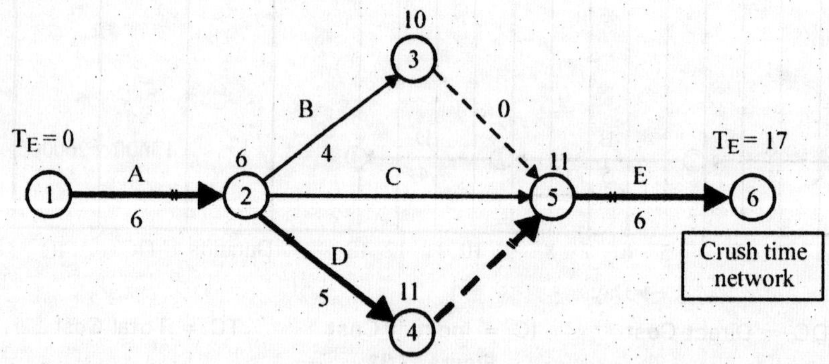

Figure 17.34

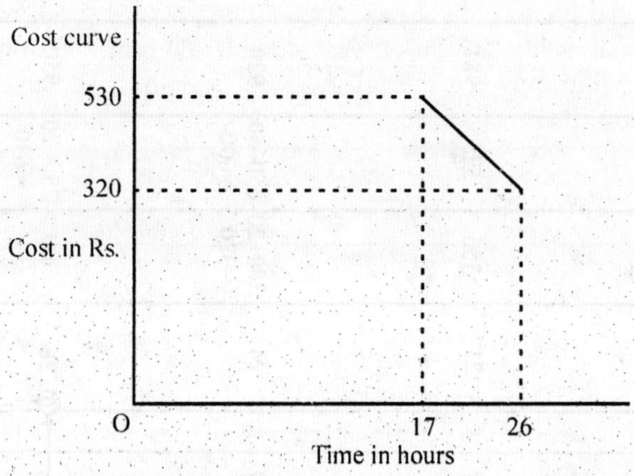

Figure 17.35

Indirect cost = Rs. 25/- per hour

Job	*Predecessor*	*Normal*		*Crash*				
		Time in days	*Cost in Rs./-*	*Cost in days*	*Cost in Rs./-*	ΔC	Δt	$\Delta C/\Delta t$
A	-	8	80	6	100	2	20	10
B	A	7	40	4	94	3	54	18
C	A	12	100	5	184	7	84	12
D	A	9	70	5	102	4	32	8
E	B, C, D	6	50	6	50	-	-	-
		Total	300		530			

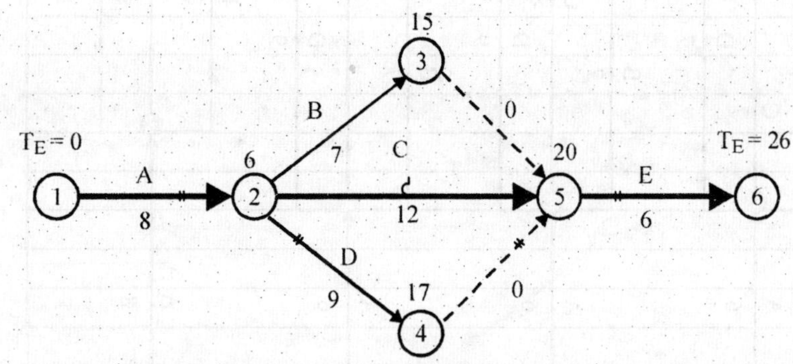

Figure 17.36

Squared network diagram is show in the next page. Refer Figure 17.37.

(*a*) Figure 17.37 shows the squared network.

(*b*) As critical activity A has got cost slope of Rs. 10/-, which is less than the indirect cost it is crashed by 2 days.

19	396	485	881
21	356	525	981
24	300+20 =320	650–50 =600	920
26	300	25 × 26 = 630	950

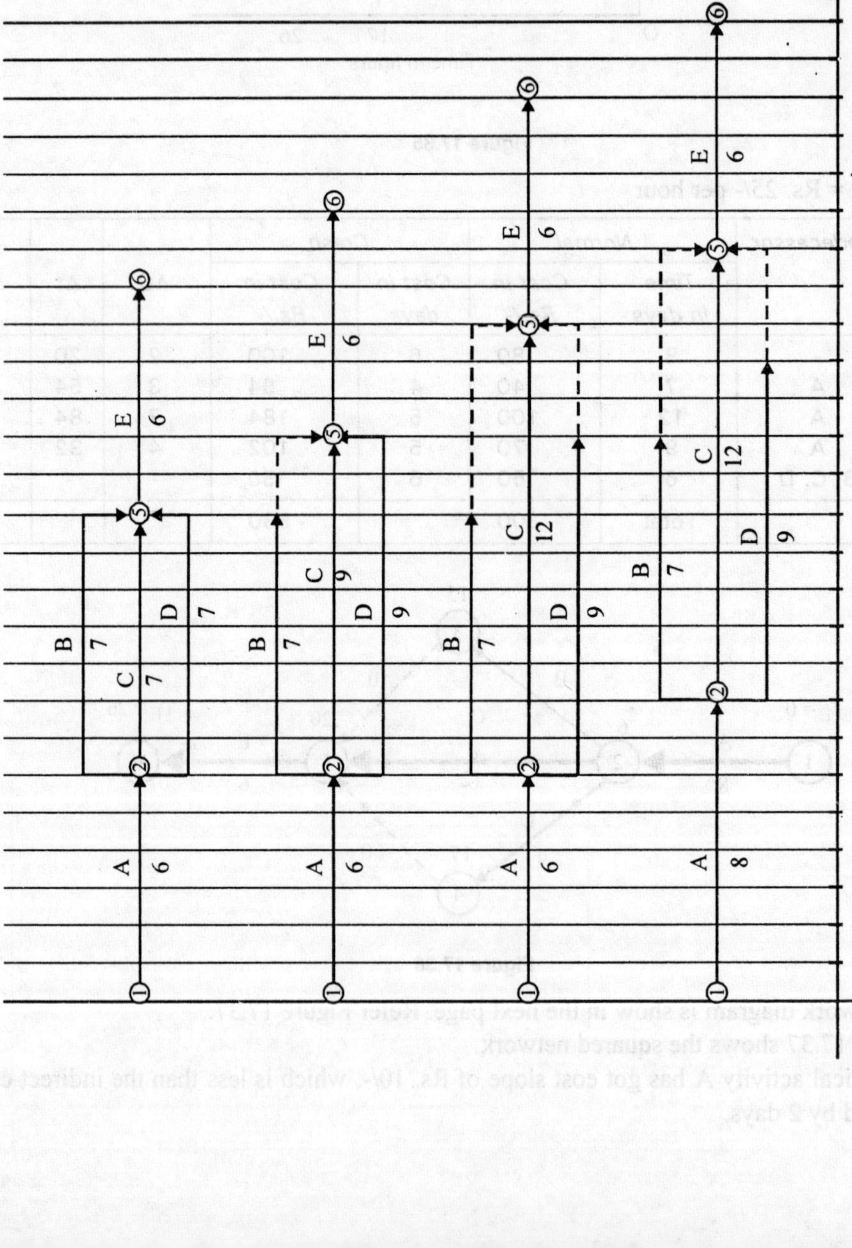

Hence duration is 24 hrs.

Direct Cost	=	Rs.300 + 2 x 10	=	Rs. 320
Indirect Cost	=	Rs.650 – 2 x 25	=	Rs. 600
		Total Cost	=	Rs. 920

(*c*) Next, critical activity *C* has got a cost slope Rs. 12/-, which is less than Rs. 25/-. This is crashed by 3 days, though it can be crashed by 7 days. This is because, if we crash further, activity *D* becomes critical activity, hence it is also to be considered for crashing. Then the cost slopes of activities C and D are taken into consideration.

Duration is 21 hrs.

Direct Cost	=	Rs.320 + 3 x 12	=	Rs. 356
Indirect Cost	=	Rs.600 – 3 x 25	=	Rs. 525
Total Cost	=	Rs. 881		

(*d*) Now cost slope of activity *C* and *D* put together = Rs.12 + 8 = 20 which is less than Rs.25/-, the indirect cost, hence both activities are crashed by 2 hours.

Duration is 19 hrs.

Direct Cost	=	Rs.356 + 2 x 20	=	Rs. 396
Indirect Cost	=	Rs.525 – 2 x 25	=	Rs. 475
Total Cost	=	Rs. 871		

As we see from the network, no further crashing can be done. Optimal time = 19 hrs and optimal cost = Rs.871 /-

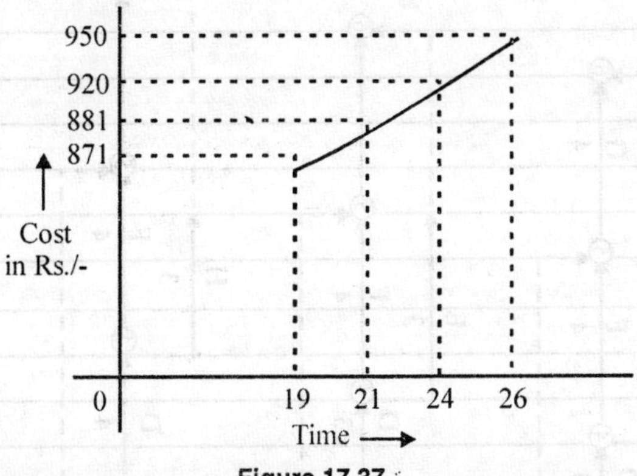

Figure 17.37

Problem 17.9 : The following details pertain to a job, which is to be scheduled to optimum cost.

Job	*Predecessor*	*Normal*		*Crash*				
		Time in days	*Cost in Rs./-*	*Cost in days*	*Cost in Rs./-*	*ΔC*	*Δt*	*ΔC/Δt*
A	-	3	1,400	2	2,100	700	1	700
B	C	6	2,150	5	2,750	600	1	600
C	-	2	1,600	1	2,400	800	1	800
D	A, B	4	1,300	3	1,800	500	1	500
E	C	2	1,700	1	2,500	800	1	800
F	D	7	1,650	4	2,850	400	3	
G	E, F	4	2,100	3	2,900	800	1	800
H	D	3	1,100	2	1,800	500	1	500
		TOTAL	13,000		18,900			

Duration Rs.	Direct Cost Rs.	Indirect Cost Rs.	Total Cost Rs.
16	14499+ 1600 =16099	17,600	33,699
18	13899+ 600 =14,499	19,800	34,299
19	13399+ 500 =13899	20,900	34,799
20	13,000+ 399 =13399	22,000	35,399
23	13,000	25,300	38,300

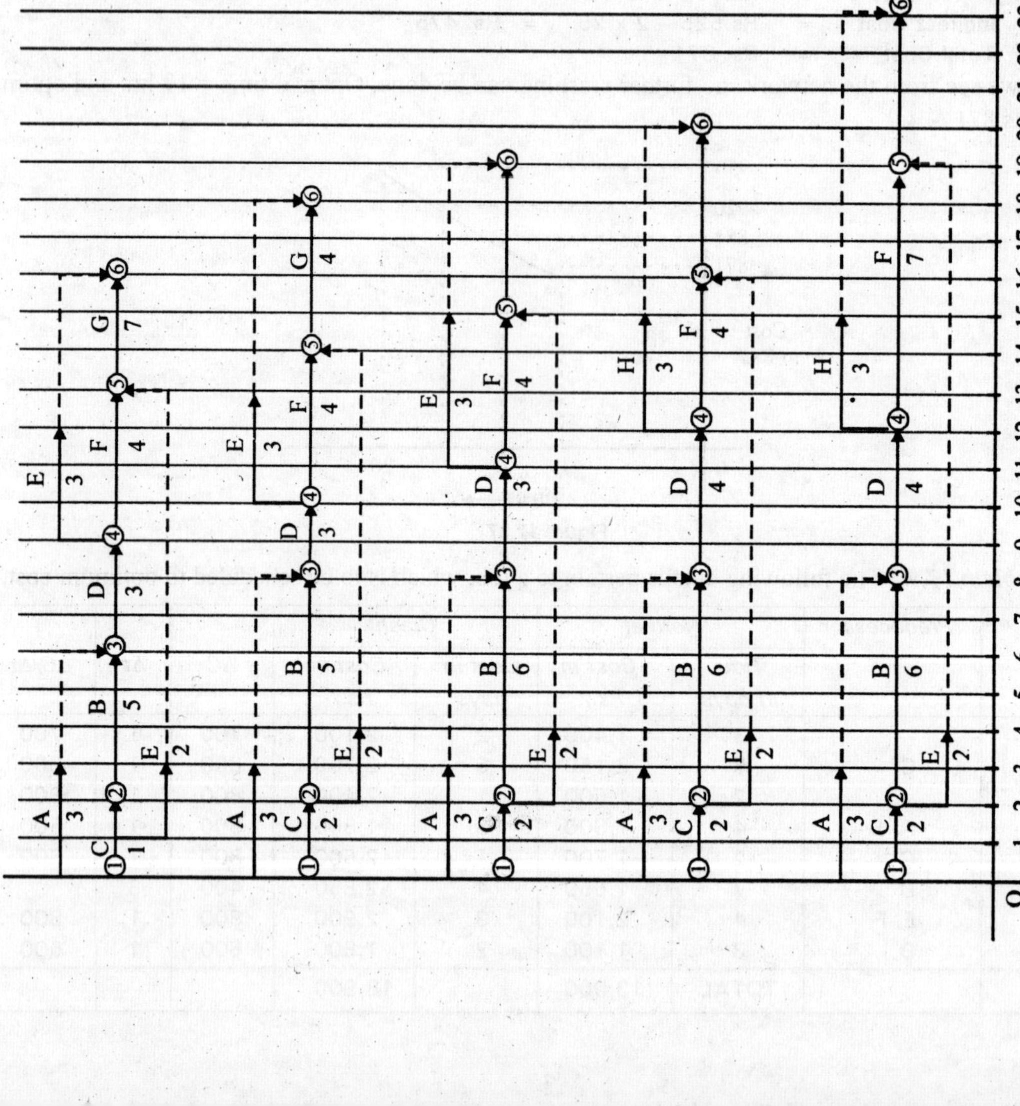

Figure 17.39

We can enter Δt in last column.

Assume the indirect cost is Rs.1100/- per day. Draw least cost schedule. The following relationship is given.

Activities *A* and *D* can be done parallel. Activity *B* follows *C*. *A* and *B* are predecessor to the activity *D*. Activity *E* starts as soon as *C* is concluded. Activities *F* and *H* starts soon after *D* is concluded. Activity *G* starts as soon as *E* and *F* are over. Activities *G* and *H* are end activities.

(**Note:** Students are advised to remember sometimes to show relationship between activities the symbols > or < is used. For example Activity *B* is < activity *A* means *B* starts after *A*. Similarly if we say *D* > *E* means *E* starts after *D* is concluded.)

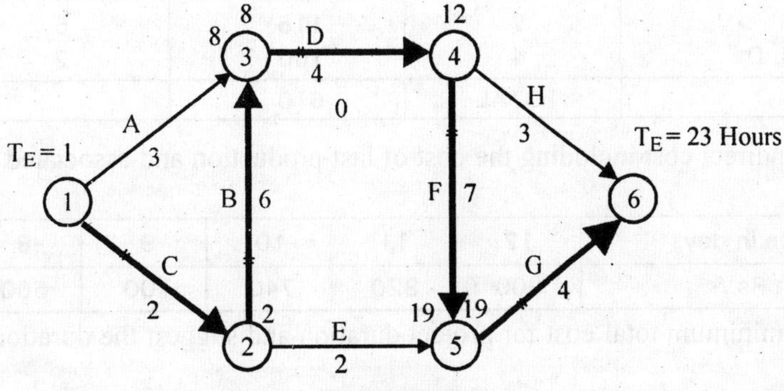

Figure 17.38

Project completion time is 23 hrs. Critical path *C–B–D–F–G*. Lowest cost slope is Rs.133 for critical activity *F* can be crashed by 3 days.

Next cost slope is Rs.500/- for activity *D*. This can be crashed by 1 day.

Next cost slope is Rs.600/- for activity *B*. This can be crashed by 1 day. Next lowest cost slope is Rs.800/- for critical activities *C* and *G*. *C* can be crashed by 1 day and *G* can be crashed by 1 day.

All critical activities have been crashed and non - critical activities have slack. Hence they are not crashed. Hence optimal cost is Rs. 33699 and optimal time is 16 days.

Squared network diagram is sown in figure 17.39 in the page 392. Cost curve is shown in figure 17.40.

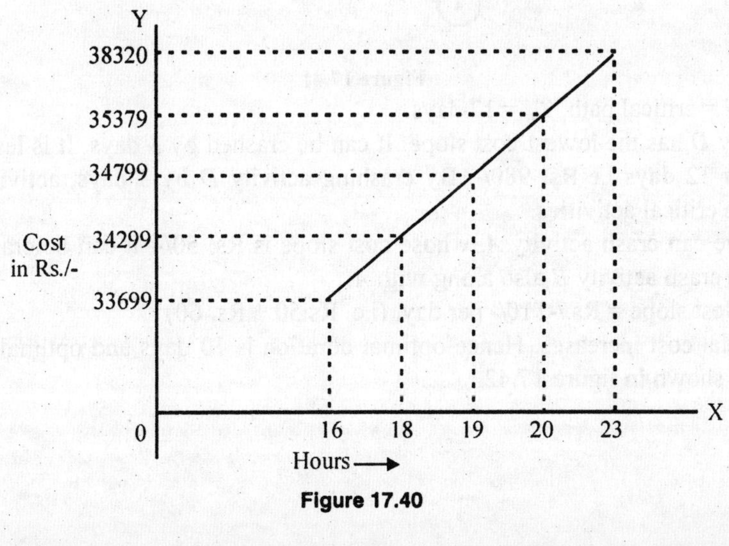

Figure 17.40

Problem 17.10 : **Given below are network data and time cost trade-off data for small maintenance work.**

Jobs	Predecessor	Normal		Crash	Cost slope
		Time in hrs	Cost in Rs./-	Time in hrs	Rs. / dayΔC
A	-	3	50	2	50
B	-	6	140	4	60
C	-	2	50	1	30
D	A	5	100	2	40
E	C	2	55	2	-
F	A	7	115	5	30
G	B, D	4	100	2	70
		TOTAL	610		

Assume that indirect cost including the cost of last production and associated costs to be as given below.

Project duration in days	12	11	10	9	8	7
Indirect cost in Rs./-	900	820	740	700	660	620

Work out the minimum total cost for project duration and suggest the duration for minimum total cost.

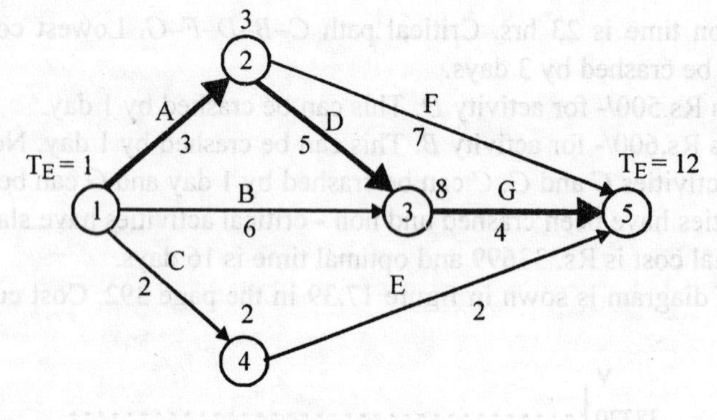

Figure 17.41

$A–D–G$ = critical path, T_E = 12 days.

1. Activity D has the lowest cost slope. It can be crashed by 3 days. It is less than the indirect cost for 12 days i.e Rs. 980/-. By crashing activity D by 3 days, activities F and B have became critical activities.
2. Next we can crash activity A, whose cost slope is Rs. 50/-, it can be crashed in 1 day. We have to crash activity B also along with A.
   Total Cost slope = Rs./-110/- per day. (i.e Rs.50 + Rs. 60)

Hence the total cost increases. Hence optimal duration is 10 days and optimal cost is Rs.1430/-. The cost curve is shown in figure 17.42.

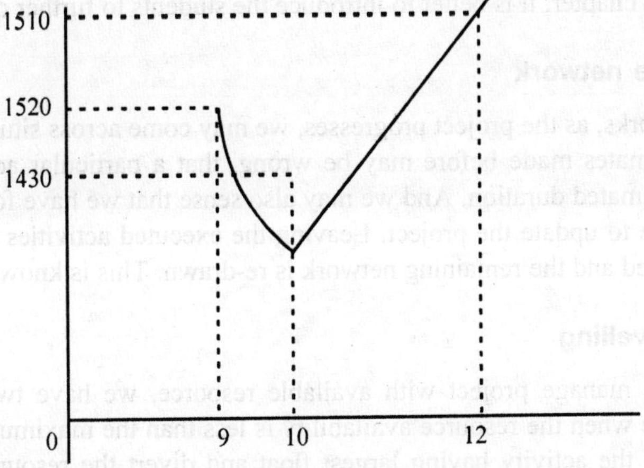
1510
1520
1430
0
9
10
12

Figure 17.42

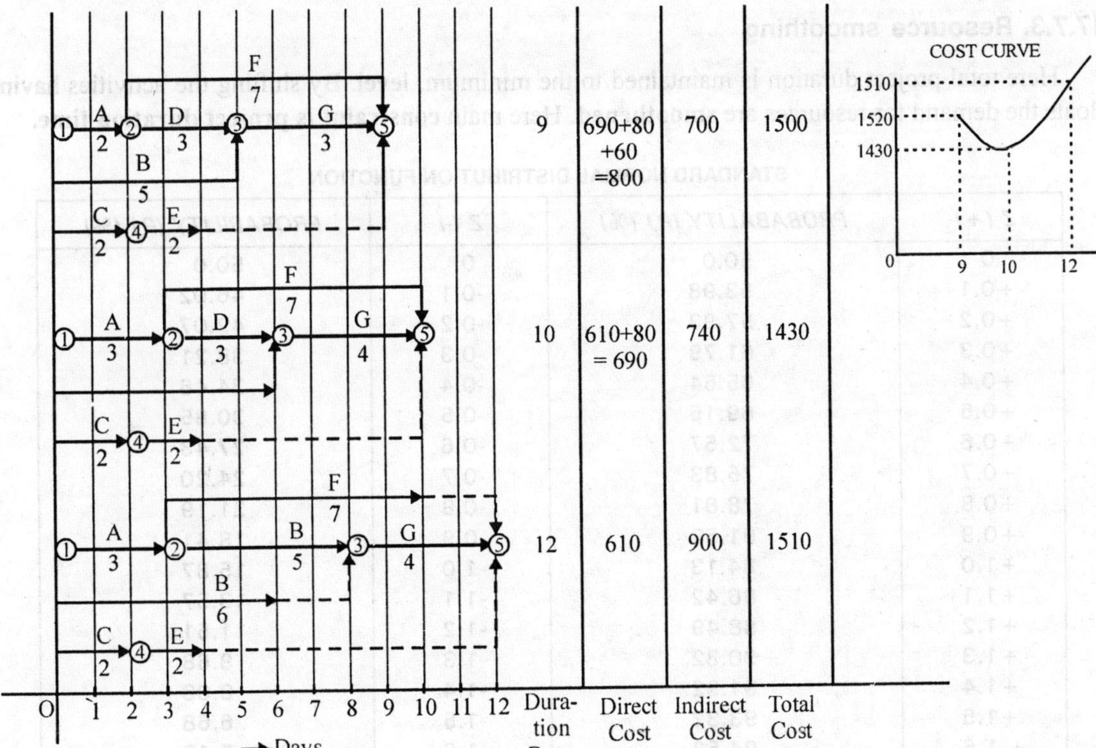
F
7
A
2
D
3
G
3
B
5
C
2
E
2
9
690+80
+60
=800
700
1500
F
7
A
3
D
3
G
4
C
2
E
2
10
610+80
= 690
740
1430
F
7
A
3
B
5
G
4
B
6
C
2
E
2
12
610
900
1510
O 1 2 3 4 5 6 7 8 9 10 11 12
→Days
Duration Days
Direct Cost Rs.
Indirect Cost Rs.
Total Cost Rs.
COST CURVE
1510
1520
1430
0
9
10
12

17.7. UPDATING AND SMOOTHENING

Before concluding this chapter, it is better to introduce the students to further development in network.

17.7.1. Updating the network

In large project works, as the project progresses, we may come across situation like:

(*a*) The time estimates made before may be wrong, that a particular activity may take less or more time than the estimated duration. And we may also sense that we have forgotten some activities. In such cases, we have to update the project. Leaving the executed activities the remaining activities may have to be modified and the remaining network is re-drawn. This is known as network **updating.**

17.7.2. Resource levelling

When we have to manage project with available resource, we have two options. First one is resource leveling. Here when the resource availability is less than the maximum resource required for an activity, then delay the activity having largest float and divert the resource to critical activities. When two or more activities compete for same resource, first try to allocate the resource to an activity, which has shortest duration and next to the activity, which is having next highest duration. Here available resource is a **constraint.** The project duration time may increase during the process. Hence project duration time will not be a constraint.

17.7.3. Resource smoothing

Here total project duration is maintained to the minimum, level. By shifting the activities having floats the demand for resources are **smoothened.** Here main **constraint is project duration time.**

STANDARD NORMAL DISTRIBUTION FUNCTION

Z (+)	*PROBABALITY (P_r) (%)*	*Z (-)*	*PROBABILITY (P_r) (%)*
0	50.0	0	50.0
+0.1	53.98	-0.1	46.02
+0.2	57.93	-0.2	42.07
+0.3	61.79	-0.3	38.21
+0.4	65.54	-0.4	34.46
+0.5	69.15	-0.5	30.85
+0.6	72.57	-0.6	27.43
+0.7	75.83	-0.7	24.20
+0.8	78.81	-0.8	21.19
+0.9	81.59	-0.9	18.41
+1.0	84.13	-1.0	15.87
+1.1	86.42	-1.1	13.57
+1.2	88.49	-1.2	11.51
+1.3	90.32	-1.3	9.68
+1.4	91.92	-1.4	8.08
+1.5	93.32	-1.5	6.68
+ 1.6	94.52	-1.6	5.48
+1.7	95.54	-1.7	4.46
+1.8	96.41	-1.8	3.59

+1.9	97.13	-1.9	2.87
+2.0	97.20	-2.0	2.28
+2.1	98.21	-2.1	1.70
+2.2	98.61	-2.2	1.39
+2.3	98.93	-2.3	1.07
+2.4	99.18	-2.4	0.82
+2.5	99.38	-2.5	0.62
+2.6	99.53	-2.6	0.47
+2.7	99.65	-2.7	0.35
+2.8	99.74	-2.8	0.26
+2.9	99.81	-2.9	0.19
+3.0	99.87	-3.0	0.13

QUESTIONS

1. Write a brief note on the history of PERT and CPM networks.
2. What do you mean by Milestone chart?
3. Explain the concept of three time estimates in PERT network.
4. Explain why PERT activity cannot be crashed.
5. Distinguish between PERT and CPM.
6. Explain what do you mean by Crashing of an activity.
7. Write a note on Resource Leveling and Resource Smoothening and Up dating of a Project network.
8. Explain what is Cost Slope. What is the significance of Cost slope in Crashing the network.
9. Explain the following terms: a) Event, b) Activity, c) Head event, d) Tail event
10. Explain why there should be only one starting point and one ending point in a network.
11. Write a short note on Dummy Activity.
12. What is a slack? How will it differ form Float?
14. Explain three different types of Floats.
15. Explain how do you find the probability of completing the project in PERT network. Why you do not do the same in CPM network?
16. The following is the information available about a project. Draw the logic diagram. Find the Project completion time and identify the critical path. Also find the slack of each event. What is the probability of completing the project one day earlier to project completion time? (Time given in days)

Activity	*Optimistic time*	*Most likely time*	*Pessimistic time.*
1 – 2	3	6	15
2 – 3	2	5	14
2 – 4	6	12	30
3 – 5	2	5	8
5 – 6	5	11	17
6 – 7	2	5	8
7 – 8	1	4	7
4 – 8	3	9	27
8 – 9	4	19	28

17. (a) Explain the following: (i) Successor event, (ii) Dummy activity, (iii) Beta distribution.
    (*b*) The following is the schedule of a project. Find the critical path of the project; and total float and free float of each activity.

Activity	*Duration in days.*
0 – 2	2
1 – 2	4
2 –3	2
3 – 4	5
2 – 5	1
4 – 5	1
0 – 6	1
3 – 7	8
6 – 7	3
5 – 8	3
7 – 8	5

18. (a) Explain the following: (i) Normal cost, (ii) Crash cost, (iii) Crash time.

    (*b*) The following table gives the list of jobs, their normal duration in days and cost in rupees, and the crash duration in days and the cost in Rs. What is the normal duration and cost of the project? If the indirect cost is Rs. 75 per day, find the minimum cost project schedule.

Activity	*Normal Duration in Days*	*Normal cost In Rs.*	*Crash Duration in Days In Rs*	*Crash cost*
1 – 2	1	25	1	25
2 – 3	3	80	2	140
1 – 3	5	125	2	225
3 – 4	3	100	2	175
4 – 5	1	30	1	30

19. For a project the detail which are given below, (*a*) Draw the network, (*b*) Determine the total duration of the project, (*c*) Determine the critical path, (*e*) Earliest Start time, Latest start time Earliest Finish time, Latest finish time for each activity. (*F*) If in the above network activity *F* depends on both *C* and *D* what would be the change in the critical path.

Activity	*Depends on in days.*	*Duration*
A	None	8
B	None	8
C	A	16
D	B and G	8
E	C and D	4
F	D	18
G	A	4
H	E	12

20. Draw a network diagram of the following project using one dummy activity, the time duration in days of each activity is given in brackets.
    (i) Activity *A* (4), *B* (8) and *E* (7) can begin at the beginning of the project.
    (ii) Activity *F* (15) can commence, once activity *A* has been completed.
    (iii) Activity *D* (6) and *G* (12) can commence only after activity *B* has been completed.
    (iv) Activity *C* (3) can start on the completion of activity F and *D* and is final activity.
    (v) Activity *K* (9) can begin on completion of activity *E*.
    (vi) Activity *H* (10) can begin on completion of activity *G* and is final activity.
    (vii) Activity *L* (11) can commence only after the completion of activities *G* and *k*.
    (viii) J (5) follows the completion of activity *L* and is a final activity.

Determine Early start time, Latest start time, Early finish Time and Latest finish time of each activity. Also determine total duration of the project and the critical path.

20 Draw the network of the following project:

Activities A and B can start at the beginning of he project.

When A is completed C and D can start.

E can start when B, C and D are completed and is a final activity.

G can start when E is finished and is a final activity.

The duration in days taken by each activity is:

A: 6 days, B: 8 days, C: 3 days, D: 4 days, E: 6 days, F: 10 days, and G: 3 days.

What is the project completion time and mark the critical path.

21. The following details pertain to a job, which is to be scheduled to optimum cost.

Job	*Normal Time in Days*	*Normal Cost in Rs.*	*Crash Time in Days*	*Crash Cost in Rs.*	*Cost of Crashing In Rs.*
A	3	1400	2	2100	700
B	6	2150	5	2750	600
C	2	1600	1	2400	800
D	4	1300	3	1800	500
E	2	1700	1	2500	800
F	7	1650	3	2900	400
G	4	2100	3	2900	800
H	3	1100	2	1600	500
	Total	13,000		18,900	

Assume indirect cost is Rs. 1100 / - per day. Develop schedule for the following assumptions:

A and *C* can be done in parallel but *D* has to start only after *A* is over.

Crash one day from job *B*.

Crash *A* and *G* by 1 day each.

Crash *B*, *D* and *F* by 1 day each.

From the above develop an optimal schedule.

OBJECTIVE TYPE QUESTIONS

UNIT : I (Production and Operations Management)

1. For a consumer the product is one which:
(a) Is available to him at cheap cost, ( )
(b) Is available when ever he needs it. ( )
(c) Is optima combination of potential utilities, ( )
(d) He can share with his friends. ( )

2. For a Production Manager, the product is:
(a) Optimal blend of uses ( )
(b) Optimal blend of services ( )
(c) Combination of surfaces ( )
(d) Combination of properties ( )

3. Product is a combination of various cost elements for a
(a) Consumer, ( )
(b) Production Manager, ( )
(c) Retail seller, ( )
(d) Financial Manager. ( )

4. For a Personal Manger, the product is a
(a) Combination of operations, ( )
(b) Combination of surfaces, ( )
(c) Combination of skills ( )
(d) Combination of costs. ( )

5. In general product can be defined as:
(a) Combination of surfaces and costs, ( )
(b) Combination of uses and costs, ( )
(c) Combination of skills and surfaces, ( )
(d) Bundle of tangible and intangible attributes along with services to satisfy consumer ( )

6. Application of technology or process to the raw material to add use value is known as
(a) Product ( )
(b) Production, ( )
(c) Application of technology ( )
(d) Combination of technology and process ( )

7. Example of production by disintegration is
(a) Automobile, ( )
(b) Locomotive, ( )
(c) Crude oil ( )
(d) Mineral water ( )

8. Crude oil is an example for
(a) Production by disintegration, ( )
(b) Production by Integration, ( )
(c) Production by assembly, ( )
(d) Production by service. ( )

9. Automobile vehicle is an example of production by
(a) Integration, ( )
(b) Disintegration, ( )
(c) Service, ( )
(d) Combination of Integration and Disintegration. ( )

10. Surface hardening is an example of
(a) Production by application of machine tool, ( )
(b) Production by disintegration, ( )
(c) Production by Integration, ( )
(d) Production by Service. ( )

11. In Production by disintegration the material undergoes
(a) Change in economic value only, ( )
(b) Change in physical and chemical characteristics, ( )
(c) Change in technology only, ( )
(d) None of the above. ( )

12. In Production by service, the product undergoes the changes in:
(a) Shape and size of the surface, ( )
(b) Shape of the surface only, ( )
(c) Size of the surface only, ( )
(d) Chemical and Mechanical properties. ( )

13. Use of any process or procedure designed to transform a set of input elements into a set of output elements is known as:
(a) Transformation process ( )
(b) Transformation of input to output, ( )
(c) Production, ( )
(d) Technology change. ( )

14. Management is
(a) Art only, ( )
(b) Science only, ( )
(c) Both Art and Science, ( )
(d) Art, Science and humanity. ( )

15. Management is
(a) Getting things done, ( )
(b) Getting things done by the people to satisfy the organisation goals, ( )
(c) Getting things done by the people to earn money, ( )
(d) Getting things done by the people to satisfy the government. ( )

16. Conversion of inputs into outputs is known as
(a) Application of technology ( )
(b) Operations management, ( )
(c) Manufacturing products, ( )
(d) Product. ( )

17. Marketing means:
(a) Selling products, ( )
(b) Searching for consumer, ( )

(c) Conversion of place and possession characteristics of a product ( )
(d) None of the above. ( )

18. Example of non physical way of production is:
(a) Production of oil, ( )
(b) Production of Mineral Water, ( )
(c) Production of Information, ( )
(d) Production of Agricultural products. ( )

19. Important aims of Production Management are
(a) Efficiency, Effectiveness and Consumer satisfaction, ( )
(b) Use of machinery carefully, and avoid accidents, ( )
(c) Use of material optimally, and avoid scrap, ( )
(d) To give whatever consumer needs and take minimum profit from him. ( )

20. The desired objective of Production and Operations Management is:
(a) Use cheap machinery to produce, ( )
(b) To train unskilled workers to manufacture goods perfectly, ( )
(c) Optimal utilisation of available resources, ( )
(d) To earn good profits. ( )

21. The scope of Production Planning and Control is
(a) Limited to Production of products only, ( )
(b) Limited to production of services only, ( )
(c) Limited to production of services and products only, ( )
(d) Unlimited, can be applied to any type of activity. ( )

22. Manufacturing system often produces:
(a) Standardised products, ( )
(b) Standardised products in large volumes, ( )
(c) Substandard products in large volumes, ( )
(d) Products and services in limited volume. ( )

23. The difference between product and service is:
(a) The demand for product can be estimated to certain accuracy where as demand service is uncertain, ( )
(b) The demand for the service is deterministic where as demand for product is highly probabilistic and cannot be estimated, ( )
(c) Service can be stored and product cannot be stored, ( )
(d) None of the above. ( )

24. The difference between product system and project system is
(a) Project system the equipment and machinery are fixed where as in product system they are movable, ( )
(b) In Product system the machinery and equipment are fixed and in project system they are not fixed, ( )
(c) Project system produces only standardized products and product system produces only unstandardised products, ( )
(d) Products cannot be stocked whereas projects can be stocked. ( )

25. Most important benefit to the consumer from efficient production system is
(a) He can save money, ( )

(b) He will have product of his choice easily available, ( )
(c) He gets increased use value in the product, ( )
(d) He can get the product on credit. ( )

26. The benefit derived by a promoter from efficient production department is
(a) They can sell all their products, ( )
(b) They get increased security for their investment, ( )
(c) Their product will become standard product, ( )
(d) None of the above. ( )

27. Important benefit that an employee gets from efficient production department is
(a) He can get any product of his choice at his place, ( )
(b) He can get products at cheapest cost, ( )
(c) He can get more products than his need, ( )
(d) He gets adequate wages and increased job security. ( )

28. Two important functions that are to be done by Production department are:
(a) Forecasting, ( ) (b) Costing ( )
(c) Scheduling and loading ( ) (d) Inspecting ( )

29. Fixing the flow lines of materials in production is known as:
(a) Scheduling, ( ) (b) Loading, ( )
(c) Planning, ( ) (d) Routing. ( )

30. The act of releasing the production documents to the production department is known as:
(a) Planning, ( ) (b) Routing, ( )
(c) Dispatching, ( ) (d) Releasing. ( )

31. The activity of specifying when to start the job and when to end the job is known as:
(a) Planning, ( ) (b) Scheduling, ( )
(c) Timing ( ) (d) Follow - up ( )

32. In an organization, generally the production management is a
(a) Line function, ( ) (b) Staff function, ( )
(c) Line and Staff function ( ) (d) None of the above. ( )

33. In an organisation the production planning and control department comes under:
(a) Planning department, ( ) (b) Manufacturing department, ( )
(c) Personal department ( ) (d) R & D department. ( )

34. In Job production system, we need:
(a) More unskilled labours, ( ) (b) Skilled labours, ( )
(c) Semi - skilled labours, ( ) (d) Old people. ( )

35. In Continuous manufacturing system, we need
(a) General purpose machines and Skilled labours, ( )
(b) Special machine tools and highly skilled labours, ( )
(c) Semi automatic machines and unskilled labours, ( )
(d) General purpose machines and unskilled labours. ( )

36. Most suitable layout for Job production is:
(a) Line layout, ( ) (b) Matrix layout, ( )
(c) Process layout ( ) (d) Product layout. ( )

37. Most suitable layout for Continuous production is:
(a) Line layout, ( ) (b) Process Layout, ( )

(c) Group technology, ( ) (d) Matrix layout. ( )

38. One of the product example for Line layout is:

(a) Repair workshop. ( ) (b) Welding shop, ( )

(c) Engineering College, ( ) (d) Cement. ( )

39. Number of product varieties that can be manufactured in Job production is:

(a) Limited to one or two, ( ) (b) Large varieties of products ( )

(c) One only, . ( ) (d) None of the above. ( )

40. Number of product varieties that can be manufactured in Mass production is:

(a) One only, ( ) (b) Two only, ( )

(c) Few verities in large volumes, ( ) (d) Large verities in small volumes. ( )

41. In general number of product verities that can be manufactured in Flow production is:

(a) One only ( ) (b) Ten to twenty verities, ( )

(c) Large verities, ( ) (d) Five only. ( )

42. Generally the size of the order for production in Job production is

(a) Small, ( ) (b) Large ( )

(c) Medium ( ) (d) Very large ( )

43. Generally in continuous production the production is carried out to:

(a) Customer's order, ( ) (b) Government orders only ( )

(c) For stock and supply ( ) (d) Few rich customers. ( )

44. Inventory cost per product in intermittent production is:

(a) Higher, ( ) (b) Lowest, ( )

(c) Medium, ( ) (c) Abnormal. ( )

45. The material handling cost per unit of product in Continuous production is:

(a) Highest compared to other systems. ( )

(b) Lower than other systems, ( )

(c) Negligible, ( )

(d) Cannot say. ( )

46. Routing and Scheduling becomes relatively complicated in

(a) Job production, ( ) (b) Batch production ( )

(c) Flow production ( ) (d) Mass production ( )

47. The starting point of Production cycle is:

(a) Product design, ( ) (b) Production Planning, ( )

(c) Routing ( ) (d) Market research. ( )

48. Most important aspect of Marketing aspect of pre planning is

(a) To plan how to sell product, ( )

(b) To see how best the product is to be transported to market, ( )

(c) To examine whether the product satisfy the user or not ( )

(d) To make arrangements for advertising. ( )

49. Length of active life of the product is known as:

(a) Life of the product, ( ) (b) Usefulness of the product, ( )

(c) Durability of the product, ( ) (d) Dependability of the product. ( )

50. Capability of product to function, when called up on to do its job is known as:

(a) Capability of the product, ( ) (b) Capacity of the product, ( )

(c) Sincerity of the product, ( ) (d) Dependability. ( )

51. Aesthetic quality of product refers to :

(a) Performance of the product, ( )
(b) Operation of the product, ( )
(c) Physical appearance of the product ( )
(d) Cost of the product. ( )

52. Aesthetic design of a product is concerned with:

(a) Designing the performance characteristics of a product, ( )
(b) Designing the operational aspects of a product ( )
(c) Decreasing the manufacturing cost of the product, ( )
(d) Designing and modeling the final shape around the basic skeleton of the product. ( )

53. One of the factors to be considered in economic analysis of product design is:

(a) Who is the customer for the product? ( )
(b) What materials are to be used to manufacture the product? ( )
(c) What is the expected production cost per product? ( )
(d) What is the life of the product? ( )

54. If an organization can not fix the extent of specialisation in the product line:

(a) It can not manufacture special products, ( )
(b) It cannot use special machine tools, ( )
(c) It will grow to unmanageable and unprofitable proportions, ( )
(d) It cannot earn profit. ( )

55. A model or a rule established by authority, custom or a general consent is known as:

(a) Special rule, ( ) (b) a rule, ( )
(c) customs rule, ( ) (d) Standard. ( )

56. Variety reduction is generally known as :

(a) Less verities, ( ) (b) Simplification, ( )
(c) Reduced verities, ( ) (d) Non of the above. ( )

57. Preferred numbers are used to:

(a) To determine the number of verities that are to be manufactured, ( )
(b) To the test the design of the product, ( )
(c) To ascertain the quality level of the product, ( )
(d) To evaluate the production cost. ( )

58. At Break-even point the organisation will have:

(a) Maximum profit, ( ) (b) No loss and no gain, ( )
(c) Maximum loss, ( ) (d) Moderate profit. ( )

59. If S = Sales revenue, P = Profit and V = Variable cost, Then S –V is known as:

(a) Profit, ( ) (b) Loss, ( )
(c) Fixed cost, ( ) (d) Contribution. ( )

60. If F = Fixed cost, V = Variable cost, S = Sales revenue, then the Break- even point is given by:

(a) $F/(S-V)$ ( ) (b) $(S-V)/F$, ( )
(c) $F/(S+V)$, ( ) (d) $(S+V)/F$ ( )

61. In Preferred number the R-10 series will have the value of '*r*' , common ratio =

(a) Fifth root of 10, ( ) (b) Tenth root of 10, ( )
(c) Fifth root of Five, ( ) (d) Tenth root of five. ( )

ANSWERS

1) c	2) c	3) d	4) c	5) d	6) b	7) c	8) a	9) a	10) d	
11) b	12) d	13) c	14) c	15) b	16) b	17) c	18) c	19) a	20) c	
21) d	22) a	23) a	24) b	25) c	26) b	27) d	28) c	29) d	30) c	
31) b	32) a	33) b	34) b	35) b	36) c	37) a	38) d	39) b	40) c	
41) a	42) a	43) c	44) a	45) b	46) b	47) d	48) c	49) c	50) d	
51) c	52) d	53) c	54) c	55) d	56) b	57) a	58) b	59) d	60) a	61) b

UNIT: II. FORECASTING

1. The act of assessing the future and make provisions for it is known as

(a) Planning, ( ) (b) Forecasting, ( )
(c) Assessment, ( ) (d) Scheduling. ( )

2. For a marketing manager, the sales forecast is:

(a) Estimate of the amount of unit sales or a specified future period, ( )
(b) Arranging the salesmen to different segments of the market, ( )
(c) To distribute the goods through transport to satisfy the market demand, ( )
(d) To plan the sales methods. ( )

3. The time horizon selected for forecasting depends on:

(a) The salability of the product, ( )
(b) The selling capacity of Salesman, ( )
(c) Purpose for which forecast is made, ( )
(d) Time required for production cycle. ( )

4. For production planning:

(a) Shot term forecasting is useful, ( )
(b) Medium term forecasting is useful, ( )
(c) Long term forecasting is useful, ( )
(d) Forecasting is not useful. ( )

5. In general, medium range forecasting period will be approximately:

(a) 5 to 10 Years, ( ) (b) 2 to 3 days ( )
(c) 3 to 6 months, ( ) (d) 10 to 20 years. ( )

6. The range of Long range forecasting period may be approximately:

(a) 1 to 2 weeks, ( ) (b) 2 to 3 months, ( )
(c) 1 year, ( ) (d) above 5 years. ( )

7. To plan for future man power requirement:

(a) Short term forecasting is used, ( )
(b) Long range forecasting is used, ( )
(c) Medium range forecasting is used, ( )
(d) There is no need to use forecasting, as future is uncertain. ( )

8. Long range forecasting is useful in

(a) Plan for Research and Development, ( )
(b) To Schedule jobs in Job production, ( )
(c) In purchasing the material to meet the present production demand, ( )
(d) To assess manpower required in the coming month. ( )

9. To determine budgetary control over expenses:

(a) Long range forecasting is useful, ( )
(b) Short term forecasting is useful, ( )

(c) Medium range forecasting is useful ( )
(d) Forecasting is not useful. ( )

10. Medium range forecasting is useful in
(a) To assess the loading capacity of the machine, ( )
(b) To purchase materials for next month, ( )
(c) To plan for capacity adjustments, ( )
(d) To decide whether to receive production orders or not. ( )

11. To decide work load for men and machines,
(a) Medium range forecasting is used, ( )
(b) Short term forecasting is used, ( )
(c) Long range forecasting is used, ( )
(d) A combination of long range and medium range forecasting is used. ( )

12. Short term forecasting is used for:
(a) To set up production run for the products, ( )
(b) To determine the dividend policy, ( )
(c) To determine expected cash flow from sales, ( )
(d) To plan for Research and Development. ( )

13. This factor influence the accuracy of forecasting:
(a) Number of competitive products in the market, ( )
(b) The sales quota fixed to each salesman, ( )
(c) Rate of labour absenteeism, ( )
(d) Availability of materials. ( )

14. Important factor in forecasting production is:
(a) Environmental changes, ( )
(b) Available capacity of machines, ( )
(c) Disposable income of the consumer, ( )
(d) Changes in the preference of the consumer. ( )

15. The following method is used for forecasting for new products:
(a) Direct survey method, ( ) (b) Method of inspection, ( )
(c) Scattered diagram method ( ) (d) Seasonal index method. ( )

16. Projection method of forecasting can be used for forecasting the demand of:
(a) New products, ( ) (b) Capital goods, ( )
(c) Inventory requirement, ( ) (d) Established products. ( )

17. The first step one has to follow while making forecasting is:
(a) To search for a product for which the forecast is to be made, ( )
(b) To determine the objective of the forecast, ( )
(c) To search for the method of forecasting, ( )
(d) To fix the forecasting horizon. ( )

18. The opinion of the marketing executives or senior managers are taken into consideration in:
(a) Extension of past history method, ( )
(b) Causal forecasting method, ( )
(c) Sales force opinion method, ( )
(d) Judgmental forecasting method. ( )

19. A method in which opinion of executives are collected in written form and examined carefully is known as:
(a) Opinion method, ( ) (b) Executive method, ( )
(c) Delphi technique ( ) (c) Linear Programming. ( )

20. A method in which executives give their opinion in open session and have brainstorming is known as:
(a) Open method, ( ) (b) Committee method ( )
(c) Delphi technique, ( ) (d) Open session method. ( )

21. Extension of past history method deals with:
(a) Previously collected data, ( ) (b) Latest data, ( )
(c) Data collected by opponent, ( ) (d) Data supplied by Government ( )

22. Cause and effect relationship is used in:
(a) Causal method, ( ) (b) Cause and effect method, ( )
(c) Scientific method, ( ) (d) Visual method. ( )

23. One source of getting primary data for forecasting is:
(a) Magazines, ( ) (b) Educational Institutions, ( )
(c) Official records, ( ) (d) Published data. ( )

24. The following is the method of collecting data by secondary source:
(b) Sales receipts, ( ) (b) Direct survey method, ( )
(c) Official records, ( ) (d) Published data. ( )

25. Where dependent variable and independent variable are tabulated chronologically it is known as:
(a) Chronological data, ( ) (b) Tabulated data, ( )
(c) Time series, ( ) (d) Quantitative data. ( )

26. A set of quantitative reading of some variable or composite of variables arranged in the order of their occurrence is known as:
(a) Time series ( ) (b) Tabulated variable data, ( )
(c) Chronological data, ( ) (d) None of the above. ( )

27. Long time growth or decay is generally is known as:
(a) Seasonal element, ( ) (b) Trend element ( )
(c) Cyclic element, ( ) (d) Random element. ( )

28. Regularly occurring periodic fluctuations are known as:
(a) Regular trend, ( ) (b) Random trend, ( )
(c) Seasonal component, ( ) (d) Trend. ( )

29. Wave like fluctuations in data is known as:
(a) Cyclic component, ( ) (b) Wave trend, ( )
(c) Wave fluctuations, ( ) (d) Seasonal trend. ( )

30. The error in collected data occurs in unsystematic way is known as:
(a) Unsystematic data, ( ) (b) Unsystematic seasonal data, ( )
(c) Irregular component, ( ) (d) Data error. ( )

31. A phenomenal growth in business or industry is known as:
(a) Phenomenal trend, ( ) (b) Secular trend, ( )
(c) Seasonal trend, ( ) (d) None of the above. ( )

32. Technological development is an :
(a) Upward trend, ( ) (b) Downward trend, ( )

(c) Seasonal trend, ( ) (d) Erratic trend. ( )

33. This factor is an example of upward trend:

(a) Decline in demand, ( ) (b) Shift in consumer preferences, ( )
(c) Improved productivity, ( ) (d) Price induced substitutes. ( )

34. The following factors are responsible for downward trend:

(a) Professional Management, ( ) (b) Innovative marketing ( )
(c) Scarcity of materials required, ( ) (d) Quality control. ( )

35. The following factors are responsible for periodic variation in data:

(a) Changes in the habits of a consumer, ( )
(b) Innovative marketing, ( )
(c) Depression phase of the business, ( )
(d) Climate and weather conditions. ( )

36. Customs, habits and traditions are responsible for:

(a) Secular trend, ( ) (b) Upward trend, ( )
(c) Seasonal variations, ( ) (d) Downward trend .( )

37. Changes in data due to Earth quake, is an example of:

(a) Loss of data, ( ) (b) Erratic data, ( )
(c) Earth quake trend, ( ) (d) Seasonal variation. ( )

38. Prospering phase, Recession phase, Depression and Recovery phases are the phases in:

(a) Trend variation, ( ) (b) Seasonal variation, ( )
(c) Cyclic variation, ( ) (d) Erratic Variations. ( )

39. One of the important point to remember while drawing trend line is:

(a) Area of the curve above the trend line must be equal to the area below the line, ( )
(b) Trend line must pass through all the points plotted, ( )
(c) The sum of areas above and below the trend line must be maximum, ( )
(d) Trend line should always be written in dotted line. ( )

40. A method in which the average of a fixed number of items in the series, which move through the series by dropping the top item of the previous averaged group is known as:

(a) Dropping method of finding averages, ( )
(b) Moving average method, ( )
(c) Semi average method, ( )
(d) None of the above. ( )

41. One of the draw back of Semi average method is:

(a) In case any one half of the series have more heavy numbers then the average we get will be shifted to heavy side, ( )
(b) It is practically impossible to calculate moving average, ( )
(c) Too many calculation procedure, ( )
(d) If we have even number of elements in the series, we cannot calculate semi average. ( )

42. One of the limitations of Moving average method is:

(a) It lacks accuracy, ( )
(b) The averages obtained do not represent the data, ( )
(c) It is very difficult to use this method, ( )

(d) Some trend values for the period in the beginning and in the end cannot be determined. ( )

43. A method in which a trend line drawn in such a way that the sum of the squares of deviations of the actual points above and below the trend line is at the minimum is known as:

(a) Squared trend method, ( ) (b) Equal square method, ( )
(c) Adjusted square method, ( ) (d) Least Square method. ( )

44. One of the advantages of Method of Least square is:

(a) It is a very easy method, ( )
(b) It does not use mathematics, ( )
(c) Trend values of all years of the series may be obtained, ( )
(d) None of the above. ( )

45. Line of Best fit is another name given to:

(a) Method of Least Squares, ( ) (b) Moving average method, ( )
(c) Semi average method, ( ) (d) Trend line method. ( )

46. New Forecast = Old forecast + a (Latest observation - Old forecast) is an equation used in:

(a) Exponential Smoothening method, ( )
(b) Method of lest squares, ( )
(c) Moving average method, ( )
(d) Correlation analysis. ( )

47. Seasonal Index for a particular month is given by:

(a) (Monthly averag) / (Yearly averag) ( )
(b) General average / Monthly average, ( )
(c) General average × monthly average, ( )
(d) (Monthly average for that particular month) × 100 / (General Averag. ( )

48. A statistical method used for expressing the relationship between two or more variables in on single figure is known as:

(a) Relationship method, ( ) (b) Statistical method, ( )
(c) Correlation method, ( ) (d) Least square method. ( )

49. This is very important in correlation method:

(a) Sufficient number of variables must be available, ( )
(b) The accurate measurement of variable is very important, ( )
(c) We apply cause and effect relationship while analyzing, ( )
(d) There must be minimum five variables to apply this method. ( )

50. When correlation between two variables are measured it is known as:

(a) Two variable correlation, ( ) (b) Simple correlation, ( )
(c) Multiple correlation, ( ) (d) Partial correlation. ( )

51. When correlation between more than two variables are studied it is known as:

(a) Three variable correlation, ( ) (b) Simple correlation, ( )
(c) Partial correlation ( ) (d) Multiple correlation. ( )

52. If the amount of change in one variable tends to bear a constant ration to the amount of change in the other variable then the correlation is said to be:

(a) Simple correlation, ( ) (b) Partial correlation, ( )
(c) Linear correlation, ( ) (d) Curvilinear correlation. ( )

53. The equation used in Karl Pearson's method of measuring the correlation (=r) is: (where dx and dy are deviations from arithmetic mean, σx and (σy are standard deviations of variables *x* and *y* respectively.

(a) $\Sigma dx.dy / (n. \sigma x . \sigma y)$ ( ) (b) $(n. \sigma x . \sigma y) / \Sigma dx.dy$ ( )

(c) $\Sigma dx / n.\sigma x$ ( ) (d) n. (x /Σdx. ( )

54. In correlation analysis, if the values of two or more variable move in the same direction, then the correlation is:

(a) Negative correlation, ( ) (b) Indirect Correlation. ( )

(c) Positive correlation, ( ) (d) Linear correlation. ( )

55. The value of correlation coefficient 'r' varies form:

(a) 0 to +1, ( ) (b) –1 to 0, ( )

(c) –1 to +1, ( ) (d) 1 to 10. ( )

56. The cause and effect relationship is more visible in:

(a) Correlation analysis, ( ) (b) Regression analysis, ( )

(c) Moving average method, ( ) (d) Method of least squares. ( )

57. In Spearman's coefficient of rank correlation is given by:

(a) $\{\pm(2C - n) / n\}^{1/2}$ ( ) (b) $\pm(2C - n) / n$ ( )

(c) $\pm 2cn / n$ ( ) (d) $(\pm 2cn / n)^{1/2}$ ( )

58. A method where, direction of change or deviation is recorded form the preceding values is known as:

(a) Rank correlation method, ( )

(b) Multiple correlation method, ( )

(c) Preceding correlation method, ( )

(d) Coefficient of concurrent deviation method. ( )

ANSWERS

1) b	2) a	3) c	4) a	5) c	6) d	7) b	8) a	9) c	10) c
11) b	12) a	13) a	14) b	15) a	16) d	17) b	18) d	19) c	20) d
21) a	22) a	23) c	24) d	25) c	26) a	27) b	28) c	29) a	30) c
31) b	32) a	33) c	34) c	35) d	36) c	37) b	38) c	39) a	40) b
41) a	42) d	43) d	44) c	45) a	46) a	47) d	48) c	49) c	50) b
51) d	52) c	53) a	54) c	55) a	56) a	57) a	58)	59) d	60)

UNIT: III. MATERIALS MANAGEMENT AND INVENTORY CONTROL

1. One of the important basic objective of Inventory management is:

(a) To calculate EOQ for all materials in the organisation. ( )

(b) To go in person to the market and purchase the materials, ( )

(c) To employ the available capital efficiently so as to yield maximum results, ( )

(d) Once materials are issued to the departments, personally check how they are used. ( )

2. The best way of improving the productivity of capital is:

(a) Purchase automatic machines, ( )

(b) Effective labour control, ( )

(c) To use good financial management, ( )

(d) Productivity of capital is to be increased through effective materials management. ( )

3. Materials management is a body of knowledge, which helps manager to:

(a) Study the properties of materials, ( )

(b) Search for needed material, ( )

(c) Increase the productivity of capital by reducing the cost of material, ( )

(d) None of the above. ( )

4. The stock of materials kept in the stores in anticipation of future demand is known as:

(a) Storage of materials, ( ) (b) Stock of materials, ( )

(c) Inventory ( ) (d) Raw materials. ( )

5. The stock of animals reared in anticipation of future demand is known as:

(a) Live stock Inventory, ( ) (b) Animal inventory, ( )

(c) Flesh inventory ( ) (d) None of the above. ( )

6. The working class of human beings is a class of inventor known as:

(a) Live stock, ( ) (b) Human inventory ( )

(c) Population, ( ) (d) Human resource inventory. ( )

7. In general the percentage of materials cost in product is approximately equals to:

(a) 40 to 50 % ( ) (b) 5 to 10 % ( )

(c) 2 to 3 % ( ) (d) 90 to 95% ( )

8. Materials management bring about increased productivity of capital by:

(a) Very strict control over use of materials, ( )

(b) Increasing the efficiency of workers, ( )

(c) Preventing large amounts of capital locked up for long periods in the form of inventory. ( )

(d) To apply the principles of capital management, ( )

9. We can reduce the materials cost by:

(a) Using systematic inventory control techniques, ( )

(b) Using the cheap material, ( )

(c) Reducing the use of materials, ( )

(d) Making hand to mouth purchase. ( )

10. The basis for ABC analysis is

(a) Interests of Materials manager, ( )

(b) Interests of the top management, ( )

(c) Pareto's 80-20 rule, ( )

(d) None of the above. ( )

11. ABC analysis depends on the:

(a) Quality of materials, ( ) (b) Cost of materials, ( )

(c) Quantity of materials used, ( )

(d) Annual consumption value of materials. ( )

12. 'A' class materials consumes:

(a) 10 % of total annual inventory cost, ( )

(b) 30% of total annual inventory cost, ( )

(c) 70 to 75% of total inventory cost, ( )

(d) 90 % of total annual inventory cost. ( )

13. 'B' class of materials consumes ---------% of annual inventory cost.

(a) 60 to 70% ( ) (b) 20 to 25% ( )

(c) 90 to 95% ( ) (d) 5 to 8% ( )

14. 'C' class materials consume -------% of annual inventory cost.

(a) 5 to 10 % ( ) (b) 20 to 30% ( )
(c) 40 to 50% ( ) (d) 70 to 80% ( )

15. The rent for the stores where materials are stored falls under:

(a) Inventory carrying cost, ( ) (b) Ordering cost, ( )
(c) Procurement cost, ( ) (d) Stocking cost. ( )

16. Insurance charges of materials cost falls under:

(b) Ordering cost, ( ) (b) Inventory carrying cost, ( )
(c) Stock out cost ( ) (d) Procurement cost. ( )

17. As the volume of inventory increases, the following cost will increase:

(a) Stock out cost, ( ) (b) Ordering cost, ( )
(c) Procuring cost, ( ) (d) Inventory carrying cost. ( )

18. As the order quantity increases, this cost will reduce:

(a) Ordering cost, ( ) (b) Insurance cost ( )
(c) Inventory carrying cost, ( ) (d) Stock out cost. ( )

19. Procurement cost may be clubbed with:

(a) Inventory carrying charges, ( ) (b) Stock out cost, ( )
(c) Loss due to deterioration, ( ) (d) Ordering cost. ( )

20. The penalty for not having materials when needed is:

(a) Loss of materials cost, ( ) (b) Loss or order cost, ( )
(c) Stock out cost, ( ) (d) General losses. ( )

21. Losses due to deterioration, theft and pilferage comes under,

(a) Inventory Carrying charges, ( ) (b) Losses due to theft, ( )
(c) Does not come under any cost,( ) (d) Consumption cost. ( )

22. Economic Batch Quantity is given by: (where, C_1 = Inventory carrying cost, C_3 = Ordering cost, r = Demand for the product)

(a) $(2C_1 / C_3)^{1/2}$, ( ) (b) $(2 C_3 / C_1 r)^{1/2}$, ( )
(c) $2C_3r / C_1$, ( ) (d) $(2C_3r / C_1)^{1/2}$. ( )

23. If ? is the annual demand, C_1 = Inventory carrying cost, i = rate of inventory carrying charges, p = unit cost of material in Rs., then EOQ =

(a) $(2C_3\lambda / ip)^{1/2}$, ( ) (b) $2C_3\lambda / ip$, ( )
(c) $(2C_3 / ip\lambda)^{1/2}$, ( ) (d) $(2\lambda / C_3 ip)^{1/2}$. ( )

24. If C_1 = Carrying cost, C_3 is the ordering cost, r = demand for the product, then the optimal period for placing an order is given by:

(a) $(2C_3/C_1r)^{1/2}$ ( ) (b) $(2C_1C_3 / r)^{1/2}$ ( )
(c) $(2C_3 r /C_1)^{1/2}$ ( ) (d) $(2C_1 C_3r)^{1/2}$ ( )

25. When C_1 = Inventory carrying cost, C_3 = ordering cost, r = demand for the product, the total cost of inventory is given by:

(a) $(2C_1 C_3 r)$ ( ) (b) $(2C_1C_3)^{1/2}$ ( )
(c) $(2C_3r /C_1)^{1/2}$ ( ) (d) $(2C_1 C_3 r)^{1/2}$ ( )

26. When λ is the annual demand for the material, *p* = unit price of the material in Rs. , C_3 is the ordering cost, *q* = order quantity, then the total cost including the martial cost is given by:

(a) $(q/2)\, ip + \lambda/q\, C_3 + \lambda p$ ( ) (b) $2C\, \lambda\, ip + \lambda p$ ( )
(c) $(q/2)\, ip + \lambda p$ ( ) (d) $(2C_3\, q\lambda\, ip)^{1/2}$ ( )

27. In VED analyses, the letter V stands for:
(a) Very important material, ( ) (b) Viscous material ( )
(c) Weighty materials, ( ) (d) Vital materials. ( )

28. In VED analysis, the letter D strands for:
(a) Dead stock, ( ) (b) Delayed material ( )
(c) Deserved materials, ( ) (d) Diluted materials. ( )

29. The VED analysis depends on:
(a) Annual consumption cost of materials, ( )
(b) Unit price of materials, ( )
(c) Time of arrival of materials, ( )
(d) Criticality of materials. ( )

30. In FSN analysis the letter S stands for:
(a) Slack materials, ( ) (b) Stocked materials, ( )
(c) Slow moving materials, ( ) (d) Standard materials. ( )

31. In FSN analyses, the letter N stands for:
(a) Non moving materials, ( ) (b) Next issuing materials, ( )
(c) No materials, ( ) (d) None of the above. ( )

32. FSN analysis depends on:
(a) Weight of the material, ( ) (b) Volume of material, ( )
(c) Consumption pattern, ( ) (d) Method of moving materials. ( )

33. MRP stands for:
(a) Material Requirement Planning, ( ) (b) Material Reordering Planning, ( )
(c) Material Requisition Procedure, ( ) (d) Material Recording Procedure. ( )

34. A system where the period of placing the order is fixed is known as:
(a) q – system, ( ) (b) Fixed order system ( )
(c) p – system ( ) (d) Fixed quantity system. ( )

35. A system in which quantity for which order is placed is constant is known as:
(a) q – System, ( ) (b) p – system , ( )
(c) Period system, ( ) (d) Bin system. ( )

36. LOB stands for:
(a) Lot of Bills, ( ) (b) Line of Batches ( )
(c) Lot of Batches, ( ) (d) Line of Balance. ( )

37. High reliability spare parts in inventory are known as:
(a) Reliable spares, ( ) (b) Insurance spares, ( )
(c) Capital spares, ( ) (d) Highly reliable spares. ( )

38. The property of capital spares is:
(a) They have very low reliability; ( )
(b) These can be purchased in large quantities, as the price is low, ( )
(c) These spares have relatively higher purchase cost than the maintenance spares. ( )
(d) They are very much similar to breakdown spares. ( )

39. Re-usable spares are known as:
(a) Multi use spares, ( ) (b) Repeated useable stores, ( )
(c) Scrap materials, ( ) (d) Rotable spares. ( )

40. JIT stands for:
(a) Just in time Purchase, ( ) (b) Just in time production, ( )

(c) Just in time use of materials ( ) (d) Just in time order the material. ( )

41. The cycle time, selected in balancing a line must be:

(a) Must be greater than the smallest time element given in the problem, ( )
(b) Must be less than the highest time element given in the problem, ( )
(c) Must be slightly greater than the highest time element given in the problem, ( )
(d) Left to the choice of the problem solver. ( )

42. The lead-time is the time:

(a) To place orders for materials, ( )
(b) Time of receiving materials, ( )
(c) Time between receipt of material and using materials ( )
(d) Time between placing the order and receiving the materials. ( )

43. The PQR classification of inventory depends on:

(a) Unit price of the material, ( ) (b) Annual consumption value of material, ( )
(c) Criticality of material, ( ) (d) Shelf life of the materials. ( )

44. The classification made on the weight of the materials is known as:

(a) PQR analysis, ( ) (b) VED analysis, ( )
(c) XYZ analysis, ( ) (d) FSN analysis. ( )

ANSWERS

1) c	2) d	3) c	4) c	5) a	6) d	7) a	8) c	9) a	10) c
11) d	12) c	13) b	14) a	15) a	16) b	17) d	18) a	19) d	20) c
21) a	22) b	23) c	24) a	25) d	26) a	27) d	28) c	29) d	30) c
31) a	32) c	33) a	34) c	35) a	36) d	37) b	38) c	39) d	40) b
41 c	42) d	43) c	44) d	45)	46)	47)	48)	49)	50)

UNIT: IV. ROUTING AND SCHEDULING.

1. Production planning deals with:

(a) What production facilities is required and how these facilities should be laid out in space available, ( )
(b) What to produce and when to produce and where to sell, ( )
(c) What should be the demand for the product in future? ( )
(d) What is the life of the product? ( )

2. Production planning will be effective when it is done:

(a) By a group of planners, ( ) (b) By an individual, ( )
(c) Progressively, ( ) (d) Combination of (a) and (b). ( )

3. The first stage in production planning is:

(a) Process Planning, ( ) (b) Factory Planning, ( )
(c) Operation Planning, ( ) (d) Layout planning. ( )

4. In Process Planning we plan:

(a) Different machines required, ( ) (b) Different operations required, ( )
(c) We plan the flow of material in each department, ( )
(d) We design the product. ( )

5. In Operation Planning:

(a) The planner plans each operation to be done at work centers and the sequence of operations, ( )

(b) Decide the tools to be used to perform the operations, ( )
(c) Decide the machine to be used to perform the operation, ( )
(d) Decide the materials to be used to produce the product. ( )

6. Before thinking of routing, the production planner has to:
(a) Decide the optimal allocation of available resources, ( )
(b) To decide what type of labour to be used, ( )
(c) To decide how much of material is required, ( )
(d) To count how many orders he has on his hand. ( )

7. The quantities for which the planner has to prepare production plan are known as:
(a) Optimal quantity of products, ( ) (b) Material planning, ( )
(c) Quantity planning, ( ) (d) Planning quantity standards. ( )

8. One of the Planning quantity standards is:
(a) Write off quantity, ( ) (b) Sales volume, ( )
(c) Quantity desired by planning engineer, ( )
(d) None of the above. ( )

9. The quantity over which the cost of special tooling must be recovered is known as:
(a) Order quantity, ( ) (b) Sanction quantity, ( )
(c) Special quantity, ( ) (d) Write off Quantity. ( )

10. The document, which is used to show planning quantity standards and production plan, is known as:
(a) Planning specifications, ( ) (b) Route sheet, ( )
(c) Bill of materials, ( ) (d) Operation sheet. ( )

11. One of the seven routing decisions is:
(a) Where to purchase the material? ( )
(b) How to purchase material? ( )
(c) When to purchase the material? ( )
(d) To make the product or buy the product? ( )

12. If the cost study shows that manufacturing cost is less than the market price of the product, then:
(a) Make the product, ( ) (b) Buy the product, ( )
(c) Buy 50% and make 50%, ( ) (d) Sub contract the product. ( )

13. If the know - how of the product suits the available resources, then
(a) Buy the product form competitor, ( )
(b) Sub contract the product, ( )
(c) Make the product, ( ) (d) Do not do anything ( )

14. If the demand for the product is steady and continuously increasing, then:
(a) Buy the product, ( ) (b) Improve marketing plan, ( )
(c) Sub contract the product, ( ) (d) Make the product. ( )

15. If a company invests Rs. 5000 /- on a new machine it will be able to make the product at a cost of Rs.2 /- per unit in variable costs. If it buys the product it would cost Rs. 3/- per unit for quantities up to 10,000 units. Then the break-even points for make or buy decision:
(a) 3000 units, ( ) (b) 1000 units, ( )
(c) 5000 units, ( ) (d) 10,000 units. ( )

16. While specifying the material shape, the designer has to specify:
(a) Whether to use alloy or plain material, ( )
(b) What are the machining allowances and special features of material? ( )
(c) The quality of material, ( )
(d) The quantity of material. ( )

17. In route sheet or operation layout, one has to show:
(a) A list of materials to be used, ( )
(b) A list of machine tools to be used, ( )
(c) Every work center and the operation to be done at that work center, ( )
(d) The cost of product. ( )

18. The cycle time in selected in balancing a line must be:
(a) Must be greater than the smallest time element given in the problem, ( )
(b) Must be less than the highest time element given in the problem, ( )
(c) Must be slightly greater than the highest time element given in the problem, ( )
(d) Left to the choice of the problem solver. ( )

19. In solving a problem on LOB, the number of workstations required is given by:
(a) Cycle time / Total time, ( ) (b) Cycle time / Element time, ( )
(c) Total time / Element time, ( ) (d) Total time / Cycle time. ( )

20. (Total station time / Cycle time × Number of work stations) × 100 is know as:
(a) Line Efficiency, ( ) (b) Line smoothness, ( )
(c) Balance delay of line, ( ) (d) Station efficiency. ( )

21. A perfectly balanced line will have its smoothness index equals to:
(a) 0, ( ) (b) 1, ( )
(c) –1 ( ) (d) 100. ( )

22. In line of balance, the balance delay is given by:
(a) 100 – Line efficiency, ( ) (b) 100 – Smoothness index, ( )
(c) Line efficiency – smoothness index, ( )
(d) Smoothness index – Line efficiency. ( )

23. Kilbridge and Wester method is used in:
(a) Solving Inventory problems, ( ) (b) Solving layout problems, ( )
(c) Solving Scheduling problems, ( ) (d) Solving Line of Balance problems. ( )

24. The station time in Line of Balance problems must be:
(a) > Than the smallest time element in the problem, ( )
(b) < Than the highest time element given in the problem, ( )
(c) > Than cycle time, ( )
(d) Should not be > than cycle time. ( )

25. Final stage of production planning, where production activities are coordinated and projected on a time scale is known as:
(a) Scheduling, ( ) (b) Loading, ( )
(c) Expediting, ( ) (d) Routing, ( )

26. Scheduling shows:
(a) Total cost of production, ( ) (b) Total material cost, ( )
(c) Which resource should do which job and when, ( )
(d) The flow line of materials. ( )

27. Scheduling deals with:
(a) Number of jobs to be done on a machine, ( )
(b) Number of machine tools used to do a job, ( )
(c) Different materials used in the product, ( )
(d) Fixing up starting and finishing times of each operation in doing a job. ( )

28. The study of relationship between the load on hand and capacity of the work centers is known as:
(a) Scheduling, ( ) (b) Loading, ( )
(c) Routing, ( ) (d) Controlling. ( )

29. Assignment problem is solved by :
(a) Johnson and Bellman method, ( ) (b) By simulation, ( )
(c) By transportation algorithm, ( ) (d) By Flood's technique. ( )

30. One of the aims of loading is:
(a) To finish the job as early as possible, ( )
(b) To minimise the material utilisation, ( )
(c) To improve the quality of product, ( )
(d) To keep operator idle time, material waiting time and ancillary machine time at minimum, ( )

31. One of the principles of Scheduling is:
(a) Principle of optimal product design, ( )
(b) Principle of selection of best material, ( )
(c) Principle of optimal operation sequence, ( )
(d) Principle of optimal cost. ( )

32. The method used in scheduling a project is:
(a) A schedule of breakdown of orders, ( )
(b) Outline Master Programme, ( )
(c) PERT & CPM ( )
(d) Schedule for large and integrated work. ( )

33. Production planning in the intermediate range of time is termed as:
(a) Production planning, ( ) (b) Long range production planning ( )
(c) Scheduling, ( ) (d) Aggregate planning. ( )

34. One of the requirements of Aggregate Planning is:
(a) Both output and sales should be expressed in a logical overall unit of measuring, ( )
(b) Appropriate time period, ( )
(c) List of all resources available, ( )
(d) List of operations required. ( )

35. In aggregate planning, one of the methods in modification of demand is:
(a) Differential Pricing, ( ) (b) Lay off of employees, ( )
(c) Over time working, ( ) (d) Sub contracting. ( )

36. In aggregate panning one of the methods used to modification of Supply is:
(a) Advertising and sales promotion, ( )
(b) Development of complimentary products, ( )
(c) Backlogging, ( )
(d) Hiring and lay off of employees depending on the situation. ( )

37. The first stage of Production control is:
(a) Dispatching, ( ) (b) Scheduling, ( )
(c) Routing, ( )
(d) Triggering of production operations and observing the progress and record the deviation. ( )

38. The act of releasing the production documents to production department is known as:
(a) Routing, ( ) (b) Scheduling, ( )
(c) Expediting, ( ) (d) Dispatching. ( )

39. One of the important production documents is:
(a) Design sheet of the product, ( ) (b) List of materials, ( )
(c) Route card, ( ) (d) Control chart. ( )

40. The act of going round the production shop and recording the actual production and inform the deviation to production department is known as:
(b) Spying, ( ) (b) Expediting, ( )
(c) Controlling, ( ) (d) Complaining. ( )

41. One of the important charts used in Programme control is:
(a) Material chart, ( ) (b) Gantt chart, ( )
(c) Route chart, ( ) (d) Inspection chart. ( )

ANSWERS

1) a	2) c	3) b	4) c	5) a	6) a	7) d	8) a	9) d	10) a
11) d	12) a	13) c	14) d	15) c	16) b	17) c	18) c	19) d	20) a
21) a	22) a	23) d	24) c	25) a	26) c	27) d	28) b	29) a	30) d
31) c	32) c	33) d	34) a	3 5) a	36) d	37) d	38) d	39) c	40) b
41) b	42)	43)	44)	45)	46)	47)	48)	49)	50)

UNIT: V. DISPATCHING.

1. The way in which we can assess the efficiency of the production plant is by:
(a) Efficient dispatching,+ ( )
(b) By manufacturing a good product, ( )
(c) By comparing the actual performance with targets specified in the specified programme, ( )
(d) By efficient production planning. ( )

2. Production control concerned with,
(a) Passive assessment of plant performance, ( )
(b) Strict control on labours, ( )
(c) Good materials management, ( )
(d) Good product design. ( )

3. Post- operation evaluation, and feedback of information is the duty of a
(a) Scheduling supervisor, ( ) (b) Production Manager, ( )
(c) Materials manager, ( ) (d) Dispatcher. ( )

4. The following is the important duty of a dispatcher,
(a) Replenishment policy of inventory, ( )
(b) Analyzing the data by comparing progress with plans. ( )

(c) To prepare schedules, ( )
(d) To draw Gantt charts, ( )

5. An activity by which the information regarding the production plan is known as:
(a) Display information, ( ) (b) Announcement, ( )
(c) Circulating, ( ) (d) Dispatching, ( )

6. In control stage, during analysis stage of cost of production we deal with,
(a) Computing costs, ( )
(b) Comparing the costs, ( )
(c) Computing costs and compare with estimates, ( )
(d) Writing cost sheet. ( )

7. To receive and filing of all shop orders and associated documents is the work of:
(a) Order clerk, ( ) (b) Schedule clerk, ( )
(c) Planking clerk ( ) (d) Dispatcher. ( )

8. One of the important duties of a dispatcher is:
(a) Selection of jobs for issue in a most favorable sequence., ( )
(b) To guide workmen on the job directly, ( )
(c) To pack up the finished jobs, ( )
(d) Just go round all the shops. ( )

9. Dispatching is toughest in:
(a) Job Production, ( ) (b) Mass production, ( )
(c) Batch production, ( ) (d) Flow production. ( )

10. One of the documents to be prepared in dispatching department is:
(a) Time series for forecasting, ( )
(b) Cost sheets of products, ( )
(c) A shop order for each component, ( )
(d) None of the above. ( )

11. In post operation analysis, production documents will help in:
(a) Deciding what to do next? ( )
(b) Deciding the future of the company, ( )
(c) Giving punishment to the workers, ( )
(d) In calculating wages and examining the cost of the job. ( )

12. The type of dispatching function to be used depends much on the:
(a) Type of product, ( )
(b) Type of production and on the size of the plant, ( )
(c) Type of materials used in production, ( )
(d) Type of management style. ( )

13. One of the aims of dispatching is:
(a) To look after the welfare of the labour, ( )
(b) To test the quality of the product, ( )
(c) To dispatch the products to different places, ( )
(d) Principle of completion of job by due date. ( )

14. When work centers are used in optimal sequence to do the jobs, we can:
(a) Minimise the set up time, ( )
(b) Minimse operation time, ( )

(c) Minimise the break down of machines, ( )
(d) Minimise the utility of facility. ( )

15. Route card and technological route card are:

(a) Different type of documents, ( )
(b) Same type of documents, ( )
(c) Route card shows route and technological route cared shows the technology used, ( )
(d) One is prepared by production manager, dispatcher prepares other. ( )

16. The card, which is prepared by dispatching department to book the labour involved in each operation, is:

(a) Labour card, ( ) (b) Wage card, ( )
(c) Credit card, ( ) (d) Job card ( )

17. The card, which shows, the number of rejected products from total quantity produced is:

(a) Quality control card, ( ) (b) Inspection card, ( )
(c) Rejection card, ( ) (d) Job card. ( )

18. The act of going round the production shop to note down the progress of work and feedback the information is known as:

(a) Follow up ( ) (b) Dispatching, ( )
(c) Routing, ( ) (d) Trip card. ( )

19. One of the activities of expediting is:

(a) To file the orders in sequence, ( )
(b) To decide the sequence of operation, ( )
(c) To record the actual production against the scheduled production, ( )
(d) To examine the tools used in production. ( )

20. The class timetable is a good example of:

(a) Route sheet, ( ) (b) Follow up chart, ( )
(c) Dispatcher's chart, ( ) (d) Gantt chart. ( )

21. 'Z' chart is a chart used in:

(a) Programme control, ( ) (b) Job control, ( )
(c) Cost control, ( ) (d) Quality control. ( )

22. Z- chart can be used to show:

(b) Process used in production ( ) (b) Quality level of the product, ( )
(c) Both the plan and the performance, and deviation from the plan, ( )
(d) To show cost structure of the product. ( )

23. Computers are used in Production control in this area:

(a) Follow up activity, ( ) (b) To control labour, ( )
(c) To disseminate information. ( )
(d) Loading, Scheduling and Assignment works, ( )

ANSWERS

1) c	2) a	3) d	4) b	5) d	6) c	7) d	8) a	9) c	10) c
11) d	12) b	13) d	14) a	15) b	16) d	17) b	18) a	19) c	20) d
21) a	22) c	23) d.							

QUESTION BANK

1. Describe with the Organization structure the importance of Production Planning and Control function and its relationship with other departments in the organization.
2. Describe the importance of various costs, which are to be considered in deciding economic lot size in production. Derive the square root formula for economic batch quantity.
3. What are the various methods of sales forecasting? What are the limitations of each?
4. What is dispatching? Give importance of dispatching activity in production control.
5. What is progressing? Describe the various aspects of Progressing.
6. What is meant by critical path? What advantages are to be associated with the use of critical path scheduling methods?
7. A firm is making an attempt to obtain an order for a complex assembly. It is necessary to determine the earliest possible delivery date so that consumers can decide on the order. The details regarding the schedule of activities and time duration for each is given in the table below:

Job	*Description*	*Preceding Activity*	*Time in Days*
A	Receiving production authorization	—	0
B	Determine part requirements	A	2
C	Determine production factors	B	4
D	Determine material availability	C	6
E	Determine equipment availability	C	3
F	Determine manpower availability	C	4
G	Prepare Operation scheduling	D, E, F	8
H	Prepare and issue shop forms	G	7

Prepare PERT network and determine the earliest delivery time. Show the critical path.

8. What are Gantt charts? Describe the Gantt machine loading chart and the Gantt order chart. Evaluate Gantt chart as a representative of the schedule problem in job shops.
9. Write note on: (a) Feed back Theory, (b) Control charts (c) Line of Balance.
10. Explain the steps in planning production in the case of :
    (a) Line Production (b) Job lot.
    What are the specific problems in each one of these and how can these be tackled?
11. Describe the methods by which you balance an assembly line. How do you achieve least balance delay?
12. Describe the fixed period ordering and fixed quantity ordering system in inventory control. Explain how you will calculate the order quantity and safety stock. What are the limitations of these systems?
13. What are the essential differences between PERT and CPM scheduling?
14. What is Line of Balance? How is it drawn? And what is its use in production?
15. Explain the advantages of using Statistical Quality Control. What is meant by Error due to assignable cause and Error due to chance? How do these errors occur?

16. What are scrapping and reworking policies adopted in production? How do you adjust the production system to these policies?
17. Recommend a suitable Production Planning and Control system for a unit undertaking design and fabrication of steel transmission towers. Each order is tailor-made to customer's requirements. Your proposal, amongst other things should cover:
    (*i*) Peculiarities of the nature of work from the point of view of Production Planning and Control.
    (*ii*) Pre production planning.
    (*iii*) Work order and feed back system.
    (*iv*) Cost estimation and control
    (*v*) Planning and control techniques particularly of importance for this type of work.
18. Write short notes on (a) Line balancing, (b) Gantt Chart, (c) Make or Buy decision.
19. (a) The production-scheduling department of a textile firm shows the following records at the end of an operation period for nine grades of a particular fabric it produces.

Grade	*Forecast For 1000 meters*	*Available stock*
M-1	43	82
M-2	93	93
M-3	152	162
M-4	20	56
M-5	27	91
M-6	61	40
M-7	90	170
M-8	120	181
M-9	60	125

Prepare a run out showing the sequence in which production orders for the several grades of fabric should be released.

(b) If all the fabrics are produced in the same production unit and this unit has a capacity of 750,000 meters per week, what quantities of each grade should be produced in order to bring all items to an equal time supply?

20. What would be the major differences in Production Planning and Control techniques used in: (a) Processing Industry, (b) Hydrogenated Vanaspathi plant, (c) Mass production engineering unit (example manufacture of Table fans.)
21. Discuss the importance of Materials Planning and scientific Procurement in a Production Planning and Control system and how proper materials policy can aid in reducing end product cost.
22. Discuss the conflicts, which normally arise in relationship between Production Planning and Control, Maintenance and Inspection departments. What organizational or other remedial steps would you suggest to overcome such conflicts?
23. What, in your opinion, should be the functions of a Production Planning and control department? How would you evaluate the performance of Production Planning and Control Department?
24. Steps involved in executing an order for a large Engine - Generator set are given below in a jumbled manner. Arrange them in logical sequence, draw a PERT network and find critical path and shortest execution period.

Activity (not in Logical order)	*Time in Weeks*
Order and receive engine	2
Prepare assembly drawing	1
Receive and study order	2
Apply and receive import license for generator	5
Order and receive generator.	3
Study enquiry for engine-generator set	2
Fabricate switchboard	3
Inspect Engine	1
Assemble Engine Generator set	2
Submit quotation with drawing and full specification	2
Prepare base and coupling	1
Order and receive Meters and Switchgear for Switchboard	3
Inspect Generator	1
Test assembly	1

25. What are the various assumptions made in the optimal lot size model with constant demand? What are the various components of the costs to be included in deriving the model? Describe the sensitivity of the model to estimation errors in arriving at the costs of ordering and inventory carrying cost.
26. What is the Assembly Line Balancing? Define the following:
    (a) Work element, (b) Work station, (c) Cycle time, (d) Station time, (e) Balance delay, (f) Smoothness index.
    List and describe briefly any two approaches to solving assembly line balancing problems.
27. What are the types of plant layout? Describe the advantages and disadvantages of each type. When is each type of plant layout is chosen? What are the various factors affecting the plant layout? Describe how these factors affect the plant layout.
29. Describe the role and need of forecasting in Production and Inventory Control. Describe each of the following forecasting methods: (a) Exponential Smoothening, (b) Correlation analysis, (c) Moving average method.
30. Write short notes on the following:
    (a) ABC analysis of Inventory, (b) Change over cost, (c) Cost of capital, (d) FIFO, LIFO (e) p-system and q-system of Inventory control, (f) (S, S) Inventory policy.
31. A company manufactures a certain chemical whose anticipated demand is the net year in tones is as follows:
    January: 300, February: 540, March: 400, April: 830, May: 760, June: 600, July: 550, August: 560, September: 760, November: 770, December: 320.
    Inventory policy of the company aims at maintaining average monthly inventory equals to 40% of the shipments or 200 tonnes, which ever is higher. Inventory at the beginning of the year was 270 tonnes.
    (a) Tabulate cumulative production requirement.
    (b) Calculate average inventory level for the year.
    (c) Plot the cumulative production requirement and graphically determine the production rate required to maintain constant level of production operations over the coming year to meet

the requirements. What would be the resultant inventory level and how do these compare with the stated inventory policies?

32. Explain the use of Statistical Quality Control in (a) Inspection of bought-out components, (b) Controlling quality of production operations.

33. The major objectives of Production Planning and Control are as follows:
   (a) To secure uninterrupted flow of work,
   (b) To ensure stable employment to workers,
   (c) To take suitable measures at the planning and control stages to ensure that the output is of the stipulated quality level, involving minimum of rework or rejections,
   (d) To assist management in formulating realistic production targets and help in achieving the same,
   (e) To affect optimum allocation of resources for producing various products in demand,
   (f) To assist sales with information for working out realistic delivery dates and to ensure fulfillment of delivery promises,
   (g) To attain highest possible effectiveness of all resources at the disposal of the production management, mainly with a view to minimizing costs or maximizing profits,
   (h) To take action to eliminate production bottlenecks, as and when they occur,
   (i) To coordinate various activities within the organization, aimed at achieving its overall objectives.

   Select those four out of the foregoing nine statements, which together indicate the widest possible coverage of he, vital objectives of Production Planning and Control. Briefly justify your choice.

34. You are to make 5000 a month of a part that requires milling machine time. The standard time for this operation is 0.0064 hours per unit.
   (a) How many machines do you need if every one works 8 hours a day for 25 days at 100% efficiency and there were no scrap loss or machine time loss?
   (b) How many items do you start into production if the scrap rate is 4%?
   (c) What is your answer if you get only 78% machine utilization from the machine and that operators are 115% effective.
   (d) How many machines (using thee production expectation arrived at in © above) will you need for the scrap indicted in (b) above.

35. (a) Customer has just sent a design change notice. You are already half way through making the parts affected and so you do not want to change. If the customer calls on you, explains as to how you would convince him about your difficulty arising out of his late change notice?
   (b) What kind of graphic and visual controls are there for use in Production control work? What are their good and bad points? When would you use them?

36. Write notes on the following:
   (a) Comparison between continuous and intermittent production systems.
   (b) Benefits of standardization, variety reduction and specialization.
   (c) Process planning, tool design and tool planning.
   (d) Master scheduling and scheduling on shop floor.
   (e) Bases of Make or Buy decision.
   (f) Forecasting techniques.

37. Make out a flow chart indicating, with your reasoning, the document that are required to facilitate Production Planning and Control in an organization where batch production is extensively adopted. The organization, it is assumed, manufactures seven hundred parts, which are fitted into one type of equipment made in large numbers by the company.
38. Explain with examples the use of Linear Programming technique in production Planning and Control functions.
39. Activities and duration in days for installation of a new lathe are given below:
    (a) Await delivery of lathe: 2 days
    (b) Install lathe: 4 days
    (c) Remove existing machine to clear the floor: 5 days.
    (d) Dispose of existing machine: 2 days.
    (e) Install power supply: 12 days
    (f) Connect power supply to lathe: 1 day
    (g) Test installation: 2 days.
        (*i*) Establish sequence in which the above activities should be performed.
        (*ii*) Draw a network and determine critical path and its duration.
        (*iii*) Workout Earliest start, Earliest Finish, Latest Start, Latest Finish and floats.
40. Distinguish in clear terms between Mass, Batch and Unit production. In what ways Production Planning and Control system differ between the three types?
41. Suggest, describe and justify a typical organization for production planning and control for a batch production unit manufacturing about 20 families of products and 15 varities in each family, having a total sales turnover of about Rs. 3 crores. Discuss also he level of reporting of such a department within the organization.
42. "Center of Production Management system is efficient organization and system of Production Planning and Control". Discuss the statement for it validity giving sufficient examples form, live situations.
43. (a) Discuss and arrive at an equation for optimum lot manufacturing.
    (b) We can manufacture a component either by manual or by an automatic process with varying time between them for set up and operation. The set up time for the manual process is 2 hours, while the time taken for manufacturing one piece is 5 minutes; for the automatic process, set up takes 11 hours, while operation time per piece is 0.50 minutes. Recommend the process for batch quantities: (*i*) 100 units, (*ii*) 120 units, and (*iii*) 250 units, in order that the total time taken for processing is minimum. What will be the time taken on the process you recommend for the quantities given above.
44. (a) How will you go about establishing Line of Balance technique for controlling batch production? Describe the same with example. Under what conditions alone LOB technique is applicable.
45. Component A requires 10 days to manufacture, while component B takes 20 days. Further 10 days are required for assembling the two components and that makes the product. The monthly production programme for the product is as follows:

Month	*Quantity (units)*
January	15
February	10
March	10
April	5
May	15
June	10

At the end March, the following progress of manufacture is observed:
Number of products completed: 25
Number of components started: A = 25
Completed: A = 20
Number of components started: B = 50
Completed: B = 40

Draw line of balance graphically as at the end of March and comment about the progress of manufacturer observed.

46. In what way PERT / CPM technique is better suited to answering the questions in Project Planning and Control? Take a practical example of your own containing at least 20 activities, draw its network and analyze the same for the critical path. Comment on the outcome of your analysis.
47. Write notes on: (a) Production control, (b) Sequencing, (c) Production reporting, (d) Process planning, (f) Dummy activities.
48. Data relating to two products in a Production schedule are given below. You have to draw a production schedule for maximum return by using overtime or additional shifts if necessary.

Products	*I*	*II*
Consumption rate 'a_c' units per day	30	24
Production rate 'a_p' per day	200	150
Constant cost 'c' per piece	6	1.6
Carrying cost factor 'k'	0.96 × 10-4	0.67 × 10-4
Set up cost in Rs.	3600	1800
Set up time t_s in days	4.8	2.4
Allowable increase in variable cost.	5%	5%
Minimum batch cost size Q_m	6120	—
Production range.	From 4470 To 8390	— —

49. You are required to determine a job-schedule given the following information:

Job	*Operation time in hours*	*Routing to machines Operation numbers* 1 2 3 4 5
A	2 4 3 7 2	3 2 1 4 5
B	3 2 5 1	1 2 4 3
C	4 2 6	5 2 1
D	3 7 8	2 4 3
E	6 4 2	1 4 5

(e.g. First operation of the job A involving 2 hours, is processed on machine No. 3)
Evolve suitable priority numbers and schedule the jobs on the assumption that the scheduler only knows of he existence of jobs which are at a machine, but has no knowledge of jobs which will arrive i.e. decentralised scheduling.

50. Write a note on: (a) Product design, (b) Production design, (c) Plant layout, (d) Production control.

51. Discuss the need for increasing productivity at the level of individual enterprise in the context of (a) Profits, (b) Wages, (c) Prices, (d) Employment.
52. Discuss the workers response, both at individual and union levels, to activities of Work Study Department and outline a strategy for securing their co-operation.
53. Draw Process layout and explain its advantages and disadvantages.
54. What information is necessary for an industrial engineer to prepare a layout of a manufacturing unit?
55. Describe what are Matrix layout and Fixed position layout. Explain where they are used?
56. Enlist the characteristics of a good layout.
57. Discuss the principles of Motion Economy as related to the design of tools and equipment. Illustrate them with suitable examples.
58. Why to study work? Explain the need and rationale for study of work. What is the scope of Works Study?
59. Explain the potential for and approach to application of Work-study in any two of the following: (a) Hospital administration, (b) A Bank, (c) A state government secretariat, (d) An automobile repair workshop.
60. "Work Measurement enables the identification and elimination of in efficient time". Discuss.
61. Briefly discuss how a company can benefit form a work measurement programme.
62. What techniques would you use to assess the workload of the house keeping staff of a luxury hotel? Justify the selection of your technique; illustrate your answer preferable with an example. (House keeping consists of making up the rooms, cleaning and sweeping the premises).
63. What are the prerequisites for launching a Work Measurement Programme?
64. What do you mean by Assignable causes and Chance causes? What do you understand by the statement that "a process is in statistical control"?
65. (a) What are control charts?
    (b) What is the basis of the X bar and R control charts?
66. What is a single sampling plan? Give the procedure of a double sampling attribute plan.
67. Write a note on: (a) Process control, (b) Lot control, (c) Producer's risk, (d) Consumer's risk.
68. List out the advantages of Statistical Quality control compared to 100 percent inspection.
69. Enumerate the merits and demerits of hundred percent inspection and sampling inspection.
70. Sales forecast is a vital key to integrated management. Comment.
71. What are the methods of Sales forecasting? Discuss.
72. Define and give examples of Use value, Time value, and Cost value.
73. Do a complete value engineering study of the pen you are using. Give complete details of the same. Give a step by step your logical development of the study. You may assume any values required.
74. Do a value engineering exercise on a Black Board.
    How do you define the value of the black board?
    List the functions of the black board.
    Evaluate the functions in terms of primary and secondary functions.
75. How do you judge the value of the following?
    (a) A bicycle, (b) A ball point pen, (c) A ready made shirt, (d) The morning news paper, (e) 1 kg. vegetable, (f) A teacup and saucer, (g) The examination you are writing.
76. Define value analysis. Explain with examples at least three different values of a product.
77. What is meant by Ergonomics and what is its area of application?
78. What is the impact of Ergonomics on Works Study and how can its application increase output?
79. Write the differences between Inspection and Quality control.